Jesus of Nazareth

Jesus of Nazareth

―――Dewey Roberts―――

Jesus of Nazareth

© 2025 Dewey Roberts

Prepared for publication by www.greatwriting.org

ISBN: 978-0-9972666-5-8

All rights reserved. No part of this publication may be reproduced, stored in a retrieval system or transmitted in any form by any means, electronic, mechanical, photocopy, recording or otherwise without prior permission of the publisher, except as provided by USA copyright law.

Cover design: www.greatwriting.org
Book layout and design: www.greatwriting.org

Unless noted otherwise, Scripture quotations are taken from the New American Standard Bible® (NASB), Copyright © 1960, 1962, 1963, 1968, 1971, 1972, 1973, 1975, 1977, 1995 by The Lockman Foundation Used by permission. www.Lockman.org

SOLA FIDE PULICATIONS
Destin, Florida

About the Author

Dr. Dewey Roberts was born in Cleveland, Mississippi, and raised in the southeastern states of the USA. He studied Bible and English at Belhaven College and earned his Master of Divinity from Reformed Theological Seminary (both institutions in Jackson, Mississippi). He is the founding pastor of Cornerstone Presbyterian Church in Destin, Florida, where he has served since 1995. He was an Army Reserve chaplain for twenty-four years and served three tours on active duty. He retired in the rank of Colonel in 2011 and spent the last eight years of his chaplain career as a writer / instructor at the US Army Chaplain School and Center in Fort Jackson, SC. In addition to his pastoral duties, he also serves as Executive Director of Church Planting International (CPI) which promotes reformed indigenous missions in Russia, Uganda, Myanmar, India, and Portugal. CPI was founded by Rev. Donald Dunkerley in 1993.

Dewey received a PhD in Historical Theology from Whitfield Theological Seminary in 2017 for his work on Historic Christianity and the Federal Vision.

Dewey and his wife, Jane, have two children and four grandchildren.

Dedication:

First, to my wife of forty-five years, Teressa Jane Ayers Roberts, who has been my most faithful friend since our first date on August 24, 1968; and,
Second, to J. Knox Chamblin who was one of my professors at Belhaven University in 1971–3.

Chapter Contents

About the Author 5
Introduction 10
1 The Fulness of Time 12
2 A Lowly Birth 23
3 Early Life in Nazareth 36
4 Jesus' Baptism and Temptations 49
5 Jesus' First Year of Ministry 66
6 Galilee of the Gentiles 87
7 Back Home in Capernaum 101
8 Do You Wish to be Well? 112
9 Jesus' True Disciples 125
10 The Second Preaching Tour in Galilee 137
11 He Has Lost His Senses 150
12 The Third Missionary Tour of Galilee 164
13 The Bread of Life 181
14 Storming the Gates of Hell 197
15 Jesus' Transfiguration 216
16 Jesus at the Feast of Tabernacles 233
17 Jesus' Ministry in Perea 261
18 Jesus' Retirement Ministry in Ephraim 290
19 Jesus' Triumphal Entry into Jerusalem 307
20 The Prelude to Jesus' Passion 316
21 Jesus' Parting Words 331
22 The Inner Sanctuary 346
23 The Garden of Gethsemane 361
24 Jesus' Arrest and Trial 379
25 Jesus' Crucifixion 398
26 Jesus' Resurrection and Ascension 421
    Bibliography 448

Dr. Dewey Roberts' latest work on the life of our God and Savior, Jesus Christ, is needed now more than ever. As the West sinks deeper into the existential mire of the secular age, believers must be strengthened to remain faithful and be witnesses for Christ. There is no greater way to do that than to focus on the very person of our Lord Jesus. The hope of the world in these times, as in every era, remains the resurrected and reigning Savior. I commend this remarkable and much-needed work to the church and to all those who would inquire into the life of the single most compelling figure in all of human history. May God use this new book to bring revival in the hearts of many.

MICHAEL A. MILTON, PhD, DMin, MPA, MDiv, President and Senior Fellow, the D. James Kennedy Institute of Reformed Leadership; President, Faith For Living, Inc.; Distinguished Professor of Missions and Evangelism, Erskine Seminary; Chancellor-President-CEO, RTS (retired); Chaplain (Colonel), US Army (Ret.)

Jesus of Nazareth is simply wonderful. It is aimed to be a classic, what every new Christian will be given, but also refreshing for the most mature believer. Roberts has highlighted every epoch in His life and with those quotes the author indicates humbly his wide reading and each chapter is casting light on our Lord. I wondered what he would do with the silent years, but I loved that chapter too. All the fruits of his wonderful library are manifest for all of us to benefit. I long to see it in print.

GEOFFREY THOMAS, Former pastor of Alfred Place Baptist Church in Aberystwyth, Wales

My friend, Dewey Roberts, has done the people of God a great service in writing his excellent work, *Jesus of Nazareth*. Dewey uses a free flowing narrative style that is factual, historically accurate, and heartwarming. He vividly captures the details of Christ's person and work which can serve as a refresher for those who have followed Jesus for many years or as an introduction for those new to the faith. This book is a must read for any who wish to follow the Lord Jesus with greater zeal.

AL BAKER, Evangelist with Reformed Evangelistic Fellowship

Dewey Roberts, a humble and faithful Presbyterian pastor of many years, provides us a full scholarly biography of our Lord in Jesus of Nazareth. Dr. Roberts' book is the first of its kind since the famous *Life and Times of Jesus the Messiah* by Alfred Edersheim. Any minister, Bible teacher, or Christian who chooses to take on this extensive yet readable biography on the life of Christ will reap rich rewards for their efforts. In the flurry of new books, this one stands out. I heartily say, "Take up and read!"—highly and warmly recommended!

MACK TOMLINSON, Providence Chapel, Denton Texas

Introduction

The greatest life ever lived was that of Jesus of Nazareth—the eternal Son of God who became flesh. His life has captured the attention of authors throughout the history of the Church and there have been countless hundreds of books written about Him. Some of those books are written, in part, as biographies, but most of them eventually focus on His teaching—instead of His life. That is understandable. It is not easy to put the life of Christ into the context of the times and places where He lived. Perhaps, the most comprehensive and most scholarly book ever written on His life is that of Alfred Edersheim, *The Life and Times of Jesus the Messiah*. Edersheim's work is a wealth of information and insight into Jewish religious and social life. No biographer of Jesus can afford to neglect his work. Yet, Edersheim also goes into such detail concerning extraneous matters that the life of Christ and the flow of the narrative often get lost in too many words.

Ever since my earliest days as a minister, there has been a desire in my heart to write a true biography of Jesus. Matthew, Mark, Luke, and John were written for specific purposes, but none of them were written to be biographies of our Lord. There are many extra-biblical facts that shed light on Jesus' life and give us the context for what He said and did. This book attempts to give His life in chronological order and to provide the historical, geographical, cultural, religious, social, and political context for it. A true chronological order of Jesus' life is a sheer impossibility. I have consulted with various chronologies of His life and what I present in this book differs from all of them in some ways. It would be wonderful if we all had more of the details of His life, but John 21:25 says—"And there are also many other things Jesus did, which if they were written in detail, I suppose even the world itself would not contain the books that would be written." We simply do not have enough facts about Jesus' life to always put events in the right order.

There certainly are details about Jesus' early life and even about His ministry that are shrouded in mystery. Almost nothing is known about Jesus' first thirty years of life outside a few details about His birth and a few remarks in the Gospel According to Luke. The emphasis in Scripture is on His three and a half year ministry and especially His death and resurrection. About forty percent of the four Gospels are focused on the last week of His life and His resurrection. That is why there is so little known about His first thirty years. Actually, the New Testament records only a small number of days out of Jesus' life and then only a small portion of those days. A true life of Christ, therefore, should not be a fictional account. There is much about His life that we do not know. We can fill in the life of Christ with extra-Biblical facts for context where they are known without writing a fictional account of His life or resorting to suppositions. Such details help to bring the story of Jesus to life. To whatever degree I have succeeded in doing that, I give the glory to the Lord. Writing this book has been the single most spiritually enlightening thing in my life.

In 2022, I began teaching the life of Jesus chronologically, as much as I understood the right order at my congregation in Destin, Florida. At first, I taught with the intention of later writing everything out in detail. I soon realized that it would be better if I wrote the book week by week as I was teaching it. I appreciate so much those faithful Wednesday evening church members who listened to me read each section and offered kind advice where needed. It has been my joy to write these pages and I hope that it is beneficial in the present and to future generations.

Dewey Roberts

1

The Fulness of Time

"In the Church of the Holy Sepulcher in Jerusalem one spot is pointed out to travelers as being the center of the world. It is a strange and rather fantastic claim. Yet there is a sense in which the corner of the earth's surface called Palestine is the geographical center. Take the three great continents of Europe, Asia, and Africa; in between them, linking them up, lies this little land bridge on the eastern shore of the Mediterranean. Clearly, if you were to start a movement whose aim was to extend out into the three great continents simultaneously, that neck of land would be a natural starting point."[1]

In *The Environment of Early Christianity*, Samuel Angus wrote the following about the time when Christ, the eternal Son of God, came to earth in human flesh:

> Christ appeared at the time when all the striving and hopes of all peoples were converging to a focus, when the vast majority of mankind were hungering for religious support, when East and West had been wedded, when men were expecting a new era, when the philosophy of Greece and the religious consciousness of the Hebrew were pointing toward a new Revelation. Christ came at the one time in history when all civilized nations lived, as it were, on the will of one, when all were able to communicate in one language, when men were unanimous to the perils and needs of the earth, when there was '*one* empire, *one* universal language, *one* civilisation, a *common* development toward monotheism, and a *common yearning* for saviours.'
>
> The advent of Christ synchronized with what is admittedly the greatest crisis in all history, 'the coming of the age of the human race,' when all that men had struggled for seemed likely to disappear from earth, when chaos threatened to reassert its primeval reign. Never before or since has the world been so utterly exhausted . . .
>
> National faiths had collapsed. The West was looking to the East for gospels . . .
>
> The incarnation of the 'Desire of all nations' answered the universal question of Seneca: . . . 'Where shall He be found whom we have been seeking for so many centuries?'[2]

---

1 James S. Stewart, *The Life and Teaching of Jesus Christ* (Nashville and New York: Abingdon Press, n.d.). 15.
2 Samuel Angus, *The Environment of Early Christianity* (London: Duckworth & Co., 1914), 222, 223, 225, 226.

The Despair of the Ancient World

The time when Jesus of Nazareth, the Messiah, was born was an age of despair in many ways. The people of all nations were longing for an answer to the moral and spiritual dilemmas of the human race, but all the older religions had produced none. Even the great moral laws of the Jews had proved powerless to reform the heart of mankind. As Paul wrote to the Romans: "For what the Law could not do, weak as it was through the flesh, God *did*: sending His own Son in the likeness of sinful flesh and as *an offering* for sin, He condemned sin in the flesh" (Romans 8:3). For many centuries, God had allowed the problem of sin to reign seemingly unchecked until the false hopes of mankind had reached the point of utter despair. Then, "in the fulness of time," He sent His Son into the world. It seemed to be late in time to the despairing cries of the world, but it was the perfect time in God's eternal plan. As Paul wrote to the Galatians: "But when the fullness of time came, God sent forth His Son, born of a woman, born under the law" (Galatians 4:4). Jesus was born at the right time, the time appointed by God, the time when the world was anxiously awaiting Him because there was hope in no other way or no one else. In his commentary on the meaning of "the fulness of time," J. B. Lightfoot wrote:

> The ideas involved in this expression may be gathered from the context. It was 'the fulness of time.' *First*; in reference to the *Giver*. The moment had arrived which God ordained from the beginning and foretold by His prophets for Messiah's coming. *Secondly*; in reference to the *recipient*. The Gospel was withheld until the world had arrived at mature age: the law worked out its educational purpose and was now superseded . . . The comparison of the child implies more than a negative effect. A moral and spiritual expansion, which rendered the world more capable of apprehending the Gospel than it would have been at an earlier age, must be assumed, corresponding to the growth of the individual; since otherwise the metaphor would be robbed of more than half its meaning.[3]

The ancient world had accomplished many noble things, but had found no way to tame the human heart. Great advances had been made by the Greeks and Romans in architecture, philosophy, science, law, and literature. The Romans had developed indoor plumbing; a

---

3 J. B. Lightfoot, *The Epistle of St. Paul to the Galatians* (Grand Rapids: Zondervan Publishing House, 1974), 167–8.

system of aqueducts to bring fresh water to cities; a road system that blanketed the trade routes of the old world; and, a stable government that prevented regional wars. The Greeks had developed a form of natural culture; and made great advances in science, art, a common language, and a system of morality.

It was the fulness of time for the ancient philosophical systems, also. It was during that period of God's silence for four-hundred years that the Greek and Roman philosophers reached their zenith under Socrates (469–399 B.C.), Plato (427–347 B.C.), and Aristotle (384–322 B.C.). The greatest thinkers of all-time only proved what Paul wrote to the Corinthians: "For since in the wisdom of God, the world through its wisdom did not come to know God" (1 Corinthians 1:21). The world had run its course in its search for God through philosophy and had come up short. The great age of philosophy was over. The fulness of time for philosophy had been reached

The ancient world had reached the zenith of all its achievements by the time the Messiah came to earth. Yet, all those achievements had not accomplished what the world had hoped they would. The heathenistic religions were powerless to curb the wildness of fallen nature; or, stifle the guilty conscience; or, rein in the moral corruption of mankind. Instead of growing better, the ancient world was getting worse, despite their intellectual advancements. As James S. Stewart asked: "What was a whole pantheon of gods worth if they had nothing to say to a man with a broken heart?"[4] The replacement of those religions with the worship of Caesar brought no improvement to the situation. It only revealed the bankruptcy of all such man-made religions. Yet, all these advances, especially in the realm of morals, had run their course and had been found wanting. As Alfred Edersheim aptly summarized the situation:

> Religion, philosophy, and society had passed through every stage, to that of despair. Without tracing the various phases of ancient thought, it may be generally said that, in Rome at least, the issue lay between Stoicism[5] and Epicureanism.[6] The one flattered its pride, the other grat-

---

[4] Stewart, *The Life and Teaching of Jesus Christ*, 20.
[5] An ancient Greek school of philosophy started by Zeno of Citium, Cyprus who taught that virtue is the highest good and is based on knowledge. Thus, man is to submit to the divine reason and be indifferent towards either pleasure or pain.
[6] A school of philosophy founded in Athens by Epicurus. This school rejected any form of determinism and advocated a hedonistic lifestyle—pleasure as the highest good.

ified its sensuality; the one was in accordance with the original national character, the other with its later decay and corruption. Both ultimately led to atheism and despair—the one by turning all higher aspirations self-ward, the other, by quenching them in the enjoyment of the moment; the one, by making the extinction of all feeling and self-deification; the other, the indulgence of every passion and the worship of matter, its ideal.[7]

The Unification of the World Under the Roman Empire

One of the greatest preparations for the coming of Christ, though, was the unification of the civilized world through the Roman government, the Greek language, and the great roads built by the Romans that connected nations with one another. All these contributed to what is called the Pax Romana, the peace of Rome. As Stewart states:

> If Christ had come a century earlier, his gospel would have been blocked at every turn, blocked on the land by closed national frontiers, blocked on the ocean by the pirates who made the high seas impassable . . . But Christ came to a generation when the Roman peace held the world, held it no doubt with an iron hand, but held it sure and far-flung and unbroken; and men could hear the Bethlehem angels sing.[8]

The natural thirst for God in the heart of every man had not yet been quenched by any of the world's paltry solutions. From the rivers of Babylon to Hadrian's wall in the British Isles, wherever the Roman Empire extended, there was a deep-seated yearning for a new answer, a new hope. As Stewart comments:

> In many parts of the world men of deeper nature and more spiritual vision were peering into the darkness for some faint flush of dawn. Among the Jews themselves the hope of the Messiah was blazing more clearly than it had done for centuries. The great mass of Jewish literature from between the period of the Old Testament and the New Testament is full of this great hope. And when any new voice rang out across the land, the voice of a John the Baptist, for instance, immediately on every lip there rose the question—"Is this the Messiah now?" The air was tense with expectation. And the Jews, penetrating as they did into every corner of the empire, took that great dream with them and handed it on. Nothing cleared the way for Christ more definitely than that passionate hope. The fulness of the time had come.[9]

---

7 Alfred Edersheim, *The Life and Times of Jesus the Messiah* (Peabody, Mass.: Hendrickson Publishers, Inc., 1995), 178.
8 Stewart, *The Life and Teaching of Jesus Christ,* 17.
9 Stewart, *The Life and Teaching of Jesus Christ,* 20–21.

The Preparation of the World by the Jewish Dispersion

The Jews, ever since the Captivity, had been a dispersed people, inhabiting most every nation of the world. Many Jews had remained in Babylon, while others were known as "the Dispersion among the Greeks" (John 7:35) because they migrated westward into Europe. "A nation, the vast majority of which was dispersed over the whole inhabited earth, had ceased to be a special, and become a world-nation."[10] Yet, the Jews were despised among the nations according to the Jewish Sibyl[11]:

> Crowding with thy numbers every ocean and country—
> Yet an offense to all around by thy presence and customs![12]

Wherever they migrated, the Jews had carried with them the same sentiments expressed in Psalm 137:4–6 which was penned by the rivers of Babylon— "How can we sing the Lord's song in a foreign land? If I forget you, O Jerusalem, may my right hand forget her skill. May my tongue cling to the roof of my mouth if I do not remember you, if I do not exalt Jerusalem above my chief joy."

Jerusalem was the mother city of all Jews and there was a deep-seated loneliness in their hearts in whatever European cities they dwelt. They were citizens of Zion, the city of God, and they had only "one metropolis—not Alexandria, Antioch, or Rome—but 'the Holy City with its Temple, dedicated to the Most High God.'"[13] The loneliness of the Jews in their dispersion made them long even more for the "fullness of time" when the Messiah would come. Their dispersion also prepared the way for the reception of the gospel of Christ in every land where they sojourned because as James declared in Acts 15:21— "For Moses from ancient generations has in every city those who preach him, since he is read in the synagogues every Sabbath."

Those Jewish communities in dispersion were unable to successfully withdraw from the influences of the Greek culture that confronted them everywhere they went—in the marketplace, in their daily occupations, and in the education of their children. Their synagogues provided them their only safe haven from the pressures of a pagan world. Yet, the Greeks were also influenced by the Jews, as Edersheim notes:

---

10 Edersheim, *The Life and Times of Jesus the Messiah*, 5.
11 The name Sibyl has its roots in the Greek word, sibylla, which means prophetess. In Greek mythology, Sibyls were women who could foresee the future.
12 Edersheim, *The Life and Times of Jesus the Messiah*, 5, footnote number 12.
13 Edersheim, *The Life and Times of Jesus the Messiah*, 5.

> Witness here the many converts to Judaism among the Gentiles; witness also the evident preparedness of the lands of this dispersion for the new doctrine which was to come to Judea.[14]

In the providence of the Lord, even the Gentiles had been informed of the coming of the Messiah. The Egyptians were informed during the four hundred years the children of Israel were slaves in their land. The Assyrians and Babylonians were informed of His coming during the period that Israel and Judah were in captivity. The Roman Empire was informed through the Jewish Diaspora and the synagogues that were erected in every city.

Part of the testimony of God to the ancients was the revelation of His attributes in nature which is suppressed by the natural man, but can never be completely denied. Natural revelation was not enough, though. Something more was needed. The special revelation of God to His chosen prophets provided an infallible written message of truth concerning the way of salvation. And that message prophesied the coming of the Messiah "whose goings forth are from long ago, from the days of eternity" (Micah 5:2). John, the beloved disciple of Jesus, therefore, describes the Messiah as follows:

> In the beginning was the Word, and the Word was with God, and the Word was God. He was in the beginning with God. All things came into being through Him, and apart from Him nothing came into being that has come into being (John 1:1–3).

Jesus, the Word of God, came in the flesh to this world as the Messiah of God. He existed before all things and was the Creator along with His Father and the Holy Spirit of everything. God gave His only begotten Son to be the Savior of the world. That truth was the great message of the Old Testament prophets and the great message of the New Testament authors. While the promise of the Messiah was primarily given to the Jews, that message also went out to the whole world even before the birth of Jesus of Nazareth. Accordingly, Paul asked and answered the following question concerning the knowledge of the gospel which the Gentiles had heard:

> But I say, surely they have never heard, have they? Indeed they have; "Their voice has gone out into all the earth, and their words to the ends of the earth." (Romans 10:18).

Malachi 4:5, the penultimate verse of the Old Testament, prophe-

---

14 Edersheim, *The Life and Times of Jesus the Messiah*, 12.

sied that the next great event of the world would be the coming of the Messiah, "the sun of righteousness" who would "rise with healing in its wings" (Malachi 4:2). The Messiah would be preceded by the Forerunner who would come in the spirit of Elijah. A four hundred year period of silence then followed Malachi's prophecy in which there were no prophets of God to address the covenant nation. As dark as the days of Malachi were, when the people obstinately said, "Everyone who does evil is good in the sight of the Lord and He delights in them" (Malachi 2:17), the world was to become darker still.

The Virgin Mary Becomes Pregnant (Matthew 1:18-25; Luke 1:26-56)
Then, suddenly, the fulness of time came and God sent forth His Son to be born of a virgin. Every Christmas, believers world-wide sing Joseph Mohr's well-beloved hymn, *Silent Night, Holy* Night, whose first stanza says in part: "Round yon virgin mother and child." J. Gresham Machen, in his magnanimous book, *The Virgin Birth*, proved that all branches of the Christian Church from her earliest days held the virgin birth of Christ to be an essential article of faith. The birth of Jesus was supernatural because it was the birth of the eternal Son of God becoming flesh. It was also prophesied in Isaiah 7:14 that the Messiah would be born of a virgin. Thus, Edward J. Young remarks concerning Isaiah's use of the word, *almah*, to describe the woman who would give birth to this Child who would be a sign to the world:

> In the light of these considerations it appears that Isaiah's choice of *'almah* was deliberate. It seems to be the only word in the language which unequivocally signifies an unmarried woman
> . . . None of these other words would have pointed to an unusual birth. Only *'almah* makes clear that the mother was unmarried.
> If however, the mother is an unmarried woman, a question arises. Was the child illegitimate or not? If the child were illegitimate, would such a birth be a sign? The whole context, indeed the whole Biblical context, rules this out. On the other hand, if the mother were a good woman, then the birth was out of the ordinary, an unusual birth. The mother is both unmarried and a good woman. When this fact is considered, it becomes apparent that in all history there is only one of whom this can be predicated, namely, Mary, the mother of the Lord.[15]

Matthew and Luke both emphasize that Jesus was born of a virgin. John emphasizes that His birth was God becoming man and dwelling among us. Taken together, the various Gospels point un-

---

15 Edward J. Young, *The Book of Isaiah* (Grand Rapids: Eerdmans, 1978), 1:288-9.

mistakably to the virgin birth as the only possible meaning of Isaiah's prophecy. As extraordinary as that seems to an unbeliever, it is the cornerstone of the Christian faith. Only a Messiah who is God can be the object of faith. Otherwise, such faith would be idolatry. Only a man who was, in the words of Martin Luther's great hymn, "A Mighty Fortress is Our God," the "right man on our side, the man of God's own choosing," could be the expected Messiah. This "right man" had to be greater than the original man, Adam, who was created in the image of God and in His likeness (Genesis 1:26, 27). Adam was upright and holy in the beginning, but was mutable. This "right man" had to be both perfect and unchangeable. He had to be everything that God intended man to be. As Geoffrey Thomas wrote to me, this "right man" had to be "God's great definition of a man, the fullest embodiment of what it means to be human, the head of a new humanity whose God-ordained destiny is eternal life in a new heavens and earth with our Creator."[16] He had to be both God and man in one Person. What a great mystery is this. Of all God's miracles, the virgin birth of Jesus is the greatest. It answers that great question of St. Anselm in his book, *Cur Deus Homo*—or, *Why God Become Man*. The Christ had to be both God and man in order to satisfy God's justice *and* redeem man. Thus, Luke's narrative transitions from Hebron to Nazareth; from the pregnancy of Elizabeth in the fifth month to Gabriel's announcement that Mary, a virgin, would conceive and bear a Son whose name would be Jesus which name means "God with us" (Matthew 1:23).

Dorothy Sayers wrote in 1937 that "the Incarnation is the most dramatic thing about Christianity, and indeed, the most dramatic thing that ever entered into the mind of man, but if you tell people so, they stare at you in bewilderment."[17] Clive Stapleton Lewis wrote something very similar in his book, *Miracles*:

> The Central Miracle asserted by Christians is the Incarnation ... Every other miracle prepares for this, or exhibits this, or results from this ... The fitness, and therefore credibility, of this particular miracle depends on the relation to the Grand Miracle, all discussion of them in isolation from it is futile.[18]

---

16 Email from Rev. Geoffrey Thomas to the author on September 12, 2024.
17 Barbara Reynolds, ed., Dorothy Sayers, *The Letters of Dorothy Sayers* (Cambridge: Dorothy L. Sayers Society, 1997), 2:43.
18 C. S. Lewis, *Miracles* (New York: Touchstone, 1996), 143.

As great as the miracle of Jesus rising from the dead is, the Incarnation is even greater. The resurrection could not have and would not have happened if Christ was not the God-man, God in the flesh. The Incarnation, therefore, should be celebrated as the ultimate act of love and humility by which the Creator, the Word of God, "became flesh, and dwelt among us" (John 1:1–3, 14) for the purpose of redeeming us by His death and resurrection. Matthew, Luke, and John emphasize the Incarnation of Christ as the essential miracle in understanding who Jesus of Nazareth was (Cf. Matthew 1, 2; Luke 1, 2; and, John 1). Augustine summed up the importance of the Incarnation as well as anyone:

> Man's maker was made man, that He, Ruler of the stars, might nurse at His mother's breast;
> that the Bread might hunger, the Fountain thirst, the Light sleep, the Way be tired on its journey;
> that the Truth might be accused of false witness, the Teacher be beaten with whips, the Foundation be suspended on wood;
> that Strength might grow weak; that the Healer might be wounded;
> that Life might die.[19]

At the time of Gabriel's announcement of the virgin birth to her, Mary was already betrothed to Joseph, a descendant of David. Betrothal in ancient Israel was the first stage of marriage and typically lasted for a year. During that time, the parties could not come together, but they were legally obligated to consummate the relationship through a formal marriage. Thus, Edersheim comments:

> From the moment of her betrothal a woman was treated as if she was actually married. The union could not be dissolved, except by regular divorce; breach of faithfulness was regarded as adultery; and the property of the woman became virtually the property of her betrothed, unless he had expressly renounced it.[20]

These facts help to explain some of the intrigue that took place before Joseph was informed by the angel that Mary's pregnancy was an act of the Lord. Gabriel first announced to Mary that she would be with child: "The Holy Spirit will come upon you, and the power of the Most High will overshadow you and for that reason the holy Child shall be called the Son of God . . . For nothing will be impossible with

---

19 Jonathan Gibson, *O Come, O Come, Emmanuel* (Wheaton, IL: Crossway, 2023), 71. Gibson quotes from a sermon of Augustine in which the Church Father expressed those words.
20 Alfred Edersheim, *Sketches of Jewish Social Life in the Days of Christ* (London: James Clarke & Co., 1961), 148.

God" (Luke 1:35, 37). Mary was informed of more than that she was pregnant. She was informed that she was pregnant in such a way that with men it would be considered impossible. Mary's response to the angel throughout this announcement was an expression of deep faith. Where she did not understand, she pondered the matter in her heart and submissively acquiesced to the Lord's will, replying: "Behold, the bond slave of the Lord; may it be done to me according to your word" (Luke 1:38). As a relative of Elizabeth, Mary probably was aware of what happened to Zacharias when he questioned the angel. Yet, Mary was in a dangerous predicament, as Hendriksen notes:

> Mary knew that becoming pregnant at this particular time, before her marriage to Joseph had been consummated, would expose her to painful criticism and ridicule; perhaps to something even worse (see Deut. 22:23 ff.). But she made a complete surrender. She placed herself, body and soul, at the disposal of the God who loved her and who, by means of the promised pregnancy and childbirth, was bestowing on her an inestimable blessing.[21]

Instead of repining in discontent or withdrawing in fearfulness, Mary took the opposite approach. Her first response was to immediately journey to Hebron, some one hundred and twenty miles south of Nazareth, to share the good news with Elizabeth. Mary probably became pregnant almost immediately following Gabriel's visit, after which "she arose and went in a hurry to the hill country, to a city of Judah" (Luke 1:39) where Elizabeth and Zacharias lived. When she arrived there, Elizabeth's baby leaped in her womb for joy and she exclaimed: "Blessed *are* you among women, and blessed is the fruit of your womb! And how has it *happened* to me, that the mother of my Lord would come to me? ... And blessed *is* she who believed that there would be a fulfillment of what had been spoken to her by the Lord" (Luke 1:42, 43, 45). Mary then responded with what is called *The Magnificat*, a heartfelt exaltation of the Lord's greatness in granting both her and all believers salvation. Mary, in contradiction of all false representations of her sinlessness, acknowledged that she "rejoiced in God my Savior" (Luke 1:47). The whole passage is filled with quotes from the Old Testament, particularly the Psalms. Mary and Elizabeth both knew that God was fulfilling His covenant promises to send a Savior to Israel. Mary spent about three months with Elizabeth be-

---

21 William Hendriksen, *Exposition of the Gospel According to Luke* (Grand Rapids: Eerdmans, 1981), 90.

fore returning home. Most likely, she stayed until John was born as a helper to Elizabeth during the more difficult days of her pregnancy.

When Mary returned home to Nazareth, it was not yet evident that she was pregnant. At some point thereafter, though, "she was found to be with child by the Holy Spirit" (Matthew 1:18) before she and Joseph had come together as husband and wife. It cannot be determined when Mary informed Joseph of Gabriel's visit and when the Holy Spirit overshadowed her. Yet, it is known that Joseph, however he first learned of it, was initially incredulous and "planned to send her away secretly" (Matthew 1:19) in order not to disgrace her. It was at that time that the angel of the Lord appeared to him in a dream and said, "Joseph, son of David, do not be afraid to take Mary as your wife; for the Child who has been conceived in her is of the Holy Spirit" (Matthew 1:20). Joseph's patience of spirit and avoidance of anything rash was rewarded by a visitation from the Lord that resolved all the apparent contradictions. He was then satisfied and willingly kept Mary as a virgin until after she gave birth to the holy Child. The angel also told Joseph in the dream to name the Child "Jesus, for He will save His people from their sins" (Matthew 1:21).

Despite all the evidences that the birth of Jesus in Bethlehem was in fulfillment of the numerous prophecies concerning the Messiah, there always have been and always will be detractors, skeptics, and mockers—whether Jews or Gentiles. Edersheim's remarks concerning such unbelief are very appropriate:

> If the claims of Jesus have been rejected by the Jewish Nation, He has at least, undoubtedly, fulfilled one part of the Mission prophetically assigned to the Messiah. Whether or not He be the Lion of the tribe of Judah, to Him, assuredly, has been the gathering of the nations, and the isles have waited for His law . . . The world has known none other, none equal. And the world has owned it, if not by testimony of words, yet by the evidence of facts . . . If He be not the Messiah, He has at least thus far done the Messiah's work. If He be not the Messiah, there has at least been none other, before or after Him. If He be not the Messiah, the world has not, and never can have, a Messiah.[22]

---

22 Edersheim, *The Life and Times of Jesus the Messiah,* 127.

2

A Lowly Birth

Alexander B. Bruce wrote the following words concerning Hebrews 2:9–18:

"The grand thought, then, in this remarkable passage is this, that Christ to be a Saviour must be a Brother, and that, as things actually stand, that means that He must be humbled, must pass through a curriculum of temptation and suffering as a man, in order that He may be in all respects like unto His brethren."[1]

The little town of Bethlehem was conveniently situated on an east-west mountain ridge about six miles south of Jerusalem with valleys both to the north and the south. The prophet Micah referred to Bethlehem in his prophecy of the Messiah: "But as for you, Bethlehem Ephrathah, Too little to be among the clans of Judah, From you One will go forth for Me to be ruler in Israel, His goings forth are from long ago, From the days of eternity" (Micah 5:2). Bethlehem, as the birthplace of King David, was a city of great importance in ancient Israel, but it never achieved the significance of Jerusalem or even Gibeah where King Saul was born. Micah's prophecy concerning Bethlehem was a poignant reminder that this little village was not included in the list of the one hundred and fifteen cities and villages given by Joshua to the tribe of Judah (Cf. Joshua 15:21–63). It was in truth "too little to be among the clans of Judah."

Bethlehem, though, was the scene of the most-anticipated event of the ancient world—the birth of Jesus the Messiah—which took place in the latter part of 5 BC or the early part of 4 BC. Herod the Great was still the King of Israel when Jesus was born, but that despot died no later than April of 4 BC.[2] A strange confluence of events had worked together in the providence of God to accomplish the fulfillment of the ancient prophecies concerning the place of the Messiah's birth. The first great event was the decree of Caesar Augustus "that

---

[1] Alexander B. Bruce, *The Humiliation of Christ* (Grand Rapids: Eerdmans Publishing Co., 1955), 25-6.
[2] Josephus tells us that an eclipse of the moon happened shortly before Herod died. The date of that eclipse was March 12-13, 4 B.C. The Passover took place that year on April 11th and Herod died before it. Thus, Herod died between March 12th and April 11th in 4 B.C.

a census be taken of all the inhabited earth" (Luke 2:1). The purpose of that census was for the better collection of taxes, especially in the lands under the rule of Herod who had fallen out of favor with Rome in 8–7 BC. At that time, Augustus decided that Rome would collect the taxes instead of using Herod as the middleman. Thus, all the citizens of Israel were required to register in the cities of their birth for this census. That decree compelled Jesus' parents to leave their home in Nazareth and journey to Bethlehem.[3] When they arrived in that little town, Joseph and Mary found that the caravansary[4] was crowded with guests and there was no room in the inn that was connected to the caravansary. Thus, Luke 2:6, 7 records:

> While they were there, the days were completed for her to give birth. And she gave birth to her firstborn son: wrapped Him in cloths, and laid Him in a manger, because there was no room in the inn.

Initially, Joseph and Mary must have slept in the courtyard of the caravansary while Joseph was fulfilling his enrollment according to law. When the time arrived, the grotto[5] below the caravansary, where the small animals were protected at night, became the birth place of the Son of God. Thus, a "manger" or a stall carved out of the rock was used as the place to lay the newborn Child. J. C. Ryle aptly remarks concerning the lowly circumstances of Jesus' birth:

> One fact should be carefully noted here, which is often overlooked. In the providence of God the birth of Christ was attended with as much publicity as a birth could possibly be attended with. It took place at an inn, and an inn crowded with strangers from all parts. Imposture was thus rendered impossible. The event was patent to many witnesses, and could never be denied. The Son of God was really incarnate, and literally and really born of woman, like any of ourselves. Had the birth taken place quietly in Nazareth, or in some private house at Bethlehem, in thirty years' time the whole would probably have been denied.[6]

---

3 Nazareth to Bethlehem would have been a three days journey under the best of circumstances. With Mary already pregnant, with the shortened days of fall and winter, and with the highways crowded by other travelers going to their own cities, the journey would have been harder and taken longer.
4 A caravansary was a "large bare building surrounding a court in eastern countries where caravans rest at night" (*Webster's New Collegiate Dictionary*, 1975).
5 A grotto is a cave which has been prepared as a shelter for animals or men.
6 J. C. Ryle, *Expository Thoughts on Luke* (Edinburgh and Carlisle, PA: Banner of Truth Trust, 2006), 1:55.

In *The Christ of the Gospels*, J. W. Shepard comments on the various stories in Matthew and Luke concerning the first few months of Jesus' life:

> The stories which cluster around the nativity of Jesus are full of idyllic charm . . . Luke desired to give a more complete account of His life and so added the beautiful narrative of his lineage; His birth, and announcement to the Judean shepherds. Matthew desiring to link the person of the Messiah up with the ancient prophecy gave his own independent account. Luke narrates in simplicity and brevity, with consummate art the circumstances of the birth, and adds the testimony of various divinely chosen witnesses, who give the interpretation of the world-wide significance of the event. Matthew adds to this testimony of universal interest, introducing the narrative of the Magi, the providential flight into Egypt, and return to Nazareth in fulfillment of God's plan revealed in prophecy . . . They agree in the Davidic descent, in the account of His humble origin, and in the profound and universal interest in the event on the part of Jew and Gentile, the royal Idumean ruler and the humble peasant class, the wise scientists and ignorant shepherds.[7]

It is generally accepted that Matthew records the lineage of Jesus through Joseph (Matthew 1:1–17) and that Luke records the lineage through Mary (Luke 3:23–38), but there are some who assert that both genealogies are through Mary.[8] It is not important for us to resolve that question because Jesus was both God and man. Mary was supernaturally impregnated by the Holy Spirit and her Child was born of a virgin, as the Scripture declares. Matthew traces Jesus' lineage back to Abraham and Luke goes back to Adam. Both writers prove that Jesus, according to the flesh, was a descendant of David and Abraham through the tribe of Judah. Interestingly, Jesus was not a pure Israelite (or Semite) because his genealogy shows that he was a descendant of both Ruth the Moabitess and Rahab the harlot who was a Canaanite. That only proves that most of the greatest men of Israel were not pure Israelites either. Thus, Jesus was not just a Jew. He was the Messiah of all people throughout the world who will believe in Him.

---

7 J. W. Shepard, *The Christ of the Gospels* (Grand Rapids: Eerdmans, 1939), 29.
8 J. Gresham Machen, *The Virgin Birth of Christ*, (Cambridge: James Clarke & Co., 2022), 203 ff. Machen believed that Matthew gave the legal descendants of David who were heirs of his throne while Luke gave the actual descendants of David down to Joseph.

The Visit of the Shepherds (Luke 2:8–20)

In Micah 4:8, there was a prophecy concerning the coming of the kingdom that was associated with "the tower of the flock," which says: "As for you, tower of the flock, hill of the daughter of Zion, to you it will come—even the dominion will come, the kingdom of the daughter of Jerusalem." The tower of the flock is a reference to a tower in the valley between Jerusalem and Bethlehem called the Migdal Eder. McClintock and Strong state about this tower in their Cyclopedia:

> Migdal-Edar ("tower of the flock"), a place on the route of Jacob (Gen. xxxv, 21), probably about two miles south of Jerusalem, near the Bethlehem road, where the cluster of ruins called Kirbet Um-Moghdala is now situated.[9]

According to the Jewish Mishna,[10] flocks tended in those fields "were destined for the Temple-sacrifices."[11] The males among the flocks became burnt offerings and the females became peace offerings. This was the most important flock among all the flocks in Israel. In these fields, David had once tended sheep. The tower of the flock was erected by Jacob in memory of his wife who died in those fields while giving birth to her youngest son, Benjamin (cf. Genesis 35:16–21). It is written that Jacob, then, "pitched his tent beyond the tower of Eder" (Genesis 35:21). The Hebrew for "tower of Eder" is Migdal Eder. Probably due to the prophecy of Micah 4:8, there was a long held belief among the Jews "that the Messiah was to be revealed from this 'tower of the flock.'"[12] Of course, a few verses later in Micah 5:2 there is that very clear prophecy that the Messiah would be born in Bethlehem Ephrathah. So, it is consistent with the Biblical prophecies that the Messiah, the Son of David and the Lamb of God, would be revealed to those very shepherds who were "staying out in the fields and keeping watch over their flock by night" (Luke 2:8). Thus, the Scriptural account of that angelic announcement to the shepherds continues:

> And an angel of the Lord suddenly stood before them, and the glory

---

9 John McClintock and James Strong, Cyclopedia of Biblical, Theological, and Ecclesiastical Literature (Grand Rapids: Baker Book House, 1981), 6:249.
10 The Mishna is the collection of the oral traditions of the Jews and is also known as the oral Torah (law).
11 Shepard, *The Christ of the Gospels*, 32.
12 Shepard, *The Christ of the Gospels*, 32.

of the Lord shone around them, and they were terribly frightened. But the angel said to them, 'Do not be afraid; for behold, I bring you good news of great joy which will be for all the people; for today in the city of David there has been born for you a Savior, who is Christ the Lord. This will be a sign for you; you will find a baby wrapped in cloths lying in a manger' (Luke 2:9–12).

The shepherds knew that the "manger" would be in the caves of the grotto under the caravansary where the unblemished ewe lambs[13] were protected shortly after their birth. Thus, the One sent forth to be the Lamb of God was laid in the very cave where the types of His sacrifice were housed when young. Yet, before they could make haste to go to Bethlehem, there suddenly appeared to them "a multitude of the heavenly host praising God and saying, 'Glory to God in the highest, and on earth peace among men with whom he is pleased'" (Luke 2:13, 14). Both Mary and Zacharias had given thanks to the Lord for the redemption and salvation that the birth of Jesus would bring to sinners (Luke 1:47, 68). Now, these holy angels announce this salvation to the shepherds. J. C. Ryle explains the significance of this truth:

> They were angels, and not men.—angels who had never sinned, and needed no Saviour,—angels who had not fallen, and required no redeemer, and no atoning blood. The first hymn to the honour of "God manifested in the flesh," was sung by "a multitude of the heavenly host."[14]

The greatest event of the world necessitated the greatest choir to sing those beautiful words. The shepherds had to have been captivated by the melodious and seraphic music being sung to them by the heavenly host. Then, as suddenly as the angels had appeared to the shepherds, they vanished from their sight. The effect on the shepherds was such that they "began saying to one another, 'Let us go straightway to Bethlehem then, and see this thing that has happened which the Lord has made known to us'" (Luke 1:15). Their journey was probably two or miles, depending on how close to the Migdal Eder they were and how far north of Bethlehem they were watching their flocks. When they arrived in Bethlehem, they soon "found their way to Mary and Joseph, and the baby as He lay in the manger. When

---

13 The lambs that were destined for Temple sacrifices had to be unblemished and, therefore, were taken out of the flocks for their protection while they were still young. The caves where they were kept were clean enough for the Child to be laid in one of the openings.
14 Ryle, *Expository Thoughts on Luke*, 1:57.

they had seen this, they made known the statement which had been told them about this Child" (Luke 2:16, 17).

In the caravansary above the grotto, there were multitudes of people gathered together and the coming of the shepherds would have been noticed by almost everyone. The remarks of the shepherds to the parents were soon known to many people with the result that "all who heard it wondered at the things which were told them" (Luke 2:18), but "Mary treasured all these things, pondering them in her heart" (Luke 2:19). When the shepherds began traveling back to the fields where their flocks lay, they were "glorifying and praising God for all that they had heard and seen" (Luke 2:20).

These shepherds became the first "preachers" of the gospel—the first messengers to the world that the Messiah had come. The angels did not appear to the crowds pressed upon one another in the caravansary. The angels did not go to the priests, scribes, lawyers, and Pharisees in Jerusalem to sing their wonderful songs. Those religious leaders were more interested in maintaining their traditions than in rejoicing in the coming of the Messiah. Instead, the angels appeared to simple shepherds. Even if they tended the flocks that would be offered in the Temple sacrifices, they still were shepherds. Even if they were not as despised as other shepherds, they were still despised by most Jews—and certainly they were despised by the religious leaders in Jerusalem. Yet, the Lord chose what men considered to be foolish things to shame the proud and the wise (cf. 1 Corinthians 1:26–29).

Jesus' Presentation in the Temple (Luke 2:21–38)
On the eighth day after a male child was born, the Mosaic law required that the baby would be circumcised (Genesis 17:12; Leviticus 12:3). Circumcision had become the sign of the Abrahamic covenant because it signified the cleansing from the sin that was transferred from one generation to the next through procreation. As the Son of God, Jesus was perfect and had no sin. Having been born of a virgin through the activity of the Holy Spirit, the sinful natures of His earthly parents were not transferred to His human flesh. But He came into this world to accomplish the redemption of His people and that required Him to both keep the law and to undergo in our place all the punishment we deserve for breaking the law. Thus, Jesus was circumcised on the eighth day in strict conformity with the Mosaic laws. He did so for two reasons. First, circumcision was "a seal of the righ-

teousness of faith," according to Romans 4:11. Adam had disobeyed God through unbelief. Jesus, as the second Adam, was full of faith at all times and always did what was pleasing to His Father. Second, circumcision was the removal of the foreskin of the flesh as a sign of the cleansing of our sinful natures through God's grace. Jesus had no sin in Himself, but as our redeemer He assumed our sinful natures when He stood in our place. As 2 Corinthians 5:21 states: "He made Him who knew no sin *to be* sin in our behalf, so that we might become the righteousness of God in Him." It was necessary for Jesus, therefore, to become our sin-bearer so that He could later offer Himself as a holy sacrifice for our sins.

Thirty-three days after His circumcision, Joseph and Mary took Jesus back to the Temple to perform the sacrifices required for a male child. Typically, the parents were to bring a one year old lamb for a burnt offering and either a pigeon or a turtle dove for a sin offering. If the parents were too poor to offer a lamb, then they could substitute two turtle doves or two pigeons. One of the birds would be the burnt offering and the other would be the sin offering. Joseph and Mary were only able to do the latter which is one more indication of their poverty. Shepard describes the scenery for this ceremony:

> Two offerings were made in the purification of the mother; the offering for Levitical defilement attached to the beginning of life, and burnt offering for restoration of communion with God. The price of the two turtle doves or pigeons was dropped in the third of the thirteen trumpet shaped collection boxes in the Court of the Women. The sacrifices were supplied by the Temple vendors. The ministrants arranged those women who had presented themselves, in the designated place beside the Nacanor gate[15], where they would be nearest the Sanctuary and the Court of Israel and could accompany the acts of sacrifice and see the cloud of incense—symbol especially of their prayers—rise from the golden altar.[16]

When these sacrifices were made, the mother was then ceremonially cleansed and restored to participation in all the other ceremonies of the Temple. The actual presentation of the Child to the priest for his blessings took place once five shekels were paid. "The priest on receiving the child would pronounce two blessings—one in thanksgiving for

---

15 The Nicanor gate was also called the Beautiful Gate (cf. Acts 3:2) and stood in front of the Temple and gave access to the Temple from the Court of Women.
16 Shepard, *The Christ of the Gospels*, 34.

the law of redemption and another for the gift of the first born son."[17] While religious worship was at a low ebb in Israel at the time of Jesus' birth and presentation, there were various devoted saints, like Simeon to whom "it had been revealed by the Holy Spirit that He would not see death before he had seen the Lord's Christ" (Luke 2:26). Another woman of faith was Anna, the prophetess, "the daughter of Phanuel, of the tribe of Asher[18]" (Luke 2:36). "She never left the temple, serving night and day with fastings and prayers" (Luke 2:37). She would have been one of those people who were fervently praying while Zacharias, the father of John, was inside the Temple performing his duties a year earlier. Of course, Zacharias and Elizabeth, and Joseph and Mary, were also among the holy remnant of devoted Israelites who were looking for the consolation of Israel. Whatever blessing the priest made over the Child, Simeon himself was filled with the Holy Spirit when he took Jesus in his arms and praised God, saying:

> Now Lord, You are releasing Your bond-servant to depart in peace, according to Your word; for my eyes have seen Your salvation, which You have prepared in the presence of all peoples, a light of revelation to the Gentiles, and the glory of Your people Israel (Luke 2:29–32).

Concerning these words of Simeon, Alfred Plummer made the following statement:

> The *Nunc Dimittis*.[19] In its suppressed rapture and vivid intensity this canticle equals the most beautiful of the Psalms. Since the fifth century it has been used in the evening services of the Church . . . and has often been the hymn of dying saints. It is the sweetest and most solemn of all the canticles . . .
>
> Symeon presents himself as a servant or watchman released from duty, because that for which he was commanded to watch has appeared.[20]

Simeon's words read like one who had a charge from the Lord for which he patiently waited until the time came when he was released from his duty station. When he saw the Christ Child, Simeon knew that in Him the Lord would accomplish salvation. Now he was released. Whether he knew of the visit of the angels to the shepherds

---

17 Shepard, *The Christ of the Gospels*, 34.
18 Asher was one of the ten so-called lost tribes. Many in those ten tribes did not return to the land after the captivity, but some of them did, as was the case of the ancestors of Anna.
19 Nunc Dimittis is the traditional "Gospel Canticle" of the evening prayer.
20 Alfred Plummer, *A Critical and Exegetical Commentary on the Gospel of S. Luke* (Edinburgh: T & T Clark, 1960), 67.

is not clarified. What is evident is that, being full of the Spirit, it was miraculously revealed to him that Jesus was the long-awaited Messiah. With that revelation, Simeon felt that he could "depart in peace" (Luke 2:29). In his blessing of the Child, He said to Mary: "Behold, this *Child* is appointed for the fall and rise of many in Israel, and for a sign to be opposed—and a sword will pierce even your own soul—to the end that thoughts from many hearts may be revealed" (Luke 2:34, 35). William Hendriksen explains the meaning of Simeon's blessing:

> Simeon now invoked God's blessing on Joseph and Mary. Having done this, he addressed to Mary words that must have startled her. In substance he told her that her child would become the great divider; not however, that events would simply turn out that way, but that in God's plan it had been so decided. Literally what he said was, "Mark well, this child is set for the falling and rising of many in Israel . . . ." In other words a person's relation or attitude toward Jesus would be absolutely decisive of his eternal destiny. Some would reject him; others would by sovereign grace accept him. The former would fall; that is, they would (unless they repented) be excluded from the kingdom. The latter would rise; that is, they would be welcomed to the kingdom and its wedding feast.[21]

On that same occasion, there was an elderly prophetess, Anna, who was constantly serving the Lord at the Temple through prayer and fasting. When she saw the Child, she immediately started telling others about Him who were also "looking for the redemption of Jerusalem" (Luke 2:38). Like Simeon and others, Anna had been waiting for the time to be fulfilled when the Lord would send forth His Son to be the redeemer of all who would believe in Him.

> And she spoke about the Child, especially to the group of righteous people in Jerusalem who were also looking forward to the redemption of God that He would bring through the Messiah. For this reason the coming of Jesus became known in a comparatively wide circle—but only among those faithful souls who had earnestly hoped for His coming.[22]

In light of these events, it is a wonder that more people in Jerusalem and Israel did not become aware of the mission of Jesus at this time. Yet, the truth was hidden from the wise and revealed to those who became like little children before the Lord.

---

21 Hendriksen, *Exposition of the Gospel According to Luke*, 169–170.
22 Norval Geldenhuys, *Commentary on the Gospel of Luke* (Grand Rapids: Eerdmans, 1960), 121.

The Visit of the Magi (Matthew 2:1–12)

In 1606, Johannes Kepler, the father of modern astronomy, wrote *De Stella Nova* (*The New Star*) in which he showed that "the most remarkable conjunction of planets—that of Jupiter and Saturn in the constellation of Pisces— . . .[took] place no less than three times in the year 747 AUC[23], or two years before the birth of Christ (in May, October and December)."[24] The following year, this conjunction was augmented by Mars, producing a supernova which was a "brilliant spectacle in the in the night-sky, such as could not but attract the attention of all who watched the sidereal heavens."[25] The astronomers-astrologers of the east would have been very observant of that amazing phenomena. Alfred Edersheim notes that there were predictions in some of the collections of three Midrashim that the Jews themselves were expecting a star to appear in the eastern sky two years before the birth of the Messiah.[26]

It is an interesting fact that Matthew, who wrote his Gospel primarily for the Jews, is the one who recorded the visitation of the "magi from the east" (Matthew 2:1). Who were these "magi"? "The term magi was used as the name for priests and wise men among the Medes, Persians, and Babylonians . . . To their number doubtless belonged the astrologers and star-gazers (Isa. xlvii, 13)."[27] "At the period in question the sacerdotal caste of the Medes and Persians was dispersed over various parts of the East, and the presence in those lands of a large Jewish diaspora, through which they might, and probably would, gain knowledge of the great hope of Israel, is sufficiently attested by Jewish history."[28] Thus, these magi were probably awaiting

---

23 747 AUC was 7 BC inasmuch as 749 BC was 5 BC and generally considered the year of Christ's birth.
24 Edersheim, *The Life and Times of Jesus the Messiah*, 148. This conjunction is acknowledged by all astronomers.
25 Edersheim, *The Life and Times of Jesus the Messiah*, 148.
26 Edersheim, *The Life and Times of Jesus the Messiah*, 147–8. Those midrashim were titled respectively, 'The Book of Elijah;' 'Chapters about the Messiah;' and, 'The Mysteries of R. Simon, the son of Jochai.' As Edersheim states: The statement is equally remarkable whether it represents a tradition previous to the birth of Jesus, or originated after that event. But two years before the birth of Christ . . . brings us to the year 747 AUC, or 7 before Christ, in which such a star should appear in the East." What that star was cannot be accurately determined, though.
27 McClintock and Strong, *Cyclopedia of Biblical, Theological, and Ecclesiastical Literature*, 5:632. Magi was used in the Scripture in both a good sense and a bad sense. Thus, Simon Magus was titled by the singular of the word.
28 Edersheim, *The Life and Times of Jesus the Messiah*, 141–2. He also notes that the kings of Yemen were Jewish from 120 B.C to the sixth century A.D. which made for close intercourse between Palestine and Arabia.

A Lowly Birth

the coming of the Messiah even as the righteous descendants of Abraham in the holy land were as well.

How was it, though, that these wise men of the east were informed of the birth of the Jewish Messiah? In the ancient world, there was a very sophisticated machine called the "Antikythera mechanism" which was used to chart the movement of the stars. That mechanism was invented by the Greeks about one hundred fifty years before Christ and has been called the world's first analog computer. It is the most technologically complex object that has been discovered from the ancient world. Recovered in 1900 from an ancient shipwreck near the tiny Greek island of Antikythera, it was studied by scientists and archaeologists for over a century. Only recently was it reconstructed—a task that had baffled modern scientists for years while enigmas still remain concerning it. Some of the design of the mechanism relied on wisdom from Middle Eastern scientists which means that the magi undoubtedly used it to chart the courses of the stars in the heaven. Observing the dazzling conjunction of stars in the sky at night several times in 7 and 6 BC, they would have learned from the Antikythera mechanism which planets were in alignment. Thus, these magi started their journey to Jerusalem sometime in 5 BC, so that they also could worship the One born King of the Jews.

When the magi suddenly appeared in Jerusalem asking where the King of the Jews was born, it was very troubling to Herod and all the people (Matthew 2:2, 3). Herod the Great was a despotic ruler who was very jealous of his kingdom. Therefore, he "called together all the chief priests and scribes of the people" and "inquired of them where the Messiah was to be born" (Matthew 2:4). Most every Jew in Jerusalem was aware of Micah's prophecy that the Messiah would be born in Bethlehem and that is what the priests and scribes told Herod. Secretly and surreptitiously in order to avoid attention, Herod "called the wise men and determined from them the exact time the star appeared" (Matthew 2:5). Thus, Herod told them, "Go and search carefully for the Child, and when you have found *Him*, report to me, so that I too may come and worship Him" (Matthew 2:8). After leaving Herod's court, "the star, which they had seen in the east, went on before them until it came and stood over the place where the Child was. When they saw the star, they rejoiced exceedingly with great joy. After coming into the house they saw the Child with His mother, and they fell to the ground and worshiped Him. Then, opening their treasures, they presented to Him gifts of gold, frankincense, and myrrh" (Matthew 2:9–11). The number of the magi cannot be determined and was probably more than the three different types of gifts given to the Child. By this time, Joseph, Mary, and Jesus were living in a house in Bethlehem and there is every reason to assume that they planned to remain in that sacred place.

The Flight to Egypt (Matthew 2:13–15)

When the magi were "warned by God in a dream not to return to Herod" but "left for their country by another way" (Matthew 2:12), everything changed for Joseph, Mary and the newborn Child. That same night, Joseph was warned in a dream that Herod was "going to search for the Child to destroy Him" (Matthew 2:12) and was told to take "the Child and His mother and flee to Egypt and remain there until I tell you" (Matthew 2:12). Joseph obeyed immediately and "got up and took the Child and His mother while it was still night, and left for Egypt" (Matthew 2:13). At that time, Jesus would have been a babe of only a few months with a hard journey ahead of Him. J. W. Shepard points us in the direction of where Joseph might have taken his family:

> The nearest place of safety to which Joseph could flee with his family was Egypt, to the nearest borders of which was a distance of seventy-five miles. Tradition says they penetrated more than a hundred miles within the country and abode for a year in a Jewish colony, in the village of Motorea[29] near Leviantapolis[30], the site of a great Jewish temple built in 150 B.C. There were more than a million Jews in Egypt at the time, and the colony was highly respectable and influential in the country. Thus the infant Saviour was snatched from the savage fury of the wicked tyrant.[31]

How much of this legend about Jesus' time in Egypt is true, we simply cannot know for certain. Yet, it does seem likely Joseph would have sought the company of other Jews dispersed in that land. Matthew saw in this event a fulfillment of the prophecy of Hosea, "Out

---

29 El Matareya (Al Matariyyah in Arabic) is a town along the Mediterranean coast in the Dakahlia Governate of Egypt. Shepard's reference to Motorea is most certainly this city. It is not to be confused with the town by the same name in the eastern area of Cairo, Egypt.
30 Perhaps Leviantapolis is Leontopolis where a Jewish temple was built over the ruins of a temple to Bubastis, the lioness-goddess. It was built during the Hellenistic and Roman period for Jewish worship and sacrifice. Josephus says it was in the district of Heliopolis. It was located along the Delta region of the lower Nile River.
31 Shepard, *The Christ of the Gospels*, 40.

of Egypt I called My Son" (Hosea 11:1). The earlier exodus of Israel from Egypt, therefore, was a type of Jesus' own exodus after the death of Herod.

Herod's Slaughter of the Male Children (Matthew 2:16–19)

The malignancy of Herod was soon manifested in the slaying of all the male children in Bethlehem under the age of two—the time when the star first appeared to the magi in the east. Perceiving that he had been tricked by the magi, "he became very enraged" (Matthew 2:16) and sent soldiers to carry out those terrible executions. By seeking to "destroy" Jesus, Herod became Satan's instrument of evil (Revelation 12:4). The little town of Bethlehem where such rejoicing had taken place only a few months earlier was now a Bochim (Judges 2:1, 5)—"a place of weepers." Matthew found in this event the fulfillment of Jeremiah 31:15—"A voice was heard in Ramah, weeping and great mourning, Rachel weeping for her children; and she refused to be comforted, because they were no more" (Matthew 2:18). Herod's vengeful action was typical of his reign, particularly of his last days. The number of male children killed was probably small in comparison to similar such deeds that despot had committed, but it was brutal nonetheless, as Edersheim comments:

> As always in the history of Christ, so here also, glory and suffering appear in juxtaposition. It could not be, that these Magi should become the innocent instruments of Herod's murderous designs; nor yet that the Infant-Saviour should fall a victim to the tyrant . . . Baffled in the hope of attaining his object through the Magi, the reckless tyrant sought to secure it by an indiscriminate slaughter of all the children in Bethlehem and its immediate neighborhood. From two years and under. True, considering the population of Bethlehem, their number could only have been small, probably only twenty at most. But the deed was none the less atrocious; and these infants may justly be regarded as the 'protomartyrs,' the first witnesses of Christ, 'the blossom of martyrdom.'[32]

---

32 Edersheim, *The Life and Times of Jesus the Messiah*, 149.

3

Early Life in Nazareth

"Nazareth was the town of Joseph and Mary, to which they returned with the infant Jesus . . . after the accomplishment of the events connected with his birth and earliest infancy (Matt. ii.22) . . . The secluded nature of the spot where it stands, together with its own insignificance, probably combined to shroud it in that obscurity on account of which it would seem to have been divinely chosen for the rearing of God's incarnate Son. As his forerunner, John the Baptist, 'was in the desert,' unnoticed and unknown, 'till the day of his showing unto Israel,' so the great Messiah himself, till his public ministry began, was hidden from the world among the Galilean hills."[1]

In the early part of 4 BC, perhaps March or April, Herod the Great died after a protracted and painful sickness at the age of 69. In his last years he suffered from chronic kidney disease, Fournier's gangrene,[2] and finally succumbed to the maggot infested disease which ravaged his body.[3] Herod, the tyrant, was dominated by paranoia, but he had undertaken colossal building programs during his earlier years. The renovation of the Second Temple and the expansion of the Temple Mount towards the north; the Tomb of the Patriarchs (considered by Jews to be the second-most important place in the world); Caesarea Maritime; and, the fortress at Masada were some of his other projects. Some of the cities that Herod built were fortifications to protect himself from the Jewish masses with whom he was unpopular. "In the temple which Herod built to Augustus in Caesarea, there were statues of the Emperor as Olympian Zeus, and of Rome as Hera."[4] Greek and Syrian worship predominated throughout these newly built towns which was

---

1 McClintock and Strong, *Cyclopedia of Biblical, Theological, and Ecclesiastical Literature*, 6:875.
2 Fournier's gangrene is a rare, but serious condition which is often life-threatening. It is a form of necrotizing fasciitis that affects the genitalia, scrotum, and anus of mostly men and kills soft tissues, including muscles, nerves, and blood vessels.
3 Amanda Onion, "Researchers Diagnose Herod the Great," (ABC News, January 7, 2006). Accessed on May 26, 2021 at: https://abcnews.go.com/Technology/story?id=98107&page=1. Jan Hirshmann was a physician at the Veterans Affairs Puget Sound Health Care System who examined all the clues found in historical documents and books, including the works of Josephus.
4 Edersheim, *The Life and Times of Jesus the Messiah*, 61.

justified by Herod as necessary for political reasons. Yet, Herod was also ruthless as testified by his slaughter of the innocent sons in Bethlehem (Matthew 2:16) and the murder of three of his own sons, as well as his second wife, Mariamne I. For their part, the Jews always "hated the Idumaean; they detested his semi-heathen reign; they abhorred his deeds of cruelty . . . So long as he lived, no woman's honor was safe, no man's life secure."[5] The weeping of Rachel for her slaughtered children at Bethlehem (Matthew 2:18; Jeremiah 31:15) was for good reason not expressed when this despotic ruler went to his grave.

When Herod died, an angel of the Lord informed Joseph through a dream and said, "Get up, take the Child and His mother, and go into the land of Israel; for those who sought the Child's life are dead" (Matthew 2:20). Joseph, Mary, and the Child had probably spent only a matter of months in Egypt before they were able to return to Israel. Once Joseph learned that Herod's son, Archelaus[6], was now the ruler of Judea, he decided to settle in Nazareth instead of Jerusalem or Bethlehem. That was a wise decision inasmuch as Archelaus began his reign by disposing of the High Priestly office for his own purposes and imitating his father's ruthlessness towards his opponents. "But he far surpassed him in cruelty, oppression, luxury, the grossest egotism, and the lowest sensuality."[7] The quaint village of Nazareth had been the home of Joseph and Mary before Jesus was born and now they returned to familiar surroundings.

Nazareth, Jesus' Boyhood Home (Matthew 2:19–23)

Nazareth, at the time Jesus lived there, was a small town of perhaps four or five hundred residents. It was situated on the northern side of the most southern range of hills of Lower Galilee. It rests in a basin among the hills and is hidden from the Plain of Esdraelon. Fifteen hilltops surround Nazareth like a natural amphitheater with the little town nestled on the lower slopes, "its narrow streets

---

5 Edersheim, *The Life and Times of Jesus the Messiah*, 90.
6 Archelaus went to Rome in 4 BC to defend his claims as the rightful heir of Herod against his brothers, Philip and Herod Antipas. Caesar Augustus conferred on Archelaus the title of ethnarch, not king, and gave him the largest portion of Herod's kingdom—Judea, Idumaea, and Samaria. The lesser title indicated his dependence on Rome for his rule. Archelaus' name means 'ruler of the people', but he was never popular with his subjects. He was half Idumaean and half Samaritan and was considered an alien oppressor by the Jews.
7 Edersheim, *The Life and Times of Jesus the Messiah* 153.

arranged like terraces."[8]. The highest of those hills are only four hundred to five hundred feet in elevation and their limestone tops are rounded. The situation of Nazareth itself among those hills has been thusly described:

> The traveller coming from the south, ascends the mountain range by a steep and rugged path, which, winding onwards and upwards through the hills, brings him suddenly into a small sequestered hollow among their summits; and, here, nestling itself close in at the base of the loftiest of the encircling heights, he beholds—what must be to the Christian one of the most profoundly interesting scenes on the face of the earth—the home for thirty years of the Saviour of the world . . . the enclosed valley is particularly rich and well cultivated: it is filled with cornfields, with gardens, hedges of cactus, and clusters of fruit-bearing trees. Being so sheltered by hills, Nazareth enjoys a mild climate. Hence all the fruits of the country—as pomegranates, oranges, figs, olives—ripen early and attain a rare perfection.[9]

Yet, magnificent scenes could also be viewed from the crest of the hill just south of Nazareth, as George Adam Smith describes:

> Esdraelon lies before you, with its twenty battle-fields—the scenes of Barak's and Gideon's victories, the scenes of Saul's and Josiah's defeats, the scenes of the struggles for freedom in the glorious days of the Maccabees. There is Naboth's vineyard and the place of Jehu's revenge upon Jezebel; there Shunem and the house of Elisha; there Carmel and the place of Elijah's sacrifice. To the east the Valley of the Jordan, with the long range of Gilead; to the west the radiance of the Great Sea, with the ships of Tarshish and the promise of the isles. You see thirty miles in three directions. It is a map of Old Testament history.[10]

It is easy to imagine Jesus climbing to the southern crest of those hills, "every village boys' playground,"[11] and spending hours viewing the scenery before Him. In one respect, there was no better place for Him to have spent His childhood than in that despised town. The Via Maris ("the way of the sea") was an ancient trade route dating from the Byzantine period and it connected Akko (also known as Acre) on the Palestinian coast with Damascus. One branch of the great highway separated near Nazareth and went towards Cana, while the other

---

8 Edersheim, *The Life and Times of Jesus the Messiah*, 103.
9 McClintock and Strong, *Cyclopedia of Biblical, Theological, and Ecclesiastical Literature*, 6:876.

10 George Adam Smith, *The Historical Geography of the Holy Land* (London: Hodder and Stoughton, 1900), 433.
11 Smith, *The Historical Geography of the Holy Land*, 433.

branch went just north of Mount Tabor towards the Sea of Galilee (also known as Lake Tiberias or the Lake of Gennesaret). From the crest of the hilltops, Jesus could watch the various traders and caravans passing below and see the commerce of the world. Sometimes, those caravans would stop in Nazareth for a respite before continuing on their journeys. "The quiet little town was not a stagnant pool of rustic seclusion."[12] Men from many nations would appear on the narrow streets of Nazareth with regularity. Or, if He ventured with His brothers or friends to the "northern edge of their hollow home, there was another road within sight,"[13] as Smith tells us, which brought other sights to view:

> The Roman ranks, the Roman eagles, the wealth of nobleman's litters and equipages cannot have been strange to the eyes of the boys of Nazareth . . . Nor can it have been the eye only which was stirred. For all the rumor of the Empire entered Palestine close to Nazareth—the news from Rome, about the Emperor's health, about the changing influence of the great statesmen, about the prospects at court of Herod, or of the Jews; about Caesar's last order concerning the tribute, or whether the policy of the Procurator would be sustained.[14]

All these things gave Jesus an opportunity to meet and converse with people from India to Egypt, as well as from Rome and Greece. He was exposed to the cultural and religious ideas of far-off nations that He would never visit. He had come to His own people, but they would not receive Him (John 1:11). Yet, the world came to Him even though He was never to venture far from Israel's borders. The world passed by that tiny village of Nazareth. It was the perfect place for the Son of Man and Savior of the world to be reared for the same reasons that it was also despised, as Frederic Farrar states:

> *Galil*, in Hebrew, means "a circle," and the name was originally applied to the twenty cities in the circuit of Kedesh-Naphtali, which Solomon gave to Hiram in return for his services in transporting timber, and to which Hiram, in extreme disgust, applied the *Cabul*, or "disgusting." Thus it seems to have been always the destiny of Galilee to be despised; and that contempt was likely to be fostered in the minds of the Jews from the fact that this district became, from very early days the residence of a mixed population, and was distinguished as "Galilee of the Gentiles." Not only were there many Phoenicians and Arabs in the cit-

---

12 Edersheim, *The Life and Times of Jesus the Messiah*, 104.
13 Smith, *The Historical Geography of the Holy Land*, 433.
14 Smith, *The Historical Geography of the Holy Land*, 433-4.

ies of Galilee, but in the time of our Lord, there were also many Greeks, and the Greek language was currently spoken and understood.[15]

The hilltops around Nazareth allowed Jesus to view the scenery of Galilee in all directions. To the north, "the view is bounded by that giant of the far-off mountain-chain, snow-tipped Hermon."[16] To the west, "lay purple Carmel; beyond it a fringe of silver sand, and then the dazzling sheen of the Great Sea. In the farthest distance, white sails, like wings outspread towards the ends of the world."[17] Indeed, the topography and climate of the whole world was represented in that tiny nation, as Samuel Bagster writes:

> The climate of Palestine is very varied, a circumstance due to the great diversity of level, which embraces a range of over 11,000 feet, extending as it does, from the summit of Mount Hermon, to the surface of the Dead Sea. The consequence of this is that among the plants and animals it contains there are representatives of the flora and fauna of every other region of the globe from the Arctic circle to the tropics. The plants of northern Europe flourish on Lebanon, those of central Europe at the level of Jerusalem and Carmel, and those of the West Indies on the plain of Jericho near the Jordan; while as for animals, some of them represent denizens of Alpine districts, and others the fauna of the plains of India and the rivers of Africa, thus supplying a natural symbolism that appeals more or less intelligibly to men of every nation.[18]

While little is known about those early days of Jesus' life, Luke records that He "continued to grow and become strong, increasing in wisdom; and the grace of God was upon Him" (Luke 2:40). Again, "And Jesus kept increasing in wisdom and stature, and in favor with God and men" (Luke 2:52). Jesus went through all the stages of mankind in order to sanctify each stage. He experienced all the same trials and endured the temptations of every stage of growth, "yet without sin" (Hebrews 4:15). When He played in the streets with the other children of Nazareth, He was the kindest playmate of all. Archaeology has discovered some of the games that amused children[19] in Nazareth:

---

15 Frederic Farrar, *Life of Christ* (USA: Bibliotech Press, 2020), 18–19.
16 Edersheim, *The Life and Times of Jesus the Messiah*, 103.
17 Edersheim, *The Life and Times of Jesus the Messiah*, 103.
18 Samuel Bagster, *Bagster's Bible Handbook* (Old Tappan, New Jersey: Fleming H. Revell Company, 1983), 136.
19 Shirley Jackson Case, "Jesus and Sepphoris," *Journal of Biblical Literature*, 1926, Vol. 45, No. 1/2, p. 15. (The Society of Biblical Literature).

Children in Jesus' day played games similar to hopscotch and jacks. Whistles, rattles, toy animals on wheels, hoops, and spinning tops have been found by archaeologists. Older children and adults found time to play, too, mainly with board games. A form of checkers was popular then.[20]

Sepphoris, a City Set on a Hill

Shortly after becoming tetrarch of Galilee in 4 BC, Herod Antipas began the rebuilding of a magnificent city near Nazareth named Sepphoris. That city had been captured by Herod the Great in a battle with Antigonus II Mattathias,[21] but the Romans later ransacked it and enslaved its inhabitants as punishment for their sedition. Previously, it had been an arms depot and a fortified city, but Herod Antipas began a major building project to make it "the ornament of all Galilee" and one of his royal residences. Four miles northwest of Nazareth, Sepphoris was made the capitol of Galilee when the Romans divided Palestine into five administrative districts upon the death of Herod the Great. All the Roman roads in that area led to it or through it. Thus, there were people from many nations who passed through Sepphoris and near Nazareth.

Tradition holds that Mary's parents were residents of Sepphoris and, if so, Mary may have grown up there herself. It became a city of beautiful stone structures during the reign of Herod Antipas and it is possible that Joseph and Jesus were employed in the various building projects there. While Joseph is typically called a "carpenter," the Greek word for his trade is *tekton*[22] which indicates work with stones, primarily, rather than wood. In fact, there were no wood buildings in ancient Nazareth or the surrounding area. Moreover, Jesus made no reference in Scripture to wood carpentry, but spoke of stone masons (Matthew 7:24; 21:42, 44). "That the village of Nazareth was a bare hour's walk from its largest city, Sepphoris, and but a half hour from its largest village, Japha, are facts whose import in this connection may be far greater than has ordinarily been supposed."

---

20 Ted Olsen, "The Life &Times of Jesus of Nazareth: Did You Know?" *Christianity Today*. Accessed on January 17, 2022 at: https://www.christianitytoday.com/history/issues/issue-59/life-times-of-jesus-of-nazareth-did-you-know.html
21 Antigonus II Mattathias, who died in 37 BC, was the last Hasmonean king of Judea, the son of King Aristobulus II of Judea.
22 Tectonic plates are large slabs of rocks. Jesus gave many illustrations concerning stones, but never spoke about wood which would be strange if Joseph was a wood carpenter.

Numerous archaeological excavations at the site of ancient Sepphoris have uncovered "some spectacular finds, including dazzling mosaics, a fine Roman-style theater, a massive underground aqueduct, and two early Christian churches."[23] Sepphoris was a mixture of Jewish, Roman, Hellenistic, and Byzantine cultures which was a school of learning for the Son of Man. It was situated on a mountain crest like a bird perched on a ledge. Thus, the name of this city was derived from the Hebrew word for a bird, zippor. From Nazareth's streets as the sun set each evening, the dazzling city of Sepphoris must have been the basis for Jesus' reference to a city set on a hill. Sepphoris was easily seen from Nazareth because it was about 1,000 feet above the surrounding valleys and basins.

Some have speculated that the various mosaics in Sepphoris indicate that "there was a much more liberal attitude towards the second commandment banning pictorial images in Judaism, and that Jews in general were much more flexible with respect to image making and artistic presentation and activity."[24] Such a suggestion overlooks the various cultures that were intermixed at Sepphoris. Idolatry and the breaking of the second commandment were sins common among all the other cultures that were melded together in that city on a hill. That does not mean that Jewish culture accepted the breaking of the second commandment nor does it mean that Jesus agreed with the Greek and Roman views of such idolatry.

The Roman amphitheater at Sepphoris, if, indeed, it existed during Jesus' childhood—and it probably did—was a place where Jesus would have learned the term "hypocrite" as actors in plays would cover their faces with a mask or a "false face." Jesus, like all Jews, did not attend Roman plays at any amphitheater, but He would have been familiar with what took place there. One cannot prevent what one sees, hears, or smells. What we do know is that the word "hypocrite" is used only by Jesus in the Scripture and He used the word several times with reference to the Pharisees (cf. Matthew 23:13–16, 23, 25, 27, 29). It is a word that comes directly from those ancient Greek and Roman plays.

---

23 Mike Mason, *Jesus: His Story in Stone* (Victoria, BC, Canada: Friesen Press, 2017), 21.
24 Eric Meyers, Professor of Religion and Archaeology at Duke University; quoted at www.pbs.org/wgbh/pages/frontline/shows/religion/jesus/sepphoris.html

Early Life in Nazareth

Jesus Visits Jerusalem at the Age of Twelve (Luke 2:41–52)

Luke the physician sheds the only light on the darkness of those silent years of Jesus' life until He was thirty. The evangelist simply states: "Now His parents went to Jerusalem every year at the Feast of the Passover. And when He became twelve, they went up there *according* to the custom of the Feast" (Luke 2:41, 42). Mount Zion in Jerusalem was the heartbeat of every true Jew. It is noteworthy, therefore, that Mary also went up to Jerusalem every year though the law only required that all males should go there (Exodus 34:23). There were many Jews dispersed throughout the ancient World who were unable to keep this requirement, but those who lived in the holy land attempted to go up at least once a year. The Passover Feast was the holiest of all the feasts because it was a perpetual reminder of their deliverance from Egypt—a type of the believer's conversion to Christ (Cf. 1 Corinthians 5:7; 10:1–5), as McClintock and Strong remind us:

> No other shadow of good things to come can vie with the festival of the Passover in expressiveness and completeness. Hence we are so often reminded of it, more or less distinctly, in the ritual and language of the Church. Its outline, considered in reference to the great deliverance of the Israelites which it commemorated, and many of the details, have been appropriated as current expressions of the truths which God has revealed to us in the fulness of times in sending His Son upon earth . . . .
>
> The deliverance of Israel according to the flesh from the bondage of Egypt was always so regarded and described by the prophets as to render it a most apt type of the deliverance of the spiritual Israel from the bondage of sin into the glorious liberty with which Christ has made us free.[25]

It is fitting that the One who came to this earth for the purpose of being sacrificed as the true Passover lamb should have spoken His first recorded words at the Passover Feast. Whether Jesus had previously gone to Jerusalem with His parents to celebrate the Passover we simply do not know. The appearance of Jesus at this Passover Feast was the time of His coming of age and becoming a "son of the law" with the responsibility to keep the annual feasts and fasts. The Passover Feast when Jesus was twelve was on Thursday, March 28, AD 9. Wicked King Archelaus had been removed as tetrarch by Caesar Augustus

---

25 McClintock and Strong, *Cyclopedia of Biblical, Theological, and Ecclesiastical Literature*, 7:750.

as a result of an embassy sent by the Jews to complain about his tyrannical reign. He was deposed by Augustus in AD 6 and banished to Vienne (Vienna) in Gaul.[26] He was succeeded by Coponius, the first Roman governor of Judea, who reigned for three years. When Coponius came to power, he was accompanied by the governor of Syria, Quirinius, who was sent to take another census of the people so that Rome could enact a more direct system of taxation. A revolt among the Jews against such taxation was led by Zadok the priest and Judah the Galilean—the latter started a nationalistic movement which became known as the sect of the Zealots. Coponius was succeeded by Marcus Ambibulus who reigned from AD 9–12. It is impossible to determine which of the two Roman prefects was in power during the Passover Feast of AD 9, but either of them was an improvement over Archelaus.

Jesus' parents would have travelled to the Passover Feast in the company of other pilgrims who made up the Nazareth caravan. There was a direct road from Nazareth to Jerusalem through the Central Range of mountains in the territory of the Samaritans, but it was not safe for Jews to travel that way. The enmity between the Samaritans and the Jews was palpable and the latter avoided traveling through their territory. Thus, Jesus' parents undoubtedly traveled from Nazareth to Jerusalem via the typical caravan route for Galilean Jews which went down the eastern side of the Jordan River. From Nazareth they traveled south past Mount Tabor until they came to the city of Jezreel—where the kings of Israel had built lavish winter palaces and where Jezebel had Naboth killed because he would not cede to her his beautiful vineyard. At Jezreel, the caravan would have traveled southeasterly towards the fortified city of Beth Shean at the junction between the valley of Esdraelon (or, Jezreel) and the Jordan River. Beth Shean was once a city of great affluence with luxurious houses, beautiful temples, and costly jewelry. It had a Roman amphitheater and stables with stone pillars for tethering the horses and cobblestone floors. It was also one of the cities of the Decapolis[27]. When King Saul was killed at nearby Mount Gilboa, "[t]he Philistines stripped [his] body, hung it on the walls of Bethshean, and placed his armor in

---

26 Plummer, *A Critical and Exegetical Commentary on the Gospel According to S. Luke*, 74.
27 Decapolis means 'ten cities.' They were then Hellenistic cities on the eastern frontier of the Roman Empire.

the temple of the goddess Ashtaroth, or Astarte."[28] At Beth Shean[29], about twenty miles south of the Sea of Galilee, the caravan would have crossed the Jordan River towards Pella, another of the cities of the Decapolis. It was founded by the Greeks and contains ruins from several historical periods. Leaving Pella, the caravan traveled the road that went south through Succoth to Bethany beyond the Jordan where they recrossed the river. They then ascended to Jericho and traveled on to Jerusalem from there. Such a route probably added another day of travel, but it was safer than going through Samaria. There were amazing scenes along that route that only a mind like Jesus's could fully comprehend.

The Jordan Valley through which that caravan traveled is a tremendous chasm in the land of Israel, unlike any other place on earth. It is from five to fifteen miles wide and is bordered on both sides by mountain ranges. To the west is the Central Range and to the east are the mountains of Gilead. The Jordan Valley is the lowest place on earth and descends seven hundred feet from the southern edge of the Sea of Galilee to the northern border of the Dead Sea. The Sea of Galilee is six hundred and eighty feet below sea level and the Dead Sea is nearly one thousand four hundred feet below sea level. This area is called El Ghor by the Arabs which means "the rift" or "the depression." Jordan itself means "descender" or "down-comer." Being below sea level, the whole valley is intensely hot from early spring to late autumn and is pocketed by numerus swamps.[30]

Jerusalem was an elevated city from every direction. Whenever a feast was celebrated, the worshipers had to go up to it. Edersheim describes what those traveling caravans would have done as they began their ascent to the city which for every Jew was the most holy of all places:

> And so, when, according to ancient wont (Ps. 42, Isa. 30:29), the festive company from Nazareth, soon swelled by other festive bands, went

---

28 Charles F. Pfeiffer and Howard F. Vos, *The Wycliffe Historical Geography of Bible Lands* (Chicago: Moody Press, 1978), 124.
29 At Beth Shean, there were three roads that crossed the Jordan. The northern road went to Damascus. The central road went towards Gadara. The southern road went to Pella and then followed along to the east of the Jordan. The caravan would have taken the southern road. Cf. George Adam Smith, The Historical Geography of the Holy Land (London: Hodder and Stoughton, 1900), 597.
30 Martha Tarbell, *The Geography of Palestine in the Time of Christ* (Indianapolis: The Bobbs-Merrill Company, 1907) 8. The information in this paragraph is taken from this work by Tarbell.

up to Jerusalem, chanting by the way those 'Psalms of Ascent' (AV 'Degrees'; Ps. 120–134) to the accompaniment of the flute, they might implicitly yield themselves to the spiritual thoughts kindled by such words.[31]

Once they arrived in Jerusalem, there was no fear of being unable to find lodging. Every home, courtyard, or rooftop became lodging to those visitors from other parts. Food was readily available as a result of all the sacrifices that were made during those feasts. Jerusalem lived out the true meaning of the hospitality endorsed by the Scripture. Yet, the Temple—not the city, nor the residents—was the central focus of those who came to worship. Surely, it would have been for Jesus also as He came to realize that His place was to be in His Father's house (Luke 2:49). Whatever others felt at that Passover Feast in AD 9, Jesus felt something more. He not only became a "son of the law" at this time, but through Him "grace and truth were to be realized" (John 1:17).

The whole Temple ground was an area that encompassed almost twenty acres and "could hold within its gigantic girdle not fewer than 210,000 persons."[32] Edersheim further describes the view of the Temple Mount which would have caught the eye of Jesus:

> The Mount itself seemed like an island, abruptly rising from out of deep valleys, surrounded by a sea of walls, palaces, streets, and houses, and crowned by a mass of snowy marble and glittering gold, rising terrace upon terrace . . . At its north-western angle, and connected with it, frowned the Castle of Antonia, held by the Roman garrison. The lofty walls were pierced by massive gates—the unused gate (*Tedi*) on the north; the Susa gate on the east, which opened on the arched roadway to the Mount of Olives; the two so-called 'Huldah' (probably, 'weasel') gates, which led by tunnels from the priest-suburb Ophel into the outer Court; and, finally, four gates on the west.[33]

Then, there were the colonnades that completely surrounded the Temple on all sides. "The most magnificent of those was the southern, or twofold double colonnade, with a wide space between; the most venerable, the ancient 'Solomon's Porch,' or eastern colonnade."[34] On the eastern side of the Temple was a tower which overlooked the Kedron Valley, four hundred feet below. From the pinnacle

---

31 Edersheim, *The Life and Times of Jesus the Messiah*, 168.
32 Edersheim, *The Life and Times of Jesus the Messiah*, 169.
33 Edersheim, *The Life and Times of Jesus the Messiah*, 169.
34 Edersheim, *The Life and Times of Jesus the Messiah*, 169.

of that tower, the priest would announce the first rising of the sun each morning. The beauty and grandeur of Jerusalem's Temple was unparalleled. There were various courtyards around it—the court of the Gentiles, the court of the women, and the court of the priests— yet, the Temple itself was the great attraction and showplace. Many could worship and pray on the larger Temple grounds, but only the priests could enter the Holy Place. And, only once a year could the high priest enter the Most Holy Place. Jesus did not enter the Temple on this occasion or on any other occasion because He was not a Levitical priest. But He kept all the laws required of the Jews and broke none of them.

After His parents had spent the full number of days at the Passover Feast, they started their journey back to Nazareth in early April of AD 9. Unbeknownst to them, Jesus remained behind. When they had traveled a day's journey, about twenty miles, they began looking for Jesus among the caravan, but He was not to be found. In such caravans, the women and small children traveled in one group and the men and older children traveled in another group. It is probable that both Joseph and Mary assumed that Jesus was with the other parent. Once they realized Jesus was not among them, Joseph and Mary returned to Jerusalem and found Him on the following day. When they found Him, He was sitting among "the teachers, both listening to them and asking them questions. And all who heard Him were amazed at His understanding and His answers" (Luke 2:46, 47). His parents were not amused, though. "When they saw Him, they were astonished; and His mother said to Him, 'Son, why have You treated us this way? Behold, Your father and I have been anxiously looking for You" (Luke 2:48). To which, Jesus simply replied: "Why have you been looking for Me? Did you not know that I had to be in My Father's *house*?" (Luke 2:49). His parents did not understand that answer, despite everything that had happened up to that time. Yet, Jesus had not been the least bit rebellious towards His earthly parents, though they were under the impression that He had not shown them proper respect. Thus, "He went down with them and came to Nazareth, and He continued in subjection to them; and His mother treasured all *these* things in her heart. And Jesus kept increasing in wisdom and stature, and in favor with God and men" (Luke 2:51, 52). The essence of Jesus' words to His parents are appropriately summed up by Ryle:

A mild reproof was evidently implied in that reply. It was meant to remind His mother, that He was no common person, and had come into the world to do no common work. It was a hint, that she was insensibly forgetting that He had come into the world in no ordinary way, and that she could not expect Him to be ever dwelling quietly at Nazareth. It was solemn remembrancer that, as God, He had a Father in heaven, and that His heavenly Father's work demanded His first attention.[35]

It is for that reason that the Scriptures are silent about almost all of the first thirty years of the life of Jesus. He was no common Person. He did not come to do common work. He dwelt quietly at Nazareth only for a season—though a long season—until the time came for Him to undertake His great work of redemption. The Scriptures, therefore, give us all the information that is necessary for us to understand what Jesus did to accomplish the great work of His Father in the redemption of the elect.

---

35 Ryle, *Expository Thoughts on the Gospels; Luke*, 1:81.

4
Jesus' Baptism and Temptations

In the fifteenth year of the reign of Tiberius Caesar, Luke informs us that "the word of God came to John, the son of Zacharias, in the wilderness. And he came into all the district around the Jordan, preaching a baptism of repentance for the forgiveness of sins" (Luke 3:2, 3). Tiberius reigned for two years with his adoptive father, Caesar Augustus, before assuming the sole reign in AD 14. Pontius Pilate was governor of Judea; Philip was tetrarch of Ituraea and Trachonitis, Lysanias was tetrarch of Abilene, and, Herod Antipas was tetrarch of Galilee and Perea. The reign of Pilate in Judea was a time of harshness and immorality. "Violence, robbery, insults, venality, murders without trial, and cruelty were charged against [his] administration."[1] Thus, there was a sense of hopelessness that filled the hearts of the godly remnant in Israel.

Then, a prophetic voice arose in the wilderness from an unexpected source proclaiming, "Repent, for the kingdom of God is at hand" (Matthew 3:2). The bearer of that message, John the Baptist, was a rugged and rough-hewn man who had spent most of his adult years in the seclusion of the desert. He wore "a garment of camel's hair and a leather belt around his waist; and his food was locusts and wild honey"[2] (Matthew 3:4). When he suddenly burst on the scene sometime in AD 26, Judeans were amazed and bewildered by both his demeanor and message. He resembled Elijah the Tishbite more than any other prophet of old which was according to prophecy: "Behold I will send you Elijah the prophet before the coming of the great and terrible day of the Lord" (Malachi 4:5). And, Isaiah 40:3 had foretold his appearance with these words: "The voice of one crying in the wilderness, make ready the way of the Lord, make His paths straight!" (Matthew 3:3).

John did not begin his ministry as the Forerunner until "the word of God came" to him, like the prophets of old. Then, he went into the

---

1 Shepard, *The Christ of the Gospels*, 59.
2 These were all signs of the poorer class of citizens in Israel. A garment of a camel's hair was like a rough sack rather than a fine piece of clothing as is the case today.

Judean wilderness where he began to preach and baptize. The wilderness area where he went was the Jordan Valley just east of Jericho in the depression below that ancient city. Centuries earlier the nation of Israel had crossed the Jordan River on dry ground at that same spot in order to occupy the Promised Land. The news of John's activities in this remote region soon spread like wildfire. "Jerusalem was going out to him, and all Judea and all the district around the Jordan; and they were being baptized by him in the Jordan River, as they confessed their sins" (Matthew 3:5, 6). McClintock and Strong describe the area of the Jordan Valley where John conducted his ministry:

> On approaching the Dead Sea, the plain of Jordan attains its greatest breadth—about twelve miles. The mountain ranges on each side are higher, more rugged, and more desolate. The plain is coated with a nitrous crust, like hoar frost, and not a tree, shrub, or blade of grass is seen except by fountains or rivulets. The glen winds like a serpent through the centre, between two tiers of banks. The bottom is smooth and sprinkled on the outside with stunted shrubs. The river winds in ceaseless coils along the bottom, now touching one side and now another, with its beautiful border of green foliage, looking all the greener from contrast with the desert above. The banks are of soft clay, in places ten feet high; the stream varies from 80 to 130 feet in breadth, and from five to twelve feet in depth.[3]

On either side of the Jordan River, the area of the plain was amply large enough for the crowds that came to be baptized by John. When they reached the Jordan River, they would necessarily have to climb down the banks of the river in order to get into the water. Those soft clay banks in some places were ten feet high. From Jerusalem, Judea, and the surrounding district of the Jordan, the people would have to descend lower and lower until they reached the waters where they would confess their sins. It was a visible picture of the green valley of humiliation which all sinners must descend to in order to manifest true repentance. Among the sincere penitents who came out to be baptized were also "many of the Pharisees and Sadducees" (Matthew 3:7a), to whom John responded:

> You brood of vipers, who warned you to flee from the wrath to come? Therefore bear fruit in keeping with repentance; and do not suppose that you can say to yourselves, 'We have Abraham for our father'; for I say to you that from these stones God is able to raise up children to

---

[3] McClintock and Strong, *Cyclopedia of Biblical, Theological, and Ecclesiastical Literature*, 4:1007.

Abraham. The axe is already laid at the root of the trees; therefore every tree that does not bear good fruit is cut down and thrown into the fire. As for me, I baptize you with water, but He who is coming after me is mightier than I, and I am not fit to remove His sandals; He will baptize you with the Holy Spirit and fire. His winnowing fork is in His hand, and He will thoroughly clear His threshing floor; and He will gather His wheat into His barn, but He will burn up the chaff with unquenchable fire (Matthew 3:7b-12).

There were some in the crowds who questioned how they could bring forth fruit in keeping with repentance, asking John, "Then, what shall we do?" (Luke 3:10b). John replied, "The man who has two tunics is to share with him who has none; and he who has food is to do likewise" (Luke 3:11). "And *some* tax collectors also came to be baptized, and they said to him, 'Teacher, what shall we do?' And he said to them, 'Collect no more than what you have been ordered to'" (Luke 3:12, 13). In that exchange with the tax collectors, there was a foreshadowing of Jesus' future ministry to sinners, harlots, and tax collectors. Finally, there were some soldiers among the penitent who asked, "'And what about us, what shall we do?' And he said to them, 'Do not take money from anyone by force, or accuse anyone falsely, and be content with your wages.'" (Luke 3:14). These three exchanges are unique to Luke's Gospel, but teach an important lesson for everyone, as Plummer notes:

> Each class is to forsake its besetting sin, and all are to do their duty to their neighbor. The stern warnings of the Baptist made the rulers leave in disgust without seeking baptism at his hands (viii. 30; Mt. xxi. 25); but they made the multitudes anxious to comply with the conditions for avoiding the threatened judgment.[4]

As impolitic as John's stern warnings to the Pharisees and Sadducees were, they were also necessary. The new work of the Messiah could not be built on the traditions and compromises of either of those sects. The very people who needed to be reached—the sickly, the diseased, the broken, the scattered, and the lost (Cf. Ezekiel 34:4)—could not be reached through any alignment with either sect. Thus, John prepared the way for Jesus to conduct His ministry outside those sects even at the expense of alienating them and provoking their hostility. They were never going to be favorable towards the Forerunner or the Messiah, anyway.

At some point during his ministry, the Holy Spirit gave John a sign

---

4 Plummer, *A Critical and Exegetical Commentary on the Gospel According to S. Luke*, 90.

by which he would know the Messiah as John 1:33 confirms—"I did not recognize Him, but He who sent me to baptize in water said to me, 'He upon whom you see the Spirit descending as a dove and remaining upon Him, this is the One who baptizes in the Holy Spirit.'" When Jesus came to be baptized, "John tried to prevent Him, saying, 'I have need to be baptized by You, and do You come to me?' But Jesus answering said to him, 'Permit it at this time; for in this way it is fitting for us to fulfill all righteousness.' Then he permitted Him'" (Matthew 3:14, 15). Unlike the others who came to be baptized by John, Jesus did not confess His sins. He was the sin bearer—not a sinner. It was necessary, therefore, for both John and Jesus to fulfill all righteousness by the Messiah receiving "a baptism intended for sinners, be anointed by the Spirit and be consecrated by the Father, at the inception of his public ministry."[5]

After His baptism, Jesus was praying as He "came up immediately from the water; and behold, the heavens were opened, and he saw the Spirit of God descending as a dove and lighting on Him, and behold a voice out of the heavens said, 'This is My Beloved Son, in whom I am well-pleased'" (Matthew 3:16, 17). That descent of the Holy Spirit in 'bodily form' was the sign to John that Jesus was the Messiah. And, that anointing of the God-man with the Holy Spirit was essential to His ministry, as Chamblin notes:

> The words of the Father, about to be quoted (Matt. 3:17), allude to Isaiah 42:1, which opens the first of the Servant songs. The major work of the Father requires of the Son—that which above all else is 'right' for the Son to do and which will entail his utter submission to the Father's will—is that he, Yahweh's righteous Servant, should save his people from their sins by himself bearing their iniquities (Isa. 53:11). That climactic event—Jesus' atoning sacrifice—is foreshadowed here at the Jordan River.
>
> The Spirit by whose power Jesus was conceived in Mary's womb (Matt. 1:18, 20), now anoints him for his manifold mission—including the imminent ordeal in the desert (4:1) . . . now the Spirit anoints the Son of David to equip him for service. The Spirit not only comes down from heaven: he 'comes upon' Jesus . . . The endowment is not only external to equip him for service, the Spirit's power floods Jesus' whole being.[6]

---

5 J. Knox Chamblin, *Matthew* (Fearn, Tain, Ross-Shire, Great Britain: Christian Focus Publications, 2010), 1:260.
6 Chamblin, *Matthew*, 1:260-3.

The Temptations of Jesus (Matthew 4:1–11; Luke 4:1–13)

Immediately following His baptism, "Jesus was led up by the Spirit into the wilderness to be tempted by the devil" (Matthew 4:1). Mark 1:12 is even more emphatic and says that He was "impelled" by the Spirit. The word Mark uses has the meaning of "throwing or casting something out." Jesus had willingly submitted to baptism in order to fulfill all righteousness and now is being led around by the Spirit to be tempted of the devil. As the second Adam, He had to undo all that the first Adam had done (Cf. Romans 5:12–21 and 1 Corinthians 15:20, 22, 45, 47). Adam in the garden of Eden had faced one temptation under the best of circumstances and failed. The second Adam, Christ, had to face every temptation in the worst of circumstances and He succeeded. Adam and Eve were cast out of the garden following their sin. Jesus was now cast or thrown out into the wilderness to face His temptations. James Henley Thornwell brings out the difference between the two temptations:

> The place. Adam's was in the garden of Eden—this in the wilderness. Adam's with a companion to relieve his solitude—Christ alone. Adam's with the beasts tamed and in harmonious subjection to his authority—Christ among beasts, wild and savage. Adam's in the midst of plenty and abundance—Christ struggling with hunger. How differently the two places! How favorable the circumstances in the one case! How unfavorable in the other.
>
> The test to Adam was condensed into a simple precept involving comparatively no self-denial . . . . Christ was open to assaults upon all points . . . . The thing to be tested in both trials was allegiance to God . . . . Adam was only a man, and the insinuation was that he was a god in capacity . . . . Christ was the Son of God, and the insinuation was that He was only a man.[7]

Matthew and Luke give us three temptations from Satan that Jesus faced "after He had fasted forty days and nights" (Matthew 4:2), but Mark tells us that "He was in the wilderness being tempted by Satan" (Mark 1:13). Part of that temptation during those forty days was being alone in the wilderness among wild animals and struggling with hunger. There were several wild animals that lived in the Judean desert—striped hyenas, lions, gazelles, leopards, mountain goats, bears, and various kinds of poisonous snakes. Most of those wild animals

---

[7] James Henley Thornwell, *The Collected Writings of James Henley Thornwell* (Edinburgh, Scotland and Carlisle, Pennsylvania: The Banner of Truth Trust, 1974), 3:296.

were unclean and were prohibited from being food by the Mosaic law. Some of them would have considered Jesus prey for their own needs. In His hunger, Jesus would have been tempted by the devil to kill and eat the unclean animals, but He did not. We are not told the extent of the temptations Jesus faced during those forty days, except that Satan was active throughout that whole period.

The place of Jesus' temptations in the wilderness has traditionally been considered as Quarantania, "a mountain which arises out of the Judean plain, fifteen hundred feet above the Jordan Valley,"[8] west of the Jordan River between Jericho and Jerusalem. To reach the mountain, Jesus would have traveled the steep road leading to Jerusalem, known as the Ascent of Blood due to the numbers of robbers who targeted passers-by.[9] It was considered the most dangerous road in Palestine. Once Jesus reached the base of Quarantania, He had to climb a mountain, barren and scarred with caves, that "rises precipitously, an almost perpendicular wall of rock."[10] John Kitto described the mountain of Quarantania as follows:

> Of the Mountain of Temptation the ascent is so difficult and perilous, that many travelers of no ordinary enterprise have desisted from the attempt to reach its summit...The way up to its top is dangerous beyond imagination...The view from the top, however, well repays the fatigue and danger of the enterprise.[11]

From the crest of Quarantania, Jesus would have had a panoramic view of much of Palestine—"Jerusalem on the West, the Jordan Valley and plains of Moab on the East, Hermon on the North . . . and highways also were visible, leading to 'all the kingdoms of the world.'"[12]

Moses was on Mount Sinai with God for forty days; Elijah fasted forty days after he fled from Jezebel's threats against his life; and, Jesus was alone in the wilderness for forty days. "Moses failed after his forty days' fast, when in indignation he cast the Tables of the

---

8 Shepard, *The Christ of the Gospels*, 73. Quaratania is 1,201 feet above sea level. Jericho is 847 feet below sea level. The Jordan River, where John baptized, is 1,365 feet below sea level. Jerusalem is 2,400–2,500 feet above sea level.
9 Shepard, *The Christ of the Gospels*, 73.
10 Edward Robinson, *Biblical Researches in Palestine, Mount Sinai and Arabia Petraea* (Boston: Crocker and Brewster, 1841), 2:303.
11 John Kitto, *Palestine: The Physical Geography and Natural History of the Holy Land* (London: Charles Knight and Co., 1841), 2:XXXIX.
12 Shepard, *The Christ of the Gospels*, 73.

Jesus' Baptism and Temptations

Law from him; Elijah failed before his forty days' fast; Jesus was assailed for forty days and endured the trial. Moses was angry against Israel; Elijah despaired of Israel; Jesus overcame for Israel."[13] At the end of His forty days in the wilderness, Jesus became hungry and the tempter, Satan, came to Him with three special trials. Hebrews 4:15 describes our high priest, Jesus, in this way: "For we do not have a high priest who cannot sympathize with our weaknesses, but One who has been tempted in all points like as *we are, yet* without sin." There is a difference in the temptations that Jesus endured and those everyone descended from Adam faces. Our sinful natures are involved in our own temptations, but that was not true of Jesus. We face three great enemies—the world, the flesh, and the devil. Jesus only faced two of those enemies because He had no weakness of the flesh. His temptations were real, but He never gave into them. Our temptations are often inward, but Jesus never was tempted in that way. He was able not to sin because He had no weakness of the flesh; because He was anointed with the Spirit above measure; and, because He was both divine and human in complete harmony, the perfect God-man. These three great temptations by Satan, therefore, are indicative of how Jesus always dealt with all other temptations by clinging to the written Word.

The special temptations of Jesus after His time in the desert were all trials of His faith and allegiance to His Father. They also appear to all be related to either His time in that desert or to His high priestly ministry. Indeed, a large part of His trials were representative in nature as He endured them in our behalf. Jesus endured far worse trials than Adam in order to show that Adam's sin was not necessary and that the human "race had not been hardly dealt with in Adam— that they might have stood, that they might have easily stood."[14] In withstanding this withering assault of the devil, the virtue of Jesus is magnified. His perfect obedience is on full display. Having caused all others to fall into temptation, the devil must have been specially irritated that he was unable to induce Jesus to fall. Jesus chose the path of suffering, as Edersheim eloquently stated:

> [T]he essence of His last three temptations; which, as the whole contest, resolved themselves into the one great question of absolute submission

---

13 Edersheim, The Life and Teachings of Jesus the Messiah, 205.
14 Thornwell, *The Collected Writings of James Henley Thornwell*, 3:297.

to the Will of God, which is the sum and substance of all obedience. If He submitted to it, it must be suffering, and only suffering—helpless, hopeless suffering to the bitter end; to the extinction of life, in the agonies of the Cross, as a malefactor; denounced, betrayed, rejected by His people; alone in very God-forsakenness.[15]

Following Matthew's order of the temptations, the first one was to change the stones into bread. Jesus was hungry and the tempter tried to entice Him to use His miraculous powers like a heathen magician in order to satisfy His appetites. Jesus did not entertain that temptation for even a moment, but rejected it categorically: "It is written, 'Man shall not live on bread alone, but on every Word that proceeds out of the mouth of God'" (Matthew 4:4). Adam had failed just at that point when the devil twisted him into knots with the question: "Indeed, has God said, 'You shall not eat from any tree of the garden?'" (Genesis 3:1). Satan first got Adam and Eve to question God's Word, then he presented his alternative narrative that God was jealous of them becoming like Him. Jesus foiled the devil's efforts against Him by refusing to depart from Scripture. The first temptation was to despair of God's help—too little faith and too little allegiance.

After that trial passed, Matthew 4:5 says, "the devil took Him into the city and had Him stand on the pinnacle of the temple." From that precipice, a priest would stand every morning to watch for the dawning of a new day, so he could signal to the people below that it was now time for the morning sacrifice.[16] Perhaps, this temptation was to place Jesus in that very spot just as the priest had descended from there. The devil tried to entice Jesus to cast Himself down from that pinnacle in a dazzling display of the power of God. It was a temptation to presumption. With this temptation, Satan quotes Scripture, Psalm 91:11, 12, but leaves out part of verse eleven, which says: "to guard you in all your ways." It was not one of the God-appointed ways of Jesus to tempt the Lord and to presume on His protection. Presumption is not faith. Thus, Jesus answered the devil by quoting Deuteronomy 6:16—"You shall not put the Lord your God to the test." This temptation by the devil was for Jesus to have too much faith—presumption. Another temptation was successfully foiled by Jesus through reference to the Scripture.

---

15 Edersheim, *The Life and Times of Jesus the Messiah*, 210.
16 Edersheim, *The Life and Times of Jesus the Messiah*, 210.

Finally, the devil took Jesus "to a very high mountain and showed Him all the kingdoms of the world and their glory" (Matthew 4:8). In this temptation, the devil makes his most audacious attempt to ruin the purpose and mission of Jesus. He said to Christ, "All these things I will give You, if You fall down and worship me" (Matthew 4:8). Satan ceased to be subtle and came straight to the point of what he desired. From the time of the fallen angels, Lucifer had always wanted to be like God. That was his first temptation to Adam and now it is his final temptation to Jesus. Yet, the devil promised to give Jesus what had already been promised to Him as the Anointed of the Lord in Psalm 2:8 by His Father—"Ask of Me and I will surely give you the nations as your inheritance, and the very ends of the earth as Your possession." That promise was made to the Anointed of the Lord immediately after God declared Him to His Son (Psalm 2:7). This third temptation was to have no faith and allegiance to the Lord. It was also a temptation to supposedly receive His inheritance without the sufferings of the Cross. It was to be gained not by sufferings, but by false worship. That was undoubtedly the greatest of the temptations Jesus endured during those forty days in the wilderness. His temptations in the wilderness, in that respect, were a foreshadowing of the great agony of soul Jesus would suffer in the garden of Gethsemane before He was arrested. Jesus answered this last temptation by saying to the devil, "Go Satan! For it is written, 'You shall worship the Lord your God, and serve Him only'" (Matthew 4:10). Knox Chamblin wrote concerning this last temptation:

> Those far-flung regions of the *kosmos* presently under the devil's tyranny are the very places Jesus' gospel of the kingdom is going to be proclaimed (Matthew 24:14; 26:13). In the end 'all the kingdoms of the world' will indeed belong to Jesus—not as a bequest from Satan (who as the very embodiment of the lie, could not be trusted to keep the promise of 4:9) but as the Father's gift to his beloved Son (28:18–20).[17]

At that point, the devil left Jesus and the angels came to minister to Him. Jesus had won a signal battle against the devil, but there were temptations still to come as that fiend bided his time. "Having suffered a major defeat in the wilderness, Satan will the more assiduously marshal his demonic host for assaults upon Jesus during his ministry in Galilee and especially during his final week in Jerusalem."[18]

---

17 Chamblin, *Matthew*, 1:284.
18 Chamblin, *Matthew*, 1:285.

The conflicts Jesus faced throughout His ministry were owing to the fact that the devil was inciting others against Him.

The Sanhedrin Sends a Deputation to John (John 1:19–34)

While Jesus was being tempted by the devil, the intrigue of the Sanhedrin continued concerning John the Baptist. They sent an unofficial deputation of priests and Levites from Jerusalem to John where he was baptizing at Bethany beyond the Jordan with the question: "Who are you?" (John 1:19). That was a question on the minds of many Jews. Through all the difficulties of the previous four hundred years, the longing for the coming of the Messiah still burned in many Jewish hearts. The promises in Malachi and Isaiah excited the hopes of the people that the day of God's visitation was close at hand when Jesus began his ministry. John's words that One was coming who would "[b]aptize them with the Holy Spirit and fire" (Matthew 3:11) and his call for them to "repent, for the kingdom of God is at hand" (Matthew 3:2) had spread like wildfire among the Judeans. Those reports reached the ears of the members of the Sanhedrin, causing them concern and confusion. That body was composed of the parties of the Pharisees and Sadducees who had been rebuked by John when they appeared for baptism: "You brood of vipers who warned you to flee from the wrath to come?" (Matthew 3:9). The religious excitement which had captured the attention of Jews throughout the whole region was not sufficiently understood by the Sanhedrin. Thus, this unofficial delegation suddenly appeared before John demanding answers.

John was not a reed shaken by the wind and he testified truly when confronted by their questions: "I am not the Christ" (John 1:20). Again, the delegation asked, "What then? Are you Elijah?" (John 1:21a). John answered them, "I am not" (John 1:21b). "Are you the Prophet?" (John 1:21c). He answered, "No" (John 1:21d). Finally, they asked him, "Who are you, so that we may give an answer to those who sent us? What do you say about yourself?" (John 1:21, 22). John answered that he was the "voice of one crying in the wilderness" (John 1:23), according to Isaiah's prophecy. John rightly denied being the Christ or the Prophet prophesied by Moses (cf. Deuteronomy 18:18, 19), who also was the Christ. While denying that he was Elijah, John claimed to be the one mentioned in Isaiah 40:3 (John 1:23). Truly, he was the voice of one crying in the wilderness.

That interview by the Jewish delegation took place on a Thursday the day before Jesus arrived back at Bethany on the Friday after His temptations were finished. When John spotted Jesus the next day walking towards him, he said to two of his disciples, "Behold, the Lamb of God who takes away the sin of the world" (John 1:29). In those words, John identified the great work of Jesus was to be the true high priest of Israel and the world (Cf. Hebrews 5:1–10). Unlike the priests after the order of Aaron, Jesus was without sin and would offer Himself as the sacrifice. John rightly called Him "the lamb of God." The Suffering Servant in Isaiah was to be an individual who would bear "the iniquity of us all" and who would offer that "guilt offering" required by God. John the Baptist, more so even than any of Jesus' disciples before His resurrection, saw that Jesus' mission was to die for sinners rather than to inaugurate a material kingdom. John, though six months older than Jesus, also acknowledged the divinity of his cousin when he said, "After me comes a Man who has a higher rank than I, for He existed before me" (John 1:30). John repeated the substance of his testimony about Jesus the next day when he once again called him "the Lamb of God" (John 1:36). Edersheim comments on John's reference to Jesus as the Lamb of God:

> For the Paschal Lamb was, in a sense, the basis of all the sacrifices of the Old Testament, not only from its saving import to Israel, but as that which really made them 'the Church', and people of God. Hence the institution of the Paschal Lamb was, so to speak, only enlarged and applied in the daily sacrifice of a lamb.[19]

As a result of John's words, two of his disciples, John[20] and Andrew, left him and started following Jesus. Jesus asked them, "What do you seek?" (John 1:38), but they only asked Him where He was staying. Where He was staying, they would stay. Where He would go, they would go. From that day, they began to be followers and disciples of Jesus. That was the Jewish Sabbath day. It was the tenth hour of the day.[21] John gives us the time of day because it was at that hour that he became a follower of Jesus. Andrew immediately sought out

---

19 Edersheim, *The Life and Times of Jesus the Messiah*, 237. Cf. Acts 7:38 where Stephen refers to the church in the wilderness.
20 John, the Beloved disciple, never refers to himself in this Gospel, but he reports things as a first-hand witness.
21 That would have either been 4 PM according to the way the Jews reckoned time or 10 AM according to the Roman measurement of time.

his brother to bring him to Jesus. John, the beloved disciple, no doubt also searched for his brother, James, but it is typical in this Gospel for him to hide any references to his own life. When Andrew found Simon, he said, "We have found the Messiah" (John 1:41). Andrew was describing that experience from his own perspective rather than from the perspective of God. Westcott shows the proper relationship between John and Jesus, the old Church and the new Church:

> The first disciples of Christ naturally came from among the Baptist's disciples. So the divine order was fulfilled, and the preparatory work had fruit. The new Church grew out of the old Church, as its proper consummation.[22]

When Simon was brought to the Messiah by Andrew, Jesus immediately discerned his true nature and changed his name to Cephas[23] which is translated as Peter. Peter means rock or stone. Jesus would transform him from a vacillating, impetuous person to a person of stability. It would not take place immediately or without many trials.

The following day, Sunday, was the inaugural day of Jesus' ministry and "He purposed to go into Galilee" (John 1:43). Along the way, He called two more disciples. First, "He found Philip" and said to him, "Follow Me" (John 1:43). Philip, like Andrew before him, described that calling in terms that were very personal when he said to Nathaniel: "We have found Him of whom Moses in the Law and also the Prophets wrote—Jesus of Nazareth, the son of Joseph" (John 1:45). That is the language of a true follower of Jesus who is describing his allegiance to the Messiah. Nathaniel was incredulous. He responded: "Can any good thing come out of Nazareth?" (John 1:46). Philip responded to Nathaniel the way Jesus had responded to the query of Andrew and John: "Come and see" (John 1:46). When Jesus saw Nathaniel coming to Him, He remarked, "Behold, an Israelite indeed in whom there is no deceit!" (John 1:47). This surprised Nathaniel and he asked the Lord how He knew him. Jesus told him that He had seen him under the fig tree. "Nathaniel . . . had, as, we often read of Rabbis, rested for prayer, meditation, or study, in the shadow of that wide-spreading tree so common in Palestine, the fig tree."[24] Such insight into the human heart caused Nathaniel to exclaim concerning

---

22 Brooke Foss Westcott, *The Gospel According to St. John* (Grand Rapids, Michigan: William B. Eerdamans Publishing Company, 1971), 24.
23 Cephas is Aramaic whereas Peter is Greek.
24 Edersheim, *The Life and Times of Jesus the Messiah*, 241.

Jesus: "Rabbi, You are the Son of God, You are the King of Israel" (John 1:49). To this remark, Jesus responded: "Truly, truly, I say to you, you will see the heavens opened and the angels of God ascending and descending on the Son of Man" (John 1:51).

Jesus' words to Nathaniel were a clear reference to the vision of Jacob's dream at Bethel, between the territory of Benjamin and Ephraim north of Jerusalem. The ladder that Jacob saw is Jesus of Nazareth. He is the only ladder between God and man. Nathaniel had referred to Jesus as the Son of God. Then Jesus claimed the words of Daniel's prophecy (Daniel 7:13, 14) applied to Him. He is the Son of Man to whom is given the kingdom by the Ancient of Days, God the Father. The place where this exchange took place between Jesus and Nathaniel may have been near either Bethel or the ford of Jabbuk where Jacob had wrestled with a man until daybreak.[25] Nathaniel[26] also joined the other disciples and became a follower of Jesus. They now numbered five—Andrew, Peter, John, Philip, and Nathanael.

The Wedding Feast at Cana (John 2:1–12)

Nazareth, the childhood home of Jesus, was approximately ninety miles north of the place where John was baptizing. In the company of His five new disciples, Jesus headed toward Nazareth via the highway that went north along the west side of the Jordan, then northwest between Mount Gerizim and Mount Ebal before turning north towards Nazareth. Monday and Tuesday of that week were hard days of travel that saw Him and His disciples traverse thirty to thirty-five miles each day. "If He were traveling expeditiously He might stop on the first night at Shiloh or Shechem; on the second day at En-Gannim; on the third day, crossing the plain of Jezreel, He could easily reach Nazareth."[27] From Nazareth, it would have taken another hour or so to reach Cana of Galilee[28], a little town that was about four miles northeast of Nazareth. The following description of the town is very enchanting:

> It is a neat village, pleasantly situated on the descent of a hill looking

---

[25] Westcott, *The Gospel According to St. John*, 28.
[26] Nathaniel is the disciple identified as Bartholomew in the Synoptic Gospels. His name in Greek is Theodore which means "Gift of God."
[27] Frederick Farrar, *Life of Christ* (Bibliotech Press, 2020), 59.
[28] Cana of Galilee has usually been identified as Kefr Kenna by most scholars, though. Another place, Kana El-Jelil, is about 8 miles from Nazareth and is favored by some scholars, but the best evidence seems to side with Kefr Kenna.

to the southwest, and surrounded by plantations of olive and other fruit-trees. There is a large spring in the neighborhood, enclosed by a wall, which, if this be the Cana of the New Testament, is doubtless that from which water was drawn at the time of the Lord's visit. It is also observable that water-pots of compact limestone are still in use in this neighborhood, and some old ones are, as might be expected, shown as those which once contained the miraculous wine.[29]

The day of the wedding was certainly Wednesday, for that was the custom for the marriage of a maiden, or virgin.[30] The wedding ceremony also would have begun at twilight, as was the custom both in Palestine and Greece.[31] Before Jewish couples could be wedded, they were required to go through a period of betrothal which was almost identical to marriage, except that they did not cohabit. "At the betrothal, the bridegroom, personally or by deputy, handed to the bride a piece of money or a letter, it being expressly stated in each case that the man thereby espoused the woman."[32] Edersheim describes what typically happened at such weddings:

> On the evening of the actual marriage, the bride was led from her paternal home to that of her husband. First came the merry sounds of music; then they who distributed among the people wine and oil, and nuts among the children; next the bride, covered with the bridal veil, her long hair flowing, surrounded by her companions, and led by the friends of the bridegroom,' and 'the children of the bride-chamber.' All around were in festive array; some carried torches, or lamps on poles; those nearest had myrtle-branches and chaplets of flowers. Everyone rose to salute the procession or join it; and it was deemed almost a religious duty to break into praise of the beauty, the modesty, or the virtues of the bride. Arrived at her new home, she was led to her husband.[33]

John 2:1 states: "On the third day[34] there was a wedding in Cana of Galilee, and the mother of Jesus was there; and both Jesus and His disciples were invited to the wedding." One or the other of the parties getting married were likely relatives of Mary which would account for the prominent part she played in the festivities. Having just completed a ninety mile trip, Jesus and His disciples would probably not have conformed to the "common Jewish custom of

---

29 McClintock and Strong, *Cyclopedia of Biblical, Theological, and Ecclesiastical Literature*, 2:61.
30 Edersheim, *The Life and Times of Jesus the Messiah*, 238.
31 Farrar, *Life of Christ*, 59.
32 Edersheim, *The Life and Times of Jesus the Messiah*, 245.
33 Edersheim, *The Life and Times of Jesus the Messiah*, 245
34 This time reference is the basis on which the days of the previous week are known.

Jesus' Baptism and Temptations

bringing with them wine and other provisions to contribute to the mirthfulness of the wedding feast."[35] It was probably for that reason that Mary informed her son that the wine had given out which would have embarrassed the groom and his parents. Mary delicately said to Jesus: "They have no wine" (John 2:3). Jesus' response is easily misunderstood. He asked, "Woman, what does that have to do with us? My hour has not yet come?" (John 2:4). Yet, Mary did not take umbrage at Jesus' words; rather, she turned to the servants and said, "Whatever He says to you, do it" (John 2:5). The word that He used to address His mother, "woman," was respectful enough to be addressed to a queen and tender enough to be addressed to someone deeply loved.[36] Jesus used the same word concerning His mother when He told John, the beloved disciple, from His cross to take Mary as his own mother. The phrase, 'what does that have to do with us?', was a common Aramaic question that was "perfectly consistent with the most delicate courtesy and the most feeling consideration."[37] It was Jesus' way to delicately inform His mother that His days of being in subjection to her authority were now at an end. He was now subject to the will of His Father. Yet, Mary also knew her son and she was convinced that He would do something to keep the wedding from being an embarrassment to the parents of the couple.

There were six stone water pots that were used for purification close by. Each one probably held twenty to twenty-five gallons of water. The Jews were meticulous with their purification laws which "was one of the main points of Rabbinic sanctity."[38] In the Mishnah, there were 126 chapters on purification with 1001 separate precepts, or compilations of precepts, concerning such cleansings. Jesus commanded the servants to fill the stone jars to the brim with water and then to draw some out and take it to the headwaiter. The headwaiter was amazed and exclaimed to the bridegroom: "Every man serves the good wine first, and when people have drunk freely, then he serves the poorer wine, but you have kept the good wine until now" (John 2:10). This was Jesus' first miracle and it tells us some very important things about Him. He did not come to man-

---

35 Farrar, *Life of Christ*, 60.
36 Farrar, *Life of Christ*, 60.
37 Farrar, *Life of Christ*, 60.
38 Edersheim, *The Life and Times of Jesus the Messiah*, 247.

date celibacy, but to commend joy in the sacred union of a man and a woman. Solomon had earlier recommended to all husbands, "Let your fountain be blessed, and rejoice in the wife of your youth . . . Be exhilarated always with her love" (Proverbs 5:16, 17). Jesus also sanctioned marriage by His attendance at this wedding. Christianity is not a gloomy religion, but it is life lived to the fullest with the blessing of God.

Jesus had refused to turn stones into bread in order to relieve His own hunger, but His heart was opened widely to turn the purification water into the best wine on this joyous occasion. How this miracle happened, we do not know. All of God's ways are a mystery to us. Yet, He brought joy to the wedding party by this sign and manifested His own glory as well. These disciples who had started to follow Him were compelled to believe in Him when they saw such a wonderful transformation of water into wine.

Following this miracle, Jesus led His disciples, His mother, and His brothers down to Capernaum (Cf. John 2:12) which was on the north side of the Sea of Galilee. That town was soon to become His home, even as it was the home of Peter and Andrew and near the home of three of His other disciples—James, John, and Philip. The Sea of Galilee is shaped like a harp, being thirteen miles long and six miles wide. That region, known as Gennesaret, is one of the most beautiful spots in all of Palestine. Gennesaret means 'garden of abundance' and the number of blossoming flowers in that area make it seem like a dazzling emerald.[39] It was a lovely place to make His home base for His ministry, as F. W. Farrar informs us:

> Josephus, in a passage of glowing admiration, after describing the sweetness of its waters, and the delicate temperature of its air, its palms, and vines, and oranges, and figs, and almonds, and pomegranates, and warm springs, says that the seasons seemed to compete for the honour of its possession, and Nature seemed to have created it as a kind of emulative challenge, wherein she had gathered all the elements of her strength.[40]

Farrar further describes what the population of that region was like:

> All along the western shores of Gennesareth Jews and Gentiles were

---

39 Farrar, *Life of Christ*, 65.
40 Farrar, *Life of Christ*, 66.

strangely mingled, and the wild Arabs of the desert might be seen side by side with enterprising Phoenicians, effeminate Syrians, contemptuous Romans, and supple, wily, corrupted Greeks.[41]

Capernaum would be the perfect place for Jesus to begin a ministry to both Jews and Greeks; to prove that He was the light of the world; and, that His death would be a sacrifice for the whole world.

---

41 Farrar, *Life of Christ*, 67.

5

Jesus' First Year of Ministry

The weather in Israel during the month of April "is seldom overcast or gloomy, except when it rains, which it does in hard thunder showers, as in the last month, but not so often. There are commonly a few days of close hazy weather, accompanied with light northerly or easterly breezes, but the winds in general are fresh westerly. The mornings and evenings hitherto remain cool; but the weather in the day begins to grow hot."[1]

The Passover Feast in AD 27 began on Friday, April 11th. It was the first Passover Jesus attended following His baptism and temptations. Jesus had called five disciples, attended a wedding, and moved his home to Capernaum, but He did not start His active ministry until He went to Jerusalem for this feast. Passover was always followed by a week-long ceremony called the Feast of Unleavened Bread. A few days after His move to Capernaum, therefore, Jesus and His disciples went up to Jerusalem for the Passover, arriving there no later than April 10th—the day of preparation. Within the precincts of the Temple, Jesus found the money changers and the sacrificial animals they sold for the travelers who attended the feast. Jesus' zealous reaction was to cleanse the Temple which He did again during the last week of His life.

Worshipers from across Europe, Africa, and parts of Asia, in addition to Israel, would gather annually for this feast. These money changers took advantage of them by exchanging their money—whether Persian, Syrian, Egyptian, Grecian, or Roman—at a charge of twelve percent for themselves. Every Jew was required to pay the annual Temple tax of a half shekel in the coinage of the Sanctuary—which fact the moneychangers used to justify their usury. On Adar 15th, thirty days before Passover, stalls were opened in every town and village throughout Israel and the Jews were allowed to pay the Temple tax for the next ten days. If they were unable to pay during that ten day window, then they had to fulfill their obligations at the Passover

---

1 Kitto, *Palestine: The Physical Geography and Natural History of the Holy Land*, 1:233.

Feast. Those Jews who lived outside of Israel typically did not have the opportunity to pay the tax except at the feast.

Additionally, the money changers also sold on the greater Temple grounds the animals needed for the sacrifices. These unholy practices were conducted "in the outer court, the court of the Gentiles, where there was a regular market, belonging to the house of Hanan (Annas)."[2] The prices were set by the priests and included a hefty profit for the Temple treasury. Worshipers always had the option of bringing their own animals for sacrifice and, as Alfred Edersheim wrote, "on the Mount of Olives there were four shops, specially for the sale of pigeons and other things requisite for sacrificial purposes"[3] Yet, every animal that was brought from outside had to be examined by the priests according to the Levitical requirements. That often led to disputes which were avoided only by purchasing the animals sold by these money changers. It was a repugnant practice which was unpopular among the common people who unduly suffered under it.

Jesus was very aware of these sinful practices and made His opposition to them the first official act of His ministry. To many people, Jesus' actions would seem unwise and not duly considered. Edersheim disagrees:

> Nor yet is there anything either 'abrupt' or 'tactless' in such a commencement of his Ministry. It is not only profane, but unhistorical, to look for calculation and policy in the Life of Jesus. Had there been such, He would not have died on the Cross. And 'abrupt' it certainly was not. Jesus took up the thread where he had dropped it on His first recorded appearance in the Temple . . . that He must be about His father's business. He was now about His Father's business, and, as we may say so, in the most elementary manner. To put an end to the desecration of the Father's House, which, by a nefarious traffic, had been made a place of mart, nay 'a den of robbers,' was what all who knew His Mission must have felt, a most suitable and almost necessary beginning of His Messianic Work.[4]

John the Baptist had earlier declared the purpose for Jesus' ministry when he exclaimed, "Behold, the Lamb of God who takes away the sin of the world!" (John 1:29). Jesus was not only the perfect sac-

---

2 Westcott, *The Gospel According to St. John*, 41. Annas was the high priest during the ministry of Jesus.
3 Edersheim, *The Life and Times of Jesus the Messiah*, 255.
4 Edersheim, *The Life and Times of Jesus the Messiah*, 258.

rifice for the sin of the world, He was also the true priest who would offer that sacrifice. His great work was to be a priest and it was as such that He consciously cleansed the Temple at the very beginning of His ministry—probably on April 10th, the day of preparation, just hours before the Passover began. Moreover, Malachi had predicted that when the Messiah came He would be "like a refiner's fire and like fuller's soap" and that He would "purify the sons of Levi and refine them like gold and silver, so that they may present to the Lord offerings in righteousness" (Malachi 3:2, 3). Those sons of Levi in Jesus' days who were permitting and endorsing these sinful practices on the Temple grounds needed to be refined and purified and that is where Jesus began His reformation. Thus, Jesus made a scourge of cords and drove the sheep and oxen out, poured out the coins of the money changers, overturned the tables, and rebuked those who were selling the doves, "Take these things away; stop making My father's house a place of business" (John 2:16). From the very beginning of His ministry, Jesus identified as closely as possible with the Father. He called Him, "My Father"—not *our* Father or *the* Father. The scourge of cords He used was as "a symbol of authority and not as a weapon of offence. The "cords" (properly of twisted rushes) was at hand . . . Jewish tradition ('Sanh.' 98 b, Wunsche) figured Messiah as coming with a scourge for the chastisement of evil-doers."[5] Edersheim commented:

> He inaugurated His Mission by fulfilling the prediction concerning Him Who was to be Israel's refiner and purifier (Mal. 3:1–3). Scarce had He entered the Temple-porch, and trod the Court of the Gentiles, than He drove thence what profanely defiled it.[6]

When His disciples observed all these things, they "remembered that it was written, 'Zeal for Your house will consume Me'" (John 2:17), a verse from Psalm 69:9. The Jewish priests who observed all these things made no effort to seize Jesus or to even rebuke Him. Instead, they asked a question: "What sign do You show us as your authority for doing these things?" (John 2:18). The Roman garrison at the Antonia Fortress was close by and would not allow a riot among the Jews. The question of authority would become the primary challenge of the Jewish authorities against Jesus, even when He performed

---

5 Westcott, *The Gospel According to St. John*, 41.
6 Edersheim, *The Life and Times of Jesus the Messiah*, 258.

signs that bore testimony to His Messiahship, as He did in the week that followed Passover (John 2:23). Jesus did not perform a miracle at the behest of the Jewish leaders, though, because His ministry was not beholden to their authority. The Jewish leaders wanted to control everything about the religious life in Israel and there was no way for Jesus to be submissive to them. His purpose was to do the will of His Father.

Jesus knew from the outset of His ministry what great events were going to unfold. He knew that an evil generation seeks for a sign (Matthew 12:38–40) and He ultimately only had one sign to give them—His resurrection from the dead. Thus, He said, "Destroy this temple, and in three days I will raise it up" (John 2:19). The Jews were incredulous, not understanding His words, and replied, "It took forty-six years to build this temple, and will you raise it in three days?" (John 2:20). Jesus' sign, which was really a parable, concerned both His death and resurrection. He spoke about His body—not about Herod's Temple. He spoke about both the destruction of His body and the raising of it up again. The Jews completely overlooked the first part of His statement. Herod's Temple was not yet finished and its purpose was fading away because of the sacrifice that Jesus would make for the sin of the world. Jesus' words were not understood by His disciples at that time and misunderstood by the Jewish leaders, who later used those words as a ground for His condemnation as a criminal. Yet, from the very beginning, Jesus knew what His mission was and He never wavered from it.

Jesus did various unnamed signs or miracles during this feast. The miracles are not specified by John, but they were probably similar to what He would do elsewhere—healing the sick, casting out demons, causing the lame to walk, and the blind to see, etc. Those days at this feast were especially filled with Jesus teaching and preaching to the crowds in the courts of the Temple He had just cleansed. Thus, "during the feast, many believed in His name, observing His signs which He was doing. But Jesus, on His part, was not entrusting Himself to them, for He knew all men" (John 2:23, 24). There were various reasons Jesus had that habitual attitude, He knew that "those who had been attracted by the miracles would have been ready to try to make an earthly king of Him."[7] Jesus knew Himself and His

---

7 Leon Morris, *The Gospel According to St. John* (Grand Rapids: Eerdmans Publishing Company,

mission; He knew the hearts of all men; and, He knew His opponents. He knew that death by crucifixion awaited Him at the end of His earthly ministry. The cross would not be the end of His mission, though, because He would rise from the dead. Yet, His disciples knew none of those things at that time and they were not yet able to be taught about Calvary at that time.

Nicodemus Comes to Jesus by Night (John 3:1–21)

It was sometime during that week of celebration that one of the rulers of Israel, Nicodemus, came to Jesus by night. John, the author of this Gospel, is believed by some to have owned a small home in Jerusalem (cf. John 19:27).[8] If so, Jesus and His other disciples probably stayed with the Beloved disciple during the Feast of the Jews. Somehow, Nicodemus found where Jesus was staying and came to Him secretly under the cloak of darkness so as to avoid persecution from his fellow members of the Sanhedrin. If others on the Council were already beginning to be antagonistic towards Jesus, Nicodemus was thoughtfully considering the possibility that Jesus might indeed be the Messiah. Manifesting great respect for Jesus, Nicodemus addressed Him: "Rabbi, we know that You have come from God as a teacher; for no one can do these signs that You do unless God is with Him" (John 3:2). Nicodemus recognized Jesus as both a teacher and a miracle worker. He knew that He had been sent from God, but he had not yet come to believe in Him and confess Him publicly. He was a sincere seeker whose heart had not yet been opened.[9] His address to Jesus was respectful, but not expressive of true faith in Him. As Westcott points out:

> According to the Jewish saying, "Rabbi was higher than Rab, Rabban than Rabbi, but greater than all was he who (like the prophets) was not called by any such title.[10]

The root word for all these titles—Rab, Rabbi, Rabban—means "great." Jesus was a great man to Nicodemus at this time, but still just a man and not even the greatest of men—certainly not as great

---

1971), 207.
8 Edersheim entertains this tradition as a possibility (as do others), but not as a fact that can be proved. Cf. *The Life and Times of Jesus the Messiah*, 265.
9 Nicodemus, while timid, did eventually come out in the daylight to express his loyalty to Jesus when Joseph of Arimathea had placed the Lord in his tomb. Nicodemus brought spices in the daytime. While the Scripture does not describe Nicodemus as believing in Jesus, yet it does commend him for coming to Jesus. Coming is a word often used in the Scripture as a metaphor for faith.
10 Westcott, *The Gospel According to St. John*, 48.

as the prophets. Jesus, knowing the hearts of all men, is described by John as possessing the "attribute of complete human knowledge."[11] When Jesus was approached by Nicodemus, He did not focus on the latter's compliment of Him, but immediately addressed the real need of this ruler's heart. Jesus said, "Truly, truly, I say to you, unless one is born again" (John 3:3). Both John the Baptist and Jesus had come preaching about the kingdom of God being near. Nicodemus wanted to learn more, but Jesus analyzed his problem as being unable to even see the kingdom of God. Jesus' reply was shocking to Nicodemus and he asked, "How can a man be born when he is old? He cannot enter a second time into His mother's womb and be born, can he?" (John 3:4). We should not assume that Nicodemus was being deliberately obtuse or argumentative, but, rather, that he "failed completely to grasp the deep meaning of the divine marshal."[12] Thus, Nicodemus asks a rhetorical question using the most extreme example which he clearly expected to be answered negatively. The term "new birth" was usually referenced concerning Gentile proselytes who had become "as a child newly born" when they were baptized from heathenism,[13] so Nicodemus was startled by Jesus' words. "The Jews understood that a proselyte must become a member of the kingdom in order to be a 'new-born child.'"[14] Nicodemus was already a member of the covenant kingdom and he did not need a new birth, or so he thought. Jesus was reversing the order: every person—including Jews—must become new born before they can even see the kingdom of God. As Leon Morris wrote:

> Nicodemus may have felt that the term appropriate to the Gentile as he entered the ranks of the chosen people was the last word that should be applied to one who was not only a Jew, but a Pharisee, and a member of the Sanhedrin.[15]

Jesus completely ignored the last question of Nicodemus, but doubled down on His emphasis on the new birth: "Truly, truly, I say to you, unless one is born of water and the Spirit he cannot enter into the kingdom of God" (John 3:5). The new birth is a contrast to the first birth which was physical. The first birth was through the moth-

---
11 Westcott, *The Gospel According to St. John*, 46.
12 William Hendriksen, *The Gospel of John* (Edinburgh, Scotland and Carlisle, Pennsylvania: The Banner of Truth Trust, 1976), 133.
13 Shepard, *The Christ of the Gospels*, 100.
14 Shepard, *The Christ of the Gospels*, 100.
15 Morris, *The Gospel According to John*, 214.

er's water in the flesh (Cf. John 3:6). The second birth is through the Holy Spirit. In this conversation with Nicodemus, Jesus is showing that the new birth must precede all else in the spiritual kingdom. A person cannot even see the kingdom of God until he is born again. He cannot believe until he has a new heart through the work of the Holy Spirit.

At that point, Jesus compared the mysterious work of the Holy Spirit to the wind that blows, especially at night, during April in Jerusalem. Sometimes, it comes from the north; sometimes from the east; but, generally, it comes from the west. Just as the sound of the wind is heard without someone knowing where it comes from and where it is going, so are those who are born of the Spirit. Despite Jesus' explanation, Nicodemus was still incredulous, asking, "How can these things be?" (John 3:9). Jesus replied, "Are you the teacher of Israel and do not understand these things?" (John 3:10). Spiritual regeneration was a subject covered in several places in the Old Testament, particularly in Ezekiel 36:26, 27: "Moreover, I will give you a new heart and put a new spirit within you, and I will remove the heart of stone from your flesh and give you a heart of flesh. I will put My Spirit within you and cause you to walk in My statutes, and you will be careful to observe My ordinances." The transformation of the heart by the work of the Spirit, Jesus asserted, was not a new doctrine, but one which should have been understood by all leaders of the Jews.

After declaring the necessity of the new birth, Jesus then emphasized the importance of saving faith. Whoever has been born again will also believe. John 3:16 is, perhaps, the most well-known verse in the Scripture and it is prefaced by a reference to an event from Numbers 21 which gives the account of the fiery serpents that bit the children of Israel in the wilderness. Moses was commanded by the Lord to make a bronze serpent and lift it up on a standard before the people. And as Scripture says, "And it came about that if a serpent bit any man, when he looked to the bronze serpent, he lived" (Numbers 21:9). Jesus associates the faith of the Israelites in Numbers 21 with the faith of believers in His atonement on the Cross. He was given as the Lamb of God who takes away the sin of the world. As the great 18th century Presbyterian minister, Samuel Davies, stated concerning this method of salvation in a sermon, "The Method of Salvation through Jesus Christ":

You see upon the whole, my brethren, you are not excluded from Christ and life by the greatness of your sins; but if you perish it must be from another cause; it must be on account of your wilful unbelief in not accepting of Jesus Christ as your Saviour. If you reject him, then indeed you must perish, however small your sins have been; for it is only his death that can make atonement for the slightest guilt; and if you have no interest in that, the guilt of the smallest sin will sink you into ruin.[16]

The historical incident from Numbers 21 referenced by Jesus in John 3:14, 15 was painted by Anthony Van Dyck in 1599 and that painting is housed in the National Gallery in London. It portrays people who had been bitten by the vipers trying various methods to save themselves or desperately looking for help from other sources, but very few of them looked to the bronzed serpent on the standard lifted up by Moses. Yet, the cross of Christ represented by that bronzed serpent is the only sacrifice acceptable to God.

John Baptizes at Aenon (John 3:22–36)

When Passover ended on April 18th, Jesus and His disciples withdrew to an area along the Jordan River where they remained for the rest of the year. The exact place where they were baptizing is not known, but it was likely not far from where He Himself had been baptized. John had moved about sixty miles north to Aenon near Salim. "In the time of Eusebius, Salim was identified with a place on the confines of Galilee and Samaria on the west of Jordan, six or eight miles south of Scythopolis."[17] The Pharisees had been successful in pushing John further and further away from Jerusalem, but closer to where Herod Antipas had his seat of government in Tiberias. A fearless reformer, like John, had reason to be concerned to be in close proximity to such a wicked ruler like Herod Antipas.

Scythopolis, or Beth Shean, was the "city of the Scythians," who were nomadic tribes from a region that is in southern Russia today. The city lies about seventeen miles south of the Sea of Galilee and had existed for several centuries. In a battle between Israel and the Philistines at nearby Mount Gilboa, Saul and his three sons had been killed and their bodies were hung on the walls of Beth Shean. The city was rebuilt in 63 BC by Aulus Gabinius, a Roman Senator and General who was a strong supporter of Pompey. It flourished under

---

16 Samuel Davies, *Sermons by the Rev. Samuel Davies* (Pittsburgh: Soli Deo Gloria Publications, 1993), 130.
17 Westcott, *The Gospel According to St. John*, 58.

the Pax Romana and was the leading city of Rome's Decapolis. The Jewish sages said about the city, "If the garden of Eden is in the land of Israel, then its gate is Beth Shean."[18] That area had fertile land and many bodies of water. That is, no doubt, why John the Baptist chose it as the place where he would continue his ministry of preaching and baptizing. The Jordan River, in comparison, sometimes overflowed its banks and other times did not have a lot of water.

When Jesus went to the Jordan to begin His ministry, He symbolically took the mantle from John. Like the Forerunner, He proclaimed the same message: "Repent, for the kingdom of God is at hand" (Matthew 4:17). Jesus' ministry was a completion of John's—not a departure from it. It was not long, though, until Jesus' ministry began to eclipse the work that John had done. Jesus and His disciples were "spending time" there and baptizing—the length of time was probably close to seven or eight months. During that period, there "arose a discussion on the part of John's disciples with a Jew about purification" (John 4:25). This is the first recorded discussion or controversy over baptism. William Hendriksen suggests that this controversy was "begun by the disciples of John who probably ascribed superior (or exclusive) *purifying* efficacy to the baptism of their teacher."[19] That may well be the case, but there is another possibility since the discussion was between John's disciples and a Jew. The Jew might have been a Pharisee or a representative of the Sanhedrin who was questioning the authority of John to be performing such baptisms. The Jews believed that baptism was a rite that belonged to the rulers of the synagogue and was to be administered to Gentile converts to Judaism. John's practice was completely out of step with the Jewish practice. They baptized Gentile converts. John called even the Jews to be baptized for the repentance of sins.

Henry Hart Milman, in his three volume set, *The History of Christianity*, showed that the Jews had contracted pagan ideas concerning the magical efficacy of sacraments during their captivity in Babylon and Assyria. The religious views of the Hindus had spread to Assyria and Babylon, influencing the Jews who were in exile there. Six centuries before Christ, the Hindus taught that the waters of baptism could bestow baptismal regeneration or make someone a "twice-

---

18 Accessed on May 11, 2022 at: https://www.bibleplaces.com/bethshean/
19 Hendriksen, *The Gospel of John*, 147.

born" man.[20] The party of the Pharisees arose after the Jews returned from their captivity and had been heavily influenced by Hinduism. It is likely, therefore, that this discussion about baptism centered on the questions of what efficacy John's baptism had for those who received it or whether it was for Gentile converts only.

After this discussion with the Jewish deputation, the disciples of John came to him and said, "Rabbi, He who was with you beyond the Jordan, to whom you have testified, behold, He is baptizing and all are coming to Him" (John 3:26). John eschewed all jealousy with a simple response: "A man can receive nothing unless it has been given him from above" (John 3:27). John's reply is very similar to what Paul wrote in 1 Corinthians 4:7—"What do you have that you did not receive? And if you did receive it, why do you boast as if you did not receive it?" John had the courage and boldness of a lion, but he was not absorbed with vainglory. He was willing for Jesus to eclipse his fame because he knew that his responsibility was simply to prepare the way for the Messiah. John's reference to the joy that the friend of the bridegroom experiences as his own joyful elation was followed by his self-effacing statement: "He must increase, but I must decrease" (John 3:30).

The last verses of John 3 are a profound statement of John's saving insight into the Divinity and mission of Jesus. He expressed his faith that Jesus was One who came "from above" and "is above all." (John 3:31). Such insight was a revelation of the Holy Spirit to John. He sets forth Jesus in these verses as primarily having a mission to teach—"What He has seen and heard, of that He testifies" (John 3:32). It is interesting that John's disciples came to him with questions about baptism and a report that Jesus was baptizing more than John, but John ignored their complaints and focused on the spiritual mission of Jesus. Paul had done the same thing in 1 Corinthians 1:17—"For Christ did not send me to baptize, but to preach the gospel, not in cleverness of speech, so that the cross of Christ would not be made void." While the Scripture plainly teaches that both John and Jesus and their disciples were baptizing large numbers of people, it gives us very little information about those baptisms. Why is that? Because the message of the Scripture is about the gospel—and sacraments are secondary to the gospel message. John the Baptist preaches one of the

---

20 Dewey Roberts, *Historic Christianity and the Federal Vision* (Destin, FL: Sola Fide Publications, 2016), 128.

greatest sermons ever in exaltation of the glory of Christ. He does not say, "He who is baptized by the Son has eternal life." He says, "He who believes in the Son has eternal life" (John 3:36). Saving faith is more important than baptism. Baptism is a sacrament that everyone who believes must receive as a sign and seal of the saving grace of God in their lives when they profess Him and unite with His church. But neither Jesus nor John ever taught that baptism saves us or regenerates us. Jesus taught that the new birth is a work of the Holy Spirit in the heart of a person and not the result of the water of baptism.

John the Baptist Imprisoned by Herod (Matthew 14:3–5; Mark 6:17–20)
Towards the end of AD 27, John the Baptist found himself increasingly on the wrong side of Herod Antipas. For a while, John had found refuge in Perea that enabled him to continue his ministry at the aforementioned Aenon near Salim. Yet, John was a faithful reformer and Herod was a cunning, sly ruler who was guilty of numerous sins, mostly of a private nature. Herod Antipas was the son of Herod the Great through his marriage to his third wife, Malthace, who was a Samaritan. He was temperamentally close to his father and acquired his vices of "craft, cruelty, and licentiousness."[21] He was also "sly, ambitious, and luxurious, only not so able as his father."[22] Frederick W. Farrar described him, thusly: "Herod Antipas—the pettiest, meanest, weakest, most contemptible of titular princelings."[23] Herod's luxury and lust soon caused problems for his kingdom that came to the attention of John the Baptist and occasioned a rebuke of the king by that great man.

Antipas had married, Phasaelis, the daughter of King Aretas IV of Nabatea,[24] a political marriage to keep the Arabians from invading his territories. There was apparently little love in the union between Herod and Phasaelis. On a visit to Rome to see his half-brother, Herod Philip, Antipas was enamored with Philip's wife, Herodias, who was the granddaughter of Herod the Great and the niece of both Phillip and Antipas. Herod Phillip and Herodias had a daughter through

---

21 Emil Schurer, *A History of the Jewish People in the Time of Jesus Christ* (London: Bloomsbury T & T Clark, 2000), 2:18.
22 Farrar, *The Life of Christ*, 289.
23 Farrar, *The Life of Christ*, 289.
24 Nabatea was an important Arabian kingdom in antiquity which stretched from Damascus in the north to the coast of the Red Sea in the south, and controlled most of the trade routes which were important to ancient Palestine.

their union, Salome. Antipas "proposed to her that she leave Phillip for him"[25] and Herodias consented under one condition: "that he divorce the daughter of Aretas."[26] Jewish law at the time permitted kings to have as many as eighteen wives, so it was not a problem for Herod to marry Herodias without getting a divorce.[27] Yet, Herodias wanted no rivals. When Phasaelis learned of this intrigue, she requested Herod "to send her to Macherus . . . without informing him of any of her intentions."[28] Machaerus was the mountain top fortress on the border between Perea and Nabatea, due east of the Dead Sea, and was under the general command of Aretas. Herod gladly sent Phasaelis to Machaerus, thinking that she was none the wiser concerning his unfaithfulness. Once she had remained there for a while, she had the general of her father's army to take her to Arabia "under the conduct of the several generals . . . and she soon came to her father, and told him of Herod's intentions."[29]

This news of Herod's scheming was the occasion of enmity between him and Aretas that resulted in both sides raising armies to prepare for war.[30] It was into that situation that John the Baptist thrust himself when he began to proclaim to Herod: "It is not lawful for you to have your brother's wife" (Mark 6:18). Herod, a weak and conflicted man, feared the Jews because of John; he feared that fearless man dressed in a garment of camel's hair; and, especially, he feared an uprising among the Jews which could jeopardize his throne. He also feared his new wife, Herodias, as well as his Arabian queen, Phasaelis, who was now living with her father at Petra. Petra was the capitol of the Nabatean kingdom and it contained both tombs and temples carved into the pink sandstone of that region. The crown was now sitting very unsteadily on the head of this Herod. Thus, he sent officers to arrest and imprison John the Baptist at Machaerus—now vacated by Phasaelis. That fortress was a natural observation post for the Roman garrison stationed there from which they could spot any

---

25 Archibald T. Robertson, *John the Loyal: Studies in the Ministry of the Baptist* (New York: Charles Scribner's Sons, 1911), 181.
26 Robertson, *John the Loyal: Studies in the Ministry of the Baptist*, 181.
27 David Smith, *The Days of His Flesh: The Earthly Life of Our Lord and Saviour* (New York: A. C. Armstrong & Son, London: Hodder and Stoughton, 1905), 71. Also, Cf. Emil Schurer, *A History of the Jewish People in the Time of Jesus Christ* (London: Bloomsbury T & T Clark, 2000), 1:18.
28 William Whiston, trans., Josephus, *Complete Works of Flavius Josephus* (Grand Rapids, Michigan: Kregel Publications, 1960), 382.
29 Whiston, trans., Josephus, *Complete Works of Flavius Josephus*, 382.
30 Whiston, trans., Josephus, *Complete Works of Flavius Josephus*, 382.

invading armies. Petra was about 120 miles due south of Machaerus and tensions between the two kingdoms continued to worsen which would eventually result in Herod's army being destroyed by Aretas.[31] That event resulted in the Roman emperor, Tiberius, sending two legions of soldiers under the command of Lucius Vitellius, governor of Syria, to attack Petra in AD 37. Yet, Tiberius died before the attack could be made and Vitellius retired to Antioch without ever engaging Aretas in battle.

The palace at Machaerus was a luxurious spectacle, 100 meters long and 60 meters wide, which utilized "natural geological features, watchtowers and a large defensive wall to protect an upper palace and lower city."[32] According to Pliny the Elder, "Machaerus was next to Jerusalem, the most strongly fortified place in Judea."[33] It could be seen as far away as Masada in the south and Alexandrium in the north while smoke signals from it were visible in Jerusalem. Originally, it was just a defensive fortress, but Herod made numerous renovations to it "including a courtyard with a garden, a Roman-style bath, a triclinium for dining and a peristyle courtyard."[34] Red roofing tiles and marble columns have also been discovered by archaeologists. Of course, the cell where John was imprisoned did not enjoy any of those luxuries. There were two dungeons for prisoners at Machaerus which were dug into the rock on which the fortress stood. "They were dark and cold and dank like the inner prison of Philippi in which Paul and Silas were confined."[35] John was able to entertain visitors who could talk with him through the bars of that dungeon on occasion. Yet, the dungeon in which he lived, cold in winter and stifling in summer, was depressive for even the most optimistic soul.

It is not known when Herod began to first listen to John or how

---

31 This did not happen until after John's death and the Jews blamed Herod's murder of the prophet for the loss of his army.
32 "Machaerus—The Palace Fortress of King Herod" online at *Heritage Daily*. Accessed on June 2, 2022 at: https://www.heritagedaily.com/2020/12/machaerus-the-palace-fortress-of-king-herod/136596
33 Gyozo Voros, "Machaerus Through the Ages" in Bible History Daily of the Biblical Archaeological Society, (Pliny the Elder, *Historia Naturalis*, 15–16). Accessed on June 2, 2022 at: https://www.biblicalarchaeology.org/issue/machaerus-through-the-ages/
34 "Machaerus: Beyond the Beheading of John the Baptist" written by Biblical Archaeology Society Staff, June 6, 2020. Accessed on June 1, 2022 at: https://www.biblicalarchaeology.org/daily/biblical-sites-places/biblical-archaeology-sites/machaerus-beyond-the-beheading-of-john-the-baptist/
35 Robertson, *John the Loyal: Studies in the Ministry of the Baptist*, 189.

the reformer had such an audience with the tetrarch wherein he could rebuke the king for his sins. The ministry of John near Salim was close enough to Tiberias, Herod's usual residence, that some of the Jews might have questioned John and then taken reports of those encounters to Herod. Josephus wrote concerning this scandal: "Herodias took upon her to confound the laws of our country, and divorce herself from her husband, while he was still alive, and was married to Herod."[36] While the priests, scribes, and Pharisees who lived in Jerusalem might have overlooked the behavior of Herod Antipas on the ground that they were under the tetrarchy of Pontius Pilate, those in Galilee and Perea were faced day by day with this adulterous and incestuous relationship. It is also possible that Herod, wily fox that he was, had summoned John to his court to ask him what he thought and, thereby, to entrap him if he opposed that marriage. However it happened, the Scripture is clear that Herod had John "arrested and bound in prison for Herodias" (Mark 6:17). John's imprisonment placed him out of the public eye and eased the tensions caused by his uncompromising stand against the ruler of Galilee and Perea. Herod was trying in vain to chart a middle path between the will of the people—who considered John to be a prophet—and the will of his wife who wanted him dead. Thus, he had John imprisoned below this fortress far removed from his palace in Tiberias, on the west side of the Sea of Galilee, where he lived in luxury with Herodias. For a while, that made life simpler for Herod, but every day was another day of suffering for John at this fortress, known as the "Black Fortress," which would prove to be his Golgotha.

The Woman at the Well in Samaria (John 4:1–30)
When John was arrested by Herod Antipas and taken to Machaerus, he was shackled and dragged down the east side of the Jordan River past where Jesus' disciples were baptizing near Bethany beyond the Jordan. John's arrest, and the likely sight of his mistreatment, were the motivations for Jesus to move the center of His ministry from the Jordan to Galilee, as Matthew 4:12 states: "Now when Jesus heard that John had been taken into custody, He withdrew into Galilee." In so doing, He avoided the trap which had led to John's imprisonment. The Pharisees had pushed John away from Judea and into Herod's kingdom by their constant criticism. The Baptist had fallen into their

---

36 Whiston, trans., Josephus, *Complete Works of Flavius Josephus*, 383.

trap and it did not end well for him. Now Jesus, knowing that His time was not yet at hand, had to retreat from any areas where He would be in direct conflict with the authorities. When the Pharisees learned that Jesus' followers were growing even larger than the number that were baptized by John (cf. John 4:1, 2), He knew it was time to depart. Thus, He returned to His homeland—Galilee. To do so, "He had to pass through Samaria" (John 4:4) in order to avoid the same territory where John had been arrested.

While there was a road that went almost straight north from the Dead Sea to the Sea of Galilee, Jesus chose the Roman road that veered northwesterly towards Nazareth—a road traveled by many, since "it was the custom of the Galileans, when they came to the holy city at the festivals, to take their journeys through the country of the Samaritans."[37] This road took Him through a region of Palestine—Samaria—that was not even acknowledged by the Pharisees as part of their nation. It was probably in late January or early February of AD 28 when this transition in Jesus' ministry took place. He and His disciples traveled north to an ancient cross road and then west-north-westerly to Sychar, a city in Samaria near to Jacob's well and between the mountains of Ebal and Gerizim. It was a "rather rough and in places steep road that Jesus traveled"[38] and also a dangerous route due to hostilities from the Samaritans. Sychar[39] was in the rich valley beneath the two mountains near where Jacob had dug a one hundred and fifty feet well almost nineteen hundred years earlier. That well was on the right side of the highway and the little town of Sychar was about a mile to the north. While He rested, Jesus sent His disciples into the town to get some food for them.

"So, Jesus, being wearied from His journey, was sitting thus by the well. It was about the sixth hour" (John 4:6). John's notation of the time was probably according to Roman calculations which would have been 6 PM. After a long day's journey, it was late in the afternoon when Jesus and His disciples reached their stopping point for the day. While Jesus was sitting there alone, a woman came out of the city to draw water at the well. "In the neighborhood there were

---

37 Whiston, trans., Josephus, *Complete Works of Flavius Josephus*, 419.
38 Shepard, *The Christ of the Gospels*, 110.
39 Westcott notes concerning Sychar: "There is at present a village, *'Askar*, which corresponds admirably with the required site." Westcott, *The Gospel According to St. John*, 67.

springs like that of El Eskor at the foot of Mt. Ebal, but their water was calcerous and unpalatable. On the other hand the water of the well was a fresh, running, cool stream, palatable and healthful."[40] To her surprise, Jesus made an unusual request of the woman: "Give Me a drink" (John 4:7). The startled Samaritan woman responded: "How is it that you, being a Jew[41], ask me for a drink since I am a Samaritan woman?" (John 4:9). The enmity of the Jews and the Samaritans limited all social contact between them, but especially between Jewish men and Samaritan women. There were a number of statements among the Jews concerning the Samaritans, such as, "May I never set eyes on a Samaritan;" or, "May I never be thrown into company with him!" Eating their bread was compared to eating swine's flesh; and, it was not lawful for a Rabbi to speak with a woman publicly, certainly not a Samaritan woman. Yet, the Samaritans were not considered as heathens either but as the lowest form of a Jew. Nonetheless, their food was considered clean which is why Jesus could send His disciples into Sychar to buy rations.

In His reply to the woman, Jesus said: "if you knew the gift of God, and who it is that says to you, 'Give me a drink,' you would have asked of Him, and He would have given you living water" (John 4:10). Living water was an idea well-known among the Jews that described the "quickening energies which proceed from God."[42] "The request which Christ had made furnished the idea of a parable; the bodily want whereby He suffered suggested an image of the spiritual blessing which He was ready to bestow."[43] Incredulously, the woman asked, "Sir, You have nothing to draw with and the well is deep; where then do You get that living water?" (John 4:11). As of yet, her eyes had not been opened to the spiritual nature of Jesus' words, but that was soon to change. Thus, Jesus responded: "Everyone who drinks of this water will thirst again; but whoever drinks of the water I will give him shall never thirst; but the water that I will give him will become a well of water springing up to eternal life" (John 4:13, 14). If Jesus had been speaking only of water, that would have begged the question: Why had He not also drunk of that living water, instead of asking a

---

40 Shepard, *The Christ of the Gospels*, 110.
41 The fringes on the shawl of a Jewish man were white whereas Samaritan shawls were fringed in blue. Also, the facial appearances of Samaritans and Jews were different.
42 Westcott, *The Gospel According to St. John*, 69.
43 Westcott, *The Gospel According to St. John*, 69.

Samaritan woman for a drink? Yet, the woman was too intrigued by the thought of obtaining "a well of water springing up to eternal life" (John 4:14), so she quickly blurted out: "Sir, give me this water, so I will not be thirsty nor come all the way here to draw" (John 4:15).

In His next words to the woman, it appears superficially that Jesus abruptly changed the subject for no apparent reason. Such is not the case, as Hendriksen notes:

> This thirst will not be truly awakened unless there be a sense of guilt, a consciousness of sin. The mention of her husband is the best means of reminding this woman of her immoral life. The Lord is now addressing himself to her consciousness.[44]

The woman responded with words that "are half sad, half apologetic, as of one who shrinks from the trial conscious of weakness, and who seeks further assurance of power before rendering complete obedience."[45] She replied with a curt remark: "I have no husband" (John 4:17a). While those words were true, they were also not the whole truth. It was her attempt to not be exposed, as surely she was so often among the people of Sychar. Jesus already knew the truth and replied: "You have correctly said, 'I have no husband'; for you have had five husbands and the one whom you now have is not your husband; this you have said truly" (John 4:17b-18). Cornered by Jesus' words, the woman attempted to turn the question away from herself and make this Jew defend an age-old controversy between the Jews and the Samaritans concerning worship. She said, "Sir, I perceive that you are a prophet. Our fathers worshiped in this mountain, and you *people* say that in Jerusalem is the place where men ought to worship" (John 4:19, 20). The ruins of the Samaritan temple on Mount Gerizim were visible to both of them when Jesus replied: "Woman, believe Me, an hour is coming when neither in this mountain nor in Jerusalem will you worship the Father. You worship what you do not know; we worship what we know, for salvation is from the Jews. But an hour is coming and now is, when the true worshipers will worship the Father in spirit and truth; for such people the Father seeks to be His worshipers. God is spirit, and those who worship Him must worship in spirit and truth" (John 4:21–24). "The Samaritans had a worship mixed

---

44 Hendriksen, *The Gospel of John*, 164.
45 Westcott, *The Gospel According to St. John*, 71.

with the idolatrous cults of Cutha[46] and Sepharvaim[47]. They did not know what they worshipped, just as the heathen, who today fall down before idols."[48] Westcott notes concerning this whole debate that:

> The rival claims of Gerizim and Jerusalem are not determined by the Lord, for they vanish in the revelation of the universal religion . . . Judaism (speaking generally) was a worship of the letter and not of spirit (to take examples from the time): Samaritanism was a worship of falsehood and not of truth. By the Incarnation men are enabled to have immediate communion with God, and thus a worship in spirit has become possible.[49]

Jesus answered the woman's statement, "I know that Messiah is coming" (John 4:25), by saying, "I who speak to you am *He*" (John 4:26). She immediately perceived that perhaps He was the Messiah. The best translation of Jesus' response to this woman is: "I that speak to you, I am," which is a form of identifying Himself with Yahweh. The woman would have understood His use of, "I am," as a reference to the sacred name of God. This is the first time Jesus identified Himself as the Messiah. Even to His disciples, He had never spoken as plainly as He did to this woman. There were reasons for Him to refrain from disclosing Himself at the beginning of His ministry. The Jewish people were looking for a political Messiah and the Jewish leaders were afraid of such a King. It was not safe for Jesus to openly reveal Himself to the Jews. He had many things to teach and do before it would be His hour to die for the sins of the world. Yet, it was relatively safe for Him to reveal Himself as the Messiah in a remote area of Israel which was generally avoided by the Jews. As strange as Jesus' words to this woman might sound to our ears, they are simply another way of inviting sinners to Himself. The woman perceived that truth and ran away to tell others about Him. She excitedly said, "Come, see a man who told me all the things that I have done; this is not the Christ, is it?" (John 4:29). She did not yet have full faith in Christ, but she was hopeful that He indeed was the Messiah.

When the disciples returned, they were surprised that Jesus had been talking with a woman. It was a rule of the Rabbis that: "A man

---

46 Cf. 2 Kings 17:30. Different tribes of Israel while in exile made idols that they worshiped.
47 Sepharvaim was the center of the worship of the god Adrammelech. Some of the people were deported to Samaria where they established this type of religion.
48 Shepard, *The Christ of the Gospels*, 113.
49 Westcott, *The Gospel According to St. John*, 72–3.

shall not be alone with a woman in an inn, not even with his sister or daughter, on account of what men may think. A man shall not talk with a woman in the street, not even his own wife, and especially not with another woman, on account of what men may say."[50] That was one reason the woman had been surprised that Jesus had asked for some water, but Jesus was dispelling with the various rules that were contrary to Scripture. This woman was a soul that needed to be rescued from a life of sin and Jesus intended to do that. Having been sent by Jesus into the village to buy food, "the disciples were urging Him, saying, 'Rabbi, eat'" (John 4:31). He responded with a metaphorical statement, "I have food to eat that you do not know about" (John 4:32). That gave Jesus the opportunity to impress on the disciples that doing the will of God is appropriate at all times and is the best food for soul winners. Jesus then quoted a saying to the disciples that gives an idea of when this event took place. He said, "Do you not say, 'There are yet four months, and then comes the harvest'?" (John 4:35a). If Jesus was referring to the barley harvest in May, then this event took place in January of AD 28. If He was referring to the wheat harvest in June, then this event took place in February of that year.

The Revival in Samaria (John 4:31–45)
While He was making these remarks to His disciples, there were men from the city who began coming to Jacob's well to find out for themselves about this interesting man of whom the woman had reported. Jesus probably looked up and saw them when He said, "Behold, I say to you, lift up your eyes and look on the fields, that they are white for harvest" (John 4:35b). As Leon Morris observed: "A harvest will not wait. Unless it is reaped while it is ripe it will spoil, and there will be no harvest."[51] Thirst can be assuaged and hunger can be satisfied at a later time, but a harvest must be gathered when it is time to do so. As Jesus said, "One sows and another reaps" (John 4:37). One person will labor for years preparing the soil for the gospel and another person will sometimes reap what the first person sowed. Yet, it is all God's work.

The men listened to everything that Jesus said and His words were not like the words of their religious leaders. They earnestly sought Him to stay with them and He stayed two more days. As a result there were

---

50 Morris, *The Gospel According to John*, 274.
51 Morris, *The Gospel According to John* 280.

many more who believed in Him, saying to the woman, "It is no longer because of what you said that we believe, for we have heard for ourselves and know that this One is indeed the Savior of the world" (John 4:42). Moreover, these Samaritans—unlike the Jews—were not seeking for signs or miracles in order to buttress their faith. Neither were they seeking for wisdom, like the Greeks. The Samaritans understanding of Jesus' work of redemption was remarkable, as Westcott notes:

> [I]t is a significant fact that this magnificent conception of the work of Christ was first expressed by a Samaritan, for whom the hope of a Deliverer had not been shaped to suit national ambition. So at last faith rose to the level the promise, v. 21.[52]

The Samaritan religion, in distinction from Judaism, held that there was only one prophet in the Old Testament—Moses—and that the next prophet would be the Messiah. Their Scripture contained only the five books of Moses and they based their view of the coming of the Messiah on Deuteronomy 18:18—"I will raise up a prophet from among their countrymen like you, and I will put My words in his mouth, and he shall speak to them all that I command him." The Samaritans considered Mount Gerizim to be the God-appointed place of worship which was also the seat of their national religion. To justify their position, they had to corrupt the text of Deuteronomy 27:4 to read "Gerizim" instead of "Ebal." Ebal was the mount where the curses of God were read when Joshua led the children into the land and Gerizim was where the blessings were read. Ebal was rocky, barren land on the top and Gerizim was fruitful, cultivated land. The Lord had commanded that the Israelites were to build an altar on Mount Ebal "of uncut stones, and you shall offer burnt offerings to the Lord" (Deuteronomy 27:6b). That was not a perpetual commandment for the Israelites to worship on that mountain. It was a commandment for them to offer "peace offerings" and to eat and rejoice there on the occasion of the success of their initial campaign to possess the land. Gerizim was also the mount of blessings. So, the Samaritans refused to offer sacrifices on Mount Ebal—the mount of curses—but chose Mount Gerizim instead for the place where they built their temple. Long after the Jews ceased to be able to offer sacrifices in Jerusalem, the sect of the Samaritans continued to do so on Mount Gerizim. As James Strong wrote in the nineteenth century:

---

52 Westcott, *The Gospel According to St. John*, 77.

[S]o likewise it is a singular historical fact, that the Samaritans have continued on this self-same mountain century after century, with the briefest interruptions, to worship according to their ancient custom ever since to the present day. While the Jews—expelled from Jerusalem, and therefore no longer able to offer bloody sacrifices according to the law of Moses—have been obliged to adopt their ceremonial to the circumstances of their destiny; here the Paschal Lamb has been offered up in all ages of the Christian era by a small but united nationality.[53]

Jesus remained there for two more days before continuing onto Galilee where the first recorded revival under Jesus' ministry took place. There is no mention in Scripture that Jesus ever visited these Samaritans again, but those few days of the Son of Man resulted in a bountiful harvest for the kingdom of God. At the end of those two days, Jesus continued His journey to Galilee where He would spend the better part of the next two years.

---

53 McClintock and Strong, *Cyclopedia of Biblical, Theological, and Ecclesiastical Literature*, 3:822.

6

Galilee of the Gentiles

"In the time of our Lord, all Palestine was divided into three provinces, Judea, Samaria, and Galilee (Acts ix, 31; Luke xvii, 11; Josephus, War, iii, 3). The latter included the whole northern section of the country, comprising the ancient territories of Issachar, Zebulun, Asher, and Naphtali. Josephus defines its boundaries, and gives a tolerably full description of its scenery, products, and population."[1]

During the days of Jesus' ministry, the territory known as "Galilee of the Gentiles" was a very populous area that was bustling with activity. There were numerous large cities; the land was "rich and well cultivated,"[2] producing an abundance of fruit and vegetables of many kinds. The Sea of Galilee was teeming with fish which supplied an industry of its own. Ever since the Captivity, though, that region of Israel had been largely inhabited by Gentiles who had moved in when the Jews were deported. Most of the towns and villages in "Galilee of the Gentiles" were in mountainous, rugged areas that were rejected by Hiram as payment for the timber and stones he provided to Solomon for the building of the temple (1 Kings 9:11–13). Despised by most Jews and considered "cabul," or "indecent," by Hiram, the whole region grew primarily through an influx of strangers and aliens. Yet, this was the territory where Jesus spent most of His short life on earth and where He started His preaching ministry.

Jesus' Ministry to the Nobleman at Cana of Galilee (John 4:46–54)
After leaving Sychar, Jesus returned to Galilee where He was readily received by the Galileans who had seen "all the things that He did in Jerusalem at the feast" (John 4:45). Before His arrival there, Jesus "testified that a prophet has no honor in his own country" (John 4:44). What was "his own country" to which Jesus was referring? Was it Galilee or was it Judea and Jerusalem? Westcott suggests that "his own country" referred to Jerusalem where He was rejected. There are reasons for us to believe that Jesus went from Sychar past Nazareth to Cana of Galilee,

---

1 McClintock and Strong, *Cyclopedia of Biblical, Theological, and Ecclesiastical Literature*, 3:717.
2 McClintock and Strong, *Cyclopedia of Biblical, Theological, and Ecclesiastical Literature*, 3:717.

the home of one of His disciples, Nathanael. Jesus was informing His disciples that He would not be returning to his hometown of Nazareth because a prophet is not welcome where he was reared.

The amount of time that Jesus spent in Cana is unknown, but the people there readily welcomed Him. During those days, a royal official from Capernaum heard that He was now in Galilee and journeyed to Cana to visit with Him. This royal official is not identified by John but there are two strong possibilities—Chuza, Herod's steward; or Manaen, Herod's foster-brother. Both of them are later identified as believers (Luke 8:3 and Acts 13:1). Chuza's wife, Joanna, was one of the women who ministered to Jesus during His Galilean ministry. And, Manaen was one of the prophets and teachers mentioned concerning the church at Antioch. Whoever this royal official was, he journeyed the twenty-five miles through the hilly country to the elevated plain where Cana was in order to make an urgent appeal to Jesus to heal his son. There are some who identify this miracle with a similar one which also took place in Capernaum—the healing of the centurion's slave. Westcott points out the differences between the two accounts:

(1) *Place*. The request was made here at Cana, there at Capernaum.

(2) *Time*. Here immediately after His return to Galilee, there after some time had elapsed.

(3) *Persons*. Here the subject was a son, there a slave: here the petitioner was probably a Jew, there a heathen soldier.

(4) *Character*. Here the faith of the father, as interpreted by the Lord, is weak; there the faith of the centurion is exceptionally strong.

(5) *Manner*. Here the request is granted in a way opposed to the prayer, there in accord with it: here the Lord refuses to go, there He offers to go to the sufferer.[3]

The two miraculous healings are complementary of one another, as so many of Jesus' words and works are. Yet, here was a Jewish official who served in the court of Herod Antipas— the very man that Jesus was trying to avoid—imploring the Lord to heal his son. Jesus' initial response did not seem hopeful, but rather slightly harsh: "Unless you people see signs and wonders, you simply will not believe" (John 4:48). That desire to see signs and wonders would become a

---

3 Westcott, *The Gospel According to St. John*, 77.

common criticism that Jesus made about the Jews. The apostle Paul distinguished Jews and Greeks in this way: "For indeed Jews ask for signs and Greeks search for wisdom, but we preach Christ crucified, to Jews a stumbling block and to Gentiles foolishness" (1 Corinthians 1:22, 23).

The royal official felt that it was imperative for Jesus to come down in order for his son to be healed. He implored the Lord, "Sir, come down before my child dies" (John 4:49). The official's faith was weak at that time because he did not yet realize that Jesus could merely speak the word and his son would be healed. Even though the royal official's faith was small, it was true faith. It was weak faith, but it was faith, nonetheless. When Jesus seemed to chide him, the royal official did not give into unbelief, but simply renewed his request for the Savior's help. God often hides behind a cloud when troubles arise in order to compel us to be more fervent in our requests for His help. When the official is not put off by Jesus' rebuke of the Jews for seeking signs, our Lord then replied: "Go; your son lives!" As Morris comments:

> Jesus' words impose a stiff test. He gives the man no sign. The officer has nothing but Jesus' bare word. But this is enough. He believes what Jesus says and goes his way.[4]

This conversation with the royal official and Jesus' miraculous healing of the son took place at about the seventh hour.[5] The return journey to Capernaum would have taken six to seven hours of hard walking, so the royal official had to wait until the next morning to start home. As he started down the hills, he was met by his servants who informed him that his son was alive. When he inquired when his son began to get better, he was told: "Yesterday at the seventh hour the fever left him" (John 4:52). Knowing that "it was at that hour in which Jesus said to him, 'Your son lives'", the father himself "believed and his whole household" (John 4:53). Morris elucidates the importance of this transformation:

> This is the third time the statement of the time coincided with the time when Jesus had told the nobleman that his son lived. This is the third time we have been told that the boy "lives." John does not want

---

4 Morris, *The Gospel According to John*, 291.
5 John probably was using Roman time, from midnight to midday, which would have been 7 PM, rather than the Jewish division of time, from sundown to sunup, which would have been 1 PM.

his readers to miss the emphasis on life, that life that Jesus gives. The servants' words were sufficient to cause the nobleman and his household to believe. In v. 50 this verb had been used of giving credence to Jesus' words. Here it is used in the sense of becoming a Christian. Previously the man had known enough about Jesus to regard him as a talented wonder-worker. But the "sign" pointed him beyond that. He plainly saw the hand of God in it, and his whole attitude was modified accordingly. The "sign" transformed his faith into a greater faith.[6]

God is a God who loves to save by families and He makes many promises in Scripture to do so. As Acts 2:39 says, "For the promise is for you and your children and for all who are far off, as many as the Lord our God will call to Himself." This miracle turned a high official of Herod's court into a follower of Jesus. The power of the Holy Spirit rested and remained on His ministry "and news about Him spread through all the surrounding district. And He began teaching in their synagogues and was praised by all" (Luke 4:14, 15). His foundational message at this time was the same message as John: "Repent, for the kingdom of heaven is at hand" (Matthew 3:2; 4:17).

Capernaum (Matthew 4:12–17)

Following this miraculous healing of the royal official's son, Jesus and His disciples went down to Capernaum—an enchanting and beautiful town on the north side of the Sea of Galilee. It was situated just south of the main highway between Damascus and the Mediterranean coast. Travelers from many nations passed by there every day without realizing what a garden spot it was. The Sea of Galilee has a special beauty which must be witnessed in order to be appreciated. From the surrounding mountain sides, there is a certain "dreariness" to the view of the lake, but "let him go down to the shore and wait till the sun declines, and he will be enchanted with the deep ethereal blue of the smooth water, and the tints of 'rose-colored, pearl-gray, and purple, blended together,' and thrown in soft shades over the sides of the encircling hills."[7]

Matthew quoted from Isaiah in giving the reason why Jesus settled there: "But there will be more gloom for her who was in anguish: in earlier times He treated the land of Zebulun and the land of Naphtali with contempt, but later on He shall make it glorious, by the way of

---

6 Morris, *The Gospel According to John*, 292.
7 McClintock and Strong, *Cyclopedia of Biblical, Theological, and Ecclesiastical Literature*, 3:719.

the sea, on the east side of the Jordan, Galilee of the Gentiles. The people who walk in darkness will see a great light; those who live in a dark land, the light will shine on them" (Isaiah 9:1, 2). As Edward J. Young wrote about Zebulun and Naphtali in his commentary on Isaiah:

> Zebulun and Naphtali, the two northeastern tribes of the land west of the Jordan (later known as upper and lower Galilee), were first devastated and depopulated by Tiglath-Pileser . . . (2 Kings 15:29) . . .
>
> A time of distress was the former time, the latter of one of glory, and the way of the sea, the way along the western side of the sea of Gennesaret, Galilee of the Gentiles, is to be honored . . . Being most remote from Judah it was nearest to the foreign countries and so subject to heathen influences. Not only the location of the district contributed to its disgrace, but it had been the first to tremble in awe before the might of Assyria. This despised district, despised even in New Testament times, was glorified when God honored it, and the fulfillment of the prophecy occurred when Jesus Christ the Son of God dwelt in Capernaum.[8]

There was a certain snobbery in Judah and Jerusalem that made them feel they were exempt from the heathen influences which infected the religious views of the Gentiles. In reality, they were simply more prone to that self-made religion and self-abasement of which Paul warned in Colossians 2:20–23—"Do not handle, do not taste, do not touch!" Jesus was exempt from such commandments and doctrines of men which made Capernaum the perfect place for the beginning of His teaching ministry. Gentiles, heathens, and demon-possessed people needed to be transformed no less or no more than the self-righteous Jews. The heathens were often guilty of drinking and eating to excess—that is, they were gluttons and wine-bibbers—but Jesus came to call sinners to repentance. Demonic possession and immorality were rampant throughout this part of Israel, but many such sinners would soon become monuments of His grace.

---

8 Young, *The Book of Isaiah*, 1:323–4.

Jesus Preaching and Healing in Capernaum (Mark 1:21–34; Luke 4:31–37)

When the Sabbath came, the congregation of Jews in Capernaum gathered at the synagogue for worship. That synagogue was built from the black basalt stones[9] that were so plentiful on the nearby mountains. Jewish synagogues permitted anyone who was approved by the rulers to exhort or teach the people. As J. A. Alexander wrote in his commentary on Mark:

> Of this truly national and sacred usage, that of meeting on the Sabbath for religious worship, our Lord availed himself, as furnishing the most direct and easy access to the more devout and serious portion of the people. The service of the synagogue appears to have been eminently simple, consisting in prayer and the reading of the Scriptures, with stated or occasional exhortation.[10]

The synagogue was both a place for worship and the school house for teaching the children. "The expositor was not an officer, but any competent Israelite who was invited by the officers. Hence the synagogue supplied invaluable opportunities to the first preachers of the Gospel."[11] Jesus availed Himself of the opportunity to preach in synagogues all across Galilee and, especially, in Capernaum. Typically, synagogue worship would begin about 9 AM on the Sabbath morning. The sermon Jesus preached on this occasion was the first time He had preached in the Capernaum synagogue. We have nothing of the content of that message given to us by the sacred writers—nor of most of the other sermons He preached. What we do know is that He preached with such boldness and authority that the crowds were mesmerized. His message was not the same kind of teaching learned by rote of which the scribes were guilty. Rather, "He was teaching with authority, and not as the scribes" (Mark 1:22b), which was a common assessment of His sermons.

There was one man who was present in the synagogue that day who was possessed of an unclean spirit. This evil spirit so controlled the

---

9 Henry Barclay Swete, *Commentary on Mark* (Grand Rapids, Michigan: Kregel Publications, 1977), 17. Swete wrote: "Tell Hum is now a wilderness of ruins, half buried in brambles and nettles; among them are conspicuous the remains of a large synagogue of white limestone." Yet, that ruined synagogue was the second synagogue built on that same site. The first, in which Jesus preached, was probably built of black stones as all the other buildings in Capernaum were.
10 Joseph Addison Alexander, *A Commentary on the Gospel of Mark* (London: The Banner of Truth Trust, 1960), 19.
11 Swete, *Commentary on Mark*, 18.

man that he would cry out by using the man's voice. Israel, in the time of Christ, had numerous different influences from the Babylonians to the Romans and many of those influences were wicked or demonic in nature. The result was that there were many who were indwelt by demons. "The frequency of such demoniacal possessions in the time of Christ is referred to an express divine appointment, intended to put honour on the Savior as the victor in that war between the seed of the woman and the seed of the serpent, which reached its crisis during his personal presence upon earth."[12] Frederick S. Leahy, in *Satan Cast Out*, comments on Jesus statement, "If I with the finger of God cast out demons, no doubt the kingdom of God is come upon you":

> In other words, where Satan's tyranny is broken, there of necessity the kingdom of God begins. Later, Peter was to proclaim the fact that Jesus of Nazareth 'went about doing good, and healing all who were oppressed of the devil' (Acts 10:38), In doing this our Lord always distinguished between the man and the demon. To the one He was compassionate and kind, to the other, stern and relentless.[13]

This is the first recorded conflict that Jesus had with someone possessed of a demon. Demons, like the devil himself, are not atheists or even agnostics. As James 2:19 says: "the demons also believe, and shudder." Even before this demon encountered the great power of Jesus, he knew enough to be afraid of the Messiah. He blurted out in defiance: "What business do we have with each other, Jesus of Nazareth? Have you come to destroy us? I know who You are—the Holy One of God" (Mark 1:24). This demon wanted Jesus to leave him alone, but that was something the Son of Man could not and would not do. As 1 John 3:8 says: "The Son of God came for this purpose, to destroy the works of the devil." There could be no détente between the devil and Jesus. Jesus came to bind the strong man armed and to cast him out. There was a sense of foreboding by this demon as he sought to be left alone. Yet, leaving the demon alone would have left the man under the dominion of that evil spirit who was causing so many problems for him. Thus, "Jesus rebuked him, saying, 'Be quiet, and come out of him!" (Mark 1:25). The demon was compelled to come out of the man, but not before "throwing him into convulsions" and crying "out with a loud voice" (Mark 1:26). The ghastly screech-

---

12 Alexander, *A Commentary on the Gospel of Mark*, 21.
13 Frederick S. Leahy, *Satan Cast Out* (Edinburgh, Scotland and Carlisle, Pennsylvania: The Banner of Truth Trust, 1975), 97.

ing of this tormented demon as he was cast out caused amazement to come over the congregation, as they debated among themselves: "What is this? A new teaching with authority! He commands even the unclean spirits, and they obey Him" (Mark 1:27). This news spread like wildfire among the surrounding district of Galilee.

Following the synagogue worship on that Sabbath, Jesus and His disciples repaired to the house of Simon and Andrew in Capernaum where Peter's mother-in-law[14] was lying sick with "a high fever" (Luke 4:38). When Jesus was informed about her, He went into the room where she was laying and "raised her up, taking her by the hand, and the fever left her, and she waited on them" (Mark 1:31). It was as though she had never even been sick. Her strength was completely restored and she was energetic enough to serve others without undergoing a period of convalescence.

As the news of these miracles continued to spread, the people waited until the sunset, ending the Jewish Sabbath, and then "they began bringing to Him all who were ill and those who were demon-possessed" (Mark 1:32). "[T]he whole city gathered at the door" (Mark 1:33) of the home where Peter and Andrew lived and Jesus "healed many who were ill with various diseases, and cast out many demons" (Mark 1:34). We are not given the details of any of those miracles, except for the man in the synagogue and Peter's mother-in-law. The demons wanted to cry out, but "He was not permitting them to speak, because they knew who He was" (Mark 1:34). There are, perhaps, two reasons why Jesus forbade them to tell everyone who He was, as Alexander wrote:

> [W]e are informed that though they recognized our Lord as the Messiah, and were ready to acknowledge him as such, he would not suffer them to do it; either because he did not need their testimony and would have been dishonoured by it, or because a premature annunciation of his Messianic claim would have defeated the whole purpose of His mission.[15]

This was one of those extraordinary days of the Son of Man when miracles seemed to be as plentiful as Solomon had once made silver in Israel. All these miracles, performed in less than twenty-four hours, were testimony to the divinity of Christ.

---

14 This verse is proof that Peter was married. Forbidding marriage is contrary to Scripture—1 Timothy 4:1–3.
15 Alexander, *A Commentary on the Gospel of Mark*, 26.

The Miraculous Catch and Fishers of Men (Matthew 4:18–22; Mark 1:35–39; Luke 5:1–11)

That first Sabbath in Capernaum, no doubt, had been an exhausting day and Jesus needed to rest. Yet, He rose early the next morning while it was still dark, in the fourth watch of the night—sometime between 3 AM and 6 AM. He quietly slipped out of the house "and went away to a secluded place, and was praying there" (Mark 1:35). That secluded place was probably the nearby mountain north of Capernaum where Jesus often resorted to commune with His Father and feed His own soul. Also, Jesus was in the habit of spending extra time in prayer before making important decisions. A large decision was now facing Him: should He stay in Capernaum where the people received Him gladly or should He go to the other synagogues of Galilee?

When the sun rose, Peter and the other disciple—who had spent the night fishing—went searching for Jesus and found Him. Peter, the natural leader that he was, said to Jesus: "Everyone is looking for You" (Mark 1:37). Those words resulted in bringing Jesus immediately back to Capernaum where "the crowds were searching for Him, and came to Him and tried to keep Him from going away from them . . . Now it happened while the crowd was pressing around Him and listening to the word of God, He was standing by the lake of Gennesaret" (Luke 4:42; 5:1). The disciples were mending their nets when Jesus got into Peter's boat and asked him "to put out a little way from the land" (Luke 5:3). From that spot, Jesus sat in the boat and began to teach the people on the shore. "When He had finished speaking, He said to Simon, 'Put out into the deep water and let down your nets for a catch" (Luke 5:4). Peter reluctantly obeyed, saying, "Master, we worked hard all night long and caught nothing, but I will do as you say and let down the nets" (Luke 5:5). The quantity of fish that were caught was so large that their nets began to break and they had to call their companions for help. (Luke 5:6, 7). Henry Baker Tristram wrote about the great quantity of fish in the Sea of Galilee:

> The density of the shoals of fish in the Lake of Galilee can scarcely be conceived by those who have not witnessed them. They sometimes cover an acre or more on the surface in one dense mass.[16]

Simon was certainly accustomed to catching large quantities of

---

16 Henry Baker Tristram, *The Natural History of the Bible* (London: Society for Promoting Christian Knowledge, 1868), 285.

fish in that lake, but the previous night had been a miserable failure. This catch was so large that Simon had to call to his companions in the other boat to help him and soon both boats began to sink. Simon's response was to "fall down at Jesus' feet, saying, 'Go away from me Lord, for I am a sinful man!'" (Luke 5:8). Hugh Martin captured the essence of this event in the following words:

> Here is a blessed and critical era in the life of Simon Peter . . . The turning point of his life, nay, of his eternal interests, is in this graphic incident, as its successive acts transpire, partly on the shore and partly on the dark blue wave of the Sea of Galilee. And when we set aside, as merely secondary and circumstantial, the external events and outward clothing of the drama—when we take up the heart and substance of the whole, as brought out in this astonished and heartbroken cry, 'I am a sinful man, O Lord,' and the Lord's most gracious reply, 'Fear not'—what have we but what must be present in every case of personal salvation?—a sinner at the feet of Jesus, stricken to the heart, self-condemned, confessed by his own lips miserable and guilty, unworthy of fellowship with God, with the grace of God lifting him up. Hence the value of the whole scene, as a very model of repentance and reconciliation.[17]

In Matthew's more abbreviated account of this same event, Jesus said to Peter and the others: "Follow Me, and I will make you fishers of men" (Matthew 4:19). Their first call, recorded in John, was to believe that He was the Messiah. Now, they were being called to become "fishers of men;" to attend Him on all His journeys and to enter into the ministry with Him—which required them to forsake their occupations for the most part. They were not yet called to discipleship or apostleship. They were fishermen, but, like many Galileans, they clung with more hope to the prophecies of the coming of the Messiah than did the Judeans. The scribes and Pharisees clung to the law as their hope of erecting a political kingdom that would be just and holy. The Galileans were less steeped in the law, but were filled with more faith and hope in the Messiah. Yet, Simon experienced a dramatic change on that day when Jesus said to him, "Put out into the deep water and let down your nets for a catch" (Luke 5:4). A child of the covenant will often not know the day or the hour of their conversion as the Lord works softly and secretly in their heart. In this instance, there was no doubt when Peter responded to the Lord's call to every-

---

17 Hugh Martin, *Simon Peter* (Edinburgh, Scotland and Carlisle, Pennsylvania: The Banner of Truth Trust, 1984), 24.

one: "Repent, for the kingdom of God is at hand" (Matthew 4:17). Plummer quotes from Paul Schanz concerning Peter's experience:

> Peter does not regard himself as a criminal, but as a sinful man; and this miracle has brought home to him a new sense, both of his own sinfulness and Christ's holiness. It is not that he fears Christ's holiness is dangerous to a sinner, but that the contrast between the two is felt to be so intense as to be intolerable . . . It frequently happens that one experience touches the heart, after many that were similar to it have failed to do so. Perhaps, without being felt, they prepare the way. Moreover, this was a miracle in Peter's own craft, and therefore was likely to make a special impression on him.[18]

Jesus' call of these fishermen to be His followers and "fishers of men" underscores a couple of important principles about the gospel ministry. As Hebrews 5:1–4 states concerning the priesthood, a minister must both be called by God (Hebrews 5:4) and he must have a knowledge of his own sins so that he can deal gently with others who are ignorant and misguided (Hebrews 5:2, 3). Whatever Peter's spiritual relationship to Jesus before this event, that day was, at the least, a deepening of that sense of sin that is necessary for every true minister of the gospel. Peter and the others were not exceptionally wicked before their conversions; and that is neither a disqualifier nor a requirement for the office. Yet, Peter had a profound and new sense of sin from this day forward that equipped him for his apostolic office despite the weaknesses of his personality.

Jesus' First Galilean Preaching Tour (Mark 1:35–45; Luke 4:42–44)

After this life-changing experience for Peter, Jesus said to him and His other followers: "Let us go somewhere else to the towns and villages nearby, so that I may preach there also; for that is what I came for" (Mark 1:38). Without hesitation, these disciples followed Him on His first preaching tour in Galilee where "He went into their synagogues . . . preaching and casting out demons" (Mark 1:39). The names of the various cities and synagogues where Jesus preached are not given to us. Yet, there were synagogues in such cities and villages as Migdal,[19] Kafr Bir'im, Sepphoris, Beth-Shean, Chorazin, Meron,[20] Marus, Bethsaida, Nazareth, Kafr Kanna (or, Cana), Japha (Haffa)

---

18 Plummer, *A Critical and Exegetical Commentary on the Gospel According to St. Luke*, 145.
19 Recent excavation has revealed that there were two synagogues in this town on the northwest side of the Sea of Galilee where Mary Magdalene once lived.
20 A city northwest of Capernaum towards Tyre and Syria. Sheep were reared there and the name of the celebrated wool, merino, may have its etymological roots from the name of the city.

on the Mediterranean coast, Beit She'arim (or, Besara),[21] and numerous other places.

Demon possession was so common throughout the whole region of Galilee that it was one of the primary afflictions that Jesus cured—just as His first miracle in Capernaum was the casting out of a demon. The elders of each synagogue could permit any adult male to preach the sermon, which made it possible for Jesus to carry on His great work of evangelization and teaching. Most synagogues throughout Israel—with few exceptions—faced towards Jerusalem with the preacher looking towards the Holy City. Thus, Hendriksen commented about Jesus' preaching tour: "It was impossible for him not to be thinking of the cross."[22] Jesus was also training His disciples on this preaching tour for the days when they would be spreading the gospel without His physical presence. It would be fascinating if we knew all the synagogues where Jesus preached, all His sermons, and all the miracles He performed on this first preaching tour. There is only one individual mentioned and we do not know his name. But he was a leper and his healing was remarkable for that reason.

In one of the synagogues, a leper in that area gathered the courage to seek help from Jesus. Lepers were outcasts from society in ancient Israel and were required to wear signs that proclaimed: "Unclean, unclean." It was thought by both Jews and Greeks that leprosy was an unmistakable sign of some great moral sin that had resulted in God's punishment with this ravaging disease. Dr. L. S. Huizenga, who was trained in both medicine and theology, stated concerning leprosy in the Bible: "I believe that Moses describes a definite disease—a disease which corresponds to what we call today leprosy, though the symptoms may not be the same."[23] Leprosy was especially common in ancient Israel and afflicted even King Uzziah towards the end of his life. Heathen writers both before and after Jesus' days represented leprosy among the Israelites as "the cause of their expulsion from Egypt."[24] That was also a convenient way for them to deny the miraculous Red Sea crossing and the drowning of Pharaoh's entire army. There can be

---

21 Located in the southwestern hills of Lower Galilee not far from Nazareth.
22 William Hendriksen, *The Gospel of Mark* (Edinburgh, Scotland and Carlisle, Pennsylvania: The Banner of Truth Trust, 1976), 76.
23 Lee Sjoerds Huizenga, *Unclean! Unclean! Or, Glimpses of the Land Where Leprosy Thrives* (Grand Rapids, Michigan: Smitter Book Company, 1927), 145-6.
24 Alexander, *A Commentary on the Gospel of Mark*, 28.

no doubt, though, from Jesus' preaching that leprosy was much more common in His day than it is today. "The lepers, therefore, were a well-defined and well-known class of sufferers, distinguished from all others by the circumstances . . . and holding a middle place between demoniacal possessions and mere ordinary ailments."[25]

This leper who came to Jesus expressed much boldness in doing so. Mark 1:40 says, "And a leper came to Jesus." They were required to stand a great distance away. The Mosaic law stated about lepers: "He shall live alone; his dwelling shall be outside the camp" (Leviticus 13:46b). This man, though "covered with leprosy. . . fell on his face and implored [Jesus], saying, 'Lord, if You are willing, You can make me clean'" (Matthew 5:12). "Lord" for this leper was more than a sign of courtesy—it was an expression of true faith. He believed that Jesus, who had cast out demons, could also heal Him—if *He* was willing. While saying those words, the leper was close enough to Jesus to be touched by Him. Thus, Jesus responded to this man's plight by stretching out His hand and touching him, saying to him, "I am willing; be cleansed" (Mark 1:41). The miraculous healings of Jesus were "complete and instantaneous."[26] This man's leprosy was totally eradicated. Mark 1:42 says, "Immediately the leprosy left him and he was cleansed."

After healing the leper, Jesus "sternly warned him and immediately sent him away" (Mark 1:43). The word translated as "sternly warned" is sometimes used for "the snorting of the horse . . . [b]ut the idea of anger is not inherent in the word."[27] Jesus was not being cold towards the leper, inasmuch as He had just been "moved with compassion" (Mark 1:41) to heal his terrible disease. Jesus certainly "Himself took our infirmities and carried away our diseases" (Matthew 8:17; Isaiah 53:4), but miracles of healing were not the primary purpose for His incarnation. He came to teach, to preach, to fulfil all righteousness, and to die for the sins of the world. Jesus also told the leper: "See that you say nothing to anyone; but go, show yourself to the priest and offer for your cleansing what Moses commanded, as a testimony to them" (Mark 1:44). The man did just the opposite and began freely

---

25 Alexander, *A Commentary on the Gospel of Mark*, 29.
26 Hendriksen, *The Gospel of Mark*, 80. The only apparent exception would be the healing of the blind man in Mark 8:23–25, but even there the healing took place within a short amount of time.
27 Swete, *Commentary on Mark*, 30.

proclaiming the news everywhere. That presented the same problem for Jesus that caused Him to go on this preaching tour through Galilee—the news about Him spread "to such an extent that Jesus could no longer publicly enter a city, but stayed out in unpopulated areas, and they were coming to Him from everywhere" (Mark 1:45).

There were additional reasons that Jesus commanded the leper to show himself to the priest. The Mosaic law specified regulations, including offerings, that were to be performed whenever a leper was cleansed. The priest was supposed to "pronounce him clean" from his leprosy which would remove the ceremonial defilement from him and from anyone who had come into contact with him (Leviticus 14:1–32). By not obeying Him, this leper put Jesus in jeopardy of being declared ceremonially unclean by the priests also. Another reason that Jesus was so stern in warning this man what to do next was so that the priests would know that He was submissive to the sacrificial system. He rejected the "traditions of man," but He obeyed every law of the Old Testament.

The length of this first preaching tour throughout Galilee is as unknown as the places where Jesus preached. When it was successively completed, though, Jesus returned to Capernaum with His disciples where He spent most of His time for the next year.

7

Back Home in Capernaum

In his travel diary of Palestine, Franz Deilitsch wrote about the ruins of ancient Capernaum:

> In one hour more we are on the great waste of ruins known as Tell Hum, and pass by oleander trees, and go through the grass and undergrowth to the surprisingly grand ruins of old Capernaum. The ruins of Chorazin, in a westerly direction among the hills, are equally grand, and those of Gamal (el-Husn) yonder on the other side are considerably grander; but the black basalt blocks and white rocks which lie scattered here in Tell Hum awakened much stronger and more vivid impressions. For here it was that the One sent of God, without an equal, made His abiding-place, in order to proclaim from this strong place the religion of love, amid the miracles of love, for the deliverance from the bonds of the old covenant. How terrible have His threats against the ungrateful and unbelieving city been fulfilled! The black and white stones of the ruined houses are like the memorial stones of those who have descended into the regions of the dead (Matt. 11:23) . . .[1]

The great Puritan author, John Flavel, wrote concerning God's providence in *Divine Conduct, or The Mystery of Providence*:

> That the affairs of the saints in this world are certainly conducted by the wisdom and care of special providence.[2]

Certainly, that special act of providence was involved in governing all the affairs of God's "Beloved Son, in whom" He was "well-pleased" (Matthew 4:17). "The circuit" of Jesus' first preaching tour was "now over, ended perhaps prematurely by the indiscretion of the leper . . .; and the Lord returns to Capernaum."[3] Yet, the closing of that stage of His ministry was no accident in the plan of God. It was all governed by that mysterious providence of God that belongs to the secret things that are unknown to men (Cf. Deuteronomy 29:29).

It was, therefore, in the early part of AD 28 that Jesus returned from His greater Galilean preaching tour to Capernaum which had

---
1 Franz Delitzsch, *A Day in Capernaum* (New York: Funk & Wagnalls, 1887), 38–9
2 John Flavel, The Works of John Flavel, "Divine Conduct, or The Mystery of Providence" (London: The Banner of Truth Trust, 1968), 4:350.
3 Swete, *Commentary on Mark*, 32.

become known as His home (Mark 2:1). His popularity throughout Galilee had become so great that He "could no longer publicly enter a city" (Mark 1:45) and He resorted to living in uninhabited regions outside the towns and villages. Capernaum may have become His home, but He never had a home of His own. Jesus probably stayed in the home with Peter, his wife, his mother, and Peter's brother, Andrew.[4] The home belonged to Peter's mother-in-law and the ruins of it in Capernaum reveal that was much larger than the other homes there. Like all the other houses in this little fishing village, it was built from the hard, black, basalt igneous rocks[5] which were in abundance on the nearby mountains just north of the village.

The ministry of Jesus at this point began to assume an "anti-Judaistic character"[6] because of the spiritual bankruptcy of the Rabbinical ministry among the Jews. Jesus did not come to be a traditionalist or a follower of men. He came with the authority of His Father to be the Light of the world. The ministry of the Rabbis, on the other hand, "stood confessedly powerless in the face of the living death of leprosy, so it had no word of forgiveness to speak to the conscience burdened with sin, nor yet word of welcome to the sinner."[7] During His Galilean tour, Jesus had healed a leper. On His return to Capernaum, He both healed a paralytic and assured him of God's forgiveness. Such a ministry was in stark contrast to what the Rabbis had performed.

Healing the Paralytic (Matthew 9:2–8; Mark 2:1–11; Luke 5:18–26)

A few days after His return, it soon became known throughout the region that Jesus was once again "at home" (Mark 2:1). Crowds came to Capernaum from as far away as Phoenicia in the north to Idumaea in the south and every part of Galilee because of the growing popularity of Jesus. "One day He was teaching, and there were some Pharisees and teachers of the law sitting there, who had come from every village of Galilee and Judea and from Jerusalem" (Luke 5:17). Controversy had already begun to swirl around Jesus and these religious leaders were, no doubt, a part of a deputation sent by the

---

4 Edersheim, The Life and Times of Jesus the Messiah, 346. The house of Peter is marked in the ruins of Capernaum today.
5 Such basalt rocks were lava rich in magnesium and iron and were formed through volcanic action. The mountains north of Capernaum are filled with many such large basalt rocks.
6 Edersheim, The Life and Times of Jesus the Messiah, 345.
7 Edersheim, *The Life and Times of Jesus the Messiah*, 345.

Sanhedrin to watch Him and to report back to them concerning His activities. Both the followers of Jesus and those who were openly hostile to Him, as well as the curious and undecided, came to the house where Jesus was teaching. This day was certainly not a Sabbath or the crowd would have assembled in the synagogue. But it was a special day because "the power of the Lord was present for Him to perform healing" (Luke 5:17). Their numbers were so large that the house was completely filled and "there was no longer room, not even near the door" (Mark 2:2). The presence of the Pharisees in Capernaum was the beginning of the open opposition to Jesus' ministry which would grow more and more hostile over the coming years.[8] As was their usual habit in religious gatherings, the Pharisees would have occupied the chief seats and those closest to where Jesus was teaching. "The general impression on our minds is, that this audience was rather in a state of indecision than of sympathy with Jesus."[9]

There was one man who was unable to enter the house, a paralytic, whose name is never given to us. He was the person who most needed to see the Lord because he had not been healed on that wonderful Sabbath day a few weeks earlier when Jesus healed so many people from all the nearby cities. This paralytic had four faithful friends who brought Him to Jesus and took great pains to get him into the presence of the Savior. Finding no way to get him into the house, they climbed the outside stairs that led to the roof of the house. The houses in Capernaum had roofs made of crisscrossed branches overlaid with tightly packed clay that had to be repaired frequently, especially during the rainy seasons. These four friends of the paralytic began to take the roof apart so that they could lower him into the very presence of Jesus. How did they do this? Shepard describes it for us:

> There is no inside stairway; so they proceed to "uncover the covering," by removing first earth and mortar, then the layer of brushwood and short sticks, leaving, between, the logs three feet apart which traversed the room from wall to wall, an aperture. This was long enough to lower through it the sick man, by the four corners of his pallet, into the presence of Jesus in the chamber below.[10]

The whole ordeal could not have been performed quietly and sure-

---
8 Shepard, *The Christ of the Gospels*, 138. Several of the observations of this paragraph are from Shepard's work.
9 Edersheim, *The Life and Times of Jesus the Messiah*, 346.
10 Shepard, *The Christ of the Gospels*, 139.

ly caused a commotion heard by everyone. Whatever some people thought of such a disturbance of Jesus' message, there is no doubt what the Savior thought of it. Our Lord perceived *their* faith in these actions; that is, He perceived the faith of all the men, especially the paralytic; and said to him: "Son, your sins are forgiven" (Mark 2:5). "And this open outburst of faith shone out the more brightly, from its contrast with the covered darkness and clouds of unbelief within the breast of those Scribes, who had come to watch and ensnare Jesus."[11] Calvin commented on Jesus seeing the faith of the paralytic and his friends, thusly:

> Only God can recognize faith, but the example of faith they gave in their tremendous effort is evident from the fact, that they would never have taken such trouble or struggled to overcome such odds, if their spirits were not supported by the firm confidence that they would succeed. The fruits of their faith were shown, in that, when their access was blocked on all sides, they were still not beaten.[12]

Jesus' absolution of the paralytic's sins did not meet with the approval of the scribes and Pharisees who were sitting in the house. They reasoned within their hearts that only God can forgive sins and they were right, but Jesus is God. Thus, He was immediately aware in His spirit what they were reasoning and asked them: "Which is easier to say to the paralytic, 'Your sins are forgiven'; or to say, 'Get up, and pick up your pallet and walk'?" (Mark 2:9). Before they could answer, Jesus commanded the paralytic, "I say to you, get up, pick up your stretcher and go home" (Luke 5:24). Chamblin comments on Jesus' question and command:

> To drive home this truth, Jesus orders the paralytic to rise and depart, a command he forthwith obeys. If Jesus' words about healing can achieve what they command (9:6b), cannot his words about forgiveness achieve what they declare (9:2b)? And if this man's sins did account for paralysis, does not his healing certify that those sins have been forgiven?[13]

Many of the people in this crowd would not have been satisfied that Jesus truly could forgive sins without the miraculous healing of

---

11 Edersheim, *The Life and Times of Jesus the Messiah*, 348.
12 John Calvin, *A Harmony of the Gospels of Matthew, Mark, and Luke* (Grand Rapids: Eerdmans Publishing Company, 1972), 1:258.
13 Chamblin, *Matthew*, 1:529–30. Chamblin also notes on page 528 of his commentary on Matthew that the Scripture warns us against universalizing the principle that all suffering is the result of personal sin.

the paralytic. When the paralytic obeyed Jesus' command, got up, picked up his pallet, and walked home, the crowds were awe-struck and glorified God that our Lord had such power. They exclaimed, "We have never seen anything like this" (Mark 2:12). Previously, Jesus had cast out demons and even healed a man of leprosy, but the connection of His power over the elements of nature with His authority to forgive sins filled the hearts of the people with amazement. The scribes had essentially accused Jesus of blasphemy by forgiving the paralytic of his sins. Jesus' statement, to them, meant that He was claiming to be equal with God—and He was. Now the gathered crowds in Capernaum were full of wonderment in contemplating that the One in their presence was indeed God with them. The Jewish rabbis were powerless either to heal the diseased or to forgive their sins. Jesus could do both. There was "the feeling of contempt which we trace in their unspoken words:"[14] "Who is this man who speaks blasphemies? Who can forgive sins, but God alone?" (Luke 5:21). They could not deny that a powerful miracle had taken place and they struggled to find grounds for an accusation to bring against Him. The amazed crowds would scarcely be convinced that Jesus was wrong to absolve the man of his sins after He had healed him. And, Jesus had not performed this miracle on the Sabbath as had been widely reported that He had done in multitudes of cases only a matter of weeks earlier. A great miracle had happened that filled most of the crowd with astonishment, fear, and a sense of God's glory, but a wary group of onlookers were already secretly plotting how to deal with Jesus.

Following the healing of the paralytic, Jesus went down to the seashore where He continued to teach the multitudes who sought Him. Despite the wariness of some, there were others who delighted in sitting at the feet of Jesus to learn.

---

14 Edersheim, *The Life and Times of Jesus the Messiah*, 349.

The Calling of Levi, or Matthew (Matthew 9:9–17; Mark 2:14–22; Luke 5:27–39)

On the same day that He healed the paralytic, Jesus passed by the tax booth located on the great Via Maris[15] trade route that was less than a mile north of Capernaum. On this trade route, there was a customs house for the collection of taxes and duties due to the Roman government. There was a tax collector in that customs house named Levi (Mark 2:14; Luke 5:27) to whom Jesus ministered. Levi, also called Matthew (Matthew 9:9), was the lowest form of tax collector[16] according to the views of the Jewish religious leaders. He was a Jew and a *publicanus*[17] who was an official in the service of the heathen Roman government. Some publicans collected real estate, income, and poll taxes, but Matthew collected "the duty on imports, exports, toll on roads, bridges, the harbour, the town tax, and a great multiplicity of other variable taxes on an unlimited variety of things, admitting of much abuse and graft."[18] Such taxes were levied by the chief tax collector who hired numerous subordinates to do that greatly despised work. Rome was paid a fixed amount and any excess collected could be kept by the tax collectors. This led to many abuses and caused such publicans to be scorned by the religious leaders of Israel who believed there was no hope for them. Matthew sat in the Roman custom house on the border between the territory of Herod Philip (to the east) and Herod Antipas (to the west). Not only the caravans of traders had to stop at this customs house where, but also all the poor fisherman had to pay taxes there. Jesus was known in Capernaum as the great Rabbi and a miracle worker, while Matthew and his fellow publicans were despised for their "frequent abuses and tyrannical spirit."[19] They were considered by the Pharisees to be outside the bounds of religious fellowship and "no better than a Gentile."[20]

As Jesus passed by this customs house, He saw Matthew and gave him a command: "Follow Me!" (Mark 2:14). Immediately, Matthew

---

15 The ancient trade route connecting Egypt with Syria, Anatolia, and Mesopotamia. The name, Via Maris, means 'the way of the sea.' It passed north along the Mediterranean Sea before turning eastward and passing just north of Capernaum and the Sea of Galilee.
16 Matthew was a Mokhes, the lowest form of tax collector.
17 *Publicanus* is the Latin word from which publican is derived. It means someone who is in the public service. In this instance, a publican was in the service of the heathenistic Romans.
18 Shepard, *The Christ of the Gospels*, 142.
19 Shepard, *The Christ of the Gospels*, 143.
20 Shepard, *The Christ of the Gospels*, 143.

left everything and followed Jesus. Matthew had probably witnessed some of Jesus' miracles and heard Him teach. With the customs house so close to Capernaum, it is also likely that Levi lived nearby. Matthew obviously knew who Jesus was and unhesitatingly complied with this call to be one of His followers. Swete comments on the call and Levi's response:

> The command was practically a call to discipleship, involving the complete abandonment of his work . . . The call was given by One Who knew that the way had been prepared for its acceptance. How the preparation had been made can only be conjectured . . . To Porphyry, who saw in Matthew's prompt obedience proof of the mental weakness of Christ's disciples, Jerome replies that it rather attests the magnetic power exerted on men by His unique personality.[21]

Jesus' call of a publican to be one of His disciples reveals the great difference between the religion of Judaism and the new things that He was ushering in. The religious leaders of the Jews still ostensibly believed in repentance for they went out to hear John's austere call to such. Yet, they looked on such tax collectors and custom officials as mostly incapable of repentance. Against that view, the preaching and ministry of Jesus was contrasted, as Edersheim aptly argues:

> Thus, in one and another respect, Rabbinic teaching about the need of repentance runs close to that of the Bible. But the vital difference between Rabbinism and the Gospel lies in this: that whereas Jesus Christ freely invited all sinners, whatever their past, assuring them of welcome and grace, the last word of Rabbinism is only despair, and a kind of Pessimism. For it is expressly and repeatedly declared in case of certain sins, and, characteristically, of heresy, that even if a man genuinely and truly repented, he must expect to immediately die—indeed his death would be the evidence that his repentance was genuine, since, though such a sinner might turn from his evil, it would be impossible for him, if he lived, to lay hold on the good and to do it (Ab. Zar. 17a[22]).[23]

The message of Rabbinical Judaism during the time of Christ was filled with hopelessness concerning the repentance and salvation of such sinners as Levi. Their fundamental problem was that they did not understand the new birth—the regeneration of the heart affected

---

21 Swete, *Commentary on Mark*, 40.
22 Ab. Zar. is a reference to the Talmudic Tractate, Abhodah Zarah, on Idolatry. The Talmud was the primary source of Rabbinic Judaism and gave the thoughts of various Rabbis on Jewish religious law and theology. The Talmud is replete with condemnations of Gentiles, publicans, and others.
23 Edersheim, *The Life and Times of Jesus the Messiah*, 355.

through the work of the Holy Spirit (cf. Jeremiah 31:31–34 and Ezekiel 36:25–27) of which even circumcision was a holy symbol (e.g., Deuteronomy 10:16 and Jeremiah 4:4). In contrast to the gloom and hopelessness of the Jewish Rabbis, Jesus called all classes of sinners to come to Him. Through this call of Matthew, Jesus was making a transparent break from the old wine of the Pharisees and Sadducees to the new wine of the gospel.

Afterwards, Matthew held a large banquet in his house for Jesus and His disciples to meet with other tax collectors and sinners. Many of them had already become followers of Jesus (Mark 2:15) by the time of this feasting. This close association of Jesus with the despised publicans and other sinners caused the scribes and Pharisees to cunningly complain to our Lord's disciples, asking: "Why is He eating and drinking with tax collectors and sinners?" (Mark 2:16). The disciples were still learning at this time and such a question was probably intended to shake their confidence in Jesus or make them distrustful of Him. The question by the Pharisees was not a sincere seeking for truth, but was a form of grumbling against the propriety and practice of Jesus (cf. Luke 5:30). From the skewed perspective of the scribes and Pharisees, this question was more than legitimate, as Hendriksen notes:

> Does not eating with a person imply sweet fellowship? . . . And had not the rabbis laid down the rule, "The disciples of the learned shall not recline at table in the company of . . . the people of the soil . . . the rabble that do not know the law."[24]

That was what the scribes and Pharisees thought of these publicans and sinners. They were "rabble;" they always would be; and, they could never be anything else. Jesus overheard the grumbling of the Jews and responded to them, "It is not those who are healthy who need a physician, but those who are sick. But go and learn what this means, 'I desire compassion, and not sacrifice,' for I did not come to call the righteous but sinners" (Matthew 9:13). In that response, the Lord stripped away the self-righteous principle of the Pharisees whereby they were aloof towards Him and condemned Him for "consorting with the diseased."[25] What physician would refuse to care for the sick and diseased? In response, Jesus directed them to their own Scriptures (cf. Hosea 6:6) which taught compassion is more import-

---

24 Hendriksen, *The Gospel of Mark*, 97.
25 Edersheim, *The Life and Times of Jesus the Messiah*, 360.

ant than sacrifice. Yet, the Talmud was more important to most of the religious leaders of Israel than the Scriptures because it taught them a legalistic approach to salvation which they thought commended them while condemning tax collectors.

Feasting versus Fasting (Matthew 9:14–17; Mark 2:18–22; Luke 5:33–38)

In the crowd Matthew invited to his large banquet, there were some Pharisees also present. Jesus effectively rebuffed their narrow and bigoted views with His statement: "I have not come to call the righteous but sinners to repentance" (Luke 5:32). Sin was an uncomfortable topic for the Pharisees. Repentance was even more uncomfortable for them. They had attempted "to bring Him into disfavor with the people and with His own disciples,"[26] but once again He had bested them. His wisdom was always superior to theirs. "But they were not to be defeated, and brought to bear again all their ingenuity to entrap Him if possible."[27] It was a hopeless task and they were continually smarting from their defeats.

A year earlier, there had risen a discussion between a Jew (probably a Pharisee) and some disciples of John over the matter of purification. When the Pharisees came to Him at Matthew's feast, they said, "The disciples of John often fast and offer prayers, the *disciples* of the Pharisees do the same, but Yours eat and drink" (Luke 5:33). Matthew says that it was the disciples of John who asked Jesus the question (Matthew 9:14). Mark says that both the disciples of John and the Pharisees were then fasting (Mark 2:18). That raised the question in their minds why Jesus and His disciples were not also fasting.

The Old Testament only required one annual fast and it was on the Day of Atonement, Yom Kippur. All of the other festivals of the Old Testament were feasts and occasions of joy, showing that Jesus was more in line with the spirit of the Old Testament than is generally realized. Yet, the Pharisees and John's disciples focused too much on mourning while failing to remember as Nehemiah once said, "the joy of the Lord is your strength" (Nehemiah 8:10). John the Baptist, despite his natural austerity, caught a glimpse of that truth when he responded to his disciples: "So this joy of mine is full" (John 3:29).

---

26 Shepard, *The Christ of the Gospels*, 146.
27 Shepard, *The Christ of the Gospels*, 146.

Though Jesus was not personally present to hear John say those words, He learned of them and He used that same argument against the Pharisees and John's confused disciples. He said, "You cannot make the attendants of the bridegroom fast while the bridegroom is with them, can you?" John had referred to Jesus as the bridegroom and now the Lord claimed that title for Himself.

It has always been a temptation for the followers of Jesus to substitute outward ceremonies for the inner joy of salvation. The Rabbis had multiplied the number of fasts until it was expected that every religious Jew would fast twice a week. Every Monday and Thursday became fast days for the Jews since it was a traditional idea that Moses went up on Mount Sinai on a Thursday and came down on a Monday, 40 days later. It was probably on one of the weekly fast days when the feast at Matthew's house was held which promoted the questions about fasting. John's disciples were surprised that Jesus and His disciples would neglect a fast day to join in revelry with sinners. Jesus replied: "But *the* days will come when the bridegroom will be taken away from them, then they will fast in those days" (Luke 5:35). Plummer commented on Jesus' expressed principle:

> This is the first intimation of His death and departure, after which fasting will be appropriate and voluntary. Its value consists in its being spontaneously adopted, not forcibly imposed.[28]

The New Testament principle concerning fasting is that it is voluntary, spontaneous, and a matter of one's conscience. Also, as Jesus taught, it is to be done in secret in order to avoid a Pharisaical spirit. Joel called for a fast day (Joel 1:14) and the church at Antioch fasted and prayed before laying hands on Paul and Barnabas as missionaries (Acts 13:3). Yet, Isaiah condemned the fasts of the Jews (Isaiah 58:1–5) as did Zechariah (Zechariah 7:5). The lesson is that the Lord desires the heart—not the outward appearance.

In His reply to the Jews, Jesus gave two parables. The first one taught the difficulty of patching an old garment with a new piece of cloth. The second parable was about putting new wine in old wine skins that had already been stretched. The wineskins were made from a single goat-skin with the neck of the animal becoming the neck of the bottle.[29] Even new wineskins are challenged by the new wine, but

---

28 Plummer, *The Gospel According to S. Luke*, 162.
29 Plummer, *The Gospel According to S. Luke*, 164.

older skins have lost their elasticity. This is how the Pharisees were when Jesus came, as Plummer notes:

> The scribes and Pharisees, wise in the letter of the law, and understanding their own cramping traditions, were incapable of receiving the free spirit of the Gospel.[30]

Or, once again, as William Hendriksen commented:

> Judaistic, legalistic, joyless fasting is out of line with the salvation Jesus is bringing.[31]

Joy alone is not a proof of salvation since the seed sown on rocky soil, in Jesus' parable, "immediately receives it with joy, yet he has no firm root in himself, but is only temporary, and when affliction or persecution arises because of the word, immediately falls away" (Matthew 13:20, 21). All Christian graces can be counterfeited by Satan. He disguises himself as an angel of light. Yet, true Christian joy survives all the turbulent tests of time. A true Christian will be characterized by such joy since joy is the second fruit of the Spirit.

---

30 Plummer, *The Gospel According to S. Luke*, 164.
31 Hendriksen, *New Testament Commentary: Exposition of the Gospel According to St. Luke*, 311.

8

Do You Wish to be Well?

"JESUS spoke to the impotent man who had been afflicted for thirty-eight years, and inquired of him, 'Wilt thou be made whole?' It seems a very strange question to ask. Who would not be made whole? Would the poor man have been lying at the pool if he had not been anxious for healing? Must there not have been in the very look of his face, as he gazed upon the Savior, an answer to that question, superseding all necessity of putting it?

Yet as our Lord spoke no superfluous words, it may be that He perceived that the paralysis of the man's body had to a very painful degree benumbed his mind and brought on a paralysis of his will. He had hoped till his heart was sick, he had waited till despondency had dried up his spirits, and now it had almost come to this, that he scarcely cared whether he was made whole or not. The bow had been bent so long that all its elasticity was destroyed. He had hungered till appetite itself was gone. He was now listless, with an indifference made up of sullen repining at his disappointments and blank hopelessness for the future.

The Savior touched a chord which needed to vibrate when He inquired as to his will. He aroused by that question a dormant faculty, whose vigorous exercise, it may be, was one of the first essentials to a cure. 'Wilt thou be made whole?' was the inquiry of a profound investigation, the scientific probe of a great physician, the resurrection from the grave of a great master power of manhood."[1]

In the "old city" of Jerusalem, there was a pool called Bethesda near the Sheep Gate that "opened from the busy northern suburb of markets, bazaars, and workshops, eastwards upon the road which led from the Mount of Olives and Bethany to Jericho."[2] Bethesda means "house of mercy" or "house of grace." This pool of Bethesda was north of the Temple Mount and it had five porticoes, or porches, with each having cloisters of colonnades. These porches were large enough that "a multitude of those who were sick, blind, lame and withered" (John 5:3) could lay there. Bethesda was a large pool, measuring "360 feet in length, 130 feet in breadth, and 75 in depth to the bottom."[3]

---

1 Charles Haddon Spurgeon, *The Metropolitan Tabernacle Pulpit* (London: Passmore and Alabaster, 1870), 16:485.
2 Edersheim, *The Life and Times of Jesus the Messiah*, 320.
3 McClintock and Strong, *Cyclopedia of Biblical. Theological, and Ecclesiastical Literature*, 1:777.

There was a legend among the people that whoever first got into the water after the stirring of the angel would be healed. One can only imagine the number of sick and infirm people who gathered every day at that pool in hopes of being first. Being near the Sheep Gate, the pool was used, according to tradition, to wash the flesh of the sacrifices before they were offered. Thus, the water of the pool was tinctured with a reddish color.[4] While the area was sufficient to hold a large multitude, there was one man in particular whose life was to be changed by Jesus at this "feast of the Jews."

The Paralytic Healed at Bethesda (John 5:1–17)

John 5:1 simply states, "that there was a feast of the Jews, and Jesus went up to Jerusalem."[5] This feast is not named, but the events of Jesus' ministry in Galilee point to a date early in the year of AD 28. John 5:9 states: "Now it was the Sabbath on that day." The Feast of Purim in AD 28 was on February 27th, a Sabbath. Purim was not one of the three annual feasts of the Old Testament—Passover, Pentecost and the Feast of Booths—in which all males were encouraged to go up to Jerusalem. Rather, Purim was a non-Mosaic feast which began as a result of the plot of Haman to exterminate the Jews throughout the whole kingdom of Assyria (which at that time extended over 127 provinces from India to Ethiopia) ruled by King Ahasuerus. Queen Esther, a Jew, convinced Ahasuerus to allow the Jews to defend themselves and the plot of Haman was foiled. The Jews, thereafter, celebrated the Feast of Purim on the fourteenth day of the month Adar with feasting and rejoicing. Thus, Jesus traveled to Jerusalem after debating the Pharisees in Galilee about fasting to celebrate in the joyous feast of Purim. If the plot of Haman had been successful, not only would the Jews as a race have been exterminated, but the Lion of the tribe of Judah—Jesus of Nazareth—would never have come in the flesh. Haman's plot was not just the plot of a jealous man. It was another of the many plots of the devil to try to foil the prophecies

---

4 McClintock and Strong, *Cyclopedia of Biblical. Theological, and Ecclesiastical Literature*, 1:777.
5 The question which feast of the Jews Jesus went to in 28 AD is very hard to determine. The timeline of Jesus' life narrows the options to either Purim or Passover. Since John gives no further information about the feast after this healing, Purim seems more likely to me. Purim is the only Jewish festival that fell on a Sabbath between AD 25 and AD 35. Yet, if this feast was Purim, there is no mention of Jesus going to the Passover in 28 AD. On the other hand, it seems very likely that John would have mentioned that this feast was Passover if it was so. Also, Jesus did not go up to Passover in AD 29 either. It is possible that Jesus avoided Passover in both AD 28 and AD 29 because He knew that it would provoke the scribes, Pharisees, priests, and rulers to attempt to kill Him before His time arrived.

about the Messiah or to kill Him once He came into the world. The real battle is always between God and Satan, as it was in the garden of Eden and has been ever since.

A few weeks before, Jesus had healed a paralytic while preaching at the home of Peter's mother-in-law in Capernaum. His claim to be able to forgive sins provoked the enmity of the Pharisees in attendance against Him. On this occasion, Jesus is even more direct by healing on a Sabbath day in Jerusalem. At a feast which celebrated the victory of God's people over their enemies, Jesus brought deliverance to a paralytic who had never given up hope of being healed. When Jesus appeared at the pool, the waters had not yet been "troubled" and anxious souls were eagerly awaiting some sign that their healing was at hand. "It was in those breathless moments of the intense suspense of expectancy, when every eye was fixed on the *pool*, that the eye of the Saviour searched for the most wretched object among them all."[6] Jesus found such a man who had been impotent for thirty-eight years and He asked him, "Do you wish to get well?" (John 5:6). This man had suffered in his misery as a "hopeless sufferer, without attendant or friend (John 5:7), among those whom misery . . . made so intensely selfish."[7] Such miserable people are quite often the least compassionate people of all. Their attention is focused solely on themselves and there is no room within their hearts for the cares of others.

J. A. Findlay reminds us that "an eastern beggar often loses a good living by being cured of his disease."[8] This query of Jesus was both appropriate and necessary. Did the impotent man wish to get well or did he want to remain in his present condition? As William Barclay notes: "The first essential towards receiving the power of Jesus is the intense desire for it."[9] Yet, even the desire for such a change must come from God. As Psalm 110: 3 says: "Your people will volunteer freely in the day of Your power." Not only must the power to be changed come from Jesus, but even the ability to "volunteer freely" comes from Him also. The response of the man indicated clearly that he wanted to be changed. He said, "while I am coming, another steps down before me" (John 5:7). As John 5:4 states: "for an angel of the

---

6 Edersheim, *The Life and Times of Jesus the Messiah*, 324.
7 Edersheim, *The Life and Times of Jesus the Messiah*, 324.
8 Morris, *The Gospel According to John* , 303.
9 Morris, *The Gospel According to John*, 303.

Lord went down at certain seasons into the pool and stirred up the water; whoever then first, after the stirring up of the water, stepped in was made well from whatever disease with which he was made afflicted." An article in *Fairbairn's Imperial Standard Bible Encyclopedia* stated the following concerning Bethesda and the angel:

> If an angel was sent to loose the chains of Peter and release him from the grasp of a persecutor; and if an angel was again sent to smite that persecutor himself, and cause him suddenly to be eaten by worms, why might not an angel be also employed at particular seasons to impart a healing virtue to the waters of a public bath, or swimming pool, such as they could not have naturally possessed, but such as the higher interests of God's kingdom might require? There is nothing improbable in this, on the supposition of angelic agency, for purposes of special interpositions being at times called into play; and at such a time as that now under consideration, there were ends—one can readily understand—that might be served by certain smaller and more fitful acts of supernatural working, as well as by those which constituted the peculiar distinction of the gospel age.[10]

The spirit of rationalism which denies the miraculous is the primary reason why John 5:4 has been considered to be of dubious trustworthiness. There are multitudes of places in the Scripture wherein the agency of angels has revealed matters to believers or delivered them from dangers or even smote those who were troublers of God's people. This angelic intervention for the healing of the people who gathered at the pool was a preparation for the greater work of Christ—which He performed on this occasion to this infirm man.

The man had often tried to get into the waters, but had failed to be the first time and again. "He explains that his failure to be cured during the long years of his illness arises from his inability to get to the water quickly enough when the waters are disturbed."[11] Jesus showed compassion on this man who would never be able to get in the water before others. Thus, He the commanded him: "Get up, pick up your pallet, and walk" (John 5:8). With the command, Jesus also gave him the power to obey so that "immediately the man became well, and picked up his pallet, and began to walk" (John 5:9). In other words, the man became well before he was able to pick up his pallet and walk home. What happened next and why is well-described by Edersheim:

---

10 Patrick Fairbairn, ed., *Fairbairn's Imperial Standard Bible Encyclopedia* (Grand Rapids: Zondervan Publishing House, 1957), 1:282.
11 Morris, *The Gospel According to John*, 303.

> The Jews saw him, as from Bethesda he carried his 'burden.' Such as that he carried were their only burdens. Although the law of Sabbath-observance must have been made stricter in later Rabbinic development, when even the labour of moving the sick into the waters of Bethesda would have been unlawful, unless there had been present danger to life, yet, admittedly, this carrying of the bed was an infringement of the Sabbatic law, as interpreted by traditionalism. Most characteristically, it was this external infringement which they saw, and nothing else; it was the Person Who had committed it Whom they would know, not Him Who had made whole the impotent man.[12]

It was at this point that the intrigue between the Jews and Jesus began in earnest. Jesus' supposed violation of the Sabbath commandment would become the chief point of contention between them. "It was on the occasion of this Feast that Jesus encountered His enemies, now thoroughly aroused, in a growing hostility of bitter antagonism in controversy about the proper observance of the Sabbath. They had attacked Him covertly at first in Galilee and afterwards more openly at Matthew's supper. They were awaiting now their chance to renew the attack in the Jerusalem feast."[13] And they found it when Jesus healed this impotent man on the Sabbath and told him to carry his bedroll home.

The Pharisees had put a hedge around the Sabbath commandment with so many man-made rules that the proper observance of the day "became wholly impossible even for themselves."[14] Thus, they had to resort to casuistry—a means of clever but unsound reasoning—in order to convince themselves that they kept it properly. The proof that they did not properly keep the Sabbath was that they faulted the Lord for His observance of the day. The Jews first told the man that it was not lawful for him to carry his pallet on the Sabbath. He replied to them that the One who made him well told him to do so. The Jews then demanded to know who that man was that had given him such a command. The impotent man who was healed did not yet know the name of Jesus. He then went to the temple where Jesus found him and revealed Himself to him while exhorting him to sin no more. The former impotent man then told the Jews that it was Jesus who had healed him. "For this reason the Jews

---

12 Edersheim, *The Life and Times of Jesus the Messiah*, 325.
13 Shepard, *The Christ of the Gospels*. 152.
14 Shepard, *The Christ of the Gospels*, 153.

were persecuting Jesus, because He was doing these things on the Sabbath" (John 5:16). Jesus' reply to their persecution was to reveal His equality with the Father: "My Father is working until now, and I Myself am working" (John 5:17).

Jesus' Equality with the Father (John 5:17–47)

The scenery changes from the pool of Bethesda to the Temple grounds. There Jesus found the man He had healed. There the Jews confronted the man. And there also Jesus answered all the objections of the Jews. The ensuing dialogue gave the Lord the opportunity to declare His equality with the Father. Jesus was more conscious of Himself and His mission than any other man ever, but His self-consciousness was always pure. He was never vain or conceited or arrogant. Likewise, Jesus was more aware of others and their inner thoughts than any other person. Yet, He was devoid of judgmentalism or faultfinding. It is impossible to study the life of Jesus without addressing both His self-consciousness and His self-disclosure. As. T. H. Root wrote concerning this subject:

> No life was ever so devoid of that which commonly goes by this term as was that of Jesus. The very intensity with which he related himself to those around him rendered such a state impossible. His intense consciousness of others is the correlative of his intense consciousness of himself. The correlation was perfect, resulting in perfect poise. In the sense that we have indicated no personality ever had a self-consciousness so deep and so all-pervading.[15]

Jesus' self-consciousness, self-disclosure, and awareness of others are truths that cannot be rightly understood apart from His divinity and His omniscience. The Jews immediately discerned that Jesus made Himself equal with God when He said: "My Father is working until now, and I am working" (John 5:17). In addition to their charges against Him of breaking the Sabbath commandment, they now "were seeking to kill Him, because He . . . was calling God His own Father" (John 5:18). In so doing, they deceived themselves into thinking that they were doing the will of God.

The charge that Jesus was breaking the Sabbath commandment was frivolous and the Jews knew it. "The Rabbis made out a system of thirty-nine works, which done rendered the offender subject to

---

15 T. H. Root, "The Self-Consciousness of Jesus, III" in *The Biblical World*, Vol. 2. No. 6 (Dec. 1893), The University of Chicago Press, 412–420.

death by stoning. Derived from these 'father-works' were numerous 'descendant-works.'"[16] Shepard further describes the result of such rabbinical rules:

> The Sabbath had become a grievous burden by the thousands of such restrictions and rules too numerous to mention.
> The excessive strictness and multiplicity of exactions heaped up by the Rabbis made the observance wholly impossible even for themselves. So they had recourse to casuistry and thought out many ways of evading the rules they themselves had made.[17]

Yet, Jesus now gave the Jews an even stronger charge against Him than Sabbath breaking. He openly claimed to be God and defended His statement with several facts. Instead of keeping this fact a secret, He disclosed Himself to this hostile crowd. While there are those who ignorantly assert that Jesus never claimed to be God, He most certainly did. It was imperative for Jesus to reveal Himself if sinners were to be drawn to Him. His self-disclosure as the Son of God was most necessary.

In response to the Jews' charges against Him, Jesus began by proving that He is entirely submissive to the Father—"the Son can do nothing of Himself, unless it is something He sees the Father doing" (John 5:19). Those "things" that the Son can do will include even "greater works than these (i.e., those works Jesus had already performed), so that you will marvel" (John 5:20). So that there will be no confusion on what He means by that assertion, Jesus clarifies that it includes raising the dead, giving life to whomever He wishes, the prerogative of judgment of every person, and the receiving of honor as God (John 5:21–23). He is not just the Son of God; He is the Son "sent" by the Father. He came with a commission from the Father. John 5:19–23 makes it clear that all His actions are coincident with the purposes of the Father.

In John 5:25–31, Jesus went beyond His relationship with the Father to the relationship of Himself to all men. It is an illustration of how the Son of God has the prerogative of judgment and the ability to give life to whomever He wishes. There are two resurrections mentioned—one of the spiritually dead who hear the voice of the Son of God and live; the other of "all who are in the tombs" (John 5:28) who will hear His voice and come forth to a resurrection of life or a resur-

---

16 Shepard, *The Christ of the Gospels*, 152–3.
17 Shepard, *The Christ of the Gospels*, 153.

rection of judgment. Instead of giving into the criticisms and charges of the Jews, Jesus becomes more emboldened to shine the light of the truth into the darkness of their hearts.

Jesus lists four witnesses to His Divinity in John 5:31–47 in addition to His own testimony. While Jesus testifies truthfully about Himself, the Scripture always requires more than a single testimony to establish every fact. The four witnesses are the testimony of John; the testimony of Jesus' works; the testimony of the Father; and, the testimony of Scripture.

The Jews were well aware of the testimony of John to Jesus because the Sanhedrin had sent a deputation to John to inquire if he was the Christ or Elijah or one of the prophets. John "confessed and did not lie" (John 1:20) that he was not the Christ, but, instead, was the "voice of one crying in the wilderness" (John 1:22). That deputation was responsible by their own acknowledgement to "give an answer to those who sent" (John 1:22) them. And John gave them an answer to take back to the Sanhedrin when he pointed to Jesus the next day and said, "Behold, the lamb of God who takes away the sin of the world!" (John 1:28). John had never retracted that statement, even while he still was languishing in Herod's prison at Machaerus.

The next witness to Jesus was the very works that He had performed—turning water into wine; healing the nobleman's son; cleansing a leper; healing numerous sicknesses and infirmities in Capernaum; healing paralytics in both Capernaum and Jerusalem; and many more. The works of Jesus were more numerous already than those performed by Elijah or Elisha. If the miracles of those prophets performed established them as true spokesmen for God, then Jesus' works established His testimony as being true also. If John was esteemed to be one about whom a deputation from the Sanhedrin would inquire, then Jesus deserved even more respect.

The third witness was the testimony of the Father concerning His Son at His baptism by John: "This is My beloved Son, in whom I am well-pleased" (Matthew 4:17). That voice of God had come out of the heavens and was heard by the others who were there. The problem for the Jews was that they were always hardening their hearts and refusing to believe the truth.

The final witness to Jesus was/is the Scripture itself. The two main sects of the Jews—both Pharisees and Sadducees—claimed to believe the Scriptures, but they steadfastly failed to understand the prophecies that were fulfilled in Jesus. The numerous Old Testament prophecies about the Messiah make it impossible that it could be anyone other than Jesus. There are three hundred and thirty-two Old Testament prophecies that were fulfilled in Him. The probability that even eight such prophecies could be fulfilled in any one person other than Jesus is one in one hundred quadrillion. The probability that all the prophecies could be fulfilled by any else is incalculable. The problem for the Jews was that they did not sincerely love God, as Jesus contended, and, therefore, were unable to receive the truth that was staring them in the face. As Jesus said, "For if you believed Moses, you would believe Me, for he wrote about Me" (John 5:46).

Two Sabbath Controversies (Matthew 12:1–14 and Mark 2:23–3:6)

Following the feast in John 5, Jesus and His disciples returned to Galilee. Jerusalem was not a safe place for Him or them at that time. While "He had defeated His antagonists in debate over the Sabbath" concerning the healing of the paralytic, "He was their prisoner virtually"[18] as long as He remained there. They were very aware of the strength of His following, so they were loath to take Him into custody. Yet, they were watching His every move and were "seeking to entrap Him."[19] It was not yet Jesus' time, so He returned to the territory where He was reared.

It was probably only a week or two later that Jesus and His disciples were passing through a grain field on the Sabbath when the disciples began to pick the heads of grain and to eat them. The Pharisees must have been following Jesus to make sure He did not travel beyond the 2,000 cubits permitted by their Rabbinical rules for a Sabbath's day journey. When they saw the disciples pluck the grains of ear, they immediately said, "Look, why are they doing what is not lawful on the Sabbath?" (Mark 2:24). By common consent, it was not against the Law for them to pluck the ears of grain on any other day: "When you enter your neighbor's standing grain, then you may pluck the heads with your hand, but you shall not wield a sickle in your neigh-

---

18 Shepard, *The Christ of the Gospels*, 160.
19 Shepard, *The Christ of the Gospels*, 160.

bor's standing grain" (Deuteronomy 23:25). The Pharisees contended that what was permissible every other day was not permissible on the Sabbath and in the absence of a prooftext from Scripture had made their own legalistic rules concerning the Sabbath day. One of those rules in the Mishna said, "He that reapeth corn on the Sabbath to the quantity of a fig is guilty; and plucking corn is reaping."[20] Other Talmudic rules concerning the Sabbath made rubbing the grain to be threshing and even walking on grass was considered a form of threshing.[21] There were several transgressions that could be committed concerning plucking of grain on the Sabbath according to the Pharisees:

> In case a woman rolls wheat to remove the husks, it is considered sifting; if she rubs the head of the wheat, it is regarded as threshing; if she cleans off the side-adherences, it is sifting out fruit; if she throws them in her hand, it is winnowing.[22]

These several transgressions of one act were rolled together, according to Rabbinical law, to make an even more serious offense that resulted in "sin, punishment, and sin-offering."[23] Interestingly, Jesus did not pluck any of the ears of grain, but He was ready with a defense of His disciples. There were five different arguments used by Jesus to dismiss the criticisms of the Pharisees. The first was the law of necessity based on the example of David when he and his companions ate the showbread that was reserved for the priests (cf. Leviticus 24:9 and 1 Samuel 21:1–6). Even Maimonides, a twelfth century Jewish philosopher, had stated that "danger to life superseded the Sabbath and all other obligations."[24] That was a principle with which the Rabbis agreed, but the Pharisees had covered it over with so many exceptions that it was seldom used. The second argument was the matter of the performance of work by the priests in the temple on the Sabbath (cf. Matthew 12:5). Worshipers could take their sacrifices to the priests on the Sabbath, but the priests had to engage in labor to offer those sacrifices. That labor was permissible which proves that there are exceptions to the requirement to desist from all work on the Sabbath.

The third argument by Jesus was the necessity of showing mercy as required by the prophets, especially Hosea 6:6—"For I delight in

---

20 Shepard, *The Christ of the Gospels*, 161.
21 Shepard, *The Christ of the Gospels*, 161.
22 Shepard, *The Christ of the Gospels*, 161.
23 Edersheim, *The Life and Times of Jesus the Messiah*, 512.
24 Shepard, *The Christ of the Gospels*, 162.

loyalty rather than sacrifice, and in the knowledge of God rather than burnt offerings." The Pharisees were engaging in a harsh, critical spirit that was the opposite of the mercy required by the Old Testament. It was also contrary to the second great commandment to "love your neighbor as yourself."

The fourth argument was based on God's purpose in giving us the Sabbath day for our rest and His worship. Jesus said, "The Sabbath was made for man, and not man for the Sabbath" (Mark 2:27). As J. A. Alexander commented on this verse:

> If God chooses mercy, i.e. kind regard to human happiness, and not (i.e. rather than) sacrifice (or other ceremonial service), we might well conclude, though it were not recorded, that the Sabbath is an institution for human benefit, and therefore to be set aside when inconsistent with it, not a necessary and inexorable law, to which the interests of man must yield, whenever they are brought into collision.[25]

The last argument was the most powerful. Jesus declared Himself to be the Lord of the Sabbath: "So the Son of Man is Lord even of the Sabbath" (Mark 2:28). "In these words He claimed not only Messiahship but final authority to change their Sabbath and rid it of the onerous burdens of their numberless traditions."[26]

Following that debate, Jesus was being watched even more carefully by the Pharisees. He entered a synagogue[27] on a Sabbath day—probably the very next Sabbath—and there was a man there with a withered hand. Luke, being a physician, records that it was the man's right hand which made it difficult for him to do anything. When Jesus saw the man with a withered hand, He asked him to come forward. Without actually touching him or doing any work of any kind, Jesus simply commanded the man to stretch forth his hand. The man did so and his hand was healed. Before performing that miracle, though, Jesus asked the congregation, "Is it lawful to do good or to do harm on the Sabbath, to save a life or to kill?" (Mark 3:4). Everyone kept silent to a question which should have evoked sympathy for the man. Thus, Jesus looked "around at them with anger, grieved at their hardness of heart" (Mark 3:5). His an-

---

25 Alexander, *The Gospel According to Mark*, 54.
26 Shepard, *The Christ of the Gospels*, 163.
27 That synagogue was probably in one of the cities of Galilee, but not Capernaum since it is not named.

ger was but for a moment while His grief was continuous and progressive.[28]

The Pharisees were not without compassion in all situations, especially when it concerned themselves, and they made various exceptions to the Sabbath commandment when it was beneficial for them. For instance, they believed that actual danger to human life required the breaking of the Sabbath. Yet, their rules for what constituted such endangerment were often preposterous. "A person suffering from toothache might not gargle his mouth with vinegar, but he might use an ordinary toothbrush and dip it in vinegar . . . Similarly, medical aid might be called in, if a person had swallowed a piece of glass; a splinter might be removed from the eye, and even a thorn from the body."[29] Angina pain was a reason to supersede the Sabbath law, but things that only affected the outside of the body—such as a withered hand—were not permitted. There were no Old Testament case laws that gave such distinctions. And these man-made laws of the Pharisees were enforced very differently for various people. Jesus healed the man without even touching him. The Pharisees did not like what He did, but there were no grounds for bringing a charge against Him. Instead, the Pharisees began to conspire with the Herodians "as how they might destroy Him" (Mark 3:6). Swete's comments on this intrigue are instructive:

> The Pharisees left the synagogue mad with rage . . . and lost no time . . . in plotting revenge . . . the consultation held that day was but one of many; the last is described in xv.1 . . . An Herodian party, so far as it found a place in Jewish life, would be actuated by mixed motives; some would join it sympathy with the Hellenising policy of the Herod family; others because they 'saw in the power' of the family 'the pledge of the preservation of their national existence.' The latter would have certain interests in common with the Pharisees, and might have joined them in an effort to suppress a teacher who threatened the *status quo* . . . The Pharisees on their part, without any great affection for the Herods, could acquiesce in their rule as the lesser of two evils . . . and . . . they were not unwilling to use Antipas as an ally against Jesus, or even to act as emisaaries of the Tetrarch.[30]

This conspiracy of the Pharisees with the Herodians was the first

---

28 The verb for 'anger' is the aorist tense which means an action completed in the past. The verb for 'grieved' is a continuous present tense.
29 Edersheim, *The Life and Times of Jesus the Messiah*, 515.
30 Swete, *Commentary on Mark*, 53-4.

active step they took jointly to "destroy" Jesus. There were things that each party gained thereby. Antipas gained the support of the Pharisees in his troubles with Rome and the continuation of "their national existence" in Galilee and Perea. The Pharisees gained the support of Antipas in their inveterate hatred of Jesus and their plot to kill Him. Jesus knew well that the Cross awaited Him because His enemies were already plotting His demise. His public ministry had scarcely begun when the plots against Him started. He had not yet even preached the Sermon on the Mount or called His apostles or trained them for their future ministry. Yet, that "twisted serpent," Leviathan, (Isaiah 27:1) was ever active in opposing the One who threatened his deception of the nations.

9
Jesus' True Disciples

In his commentary on Matthew, Craig L. Blomberg wrote concerning the possible site where Jesus delivered His message called the Sermon on the Mount:

Though 'we cannot determine exactly where Jesus delivered his message,' the 'traditional site on the. . . shore of the Sea of Galilee, known as the Mount of Beatitudes, at least gives a good acoustical illustration of how a speaker could address a large crowd on a plateau in the hills overlooking the lakeside and be heard by thousands at once.'[1]

While the Pharisees and Herodians were plotting to destroy Him as a result of the Sabbath disputes (Mark 3:6 and Luke 6:11), Jesus and His disciples withdrew to the shore of the Sea of Galilee (Mark 3:7–11). "This retreat before his enemies was prompted, not by fear, but by that wise discretion which was constantly employed in the selection and the use of necessary means for the promotion of the great end which he came to accomplish."[2] Our Lord then made a request to His disciples carrying the force of a command that a small boat "stand ready for Him because of the crowd" (Mark 3:9). The Greek word for this boat indicates a vessel smaller than the typical fishing boat. Jesus wanted a boat that could be easily maneuvered and ready at a moment's notice to take Him away from danger. Teaching and healing on the northern shore of the Sea of Galilee afforded Him more protection from a plot to kill Him than the narrow streets of Capernaum did. It would be much more difficult for those conspirators to seize Him in the open air with crowds of His followers all around.

---

1 Craig L. Blomberg, *Matthew* (Nashville: Broadman Press, 1992), 97. Blomberg is correct in his description of that site, but it is actually the northwest shore of the Sea of Galilee, not the northeast shore as Blomberg wrote.
2 Alexander, *The Gospel According to Mark*, 60.

Miracles by the Sea (Matthew 12:15–21; Mark 3:7–27 and Luke 6:17–19)

There was a great multitude that had gathered in Capernaum from all over Galilee, Judea, Jerusalem, Idumea, beyond the Jordan in Perea, and the vicinity of Tyre and Sidon (Matthew 4:25; Mark 3:7, 8; and, Luke 6:17–19). The crowd was a mixture of both Jews and Gentiles. Idumea was the region east of the Dead Sea all the way down to the Red Sea. It was the land of Esau known as Edom. During the Captivity of the Jews, these Edomites had encroached on the territory of Israel and were later mixed with them in marriages. The Herods who ruled Israel came from Idumea and were mixed both in their racial heritage and their religious views. Perea was that area east of the Jordan River stretching from the Dead Sea to the Sea of Galilee which the tribe of Gad had inherited. Tyre and Sidon were mostly Phoenician cities dominated by paganism, but had formerly been on the borders of the territory of the tribe of Asher. Many of the people in this crowd were Gentiles who were eagerly seeking the relief that only the Messiah could give. A large number of them were afflicted with diseases and scourges. The impression is that everyone who eagerly sought Jesus, believing in His power to heal them, had their diseases taken away. Thus, they were pressing "around Him in order to touch Him" and be healed (Mark 3:10).

During the miraculous healings that were taking place, there were also many unclean spirits that were cast out. Those unclean spirits were among the first beings to acknowledge Jesus as divine, reluctantly falling on their knees and shouting out, "You are the Son of God!" (Mark 3:11). Jesus sternly warned them not to tell anyone who He was (Mark 3:12). That begs the question why Jesus did not want them to make Him known. There are a couple of reasons. First, they acknowledged Him out of a grave sense of dread and tremblingly believed in Him. They were not giving glory to Him as God, but blurted out who He was from extreme fear. Second, Jesus wanted the revelation of His Sonship to be spread by people who had come to worship Him and had seen His glory. The glory of Christ could never be rightly spread by demons, but only by true believers. Thus, Henry Barclay Swete expounds on this point:

> The purpose of the censure was to prevent a premature divulgence of His true character . . . it was not yet time for a general manifestation . . .

and the [demons] were possibly aware that their revelations could only work mischief at this stage.³

The revelation of the demons was another instance of the ongoing battle between Satan and Jesus. This was one of those more opportune times (cf. Luke 4:13) that the devil sought in order to gain the advantage over our Lord. Yet, once again, his fiendish plan was foiled.

The Calling of the Twelve (Matthew 10:1–15; Mark 3:13–19; and, Luke 6:12–16)

Following these miracles by the sea, Jesus "went up on the mountain" (Mark 3:13) to pray before selecting the Twelve to follow Him and to be His apostles. The mountain in question was certainly one of the mountains in the area just north of Capernaum where Jesus often resorted to commune in private with His Father. It was probably that "gentle, grassy slope just west of Taghba."⁴ Jesus' dependency on prayer before making a major decision is an example to all believers. Thus, "He spent the whole night in prayer to God" (Luke 6:12) before summoning "those whom He Himself wanted, and they came to Him" (Mark 3:13). The men Jesus chose were mostly ordinary men by trade and profession. Several of them were fishermen. One was a tax collector. Another was a zealot—a sect that rebelled against the rule of the Romans. Six or seven of them had been with Jesus from almost the beginning of His ministry. The others had certainly followed Him for a while, so that it was little surprise to most of them when they were chosen. Five of the Twelve had not been mentioned in any of the Gospels previous to this momentous day. Henry Latham describes the importance of that vigil of prayer:

> A way was prepared in that night of prayer upon the hills whereby an organic life was imparted to the little community . . . Our Lord takes counsel of the Father alone, ... when morning comes . . . His resolve is distinct and it is forthwith carried out.⁵

The twelve apostles would be the men through whom Jesus would continue to build His church. By bringing these men into closer fellowship with Himself, Jesus could impart to them the special training that they needed. As J. A. Alexander remarked:

---

3 Swete, *Commentary on Mark*, 57.
4 Hendriksen, *Exposition of the Gospel According to Luke*, 326.
5 Swete, *Commentary on Mark*, 57. .

It formed, as we have seen (on I, 16), no part of our Lord's personal errand upon earth to reorganize the Church. For the same reason, he did not develop the whole system of Christian doctrine, but left both these tasks to be accomplished after his departure, yet preparing the way for both, by teaching the true nature of his kingdom, and by training those who should complete the Church, both as to its organization and its creed.[6]

There were two specific purposes in their ordination as apostles by Jesus. First, they would be discipled in the message that they were to preach to the world. Second, they would be given the authority to heal and work miracles as proofs of their apostolic commission (cf. Hebrews 2:4). There are four times in the New Testament that the list of the apostles is given. Peter is always the first listed; Philip is the fifth; James is the ninth; and, Judas is always the last (except in Acts where he had already betrayed Jesus and killed himself). These men did not call themselves. They were called by Jesus and ordained by Him. Now, ordination is a matter of the true church to set apart those who exhibit the qualities and graces required of officers. Like King David, Jesus had to take as disciples those who were willing to follow Him. Thus, A. B. Bruce states:

> The truth is, that Jesus was obliged to be content with fishermen and publicans, and quondam[7] zealots, for apostles. They were the best that could be had. Those who deemed themselves better were too proud to become disciples, and thereby they excluded themselves from what all the world now sees to be the high honor of being chosen princes of the kingdom The civil and religious aristocracy boasted of their unbelief. The citizens of Jerusalem did feel for a moment interested in the zealous youth who had purged the temple with a whip of small cords; but their faith was superficial, and their attitude was patronizing, and therefore Jesus did not commit Himself unto them, because He knew what was in them. A few of good position were sincere sympathizers, but they were not so decided in their attachment as to be eligible for disciples. Nicodemus was barely able to speak a timid apologetic word in Christ's behalf, and Joseph of Arimathea was a disciple "secretly," for fear of the Jews.[8]

The training of these twelve men over the next two years would be the great work of Jesus in preparation for His atoning sacrifice. These disciples—minus Judas—would be shaped into apostles through the teaching of Christ and the ministry of the Spirit.

---

6 Alexander, *The Gospel According to Mark*, 63.
7 Quondam means 'former.' Simon the Zealot was a zealot no more after being called by Jesus.
8 A. B. Bruce, *The Training of the Twelve* (Grand Rapids: Kregel Publications, 1971), 37–8.

The Sermon on the Mount (Matthew 5–7)

The view of the Sea of Galilee from the gently sloped plain of the Korazim Plateau on Mount Eremos is beautiful and serene. Many Biblical scholars believe that plateau is where Jesus delivered His Sermon on the Mount. Eremos is 574 feet above the Sea below, but over 100 feet below the Mediterranean Sea. It is one of the lowest mountain peaks in the world. Taghba is to the southwest and Capernaum is to the southeast. This mountain is probably the place where Jesus had prayed all night before calling the Twelve. Thus, Matthew 5:1 states: "When Jesus saw the crowds, He went up on the mountain; and after He sat down, His disciples came to Him." Matthew refers to a specific mountain, 'the mountain,' which came to be the place where Jesus often retired for solitude, meditation, and prayer.

The setting of the Sermon on the Mount has been compared to the giving of the Law to Moses at Mount Horeb. Hendriksen makes the following comparison and contrast:

> On the one hand, Mount Horeb: cold, bleak, barren, almost inaccessible, situated in the midst of a howling wilderness with its fiery serpents. On the other hand, the Mount of Beatitudes with its smiling landscapes and grassy slopes, as it were extending a hearty welcome to all and spreading delight by means of its lilies, daisies, hyacinths, and anemones. At Horeb, God appearing in thunder and lightning, and the people overcome with fear. In Galilee: Immanuel, grace and truth proceeding from his lips, sitting down in the midst of his disciples without fear or trembling.[9]

Yet, the differences must not be pressed too closely because Jesus is both a gentle Savior and a Righteous Judge who will mete out vengeance in the Last Day. The same Lord who thundered from Mount Sinai also repeatedly expresses His love for His people in the Old Testament. And, the Sermon on the Mount does not abrogate the Ten Commandments, but, rather, unfolds their true, spiritual meaning. As John 1:17 says: "For the Law was given through Moses; grace and truth were realized through Jesus Christ." The face of Moses was so filled with glory whenever he came back down from the mountain that they could not look on him directly. Yet, the crowd beheld Jesus face-to-face and listened to His voice with raptured attention even though He had more glory than Moses.

---

9 Hendriksen, *Matthew*, 261.

This sermon, which rightfully deserves to be considered the greatest sermon ever, was first of all delivered by Jesus to His disciples. Having just called them as His disciples, the Sermon on the Mount is partly an ordination sermon for them and partly a sermon that defines His true followers. This sermon does not tell the crowds what they are to do to become Jesus' disciples, but, rather, it describes the character of those who are His disciples. In his magnanimous work, *Studies in the Sermon on the Mount*, D. M. Lloyd-Jones wrote the following overall analysis of that sermon:

> What is of supreme importance is that we must always remember that the Sermon on the Mount is a description of character and not a code of ethics or of morals. It is not to be regarded as law—a kind of new 'Ten Commandments' or set of rules and regulations which are to be carried out by us—but rather as a description of what we Christians are meant to be, illustrated in certain particular respects. It is as if our Lord says, 'Because you are what you are, this is how you will face the law and how you will live it.'[10]

The Sermon on the Mount is found in its fullness only in Matthew 5–7, but various parts of are recorded in Luke 6:20–49, including several verses that are not found in Matthew. For instance, the Beatitudes are stated both as blessings for the true disciples of Christ in Matthew and as woes for those who disobey the truth in Luke (Cf. Matthew 5:1–12 and Luke 6:20–26). This sermon is the fullest and best representation of the preaching of Jesus that startled Galilee and resulted in so many people hanging on His words. His miracles had already had the impact of attracting crowds from everywhere. Matthew Henry wrote concerning the setting for this sermon:

> *The place* was a mountain in Galilee. As in other things, so in this, our Lord Jesus was but ill-accommodated: He had no convenient place to preach in, any more than *to lay His head on*. While the scribes and Pharisees had Moses' chair to sit in, with all possible ease, honour, and state, and there corrupted the Law, the great Teacher of truth, is driven out to the desert, and finds no better place than *a mountain* can afford.[11]

The value of such open air preaching as our Lord used on this occasion is that the large multitudes could be reached in one setting

---

10 D. Martyn Lloyd-Jones, *Studies in the Sermon on the Mount* (Grand Rapids: Eerdmans Publishing Company, 1972), 1:28.
11 Matthew Henry, *Commentary on the Whole Bible* (Old Tappan, New Jersey: Fleming Revell, n.d.), 5:46.

whereas there were no synagogues large enough to hold them all. The scribes and Pharisees taught: "Do this and live." Jesus taught: "Live by faith and do this." The gospel is just the opposite of the law. As Paul wrote in Romans: "For Christ is the end of the law for righteousness to everyone who believes. For Moses writes that the man who practices the righteousness which is based on law shall live by that righteousness" (Romans 10:4, 5). On the other hand, the Sermon on the Mount was not a call to strive to be good in order to attain salvation. Rather, Jesus began this sermon by proclaiming a benediction, which means "good words," on those who are His disciples. He did not give them directions on how to work for their salvation, but rather how to live as those who are redeemed. He describes the character of those who are His disciples. They are poor in spirit, they mourn, they are gentle, they hunger and thirst for righteousness, they are merciful, they are pure in heart, they are peacemakers, and they are persecuted. The last Beatitude is the key for interpreting the whole sermon. Jesus' disciples are persecuted for who they are—followers of Jesus—not for what they do. Such followers of Jesus will receive the kingdom of heaven, will be comforted, will inherit the earth, will receive satisfaction, will receive mercy, will see God, will be called sons of God, and will receive a great reward in heaven. The words of Jesus in these Beatitudes read like the blessing He will give to the sheep on the day of Judgment: "Come, you who are blessed of My Father, inherit the kingdom prepared for you from the foundation of the world" (Matthew 25:34).

Following the Beatitudes, Jesus then makes certain statements about His disciples in Matthew 5:13–20—"You are the salt of the earth"; "You are the light of the world"; "Let your light shine before men." Chamblin commented on this section:

> He speaks of what they are, not of what they ought to be . . . Yet because nature and function are inseparable in both salt and light, the text also contains exhortations implicit (5:13b, 15) and explicit (5:16). What the disciples do discloses what they are; 'Salt salts because it is salt, and light illumines because it is light.' As salt and light are eminently useful so can the disciples be.[12]

The rest of Matthew 5 (verses 21–48) is taken up with various statements of Jesus that either expound the spirituality of the law

---

12 Chamblin, *Matthew*, 1:331.

or contradict the wrong interpretation of it. Six times Jesus quotes an Old Testament verse and then states: "But I say to you . . ." In so doing, Jesus asserts His authority as opposed to the traditions of the Jews. "He shows us that the Law, as expounded by Him, was a far more spiritual and heart-searching rule than most of the Jews supposed."[13] For instance, the sixth commandment about murder is broken by being angry with your brother; the seventh commandment against adultery is broken by the look of lust; the certificate of divorce that Moses allowed (Deuteronomy 24:1, 3) for "indecency" is limited by Jesus to adultery; the third commandment against false vows is hedged in by Jesus to making simple yes and no responses; the rule of equity for judges, "an eye for an eye, and a tooth for a tooth," cannot be used for personal revenge, but they are taught to "turn the other cheek"; and, the negation of the second great commandment, "You shall love your neighbor," by adding, "and hate your enemies," is overcome by "loving your enemies and praying for those who persecute you." What Jesus encouraged His disciples to do truly surpassed the merely outward standard of righteousness taught by the scribes and Pharisees (Cf. Matthew 5:20). The righteousness which Jesus commended to His disciples is described by A. B. Bruce:

> In the one aspect He characterized pharisaic righteousness as superficial and technical; in the other as ostentatious, self-complacent, and censorious. In contrast, thereto, He described the *ethics* of the kingdom as a pure stream of life, having charity for its fountainhead; a morality of the heart, not merely of outward conduct; a morality also broad and catholic, overleaping all arbitrary barriers erected by legal pedantry and natural selfishness. The *religion* of the kingdom He set forth as humble, retiring, devoted in singleness of heart to God and things supernatural; having faith in God as a benignant gracious Father for its root, and contentment, cheerfulness, and freedom from secular cares for its fruits; and finally, as reserved in its bearing towards the profane, yet averse to severity in judging, yea, to judging at all, leaving men to be judged by God.[14]

The righteousness of the Pharisees was superficial and consisted in performing outward duties while neglecting the heart. The righteousness Christ commended begins with poverty of spirit—which

---

13 John Charles Ryle, *Expository Thoughts on the Gospels: Matthew* (Cambridge: James Clarke & Co., 1974), 40.
14 Bruce, *The Training of the Twelve*, 43

is the mark of true repentance—and bears "fruit in keeping with repentance" (Matthew 4:8). Thus, the message of Jesus commended both the root and fruit of true saving grace in keeping with the basic teaching of John the Baptist.

The Sermon on the Mount divides into three general parts. The first section in Matthew 5:1–16 deals with the characteristics of the followers of Jesus. The second section, Matthew 5:17 to 7:12, unfolds the true meaning of the law and how Jesus' followers are to exhibit their works of righteousness which evidence their faith in Him—in personal relationships (5:21–48); in almsgiving (6:1–6); in private prayer (6:7–15); in fasting and the use of possessions (6:16–24); in resisting worry (6:25–34); in not judging others (7:1–6); and, in importunate prayer and following the golden rule (7:7–12). The final section, gives three exhortations for the hearers to make sure they are the true children of God by entering the narrow gate (7:13, 14); by bearing good fruit (7:15–23); and by building on the right foundation (7:24–27). "When Jesus finished these words, the crowds were amazed at His teaching; for He was teaching them as one having authority, and not as their scribes" (Matthew 7:28, 29). The people in Capernaum had responded with the same words when He preached His first sermon in their synagogue a few months earlier. The great Puritan preacher, William Perkins, rightly said about this sermon; "It may be justly called the key of the whole Bible, for here Christ openeth the sum of the Old and New Testaments."[15] And Matthew Henry praised the practical use of this sermon: "There is not much of the credenta of Christianity in it—the things to be believed; but it is wholly taken up with the agenda—the things to be done, for 'If any man will do His will, he shall know of the doctrine' (John vii.17)."[16] Indeed, all of Jesus' teaching was of the same kind—practical and spiritually edifying.

---

15 Arthur W. Pink, *An Exposition of the Sermon on the Mount* (Grand Rapids: Baker Book House, 1974), 13.
16 Pink, *An Exposition of the Sermon on the Mount*, 13.

Healing the Centurion's Slave (Matthew 8:5–13 and Luke 7:1–10)

Following the Sermon on the Mount, Jesus returned to Capernaum where he was almost immediately visited at His home by a deputation of Jewish elders who were sent by the centurion of that area. The Jewish elders informed Jesus of the desperate situation of the centurion's slave who "was sick and about to die" (Luke 7:2). Concern for a slave was unusual in the ancient world inasmuch as slaves were often considered little more than property. Such concern by this centurion for his slave touched the sympathetic heart of Jesus. This unnamed centurion was a Roman officer who was a fellow-official of the Court of Herod Antipas with the royal official whose son Jesus had healed from a distance (John 4:46–54). He commanded a company of one hundred soldiers quartered in Capernaum. He also had built the synagogue in Capernaum at his own expense and probably attended the services there even though he was not a convert to Judaism. Rather, he appears to have been a God-fearing Gentile like Cornelius (Acts 10:1, 2).. As the centurion for that area, he would have been aware of what was happening among the people. Yet, he also had a deeper spiritual interest because, as the Jewish elders relayed to Jesus, he was one who "loves our nation" (Luke 7:5). The circumstances of the centurion's household now required a miracle to be performed and he knew of the One who was healing multitudes of every sickness and disease in Capernaum. Thus, he decided to "ask, seek, and knock" to find out if Jesus would grant his request. While the Jewish elders were probably the main speakers, Matthew clearly notes that centurion himself "came to Him, imploring Him" (Matthew 8:5). True saving faith can never be expressed through a proxy alone, but is evidenced by personal and humble dependence on Christ.

When the Jewish elders came to Jesus, they also "earnestly implored Him, saying, 'He is worthy for you to grant this to him'" (Luke 7:4). Jesus immediately began to go with the Jewish elders to the centurion's home that was probably somewhere outside of Capernaum. The reluctance of the centurion to approach Jesus directly indicates clearly that he was not one who was a "proselyte of righteousness." A "proselyte of righteousness" had all the same privileges as the Jews and were considered their equal in most respects. It was different with those who had not taken that vital step. The Jews viewed such unbelieving Gentiles as unclean and their homes "were considered as defiled, and as defiling those who entered them."[17] For His part, Jesus had not hesitated to traverse to the centurion's home and was without a doubt willing to enter into it. Jesus was not bound in His conscience by such Talmudic rules and He was not afraid of becoming ceremonially defiled by close contact with Gentiles.

Seeing Jesus approaching his home, the centurion hastily dispatched some of his friends with this message, "Lord, do not trouble Yourself further, for I am not worthy for You to come under my roof; for this reason I did not even consider myself worthy to come to You, but just say the word and my servant will be healed. For I also am a man under authority, with soldiers under me; and I say to this one, 'Go!' and he goes, and to another, 'Come!' and he comes, and to my slave, 'Do this!' and he does it" (Luke 7:6b-8). Marveling at these words, Jesus turned to the crowd following Him and said, "Truly, I say to you, I have not found such great faith with anyone in Israel. I say to you that many will come from east and west, and recline at the table with Abraham, Isaac, and Jacob in the kingdom of heaven; but the sons of the kingdom will be cast into outer darkness; in that place there will be weeping and gnashing of teeth" (Matthew 8:10–12). In those words, the Lord swept away all the wrong presumptions of the Jews that the great Messianic banquet feast would honor them while the Gentiles would receive only the left-over crumbs. Instead, Jesus said that the "sons of the kingdom" would be cast into outer darkness, while such Gentiles as this centurion would sit down with Abraham, Isaac, and Jacob.

Thus, to the centurion, Jesus said, "Go; it shall be done for you as you have believed." The words of the centurion when juxtaposed against the pleas of the Jewish elders indicated his great humility. They had implored Jesus' help for him on the basis of his worthiness, but the centurion told Jesus: "I did not even consider myself worthy to come to You" (Luke 7:7). J. C. Ryle commented on the centurion's expressed humility:

> Humility like this is one of the strangest evidences of the indwelling of the Spirit of God. We know nothing of it by nature, for we are all born proud. To convince us of sin, to shew us our own vileness and corruption, to put us in our right place, to make us lowly and self-

---

17 Edersheim, *The Life and Times of Jesus the Messiah*, 377.

abased,—these are the principal works which the Holy Ghost works in the soul of man.[18]

Such Spirit produced humility always issues forth into saving faith as well and Jesus focused particularly on the faith of the centurion. The centurion clearly expressed his faith in the authority of Jesus to perform whatever miracle that was necessary. He saw with clear vision that all authority had been given to Jesus in heaven and on earth. As a result, the centurion's servant was immediately raised up from the bed of sickness and found to be in "good health" (Luke 7:10).

---

18 Ryle, *Expository Thoughts on the Gospel of Luke*, 1:202.

10

The Second Preaching Tour in Galilee

"The selection by Jesus of the twelve from the band of disciples who had gathered around His person is an important landmark in the Gospel history. It divides the ministry of the Lord into two portions, nearly equal, probably, as to duration, but unequal as to the extent and importance of the work. In the earlier period Jesus labored single-handed; His miraculous deeds were confined for the most part to a limited area, and His teaching was in the main of an elementary character. But by the time the twelve were chosen, the work of the kingdom had assumed such dimensions as to require organization and division of labor; and the teaching of Jesus was beginning to be of a deeper and more elaborate nature, and His gracious activities were taking on ever-widening range."[1]

One of the first things Jesus did after calling the twelve to be His disciples was to take them on a mission trip where they would be trained in evangelism. They were now His apprentices and He modeled for them what they would be later doing apart from Him. Luke 7:11 tells us concerning this trip: "Soon afterwards He went to a city called Nain; and His disciples were going along with Him, accompanied by a large crowd." Among that crowd were some women: "Mary who was called Magdalene, from whom seven demons had gone out, and Joanna the wife of Chuza and Susanna, and many others who were contributing to their support out of their private means" (Luke 8:2, 3). Whether this trip started that same day or a following day cannot be determined, but it was "soon afterwards." Nain is twenty-five miles southwest of Capernaum. The most direct land route would have taken Jesus through Tiberias where Herod Antipas had his primary dwelling. It is all but certain that the Lord did not choose that route for this trip. Jesus also could have traveled by boat to the most southwestern part of the Sea of Galilee before beginning His journey on foot. That would have made it more difficult for "the sizable crowd." There were other routes Jesus could have taken, but the Scripture simply does not tell us how they all traveled.

---

1 Bruce, *The Training of the Twelve*, 29.

Nain was a city on the north slopes of the mountain called the Little Hermon (also known as Mount Moreh), and was about four miles south of Mount Tabor. The elevation of the Little Hermon is approximately 1,600 feet above sea level whereas the Sea of Galilee is 700 feet below sea level. Nain means "pleasant" which, according to the ancient Rabbis, fulfilled that promise to Issachar who "saw the land that was pleasant."[2] That little city still remains today and "tombs in the rock have been found before the eastern gate of the village along the road that leads to Capernaum."[3] McClintock and Strong describe the location and setting of Nain:

> It stands on a bleak, rocky slope. On the northern declivity of Jebel ed-Duhy (the "hill Moreh" of Scripture and the "Little Hermon" of modern travelers), directly facing Tabor, from which it is four miles distant, and two and a half miles south-west of Endor . . . At the foot of the slope on which it stands is the great plain of Esdraelon, bounded on the north by the graceful wooded hills of Galilee, over which the snow-capped summits of Hermon and Lebanon appear.[4]

The fertile Valley of Jezreel ("God's seeding place") lay between Nain and Nazareth where Jesus was reared. That valley had been the scene of so many important battles and events in Israel's history. Close by were the cities of Shunem where Elisha raised the Shunammite's son; Zarephath where Elijah raised the widow's son; and, Endor where Saul consulted the witch. Jesus' journey to this formerly walled city with His disciples and the large crowd would have taken the better part of the day. They probably arrived at Nain in the early evening when funeral processions typically took place. The burial ground was about ten minutes by foot to the east of Nain and the large entourage with Jesus was coming from the northeast. Thus, in the providence of the Lord the two groups met up on the east side of Nain. Edersheim describes what such a funeral procession was like:

> We can follow in spirit the mournful procession, as it started from the desolate home . . . Outside, the funeral orator, if such was employed, preceded the bier, proclaiming the good deeds of the dead . . . Immediately before the dead came the women . . . The body was not . . . carried in an ordinary coffin . . . but laid on a bier, or in an open coffin. Commonly . . . the face of the dead body was uncovered.[5]

---

2 Edersheim, *The Life and Times of Jesus the Messiah*, 382.
3 Geldenhuys, *The Gospel of Luke*, 222.
4 McClintock and Strong, *Cyclopedia of Biblical, Theological, and Ecclesiastical Literature*, 6:833.
5 Edersheim, *The Life and Times of Jesus the Messiah*, 384.

The Second Preaching Tour in Galilee

Thus, there were two large groups of people who met at the gate of the city as the funeral procession was headed to the burial grounds. One group was full of rejoicing as they were following the Prince of Life. The other group was full of mourning, loud lamentations, and somber music from flutes, cymbals, and trumpets as they had been visited by the Angel of Death. The crowds following Jesus quickly ceased their rejoicing as was the custom for funeral processions then, even as it is today. Jesus surveyed the procession and quickly spotted the grieving mother who was also a widow. Dismissing protocol, He interrupted the procession and spoke to the bereaved mother: "Do not weep!" (Luke 7:13). He then "came up and touched the coffin and the bearers came to a halt. And He said, 'Young man, I say to you, arise!'" (Luke 7:14). Immediately the "dead man sat up and began to speak. And *Jesus* gave him back to his mother" (Luke 7:15). Jesus, once again, was unconcerned about becoming ceremonially unclean. He took the action that was needed to turn mourning into rejoicing. He was moved with compassion for this widow who had lost her only son and He gave him back to her. The result was that great fear seized the hearts of all the people as they realized that a great prophet was in their midst and they said: "God has visited His people!" (Luke 7:16) Elijah and Elisha had performed great miracles near to Nain in days past through their fervent prayers, but Jesus performed His miracle with a mere word and the saving touch. This report went out throughout all Judea and all the surrounding district of Galilee. "After the weary centuries during which no Prophet had appeared, it was indeed a proof of Jehovah's visiting His people that one who excelled the greatest prophets was among them. No one in the O. T. raised the dead with a word."[6] As Geldenhuys wrote:

> In this story the Saviour's sympathy with the sorrowing and His absolute divine power over the invisible spirit-world are gloriously revealed. We see Him here as the loving Comforter, the Victor over death, and the Reuniter of separated dear ones. What He did here for that widowed mother and son He will one day do for all the faithful in a perfect and final form.[7]

---

6 Plummer, *A Critical and Exegetical Commentary on the Gospel According to S. Luke*, 200.
7 Geldenhuys, *Commentary on the Gospel of Luke*, 223.

The Deputation from John (Luke 7:18–30)

The disciples of John heard of the many miracles Jesus was doing, especially this miracle, and "reported to him about all these things" (Luke 7:18). John had baptized many people in Judea, but he had never performed miracles. As he was languishing in his darkened prison cell at Machaerus, this news raised John's hopes. Could Jesus be the Messiah? Perhaps, even most likely, John was troubled by the prophecies concerning Yahweh's Servant found in Isaiah 42:7 which states: "I am the Lord, I have called You in righteousness, I will also hold You by the hand and watch over You, and I will appoint You as a covenant to the people, as a light to the nations, to open blind eyes, to bring out prisoners from the dungeon and those who dwell in darkness from the prison." John was even then languishing in the dungeon of the Machaerus prison. If Jesus was the Messiah, John must have thought, then why was he still imprisoned?

At an earlier time, John had been confident that Jesus was the coming Messiah. Months of imprisonment at Machaerus had dashed the hopes of John that "the kingdom of heaven" he had proclaimed to be "close at hand" (Matthew 3:2) was really close at all. Had he been mistaken? Then, John's disciples came to visit him at Machaerus and reported to him what Jesus was doing—healing the sick, restoring sight to the blind, casting out demons, cleansing lepers, making the lame walk, and raising the dead. No one had ever performed more miracles than John's cousin. Could He be the Messiah? Yet, John was imprisoned still and that gnawing thought tormented his soul and perplexed his mind.

John had, undoubtedly, engaged in some serious searching of his soul over his ministry in the bleakness of his prison cell. He still preached occasionally to Herod who seemed to hear him gladly, but that despot remained unchanged. John's boldness was both his strength and his weakness. His ideas of the coming kingdom which he had announced were imperfect. He seemed to expect an idyllic state to suddenly descend on Israel similar to the ideas expressed in the Talmud. Thus, he sent his disciples back to Jesus with a question: "Are You the Expected One, or do we look for someone else?' (Luke 7:19). There was probably a failure both of faith and patience on John's part. Incarceration in a gloomy prison month after month could certainly have had that effect on him. Hendriksen captures both ideas in his comments on John's state at this time:

So, the imprisoned herald may have been wondering, "If Jesus is that powerful, why does he not do something about my incarceration?" But especially: as John saw it, the gracious words that fell from the lips of the Savior and the miracles he performed did not harmonize with the manner in which he, the Baptist, had pictured him before the public. He had presented him as One who had come to punish and destroy (Matt. 3:7, 10; Luke 3:7, 9).

John's words had been true and inspired, the very "word of God" (Luke 1:76; 3:2). What Christ's herald missed was this: he failed to discern that this prophecy of doom would go into fulfillment not now but at Christ's second coming. He had not seen the present and the future in true perspective.[8]

This was the gracious period of Jesus' ministry when the offer of salvation was given to all who would repent and believe. In the future, there would be the day of judgment that would come. Jesus, therefore, answered John's disciples with quotes from Isaiah 35:5, 6 and Isaiah 61:1 about the ministry of the Messiah. Jesus then told the disciples of John: "Go and report to John what you have seen and heard" (Luke 7:22). After quoting from Isaiah, He then spoke words as a tonic for John's troubled soul: "Blessed is he who does not take offense at Me" (Luke 7:23). There were many who were taking offense at Jesus. As Edersheim remarked concerning John's struggle:

> In that terrible conflict John overcame, as we all must overcome. His very despair opened the door of hope. The helpless doubt, which none could solve but One, he brought to Him around Whom it had gathered. Even in this there was evidence for Christ, as the unalterably True One. When John asked the question: Do we wait for another? light was already struggling through darkness. It was incipient victory even in defeat. When he sent his disciples with this question straight to Christ, he had already conquered; for such a question addressed to a possibly false Messiah has no meaning. And so must it ever be with us. Doubt is the offspring of our disease, diseased as its paternity. And yet it cannot be cast aside. It may be the outcome of the worst, or the problems of the best souls. The twilight may fade into outer night, or it may usher in the day. The answer lies in this: whether doubt will lead us *to* Christ, or *from* Christ.[9]

Once John's deputation of disciples had left, Jesus turned His attention to the spiritual needs of the crowds of people who had fol-

---

8 Hendriksen, *Exposition of the Gospel According to Luke*, 392-3.
9 Edersheim, *The Life and Times of Jesus the Messiah*, 459.

lowed Him from Capernaum to Nain. His questions were especially searching for those who had once been followers of John and who had gone out into the wilderness to be baptized by him. "What did you go out into the wilderness to see? A reed shaken by the wind? But what did you go out to see? A man dressed in soft clothing? Those who are splendidly clothed and live in luxury are found in royal palaces? But what did you go out to see? A prophet? Yes, I say to you, and one who is more than a prophet" (Luke 7:24b-26).

Jesus declared John to be the forerunner prophesied by Isaiah and Malachi. Then, He praised John as the greatest man of the Old Testament era, though less than the "least in the kingdom of God" (7:28). John prepared the way for Jesus, but would not live to see the glorious days of the Son of Man after His death and resurrection. The common people and tax collectors gladly were baptized by Jesus while confessing their sins, but the proud Pharisees and cunning lawyers rejected God's purpose for themselves by refusing to be baptized (Luke 7:29, 30).

Having exonerated John's doubts, Jesus then turned his attention to the "men of this generation" about whom He frequently had unkind words. The fickleness of that generation was a constant source of displeasure for Jesus. That same fickleness seems to characterize every generation. John and Jesus were two very different types of people. In some respects, they were polar opposites. The chief exhibit of that generation's fickleness was their response to both John and Jesus. John came in great austerity and the people complained that he neither danced when they played the flute nor wept when they sang a dirge (Luke 7:32). John came "eating no bread and drinking no wine" but they said, "He has a demon!" (Luke 7:33). On the other hand, Jesus came "eating and drinking" but they said about Him, "Behold, a gluttonous man and a drunkard, a friend of tax collectors and sinners!" (Luke 7:34). The Jews had wanted John to be less stern and Jesus to be more austere. Jesus also would be accused of having a demon by the Pharisees. To the men of that generation, Jesus was too loose and John was too tightly wound. Thus, they were like children who could not be satisfied.

The Second Preaching Tour in Galilee

Jesus Forgives the Immoral Woman (Luke 7:36–50)

Following the visit of the disciples of John to Jesus, our Lord was invited by a Pharisee named Simon to come dine at his house. The town where this Pharisee lived is not mentioned in Scripture and neither is the repentant woman identified. All we know is that she was an immoral woman. Some have speculated that she was Mary Magdalene and the place where this meeting took place was in Magdala. The assumption is that the disciples of John came to where Jesus was shortly after He raised the man at Nain.

This Pharisee undoubtedly had heard Jesus speak so glowingly about John the Baptist. Since the Pharisees had for the most part rejected John and had refused to be baptized—or, perhaps, John had refused to baptize them until they were repentant. As John had said when he saw many of the Pharisees and Sadducees coming to him for baptism: "You brood of vipers, who warned you to flee from the wrath to come?" (Matthew 3:7). This Pharisee named Simon must have been intrigued by the crowds declaring Jesus to be some great prophet (Luke 7:16) and, especially, by Jesus' words of praise for John. Thus, he invited Jesus to dine with him for the purpose of being able to make a better judgment about Him. Things did not develop as he had hoped. The diffidence of Simon towards Jesus was manifested immediately in that the normal and customary ways that hosts treat their guests were ignored by him. As Shepard wrote:

> Simon coldly omitted all the ordinary attentions shown usually to invited guests. Jesus was received with hauteur[10]; no one brought water to wash His sandalled feet; no kiss of welcome was given to Him by the host; no cool fragrant perfume was poured on His head. Simon felt that he was conferring a great honor on the visiting Rabbi.[11]

Jesus was an invited guest, but not a very welcome guest. The tension between Jesus and this Pharisee was so thick it could be cut with a knife. Jesus had been in many such situations and always knew how to navigate His way through them. The narrowness of the Pharisees stood in sharp contrast with the enlarged heart of Jesus. He would eat not only with sinners and tax collectors, but also with proud Pharisees. Making Himself at home, Jesus reclined at Simon's table in the typical manner that the Jews had learned during their captivity.

---

10 Hauteur means "haughtiness of manner; disdainful pride."
11 Shepard, *The Christ of the Gospels*, 203.

"Each person, facing the table, would be lying slantwise, with his feet stretched backward. He would be leaning on his left arm, in order to keep his right hand free to handle the food."[12] Thus, the feet of all the guests while dining would be exposed to someone from behind.

Into Simon's house suddenly appeared a woman—a notorious woman—who was evidently known for her many immoralities. Such an intrusion by uninvited guests was common in Palestine during that time, especially when dinner was being served. Hospitality was much more common in that day than it is now. Yet, here was an unclean woman entering into the supposed holy abode of a self-righteous Pharisee. Moreover, she was not wanting food. She wanted something else. She wanted to express her deep repentance to that "great prophet" whose words had touched her heart very deeply. As one who was truly in earnest, she found expression for her emotions with the only thing she had—an alabaster vial of perfume. Standing behind Jesus, she wet His feet with her abundant tears, wiped them with her unfurled hair, and anointed them with her perfume. "Among the Jews it was a shameful thing for this woman to let down her hair in public."[13] The unfurled hair of this woman clearly identified her as a woman of loose morals. Perhaps, she had only come to anoint Jesus' feet with her perfume and then to kiss them. "Kissing the feet was a common mark of deep reverence, especially to leading Rabbis."[14] But then she was overcome with emotion and began to cry, dripping her tears on His feet. "As she stood behind Him at His feet, reverently bending, a shower of tears, like sudden, quick summer-rain, that refreshes air and earth, 'bedewed' His feet."[15] She did what she could and wiped them with her hair. Yet, that act to the Jews gathered around Simon's table was another proof that she was a sinner. This woman's perfume was very costly. As Edersheim noted:

> We have evidence that perfumed oils . . . were largely manufactured in Palestine . . . A flask was worn by women around the neck, and hung down below the breast . . . So common was its use as to be allowed even on the Sabbath . . . The 'flask' not always of glass, but of silver or gold, probably also of alabaster . . . was used to sweeten the breath and perfume the person.[16]

---

12 Hendriksen, *Exposition of the Gospel According to Luke*, 406.
13 Plummer, *A Critical and Exegetical Commentary on the Gospel According to St. Luke*, 211.
14 Plummer, *A Critical and Exegetical Commentary on the Gospel According to St. Luke*, 211.
15 Edersheim, *The Life and Times of Jesus the Messiah*, 390.
16 Edersheim, *The Life and Times of Jesus the Messiah*, 390.

The Second Preaching Tour in Galilee

It was at this point that the whole matter reached a critical point for Simon. Reasoning in his heart, he said to himself, "If this man were a prophet, He would know who and what sort of a person this woman is who is touching Him, that she is a sinner" (Luke 7:39). Social contact with women in public, no matter how virtuous, was strictly forbidden by Jewish customs. Thus, Simon was offended by the disregard for those customs by Jesus. Surprisingly to Simon, what he thought in his heart, Jesus perceived because He was indeed more than prophet. Jesus then told Simon a parable of two debtors— "one who owed five hundred denarii, and the other fifty" (Luke 7:41). The basis for Jesus' parable was a truism among the rabbis. If both debtors were unable to repay their debt, then it might seem that they would have an equal love for their master. Yet, that was not according to the standard reasoning of the Rabbis in ancient Israel. "A *Rabbi* would, according to Jewish notions, say, that he would love most to whom most had been forgiven . . . If there were much benefit, there would be much love; if little benefit, little love."[17] Thus, Jesus used even the sayings of the rabbis to refute the false notions of the Pharisees.

After giving His parable, Jesus asked Simon which of the two debtors would love the most and he replied: "I suppose the one whom he forgave more" (Luke 7:43). Jesus commended Simon for his answer, but immediately contrasted the treatment He had received from him with His treatment by this woman. According to the Rabbinic principle stated above, the overflowing of emotion by this woman indicated clearly that she loved much because she had been forgiven much. And the haughty indifference of Simon indicated that he did not even realize that he owed a debt at all. Jesus then rebuked Simon while publicly declaring that the woman's sins were forgiven. What Jesus spoke with words was apparent by the actions of the two parties. The others reclining at Simon's table were amazed by Jesus' statements to the woman and began to ask: "Who is this man that even forgives sins?" Jesus' message to this woman was the same as it was to Simon: salvation is found in repentance and faith.

---

17 Edersheim, *The Life and Times of Jesus the Messiah*, 391.

Jesus Preaches at Nazareth (Matthew 13:54-58; Mark 6:-6; and, Luke 4:16-30)

From Nain, Jesus "*began* going around from one city and village to another, proclaiming and preaching the kingdom of God" (Luke 8:1). It was during this second preaching tour of Galilee that Jesus began to teach by parables. As Luke 8:4 notes: "When a large crowd was coming together, and those from various cities were journeying to Him, He spoke by way of a parable." The first parable He taught was the Parable of the Sower and the Soils.[18] Matthew 13 gives numerous other parables the Lord taught in Capernaum, including the Parable of the Sower and the Solis. The purpose of teaching by parables was given by Jesus in Matthew 13:11, 13—"To you it has been granted to know the mysteries of the kingdom of heaven, but to them it has not been granted . . . Therefore I speak to them in parables; because while seeing they do not see, and while hearing they do not hear, nor do they understand." While the ability to understand and believe come solely through the unmerited grace of God, Jesus focused on the responsibility of each person in those words and the use they make of every gracious work of the Lord. Through the natural hardness of heart of all men, even things that should lead them to salvation cause their hearts to be even more hardened. As Hendriksen notes:

> My parables, says Jesus as it were, will therefore lead to further obfuscation. That is the punishment which these people deserve and receive. They have brought it upon themselves.[19]

After a preaching tour to various towns and villages near Nazareth, Jesus finally visited the village of his youth. The reports of His teaching and miracles were well-known there. Geldenhuys suggests the following narrative to harmonize the various accounts in the Gospels:

> A few days before the Sabbath Jesus had come there, healed only a few sick (Mark vi.5) owing to the sceptical attitude of the inhabitants (the old acquaintances of a great person are but too often his keen critics and slow to believe in his greatness). For the time being, however they had not yet clashed with Him, but adopted a waiting attitude until the Sabbath.[20]

---

18 Some of these parables were taught on this mission trip and others were taught back in Capernaum. Jesus sometimes taught the same things more than once or to different audiences.
19 Hendriksen, *The Gospel of Matthew*, 554.
20 Geldenhuys, *Commentary on the Gospel of Luke*, 167.

The Second Preaching Tour in Galilee

It might seem strange that Jesus, who was able to raise even the dead, "could do no miracle there except that He laid His hands on a few sick people and healed them" (Mark 6:5), but the absence of faith on the part of the people was decisive. As Swete remarks:

> To work a miracle upon a responsible human being it was necessary that faith on the part of the recipient should concur with Divine power; neither was effectual without the other . . . .Faith was necessary on the part of the worker of the miracle . . ., but in our Lord's case this condition was always satisfied.[21]

The passage from the prophets for that day was from Isaiah 61:1, 2—"The Spirit of the Lord is upon Me, because He anointed Me to preach the gospel to the poor . . ." The marvelous providence of God can be seen even in the selection of that passage from which Jesus preached. Jesus had returned "to Galilee in the power of the Spirit" (Luke 4:14) and in His first sermon to the synagogue in Nazareth was preaching about the Spirit of God being on Him as an evidence of His Messiahship (Matthew 13:54–58, Mark 6:1–6; and Luke 7:16–30).[22] The elders and members of that synagogue were eager to hear from Jesus, the hometown boy who had become such a Wonder throughout Galilee.

When Jesus began His sermon at Nazareth, "the eyes of all in the synagogue were fixed on Him . . . And all were speaking well of Him and wondering at the gracious words which were falling from His lips" (Luke 4:20, 22). Yet, there was a spirit of unbelief already at work in their hearts inasmuch as they were also questioning, "Is not this the carpenter, the son of Mary, and brother of James and Joses and Judas and Simon? Are not His sisters here with us?" (Mark 6:3). As a result, the people began to take offense at Him (Mark 6:3). The members of this synagogue were mesmerized by His words concerning the Messiah and the Year of Jubilee that He was announcing. As E. J. Young commented on these verses from Isaiah:

> What is pictured here reflects partly upon the exile but describes also

---

21 Swete, *Commentary on Mark*, 114.
22 Augustine and many expositors take the three accounts of Jesus' ministry in Nazareth as pointing to the same events. For instance, Knox Chamblin considered the account in Matthew 13:54-58 to be the same one as Luke records in Luke 4:16-30. That is the view that I also have. I do not believe that Jesus would have ever returned to preach at Nazareth after the citizens tried to kill Him. His disciples would also have advised Him against doing so. Additionally, there is great similarity in the preaching of all the accounts of His ministry in Nazareth which pints to the same time for all.

New Testament and eternal relationships. It is the Messianic work, which no prophet in himself could carry out; hence the speaker not merely announces but also dispenses the great gifts of God . . . healing is accomplished through the proclaiming of *liberty to the captives*. Isaiah employs a phrase used in the law of the year of jubilee, which occurred every fiftieth year . . .

When Christ said that *this day this prophecy is fulfilled in your ears*, He did not mean the prophecy was exhausted on that particular day, but rather that the time had now come of which Isaiah spoke, and which the prophecy would be fulfilled throughout the course of the Church upon earth. The passage brings to the forefront the great work of redemption that the Messiah would accomplish and the proclamation of the Gospel that he and the disciples under His authority would carry out.[23]

Jesus, aware of what they were thinking and saying, confronted the blindness of their hearts by saying to them: "No doubt you will quote this proverb to Me, 'Physician heal yourself!' Whatever we heard was done at Capernaum, do here in your hometown as well." (Luke 4:23). He then gave two illustrations from the ministries of Elijah and Elisha to show how those prophets had worked their miracles on people outside Israel. As William Hendriksen wrote: "Jesus refutes the people's mistaken opinion that Nazareth had a special claim on him since that was the place where he had been raised."[24] Jesus' words touched off a near riot on the part of the congregants of the synagogue. His words on that occasion might seem impolitic to some, but they were necessary in light of the unbelief in that city which hindered His ability to work the miracles He had elsewhere. When they began to manifest that same skeptical, unbelieving attitude during His sermon, Jesus rebuked them for their unbelief. Thus, they immediately got up from their seats in a rage, "drove Him out of the city, and led Him to the brow of the hill . . . in order to throw Him down the cliff" (Luke 4:28, 29). The spot was probably on the west side of the city where a cliff overhangs a valley forty feet below it.[25] They intended to push him down the hill and hope that he was killed from the fall on the sharp rocks. "Nazareth was (and still is) situated in a hollow, high up against the slopes of a mountain, in such a manner that it is enclosed on three sides by more elevated portions of the mountain. The Jews, after they

---

23 Young, *The Book of Isaiah*, 3:459–460.
24 Hendriksen, *Exposition of the Gospel According to Luke*, 257.
25 Edersheim, *The Life and Times of Jesus the Messiah*, 316.

had driven Jesus out of the synagogue and the town, brought Him to one of the mountain peaks to throw Him down the cliffs."[26] This whole matter reveals how the natural hearts of all men are filled with inveterate enmity of Christ. People who had known Him for thirty years took such offense at His words on one occasion that they could think of nothing else than killing Him. Yet, they did not accomplish their desire. Jesus passed "through their midst" and "went on His way" (Luke 4:30). There is no evidence that Jesus ever visited that city again or even mentioned them to anyone. If there was any lesson to be learned by the disciples from the treatment of Jesus in His own hometown and in the synagogue where He once worshiped it was, as Jesus said, "Truly, I say to you, no prophet is welcome in his hometown" (Luke 4:24). A greater judgment cannot be conceived than a congregation that becomes so enraged at the words of Christ that they actively seek to kill the Lord of glory. They were unsuccessful in their fitful rage because "passing through their midst, He went His way" (Luke 4:30). By what means Jesus was able to escape is not told us, but it was certainly by the providential protection of His Father. Another plot of the devil to destroy Jesus was foiled because His time had not yet come.

---

26 Geldenhuys, *Commentary on the Gospel of Luke*, 169.

11

He Has Lost His Senses

Jesus' rejection by the citizens of Nazareth was apparently the end of His second Galilean missionary tour. The disciples were not yet ready for the great work of evangelism—they were disciples or trainees at this point—and that experience in Nazareth unnerved them. It could have destroyed their confidence prematurely if Jesus had not withdrawn from there or if He returned there at a later time.[1] Thus, He returned to the city that had become His home—Capernaum—where "the crowd gathered again, to such an extent that they could not even eat a meal" (Mark 3:20). They were at the door and probably even in the house (Cf. also Mark 1:33; 2:2). At this time, there was a deputation of scribes and Pharisees who came to Capernaum from Jerusalem. It is likely that a report from people in Nazareth was sent to Jerusalem informing them of the *irregular* things Jesus was doing. When that deputation arrived in Capernaum, Jesus was just then involved in healing a deaf and mute man who was possessed of a demon. When the mute man was able to speak and see, there was no denying that something extraordinary had happened, but just what? And by whom? "The crowds were amazed, and were saying, 'This man cannot be the Son of David, can he?'" (Matthew 12:23). The very question was anathema to the Pharisees who immediately responded, "This man casts out demons only by Beelzebul the ruler of the demons" (Matthew 12:24). With that accusation, they were calling Jesus an agent of Satan.[2] His miracles, they alleged, were performed by the power of the "prince of darkness." The lynchpin in the Pharisee's argument was that Jesus was a sinner because He did not observe the sabbath according to their rules. Since a sinner could not perform such works by the power of God, that meant Jesus was under the power of the devil. As Edersheim notes:

---

1 Jesus' response to the various attempts to kill Him in other parts of Scripture convince me that there was only one time that He preached at Nazareth. Cf. John 7:1. They were not ready for the Crucifixion.
2 Beelzebul is a combination name which means 'master' of the 'abode or dwelling.' It is a name for Satan.

He Has Lost His Senses

The charge of Satanic agency was, indeed, not quite new. It had been suggested, that John the Baptist had been under demoniacal influence, and this cunning pretext for resistance to his message had been eminently successful with the people. The same charge, only in much fuller form, was now raised against Jesus. As 'the multitude marvelled, saying, it was never so seen in Israel,' the Pharisees, without denying the facts, had this explanation of them, to be presently developed to all its terrible consequences.[3]

Jesus, "knowing their thoughts said to them, 'Any kingdom divided against itself is laid waste; and any city or house divided against itself will not stand. If Satan casts out Satan, he is divided against himself, how then will his kingdom stand? . . . But if I cast out demons by the Spirit of God, then the kingdom of God has come upon you'"(Matthew 12:25, 26, 28). In His further reply to that malignant accusation, Jesus uttered His well-known statement about the unpardonable sin which is "blasphemy of the Spirit" (Matthew 12:31). Then, He called the Pharisees a "brood of vipers" (Matthew 12:34), after the manner of John the Baptist. Sensing that they were losing the argument and, as well, losing their face before the crowds, the scribes and Pharisees switched course. Some of them said to Jesus, "Teacher, we would like to see a sign from You" (Matthew 12:38b). He would not allow their hypocrisy, but replied to them, "An evil and adulterous generation craves for a sign; and yet no sign will be given it but the sign of Jonah the prophet" (Matthew 12:39). That sign would point to His death and resurrection, but it was so veiled at this time that they did not understand what He had said—neither did His disciples.

Jesus' Mother and Brothers (Matthew 12:46–50; Mark 3:31–35; and, Luke 8:19–21)

"While [Jesus] was still speaking to the crowds, His mother and brothers were standing outside, seeking to speak with Him" (Matthew 12:46). They had, no doubt, heard the reports of all His followers and came to take Him into custody, perhaps for His own protection, but certainly because they said, "He has lost His senses" (Mark 3:21). They had been, no doubt, in the Nazareth synagogue when Jesus preached there and were witnesses to the attempt by the citizens to throw him off a cliff. The scribes and Pharisees had earlier tried to convince the disciples of Jesus that He was wrong for eating with sinners and tax collectors (Matthew 9:11), so they may well have

---

3 Edersheim, *The Life and Times of Jesus the Messiah*, 397.

had some input into convincing Jesus' immediate family members to take Him into their custody. Once again, Edersheim states concerning their visit to Capernaum at this time:

> We place this visit of the 'mother and brethren' of Jesus immediately after His return to Capernaum, and we attribute it to Pharisaic opposition, which either filled those relatives of Jesus with fear for His safety, or made them sincerely concerned about His proceedings. Only if it meant some kind of interference with His Mission, whether prompted by fear or affection, would Jesus have so disowned their relationship.[4]

Of all the calumnies Jesus suffered during His ministry, this reaction by His own family members had to hurt worse than all others. "The family of Jesus were doubtless inspired by a desire for His safety, but their interpretation of His enthusiasm implied want of faith in Him."[5] How often is Spirit-filled enthusiasm mistaken for zeal born of natural affections—or, even worse, for insanity. This was one of the most direct fulfillments of those words in John 1:11— "He came to His own, and those who were His own did not receive Him." In every age of religious formality and indifference to true spirituality, those who have been the subjects of a spiritual awakening have been falsely maligned as hysterical or insane. Jesus was now being accused of insanity by His own brethren who were spreading that report openly to others. Alexander's comments on the word that was used to describe Jesus' mental state is worth noting:

> The Greek verb is the same employed above (2, 12) to signify extreme amazement, but intrinsically applicable to any derangement or disorder, whether bodily or mental, and actually used by the classics and Josephus, with the mind or senses, to denote insanity, in which sense Paul elliptically makes use of the verb alone (2 Cor. 5, 13). Some interpreters prefer the sense of bodily exhaustion, and suppose these friends to have gone out, either to sustain (support) him, or to hold him back from such injurious exertion. It is commonly agreed, however, that the reference is to mental disorder or extreme excitement.[6]

Undoubtedly, the exhaustion of the body has a large effect on the mind and Jesus was greatly overworked, including spending many nights in prayer, as He did before the calling of His disciples. Yet, the words that were broadcast about Him were in reference to His mental state. His own family members were concerned that He was insane.

---

4 Edersheim, *The Life and Times of Jesus the Messiah*, 397.
5 Swete, *Commentary on Mark*, 64.
6 Alexander, *The Gospel According to Mark*, 72.

There was growing opposition to Jesus at this time as a result of the envy and malignancy of the Pharisees and the scribes. They had been watching His every move very carefully for some months—ever since the arrest and imprisonment of John the Baptist. Thus, there was a new deputation from Jerusalem that came to Capernaum with new accusations—"'He is possessed by Beelzebul,' and 'He casts out the demons by the ruler of the demons'" (Mark 3:22). Luke described these accusations as arising from the people who saw His miracles; Matthew said it was the Pharisees who thus accused Him; and, more specifically, Mark wrote it was the scribes. Of course, all three writers are correct. These scribes were from the strict Jewish sect of the Pharisees and they had seen many of Jesus' miracles. After being embarrassed by Jesus concerning fasting and the Sabbath day observance, they probably sent a party back to Jerusalem to ask advice from the Sanhedrin. The decision was made by those religious leaders to accuse Jesus of being possessed by a demon and performing His miracles by that underworld power. Galilee was an area of Israel that was especially infiltrated by all kinds of pagan ideas and this charge seemed to have enough plausibility to persuade the masses to turn against Jesus. Moreover, it was ultimately successful in doing that very thing. As William Lane commented in his commentary on this passage:

> The charge leveled against Jesus is that "he has lost his mind." The Marcan term describes one who is ecstatic in the sense of psychic derangement. Reflection on Jesus' eschatological sense of mission, his urgent drive to minister, his failure properly to eat and sleep undoubtedly led the family to their conviction, but it reveals both misunderstanding and unbelief.[7]

Can Satan Cast Out Satan? (Matthew 12:22–32; Mark 3:20–27; and Luke 11:14–22)

Jesus did not ignore those very serious accusations against His ministry that He cast out Satan by the power of Satan. Instead, He called the scribes together and began to speak to them in parables. It is not clear whether Jesus actually heard the scribes say such things about Him or simply received reports of them doing so. Beelzebul was the Lord of the flies or, more accurately, the Dung-god. Nothing could have been more odious than for these scribes to make such a charge against Jesus. On the one hand, the scribes were aware of the proto-

---

[7] William L. Lane, *The Gospel According to Mark* (Grand Rapids: Eerdmans Publishing Company, 1974), 139.

evangelium from Genesis 3:15, the ongoing conflict between God and Satan which would be carried out in "two antagonistic races."[8] They were right to hold that the devil was not an occasional enemy, but an ever-present adversary. Yet, Jesus showed them how absurd their charge against Him was. As He asked, "How can Satan cast out Satan?" (Mark 3:23). Alexander commented on that question:

> This simple question contains the sum of the whole refutation. It implies, as previous questions, who is Satan? What is the meaning of the name? What relation does it necessarily denote? How can the adversary be a friend? How can the leader of one party, in a war which has been going on for ages, be the ally of his enemy and conqueror? Christ came avowedly, as well as really, to destroy the works of the devil (1 John 3:8), not as an incidental or collateral effect, but as the very object of his work and mission. Of this mission his credentials were his miracles.[9]

Those simple and direct questions that Jesus asked the scribes were never answered and remain unanswerable. No one needs to have such statements explained to him. Jesus then used those questions to state another great truth—the possibility of committing the unpardonable sin. The unpardonable sin is the blasphemy of the Holy Spirit. Instead of openly rebuking the scribes, Jesus indirectly described for them the nature of the sin which they were in danger of committing. Jesus' declaration begins with "a solemn form of affirmation."[10] It indicates a solemn form of attesting to what has been said or what will be said. In these words, Jesus warns the scribes of their dangerous position—the danger of eternal fire and the refusal of all forgiveness.

There are some things to notice about the blasphemy of the Spirit. First, it is called the "blasphemy of the Spirit" which means that only those who have been wooed by the Holy Spirit and refused Him can be guilty of this sin. Second, it is not just any sin or blasphemy. Jesus said, "all sins shall be forgiven the sons of men, and whatever blasphemies they utter" (Mark 3:28). Third, the blasphemy of the Spirit is nowhere in Scripture described in detail and that is for a reason. If men knew the exact boundary lines of the blasphemy of the Spirit—or, the unpardonable sin—they would be prone to get as close to it without committing it as possible. Instead, the Scripture simply warns us of a great danger that must be avoided. The wise

---

8 Alexander, *The Gospel According to Mark*, 75.
9 Alexander, *The Gospel According to Mark*, 76.
10 Alexander, *The Gospel According to Mark*, 79.

will take heed and stay clear of the danger, but the foolish will fall into the pit heedlessly.

At that point, Jesus' mother and brothers arrived in Capernaum and the crowds told Him that His family was looking for Him. Swete describes the situation well for us:

> They were crowded out, as in the case of the paralytic . . . Naturally, they were unwilling to disclose their errand (iii, 21), and therefore contented themselves with asking for an interview.[11]

Jesus, knowing all things, knew the purpose of this request for an interview. Mary had probably given into the pressures placed on her by her other sons, but Jesus knew that their requested interview was for the purpose of trying to put an end to His mission. Satan was using many different methods to try to interrupt and stop Jesus' ministry. After the revolting accusations of the scribes did not work, then the devil tried to entice Jesus through His own mother. The actions of Jesus might seem harsh and unfeeling to us until we focus on why He responded as He did.

Jesus Teaches by Parables (Matthew 13:1–52; Mark 4:1–34; and Luke 8:4–21)

On that same day, Jesus and His disciples went out of the house and were sitting by the seaside (Matthew 13:1, 2). Such large crowds gathered around Him that Jesus got into a boat[12] and began to teach them in parables. The first parable He taught was the Sower and the Soils. There were four types of soil: soil trampled down by the roadside, the rocky soil, the soil covered with thorns; and good soil. All four soils would have been familiar to the people in Capernaum. Only the good soil produced good fruit. The disciples needed this parable as much as anyone to keep them from being depressed following the persecution at Nazareth. They needed to understand that there would be many people who would turn against them or refuse to hear their message of the gospel. If not all are converted when Jesus sows the seed, then the disciples need not expect their sowing to be any different.

---

11 Swete, *Commentary on Mark*, 69.
12 A visit to Capernaum reveals why Jesus did what He did. The land around the Sea of Galilee at Capernaum forms a natural amphitheater for someone sitting in a boat. Thus, Jesus could be seen and heard better from there.

There were eight[13] different parables Jesus taught on that morning in AD 28. They form what are called the kingdom parables. The other parables He taught at this time were: the Tares and the Wheat; the Mustard Seed; the Leaven; the Hidden Treasure; the Pearl of Great Value; the Dragnet; and, the Lamp. Six of these parables are given in Matthew 13 and begin with these words: "the kingdom of heaven is like . . ." "Two of six describe the incomparable joy of those who presently discover the kingdom (13:44–46), Two others speak of the kingdom's growth from its inaugural to its consummation (13:31–33). The remaining two focus especially on the final judgment (13:24–30, with vv. 36–43 and 13:47–50). Given the separation that will then occur, it matters terribly how people respond to the message of the kingdom—and whether they believe Jesus (13:51–52) or not (13:53–58)."[14] The Parable of the Lamp emphasizes that nothing can be hidden that will not be revealed. No one puts a lamp under a bushel. Thus, the true follower of Christ will let his light shine before the world. As Geldenhuys writes:

> Only when our own lives are brightly illuminated, shall we be able to let our light shine upon others. Every believer is called upon to "take heed how he hears" and to let His light shine in and through our life—in word and act.[15]

The Storm on the Sea (Matthew 8:18, 23–27; Mark 4:35–41; and Luke 8:22, 25)

"On that day, when evening came, He said to His disciples, 'Let us go over to the other side.' Leaving the crowd, they took Him along with them in the boat, just as He was; and other boats were with Him" (Mark 4:35, 36). Their destination was the area called Gadara, which was located on the southeastern shore of the Sea of Galilee in an area where the hills drop precipitously into the sea.[16] The city of Gadara[17] was one of the most strongly-fortified cities in the whole area and was inhabited primarily by Gentiles. It was approximately six miles southeast of the Sea of Galilee, but that whole area was called Gadara.

---

13 Matthew lists seven of them and Luke 8:16–19 supplements that number with another one on the Lamp.
14 Chamblin, *Matthew*, 1:707.
15 Geldenhuys, *Commentary on the Gospel of Luke*, 248.
16 Gadara (or, Gerasa) is usually identified with the town in Jordan called Umm Qais which was a little inland and southeast of the sea.
17 "Pliny states that the original members of the Decapolis were Scythopolis, Pella, Dion, Gerasa, Philadelphia, Gadara, Raphana, Kanatha, Hippos, and Damascus." Pfeiffer and Vos, *The Wycliffe Historical Geography of Bible Lands*, 177.

Jesus and His disciples probably left in the first part of the evening, shortly after 6 pm, while there was still a little bit of daylight. The trip by boat from Capernaum would not have taken long in ideal circumstances. On this occasion, though, a fierce storm blew up on the sea. Mark 4:37, 38 describes the scene for us: "And there arose a fierce gale of wind, and the waves were breaking over the boat so much that the boat was already filling up. Jesus Himself was in the stern, asleep on the cushion; and they woke Him and said to Him, 'Teacher, do you not care that we are perishing?'" The storm must have been unusually fierce for these disciples, many of whom were fishermen by trade, to be so afraid and fear for their lives. George Adam Smith describes what such fierce winds can do to the surface of the Sea of Galilee:

> The sea-winds, which freshen all Galilee . . . , blow over this basin, and the sun beats it with unmitigated ardour. The atmosphere, for the most part, hangs still and heavy, but the cold currents, as they pass from the west, are sucked down in vortices of air, or by the narrow gorges that break upon the lake. Then arise those sudden storms for which the region is notorious.[18]

In *The Training of the Twelve*, A. B. Bruce gives additional insight into the violent storms on the lake:

> The Sea of Galilee, though but a small sheet of water, some thirteen miles long by six broad, is liable to be visited by sharp, sudden squalls, probably due to its situation. It lies in a deep hollow of volcanic origin, bounded on either side by steep ranges of hills rising above the water from one to two thousand feet.[19]

The great difference in temperatures between the surrounding mountains and the sea resulted in terrible storms as winds would come crashing down the steeply sloped hills and descend on the lake. The clash of the cold winds from the hills with the warm air at the sea often caused violent storms. One moment the sea was as calm as glass; the next it was covered with white foam and columns of violent waves.[20] The disciples had been in many such storms before, but this one must have been unusually fierce to cause panic for these fishermen. The crashing waves soon began to fill up their boat and a sense of desperation overcame the disciples. Thus, they awakened their Master and said to Him, "Teacher, do You not care that we are

---

18 Smith, *The Historical Geography of the Holy Land*, 441–2.
19 Bruce, *The Training of the Twelve*, 129.
20 Bruce, *The Training of the Twelve*, 129.

perishing?" (Mark 4:38). Matthew records that they also cried out to Him, "Save us, Lord; we are perishing!" (Matthew 8:25). Probably one or another cried out to Him in fear of perishing. Jesus, being awakened out of His sleep, immediately rebuked the wind and waves: "Hush, be still" (Mark 4:39a). When "the wind died down" and the sea "became calm" (Mark 4:39b), He then asked His disciples: "Why are you afraid? How is it that you have no faith?" (Mark 4:40). That miracle and Jesus' question caused the disciples to become even more afraid as they asked one another, "Who then is this, that even the wind and the sea obey Him" (Mark 4:41). This second fear is defined rightly by Swete:

> An awe of the Presence of Christ generically different from the fear which sprang from want of faith in Him—indeed its direct opposite. This miracle came home to the Apostles above any they had witnessed. It touched them personally: they had been delivered by it from imminent peril. It appealed to them as men used to the navigation of the Lake. Thus, it threw a new and awful light on the Person with Whom they daily associated.[21]

This storm and Jesus' rescue of His disciples from danger was a necessary part of their training. There would be worse storms they would face than the dangers of shipwreck and they needed to experience how the Lord would deliver them. In all the other miracles they had witnessed, it was other people who were rescued. This time, they were the recipients of His saving power and it deeply impressed their hearts.

The Gadarene Demoniac (Matthew 8:28–34; Mark 5:1–20; and Luke 8:26–37)

Soon the boat came to the other side, where Jesus was met by two men who were demoniacs. This was the first time Jesus and His disciples went into Gentile territory, into the region known as the Decapolis. Gadara was southeast of the Sea of Galilee about six miles. In the southeast corner of the Sea of Galilee, there was once a splendid harbor with a 500 meter pier. "Coins from Gadara were discovered which depict boats commemorating the 'Naumachia,' or naval battles reenacted by the people of Gadara."[22] Between this harbor, which serviced the whole region of Gadara, and the town of Gadara (mod-

---

21 Swete, *Commentary on Mark*, 90–1.
22 Accessed on April 29, 2024 at: https://biblearchaeology.org, "Life & Ministry of Jesus: Demoniacs of Gadara."

ern Umm Qais) lay the deep and nearly impassable Yarmuk River gorge—a tributary of the Jordan River. Gadara was on the crest of a hill which was 1,240 feet above sea level. The modern city of Umm Qais is "surrounded by very extensive ruins, all bearing testimony to the splendor of ancient Gadara."[23] "The ruins include those of 'baths, two theaters, a hippodrome, colonnaded streets and under the Romans, aqueducts, a temple, a basilica and other buildings, telling of a once splendid city."[24] The ruins of a black basalt amphitheater are also still standing. McClintock and Strong make the following statement concerning Gadara:

> The most interesting remains of Gadara are its tombs, which dot the cliffs for a considerable distance round the city, chiefly on the northeast declivity; but many beautifully sculptured sarcophagi are scattered over the surrounding heights. They are excavated in the limestone rock, and consist of chambers of various dimensions, some more than 20 feet square, with recesses in the sides for bodies.[25]

There were many such tombs that dotted the abundant cliffs throughout the whole area of Gadara. When Jesus and His disciples reached the shores of that territory, Mark states that "immediately a man[26] from the tombs with an unclean spirit met Him, and he had his dwelling among the tombs. And no one was able to bind him anymore, even with a chain" (Mark 5:2, 3). He had often been shackled and chained, but he would break the shackles and tear apart the chains so that "no one was strong enough to subdue him" (Mark 5:4). He both tormented others and was a torment to himself. He would scream "among the tombs and in the mountains . . . gashing himself with stones" (Mark 5:5). Those horrible sounds reverberated throughout the mountains and could probably be heard by fishermen on the lake below. All the people of the nearby town[27] were afraid of this demoniac because he was "so extremely violent that no one could pass that way" (Matthew 8:29). Yet, here was Jesus with His disciples and the demoniac immediately recognized Him. Then, the demoniac saw "Jesus from a distance" and "ran up and bowed down

---

23 Accessed on April 29, 2024 at: https://christiananswers.net "Gadara."
24 Accessed on April 29, 2024 at: https://en.m.wikipedia.org "Gadara."
25 McClintock and Strong, *Cyclopedia of Biblical, Theological, and Ecclesiastical Literature*, 3:707.
26 Matthew says there were two demoniacs who met Jesus. Mark and Luke focus only on Jesus' interactions with one of the two.
27 The particular town is unknown, but it was not Gadara as it was six miles away across a deep river gorge.

before Him; and shouting with a loud voice, he said, 'What business do we have to do with each other, Jesus, Son of the Most High God? I implore You by God, do not torment me!'" (Mark 5:6, 7). Swete comments on the whole scene:

> The onrush of the naked yelling maniac must have tried the newly recovered confidence of the Twelve. We can imagine their surprise when, on approaching, he threw himself on his knees.[28]

This demoniac was possessed of a legion of demons who had taken control of him and were terrified by the command of Jesus to them: "Come out of the man, you unclean spirit!" (Mark 5:8). They were tormented by the thought of coming under God's wrath before the final judgement. William Hendriksen comments on this verse:

> Though men will at times do their utmost to deny Jesus' deity, the demons do not; note the exalted title given to the Master by the spokesman of the unclean spirits that inhabited this man. He calls Jesus "Son of the Most High God," nothing less! And Jesus was and is exactly that...The demonic world realizes that on the day of final judgment its relative freedom to roam about on earth and in the sky above it... must cease forever. And that its final and most terrible punishment is destined to begin at that time. Its representative who is now speaking to Jesus knows that right now he is face to face with the One to whom the final judgment has been committed, and he is afraid that even now—"before the appointed time"—Jesus might hurl him and his partners into "the abyss" or "dungeon," that is, into hell, the place where Satan is kept.[29]

Thus, the demons implored Jesus to send them into a nearby herd of swine. Jesus permitted them to enter the swine when He cast them out of the man and they quickly drove the swine into the lake. The steep, lofty bank above the shore was very hazardous for those descending to the lake and once the swine started rushing downwards there was no way for them to stop. There were about two thousand of them and their demise caused the herdsmen to rush into the nearby city and report what had just happened. Thus, a crowd of men soon "came to Jesus and observed the man who had been demon-possessed, clothed and in his right mind, the very man who had had the 'legion'; and they became frightened" (Mark 5:15). "The man...was free from the slavery of headstrong passions, master of himself again."[30] He had been constantly driven by the demons into torturous acts against others and

---

28 Swete, *Commentary on Mark*, 94.
29 Hendriksen, *Mark*, 191.
30 Swete, *Commentary on Mark*, 98.

himself, but now he was sane for the first time in years. The townspeople listened as "those who had seen it described to them how it had happened . . . and *all* about the swine" (Mark 5:16). Their fear was the very opposite of what the disciples had experienced on the sea shortly before. Their fear of Jesus was increased by seeing the man in his right mind and "they began to implore Him to leave their region" (Mark 5:17). Having lost a considerable herd of swine, they did not want to suffer an even greater economic loss. Yet, their fear of Jesus was more than just a fear of economic ruin. It was the same type of fear that the demoniac had experienced before he was delivered from the "Legion."

The healed demoniac, unlike the townspeople, was now willing to be a follower of Christ and implored Jesus "that he might accompany Him" (Mark 5:18). Jesus had other plans for the man and told him, "Go home to your people and report to them what great things the Lord has done for you, and *how* He had mercy on you" (Mark 5:19). That advice was opposite of what Jesus typically gave. Different circumstances required different strategies. Swete explains why Jesus refused the man's request to go with Him:

> The request is refused, because the man is wanted for immediate service. The eastern shore of the Lake was for the present closed against Jesus and the Twelve. A preparatory publication of the demoniac's story was necessary in anticipation of a later visit (vii. 31 ff.). What had been prohibited in Galilee (1.43 f.) is under different circumstances not only permitted but commanded in Decapolis . . . The man's first duty was his own house (where he had long been a stranger, Lc. viii. 27), and his relatives and acquaintances.[31]

As Jesus and His disciples returned to their boat, the former demoniac was left behind to be the first witness to Jesus in that region. A more dramatic conversion can scarcely be imagined. Nothing more is ever heard from that man, but we can be sure that the circumstances of his former life, which were well-known, required him to continually testify to the mercy and salvation he had received from Christ. Meanwhile, Jesus "crossed over again in the boat to the other side" where "a large crowd gathered around Him; and so He stayed by the seashore. One of the synagogue officials named Jairus came up, and on seeing Him, fell at His feet and implored Him earnestly, saying, 'My little daughter is at the point of death, please come and lay Your

---

31 Swete, *Commentary on Mark*, 99.

hands on her, so that she will get well and live'" (Mark 5:21–23). Jesus immediately started off with Jairus, with the large crowd following, when suddenly a woman pressed close to Him and touched His garment. The woman had been sick with a hemorrhage for twelve years "and had endured much at the hands of many physicians, and had spent all that she had and was not helped at all, but rather had grown worse" (Mark 5:26). Having heard "about Jesus, she came up in the crowd behind *Him* and touched His cloak. For she thought, 'If I just touch His garments, I will get well.' Immediately, the flow of blood was dried up and she felt in her body that she was healed of her affliction"(Mark 5:27–29). Jesus perceived that someone had touched Him with the hand of faith and asked, "Who touched Me?" (Mark 5:31). While all the crowd denied touching Him, "Peter replied, 'Master, the people are crowding and pressing in on You'. But Jesus said, 'Someone did touch Me, for I was aware that power had gone out of Me" (Luke 45b-46). Jesus looked around and focused on the woman. When she realized "she had not escaped notice, she came trembling and fell down before Him" (Luke 8:47). Her trembling was not slavish fear, but reverent awe of Jesus and her faith was rewarded by the Lord with these words: "Daughter, your faith has made you well; go in peace and be healed of your affliction" Mark 5:34). J. A. Alexander's comments on this miracle are helpful:

> As he had not asked for information, but to make the subject of the miracle come forward and disclose herself; so even this exposure was intended not to punish or deprive her of the benefit she had sought to gain in secret, but by one consummate stroke of justice and of mercy, to reprove her fault and yet reward her faith; requiring her to give God the glory and come to Christ as others came, but at the same time to assure her of a permanent deliverance from her former sufferings, if not from sin.[32]

While this healing was taking place, some people came from Jairus' home with the news: "Your daughter has died; why trouble the Teacher anymore? But Jesus, overhearing what was being spoken, said to the synagogue official, 'Do not be afraid any longer, only believe.'" (Mark 5:35, 36). When Jesus and Jairus arrived at his house, there was "a commotion, and people loudly weeping and wailing" (Mark 5:38). Their tears quickly turned to mocking laughter when Jesus told them, "The child has not died, but is asleep" (Mark 5:39). Their too sudden

---

32 Alexander, *The Gospel According to Mark*, 131.

change of emotions showed the shallowness and insincerity of their expressions. As Swete comments:

> The mourners were probably professional; among them were musicians . . ., and wailing women . . .; "even the poorest of Israel will afford his dead wife not less than two minstrels and one woman to make lamentations" . . . and this was the house of [a ruler of the synagogue].[33]

Jesus put all of them out of the house, including Jairus and his wife and His own disciples. Then, He went into the child's room and "taking the child by the hand, He said to her, 'Talitha kum!' (which translated means, 'Little girl, I say to you, get up!')" (Mark 5:41). The girl was immediately healed; got up, and began to walk. All the people, including the weepers and wailers, "were completely astounded" (Mark 5:42). Jesus charged them to tell no one what had happened, but that "something should be given her to eat" (Mark 5:43). Once again, Jesus told them to do the very opposite of what He had just earlier told the demoniac, for reasons Alexander unfolds:

> Mark here describes our Lord as exercising that divine discretion which in every case determined whether the publication of the miracle required to be stimulated or retarded, though the grounds of the distinction may be now, and may have been at first, inscrutable to human wisdom.[34]

While enduring the accusation by His own family members that He had "lost His senses" and being accused by the Pharisees of casting out demons by the power of Satan, Jesus ignored their caviling. Instead, He left Capernaum to go restore a man who had truly lost his senses to his right mind. And, in that same miracle, He also cast out demons—a "Legion" of them. Instead of bringing the demoniac back to Capernaum as a display of His power, Jesus was content to let him remain behind as a witness. When He returned to Capernaum, He carried on His ministry as before without any mention of the previous differences. Yet, He charged them that they should not spread around the miracle of the raising of Jairus' daughter. Despite His command, "this news spread throughout all that land" (Matthew 9:26).

---

33 Swete, *Commentary on Mark*, 108.
34 Alexander, *The Gospel According to Mark*, 138.

12

The Third Missionary Tour of Galilee

During His second missionary journey through all the cities and villages of Galilee, Jesus was struck by the hopelessness and helplessness of the common people who heard Him gladly. "He felt compassion for them, because they were distressed and dispirited like sheep without a shepherd" (Matthew 9:36). In that spirit, He remarked to His disciples, "The harvest is plentiful, but the workers are few. Therefore beseech the Lord of the harvest to send out workers into His harvest" (Matthew 9:37, 38). Jesus, the Lord of the harvest, now commissioned the Twelve to "go to the lost sheep of the house of Israel" and to "preach . . . 'The kingdom of heaven is at hand'" (Matthew 10:6, 7). That had been the message of both John the Baptist and Jesus and now it was the commission of the Twelve.[1] Alexander aptly informs us that:

> Their original commission was not ecumenical or catholic, but strictly national and theocratical, because the Christian church was to be founded on the Jewish.[2]

The time was not ripe for the apostles to go beyond the realm of Galilee in their ministry. They were still evangelists in training. They still had several Jewish prejudices that made them unfit to carry the good news to Gentiles, or even Samaritans. As Bruce wrote:

> The Twelve at the period of their first trial mission, were not fit to preach the gospel, or to do good works, either among Samaritans or Gentiles. For the catholic work of the apostleship they needed a new divine illumination and a copious baptism with the benignant spirit of love. Suppose these raw evangelists had gone into a Samaritan village, what would have happened? In all probability they would have been drawn into disputes on the religious differences between Samaritans

---

1 It is always difficult to exactly pinpoint the time when Jesus did anything. After careful consideration of everything, I am convinced that Jesus' third missionary tour must have taken place sometime during the latter part of AD 28 and/or the early part of AD 29. After Jesus' feeding of the 5,000 and His subsequent sermon at Capernaum, our Lord withdrew there and took the gospel to the Gentiles, before finishing His ministry in Judea and Perea.
2 Joseph Addison Alexander, *The Gospel According to Matthew: Explained* (Lynchburg, VA: James family Christian Publishers, n.d.), 283.

and Jews, in which, of course, they would have lost their temper; so that instead of seeking the salvation of the people among whom they had come, they would rather be in a mood to call down fire from heaven to consume them, as they actually proposed to do at a subsequent period.[3]

The Disciples Sent Out (Matthew 10:1–15; Mark 6:7–13; and Luke 9:1–6)

In light of the disciples' inexperience, Jesus wisely limited the sphere of their mission to "the house of Israel" with further instructions to them: "Do not go in the way of the Gentiles, and do not enter any city of the Samaritans" (Mathew 10:5). Bruce comments on this mission are helpful:

> This mission of the disciples as evangelists or miniature apostles was partly, without a doubt, an educational experiment for their own benefit; but its direct design was to meet the spiritual necessities of the people, whose neglected condition lay heavy on Christ's heart. The compassionate Son of man, in the course of His wanderings, had observed how the masses of the people were, like a shepherdless flock of sheep, scattered and torn, and it was His desire that all should know that a good Shepherd had come to care for the lost sheep of Israel.[4]

There is a mixture of the present and the future throughout Jesus' commission to the Twelve which makes it impossible to restrict His words to one or the other. The basic commission, included in all the Synoptic Gospels, was to limit their ministry to Israel and, even more specifically, to Galilee. They were not to go north, east, or west into the Gentile cities within Galilee, such as Tiberias or Sepphoris; nor south into the areas populated by the Samaritans. They were to restrict themselves to the Galilean towns and villages where those sheep without a shepherd were languishing. "But their field of labor was wisely limited, because the time was not yet ripe for the institution of the world-wide campaign, mainly because the workers were not yet sufficiently trained and instructed in the universalism of the gospel."[5] The fuller version of Jesus' commission to the disciples in Matthew 10 is given to the Church in all ages and all circumstances. As Edersheim notes:

> It is evident, that the Discourse reported by St. Matthew goes far beyond that mission of the Twelve, beyond even that of the Early Church,

---

3 Bruce, *The Training of the Twelve*, 101.
4 Bruce, *The Training of the Twelve*, 99.
5 Shepard, *The Christ of the Gospels*, 247.

indeed, sketches the history of the Church's Mission in a hostile world up 'to the end.' . . . For St. Matthew himself could not have intended to confine the words of Christ to this first journey of the Apostles, since they contain references to division of families; persecutions; and conflict with the civil power (vv.16–18), such as belong to a much later period of the Church; and, besides, contain also that prediction which could not have applied to this first Mission of the Apostles, 'Ye shall not have gone over the cities of Israel, till the Son of Man be come' (v.23).[6]

A striking feature of Jesus' commission is "that this Discourse, while so un-Jewish in spirit, is more than any other, even more than that on the Mount, Jewish in its forms and modes of expression."[7] Many of the charges that Jesus gave to the disciples were truly Jewish in nature. Several of them are found in the Hebrew Midrash. The phrase, "sheep in the midst of wolves," was used in the Midrash to describe the nation of Israel in the midst of a hostile world. The charge to be as "wise as serpents and harmless as doves" was used by the Midrash to describe the nation of Israel as harmless towards God, but wise as serpents toward the Gentile nations. The phrase, "freely you have received, freely give," was a common saying among the Rabbis based on the example of Moses in Deuteronomy 4:5. "Again, the directions about not taking staff, shoes, nor money-purse, exactly correspond to the Rabbinic injunction not to enter Temple-precincts with staff, shoes, . . . and a money girdle."[8] Yet, the message of these evangelists was different than what the Rabbis, scribes, and Pharisees were teaching. The outward forms and modes of expression were often similar, but the spirit of Jesus' teaching was altogether different. Thus, the wisdom of Christ was displayed even in this respect.

The disciples were commanded to go "forth and proclaim the kingdom of God and to perform healing" (Luke 9:2). They were to: "heal the sick, raise the dead, cleanse the lepers, cast out demons" (Matthew 10:8). They did not perform these miracles in their own power, but Jesus empowered them even as He commanded them to do so. The Scripture records that they were faithful to this commission and both preached repentance and performed many miracles. "[T]hey were casting out many demons and were anointing with oil many sick people and healing them" (Mark 6:13). "All the miracles wrought by the Twelve were

---

6 Edersheim, *The Life and Times of Jesus the Messiah*, 440, 441, and 443.
7 Edersheim, *The Life and Times of Jesus the Messiah*, 441.
8 Edersheim, *The Life and Times of Jesus the Messiah*, 442.

really wrought by Jesus Himself, their sole function consisting in making a believing use of His name."[9] Thus, the report about these miracles caused the people, and even Herod's court, to ascribe them to Jesus (Mark 6:14). Not even Moses had ever been able to impart miraculous powers to others which surely pointed to Jesus as the long-expected Messiah. Edersheim notes concerning the disciples:

> They were itinerant preachers, who were to go on heralding the kingdom at the gates of the walled towns and in the presence of the smaller groups of the villages . . . Their message was to be backed by their work of healing the sick, raising the dead, cleansing the lepers, and casting out demons.[10]

Jesus' several instructions to them in Luke 10:9–15, and the other Synoptic Gospels, enforce two very important rules for Christian pastors, evangelists, and missionaries. First, Jesus says: "Do not acquire gold, or silver, or copper for your money belts" (Matthew 10:9). "The love of money is the root of all sorts of evil" (1 Timothy 6:10) and those who are workers in Christ's field are to turn away from such false love. Rather, they are to be wholly dependent on the Lord to supply their needs. As Chamblin commented on this verse:

> Those who seek first God's kingdom—as the Twelve are to do in this mission—surely need not fret about what they will eat and drink and wear.[11]

Second, Jesus tells them to depend on the faithful hospitality of those who are worthy in any town or village where they journey. They are then to remain in those homes until they leave that city. "If the house is worthy, give it your blessing of peace. But if it is not worthy, take back your blessing of peace . . . and shake the dust off your feet" (Matthew 10:13, 14). Jesus' words apply to churches also that persecute the true preachers of the gospel. Where there is greater light through the more perfect revelation of the gospel there will also be greater condemnation for those who reject that light. As Jesus said, "This is the judgment, that the Light has come into the world, and men loved darkness rather than the Light, for their deeds were evil" (John 3:19).

---

9 Bruce, *The Training of the Twelve*, 102.
10 Edersheim, *The Life and Times of Jesus the Messiah*, 248.
11 Chamblin, *Matthew*, 1:571-2.

The Difficulties of Discipleship (Matthew 10:16–42 and Luke 10:1–12)

In addition to commissioning the apostles, Jesus did the same for the Seventy who had also followed Him. He gave them the same directions and the same commission. They also were given the power to heal the sick and to cast out demons. As He had done with the apostles, Jesus sent them out two by two into all the cities of Galilee. Galilee was soon blanketed with evangelists and all the towns heard the message of Jesus: "Repent, for the kingdom of God is at hand" (Matthew 4:17). In commissioning both the Twelve and the Seventy, Jesus was identifying the New Testament church as an outgrowth of Judaism which had twelve tribes and seventy members of the Sanhedrin.

In Matthew 10:16–23, Jesus warned His followers of the various trials they would face. "Some of these warnings point forward undoubtedly to the religious bigotry and bitter persecutions suffered at the hands of heathen governors and kings by His workers after the Ascension."[12] Jesus was already facing increasing persecution in Galilee which would become more intense in the months ahead of Him. His disciples and followers needed this timely warning that they were being sent out "as sheep in the midst of wolves" (Matthew 10:16). If they were to be true followers of Jesus, they needed to exhibit His patience towards all and to not strike back at others. Jesus' admonition to them to be as "shrewd as serpents and as innocent as doves," a phrase which was taken from a comment in the Jewish Midrash on Song of Solomon 2:14.[13]

The warning that men will "hand you over to the courts and scourge you in their synagogues; and you will even be brought before governors and kings for My sake, as a testimony to them and to the Gentiles" did not take place during this Galilean phase of the ministry. The very opposite happened. Some of the seventy returned to Jesus "with joy, saying, 'Lord, even the demons are subject to us in Your name'" (Luke 10:17). Yet, after Jesus rose from the dead and ascended to heaven, great persecution came on the church both in Palestine and among the Gentiles. Chamblin commented on this section:

---

12 Shepard, *The Christ of the Gospels*, 250.
13 Edersheim, *The Life and Times of Jesus the Messiah*, 442.

Beset with such persecution and perfidy, the twelve and other missionaries are to maintain their innocence ... They are not to return evil for evil (5:39) or hatred for hatred (5:43) by persecuting their persecutors (5:44), or mounting a *jihad* of their own ... Prudence may well counsel you to flee from one place to another (10:23a; the verb *pheugo*, whence 'fugitive'), rather than to tarry in the ideal but vain hope of making peace with an implacable enemy.[14]

When the inevitable was to happen and the disciples would have to stand before kings and governors, they were not to worry about what they were supposed to say. As Jesus said, "for it will be given to you in that hour what you are to say" (Matthew 10:19b). Jesus' words are not to be understood as countenancing laziness. Rather, He gives a promise for extraordinary circumstances that they would be given extraordinary grace. Leon Morris once said that the promise of Matthew 10:19–20 is "an emergency ration, not a staple diet."[15] The Spirit of their heavenly Father would speak in them and through them.

This persecution would be the result of men's natural hatred of Jesus. As He said, "If they called the head of the house Beelzebul, how much more will they malign the members of His household" (Matthew 10:24). Psalm 2:1–3 predicted this enmity against Christ when the psalmist asked: "Why are the nations in an uproar and the peoples devising a vain thing? The kings of the earth take their stand and the rulers counsel together against the Lord and against His Anointed, saying: 'Let us tear their fetters apart and cast away their cord from us!'" Yet, Psalm 2:4 says, "He who sits in the heavens laughs, the Lord scoffs at them." It is for that reason that Jesus counseled His followers: "do not fear them" (Matthew 10:26). The raging of the heathen is for a brief moment. The rejoicing of Christians is for all eternity. The Father of believers considers His children to be much more valuable than the hairs of their heads or the sparrows of the air both of which He governs by His providential care (Matthew 10:29–31).

After His counsel to the disciples to not fear, Jesus makes a definitive statement about confessing Him that is found in all the Synoptic Gospels: "Therefore everyone who confesses Me before men, I will

---

14 Chamblin, *Matthew*, 1:577.
15 Chamblin, *Matthew*, 1:577.

also confess Him before My father who is in heaven. But whoever denies Me before men, I will also deny him before My Father who is in heaven" (Matthew 10:32, 33). Calvin expounds the importance of Jesus' words to us:

> Christ now fits what He had previously said about the disregard for death to His present purpose, that we should resist the fear of death, in case it should divert us from that frank confession of our faith, which God strictly demands, and which the world cannot endure. So the reason why Christ's disciples must be brave and stout-hearted is that they must ever be ready for martyrdom. Now the confession of Christ, though it be treated by the majority of men as a negligible thing, is here reckoned in the forefront of the honour paid to God, and as a unique practice of religion; and deservedly so . . . If a man runs away or keeps silence, is he not, by frustrating the work of the Son of God, taking himself out of the family of God?[16]

In concluding His discourse, Jesus makes it abundantly clear that the greatest obstacles to the confession of Christ will be the attachment to the members of one's own family—father or mother, son or daughter, etc. "And a man's enemies will be the members of his own household" (Mathew 10:36). That is why John Bunyan began *The Pilgrim's Progress* with Christian fleeing the City of Destruction where he lived and leaving his wife and children behind, though they begged him with tears not to go away. As Jesus said, "And he who does not take his cross and follow after Me is not worthy of Me" (Matthew 10:38). Chamblin elucidates the meaning of Jesus' call for His followers to lose their lives for His sake:

> Doing so is yet more demanding than going to a martyr's death; the one thing harder than dying for Jesus is living for him in the way here prescribed—namely, willingly denying *oneself* (as distinct from denying oneself things), and surrendering oneself utterly to Christ, at whatever cost, every single day. It may be agonizing to die in a relationship that obstructs one's service to Christ; but genuinely and voluntarily dying to oneself—in Pauline terms, crucifying the flesh (Gal. 5:24)—will almost certainly be excruciating . . . Is not the relinquishing of a proud ego to the Lordship of Jesus a stupendous miracle of sovereign grace?[17]

---

16 Calvin, *A Harmony of the Gospels Matthew, Mark and Luke*, 1:308–9.
17 Chamblin, *Matthew*, 1:596.

Woes on Chorazin, Bethsaida and Capernaum (Matthew 11:20–24 and Luke 10:13–15)

After the commissioning of the apostles and the other seventy,[18] Jesus Himself began to travel throughout Galilee "to teach and preach in their cities" (Matthew 11:1). The whole area was blanketed with eighty-three evangelists empowered to heal, perform miracles and preach the gospel. The world had never seen anything like it before this time nor since those days. The religious excitement caused by all these mighty works reached the ears of people throughout Galilee and even was heard by John the Baptist as he languished in the prison at the Machaerus fortress. J. A. Alexander commented on Matthew 11:1, as follows:

> The verse before us is a winding down up of the preceding chapter by the statement that our Lord, after organizing and commissioning the twelve, did not allow that act to interrupt his own itinerant labours, but as soon as he *finished charging or instructing* them (a military term in Greek, originally denoting the array and disposition of the of armed forces), he passed on thence, i.e. from the place where these instructions were delivered, and which cannot now be ascertained, though commonly supposed to be Capernaum or its neighborhood. The design of this departure was not rest but labour, to teach and preach.[19]

This commission of the apostles and the seventy was not at this time a diminishing of the great work of Jesus or of His own labors. He was still the primary herald of the coming Messianic kingdom. Instead, there was a dual purpose in what Jesus was doing. First, by sending them out to all the Jewish cities of Galilee, they were preparing the way for Him and He soon followed behind them in all those same places. Second, He was also preparing them for the great work they would do after His death, resurrection, and ascension. Chamblin opined on the importance of Matthew 11:1 stating that Jesus went out to teach and preach in all those cities:

> I believe Matthew, anticipating 11:2–6, is implying that Messiah's

---

18 Many scholars place the sending out of the Seventy during the Judean and Perean part of Jesus' ministry in the late Fall of AD 29 or early AD 30. There is no Scriptural evidence to support that view of the chronology of Jesus' life. At that point of His ministry, "Jesus...was unwilling to walk openly in Judea because the Jews were seeking to kill Him" (John 7:1). If He had sent out seventy evangelistic workers throughout Judea during that period, even more hostility against Him would have been provoked. Thus, I take this commission of the Seventy as happening in Galilee before Jesus turned His attention to the Gentiles and, therefore, coincident with or shortly after the apostles were commissioned to preach the Gospel to the lost sheep of Israel in Galilee.
19 Alexander, *The Gospel of Matthew Explained*, 301.

foremost work is not visible but verbal—proclaiming the gospel of the kingdom to the poor (11:5; 4:23; 9:35)[20]

It was at this time, as Jesus was about to set out on His third and last preaching tour throughout Galilee, that He began to denounce the very cities where He had done most of His great miracles. Over the previous year, there had been a developing hostility towards Jesus by the Pharisees who incited the people against Him, including the people of His "hometown," Capernaum. As shocking as Jesus' words might seem, He was actually doing exactly what He instructed His disciples to do. "If the house is worthy, give it your blessing of peace. But if it is not worthy, take back your blessing of peace. Whoever does not receive you, nor heed your words, as you go out of that house or that city, shake the dust off your feet. Truly I say to you, it will be more tolerable for the land of Sodom and Gomorrah in the day of judgment than for that city" (Matthew 10:13–15). Luke 10:13–15 records those denunciations of Jesus which stand in stark contrast to the generally mild language of our Lord:

> Woe to you, Chorazin! Woe to you, Bethsaida! For if the miracles had been performed in Tyre and Sidon which occurred in you, they would have repented long ago, sitting in sackcloth and ashes. But it will be more tolerable for Tyre and Sidon in the judgment than you. And you, Capernaum, will not be exalted to heaven, will you? You will be brought down to Hades!

The harshness of Jesus' words is both striking and unusual. Jesus preferred to assume the posture of a weeping prophet, like Jeremiah, and tenderly call Israel to repentance, as He would later weep over Jerusalem. Yet, now He was shaking the dust off His feet after a rather fruitless year that had been spent in Capernaum. The reaction of that city to the charge by the Pharisees that he was performing His miracles by the power of Satan was probably the last straw in Jesus' patience with their unbelief. There had been many miracles performed and many great works done there, but a revival of that fishing village was still lacking. The Capernaum synagogue had been graced with the very words of the Son of Man on numerous occasions, but now their day of grace was drawing to an end. The cities of Chorazin and Bethsaida were in close proximity to Capernaum and, thus, shared in the condemnation that Jesus denounced against Capernaum. Bethsaida was about five miles east of Capernaum on the other side of the Jordan River and Choraz-

---

20 Chamblin, *Matthew*, 1:602–3.

in was two and a half miles north of Capernaum on a hill in the area known as the Korazim Plateau. Jesus' celebrated Sermon on the Mount was preached near to that area where Chorazin was located. The ruins of an ancient synagogue at the village nearby to Khirbat Karazza can still be seen there which dated from the second century AD. An earlier synagogue was located six hundred and fifty feet away and was described by G. Foerster as follows:

> A square colonnaded building of small dimensions, of a disposition similar to the interior of arrangement of the synagogue, 7 columns, 3 on each side . . . with sitting benches in 5 courses.[21]

Jesus must have preached at the synagogue in Chorazin on many occasions, since it was so close to where He was headquartered for a year. Jesus performed various miracles at Bethsaida also and surely would have preached in any synagogue in that area. As Calvin notes concerning what must have inspired Jesus' words of denunciation of these three cities:

> He was thinking of the ingratitude of those among whom He had for a long time fruitlessly performed the office of Prophet and done many wonderful works, and He broke out into these words, as if saying that the time had come for Him to turn to other cities, now that He had found the inhabitants of that shore, where He had begun to preach the Gospel and to do miracles, so unteachable and terribly malicious. Without mentioning His teaching, however, He blames them that His miracles had not led them to repentance. For it is certain that the Lord put forth signs of His power to invite men to Himself. But since by nature all are turned away from Him, it is necessary to start at repentance.[22]

What is most shocking about Jesus' words is that He compares their coming judgment unfavorably to people considered by the Jews to be the worst examples of humanity. Tyre and Sidon, along the Mediterranean seacoast, were "notorious for ungodliness, pride, extravagance and other vices."[23] False worship, even demonism, was common among the citizens of those two cities, Yet, Jesus says that "it will be more tolerable for Tyre and Sidon in the day of judgment" (Matthew 11:22) than for Chorazin, Bethsaida, and Capernaum.[24]

---

21 Lee I. Levine, ed., *Ancient Synagogues Revealed* (Jerusalem, Israel Exploration Society, 1981),
26. Cf. also, G. Foerster, "The Synagogues at Masada and Herodium", pp. 24-29).
22 Calvin, *A Harmony of the Gospels Mathew, Mark, and Luke*, 2:15.
23 Calvin, *A Harmony of the Gospels Mathew, Mark, and Luke*, 2:15.
24 A visit to those cities today reveals only ruins. No one lives there. Other cities in Israel have grown, but those once flourishing cities are completely gone.

Capernaum will "descend to Hades" (Matthew 11:23), rather than be escorted into heaven. Several of Jesus' disciples, including His inner circle, were from that region. Peter's wife had a home in Capernaum. Yet, all those facts are external. Jesus' preaching was a call to the renovation of the heart and those three cities had failed to truly come to Him. Thus, they would be severely condemned.

Come to Me (Matthew 11:25–30)
Following His denunciation of Chorazin, Bethsaida, and Capernaum, Jesus began to reveal Himself more fully than ever before. Matthew 11:25 states: "At that time Jesus said, 'I praise You Father. Lord of heaven and earth, that You have hidden these things from *the* wise and intelligent and have revealed them to infants." Then Matthew 11:28 says: "Come to Me, all who are weary and heavy-laden, and I will give you rest." In calling people to come to Him, He put His finger on what was missing in the response of those cities to His ministry. They knew about Him. They saw His miracles. They rejoiced in all the great things He was doing. But . . . they simply refused to come to Him. Come to Him they must or else they could not find rest for their souls or be saved. In calling them to come to Him, Jesus revealed that He is the Son of God, the author of salvation. At this point in His ministry, Jesus engages in more self-disclosure to the Jews than He had at any point up to this time. Others had pointed to Jesus as the Messiah of God—the Expected One—but He had not been so straight forward to the Jews.

Jesus had not fully opened Himself up to the people in Galilee before this time. Like a flower that opens slowly to reveal the inner beauty, Jesus performed many great works and preached the most eloquent sermons ever, but He had withheld—for a time—the full truth about Himself. This invitation in Matthew 11:28–30 is the first time Jesus said, "Come to Me." Now He was identifying that true salvation was not just in His words, but in Himself.

The last three verses of Matthew 11 give us one of the most precious invitations of the gospel to be found anywhere in Scripture. In those verses, the mild and gentle Jesus invites weary, heavy-laden sinners to come to Him. He does not offer hard terms for them to get relief. He does not require heroic efforts on their part before they can be unburdened. He does not chide them or speak harshly to them. Rather, He makes a simple request that every person outside of Christ should gladly heed. He says:

> Come to Me, all who are weary and heavy-laden, and I will give you rest. Take My yoke upon you and learn from Me, for I am gentle and humble in heart, and you will find rest for your souls. For My yoke is easy and My burden is light (Matthew 11:28–30).

The yoke of which Jesus speaks refers to the burden and the heavy load that is being born by those He invites. Chamblin expounds on the meaning of this verse:

> A yoke . . . on one's neck and shoulders was a means for bearing a load. Used figuratively, the term could denote both servitude to an oppressive master and service to Yahweh—who is also praised as the One who frees His people from the yoke of slavery. Jewish sources from Jesus' time and afterwards speak of serving Yahweh as accepting 'the yoke of the law' or 'the yoke of the kingdom.' . . . The expression 'my yoke' . . . reflects Jesus' unique authority as Yahweh incarnate to establish that rule and to interpret that law.[25]

The Puritan author, John Bunyan (1628–1688), in *Pilgrim's Progress*, described sin as an insufferable burden for Christian—the chief character of his allegory—from which he eagerly longed to be free. Bunyan wrote, as if in a dream:

> *I saw a Man clothed with Raggs, standing in a certain place, with his face from his own house, a Book in his hand, and a great burden upon his Back.* I looked and saw him open the Book, and Read therein; and as he read, he wept and trembled: and not being able to contain, he brake out with a lamentable cry; saying, *what shall I do?*[26]

There are so few who come to Christ because so few are truly burdened with their sins. Few people see their sins as dirty rags draped over their bodies and heavy burdens weighing down their backs. Sin is a friend to them, a dear companion, whom they cherish and from whom they never want to part. Yet, sin is actually a deadly enemy which destroys the soul. If that terrible enemy is not removed by coming to Christ, it will hang around a person's neck and be strapped to their back through all eternity. That burden will remain with them forever in that place of torment to which all unrepentant sinners are doomed. The excruciating sufferings they experience there will only be increased by the burden that remains on their backs. Thus, the invitation of Christ for all sinners to come to Him is conditioned in this respect: They must feel that sin is a heavy and wearisome burden from which they must be

---

25 Chamblin, *Matthew*, 1:635–6.
26 John Bunyan, *The Pilgrim's Progress: From This World To That Which Is To Come* (Oxford, England: Oxford University Press, 1960), 8.

relieved. Those who are "weary and heavy-laden" by their sins are particularly invited because no one else will ever come to Him.

In the verses previous to this wonderful invitation to come to Christ, our Lord had spoken of the possibility of knowing the Son by revelation of the Father. Alexander comments on how those verses impact the invitation of Christ to come to Him:

> [O]ur Lord offers, as it were, to exercise this gracious function, by inviting men to come to him, not in the way of speculation but of penitent submission, not as philosophers to be enlightened, but as sinners to be saved.[27]

Jesus promises that whoever comes to Him will find "rest for your souls" (Matthew 11:29). This rest is that great spiritual rest promised in the Scripture. It is the rest of which Hebrews 4:9, 10 speaks: "So there remains a Sabbath rest for the people of God. For the one who has entered His rest has himself rested from his works, as God did from His." John Brown gives the meaning of this rest that is offered to us:

> The rest here is that state of holy happiness which Christians enjoy on earth as well as in heaven, and into which they enter by the "belief of the truth."[28]

Jesus promises with this invitation to replace their burdens with a yoke that is easy and light; a yoke in which they will find rest, instead of labor. The only thing required in this invitation to come to Christ is that a sinner must feel the weight of his sins and realize that no one but Jesus can take that burden away. Davies passionately urged sinners to flee to Christ and accept His gracious invitation with these words:

> Suppose one should ask you upon your return home, "What were you doing today?" You must answer, "I was engaged in a treaty with the Proprietor of the universe, and the Redeemer that bought me with his blood, about becoming his servant, and acknowledging his right to me." "Well, and what was the issue? Certainly you did not dare to refuse. Certainly you are now the willing servant of God."—"No, I refused, and so the treaty broke up."[29]

Once again, Bunyan describes how Christian finally found relief from his burden:

---

27 Alexander, *The Gospel According to Matthew, Explained*, 320.
28 John Brown, *Hebrews* (London, England and Carlisle, Pennsylvania: The Banner of Truth Trust, 1972), 208.
29 Davies, Sermons by the Rev. Samuel Davies, 2:140.

The Third Missionary Tour of Galilee

> He ran till he came at a place somewhat ascending; and upon that place stood a *Cross*, and a little below, a Sepulcher. So, I saw in my Dream, that just as Christian came to the Cross, his burden loosed off his shoulders, and fell from his back; and began to tumble; and so continued to do, till it came to the mouth of the Sepulcher, where it fell in and I saw it no more.[30]

Christian's burden was not taken away until he came to the cross and to Jesus. Then it fell off and was buried with Christ, so that Christian could also rise with Him. That is why Jesus invites weary and heavy-laden sinners to come to Him. He will take away your burdens and give you rest.

The Seventy Return Rejoicing (Luke 10:17–20)

When the larger body of disciples, the Seventy, returned from their missionary work in Galilee, their hearts were full of joy. Coming to Jesus, they said, "Lord, even the demons are subject to us in Your name" (Luke 10:17). Jesus had distinctly given the Twelve authority to cast out demons, but nowhere is it specifically stated in Scripture that He had given that same power to the Seventy. Yet, they found during their mission that the demons were subject to them in Jesus' name. Demonic influence was prevalent throughout Galilee and Judea and always had been. There were many people who were demon-possessed. The disciples of Jesus had observed His miracles of casting out demons on previous occasions. Now, they had the same power over demons as their Lord, in His name.

Their rejoicing over this miraculous power was sincere, but it was misplaced. They were focused on the wrong thing. Jesus abruptly refocused their attention on the more important truth. First, He told them that while they were casting out demons, He was observing something even more spectacular—the fall of Satan from heaven. He said, "I was watching Satan fall from heaven like lightning" (Luke 10:18). The fall of Satan that Jesus referenced was neither that fiends first fall before the creation of the world nor his last fall at the end of all time. Rather, it was a fall in conjunction with the power given to the seventy over the demons. As Edersheim notes:

> So to speak, the fall of Satan is to the bottomless pit; ever going on to the final triumph of Christ. As the Lord beholds him, he is fallen from heaven—from the seat of power and of worship; for, his mastery is

---

[30] Bunyan, *Pilgrim's Progress*, 38.

broken by the Stronger than he. And he is fallen like lightning, in its rapidity, dazzling splendour, and destructiveness (Rev. 12:7–12). Yet, as we perceive it, it is only demons cast out in His Name.[31]

Jesus' words are profound. "As one has aptly paraphrased it: 'While you cast out his subjects, I saw the prince himself fall.'[32]" The demons could not have been cast out unless Satan himself was bound by One more powerful than him.

Then, Jesus gave a promise to them of what awaited His church in the future. Certainly, there would be great trials, but there would also be great power given to them. Jesus said, "Behold, I have given you authority to tread on serpents and scorpions, and over all the power of the enemy, and nothing will injure you" (Luke 10:19). This verse is to be understood primarily in the symbolic sense. Satan himself is called a serpent in the Scripture. Once again, Edersheim elucidates the meaning of this verse for the Church:

> The authority and power over 'the demons,' attained by faith, was not to pass away with the occasion that called it forth . . . As already indicated, the sight of Satan fallen from heaven is the continuous history of the Church . . . For the words in which Christ gave authority and power to tread on serpents and scorpions, and over all the power of the Enemy. And the promise that nothing would harm them, could not have been addressed to the Seventy for a Mission which had now come to an end, except in so far as they represented the Church Universal.[33]

After making that promise, Jesus then pointed them to the more important spiritual truth—"Nevertheless do not rejoice in this, that the spirits are subject to you, but rejoice that your names are recorded in heaven" (Luke 10:20). "The casting out of demons gives no security for the possession of eternal life . . . A Judas might cast out demons."[34] Indeed, Jesus said in the Sermon on the Mount: "Many will say to Me on that day, 'Lord, Lord, did we not prophesy in Your name, and in Your name cast out demons, and in Your name perform many miracles?' And then I will declare to them, 'I never knew you; Depart from Me, you who practice lawlessness.'" (Matthew 7:22, 23). The greater gift is eternal life and that is what is to be our joy at all

---

31 Edersheim, *The Life and Times of Jesus the Messiah*, 570.
32 Edersheim, *The Life and Times of Jesus the Messiah*, 570.
33 Edersheim, *The Life and Times of Jesus the Messiah*, 570–1.
34 Plummer, *A Critical and Exegetical Commentary on the Gospel According to St. Luke*, 280.

times. Peter wrote that true believers "greatly rejoice with joy inexpressible and full of glory" (1 Peter 1:8c). Jesus always knew the right words to speak to every person, whether they were rejoicing or weeping. As William Hendriksen commented on this verse:

> What the Master must have meant was that authority over demons was, after all, insignificant in comparison with having one's name recorded in heaven's book of life.[35]

After redirecting the Seventy to focus on their eternal salvation, Jesus Himself rejoiced greatly in the Lord, praying, "I praise You, O Father, Lord of heaven and earth, that You have hidden these things from the wise and intelligent and have revealed them to infants. Yes, Father, for this was well-pleasing in Your sight" (Luke 10:21). The Greek used in this verse indicates that Jesus prayed that prayer in that "same hour" as when the Seventy were rejoicing in their newly given authority over the demons. Jesus' prayer reminds us that heavenly citizenship is not the result of superior gifts or intelligence, but is bestowed by the sovereign grace of God. It is off-putting to some that Jesus says the Father hides the truth from the intelligent and gives that knowledge to infants. Yet, that is what is taught in other places in the Scripture. Paul wrote: "For consider your calling, brethren, that there were not many wise according to the flesh, not many mighty, not many noble; but God has chosen the foolish things of the world to shame the wise, and God has chosen the weak things of the world to shame the things which are strong" (1 Corinthians 1:26, 27). And God told the Jews in the Deuteronomy: "The Lord did not set His love on you nor choose you because you were more in number than any of the peoples, for you were the fewest of all peoples, but because the Lord loved you and kept the oath which He swore to your forefathers" (Deuteronomy 7:7, 8a). What Jesus praised the Lord for was what the Scripture teaches everywhere. The Church is not an elite body where only the strongest or smartest or richest are included. As Geldenhuys wrote on these verses:

> From these words it appears that the Saviour rejoiced in the fact that God in His wisdom, omnipotence and love has so arranged matters that insight is given into the redeeming truths of the kingdom not to those who are self-righteous and wise in their own esteem (as so many Pharisees and scribes were at that time), but to those (like His faithful

---

35 Hendriksen, *Exposition of the Gospel According to Luke*, 582.

disciples) who in childlike simplicity and humility feel their utter dependence on the Lord and accept without intellectual arrogance the truths revealed by God through Him.[36]

After that brief prayer, Jesus turned to His disciples and said to them in private: "Blessed are the eyes which see the things that you see, for I say to you, that many prophets and kings wished to see the things which you see, and did not see them, and to hear the things which you hear, and did not hear them" (Luke 10:23, 24). Once again, Geldenhuys elucidates the importance of those words of Jesus words for us today:

> However great the privileges of those disciples was, we who possess in the New Testament the completed revelation of God in Christ have a still greater privilege. They indeed saw Him in the flesh, but we see Him in the New Testament not merely as the Incarnate Son of God but also as the Crucified One, and as the Risen Redeemer and the glorified King of His church. And because our privilege is so great, a great responsibility likewise rests on us. The people of that time who rejected the revelation of God in Christ did not escape the divine judgment. So much the more will those who reject the completed revelation of God in His Word also bring judgment upon themselves.[37]

The disciples did not yet understand why some people were rejecting Jesus despite seeing His miracles and hearing His teaching, but they would soon understand.

---

36 Gendenhuys, *Commentary on the Gospel of Luke*, 360.
37 Gendenhuys, *Commentary on the Gospel of Luke*, 307–8.

13

The Bread of Life

"It is, however, not merely as incarnate that the Son of God is the bread of eternal life. Bread must be broken in order to be eaten. The Incarnate One must die as a sacrificial victim that men may truly feed upon Him. The Word become flesh, and crucified in the flesh, is the life of the world."[1]

It was in the Spring of AD 29, shortly before the Passover, that the brief life of John the Baptist came to an end. Ever since his imprisonment at Herod's Machaerus palace the previous year, the destiny of John had been very tenuous. Herod was severely conflicted over John. Herodias had a Jezebel-like hatred of him and an inveterate determination to have him killed. Herod was inclined to placate his wife, but he feared the people who revered the Forerunner as a prophet. Thus, Herod would often hear John preach which perplexed him though he enjoyed listening to the Baptist (Mark 6:20). Whereas Herodias had an implacable grudge against him, "Herod was afraid of John, knowing that he was a righteous and holy man, and he kept him safe" (Mark 6:20). There was a part of Herod that wanted to release John, but Herodias was passionate in her intentions for his death. Despite this palace intrigue, John remained unflinching in his rebuke of Herod: "It is not lawful for you to have your brother's wife" (Mark 6:18). This triangular battle of wills was soon to be decided in favor of Herodias as the spouse who was most determined to get her way. No doubt, she was constantly scheming of how to rid herself of this zealous reformer. Such a strategic day arrived in the form of Herod's birthday[2] party. This was the opportunity for which Herodias was longing. Edersheim describes the setting:

A fit time this for a Belshazzar-feast, when such an one as Herod would

---

1 Bruce, *The Training of the Twelve*, 138.
2 Edersheim, *The Life and Times of Jesus the Messiah*, 461, footnote 38. Edersheim suggests that the Greek word, genesia, can mean either birthday or anniversary of his accession. If it is the latter, it would refer to Herod's accession to the Tetrarchy at the death of his father, Herod the Great. That took place in early April of 4 B.C. Thus the anniversary every year would have been shortly before Passover.

gather to a grand banquet 'his lords,' and the military authorities, and the chief men of Galilee. It is evening, and the castle-palace is brilliantly lit up. The noise of music and shouts of revelry come across the slope into the citadel, and fall into the deep-dungeon where waits the prisoner of Christ.[3]

These ancient state banquets were celebrations to which only men were invited. It was unacceptable for women to recline at table with the men on such occasions. Herodias was well-aware of these mores and, thus, this banquet was just "the strategic day" (Mark 6:21) for which she had been eagerly waiting. All the men would drink until they were inebriated. Then, some woman or women would be summoned to provide entertainment for the king and his guests. In ancient Persia, Queen Vashti had refused King Ahasuerus when he summoned her to his banquet (Esther 1:10–12), but cunning Herodias, ever lurking in the background, was prepared for this very opportunity. Herodias had groomed Salome, her daughter through marriage to Herod Phillip, to perform a dance at these festivities. Salome was then about fourteen to sixteen years of age. The fact that she was the step-daughter of Herod Antipas did not give sanction to her performance or lessen its repulsiveness. Were the king and his guests "even sober as they watched Salome go through her rhythmic movements, dancing bewitchingly and seductively?"[4] Edersheim elaborates on the feelings that must have overcome Herod during this performance:

> She has come, and she has danced, this princely maiden, out of whom all maidenhood and all princeliness have been brazed by a degenerate mother, wretched offspring of the once noble Maccabees. And she has done her best in that wretched exhibition, and pleased Herod and them that sat at meat with him. And now, amidst the general plaudits, she shall have her reward—and the king swears to it to her with loud voice, that all around hear it—even to the half of his kingdom.[5]

Salome had been "prostituted by her mother to the low level of a scenic dancer . . . and 'executed a *pas seul*[6] in the midst of these dissolute and half-intoxicated revelers.'"[7] While the many guests lounging on the divans all enjoyed her lewd, licentious movements, her dance was aimed at pleasing only one person—Herod. She danced, at the

---

3 Edersheim, *The Life and Times of Jesus the Messiah*, 461.
4 Hendriksen, *Matthew*, 588–9.
5 Edersheim, *The Life and Times of Jesus the Messiah*, 462.
6 Pas seul is a dance for one person.
7 Shepard, *The Christ of the Gospels*, 257.

behest of her mother, to seduce this vain king who was easily enticed by voluptuous pleasures. In the beautiful seven thousand square foot courtyard where Herod sat on his throne, with music playing and large numbers of drunken guests cheering, Salome went through all the gyrations of her well-choreographed dance with the singular aim of enticing Herod's heart. She performed her part well, though she apparently did not understand the end-game. Like a poisoned arrow aimed at his heart, Salome's dance accomplished its purpose. Herod's resistance was broken and he hastily blurted out his ill-considered promise to his attractive and seductive step-daughter. He promised her whatever she wanted and then swore with an oath to give her up to half his kingdom. All the dinner guests heard the king's rash oath. There could be no retraction of his promise at that point. Salome, immediately rushed to her mother, who counseled her to reply, "Give me here on a platter the head of John the Baptist" (Matthew 14:8). Caught off guard, Herod then realized he had fallen into the trap set by Herodias which grieved him. Yet, because of his oaths and dinner guests "he sent and had John beheaded in prison. And the head was brought on a platter and given to the girl, and she brought it to her mother" (Matthew 14:10, 11). Edersheim describes what happened when Salome made her request:

> It has been but the contest of a moment. "Straightway" the king gives the order to one of the body-guard. The maiden hath withdrawn to await the result with her mother. The guardsman has left the banqueting-hall. Out into the cold night, up that slope, and into the deep dungeon. As its door opens, the noise of the revelry comes with the light of the torch which the man bears. No time for preparation is given, nor needed. A few minutes more, and the gory head of the Baptist is brought to the maiden in a charger, and she gives the ghastly dish to her mother.[8]

Too late, Herod realized what had happened. For months he had refused to kill John, but now here was his head on a platter. "Antipas, half-drunk, was caught in the snare of Herodias. What she had failed to get by entreaty she secured by craftiness... At last Herodias had triumphed, and now in fiendish delight receives the head of the prophet, whose words had made many hearts quail because of their sins."[9] It was a sobering and horrifying moment for Herod, though. His heart was shaken by this event and the gruesome view of John's

---

8 Edersheim, *The Life and Times of Jesus the Messiah*, 463.
9 Shepard, *The Christ of the Gospels*, 258.

head would haunt this Tetrarch for the rest of his days. John had lost his head, but he never lost his composure; he never lost his courage; he never lost his boldness; he never lost his reputation; and, he never lost his Savior. He died as he had lived.

Matthew 14:12 says, "His disciples came and took away the body of John and buried it, and they went and reported to Jesus." Whether true or not, "tradition says that Herodias ordered the headless trunk to be flung over the battlements of the castle-dungeon to be devoured by dogs and vultures in the ravines below."[10] Before the swirling vultures and ravenous dogs could destroy the body of John, though, his disciples were able to find it and give it the burial[11] that great man deserved. John's death had a powerful impact on Jesus and His ministry from that time forward. This was a turning point in bringing Jesus' Galilean ministry to a conclusion just as John's arrest by Herod had ended His Judean ministry.

Henry Wadsworth Longfellow wrote a poem about John's beheading called *Under the Walls of Machaerus*. Some of those lines are as follows:

> The Prophet of God is dead! At a drunken monarch's call,
> At a dancing-woman's beck, They have severed that stubborn neck,
> And into the banquet-hall Are bearing the ghastly head!
> A torch of lurid red, Lights the window with its glow;
> And a white mass as of snow Is hurled into the abyss
> Of the black precipice, That yawns for it below!
> O hand of the Most High, O hand of Adonai!
> Bury it, hide it away, From the birds and beasts of prey,
> And the eyes of the homicide, More pitiless than they,
> As thou didst bury of yore, The body of him that died
> On the mountain of Peor!

Herod's Troubled Conscience (Matthew 14:1, 2; Mark 6:7–16; and, Luke 9:7–9)

The lives of Jesus and Herod Antipas were entwined in many different ways though they had never met when reports of the miraculous works of the Galilean began to filter back to the Tetrarch. Herod Antipas could not have been oblivious to the intrigue of Jesus' birth and the extreme paranoia of his father—even if he never associated those events with Jesus of Nazareth—the Galilean. Yet, for most of the next

---

10 Shepard, *The Christ of the Gospels*, 258.
11 Jerome and others believed that the body of John was interred at Sebastia, near Nablus and the scene of Jesus' ministry to the woman at the well.

thirty-two years both Jesus and Herod Antipas had lived within twenty miles of one another without ever meeting.

The ghastly beheading of John the Baptist at the Machaerus fortress near the Dead Sea had happened only a matter of days or a few weeks before Herod received word of some amazing things that were happening in his territory through the ministry of Jesus and His disciples. For nearly a year, Jesus had been conducting His ministry in Capernaum, but now He had trained and commissioned His disciples to do the same things He had been doing—healing the sick, casting out demons, cleansing the lepers, and raising the dead (Matthew 10:8). When the disciples returned to Jesus in Capernaum, the news of their success spread like wildfire throughout the region. J. W. Shepard describes what was the result:

> The fame of the name of Jesus spread over Galilee as never before and penetrated into the golden Palace of Herod Antipas in Tiberias.[12]

Tiberias was a city built in AD 18 according to Roman architectural styles with all the roads crossing at right angles. It became the primary residence of this wicked king who was more concerned with luxury and pleasure than with ruling equitably for the advantage of his subjects. Herod's palatial and grandiose residence itself was built, wittingly or unwittingly, on the ruins of a Jewish cemetery which caused that wicked ruler to fall even more out of favor with the Jews. The city was lined with markets, shops, statues of Herod, a luxurious bathhouse, and that magnificent royal palace. Galileans were enticed to move there by the promise of free land, free housing, and various tax exemptions, but the desecration of the cemetery kept most of them away. Jesus was apparently among the Jews who stayed away from Tiberias because there is no mention in Scripture of Him ever passing through that city for any reason.

There were many pressing concerns that had occupied the attention of Herod over the previous years—his trip to Rome where he met and married his brother's wife, Herodias; his troubles with his former wife, Phasaelis of Nabatea; and the resulting war with Aretas, Phasaelis's father, that ended in Herod's defeat. In such circumstances, Herod tried to find solace from the troubles of his kingdom by immersing himself in sinful pleasures, in vanity and in his numerous

---

12 Shepard, *The Christ of the Gospels*, 254.

building projects. What was happening among the religious segment of his populace was not a high priority for him at this time. "A palace is late in hearing spiritual news"[13] and, thus, Jesus had been conducting a powerful ministry without arousing the suspicion of Herod—until now.

Yet, within a short time after the death of John the Baptist, reports reached Herod's ears that caused him a great deal of consternation. Luke 9:7, 8 says that Herod heard what "was happening; and he was greatly perplexed, because it was said by some that John had risen from the dead, and by some that Elijah had appeared, and by others that one of the prophets of old had risen." Indeed, Herod was very perplexed and more than perplexed. He "was 'utterly at loss' as to what he was to think of Jesus . . . He had no doubt heard of Christ before. It was the startling theories about Him which perplexed Herod."[14] The crown always rests very insecurely on the heads of wicked, despotic rulers whose god is their belly. And so it was with Herod. Like his father, Antipas was troubled by any challenge—real or imagined—to his rule, especially in light of his recent defeat by the armies of Aretas. Yet, Herod was troubled also at a deeper level. His conscience was accusing him every day and he could not be reassured no matter how hard he tried. These circulating reports did not originate with Herod, but they came to him through others. Immediately, Herod seized on one only as the true explanation for Jesus' miraculous powers. Mathew 14:2 records that he "said to his servants, 'This is John the Baptist; he has risen from the dead, and that is why miraculous powers are at work in him.'" That must have been a terrifying thought for the despot. The suggestion that Jesus' miracles were the result of John rising from the dead was probably due to the popular revolt of the people following Herod's terrible deed of the beheading. As Calvin remarked on these reports:

> I have no doubt that the hatred of this tyrant and loathing for the wicked murder was, as often happens, the cause of this rumour. The superstition that the dead return to life in another person was firm in men's minds, as I have said elsewhere. Now they seize on a cognate idea, that when Herod cruelly put this holy man to death he did not achieve his end, for John was suddenly raised from the dead by the

---

13 Shepard, *The Christ of the Gospels*, 255.
14 Plummer, *A Critical and Exegetical Commentary on the Gospel According to St. Luke*, 241.

wonderful power of God, and would be a fiercer avenger of his enemy's wickedness . . . It is surprising that when they put forward these different opinions the true one did not occur to any of them, especially since the contemporary situation pointed them to Christ.[15]

These servants of Herod were most likely his court ministers or counselors. They were the people with whom he was in the habit of unburdening his heart and revealing his thoughts. In this instance, he shares with them how guilty his conscience was. As David Brown commented, "The murdered prophet haunted his guilty breast like a spectre, and seemed to him alive again and clothed with unearthly powers in the person of Jesus."[16] Amazingly, though, John had never performed any miracles and his resurrection from the dead would not have explained the wondrous reports of what Jesus and His disciples were doing.

In overlooking the obvious and true opinion of the origin of the miracles that Jesus was doing, Herod and others manifested the blindness of their own hearts. Both Herod and many of the people overlooked the obvious explanation for the cause of Jesus' miracles—that He was indeed the Messiah of prophecy. Once again, Calvin explains the situation concerning John for us:

> But what they are thinking is that he is performing miracles for the first time to prove his resurrection and to witness that he had been a holy prophet of God irreligiously killed by Herod and that now he came forth, so to say sacrosanct, that none might dare to hurt him again.[17]

There is no reasoning that could calm the troubled conscience of Herod, though. He remained impenitent, but deeply troubled. His perplexity was not of the inquisitive type, but his mind was filled with terror that his deeds had been found out. As Calvin says, "As for Herod, as I mentioned earlier, it was not his own idea that John was risen; but as bad consciences waver in terror and bend at every breeze, he easily conceived what he feared. And God often alarms the ungodly with blind terrors. They try to harden themselves against outside assaults, but they cannot get any rest from the harsh punishment of their inward tormentor."[18]

These reports of Jesus' ministry and His disciples placed Him above

---

15 Calvin, *A Harmony of the Gospels: Matthew, Mark and Luke*, 2:137–8.
16 David Brown, *The Four Gospels* (London, England: The Banner of Truth Trust, 1969), 83.
17 Calvin, *A Harmony of the Gospels: Matthew, Mark and Luke*, 138.
18 Calvin, *A Harmony of the Gospels: Matthew, Mark and Luke*, 138.

all the great prophets of the Old Testament "because He manifested in Himself the greatness of all combined."[19] These popular reports were so stupendous that Herod continued to seek an opportunity to meet Jesus face-to-face, but not with the desire of a true penitent who wanted to bow his knees before the King of Kings. Yet, that meeting with Jesus would not take place for another year. As long as it was day, Jesus continued to labor and to finish the work that the Lord had given Him.

Feeding the 5,000 (Matthew 14:13–21; Mark 6:32–44; Luke 9:10–17; and, John 6:1–14)

The feeding of the 5,000 is the only miracle, with the exception of the resurrection of Jesus, that is recorded in all four Gospels. This miracle comprehends more of the purpose of Christ towards His people as a whole than any other miracle. It shows how He provides for all our needs and how He invites us to eat with Him. It is parallel, in that sense, to those words of invitation found in Revelation 3:18—"Behold, I stand at the door and knock; if anyone hears My voice and opens the door, I will come in to him and will dine with him and he with Me."

The disciples of Jesus had just returned to Capernaum with the reports of their success. With a gentle admonition, Jesus called His disciples to come away with Him for a well-needed rest: "Come away by yourselves to a secluded place and rest a while" (Mark 6:31). Besides, "there were so many people coming and going that they did not have time to eat" (Mark 6:31). The secluded place where Jesus took them was Bethsaida Julias[20] on the northeast shore of the Sea of Galilee. It was just on the other side of the Jordan River from the territory of of wicked Herod.

Jesus and the twelve left Capernaum and went by boat to that secluded place, but the crowds were following Him on foot. At Bethsaida Julias, "there was a fertile but sparsely populated plain to the south . . . which narrowed down at the southern end where there were grassy slopes."[21] This town straddled the area where the Jordan River entered into the Sea of Galilee and the "eastern portion was built up into a beautiful city by Herod Philip, and named . . . after Julia, the daughter of the Roman emperor, Tiberius."[22]

The crowds of people recognized Jesus and His disciples as they

---

19 Shepard, *The Christ of the Gospels*, 256.
20 This city was named in honor of Empress Julia by Philip the Tetrarch.
21 Shepard, *The Christ of the Gospels*, 261.
22 Article on Bethsaida accessed at: www.biblebento.com on October 9, 2022.

tried to slip away in a boat to that secluded place, but some of the crowds arrived there first and were waiting on the Teacher as He came ashore. Jesus was moved with compassion for such a large crowd of people—men, women, and children—"because they were like sheep without a shepherd; and He began to teach them many things" (Mark 6:34). Passover was close at hand and there were also a large number of travelers to Jerusalem who were passing through this area to celebrate that feast. Jesus, apparently, did not go up to Jerusalem for this Passover because of the level of hostility against Him by the scribes and Pharisees. This miraculous feeding of the 5,000, therefore, was more than just a meal for a day. It was the fulfillment of everything that the Old Testament Passover feast symbolized. Jesus' disciples did not need to go to the Passover feast in Jerusalem because One greater than Moses was in their midst and He would provide them bread greater than the manna of the Old Testament. Just as the fathers did not have to work for the manna by the sweat of their brow, so this great multitude received this bread by a miracle of Christ's grace.

After teaching the crowds and healing their diseases, Jesus took His disciples up on a nearby mountain from which height he looked over the crowd and felt compassion for their bodily needs. When it was getting quite late, the disciples advised Jesus as follows: "This place is desolate and it is already quite late, send them away so that they may go into the surrounding country side and villages and buy them something to eat" (Mark 6:35, 36). Jesus then turned to Philip, testing his faith, and asked, "Where are we to buy bread, so that these may eat?" (John 6:5). Philip—the matter of fact and coldly calculating disciple[23]—quickly answered Him, "Two hundred denarii is not sufficient for them, for everyone to receive a little" (John 6:7). Jesus then commanded the disciples, "You give them something to eat" (Mark 6:37), but they responded, "Shall we go and spend two hundred denarii on bread, and give them something to eat?" The disciples' query revealed that they all, like Philip, surveyed the problem only in terms of a monetary answer. Having seen the miracles that Jesus performed on many occasions—and even this very day—their thoughts were fixated on the material. Andrew, though, was a man of action and he came to Jesus with a possible solution—"There is a lad here who has five barley loaves and two fish, but what are these for so many people?"

---

23 Shepard, *The Christ of the Gospels*, 262.

Jesus then said, "have the people sit down" (John 6:10). And they had the people sit down in groups of about fifty people each. "Thus arranged, the multitude, dressed in Oriental costumes of various colors, looked like garden-beds in bright colored flowers against the green background of abundant grass. Already it was evening and the sun was descending toward the western horizon."[24]

"Jesus then took the loaves, and having given thanks, He distributed to those who were seated; likewise of the fish as much as they wanted" (John 6:11). While the specific prayer Jesus offered on this occasion is unknown, it surely was not a customary table prayer, as Hendriksen notes:

> It must be borne in mind in this connection that our Lord's addresses to the people were always characterized by freshness and originality—he never spoke like the scribes, merely copying words of former rabbis.[25]

The result of this miracle was that "they all ate and were satisfied" (Luke 9:17). For the people, it was more than a snack. It was a meal in which they ate to their hearts content. From "five little barley cakes like crackers and two little sardine-like fish,"[26] Jesus had fed 5,00 men, plus women and children, to the fullness of satisfaction. After everyone was well-fed, there were twelve large wicker baskets gathered of the broken pieces that had not been served. That was a lesson to all the people that Jesus was able to give them living bread and to supply all their needs. "But though there was abundance there was no waste, for Jesus commanded the fragments to be gathered up."[27] There is more emphasis in this miracle on the loaves of bread because Jesus was set forth as greater than the manna of the wilderness. "Thus the miracle was the preparation for the sermon to follow in Capernaum"[28] the following day. This miracle was certainly one of the greatest that Jesus ever performed, next to His resurrection. It is a miracle that ministers to the needs of every person. We all need to come away with Christ to a solitary place where we can rest in Him. We all need to feed on Him by faith and to find in Him the true meaning of the Paschal Lamb.

---

24 Shepard, *The Christ of the Gospels*, 264.
25 Hendriksen, *The Gospel of John*, 222.
26 Shepard, *The Christ of the Gospels*, 263.
27 Morris, *The Gospel According to John*, 345.
28 Shepard, *The Christ of the Gospels*, 264.

Jesus Walking on the Water (Matthew 14:22–33; Mark 6:45–51; and, John 6:15–21)

Following the miraculous feeding of the 5,000, there were many who misunderstood Jesus' teaching on the kingdom of God (Luke 9:11). They came to Jesus with the intention of making a political king out of Him—by force, if necessary. Their enthusiasm "was not limited to a recognition of the Lord's prophetic office: they were on the point of seizing His person and proclaiming Him King."[29] This represented the greatest threat yet to the ministry of Jesus, as Henry Latham acknowledged:

> No malice on the part of the scribes could have been so fatal . . . as their giving of a political turn to the movement . . . He hurried the disciples on board that they might not catch the contagion of the idea.[30]

The well-intentioned directive of Jesus for His disciples to "come away by yourselves to a secluded place and rest a while" (Mark 6:31) never materialized. A day of incessant labors in healing the sick and teaching them was concluded by the great miracle of the multiplication of the loaves. Now Jesus perceives the danger of this situation. Perhaps, the crowds thought the only way to counteract Herod was to replace him a greater king. Thus, Jesus gathered His disciples together and sent them ahead of Him in the boat to the other Bethsaida on the western shores of the Sea of Galilee. After convincing the crowds to go home, Jesus retired to the nearby mountain where He spent several hours in prayer. Swete describes the scene:

> Another crisis had come; the way to further usefulness in Galilee seemed blocked, partly by the attitude of Antipas, partly by the unreasoning enthusiasm of the people; He needed counsel and strength for the immediate future.[31]

Additionally, the hostility of the scribes and Pharisees and Sadducees and Herodians presented another obstacle for Jesus. In this crisis, Jesus sought and found the solace He needed in communion with His Father. Meanwhile, the scene on the Sea of Galilee was becoming treacherous for the disciples. Spring is a time of unusual storms on that body of water. This particular storm must have been even more violent than normal because these fishermen were greatly distressed by it. No mat-

---

29 Swete, *Commentary on Mark*, 136.
30 Henry Latham, *Pastor Pastorum of the Schooling of the Apostles by our Lord* (New York: James Pott & Co. Publishing, 1891), 307.
31 Swete, *Commentary on Mark*, 137.

ter how hard they rowed, they were not making much headway against the winds and waves. The Sea of Galilee is small enough so that all boats can be observed from the hills and mountains during periods of light. On this occasion, "the Paschal moon gave light enough to reveal the boat struggling with the waves and well out to sea . . . The Lord, who was alone on the land, broke off His vigil and went down to the sea"[32] to rescue His disciples. He had prayed through three watches of the night from 6 PM to 3 AM. For nearly nine hours, the disciples had rowed feverishly to get to Bethsaida, but had only gone four miles on the water. Now, sometime during the fourth watch of the night, Jesus came to the boat via the miracle of walking on the water.

Yet, they were continually being pushed away from their destination by the winds and waves. Neither their sails nor their rowing was accomplishing any good. No doubt, they began to feel desperate. Mark 6:48 says that Jesus "seeing them straining at the oars" while He was on land and then decided to go help them. Then, the disciples saw Jesus walking on the water and it appeared to them that "He intended to pass by them" (Mark 6:48).

They thought they were seeing a ghost. The reaction of the disciples was fear, causing them to cry out for help. Jesus quickly comforted them that it was Him, "Take courage. It is I, do not be afraid" Mark 6:50). "Jesus begins with an imperative of command and closes with an imperative of prohibition."[33] Peter immediately said to the Lord, "Lord, if it is You, command me to come to You on the water" (Matthew 14:28). Jesus invited him to "Come" (Matthew 14:29), "and Peter got out of the boat and walked on the water and came toward Jesus" (Matthew 14:29). As amazing as it was for Jesus to walk on the water, it is an even greater miracle that Peter was able to do so. Peter was able to walk some of the way to Jesus, but soon became frightened by the winds and began to sink, crying out, "Lord, save me!" (Matthew 14:30). "Immediately. Jesus stretched out His hand and took hold of him, and said to him 'You of little faith. Why did you doubt?'" (Matthew 14:31). Ryle's comments on Peter's experience are worth noting:

> What a lively picture we have here of the experience of many a believer! How many there are who have faith to take the first step in following

---

32 Swete, *Commentary on Mark*, 137.
33 Chamblin, *Matthew*, 2:764.

Christ, but not faith enough to go on as they began. They take fright at the trials and dangers which seem to be in their way. They look at the enemies that surround them, and the difficulties that seem likely to beset their path; they look at them more than Jesus, and at once their feet begin to sink; their hearts faint within them; their hope vanishes away; their comforts disappear.[34]

When Jesus got into the boat, the storm completely died down and they almost immediately made it to shore. Yet, it was Gennesaret where they landed—not Bethsaida. Gennesaret was an area about four miles in length and three miles in width. It was a beautiful and fertile area that has been described as follows:

> It is exceedingly fertile and well watered: the soil, on the southern part at least, is a rich black mould, which in the vicinity . . . is almost a marsh. Its fertility, indeed, can hardly be exceeded; all kinds of grain and vegetables are produced in abundance, including rice in the moister parts.[35]

Jesus' Last Sermon at Capernaum (John 6:22–71)

The ministry of Jesus in Capernaum had now reached a great turning point. In the synagogue at Capernaum, Jesus had preached for almost a year and half with the exception of His preaching tours throughout Galilee. We are left with only a few scattered statements from those sermons by Jesus, but those glorious days of the Son of Man were certainly the high-water mark for that town and that whole region. When the nearby towns all gathered together the previous day and were fed by Jesus at Bethsaida-Julias, little did they realize that His ministry among them was winding down. When those crowds came searching for Jesus the next day (after attempting to make Him their King by force the previous day), they did not discern the impending crisis of the moment. They wanted a "sign" that He was the Messiah for whom they had waited. They, therein, revealed that they had no real insight into the events of the previous day—or of the events of the previous eighteen months. They especially did not realize that this would be the last time Jesus would ever preach in Capernaum. How often that is the case. These Galileans who lived along the northside of the lake were like that. They wanted answers, but they did not realize that their demands for such were establishing the great turning point in Jesus' Galilean ministry.

---

34 Ryle, *Expository Thoughts on the Gospels: Matthew*, 169.
35 McClintock and Strong, *Cyclopedia of Biblical, Theological, and Historical Literature*, 3:787.

The narrative of John 6:41–71 does not inform us what conversations were held by the sea shore and what were held in the city and what were held in the synagogue. It seems like a long discussion in one spot, but John 6:59 says: "These things He said in the synagogue as He taught in Capernaum." The discussions began on Friday morning and continued throughout the day until the setting of the sun ushered in the Jewish Sabbath with Jesus teaching and preaching at the synagogue. They began by the seashore and continued in the city and in the synagogue. What John has recorded for us is only a part of the bantering back and forth that must have taken place between the people and Jesus. They wanted to force Jesus by their words to make it clear to everyone that He was the Messiah by performing some sign greater than His feeding of the multitudes. As great as Jesus' miracle was, the Lord had provided manna in the wilderness every day for forty years that fed millions of Israelites. Thus, the doubting crowds were guilty of minimizing the greatness of Jesus' miracle the previous day. If He was really the Messiah, then why was He reluctant to accept the Kingship which they associated with that position, they must have thought. As Alfred Edersheim acknowledges:

> What brought them, was not that they had discerned either the higher meaning of that miracle, or the Son of God, but those carnal Judaistic expectancies which led them to proclaim Him King. What they waited for, was a kingdom of God—not in righteousness, joy, and peace in the Holy Ghost, but in meat and drink—a kingdom with miraculous wilderness-banquets to Israel, and coarse miraculous triumphs over the Gentiles. Not to speak of the fabulous Messianic banquet which a sensuous realism expected, or of the achievements for which it looked, every figure in which prophets had clothed the brightness of those days was first literalised, and then exaggerated, till the most glorious poetic descriptions became the most repulsively incongruous caricatures of the Messianic expectancy. The fruit trees were every day, or at least every week or two, to yield their riches, the fields their harvests (Shabb. 20b; Jer. Shequal. 6.2); the grain was to stand like palm trees, and to be reaped and winnowed without labour (Kethub. 111b). Similar blessings were to visit the vine; ordinary trees would bear like fruit trees, and every produce, or every clime, would be found in Palestine in such abundance and luxuriance as only the wildest imagination could conceive.[36]

In their "incongruous caricatures of the Messianic" kingdom, those unbelieving Jews failed to realize how greatly the Lord had

---

36 Edersheim, *The Life and Times of Jesus the Messiah*, 494.

The Bread of Life

already blessed them by giving them that good land in which they dwelt. They already had the produce and the climate of every part of the globe. The Messianic kingdom would not simply be more of the same, though in greater measure. It would be something entirely different. It would be the spiritual reality of the earthly things they had already experienced. Jesus described it as "the food which endures to eternal life" (John 6:27).

The words of Jesus did not answer the various queries of the Jews to their satisfaction Instead, they began to grumble among themselves because He said, "I am the bread that came down out of heaven" (John 6:41). That claim by Jesus appeared to be nonsense to them, as they stated: "is this not Jesus, the son of Joseph, whose father and mother we know? How does He now say, 'I have come down out of heaven.'" (John 6:42). That was the same type of complaint about Jesus that led the people at Nazareth to reject the One who should have been their favored son (Matthew 13:55; Luke 4:22) and would lead the Jews later to reject Him at the Feast of Tabernacles in Jerusalem (John 7:21ff.). Jesus, thus, traced the problem back to the fact that they had not been drawn by the Father: "No one can come to Me unless the Father who sent Me draws Him; and I will raise Him up on the last day" (John 6:44). They were not taught by the Father (John 6:45) and, therefore, could not discern the spiritual truths He was teaching. William Hendriksen elaborates on this drawing of the Father:

> The drawing of which these passages speak indicates a powerful—we may say, an irresistible—activity. To be sure, man resists, but his resistance is ineffective. It is in that sense that we speak of God's grace as being irresistible.[37]

As Jesus further emphasized the necessity of eating His flesh and drinking His blood, the crowds grew impatient with inner torment. Their response was: "This is a difficult statement; who can listen to it?" (John 6:60). Jesus' words had at least a secondary reference to the great Christian feast of the Lord's Supper as our Lord, the true paschal Lamb, would give His body and blood as an atonement for our sins. True salvation is found through faith in His great work of salvation by eating His flesh and drinking His blood. As a result of these words, many of the larger number of disciples of Jesus withdrew from Him and followed Him no more. In words full of heart-felt

---

37 Hendriksen, *The Gospel of John*, 238.

pathos, Jesus turned to the twelve and asked them, "You do not want to go away also, do you" (John 6:67). Peter, ever the spokesman for the disciples, replied: "Lord, to whom shall we go? You have words of eternal life. We have believed and have come to know that you are the Holy One of God" (John 6:68–9). Peter's words indicate that his understanding of Jesus was on the very cusp of true spiritual insight—but not quite. Peter and the other disciples did not yet understand fully the purpose for which Jesus came. They did not yet realize that His mission necessitated that He would have to be handed over to the Gentiles, suffer, and be crucified, only to rise from the dead on the third day. They would still be slow in assimilating those thoughts into their minds. Yet, they had made their decision and they would remain with Jesus notwithstanding the defections of others.

Jesus did not allow Himself to be flattered by Peter's words, but responded: "Did I Myself not choose you, the twelve, and yet one of you is a devil?" (John 670). Those words pointed to Judas as the one who would betray Jesus. With the falling away of many the fickleness of Judas was manifested more and more. The demonic activity began to work in his heart more and more.

With the conclusion of this discourse, the ministry of Jesus to Capernaum came to a sudden and unexpected ending. Never again would Jesus preach at the synagogue in Capernaum. A more ignoble ending to a gospel ministry there has never been. It reminds us once again that the pupil is not above the teacher. Jesus suffered all the contradiction of sinners against Himself that any of the rest of us can ever endure.

14

Storming the Gates of Hell

Passover in AD 29 began on Monday, April 18th. There is no evidence Jesus went to Jerusalem during the feast, though. Following that great festival, some Pharisees and scribes from Jerusalem returned to Capernaum in late April or early May. Soon they sought to embroil Jesus in a frivolous cavil over the Rabbinical tradition of washing hands before eating. With the growing hostility of the Jewish religious leaders toward Jesus, the Lord had probably decided to not go up to Jerusalem on that occasion. That would have also prevented the Jews from slandering and verbally attacking Him during the feast.[1] Thus, those spiritual abusers returned to Capernaum after the Passover to stir up this controversy with Him since He had not allowed them that opportunity at the feast.

Both Matthew and Mark simply note that the "Pharisees and some of the scribes gathered around [Jesus] when they had come from Jerusalem" (Mark 7:1). This group of Jewish religious leaders had, no doubt, left the Sea of Galilee for Jerusalem in order to attend the feast. The religious leaders of the Jews were intent at this point in finding a reason to entrap Jesus and to be done with Him. He was doing many things that they considered to be contrary to their Rabbinic laws—not observing their weekly fasts, healing on the Sabbath, plucking ears of grain on the Sabbath, eating with publicans and sinners, and many more. Most of all, He simply did not walk according to their traditions. This particular confrontation probably took place in or

---

1 Many scholars believe that Jesus went to the Passover every year of His three and a half year ministry, but there is no clear Scriptural evidence that He went to Passover in either AD 28 or AD 29. There are reasons it would have been unwise for Him to do so in AD 29. For one thing, John the Baptist had just been beheaded by Herod Antipas about a month before the Passover. Then, there was growing hostility towards Him by both the Jewish religious leaders and the political leaders of Israel. If Jesus had gone up to Jerusalem for the Passover in AD 29, the Jews would have tried to have Him crucified that year. But AD 29 was not the right year for His death. Passover was on a Monday. His resurrection would have then been on Wednesday or Thursday of the week. The first day of the week would then not have been the Lord's Day as a result of His resurrection. Nothing would have worked right. AD 30 was the right year in every respect. AD 29 was the wrong time. Jesus' time had not yet come that year. Thus, He probably—almost certainly—avoided that conflict altogether.

near Capernaum shortly after the great defection of many of those who had followed Jesus for a couple of years (cf. John 6:59–71). The date for this conflict, therefore, would have been in the latter part of April, probably within a few days after He preached His last sermon in the synagogue at Capernaum.

Coming to Jesus, they asked a simple question: "Why do Your disciples break the tradition of the elders? For they do not wash their hands when they eat bread" (Matthew 15:2). Those words of confrontation "stand out all the more harshly and provocatively ... [and] seem extraordinarily pedantic in the wake of Jesus' disclosures to the disciples and service to the crowds."[2] Such a question seemed extremely trite, but it was considered a matter of great importance to the Jews. "Although the cavil of the of the Jerusalem Scribes may have been occasioned by seeing some of the disciples eating without first having washed their hands, we cannot banish the impression that it reflected on the miraculously provided meal"[3] when Jesus fed the 5,000. While the Jews asked Jesus for a sign, they rejected his miracles and were constantly trying to prove that He was sinning by doing them or, else, that He accomplished His miracles by the power of Beelzebub. The Pharisees thought they had an irrefutable charge to bring against Jesus concerning their oral tradition which they had elevated to the same level as the Laws of Moses. As Herbert Danby notes:

> The Law (*Torah*) throughout post-biblical Jewish religious literature has the three-fold connotation of (a) the Pentateuch, the "Written Law"; (b) the "traditions of the elders"—rules of Jewish life and religion which in the course of centuries had come to possess a validity and sanctity equal to that of the Written Law and which, as the "Oral Law," were deemed, equally with the Written Law, to be of divine origin and therefore consonant with, and for the most part deducible from the Written Law; and (c) the study of the Law in its twofold aspect, a study which sought to sanction by deeper understanding the seeming violations between Oral and Written Law, to apply the Law to present-day life, and by successive interpretations to solve new problems by the authority of the Law, written and oral.[4]

The Jews of Jesus' days had already begun to develop the theory that the oral law was composed of those commandments of God that

---

[2] Chamblin, *Matthew*, 2:772.
[3] Edersheim. *The Life and Times of Jesus the Messiah*, 480.
[4] Herbert Danby, *The Mishnah. Translated from the Hebrew with Introduction and Brief Explanatory Notes* (London: Oxford University Press, 1964), 446, n. 2.

were not written down by Moses. Yet, that view is specifically in opposition to the plain statements of Scripture that Moses wrote down all the words of the Lord (Exodus 24:4; 34:27: Deuteronomy 31:9). There is not one verse of Scripture that indicates some of the words of the Lord to Moses became oral traditions which had the same binding authority as the written Law. The problem with such oral traditions is that there is no objective way to dispute any claim by the Jews to their traditions. In their commentary on Exodus 24:4, C. F. Keil and F. Delitzsch state:

> It was necessary that the people should not only know what the Lord imposed on them, but that they should also declare their willingness to perform what was imposed upon them. The covenant itself was commenced by Moses writing all the words of Jehovah in *"the book of the covenant"* (vers. 4 and 7), for the purpose of preserving them in an official record.[5]

The problem with the "tradition of the elders" claimed by the scribes and Pharisees is that those alleged words spoken to Moses by Jehovah were no longer simply oral tradition, but had been written down by the Rabbis. That begs the question why Moses did not write them down and include them in the Five Books of Moses also if, indeed, the Lord had spoken them to him? There are passages in Exodus and Deuteronomy that required the washing of hands for the priests and the elders, but the Pharisees made those rules obligatory for all Jews. And the Babylonian Talmud has a benediction which says: "Blessed be Thou, O Lord, King of the Universe, who sanctified us by thy laws and commanded us to wash the hands."[6]

This question by the scribes and Pharisees was an attack on Jesus' teaching and ministry—not the disciples. They were His followers and were doing what He permitted. It was another attempt to find grounds of bringing a charge against Him. Our Lord addressed their question indirectly—not directly. In so doing, He showed that their oral traditions were not Scripture. Jesus appealed to the Ten Commandments—the fifth commandment, "Honor your father and mother" (Exodus 20:12; Deuteronomy 5:16). He also referenced an interpretation of the meaning of the fifth commandment found in Exodus 21:17 and Leviticus 20:9—"He who speaks evil of father or mother is

---

5 C. F. Keil and F. Deilitzsch, *The Pentateuch* (Grand Rapids: Eerdmans Publishing Company, 1975), 2:156.
6 Chamblin, *Matthew*, 2:776.

to be put to death." Jesus did not allow the Jews to entangle Him in a debate over whether the oral "tradition of the elders" was equal with the law. Instead, He proved to them that they were law-breakers, not law-keepers, by their annulment of the fifth commandment through the korban tradition. As Chamblin comments:

> The korban tradition, while ostensibly honoring the first commandment above the fifth, actually fosters human selfishness. 'In the hypothetical situation proposed by Jesus, if the son declared his property *qorban* to his parents, he neither promised it to the Temple nor prohibited its use to himself, but he legally excluded his parents from the right of benefit.' 'Behind the declaration [of 15:5–6a] stands the purpose of retaining one's own use of the item, i.e., of avoiding the obligation to give it to meet the need of someone else, such as a parent.' Thus, this oral tradition 'puts casuistry above love,' love both for God (whose command is being disobeyed) and for some of one's closets neighbors (his or her parents).[7]

Thus, Jesus accuses them of invalidating "the word of God for the sake of your tradition" (Matthew 15:6). That verse effectively dismisses the whole question of whether there is such a thing as oral tradition that is equal to the Law and/or the Scripture.

Cleansing the Heart (Matthew 15:10–20)
In His response to the cavil of the Pharisees, Jesus neither condemned His disciples nor rejected the teaching of the elders. Instead, He showed the inconsistency of the Rabbinical laws with the clear teaching of Scripture. The fifth commandment is permanent and was not devised by men. The issue for the Jews was ritual purity—not personal hygiene. Their rules were first implemented as a way to guarantee that the Jews walked in holiness. They had strict and minutes rules on when and how to wash before eating. A person had to have water poured over both hands up to the wrist. Anything less than that was not acceptable.

After summarily dismissing the frivolous complaint of the Pharisees, Jesus turned to the crowds that gathered around Him, stating, "Hear and understand. It is not what enters into the mouth that defiles the man, but what proceeds out of the mouth, this defiles him" (Matthew 15:10b-11). In that antithetical parallelism, Jesus defined

---

7 Chamblin, *Matthew*, 2:779–780. The two quotes in this quote from Chamblin are identified by him as being from William Lane, *Commentary on the Gospel of Mark* (1974), and Robert H. Gundry, *The Use of the Old Testament in St. Matthew's Gospel* (1967).

true spirituality better than anyone ever had before or since. The Pharisees emphasized outward purity and ritualism. Jesus, as well as the rest of Scripture, emphasized inner purity. The issue for Jesus was neither ritual purity nor physical cleanliness, but moral purity.

Following those words, the disciples came to Jesus with this question, "Do you not know that the Pharisees were offended when they heard this statement?" Their reaction to Jesus' simple statement was a fulfillment of what He said. They were defiled by the thoughts of their hearts and the words expressing those thoughts that proceeded out of their mouths. When John's disciples had come to Him with the query if He was the Messiah, Jesus concluded His answer to them with this statement: "And blessed is he who does not take offense at Me" (Matthew 11:6). It is the same word as in Matthew 15:12. Thus, Jesus replied in an unusual way: "Every plant which My heavenly Father did not plant shall be uprooted" (Matthew 15:13). John Calvin's comments are noteworthy:

> Moreover, because salvation is of God's election alone, it is necessary that the reprobate shall in some way or another perish. For although it is set before all for their salvation, it has this result only in the elect. It is for the faithful and good teacher so to adapt what he puts forward that all may profit from it. But whenever things turn out differently let us be consoled by Christ's reply. The parable expresses beautifully the fact that the cause of destruction does not lie in the doctrine but that when reprobates, without any root in God, are confronted with the doctrine, they vomit out their hidden poison and hasten their death to which they were appointed.[8]

The Father's planting of grace in the hearts of His elect is a comfort—not a terror—to all true believers. None are excluded by His sovereign grace from coming to Christ, if they desire to do so. Rather, God's free grace alone enables anyone to come to Christ. As Isaiah 1:9 says: "Unless the Lord of hosts had left us a few survivors, we would be like Sodom, we would be like Gomorrah." The gospel is a terror to the unbeliever who refuses to believe. It convicts him of his sin and threatens him with eternal damnation. Jesus' reply is consistent with what Paul wrote in 2 Corinthians 2:15, 16— "For we are a fragrance of Christ to God among those who are being saved and among those who are perishing. To the one an aroma from death to death, to the other an aroma from life to life. And who is adequate for these

---

8 Calvin, *A Harmony of the Gospels Matthew, Mark and Luke*, 2:163.

things?" Jesus' disciples were, no doubt, perplexed by the offense of the Pharisees, even though they had observed that same offense from them on other occasions. At this point in their training, the disciples did not yet understand that the same message of the gospel both heals and kills, it gives eternal life and brings eternal destruction. Thus, Jesus gave them a command in a few words: "Let them alone" (Matthew 15:14). The reason Jesus told His disciples to leave the Pharisees alone is because, as He said, "they are blind guides of the blind" (Matthew 15:14). Once again, Calvin's comments are helpful:

> This is the basis for the common distinction in the avoidance of offences, that we should take care not to give offence but that if anyone takes offence out of obstinacy and malignity there is no help for it . . . Therefore it is important to make a distinction between the weak who take offence out of ignorance and soon return to their senses and the proud and hypocritical who voluntarily seize on offences. Let the wicked obstinately seize on offences, but let us go on quietly in the midst of offences.[9]

There is a difference between an offense given and an offense wrongly taken. The first is based on something wrong that we did. The second arises from the malignancy and obstinacy of an unregenerate heart. Also, there are some who take momentary offense because they are weak in their understanding and others take offense because their hearts are hardened. Thus, Jesus' words of advice to His disciples were timely and necessary. The gospel must not be compromised by placating the obstinacy of the enemies of Christ.

At that point, Peter spoke for the disciples and asked Jesus to explain the parable to them. Jesus' reply cannot be understood correctly without bearing in mind the distinction He was making between moral purity on the one hand and ceremonial or hygienic purity on the other. It is certainly true that unwashed hands may indeed cause problems for a person and defile his stomach. Good hand washing before eating is not dismissed by Jesus. There are many illnesses that can be acquired through contaminated hands or foods. Rather, He dismisses the idea that the washing of the hands before eating is the great problem facing mankind. A person can be very punctilious about hand washing while neglecting the heart. The matter of the heart is the heart of the matter, according to Jesus.

---

9 Calvin, *A Harmony of the Gospels Matthew, Mark and Luke*, 2:164.

Jesus identified those things that defile a man as "evil thoughts, murders, adulteries, fornications, thefts, false witnesses, slanders" (Matthew 15:19) and many such similar things. The Gospel of Mark states parenthetically concerning those words of Jesus: "Thus He declared all foods clean" (Mark 7:19). It is interesting that when the Lord wanted Peter to preach the gospel to the Gentiles in Caesarea, He showed him a sheet full of unclean animals and said to him, "Get up Peter, kill and eat!" (Acts 10:13). When Peter refused to eat the unclean animals, the Lord said to him, "What God has cleansed no longer consider unholy" (Acts 10:15). Jesus was teaching His disciples that the cleansing of the heart by grace is more important than the washing of the hands. The latter does not affect the heart.

After the dispute with the Pharisees over the washing of hands, Jesus and His disciples left Galilee and retired to distinctly Gentile territory—Tyre and Sidon. Those cities were outside of Israel along the Mediterranean Sea and represent the only occasion when Jesus traveled outside the boundaries of ancient Israel. Mark simply records, "Jesus got up and went away from there to the region of Tyre" (Mark 7:24). The particular route He and His disciples took cannot be known inasmuch as there was no direct route. It is likely that they traveled west to the Mediterranean Sea and then north to Tyre by the road known as the Via Maris—'the way of the sea.' There are several things that stand out about this trip, as Knox Chamblin's comments on Matthew 15:21 inform us:

> This verse marks a threefold shift. *Socially*, Jesus moves from the company of Jews (15:1–20) into encounters with Gentiles—first an individual (15:21–28), then a crowd (15:29–39). *Geographically*, he leaves 'there,' where Pharisees and scribes met him (15:1; probably in or around Capernaum), travels to the northwest, and enters the vicinity . . . of coastal towns identified in 11:21–22 as pagan. *Theologically*, the teachings in previous verses about clean and unclean foods are now superbly applied to relations between Jews and Gentiles—even though the apparent reason for Jesus' withdrawal . . . is not to serve Gentiles but to seek privacy.[10]

The Pharisees were even more zealous about not associating with the Gentiles than they were about washing their hands before eating. There can be little doubt that Jesus retired to the coastal area where paganism predominated in part because He wanted to illustrate a les-

---
10 Chamblin, *Matthew*, 2:792.

son to the disciples. Jesus was also consciously making an attempt not to provoke the rulers of Israel. It was a practice He has had throughout His ministry. His actions were not cowardice, but prudence. He knew there was an appointed hour for His death. And He knew that Satan was always attempting to provoke the rulers and the crowds before that hour arrived. Thus, He went to a city which represented the worst of heathen religious practices. As 1 John 3:8 says: "The Son of God appeared for this purpose, to destroy the works of the devil" (1 John 3:8b). Robert Candlish made the following comment on that verse:

> It was a great blow to the works of the devil; it cut up by the roots the very pith and staple of his power to work at all; when the Son of God was thus manifested; when it was made patent to all the universe that it was no degradation or bondage for the Son himself to be the servant of the Father; when it was seen that his being so was not incompatible with sonship, but was in fact its very perfection.[11]

Tyre, which means "rock," was both along the coast of Syro-Phoenicia and on the rocky island stronghold a few miles out in the Mediterranean Sea. It was famous in the days of David and Solomon for timber and skilled artisans. David formed an alliance with the King of Tyre, Hiram, to exchange grain for timber. Yet, Tyre was a heathen city and had contributed to the introduction of Baal worship in Israel. The imagination of the devil as a red being with a pitchfork comes from the depictions of Baal by the Phoenicians. He was, supposedly, the god of the weather, fertility, and life, but immorality became the norm for those who worshiped him. Jesus' retirement to this area, with His disciples, should be considered as Him storming the gates of hell.

Jesus came to seek and to save the lost and none were so lost as these heathens in Tyre and Sidon. Psalm 87 speaks of the citizens of Zion, God's holy mountain, and mentions that people from Tyre would be among those who know the Lord. Jesus' visit to this area was the first fruits of the blessings of the gospel in that region.

When Jesus and His disciples reached their destination, He entered a house and "wanted no one to know of it, yet He could not escape notice" (Mark 7:24). There were many in that region who

---

11 Robert S. Candlish, *A Commentary on 1 John* (London and Carlisle, Pennsylvania: The Banner of Truth Trust, 1973), 1:334.

had heard of Jesus and the mighty miracles He performed. One unnamed woman from Syro-Phoenicia, in particular, was encouraged enough to earnestly seek the Savior's help for her daughter who was demon-possessed, a monstrous situation that was especially prevalent in that region during those days. Coming to the house where Jesus was staying, she overcame all the obstacles to her faith—she was a Greek, a woman, and she lived in a pagan area. Yet, she kept petitioning Jesus: "Have mercy on me, Lord, Son of David; my daughter is cruelly demon-possessed" (Matthew 15:22). While Jesus answered her not a word at first, His disciples were cold and heartless towards her. They implored the Lord: "Send her away because she keeps shouting at us" (Matthew 15:23). The disciples considered her a nuisance and thought they were protecting the privacy of Jesus and His desire for rest. Too often, the followers of Christ are less compassionate than their Savior, as Ryle stated:

> The woman about whom we are reading found small favour with our Lord's disciples . . . Peter, and James, and John may say to the afflicted soul, "Send her away;" but such a word never came from the lips of Christ. He may sometimes keep us long waiting as He did this woman; but He will never send us empty away.[12]

The widow of Zarephath in this same area had once appealed similarly to Elijah and was likewise rewarded (1 Kings 17:17–24) when the prophet raised her son from the dead. This woman in the Gospels is called a Syro-Phoenician by Mark and a Canaanite woman by Matthew. She was both. She was a Canaanite living within the bounds of Syro-Phoenicia. The Canaanites lived within the land of Israel and had been the mortal enemies of the Jews for centuries. As a Canaanite, she probably understood something of the Scripture promises and was, thus, encouraged to present her case to the Lord. He did not disappoint her, even though neither did He immediately answer her.

When she prayed, "Have mercy on me, O Lord, Son of David . . . ," Jesus seemed indifferent to her at first. Then, He answered her after the complaint of the disciples: "I was sent only to the lost sheep of the house of Israel" (Matthew 15:24). Jesus' apparent disinterest in her prayer is in stark contrast to the Scriptural picture of Him as the "Good Shepherd" (John 10) who seeks for the lost sheep. In His commission to both the Twelve disciples and the Seventy, He had com-

---

12 Ryle, *Expository Thoughts on the Gospels: St. Matthew*, 181.

manded them to not go to the Gentile areas of Galilee. "Do not go in the way of the Gentiles, and do not go in any city of the Samaritans, but rather go to the lost sheep of the house of Israel" (Matthew 10:5, 6). Thus, Jesus' words were in harmony with what He had previously told His disciples to do which kind of exonerates them from blame. Jesus' words seemed to be saying that the doors of the gospel were not yet open to the Gentiles. Yet, He was in that pagan city and this Gentile woman needed help.

Despite the seemingly unfavorable response of Jesus to her petition, the woman was not to be put off. She came and bowed down before Jesus, imploring Him, "Lord, help me!" (Matthew 15:25). Calvin elucidates the response of the woman:

> The woman looks as if she is wrestling with a sort of obstinacy in Christ and trying to wring something out of Him unwillingly. But there is no doubt that what inspired her was the faith she had conceived in the goodness of the Messiah. When Christ directly denies that this is His office, the repulse does not frighten her or turn from her purpose. And this is because, as I said, her original feeling of faith was deeply fixed in her and rejected everything contrary to her hope. And this is the true proof of faith, when we do not permit the general principle of our salvation, which is founded in the Word of God, to be shaken away from us in any way.[13]

Even this fervent petition by the woman did not seem to open wide heart of Jesus towards her. But He was testing her faith to the fullest before He would bless her. Jesus' response was: "Let the children be satisfied first, for it is not good to take the children's bread and throw it to the dogs" (Mark 7:27). Many people would have been so offended that they would have walked away in disgust at such an answer. This woman, despite all the obstacles in her path, continued to press her request, as Chamblin notes:

> While the language is not complimentary (Gentiles, human beings made in God's image, are termed 'dogs'), it is not so disparaging as it might be. The statement itself is proverbial: Jesus does not directly call the woman herself a dog. Moreover, he speaks not of 'street-roaming scavengers' but of 'household pets,' as is evident from his use of the diminutive kynaria . . . and from the woman's words in 15:27.[14]

The woman quickly replied, "Yes, Lord, but even the dogs under

---
13 Calvin, *A Harmony of the Gospels Matthew, Mark and Luke*, 2:169.
14 Chamblin, *Matthew*, 2:795.

the table feed on the children's crumbs" (Mark 7:28). Jesus' granting of her petition was even quicker. He said, "O woman, your faith is great; it shall be done as you wish" (Matthew 15:28) and, "Because of this answer go; the demon has gone out of your daughter" (Mark 7:29). J. A. Alexander notes the wisdom of Christ' dealings with this woman:

> His discouraging reception of her prayer at first had served both to strengthen and illustrate, and was therefore no more unkind than the similar processes continually going on in true believers, though of course unknown to the experience of those skeptical interpreters, who either sneer at this as cruel treatment, or assume a real change or purpose wrought in Christ by her persistent importunity.[15]

Jesus' Ministry in Decapolis (Matthew 15:29–39 and Mark 7:31–8:13)

Following His brief stay in Tyre where He found no rest, Jesus and His disciples traveled twenty miles north to Sidon along the Via Maris before returning to the region of the Sea of Galilee. The route they took from Sidon (Mark 7:31) was circuitous because of the mountains between Sidon and Decapolis, on the eastern side of the Jordan River, which was His destination. Swete describes for us the probable route Jesus and His disciples took:

> From Sidon and the Mediterranean coast, He returned to . . . the Sea of Galilee. But to its eastern shore . . . A road led from Sidon across the hills . . .; it crossed the Leontes near the modern Belfort, and climbing the ranges of the Lebanon, passed through the tetrarchy of Abilene, and eventually reached Damascus. The Lord probably left it where it skirted Hermon, and striking south kept on the east bank of the Jordan till He reached the Lake.. . The long *detour* may have served the double purpose of defeating the immediate designs of His enemies and providing "for the Apostles the rest which He had desired to give them before."[16]

The tetrarch of Abilene was Lysanias (Luke 3:1), a relative of Zenodorus[17], who had probably reigned as tetrarch for 47 years or more by this time. Abilene provided the only east-west passage through the mountains of Lebanon and was well-traveled. Yet, its territory was almost indefensible from invaders who were attracted to that

---

15 Alexander, *The Gospel According to Mark*, 199–200.
16 Swete, *Commentary on Mark*, 159. Swete's quote within the quote is taken from Henry Latham, *Pastor Pastorum*, p. 333.
17 Zenodorus was the son of the first Lysanias who was killed by Mark Antony in 36 BC and had been tetrarch of Abilene. The exact date when the Lysanias mentioned in the Gospel of Luke becamse tetrarch of the same territory cannot be known for certain.

enchanted and beautiful land. The Leontes River flowed through a deep chasm between the mountains of Lebanon which ran southwesterly for 110 miles before sinking into the hills of Galilee. Jesus and His disciples would have followed that river through the mountains to the great road that led to Caesarea-Philippi at the southern base of Mount Hermon (9,232 feet above sea level) where they continued their descent towards Galilee along the eastern side of the Jordan River. In this way, they avoided direct contact with Herod Antipas, the Pharisees, and the people of Capernaum—which city had probably become unsafe after Jesus' last sermon in that synagogue.

When Jesus returned to the Sea of Galilee, He went to distinctly Gentile territory in Decapolis. Those ten cities called Decapolis "resembled each other in being inhabited mostly by Gentiles, and in their civic institutions and privileges."[18] Jesus' exact location for this part of His ministry is unknown inasmuch as the territory encompassing those ten cities was about 60 miles wide and 200 miles from north to south. What is known is that He moved from one pagan and Gentile stronghold to another—from Tyre to Decapolis. Most of that region had once been a part of the tribe of Manasseh (one of the two sons of Joseph) and there were still many Jews who lived in that area, but things had changed dramatically in one of the Jewish wars. "Immediately after the conquest of Syria by the Romans (B.C. 65), ten cities appear to have been rebuilt, partly colonized, and endowed with peculiar privileges."[19] Roman culture with all its privileges and vices, its learning and paganism, was transported into this region. Most of the great palaces and Roman architecture of those cities have now been lost except for the magnificent ruins that have been unearthed by archaeologists. Roman rule had allowed the citizens of those cities to worship the Greek and Roman gods and goddesses and no longer chafe under the efforts of the Jews to convert them. Yet, Jesus' visit to this area was the beginning of a spiritual transformation.

The first thing Jesus did in Decapolis was to heal a deaf man who "spoke with great difficulty" (Mark 7:32). He did so by taking the man "aside from the crowd, by himself, and put His fingers into his ears, and after spitting, He touched his tongue with the saliva" (Mark 7:33). After He said, "Ephphatha!" the man's ears were un-

---

18 McClintock and Strong, *Cyclopedia of Biblical, Theological, and Ecclesiastical Literature*, 2:721.
19 McClintock and Strong, *Cyclopedia of Biblical, Theological, and Ecclesiastical Literature*, 2:721.

stopped and his tongue was loosened. Jesus' manner of healing this man was, no doubt, to defeat the idea that He had to perform certain external actions in the same way in order to heal. Yet, sometimes He merely spoke the word. Other times, he laid His hands on people. On this occasion He used His own spit as a medium for the healing. The power was in His Person—not in His actions. There were other sick and diseased people who were also brought to Jesus in Decapolis. He healed them all—the lame, the crippled, the blind, the mute, and many others (Matthew 15:30). The crowd was amazed by such a display of Jesus' mighty power and "glorified the God of Israel" (Matthew 15:31).[20] Jesus instructed them not to tell anyone what He had done for the man or the others, "but the more He ordered them, the more widely they continued to proclaim it" (Mark 7:36). It might seem strange that Jesus would give such an order. Yet, His life was in danger and His time had not yet arrived. "If He safeguarded it, the motive was that it might be freely given in due time (Jo. X. 11, 15, 18). It was saved for the Cross."[21]

Jesus' ministry on the mountainside continued for three days in which the Scripture only records that He performed healings. Then, came the day when He revealed to His disciples the "compassion" He had for the people who had remained with Him for three days. While there are some general similarities between the feeding of the 4,000 with the earlier feeding of the 5,000, there are more differences. The 5,000 were Jews—the 4,000 were Gentiles. Jesus had earlier displayed His compassion[22] for the lost sheep of Israel, but now Gentiles are the objects of it. In the earlier miracle, the disciples had come to Jesus with concerns for the people. In this miracle, Jesus calls His disciples to come to Him and tells them, "I do not want to send them away hungry, for they might faint on the way" (Matthew 15:32). The phrase, "send them away," is striking because it is the very words the disciples had used concerning the Syro-Phoenician woman. They had said to Jesus, "Send her away, because she is

---

20 The phrase, "the God of Israel", is a clear indication that the people who were being healed were Gentiles. Formerly, they had been prejudiced against the God of Israel, but now they praised Him.
21 Swete, *Commentary on Mark*, 155.
22 These are the only two instances in which Jesus is identified as having compassion on people. That does not mean He did not have compassion on other occasions, though. In both instances, the final result was that He fed large crowds with a few loaves of bread and a few fish. Cf. Knox Chamblin, *Matthew*, 2:799.

shouting at us" (Matthew 15:23). In this way, Jesus was teaching the disciples to have compassion on the lost people of every nation. In both instances, only the men—not the women and children—are included in the numbers given. So, there were much more than 4–5,000 people who were fed on each occasion. Also, in both instances, the people were asked to sit down on the grass or the ground before they were fed.[23]

Having witnessed all His miracles and the feeding of the 5,000, the disciples were still perplexed by this dilemma. They seemed to have forgotten how Jesus provided food on the earlier occasion. Thus, they query Jesus: "Where would we get so many loaves in this desert place to satisfy such a large crowd?" (Matthew 15:33). This miraculous feeding was an indication that His ministry in Decapolis was about to close, as Edersheim notes:

> And here it is remarkable, that each time His prolonged stay and Ministry in a district were brought to a close with some supper, so to speak, some festive entertainment on his part. The Galilean Ministry had closed with the feeding of the five thousand, the guests being mostly from Capernaum and the towns around, as far as Bethsaida (Julias), many in the number probably were on their way to the Paschal feast at Jerusalem. But now at the second provision for the four thousand, with which His Decapolis Ministry closed, the guests not strictly Jews, but semi-Gentile inhabitants of that district and neighborhood. Lastly, His Judean Ministry closed with the Last Supper ... Thus these three suppers seem connected, each leading, as it were, to the other.[24]

In each feeding of the multitudes, both bread and fish were distributed, as those were the staples of their diet. The miraculous increase of the food stopped only when everyone had been served. In both instances, there were a number of baskets filled with the left overs even though there had been only a few fish and a few loaves of bread that were distributed. And at the end of each feeding, Jesus and the disciples left that area to travel elsewhere. In this case, both Jesus and His disciples got into a boat and traveled to Magadan,

---

23 The feeding of the 5,000 took place shortly before the Passover in 29 AD which was on April 18th that year. That means that the feeding of the 4,000 probably took place not earlier than late May or even later in the year. Whereas, the Jews sat "down on the green grass" (Mark 6:39) in the feeding of the 5,000, the Gentiles sat "down on the ground" (Mark 8:6)—or the 'dirt'—which indicates that the heat of summer had burned up the green grass.
24 Edersheim, *The Life and Times of Jesus the Messiah*, 517.

or the region of Dalmanutha. Jesus leaving the people after feeding them was not a cessation of His grace to them, but a prelude to what awaits those who believe in Him and who will be invited to the marriage feast of the Lamb and the bride (Revelation 19:7–10).

Beware of the Leaven of the Pharisees (Matthew 16:1–12 and Mark 8:11–26)

Once the people in Decapolis were well-nourished, Jesus sent them to their homes. Then, He and His disciples got into a boat and traveled to the other side of the Sea of Galilee to the "district of Dalmanutha" (Mark 8:10) or the "region of Magadan"[25] (Matthew 15:39). "There is some evidence to support the belief that Dalmanutha was located south of the Plain of Gennesaret, on the southwestern side of the Sea of Galilee. In this vicinity a cave was found bearing the name 'Talmanutha.'"[26] There is "a site . . . near the junction of Yarmuk[27] with the Jordan, some five miles S[outh] of the Lake."[28] That region was still in Decapolis which provided Jesus and His disciples some protection from the tyranny of Herod Antipas and the religious sects of the Jews. Galilee was not a safe place[29] for Jesus at this time and would grow increasingly hostile to Him.

When Jesus arrived at Dalmanutha, some of the Pharisees and Sadducees[30] came to where He was "and began to argue with Him, seeking from Him a sign from heaven, to test Him" (Mark 8:11). It was the same request for a sign which they had demanded on an earlier occasion: "Teacher, we want to see a sign from You" (Matthew 12:38). These Pharisees and Sadducees were not denying the miracles Jesus was performing, but, instead, they were insinuating that such works were not sufficient. The scribes and Pharisees had seen Him heal and perform many miracles, but they attributed those powers to Beelze-

---

25 Edersheim, *The Life and Times of Jesus the Messiah*, 520. "Accordingly, we would seek Magadan south of the Lake of Tiberias, and near the borders of Galilee, but within Decapolis."
26 William Hendriksen, *The Gospel of Mark* (Edinburgh: The Banner of Truth Trust, 1976), 313.
27 The Yarmuk (Yarmouk) River is a tributary that feeds into the Jordan downstream from the Sea of Galilee. It begins in the high eastern plains of Jordan (Huran Plateau) and is fed by the wadis of Allan, Ruqqad, Ehreir, and Zeizun. The Jordan flows south from the base of Mount Hermon, whereas the Yarmuk flows southwesterly.
28 Swete, *Commentary on Mark*, 167.
29 There are many scholars who place Magadan and Dalmanutha in the area of Magdala, between Tiberias and Capernaum, but that would have placed Jesus in the jurisdiction of Herod at a time when that despot was eagerly seeking to see Him following the execution of John. Jesus typically avoided hostility which is an argument against that being a site where He purposely retired.
30 The Sadducees were primarily composed of priests and aristocrats and resided in and around Jerusalem.

bub—not Jehovah (cf. Luke 11:14–23). The presence of the Sadducees with the Pharisees "on this occasion indicates the extent to which the hostility of the latter was now carried."[31] These two sects seldom worked in tandem on any matter, but the Pharisees at this point realized that they would need the Sadducees in order to make their case against Jesus that He was a false prophet (Deuteronomy 13:1–5). Their plan was simple. They wanted to entrap Jesus and, thereby, to prove that He was not the Messiah. They wanted to "test" Him by any means possible and accuse Him of false signs. The verb for "test" is peirazo, which was last used in Matthew's Gospel concerning the temptations of Jesus. Chamblin astutely remarks: "here, as there, the intent is diabolical."[32] Their arguments against Jesus were both cunning and sinister. Jesus was well aware of the thoughts and intents of their hearts. Henry Barclay Swete rightly describes their arguments:

> The demand was for a [sign] of a higher order than the miracles—a visible or audible interposition of God . . . The manna is cited in [John 6:30ff.] as such a sign; the Bath Qol[33] might have been regarded as another. Such wonders had more than once signalized the ministry of Elijah (1 Kings xviii. 38, 2 Kings i.10ff.). The more fruitful but more human and less startling miracles of the Gospel appealed less forcibly to a generation which was possessed by a passion for display.[34]

Jesus, for His part, never allowed Himself to be entrapped by the devious plans of those who would soon prove to be His mortal enemies. He ignored their demands for signs of a sufficient order to compel their faith in Him. Rather, He knew their problem was much deeper than signs of any order. Thus, He immediately countered their arguments with this statement: "When it is evening, you say, '*It will be* fair weather, for the sky is red.' And in the morning, '*There will be* a storm today, for the sky is red and threatening.' Do you know how to discern the appearance of the sky, but cannot discern the signs of the times?" (Matthew 16:2, 3). Then, He concluded: "An evil and adulterous generation seeks after a sign; and a sign will not be given it, except the sign of Jonah" (Matthew 16:4). Jesus' response has been made into an oft-repeated poetic proverb: "Red sky at night, sailors' delight. Red sky at morning, sailors take warning." In His remarks,

---

31 Swete, *Commentary on Mark*, 167.
32 Chamblin, *Matthew*, 2: 805.
33 A 'Bath Qol' is an audible divine voice apart from any visible divine manifestation, such as the Lord's thundering at Mount Sinai and later His voice on the Mount of Transfiguration.
34 Swete, *Commentary on Mark*, 167–8.

Jesus visibly displayed the true meaning of Proverbs 26:4, 5. He did not answer the Pharisees and Sadducees according to their folly, but He did expose their folly.[35] Apparently, Jesus did not wait for them to reply, but "left them and went away" (Matthew 16:4). Wisdom is the better part of valor and withdrawing from these schemers was the wisest course of action Jesus could have taken. As Knox Chamblin notes:

> While the disciples are blind to the truth about Jesus, these two groups deliberately seek to impede and suppress that truth. So strong is their combined influence, and so insidious are their methods, that Jesus knows they pose grave danger even to his closest followers—especially given the disciples' present state of mind.[36]

Jesus never took His eyes off two targets of great importance. First, He knew when was the right time—the appointed hour—for His atoning death, so He protected His life against any attempts to kill Him before that hour. Second, He always watched over His disciples with a holy jealousy. Thus, leaving those two groups of accusers, "he again embarked and went away to the other side" (Mark 8:13). He had spent only a short while, perhaps only a matter of a few hours, at Dalmanutha before He realized that He and His disciples were not safe there. They traveled northeasterly[37] by boat back to where their trip had begun, probably very near to Bethsaida Julias. Their departure was so hasty that the disciples, no doubt, mistakenly left their bread behind—those seven large baskets of fragments they had gathered following the feeding of the 4,000. When they got to the other side, Jesus warned them: "Watch out and beware of the leaven of the Pharisees and Sadducees" (Matthew 16:6).[38]

The disciples immediately thought that Jesus' warning was because they had forgotten the baskets of bread: "*He said that* because we did not bring any bread" (Matthew 16:7). Jesus was compelled to chide them for the smallness of their faith: "You men of little faith. Why do you discuss among yourselves that you have no bread?" (Matthew 16:8). And, after reminding them of the two miracles of feeding multitudes, He asked them: "How is it that you do not understand

---

35 Chamblin, *Matthew*, 2:806.
36 Chamblin, *Matthew*, 2:804.
37 Chamblin, *Matthew*, 2:807.
38 Mark 8:15 warns them: "Beware of the leaven of the Pharisees and the leaven of Herod." These accounts are supplementary—not contradictory.

that I did not speak to you concerning bread? But beware of the leaven of the Pharisees and Sadducees" (Matthew 16:11). "Then, they understood that he did not say to beware of the leaven of bread, but of the teaching of the Pharisees and Sadducees" (Matthew 16:12). As Calvin comments on this verse:

> It is quite clear that Christ was setting the word 'leaven' in opposition to the simple and pure Word of God. Earlier Christ had used the word in a good sense saying that the Gospel was like leaven; but generally Scripture indicates by this word a foreign element which infects the native purity of something . . . From this it follows that it is anything mixed in from outside that is called leaven; just as Paul tells us that faith is adulterated as soon as we are led away from the simplicity of Christ (II Cor..3).[39]

When they arrived at Bethsaida, a blind man who was brought to Jesus and the people were imploring Him to heal his blindness (Mark 8:22). Once again, Jesus showed the variety of ways at His disposal to heal people. He was not stuck to a set regimen that had to be closely followed. In this instance, He took the man outside the town; spat on his eyes; laid His hands on him; and asked, "Do you see anything?" (Mark 8:23). The man replied: "I see men, for I see them like trees, walking around" (Mark 8:24). Jesus again laid His hands on the man and "he looked intently and was restored, and began to see everything clearly" (Mark 8:25). Once he could see, Jesus immediately sent him back to his house with the admonition, "Do not even enter into the village" (Mark 8:26). Jesus healed this man's blindness in two stages, most likely, as an illustration of how the Spirit of God affects conversion in our souls, as Ryle submits to us:

> We are all naturally blind and ignorant in matters which concern our souls. Conversion is an illumination, a change from darkness to light, from blindness to seeing the kingdom of God. Yet few converted people see things distinctly at first. The nature and proportion of doctrines, practices, and ordinances of the Gospel are dimly seen by them, and imperfectly understood. They are like the man before us, who at first saw men as trees walking. Their vision is dazzled and unaccustomed to the new world into which they have been introduced. It is not till the work of the Spirit has become deeper, and their experience been somewhat matured, that they see all things clearly, and give to each part of religion its proper place.[40]

---

39 Calvin, *A Harmony of the Gospels Matthew, Mark and Luke*, 2:181.
40 Ryle, *Expository Thoughts on the Gospels: Mark*, 162.

Perhaps Jesus healed this man of his blindness in two stages as an object lesson for His disciples who had been so slow to see clearly the dangers of the Pharisees and Sadducees. They saw the Pharisees and Sadducees as men walking like trees, but could not discern the specific dangers of their teaching. With this healing of the blind man, the truth dawned on them a little more and would do so to an even greater degree over this final year of Jesus' life on earth.

15

Jesus' Transfiguration

After sending the blind man He had healed to his home, Jesus left Decapolis and took His disciples into the region of Caesarea Philippi which was about thirty miles north of the Sea of Galilee. There was an ancient Roman road between Bethsaida Julias and Caesarea Philippi that skirted Lake Merom (or, Lake Huleh) on the eastern side and traversed through the undulating plains between the mountain ranges on both sides. The hills rise to the north and the Sea of Galilee recedes to the south as the traveler gradually ascends higher on the journey to Caesarea Philippi. Edersheim describes what the two-day journey for Jesus and His disciples would have been like:

> As we climb the steep hill above the marshes of Merom, we have before us one of the richest plains of about two thousand acres. We next pass through olive-groves and up a gentle slope. On a knoll before us, at the foot of which gushes a copious spring, lies the ancient Kedesh.
>
> The scenery is very similar, as we travel on towards Caesarea Philippi . . . We are now amidst vines and mulberry trees. Passing through a narrow rich valley, we ascend through a rocky wilderness of hills, where the woodbine luxuriantly trails around the plane-trees. On the height there is a glorious view back to Lake Merom and the Jordan-valley; forward, to the snowy peaks of Hermon; east, to height on height, and west, to peaks now only crowned with ruins . . . Another hour, and we are in a plain where all the springs of the Jordan unite. The view from here is splendid, and the soil most rich, the wheat crops being ripe in the beginning of May. Half an hour more, and we cross a bridge over the bright blue waters of the Jordan . . . which, under a very wilderness of oleanders, honeysuckle, clematis, and wild rose, rush among huge boulders, between walls of basalt . . . Dan lies on a hill above the plain . . . And from Dan olive-groves and oak-glades slope up to Banias, or Caesarea Philippi.[1]

Caesarea Philippi was enlarged and beautified by Herod Philip, who was tetrarch of Trachonitis, in honor of Caesar Augustus. The town was a very fertile and attractive spot because of the underground spring which gushed forth from a cave at the foot of Mount Hermon.

---

1 Edersheim, *The Life and Times of Jesus the Messiah*, 523–4.

That spring, known as Wadi Baneas (or Paneas in Greek) was also the main headwater of the Jordan River. Once He and His disciples arrived in that region, Jesus immediately resorted to prayer (cf. Luke 9:18) against the backdrop of one of the most picturesque spots in ancient Israel. His disciples were close by but did not join Him in this prayer.

The Greek god, Pan, was the half-man, half-goat god of fright or panic who was often depicted playing a flute. There was an open-air sanctuary built to Pan by the Greeks next to the source of water and sacrifices were offered to him in the cave from the third century BC onwards. When the city was given to Herod the Great by Caesar Augustus in 20 BC, he erected a marble temple for Pan worship and dedicated it to the Roman Emperor. Craig Keener rightfully notes that Caesarea Philippi "was as pagan a territory as one could find."[2] Pan was the god of nature and Caesar was the self-proclaimed deity of mankind. The region of Caesarea Philippi, therefore, was the commingling of Judaism and heathenism with the Gentiles outnumbering the Jews. It was the right spot for Jesus to ask His disciples the question: "Who do people say that the Son of Man is?" (Matthew 16:13b). As Plummer notes:

> Thus, just where Judaism touched both the worship of nature and the worship of man, Jesus called upon His disciples to answer for mankind and for themselves as to what His claims upon the conscience were as against the claims of these conflicting worships.[3]

The worship of Pan was the worship of demons, as Paul wrote in 1 Corinthians 10:20: "the things which the Gentiles sacrifice, they sacrifice to demons and not to God." Immoralities were often committed in the worship of these false gods. Nowhere was it truer than at Caesarea Philippi. The Grotto of Pan was considered the gateway to the underworld (Hades) where the fertility gods took residence during the winter months. Worshipers committed their detestable acts at the nearby pagan temple. The scenery around Caesarea Philippi is among the most beautiful that can be found. It is situated on a terrace 1,150 feet above the well-watered and lush valley below. The contrast between light and darkness is not always obvious or easy to

---

2 Craig S. Keener, *A Commentary on the Gospel of Matthew* (Grand Rapids: Eerdmans Publishing Company, 1999), 424.
3 Alfred Plummer, *An Exegetical Commentary on the Gospel According to S. Matthew* (London: James Clarke & Co., LTD., n.d.), 224.

determine because Satan disguises himself as an angel of light. Jesus had to resist the temptation of the devil who "took Him to a very high mountain and showed him all the kingdoms of the world and their glory" (Matthew 4:8). Caesarea Philippi was such a glorious spot even though it was very paganistic. Archeologists have discovered the remains of fourteen temples to Baal worship in this region. Before Pan was worshiped there, it had been a shrine to Baal worship. Centuries earlier, Joshua had conquered all the land of northern Palestine "from Mount Halak, that rises toward Seir, even as far as Baal-Gad in the valley of Lebanon at the foot of Mount Hermon" (Joshua 11:17; Cf. also Joshua 12:7; 13:5; Judges 3:3; and, 1 Chronicles 5:23). Baal worship predated Joshua at this place. Baal-Gad means "the god of luck" or "the god of fortune." It is a denial of the sovereignty of God to believe that life's events are the result of fortune, whether good or bad. This worship of nature and good fortune had been a thorn in Israel's side for centuries. There was no better place for Jesus to challenge His disciples about His deity and His mission than at Caesarea Philippi. Elijah had challenged Israel on Mount Carmel: "If the Lord is God, follow Him; but if Baal follow him" (1 Kings 18:21b). Now, the One greater than Elijah makes the same type of challenge to His disciples.

Peter's Confession of Christ (Matthew 16:13–20; Mark 8:27–30; and, Luke 9:18–20)

So, the disciples answered Jesus' question: "Some say John the Baptist, and others, Elijah; but still others, Jeremiah, or one of the prophets" (Matthew 16:14). Herod Antipas, with a guilt laden conscious for his treachery against John, had already declared that Jesus was John the Baptist risen from the dead. The connection of Jesus with Elijah, inasmuch as both worked miracles, made sense to some people—especially since John did not work miracles. Both Mark and Luke have the disciples refer to the prophets in general, but only Matthew speaks about Jeremiah. The connection between Jeremiah and Jesus is brought out well by Chamblin:

> It is easy to see why the two were associated: both employed verbal and visible parables; both exposed Israel's manifold sin, spoke against the temple, and warned of imminent judgment; both suffered greatly on that account, especially at the hands of the nation's leaders; and both promised saving grace from Israel's covenant-keeping God.[4]

---

4 Chamblin, *Matthew*, 2:815.

None of those answers was what Jesus wanted from His disciples. Thus, He asked them once more: "But who do you say that I am?" (Matthew 16:15). Simon Peter immediately responded: "You are the Christ, the Son of the Living God" (Matthew 16:16). That confession was another step beyond what Peter had stated in John 6:69—"We have believed and have come to know that You are the Holy One of God." This is the first time in the Gospels that "a figure in the story directly affirms the Messiahship of Jesus."[5] Peter goes beyond just affirming that Jesus is the Christ. He also says that He is "the Son of the Living God." "Moreover the Greek construction at the close of 16:16 . . . expresses Peter's conviction that the Father of Jesus is the true and living God, language that has special poignancy in a place devoted to the worship of Pan."[6]

Jesus commends Peter's great confession as follows: "Blessed are you, Simon Barjona, because flesh and blood did not reveal this to you, but My Father who is in heaven" (Matthew 16:17). It was the same message delivered under different circumstances that Jesus had spoken to Nicodemus: "Truly, truly, I say to you, unless one is born again he cannot see the kingdom of God" (John 3:3b). Spiritual insight is given only by the grace of God. Only the Father of glory can "give to you a spirit of wisdom and revelation in the knowledge" (Ephesians 1:17) of Christ. The greatness of Peter was owing to the greatness of God's revelation to him.

The next statements of Jesus are the most debated, perhaps, of all His words in the Scripture. The great question is whether Peter is the rock on which Christ promises to build His church or whether it is something else intended by the words, "upon this rock I will build My church?" (Matthew 16:18a). It is important to note that Jesus does not say to Peter: "upon you I will build My church." If Jesus had said that, the debate would have easily concluded. Rather, Jesus says He will build His church "upon this rock." In the Scripture, God is very frequently called the rock of our salvation (cf. Psalm 19:14; Romans 9:33; 1 Corinthians 10:4; and 1 Peter 2:8). Also, Ephesians 2:19–22 says: "So then you are no longer strangers and aliens, but you are fellow citizens with the saints, and are of God's household, having been built on the foundation of the apostles and prophets, Christ Jesus

---

5 Chamblin, *Matthew*, 2:816.
6 Chamblin, *Matthew*, 2:817.

Himself being the corner *stone*, in whom the whole building, being fitted together, is growing into a holy temple in the Lord, in whom you also are built together into a dwelling of God in the Spirit." Peter is a rock. Jesus is the Rock.[7] The testimony of the apostles and prophets are a part of the foundation of this church, but Jesus Christ is the corner stone. The whole dwelling is a work of God's Spirit. Jesus is the One who builds His church.

At the mouth of that cave called "the gates of hell," Jesus emphatically declared that those gates of the enemy would not prevail against His church. Try though the devil might, he has never been able to destroy God's church on this earth. Even when the blood of martyrs has been spilled like rivers, it has proved to be the seed of the church. Death would not be the end of Christ's mission and Church, but the beginning. Death would not keep Christ imprisoned, but He would rise victorious over death and the grave.

In conclusion, Jesus strictly warned His disciples not to tell anyone that "He was the Christ" (Matthew 16:20). There would come a time when the message would be broadcast everywhere, but the present hour was not that time. There were forces of evil who wanted to destroy the work of Jesus and they must not be allowed to do so. As Alexander commented:

> This prohibition is to be explained . . . not as an absolute suppression of the truth, but such a gradual disclosure as might best secure the great ends of his advent, and especially postpone its final issue or catastrophe till all intermediate ends had been accomplished.[8]

Jesus Foretells His Death (Matthew 16:21–28; Mark 8:31–9:1; and, Luke 9:22–27)

At the foot of Mount Hermon, Jesus first revealed to His disciples the grand purpose of His life—"to suffer many things . . . to be killed . . . and be raised up on the third day" (Matthew 16:21). There are, perhaps, two primary reasons why Jesus chose that particular time and that place to make this revelation to the Twelve. First, Jesus would be gloriously transfigured in six days and the disciples could not understand that coming event without knowing that sufferings awaited Him. Second, Caesarea Philippi represented the mixture of Jews and

---

7 Alexander, *The Gospel According to Matthew Explained*, 436–441. His arguments about Peter's words are more convincing to me than those of anyone else I have consulted.
8 Alexander, *The Gospel According to Matthew Explained*, 442.

Jesus' Transfiguration

Gentiles together which the church of our Lord would be. As Ephesians 2:13, 14 states: "But now in Christ Jesus you who formerly were far off have been brought near by the blood of Christ. For He Himself is our peace, who made both groups into one and broke down the barrier of the dividing wall." This reconciliation of Jews and Gentiles together would be better understood in days to come because of where the sufferings of Jesus were first reveled to the disciples.

Matthew states that it was "[f]rom that time that Jesus began to show His disciples that He must go to Jerusalem, and suffer many things . . ." The time reference is definitive. The cross was eight or nine months away and it was an opportune time—the right time—for Jesus to begin to disclose to them "the greatest secret of His death."[9] Peter's great confession had opened the door for Jesus to make this self-disclosure to them. Jesus will repeat this warning two more times with further information each time. "They must know it now to be ready then."[10] Even if they did not have the capacity yet to understand what was going to happen, they needed to hear the words. They needed to grapple with the ideas involved.

Peter, as the leader of the twelve, was the first to make a confession that Jesus was the Son of God, but he is also the first to rebuke Jesus and to tempt Him to not undertake the way of suffering. The Gospel of Mark gives a more complete understanding of the exchange which took place between Jesus and Peter at this time. Mark 8:32 says: "And He was stating the matter plainly. And Peter took Him aside and began to rebuke Him." It was necessary that Jesus would state the matter plainly because the idea of a suffering Messiah was anathema to the Jewish mind. Jesus' words were immediately met with resistance by Peter, who took the Lord aside in order to correct Him in private. The word for "rebuke" in Mark 8:32 "is used of the stronger or wealthier coming to the help of the weaker or poorer . . . and carries here an air of conscious superiority . . . Something of this officiousness had shown itself already in Simon Peter's relations to His Master . . ., the tension of his recent act of faith and exaltation of feeling which followed it probably exaggerated a fault of natural character, and led to the astounding conduct

---

9 Archibald Thomas Robertson, *Word Pictures in the New Testament, The Gospel According to Matthew, The Gospel According to Mark* (Nashville, Tennessee: Broadman Press, 1930), 1:135.
10 Robertson, *Word Pictures in the New Testament, The Gospel According to Matthew, The Gospel According to Mark*, 1:135

described in the next words."[11] Those next words were: "God forbid it, Lord! This shall never happen to You" (Matthew 16:22b). Peter, no doubt, felt that Jesus was suffering from a momentary weakness due to the recent hostilities against Him and the departure of many who had once followed Him. Thus, Peter thought "it was his duty as the senior of the Twelve to remonstrate"[12] and to attempt to buttress what he thought was weakness of faith on Jesus' part. In so doing, Peter completely rejected Jesus' frankness of speech as simply "premonitions of failure" that "were at variance with all his conceptions of the Christ."[13] Therein was the problem for both Peter and the other members of the Twelve. There was no room in their theology for a Messiah as described in Isaiah 53. A warrior king like David or a peaceful reign like that of Solomon were both possible in the minds of the disciples, but a Messiah who was put to death was unthinkable to them.

Peter and Jesus both had their backs to the rest of the Twelve during this exchange. Upon receiving Peter's rebuke, Jesus turned to face him and saw the other disciples. Something in the look of those other disciples revealed to Jesus that they also had sympathy with Peter's views. A tender look or a private rebuke would not be sufficient. "A public reproof was therefore necessary, and the Lord did not spare His first Apostle."[14] Thus, Jesus said, "Get behind Me, Satan; for you are not setting your mind on God's interests, but man's" (Mark 8:33). Jesus had spoken a simplified form of this command to Satan when He was tempted by that evil one (Cf. Matthew 4:10). Swete's comments on these words spoken to Peter are enlightening:

> [T]he words in which the Lord before the beginning of His public work dismissed the Tempter, when he offered the kingdoms of the world on condition of receiving homage for them. This temptation was now renewed by Satan in the person of the Apostle who desired his Master to put from Him the prospect of the Cross. It is unnecessary to suppose either that Peter is called 'Satan' (cf. Jo. vi. 70) or that the word is to be understood simply in the etymological sense, 'adversary' . . . The Lord recognizes His great adversary in Peter, who for the moment acts Satan's part . . . If Peter identified himself with Satan, he must share Satan's repulse and exile.[15]

---

11 Swete, *Commentary on Mark*, 180.
12 Swete, *Commentary on Mark*, 180.
13 Swete, *Commentary on Mark*, 180.
14 Swete, *Commentary on Mark*, 180.
15 Swete, *Commentary on Mark*, 180–1.

Jesus' public rebuke of Peter, though sharp, was also loving. He was calling His disciple back from the imitation of Satan for which there could only be banishment from the Lord. As Paul asked in 2 Corinthians 6:15—"Or what harmony has Christ with Belial?" A suffering Messiah was a hard concept for the disciples to grasp which Jesus understood very well. Even He had to come slowly and incrementally to the knowledge of what awaited Him. Plummer's comments on Matthew 16:21 elucidate this truth for us:

> Like the time when He became conscious that He was the Messiah, the time when Jesus became conscious that He must suffer many things and be killed, is hidden from us. We have no right to assume (see Jn. Iii.14) that He had only just become aware of it, when He revealed the fact to His disciples. On the other hand, we need not suppose that He had known it from childhood. We may reverently believe that even He required to be trained for such a future, and that perhaps not until His baptism, and then only gradually, was the will of God, in this respect, revealed to Him. A childhood overshadowed by the prospect of sufferings from which even His ripe manhood shrank, would indeed be a mystery.[16]

Jesus was, and now eternally is, both God and man. As the Godman, Jesus had two complete natures—one divine and the other human. Both natures acted according to what was proper for each. As God, Jesus could read the hearts of all men. As man, He underwent growth in many respects, as Luke 2:52 says—"And Jesus kept increasing in wisdom and stature, and in favor with God and men." This subject is shrouded in mystery, but it is evident from Jesus' prayers that he sought answers and guidance from God. He spent the whole night in prayer before calling His disciples (cf. Luke 6:12–16) which was not an exercise in play acting. One of those disciples, Judas, was a "devil" (John 6:70) whom Jesus would not have called to be among the Twelve without knowing that was the will of His Father. His night in prayer would have confirmed that to Him. There are other examples of His prayers confirming the will of God to Him as well, especially in the garden of Gethsemane. In the end, though, Deuteronomy 29:29 applies to this subject: "The secret things belong to the Lord our God, but the things revealed belong to us and to our sons forever, that we may observe all the words of this law." We do not know how the divine and human natures of Christ cooperated together in all things

---

16 Plummer, *An Exegetical Commentary on the Gospel According to Matthew*, 234.

for our salvation, but we do know that Jesus was the most prayerful and the only perfect man who ever lived.

After rebuking Peter, Jesus then challenged the twelve, and all Christians, with the costs of discipleship. "And He summoned the crowd with His disciples, and said to them, 'If anyone wishes to come after Me, he must deny Himself, and take up His cross and follow Me. For whoever wishes to save his life will lose it, but whoever loses his life for My sake and the gospel's will save it" (Mark 8:34, 35). Even when Jesus was ministering to the Twelve, the crowds were never very far away from Him. If they could not hear everything He said, they at least saw the interactions. So, it was easy for Jesus to summon the larger group of followers when He had things to teach that were universally applicable. The idea of taking up the cross was "a reference to the common practice of compelling malefactors to convey their own cross to the place of execution. Crucifixion being commonly regarded as at once the most powerful and disgraceful way of dying, is here put for the worst form of suffering, and carrying the cross for humble, patient submission to it . . . As if He had said, 'let him follow me to Golgotha.'"[17] Jesus' admonition requires three things of all His followers—self-denial, taking up the cross of their "crucifixion," and persevering in following Christ. With the disciples, Jesus had started with His own crucifixion. With the crowds, He begins with their crucifixion as proof of being His followers. This is why Dietrich Bonhoeffer titled his book, *The Cost of Discipleship*. It is costly to be a follower of Christ. We must die to self and live for Christ.

Jesus concluded this call to discipleship with these words: "For the Son of Man is going to come in the glory of His Father with His angels, and will then repay every man according to his deeds. Truly I say to you, there are some of those standing here who will not taste of death until they see the Son of Man coming in His kingdom" (Matthew 16:27, 28). The finding or losing of the soul by anyone is ultimately determined by the Son of Man when He comes "in the glory of His Father." It is the same thing, essentially, that Psalm 2:12 says—"Do homage to the Son, that He not become angry, and you perish *in* the way, for His wrath will soon be kindled. How blessed are all those who take refuge in Him!" Life, eternal life, true life can only be found in Jesus. Satan tempted Jesus with all the kingdoms of the world if He would only serve that fiend.

---

[17] Alexander, *The Gospel According to Mark*, 226.

Jesus teaches that the soul is of far more worth than the whole world, but it can only be found or saved in Him. Jesus mentions two comings in these verses—the coming at the end of all days and the coming that some standing there would see before they die. As Chamblin notes:

> This coming (a participle of the verb erchomai) is not the one of Matthew 16:27, but an anticipation of that event in Jesus' own generation, most notably in his coming to execute judgment against the Jewish nation in A.D. 70.[18]

Jesus' Transfiguration (Matthew 17:1–8; Mark 9:2–8; and, Luke 9:28–36)
The six days[19] between Peter's confession of Jesus as the Son of God and Jesus' transfiguration on the majestic Mount Hermon were no doubt spent in despondency by the saddened apostles. Jesus' forewarning of what awaited Him in Jerusalem was exactly opposite of what they were expecting. While the four Gospels do not give us a day-by-day account of Jesus' ministry, the silence is deafening concerning those days following Jesus' first warning of His crucifixion and resurrection. Those depressive days were undoubtedly spent at the foot of Mount Hermon and in that very region where Jesus had made His prediction.[20] The road to the top wound around the mountain for several miles of intense, uphill climbing.

It was late July or early August of AD 29 when these events took place. The heat of a summer's day was not the right time to climb such a mountain. Moreover, Jesus was accustomed to praying on mountain heights in the evening (e.g., Matthew 14:23; Luke 6:12). Therefore, Edersheim is surely correct in what he suggests concerning their mountain hike:

> It was evening, and, as we have suggested, the evening after the Sabbath, when the Master, and those three of His disciples, who were most closely linked to Him in heart and thought, climbed the path that led up to one of the heights of Hermon.

---

18 Chamblin, *Matthew*, 2:840.
19 Luke 9:28 says it was 8 days after the various saying by Jesus at Caesarea Philippi. Matthew and Mark state that it was six days afterwards. The obvious explanation is that Matthew and Mark were referencing the days between those events while Luke was including both the day of the sayings and the day of the transfiguration.
20 An ancient tradition says that Jesus was transfigured on Mount Tabor (southwest of Nazareth), but there was a fortress at the top of that mountain at that time. It would not have provided the opportunity for rest and reflection that Mount Hermon did. There is no indication that Jesus and the disciples left the area of Caesarea Philippi until after the transfiguration. Plus, Luke simply wrote that Jesus "took along Peter and John and James, and went up on the mountain to pray" (Luke 9:28) which indicates it was the mountain where Jesus had forewarned them.

> The Sabbath-sun had set, and a delicious cool hung in the summer air, as Jesus and the three commenced their ascent . . . [T]here is only one road that leads from Caesarea Philippi to Hermon, and we cannot be mistaken in following it. First, among vine-clad hills stocked with mulberry, apricot and fig-trees; then, through corn-fields where the pear tree supplants the fig; next through oak coppice, and up rocky ravines to where the soil is dotted with dwarf shrubs. And if we pursue the ascent, it still becomes steeper, till the first ridge of snow is crossed, after which turfy banks, gravelly slopes, and broad snow patches alternate. The top of Hermon in summer . . . is free from snow, but broad patches run down the sides expanding as they descend.
>
> As they ascend to the cool of that Sabbath evening, the keen mountain air must have breathed strength into the climbers, and the scent of snow—for which the parched tongue would long in summer's heat (Prov. 25:13)—have refreshed them.[21]

A journey to the highest peak of Mount Hermon would have been "an Alpine ascent"[22] and would have required time which the Scripture records do not indicate. Additionally, spending the night among the snow covered peaks of Hermon would have been virtually impossible in late summer due to the extreme difference in temperature.[23] Thus, Jesus and His inner circle of disciples probably went to a lower part of the mountain where they first engaged in prayer.

As Jesus was praying, "He was transfigured before them, and His face shone like the sun, and His garments became as white as light—as no launderer on earth can whiten them" (Matthew 17:2 and Mark 9:3). The disciples, following their mountain climb, were "overcome with sleep; but when they were fully awake, they saw His glory and the two men standing with Him" (Luke 9:32). The two men were Moses and Elijah, the leading representatives of the law and the prophets, which Jesus came to fulfill. They were conversing with Jesus about "His departure which He was about to accomplish at Jerusalem" (Luke 9:31). Plummer comments on what Jesus discussed with Moses and Elijah:

> His departure from this world by means of the Passion, Resurrection, and Ascension . . . That the Apostles heard this subject being discussed explains part of the meaning of the Transfiguration. It was to calm their minds, which had recently been disturbed by the prediction of Christ's sufferings and death . . . It is all ordained by God,

---

21 Edersheim, *The Life and Times of Jesus the Messiah*, 538–9.
22 Edersheim, *The Life and Times of Jesus the Messiah*, 539.
23 Edersheim, *The Life and Times of Jesus the Messiah*, 539.

Jesus' Transfiguration

and is sure to take place; and when it takes place it may be regarded as a fulfilment . . . , and also as a filling full. There were types and prophecies shadowing the divine purpose, every detail of which must be gone through.[24]

Whenever Moses ascended Mount Sinai to converse with God, his face would begin to shine brilliantly. Then he would have to veil his face before he descended back to the camp of the Israelites (Exodus 34:29–35). On Mount Hermon, Jesus' face shone more brilliantly than even Moses' face had once shone. Luke 9:29 records that His "face became different." This difference was the result of "[t]he 'form of God' shining through 'the form of a servant.'"[25] Jesus, the Son of God, had been veiled in human flesh during His tabernacle on this earth, but on the Mount His glory was manifested in great measure to those three disciples. They saw Him in a new way. Peter would later write of that experience in 2 Peter 1:17, 18—"For when He received honor and glory from God the Father, such an utterance was made to Him by the Majestic Glory, "This is My beloved Son with whom I am well-pleased'—and we ourselves heard the utterance made from heaven when we were with Him on the holy mountain."

When Peter was roused out of his half-stupor, he saw the glory of Christ but quickly blurted out: "Master, it is good for us to be here; let us make three tabernacles; one for You, and one for Moses, and one for Elijah" (Luke 9:33a). The tabernacle was the representation of God's presence among His people. Jesus tabernacled among us (John 1:14), but the same cannot be said about either Moses or Elijah. Thus, Luke 9:33b says, Peter spoke those words without "realizing what he was saying." Matthew 17:5 tells us what happened next:

> While he was still speaking, a bright cloud overshadowed them, and behold a voice out of the cloud said, 'This is My beloved Son, with whom I am well-pleased, listen to Him!'"

The disciples were afraid at the sight of the glory of Christ (Mark 9:6) and the cloud that enveloped them, but were even more terrified when the voice of God spoke from heaven. John, who was one of the three disciples with Jesus on the holy mountain, had a similar experience when he saw the glory of the Son of Man in Revelation

---

24 Plummer, *A Critical and Exegetical Commentary on the Gospel According to St. Luke*, 251.
25 Edersheim, *The Life and Times of Jesus the Messiah*, 540.

1:17, 18—"When I saw Him, I fell at His feet as a dead man. And He placed His right hand on me, saying, 'Do not be afraid; I am the first and the last, and the living One; and I was dead, and behold I am alive forevermore, and I have the keys of death and of Hades.'" Alexander comments on the fear that overtook Peter, causing him to blurt out his words about the tabernacles, and the fear of the disciples at the sight of the cloud:

> The cause of both effects was fear, not mere alarm or dread, but also a religious awe, occasioned by the supernatural character of the whole transaction. This effect was common to the three disciples . . . [26]

While the disciples were lying face down on the ground in fear, Jesus spoke to them: "Get up, and do not be afraid" (Matthew 17:7b). That message of comfort was similar to what He had spoken when He came walking on the water and the disciples thought He was a ghost. When the disciples lifted "up their eyes, they saw no one except Jesus alone" (Matthew 17:8). As Chamblin writes:

> Both the *presence* of Jesus and the *absence* of Moses and Elijah are accentuated . . . Moses and Elijah are by no means obsolete; their testimony remains vitally important . . . But their personal and visible presence is no longer needed, now that the Son has come.[27]

As Jesus and His disciples traveled down the mountain, Jesus commanded them: "Tell the vision to no one until the Son of Man has risen from the dead" (Matthew 17:9). That was the third time the disciples were confronted with the truth of Jesus' resurrection, including the conversation of Jesus with Moses and Elijah on the Mount. It was a truth that apparently, once again, did not register with the disciples. Instead of focusing on Jesus' new command to them, they asked Him, "Why then do the scribes say that Elijah must come first?" (Matthew 17:10). Jesus' answer to them made it clear to the disciples that John the Baptist had been the Elijah of prophecy (Matthew 17:13). The fact that they "did to [John] whatever they wished" (Matthew 17:12) was a foreshadowing of the death of Christ. What Jezebel had threatened to do to Elijah, Herod Antipas actually did to John, the forerunner of the Messiah.[28] Thus, Chamblin notes about the Forerunner:

---

26 Alexander, *The Gospel According to Mark*, 237.
27 Chamblin, *Matthew*, 2:851.
28 Morna D. Hooker, *The Gospel According to Saint Mark* (Peabody, MA: Hendrickson Publishers, 1991), 221.

It is precisely by the Son of Man's suffering and death that he will save his people and establish God's rule. John heralds Messiah's work by his life no less than by his preaching and baptizing. John's most poignant witness to Jesus is his martyrdom; the Elijah of Malachi, far from forestalling Messiah's death, would foreshadow it.[29]

The Valley of Humiliation

In *The Pilgrim's Progress*, John Bunyan describes Christian having to descend down into the Valley of Humiliation after enjoying the beautiful scenery on the delectable Mountains—Immanuel's Land and the Celestial City. Yet, Christian could not stay on the mountain top. He had to descend to the valley once again. Bunyan describes the conversation between Christian and his companions—Discretion, Piety, Charity, and Prudence:

> Then said *Christian*, as it was *difficult* coming up, so (so far as I can see) it is *dangerous* going down. Yes, said *Prudence*, so it is; for it is an hard matter for a man to go down into the valley of *Humiliation*, as thou art now, and to catch no slip by the way . . .
>
> But now in this Valley of *Humiliation* poor *Christian* was hard put to it, for he had gone but a little way before he espied a foul *Fiend* coming over the field to meet him; His name is *Apollyon*.[30]

Bunyan could have been writing about the spiritual warfare that was about to engage Jesus' twelve disciples, and probably was. Yet, there is a spiritual parallel in the experience of all true believers which Bunyan discerned. Mountain top experiences are not the best place for Christian growth. Oftentimes, grace grows best in winter. The Twelve were soon to learn that truth by heart. The next eight months or so would be the most challenging period in being followers of Jesus. Unbelief, jealousy, vindictiveness, pride, and other sins would soon be obstacles to their growth in grace. Those problems manifested themselves immediately at the foot of Hermon. Not only the three disciples—Peter, James, and John—who comprised the inner circle of Jesus and were eyewitnesses to His transfiguration, but all the other disciples were part of this spiritual declension.

It was the next morning when Jesus and His three disciples began their descent from the Mount of Transfiguration. They were to find a crowd awaiting them at the bottom of the hill composed of the rest of the disciples, some scribes, and a large crowd of people who probably

---

29 Chamblin, *Matthew*, 2:854.
30 Bunyan, *The Pilgrim's Progress: From this World to That which is to Come*, 55–56.

lived in that area. As was typical of them, the scribes were arguing with the disciples. When the crowd spotted Jesus and His inner circle, they began running up to them. Jesus was aware that they had been discussing something with the scribes so He asked, "What are you discussing with them?" (Mark 9:16). Before the disciples could answer, a man blurted out: "Teacher, I brought You my son, possessed with a spirit which makes him mute; and whenever it seizes him, it slams him to the ground and he foams at his mouth, and grinds his teeth and stiffens out. I told Your disciples to cast it out, and they could not do it" (Mark 9:17, 18). Luke records that the man begged Jesus for His help and had likewise begged the disciples to cure him to no avail. Jesus' response was an expression of exasperation: "O unbelieving generation, how long shall I be with you? How long shall I put up with you? Bring him to Me!" (Mark 9:19). Swete astutely remarks on this reproof:

> The Lord replies to all whose feeling the father had voiced . . . ; the reproof . . . is general, perhaps purposely so, including Scribes, the people, and the father (vv. 22, 23) so far as their faith had been at fault, and the disciples not the least (v. 29).[31]

The first manifestation of the disciples' spiritual declension was their inability to cast out the demon of this little boy at the bottom of the hill. Jesus had previously given them power to cast out demons and they had exercised that gift when they went throughout Galilee preaching and teaching (Matthew 10:8). Even the seventy other disciples had been given the same power to cast out demons and they had returned to Jesus, joyously exclaiming: "Lord, even the demons are subject to us in Your name" (Luke 10:17). Perhaps there was an element of pride that overcame the Seventy and the Twelve even before the Transfiguration. It was true of all of them even as it is true of all Christians what Jesus said in John 15:5c—"for apart from Me you can do nothing." That seems to be a lesson they were still learning.

Immediately, the boy was brought to Jesus and he began rolling around on the ground, foaming at the mouth, and convulsing (Mark 9:20). Jesus asked the father, "How long has this been happening to him?" (Mark 9:21) and He was told, "From childhood." Then, the father manifested some of that unbelief Jesus had just rebuked by saying, "But if You can do anything, take pity on us and help us!" (Mark

---

31 Swete, *Commentary on Mark*, 198.

9:22). Jesus swiftly responded, "If you can? All things are possible to him who believes" (Mark 9:23). Calvin unfolds the meaning of Jesus' promise in these words:

> From this we gather the useful lesson, which applies to us all alike, that it is not the Lord's fault if a great abundance of blessings does not flow from Him to us, but it must be imputed to the narrowness of our faith, that it only comes drop by drop—sometimes, indeed, we do not even feel a drop, because unbelief blocks up our hearts.[32]

At that point, Jesus "rebuked the unclean spirit, 'You deaf and dumb spirit, I command you, come out of him, and do not enter him again'" (Mark 9:25). At first, the boy became like a corpse, but Jesus took him by the hand and raised him up (Mark 9:26, 27). Afterwards, the disciples came to Jesus and quizzed Him on why they could not do the same? Jesus replied: "This kind cannot come out by anything but prayer" (Mark 9:29). Once again, Calvin's comments are helpful"

> The meaning therefore is that, when we have to fight earnestly against Satan, any sort of faith is not enough. Strenuous efforts are required. As the remedy for a languid faith He prescribes prayer, to which He adds fasting as an assistance . . . But since He affirms that that kind of demon can only be cast out by prayers and fasting, the meaning is that where Satan fixes deep roots and has ruled by a long possession, or where he attacks with unbridled fury, victory is hard and difficult and we must fight with all our strength.[33]

The disciples who had remained at the foot of the mountain while Jesus was transfigured before His inner circle had been arguing with the scribes. They also had probably been overwhelmed by the unbelieving spirit of the scribes. Thus, the first sign of spiritual declension in the disciples was their inability to minister in faith—though they had done so previously.

Following this miracle, Jesus and His disciples left Caesarea Philippi and began the journey back to Capernaum through Galilee (Mark 9:30). While on their way, Jesus was once again giving them warning of what awaited Him in Jerusalem: "The Son of Man is to be delivered into the hand of men, and they will kill Him, and when He has been killed, He will rise three days later" (Mark 9:31). The disciples, though, "did not understand this statement, and they were afraid to ask Him" (Mark 9:32). Luke 9:45 adds that "it was concealed from

---

32 Calvin, *A Harmony of the Gospels Matthew Mark, and Luke*, 2:208.
33 Calvin, *A Harmony of the Gospels Matthew Mark, and Luke*, 2:210.

them so that they would not perceive it." The time was not right for them to understand the meaning of His passion and resurrection and ascension.

Instead of pondering Jesus' words carefully, the disciples became embroiled in an argument as to which of them was the greatest (Luke 9:46). This was the second evidence of their spiritual declension. They were overcome with vainglory and pride. They were guilty of wanting to be pre-eminent. Yet, they were concealing this fact from Jesus as they traveled back to Capernaum. When they arrived at the house, Jesus quizzed them: "What were you discussing on the way?" (Mark 9:33). They kept silent (Mark 9:34), not realizing that Jesus already knew. So, Jesus said to them, "If anyone wants to be first, he shall be last of all and servant of all" (Mark 9:35). He then placed a little child in their midst as an object lesson on humility and serving one another. Alexander unfolds the meaning of the word "servant":

> The Greek noun is not that which means a slave . . ., but one which properly denotes a waiter or attendant on the table, one who waits upon the person and supplies the wants of his employer or master . . . If anyone wishes to truly be first, he must become so, not by caring for himself, but by ministering to the wants of others.[34]

---

34 Alexander, *The Gospel According to Mark*, 258-9.

16

Jesus at the Feast of Tabernacles

The Feast of Tabernacles in AD 29 was from October 11–17. Initially, Jesus had not planned to go to that feast because the Jews in Jerusalem "were seeking to kill Him" (John 7:1b). Yet, His brothers—James, Joseph, Simon, and Jude—chided Him:

> Leave here and go into Judea, so that Your disciples may see your works which You are doing. For no one does anything in secret when he himself seeks to be known publicly. If you do these things, show Yourself to the world (John 7:3b-4).

John, the beloved disciple, wrote that the brothers gave Jesus this advice because "not even [they] were believing in Him" (John 7:5). Indeed, they had wanted to put Him away only a few months earlier. Their words show that "they were charging him with inconsistency, and that they, in common with many others, harbored secular ideas with reference to the coming and office of the Messiah."[1] They did not really believe what they were saying to Him. Their position about Him had not changed. They still thought He was a lunatic. They had only changed the form of their argument. Thus, Jesus replied to them:

> My time is not yet here, but your time is always opportune. The world cannot hate you, but it hates Me because I testify of it, that its deeds are evil. Go up to the feast yourselves; I do not go up to this feast because My time has not yet fully come (John 7:6b-8).

For that reason, Jesus remained in Galilee after His brothers began their journey to Jerusalem. He was keenly aware that the Passover in AD 30, would be His time of suffering, crucifixion, and resurrection. The open hostility of the Jews in Jerusalem towards Him made Him reluctant to do anything which would result in His premature death before His appointed time.[2] Nonetheless, Jesus and His disciples went up to this feast afterwards, but they did so in secret. On their journey from Galilee, He sent some messengers ahead of Him into a

---
1 Hendriksen, *The Gospel of John*, 2:5.
2 There was an appointed time for Jesus' crucifixion, but our Lord did not risk His death before that time. He understood the dynamic tension between God's sovereignty and man's responsibility.

Samaritan village in order to make preparations for His coming there (Luke 9:52). "But they did not receive Him, because He was traveling to Jerusalem" (Luke 9:53). There was enmity between the Jews and the Samaritans on both sides as Plummer notes:

> The fact that He was on His way to keep a feast at Jerusalem, thus repudiating the Samaritan temple on Mount Gerizim, increased the animosity of the Samaritans.[3]

The Sons of Thunder (Matthew 20:20–28; Mark 10:35–45; and, Luke 9:51–56)

This inhospitality of the Samaritans was the result of age-old differences between them and the Jews over the true temple and its worship. Yet, it struck a nerve in the hearts of the sons of Zebedee—James and John—who became known as "sons of thunder." When they saw the response of the Samaritans, they asked Jesus: "Lord, do you want us to command fire to come down from heaven and consume them?" (Luke 9:54). No doubt, the brothers were thinking of the time when Elijah called down fire from heaven to consume one hundred soldiers of King Ahaziah of Samaria (cf. 2 Kings 1:9–16). It seemed natural to the brothers who had recently seen Elijah at Jesus' transfiguration to think of that incident. Their misplaced zeal was an evidence of their intense and even fiery loyalty to Jesus, but it was sinful just the same. Jesus immediately turned and rebuked them, saying: "You do not know what kind of spirit you are of; for the Son of Man did not come to destroy men's lives, but to save them" (Luke 9:56). "Jesus, too, all gentle as He was, had His thunderbolts; but He reserved them for other objects than poor, benighted, prejudiced Samaritans. His zeal was directed against great sins, and powerful, privileged, presumptuous sinners; not against little sins, or poor, obscure, vulgar sinners."[4]

Jesus' words in gently rebuking His disciples had their desired effect and they moved on to another village for their rest while traveling to Jerusalem. Geldenhuys' comments are on target:

> Just as they have to act with unanimity (verse 50) towards persons acting in His name but not following Him precisely as they did, so also they must act tolerantly towards persons who are hostile to Him and His followers. With His followers there must never be anything like revenge or violence against enemies. Jesus came not to destroy men

---

3 Plummer, *A Critical and Exegetical Commentary on the Gospel According to S. Luke*, 263.
4 Bruce, *The Training of the Twelve*, 246.

through divine power but to save them.[5]

The route Jesus was following was the more direct road through Samaria which was generally avoided by Jewish pilgrims because of the animosities with the Samaritans. Yet, Jesus wanted to go to the feast in secret due to the hostilities against him in Jerusalem. If He and His followers had traveled the normal route through Perea,[6] there would have been numerous caravans of pilgrims going up to that festival. He and His disciples would have been quickly detected by those crowds; and His secrecy would have been impossible.

The Cost of Discipleship (Matthew 8:19–22 and Luke 9:57–62)

After the rebuff of Jesus and His disciples by the Samaritan village, they continued their travels southward. Soon there were three different men "along the road" (Luke 9:57) who expressed some interest in being Jesus' disciples. The first one said to Him, "I will follow you wherever You go" (Luke 9:58a). Matthew identified that man as a scribe which is puzzling why he had not already gone to the feast, but was tarrying with Jesus. Such an expression of wholehearted devotion that he made would typically be welcomed by most people with open arms. Jesus was different. He did not readily entrust Himself to such people because "He Himself knew what was in man" (John 2:24, 25). Thus, Jesus replied to this man's overture, "The foxes have holes and the birds of the air have nests, but the Son of Man has nowhere to lay His head" (Luke 9:58b). Having just been denied the customary Oriental hospitality, Jesus had neither a place to sleep nor a place to eat. As the Son of Man, His was a life "of utter homelessness . . . in this world,"[7] especially at this juncture in His ministry. For a while, Capernaum had been His home—at least His residence. Those days were now over and for the rest of His time in the flesh Jesus would be without a place to lay His head—except when His friends infrequently supplied His needs. Geldenhuys' comments are enlightening:

> On the journey someone tells the Saviour that he will follow Him whithersoever He may go. He spoke with so much self-confidence because he had no inkling of the way of sorrows and death which the Lord would yet follow and also because he did not realize his own weakness and instability. In answer to his declaration of loyalty to the Master, the Saviour calls

---

5 Geldenhuys, *Commentary on the Gospel of Luke*, 293.
6 That travel would have been along the eastern side of the Jordan River in the area called Perea.
7 Edersheim, *The Life and Times of Jesus the Messiah*, 565.

attention to the naked reality of His life of extreme privation. For Him there is no rest such as is to be found even for the foxes and the birds of heaven, for He has continually to proceed from one town to another because He is repeatedly rejected or because there are again and again new cases of need where He has to bring salvation, or because the multitude is constantly pursuing Him so that He gets no opportunity of resting from His labour or from the endless conflict with the power of evil.[8]

This man who pledged his loyalty so readily could not have been prepared for the hardships that awaited Jesus and His disciples in just a few short months. Thus, there is no indication that his offer to follow Jesus went any further. Jesus then turned a little later to another man and said, "Follow Me" (Luke 9:59a). The Lord's actions were not contradictory, but supplementary. After showing the demands of being one of His followers, He wanted to illustrate to the disciples the unwillingness of most people to comply with those stringent requirements. This second man, therefore, responds: "Lord, permit me first to go and bury my father" (Luke 9:59b). Excuses for delaying discipleship are so many impediments in the way of following Jesus. Jesus replied in words that might seem harsh or unnecessary: "Allow the dead to bury their own dead; but as for you, go and proclaim everywhere the kingdom of God" (Luke 9:60). Jesus only had a few months to live and He knew it. He could not wait for people to decide whether they would be His followers or not. As Plummer notes:

> "I must first bury my father" is an almost brutal way of saying, "I cannot come so long as my father is alive"; and to put off following Jesus for so indefinite a period would have seemed like trifling.
>
> This disciple needs to be told, not of the privations of the calling, but of its lofty and imperative character. The opportunity must be embraced directly it comes, or it may be lost; and therefore even sacred duties must give way to it . . . By the time that the funeral rites were over, and he cleansed from pollution, Jesus would be far away, and he might have become unwilling to follow Him.[9]

The first man was too eager to follow Christ before considering the cost. The second man considered that the cost of discipleship was too great in his present circumstances. Neither man was a true disciple. Another man then offered to follow Jesus if He would allow one condition: "first permit me to say good-bye to those at home" (Luke

---

8 Geldenhuys, *Commentary on the Gospel of Luke*, 295.
9 Plummer, *A Critical and Exegetical Commentary on the Gospel of Luke*, 266–7.

9:61b). This man had, no doubt, heard Jesus' prohibition against waiting until one's parents are deceased. All he wanted was just to say good-bye to them. Yet, the time was short and those who would be Jesus' disciples must become so at that hour. Jesus replied: "No one, after putting his hand to the plow and looking back, is fit for the kingdom of God" (Luke 9:62). Alfred Edersheim elucidates what was the essential error of this third would be disciple:

> It shows, that to follow Christ was regarded as a *duty*, and to leave those in the earthly home as a *trial*; and it betokens, not merely a divided heart, but one not fit for the kingdom of God. For, how can he draw a straight furrow in which to cast the seed, who, as he puts his hand to the plough, looks around or behind him?[10]

The Feast of Tabernacles in AD 29 (John 7:1–53)

The Feast of Tabernacles had already started when Jesus and His disciples arrived in Jerusalem. They had missed the holy convocation of the first day of the feast—the opening ceremony—on which no laborious work could be done (Leviticus 23:34). Their arrival was during "the non-sacred part of the festive week," which "the half-holy days were called."[11] Jesus' absence at the beginning was well-noted and there was a general murmuring throughout Jerusalem as everyone was looking for Him. The Jews were asking, "Where is He?" (John 7:11). Among the crowds, there was disagreement about Jesus. Some said, "He is a good man" (John 7:12a), while others contradicted that view: "No, on the contrary, He leads the people astray" (John 7:12b). Yet, all were hesitant to speak about Him openly for fear of the Jews. Thus, they spoke about Him in hushed tones when in public.

The Feast of Booths, as it is also called, "was pre-eminently the Feast for foreign pilgrims, coming from the farthest distance, whose Temple-contributions were received and counted."[12] Jews who were dispersed both to the East and to the West were more able to attend this feast than any of the others since it was after harvest. Their presence in Jerusalem represented the influences of their pagan lands both in the strange costumes that suddenly appeared on the streets of the city and in the change of the opinions of these "swarthy strangers."[13]

---

10 Edersheim, *The Life and Times of Jesus the Messiah*, 566. The original used 'cat' where 'cast' was obviously intended and has been corrected in this quote.
11 Edersheim, *The Life and Times of Jesus the Messiah*, 576.
12 Edersheim, *The Life and Times of Jesus the Messiah*, 576.
13 Edersheim, *The Life and Times of Jesus the Messiah*, 576.

These members of the Diaspora would come from Media, Arabia, Persia, and India in the East; and, Italy, Spain, modern Crimea, and the banks of the Danube in the West.[14] Edersheim describes the changes in Jerusalem during this festive season:

> Then it was, indeed, a scene of bustle and activity. Hospitality had to be sought and found; guests to be welcomed and entertained; all things for the feast to get ready. Above all, booths must be erected everywhere—in court and on housetop, in street and square, for the lodgment and entertainment of that vast multitude; leafy dwellings everywhere, to remind of the wilderness-journey, and now of the goodly land.[15]

Having finally arrived in Jerusalem during "the midst of the feast Jesus went up into the temple and *began* to teach" (John 7:14). The place where Jesus taught His disciples and all interested people was probably Solomon's portico which was the eastern-most colonnade on the south side of the Temple. The columns that comprised these colonnades were twenty-seven cubits or forty feet high and were monoliths of white marble. Edersheim gives more details about them:

> These colonnades, which, from their ample space, formed alike places for quiet walks and for larger gatherings, had benches in them—and from the liberty of speaking and teaching in Jerusalem, Jesus might address the people in the very face of His enemies.[16]

Jesus' teaching astonished the Jews, particularly the scribes and Pharisees, who asked, "How has this man become learned, having never been educated?" (John 7:16). For the rulers of Israel, the only true learning was to sit at the feet of the Rabbis which Jesus never did. While asserting that His teaching came from the One who sent Him, Jesus answered the Jews query: "If anyone is willing to do His will, he will know of the teaching, whether it is of God or whether I speak from Myself" (John 7:17). After accusing the Jews of not carrying out the law given to them by Moses, He then asked: "Why do you seek to kill Me?" (John 7:19). "The crowd responded, 'You have a demon! Who seeks to kill You?'" (John 7:20). Yet, the Jews had indeed tried to kill him at the Feast of Purim in AD 28 when he healed the paralytic at the Pool of Bethesda (Cf. John 5:18) on the Sabbath and for claiming to be equal with the Father. And, there would soon be even further plots against Him. The accusation that Jesus had a demon was, un-

---

14 Edersheim, *The Life and Times of Jesus the Messiah,* 576.
15 Edersheim, *The Life and Times of Jesus the Messiah* 576–7.
16 Edersheim, *The Life and Times of Jesus the Messiah* 578.

doubtedly, because the Jews had dismissed his miracles of casting out demons as a manifestation of the power of Beelzebub. Some of the people were aware that the rulers were trying to kill Jesus (John 7:25) and, therefore, they exclaimed, "Look, He is speaking publicly, and they are saying nothing to Him. The rulers do not really know that this is the Christ, do they? However, we know where this man is from, but whenever the Christ may come, no one knows where He is from" (John 7:26, 27).

In reply, Jesus cried out: "You both know Me and where I am from; and I have not come of Myself, but He who sent Me is true, whom you do not know" (John 7:28b). He was, in essence, saying to them that they knew everything *and* they knew nothing at the same time. As Calvin wrote about these verses:

> And indeed there is no worse plague than when men are so drunk with their belief in their little learning that they boldly reject everything contrary to their opinion.[17]

The Jews were incensed by Jesus' depiction of them as people who do not know God. How could such an unlearned man as Him make such a statement about them? Thus, they were antsy to seize Him that very hour, but could not do so because it was not yet His "hour." Many in the crowd believed in Him "and they were saying, 'When the Christ comes, He will not perform more signs than those which this man has, will He?'" (John 7:31). This muttering of the crowds compelled "the chief priests and Pharisees to send officers to seize Him" (John 7:32).

Jesus, knowing that His days were few on this earth, began to inform even the crowds that He would only be with them "[f]or a little while longer" (John 7:33) and that soon they would not be able to find Him. Those remarks piqued the interest of the crowds, who asked, "Where does this man intend to go that we will not find Him? He is not going to go to the Dispersion among the Greeks, and teach Greeks, is He?" (John 7:35). The Jews were at this time clueless concerning the true mission of Jesus. They did not expect a Suffering Savior as Isaiah 53 depicted. Thus, it is interesting that at the very time that more of the Dispersion was gathered in Jerusalem than at any other time of the year the Jews could only think that Jesus would

---

17 John Calvin, *The Gospel According to St. John, 1-10*, (Grand Rapids: Eerdmans Publishing Co, 1959), 191.

go away from them by going to the Dispersed Jews. They had no conception of the Messiah as "the Lamb of God who takes away the sin of the world" (John 1:29).

"Now on the last day, the great *day* of the feast, Jesus stood and cried out, saying, 'If anyone is thirsty, let him come to Me and drink. He who believes in Me, as the Scripture said, 'From his innermost being will flow rivers of living water'" (John 7:37, 38). On that day, there was a "ceremony of the outpouring of water, which was considered of such vital importance as to give the whole festival the name of 'House of Outpouring,'" and "was symbolical of the outpouring of the Holy Spirit."[18] Andrew Bonar describes the rejoicing that occasioned the last day of every Feast of tabernacles:

> As it was said of the day of Atonement, that 'a man had never seen sorrow who never saw the sorrow of that day;' so, on the contrary, it was said of the feast of Tabernacles, and especially of its last day, that 'he who never saw the rejoicing of drawing water, never saw rejoicing in his life.' It fell at the time of vintage, and when all kinds of increase were gathered in. It was, however, apt to be a rainy month: it was not in itself the best suited for dwelling in booths. Hence the Jews say that this season of the year was fixed upon as being on this very account the better suited to shew that in keeping it they acted from regard to a Divine command. Had it been in spring-time, it might have been thought the suggestion of natural feeling.[19]

Thus, even the Old Testament festivals pointed to the Messiah's work of redemption and the sending of the Holy Spirit. Morris amplifies the meaning of Jesus' cry on the last day of the feast:

> In words reminiscent of 4:10 Jesus gives the invitation to the thirsty to come to Him and drink. There is the implication that the thirsty soul will find supplied in Him the need which could not be supplied elsewhere. The appropriateness of the words at this feast is that throughout the seven days libations were made in the temple with water drawn from the pool of Siloam ... But on the eighth day no water was poured, and this would make Jesus' claim all the more impressive. At the same time His primary reference may not be the temple rite, but to the supply of water from the rock in the wilderness. The water supplied the physical needs of the Israelites, whereas no one drank from the water poured out of the golden ewer.[20]

---

18 Edersheim, *The Life and Times of Jesus the Messiah*, 577.
19 Andrew A. Bonar, *Leviticus* (London and Carlisle, Pennsylvania: The Banner of Truth Trust, 1972), 420.
20 Morris, *The Gospel According to John*, 422.

Jesus' words on this last day of the feast led to a division among the crowd. Some said, "This certainly is the Prophet" (John 7:40b). Others said, "This is the Christ" (John 7:41a). Still others quizzically responded, "Surely the Christ is not going to come from Galilee, is He?" (John 7:41b). There were others who wanted to seize Him and officers had been sent from the Sanhedrin to do that very thing. Yet, they returned to the chief priests without Jesus in their custody. The chief priests and Pharisees then asked them, "Why did you not bring Him?" (John 7:45b). The answer of the officers was as profound as it was simple: "Never has a man spoken the way this man speaks" (John 7:46). The Pharisees were not impressed by that response and immediately countered, "You have not also been led astray, have you?" (John 7:47). "Nicodemus, still a night-disciple, even in the brightest noon-tide . . . could not hold his peace, and yet he dared not speak for Christ. So he made compromise of both by taking the part of, and speaking as, a righteous, rigid Sanhedrist:"[21] "Our Law does not judge a man unless it first hears from him and knows what he is doing, does it?" (John 7:51). Certainly, defending the rights of due process are important for justice, but Nicodemus missed this opportunity to confess Christ before men. Jesus was not helped by his words and Nicodemus was easily recognized as an advocate for the Galilean. Thus, the Pharisees were dismissive in their answer to Nicodemus: "You are not also from Galilee, are you? Search and see that no prophet arises out of Galilee" (John 7:52). Yet, their challenge was not true, as Morris cites:

> They were angry men, and men who had been baulked of their prey, so their answer is not a careful one. They ignore Jonah, who was a Galilean (other prophets may also have come from there; there is uncertainty about the origin of some). And they ignore the power of God to raise up His prophets where He will.[22]

---

21 Edersheim, *The Life and Times of Jesus the Messiah*, 586.
22 Morris, *The Gospel According to John*, 434.

The Woman Caught in Adultery (John 8:1–11)

Following the events of the last day of the feast, "everyone went to his home" (John 7:53), "but Jesus went to the Mount of Olives" (John 8:1)[23]. Some speculate that He spent the night in Bethany—with Lazarus, Martha, and Mary—on the eastern slopes of the Mount of Olives, but there is no indication of that in the Scriptures. It is most likely that Jesus, in typical Eastern fashion, "simply slept . . . on the green turf under those olive trees"[24] in the Garden of Gethsemane, since the Son of Man had no other place to lay His head.

The Mount of Olives is the southernmost of three limestone mountain ridges east of Jerusalem's Old City across the Kedron Valley. Its western slopes have been used as burial grounds for centuries. Olive trees grew plentifully on this Mount and there was a garden spot for retirement there which Jesus used often during the last months of His life.

The great day of the feast had just passed and the following morning would be the beginning of their homeward journey for many pilgrims back to their native lands. The Garden of Gethsemane would have allowed Jesus to return to the city at the break of dawn and engage the people in one more spiritual lesson. Jesus arrived at the Temple grounds "early in the morning" (John 8:2) the next day and many people gathered around Him. As He was starting to teach the people, suddenly the scribes and Pharisees arrived with "a woman caught in adultery" (John 8:3) in tow. This self-righteous group of men placed the woman "in the center *of the court*" (John 8:3) and quickly said to the Lord, "Teacher, this woman has been caught in adultery, in the very act. Now in the Law Moses commanded us to stone such women, what do you say?" (John 8:4, 5).

That many such cases of adultery took place during the Feast of Tabernacles (and the other feasts) cannot be doubted. With people living in such close proximity to one another on Jerusalem's streets, courts, and housetops, temptation and sin was everywhere. As Farrar wrote:

---

23 While John 7:53 to 8:11 is not found in the earliest manuscripts, everything it says about Jesus is consistent with how the rest of the Bible describes our Lord and His interactions with both sinners and the Pharisees. John 8:15 and 17 give indirect support for this account to be both Scriptural and in the right place.
24 Farrar, *The Life of Christ*, 204.

Jesus at the Feast of Tabernacles

It is probable that the hilarity and abandonment of the Feast of Tabernacles, which had grown to be a kind of vintage festival, would often degenerate into acts of license and immorality, and these would find more numerous opportunities in the general disturbance of ordinary life caused by the dwelling of the whole people in their leafy little booths.[25]

A week of feasting and drinking would no doubt result in many situations of immorality. It was not surprising, therefore, that the Jews were able to bring a woman into the presence of the Lord who was allegedly caught in the act of adultery. Yet, there was a problem with this situation. Certainly, the Mosaic Law commanded that both the man and the woman be stoned. If the woman was caught in the "very act" how was it that the man was not also caught?

As the Jews had done on several other occasions, they were obviously trying to present a conundrum to Jesus which they could use against Him either way He responded to their questions. Jesus was not the person to whom they should have taken this woman if they were truly interested in justice. Westcott succinctly states the issue at hand:

> To affirm the binding validity of the Mosaic judgment would be to counsel action contrary to the Roman law. To set the Mosaic judgment aside would be to give up the claim to fulfil the Law. In either case there was material for accusation, practically fatal to the assumption of the Messiahship to which the Lord's teaching evidently pointed.[26]

There is another way to consider this apparent conundrum. If Jesus affirmed the Mosaic law, He would act in contradiction of his well-deserved reputation as the compassionate friend of sinners which would shock the multitudes who gathered around Him. If He denied the validity of the Mosaic law, there would be grounds for bringing charges of heresy against Him. The hypocrisy of the Jews in bringing this woman to Jesus is easily discerned as Farrar notes:

> But the spirit which actuated these scribes and Pharisees was not by any means the spirit of a sincere and outraged purity. In the decadence of national life, in the daily familiarity with heathen degradations, in the gradual substitution of a Levitical scrupulosity for heartfelt religion, the morals of the nation had become corrupt.[27]

---

25 Farrar, *The Life of Christ*, 205.
26 Westcott, *The Gospel According to St. John*, 126.
27 Farrar, *The Life of Christ*, 205. One example of what Farrar was stating is the fact that Joseph was willing to put Mary away privately when he thought she had committed adultery after their

Jesus did not respond to their persistent queries in the way they had hoped or expected. Instead of engaging them in dialogue, He merely stooped down and began to write something on the ground. What He wrote can never be determined, but it must have been some verse or verses from the Mosaic law that were selected to produce conviction of sin. Thus, when the Jews persisted in pushing Him for an answer, "he straightened up and said to them, 'He who is without sin among you, let him *be the* first to throw a stone at her'" (John 8:7). Deuteronomy 17:7 says: "The hand of the witnesses shall be first against him to put him to death, and afterward the hand of all the people. So you shall purge the evil from your midst." There are unanswerable questions concerning this woman. First, was she really caught in the very act of adultery? Second, who were the witnesses? Third, as Jesus pointedly stated, were the witnesses without sin? Indeed, were the witnesses themselves the ones who were guilty of adultery with the woman?

The scribes and Pharisees never answered Jesus a word and did not throw a stone at the woman. So, Jesus bent down and began to write again. The symbolism of Jesus writing on the ground twice was reminiscent of God twice writing the Ten Commandments on the tablets of stone with His finger (Cf. Exodus 24:12; 31:18; 32:16; 34:1). The result was that the Jews "began to go out one by one, beginning with the older ones, and He was left alone, and the woman, where she was in the center *of the court*" (John 8:9). For whatever reason, the Jews were all convicted in their hearts of their own sin and each of them left the woman alone in the presence of Jesus.

The difference between the law and the gospel is revealed in this situation. The Jews were not capable of judging others rightly because they themselves were not without sin. In this instance, especially, they were not even interested in justice, but were simply trying to entrap Jesus. As Westcott wrote concerning Jesus' requirement that the sinless person throw the first stone:

> In this way the words of the Lord revealed to the men the depths of their own natures, and they shrank in that Presence from claiming the prerogative of innocence. At the same time the question as to the woman's offence was raised at once from a legal to a spiritual level. The judges were made to feel that freedom from guilt is no claim to sinless-

betrothal. Cf. Matthew 1:18, 19.

ness. And the offender in turn was led to the see that flagrant guilt does not bar hope. The Law as in a figure dealt with that which is visible; the Gospel penetrates to the inmost soul.[28]

The conflict between conformity to the law and the inner love of the truth was at the heart of most every dispute Jesus had with the Pharisees. And so it was in this case also. After all the men left, Jesus addressed the woman with a question: "Woman, where are they? Did no one condemn you?" (John 8:10). She answered, "No one, Lord" (John 8:11a) to which Jesus replied, "I do not condemn you, either. Go. From now on sin no more" (John 8:11b). Jesus' words are a call of this woman to repent and believe. As Morris wrote:

> Jesus does not refer specifically to adultery, though there cannot be any doubt that that is primarily in mind. His words are perfectly general. He is calling the woman to amendment of life, the whole of life. It should not be overlooked that He says nothing about forgiveness. The guilty woman has given no sign of repentance or faith. What He does is to show mercy and call to righteousness.[29]

The Light of the World (John 8:12–59)

The first night of the Feast Tabernacles was celebrated each year by the lighting of the golden candelabras in the court of the women. The successive nights of the feast probably observed the same lighting of the candelabras. Jesus probably made an illusion to that observance when He said, "I am the Light of the world" (John 8:12). Westcott unfolds the meaning of the lighting of the candelabras:

> But the lamps themselves were only images of the pillar of light which had guided the people in the wilderness, just as the libations (vii.38) recalled the supply of water from the Rock. And it is to this finally that the words of the Lord refer. The idea of that light of the Exodus—transitory and partial—was now fulfilled in the living Light of the world . . . The same title in all its fulness was given by the Lord to His disciples.[30]

The feast had officially ended the previous day, but the Jews who gathered around Jesus on the following day had that ceremony still fresh in their minds. Jesus' reference to being the "Light of the world" would have also caused them to reflect on the Messianic hopes of the Jews (Cf. Isaiah 42:6; 49:6; and Malachi 4:2). Simeon had prophesied

---

28 Westcott, *The Gospel According to St. John*, 127.
29 Morris, *The Gospel According to John*, 891.
30 Westcott, *The Gospel According to St. John*, 128.

about Jesus at His presentation in the Temple, that He would be: "A light of revelation to the Gentiles, and the glory of Your people Israel" (Luke 2:32). Even the Jewish Midrash, according to Edersheim, explained the relationship of light with the Messiah as follows:

> In Messianic times God would, in fulfillment of the prophetic meaning of this rite,[31] 'kindle for them the Great Light,' and the nations of the world would point to them, who had lit the light for Him Who lightened the whole world.[32]

The place where Jesus engaged the Jews in this discourse of John 8 was the same court of women where the candelabras were lit every evening. In that colonnade, which was also called "the treasury" (John 8:20), there were several "receptacles for charitable contributions" and it was "the common meeting-place of the worshippers, and . . . the most generally attended part of the Sanctuary."[33] It was for that reason that Jesus often went to this court in order to teach the people. This was Jesus' first discourse with the Pharisees in the Temple and His teaching was unmistakable. There was no longer any pretense that the Jews did not want to kill Jesus. Even the crowds knew of their hostility and openly discussed that fact (John 7:1; 11; 19; 26; 30, 32). Jesus warned the Twelve that He would be handed over to the Gentiles by the Jews, scourged, and crucified. They had heard Jesus' words, but did not believe it could be true. This discourse was the claim by Jesus that He was the One sent by the Father as the Messiah. Having announced Himself as "the Light of the world," He next said, "He who follows Me will not walk in the darkness, but will have the Light of life" (John 8:12b). The Pharisees quickly contradicted Jesus' statements: "You are testifying about Yourself; Your testimony is not true" (John 8:13).

The response of the Pharisees was true in judicial cases where the testimony of two is necessary to establish every fact, but Jesus was not formally under investigation. Thus, their objection was another of their attempts to cause a conundrum for Him. It was tantamount to the various times when they had asked Him to give them a sign from heaven that He was the Messiah. They knew that He could not supply such an external, visible testimony for their own self-ap-

---

31 The rite which Edersheim references was the lighting of the candelabras at the Feast of Tabernacles.
32 Edersheim, *The Life and Times of Jesus the Messiah*, 589.
33 Edersheim, *The Life and Times of Jesus the Messiah* 588.

pointed court. That would be the miraculous sign the Pharisees were seeking, but even that would not have turned their malignity against Him into benignity—much less into discipleship. Thus, Jesus wisely ignored their demand, as Edersheim observes:

> If Christ had yielded to their appeal, and transferred the question from the moral to the coarsely external sphere, He would have ceased to be the Messiah of the Incarnation, Temptation, and Cross, the Messiah-Saviour. It would have been to un-Messiah the Messiah of the Gospel, for it was only in another form, a repetition of the Temptation.[34]

The devil was as much behind these temptations by the Pharisees as he was when he wanted Christ to cast Himself down from the pinnacle of the temple. Jesus performed many miracles, but He never did so for display. Jesus' retort to the Pharisees was: "Even if I testify about Myself, My testimony is true, for I know where I came from and where I am going; but you do not know where I came from or where I am going" (John 8:14). Such a statement was unanswerable by the Pharisees, especially when so boldly proclaimed by Jesus. Then, He laid out the first of His accusations against them: "You judge according to the flesh" (John 8:15a). The moral and spiritual corruption of human nature is interspersed by Jesus throughout this discourse. The Pharisees, despite their haughtiness and self-righteousness towards Jesus in this chapter, never understood His statements because they were deficient in the history of their own Bible. "Only he who has, in some measure, felt the agony of the first garden, can understand that of the second garden."[35] The Cross of Christ made no sense to them because they did not adequately understand the fall of our first parents into sin. Thus, when Jesus claimed to have the testimony of His Father, the Jews sarcastically queried Him: "Where is Your Father?" (John 8:19a). Their insinuation was a charge they would later openly allege against Him when they said, "We were not born of fornication; we have one Father, God" (John 8:41b).

Much of this discourse appears to be two parties accusing the other of the same things alleged against them and talking past one another. Both claimed to have God as their Father and both accused the other of being possessed of a demon. In John 8:44, Jesus says to the Pharisees, "You are of your father the devil." The Pharisees replied a

---

34 Edersheim, *The Life and Times of Jesus the Messiah*, 591.
35 Edersheim, *The Life and Times of Jesus the Messiah*, 590.

few verses later, "Do we not say rightly that You are a Samaritan and have a demon?" (John 8:48). The Pharisees knew very well that Jesus grew up in Galilee, but the accusation of being a Samaritan probably meant that He, like the Samaritans, only observed those parts of their tradition that He liked. The Jews also considered that demonology came into the land through the corruption of the Samaritans. Thus, they were essentially making the same charge against Him of having a demon by accusing Him of being a Samaritan. That is probably why Jesus only responded to the charge of having a demon, by saying: "I do not have a demon, but I honor My Father, and you dishonor Me" (John 8:49).

While accusing the Jews of not knowing Him or where He was from, Jesus said: "And you will know the truth, and the truth will make you free" (John 8:32). The Jews quickly retorted, "We are Abraham's descendants and have never yet been enslaved to anyone; how is that You say, 'You will become free'?" (John 8:33). Their answer was a denial of the facts of their history, as Westcott points out:

> The episodes of Egyptian, Babylonian, Syrian, and Roman conquests were treated as mere transitory accidents, not touching the real life of the people, who had never accepted the dominion of their conquerors or coalesced with them.[36]

The Jews had been in Egypt for four hundred years and in Babylon for seventy years. Plus they were under the dominion of the Romans at the present time. Yet, they claimed to never have been enslaved to anyone. Such a claim was nonsensical. It was also an attempt to avoid the freedom that Jesus was pressing on them—spiritual freedom. Thus, Jesus responded: "Truly, truly, I say to you, everyone who commits sin is the slave of sin"(John 8:34). Later, Jesus made two profound statements concerning Abraham: "Your father Abraham rejoiced to see My day, and He saw it was glad . . . Truly, truly, I say to you, before Abraham was born, I am" (John 8:56, 58). The first statement was another claim by Jesus to be the Messiah. Abraham saw the day of Christ on Mount Moriah when God commanded him to offer Isaac on the altar and then provided a ram as a substitute. Abraham in that exchange came to understand the gospel hereby God the Father gives His Son as the atonement for their sins. The second statement is Jesus claiming to be God. It is one of those "I am" statements that referred

---

36 Westcott, *The Gospel According to St. John*, 134.

to Jesus as Jehovah—"I am that I am" (Cf. Exodus 3:14). As Westcott once again states:

> The phrase marks a timeless existence. In this connexion "I was" would have expressed simple priority. Thus there is in the phrase the contrast between the created and the uncreated . . .[37]

Jesus was not created. Instead, He is the Creator of all things (John1:1–3). The Jews immediately understood the impact of Jesus' words and "they picked up stones to throw at Him, but Jesus hid Himself and went out of the temple" (John 8:59).

Healing the Man Born Blind (John 9:1–41)

Leaving the temple grounds to escape the mob trying to stone Him,[38] Jesus passed by a man who was blind from birth. His disciples immediately asked Him: "Rabbi, who sinned, this man or his parents, that he should be born blind?" (John 9:2). That was an age-old question based on the assumption that all suffering is due to personal sin. It was essentially the same question that was considered and argued by Job and his three friends. Jesus, therefore, answers this query of His disciples: "*It was* neither that this man sinned nor his parents; but *it was* so that the works of God might be displayed in him" (John 9:3). Jesus was not concerned with the cause of the suffering, but with its cure which provided an opportunity to glorify God. As Hendriksen wrote:

> All things—even afflictions and calamities—have as their ultimate purpose the glorification of God in Christ by means of the manifestation of his greatness.[39]

Jesus then said: "We must work the works of Him who sent Me as long as it is day; night is coming when no one can work. While I am in the world, I am the Light of the world" (John 9:5).[40] The Temple or its courts was "the chosen spot for those who, as objects of pity, solicited charity."[41] Thus, "we can scarcely doubt that the miracle took

---

37 Westcott, *The Gospel According to St. John* 140.
38 There are different opinions among commentators concerning when this healing took place, whether it was at the Feast of Tabernacles or the Feast of Dedication (which is also called the Feast of Lights). I agree with William Hendriksen who wrote: "But if the blind man was not cured on the day Jesus escaped being stoned to death, the miracle must have taken place very soon afterward (perhaps, the next day)." (Hendriksen, *The Gospel of John,* 72.
39 Hendriksen, *The Gospel of John,* 73.
40 Cf. John 8:12 where Jesus also referred to Himself as the Light of the world. John 8:12 and 9:5 connect these chapters together as having happened at the same feast.
41 Edersheim, *The Life and Times of Jesus the Messiah,* 597. Cf. Acts 3:10.

place at the entering to the Temple or the Temple-Mount."[42] Seeing the man's situation, Jesus spat on the ground, made a clay paste of it which He applied to the blind man's eyes with the command: "Go, wash in the pool of Siloam" (John 9:6). Siloam is the pool where Jesus healed the infirm man in John 5. The blind man, therefore, did as Jesus commanded him and came back seeing. "[T]he neighbors, and those previously saw him as a beggar, were saying, 'Is this not the one who used to sit and beg?'" (John 9:8). There was disagreement among them concerning his identity, but he kept saying to them, "I am the one" (John 9:9). When questioned intensely how his eyes were opened, the man replied: "The man who is called Jesus made clay, and anointed my eyes, and said to me, 'Go to Siloam and wash'; so I went away and washed, and I received sight" (John 9:12).

The Feast of Tabernacles ended on October 17th and the weekly Sabbath began at 6 PM on October 21st. John 9:14 simply says, "Now it was a Sabbath on the day when Jesus made the clay and opened his eyes." Leviticus 23:36 says concerning the eight day of the Feast of tabernacles: "For seven days you shall present an offering by fire to the Lord. On the eighth day you shall have a holy convocation and present an offering by fire to the Lord; it is assembly. You shall do no laborious work." The Pharisees thought that this miracle performed on the holy convocation of the eighth day gave them a charge against Jesus as a Sabbath breaker. The Talmudic rules against doing good on the Sabbath are given to us by Edersheim:

> The ground on which the present charge against Jesus would rest was plain: the healing involved a manifold breach of the Sabbath-law. The first of these was that He had made clay (Shabb. 24.3). Next, it would be a question whether any remedy might be applied to the holy day. Such could only be done in diseases of the internal organs (from the throat downwards), except when danger to life or the loss of an organ was involved (Jerus. Shabb. 14d). It was, indeed, declared lawful to apply, for example, wine to the outside of the eyelid, on the ground that this might be treated as washing; but it was sinful to apply it to the inside of the eye. And as regards saliva, its application to the eye is expressly forbidden, on the ground that it was evidently intended as a remedy (Jer. Shabb. 14d).[43]

After the crowd brought the man to the Pharisees, they declared

---

42 Edersheim, *The Life and Times of Jesus the Messiah*, 597.
43 Edersheim, *The Life and Times of Jesus the Messiah*, 600.

concerning Jesus, "This man is not from God, because He does not keep the Sabbath" (John 9:16a). That response by the Pharisees did not satisfy the crowd and there was a division among them with some saying, "How can a man who is a sinner perform such signs?" (John 9:16b). There were two different theories that were debated. The Pharisees started with the conviction that everyone who is righteous keeps the Sabbath commandment according to their Pharisaic rules. Many in the crowd started with the conviction that a sinner could not perform such miracles. The Sanhedrin had already made a decision that if anyone confessed Jesus "to be the Christ, he was to be put out of the synagogue" (John 9:22). That decision was, without doubt, in response to the conflicts that they had with Him in John 8. Many had come to believe in Him (John 7:31 and 8:30) at the Feast of Tabernacles which was making the Sanhedrin paranoid about losing their control over the religious worship of the people. The formerly blind man was specifically asked what he thought about Jesus and replied, "He is a prophet" (John 9:17b). He did not yet have faith to believe that Jesus was the Messiah, but he proved to be unafraid of the threats of the Sanhedrin and Pharisees. His parents timidly answered, "He is of age; ask him" (John 9:23). They were afraid of the Jews and the threat of being put out of the synagogue (John 8:22). In ancient Jerusalem, ex-communication from the synagogue carried frightful consequences in every area of Jewish life. Such a judgment could result in the loss of a job and the means to support one's family. The cowardice of the parents, while understandable on one level, was still wrong. F. L. Godet observes concerning their refusal to answer the rulers of the synagogue:

> The cowardice of the parents is, as it were, the prelude of that of the whole people.[44]

The Sanhedrin had been stumbling around trying to determine the best way to deal with both Jesus and the crowds that followed Him. Putting His followers out of the synagogue was "a new landmark on the path of hostile measures adopted with regard to Jesus; it is the transition between the sending of the officers (chap. viii.) and the decree of death in chap xi."[45] If they could not make Jesus heel

---

44 Frederick Louis Godet, *Commentary on the Gospel of John*, (Grand Rapids: Zondervan Publishing House, 1970), 2:133.
45 Godet, *Commentary on the Gospel of John*, 2:133

to their commands, then they would frighten His followers and turn the crowds against Him. Thus, they questioned the man born blind for the second time and said to Him, "Give glory to God; we know that this man is a sinner" (John 9:24). Their bullying methods did not work on him, though. He knew one thing and he knew it well: "one thing I do know, that though I was blind, now I see" (John 9:25). The more they tried to subdue this man, the bolder he became in his attachment to Jesus. When they asked him once again how Jesus healed him, he responded: "I told you already and you did not listen; why do you want to hear it again? You do not want to become His disciples too, do you?" (John 9:27). The half-ironic question of the formerly blind man stung the Pharisees to the quick,[46] causing them to lose "all self-possession" and to suffer a moral defeat.[47] Their sardonic reply was defensive in nature and they surely had the realization that they were losing the debate when they said, "You are His disciple, but we are disciples of Moses. We know that God has spoken to Moses, but as for this man, we do not know where He is from" (John 9:28, 29). Their self-conceit of moral superiority was gone and even their claims about Jesus were meekly expressed. Leon Morris' comments on their arguments are enlightening:

> They regard their ignorance of Jesus' origin as damaging to His cause. But in 7:27 it was said that when the Christ comes no one will know whence He comes. Their argument was less consistent than they may have thought. Had they considered its implications they might have been led to the truth.[48]

Some of the people were debating whether Jesus was the Christ and said concerning Him: "However, we know where this man is from; but whenever the Christ may come, no one knows where He is from." Even the Sanhedrin had said concerning Jesus to the officers who failed to arrest Him: "Search and see that no prophet arises out of Galilee" (John 7:52). Yet, now that same body says, "We do not know where He is from." After all the accusations they had brought against Jesus, how ironic that they now admit that they do not know where He was from. If they did not know that, how could they know that He was a sinner? The man pounced on their words and replied, "Well here is an amazing thing, that you do not know where He is

---

46 Edersheim, *The Life and Times of Jesus the Messiah*, 602.
47 Edersheim, *The Life and Times of Jesus the Messiah*, 602.
48 Morris, *The Gospel of John*, 492.

from, and yet He opened my eyes. We know that God does not hear sinners; but if anyone is God-fearing and does His will, He hears him. Since the beginning of time it has never been heard that anyone opened the eyes of a person born blind. If this man were not from God, He could do nothing" (John 9:30–33). The Pharisees had no response to those words except to retort abusively: "You were born entirely in sins, and are you teaching us?" (John 9:34). Then, they put the man out of the synagogue.

Jesus heard what had happened to the man and found him, probably near the spot where He first saw him. He then asked the man a question: "Do you believe in the Son of Man?" (John 9:35). That was followed by the man's question: "Who is He, Lord, that I may believe in Him?" (John 9:36). Jesus then indirectly revealed Himself to the man with this reply: "You have both seen Him, and He is the one who is talking to you" (John 9:37). The man simply responded, "Lord, I believe" and he worshiped Jesus (John 9:38). Thus, the eyes of his understanding were enlightened in the gospel.

The final words of this discourse are very telling. Jesus made the statement: "For judgment I came into this world, so that those who do not see, and that those who see may become blind" (John 9:39. The bold accusations of the Pharisees that Jesus was a sinner were all now gone. Instead of doubling down on their assertions about Jesus, they reveal the introspective doubts of their own hearts when they weakly ask, "We are not blind too, are we?" (John 9:40). As Morris comments:

> Their reaction was an incredulous question: "Are we also blind?" They are the embodiment of the condemnation of which Jesus was speaking. It never occurs to them that they can possibly be blind.[49]

As in so many similar instances, Jesus did not directly either confirm or deny that they were blind. If He had acquitted them, He would have done no good for the future generations who would read His words. Rather, he threw the whole question back in their laps: "If you were bind, you would have no sin; but since you say, 'We see', your sin remains" (John 9:41). The Pharisees had simply asked if they were blind also. Jesus replied, in effect, "If you think you see, you are blind." Ryle expresses the meaning of Jesus' words very well:

---

49 Morris, *The Gospel of John*, 497.

Our Lord's answer to the Pharisees is a very remarkable and elliptical one. It may be thus paraphrased: "Well would it be for you, if you were really blind and ignorant. If you were really ignorant, you would be far less blameworthy than you are now. If you were really blind, you would not be guilty of the sin of wilful unbelief, as you are now. But unhappily, you say that you know the truth, and see the light, and are not ignorant, even while you are rejecting Me. This self-satisfied state of mind is the very thing that is ruining you. It makes your sin abide heavily on you.[50]

For all their boasts and pretenses to be knowledgeable, there was a deep-seated doubt in the hearts of these Pharisees. They had gone from boldly accusing Jesus of sin to questioning their own spiritual status. Yet, they had not gone nearly far enough and were still in darkness.

The Good Samaritan (Matthew 22:34–40; Mark 12:28–34; and, Luke 10:25–37)

Following the conclusion of the Feast of Tabernacles, Jesus and His disciples began a journey on the main road between Jerusalem and Jericho, a "road notorious for its danger and difficulty."[51] Soon, there was a conversation with a Jewish lawyer along the journey who asked Jesus, "Teacher, what shall I do to inherit eternal life?" (Luke 10:25). The Lord asked him for a summary of the Ten Commandments. The lawyer summed up the law as follows: "You shall love the Lord your God with all your heart, and with all your soul, and with all your strength, and with all your mind; and your neighbor as yourself." (Luke 10:27). The first part of that answer concerning the love of God was given in Deuteronomy 6:5, which was known as the great Shema[52] for the Jews which was recited twice every day with their prayers. The second part, concerning loving your neighbor as yourself, is almost verbatim from Leviticus 19:18b—"but you shall love your neighbor as yourself; I am the Lord." Jesus then replied, "You have answered correctly; do this and you will live" (Luke 10:28).

Jesus was not advocating salvation by works with that response. Rather, He simply quoted Deuteronomy 18:5 which taught that the only way to obtain salvation through the law was to obey perfect-

---

50   John Charles Ryle, *Expository Thoughts on the Gospels: St. John*, (Cambridge and London: James Clarke & Co., LTD., 1969) 2:193.
51   Maura Sala, "The Road to Jericho," accessed at: www.bibleodyssey.org on September 7, 2023.
52   Shema is a Hebrew word which means 'hear.' It was a call for the Jews to hear and listen to these truths.

ly and unendingly.[53] This lawyer, obviously, belonged to that school of thought of Rabbi Hillel which taught that salvation could only be attained by keeping the law. Hillel had summarized the law in its briefest form as follows: "What is hateful to thee, do not to another. This is the whole Law; the rest is only explanation."[54] In Matthew 22:40, Jesus said something almost like Hillel's statement: "On these two commandments depend the whole Law and the Prophets." Likewise, Hillel's summary of the Law is turned into a positive statement in the Golden Rule—"In everything, therefore, treat people the same way you want them to treat you, for this is the Law and the Prophets" (Matthew 7:12). Jesus knew how to separate the dross from the gold and was able to bring forth both new and old things to teach the people. The Rabbis were often wrong, but not always and not in every circumstance. Jesus was capable of extracting the truth from all their wearying statements.

Yet, this lawyer quickly evidenced he had learned the dialectical subtlety of the Rabbis when he tried to justify himself by asking, "And who is my neighbor?" (Luke 10:29). It was the standard practice among the various schools of the Rabbis to ask one another a question that would require the other to engage in subtle distinctions that revealed the weakness of their positions. Moreover, the Middle Ages philosopher and Torah expert, Moses Ben Maimon or Maimonides, later wrote concerning the lawyer's question: "he excepts all Gentiles when he saith, His neighbor. An Israelite killing a stranger inhabitant, he doth not die for it by the Sanhedrin; because he said, 'If any one lift up himself against his neighbor.'"[55] Among the Jews during Jesus' days, it was a serious question whether a Gentile was a neighbor of a Jew. This parable is one of the best remembered of all Jesus' parables. Indeed, this parable might even have a factual basis, as Plummer notes:

> We may believe that the parable is not fiction but history. Jesus would not be likely to invent such behaviour, and attribute it to priest, Levite, and Samaritan, if it had not actually occurred. Nowhere else does He speak against priests or Levites. Moreover, the parable would have far more point if taken from real life.[56]

---

53 Jesus uses the present imperative verb form which has the meaning of "continually do this."
54 Edersheim, *The Life and Times of Jesus the Messiah*, 637-8.
55 Plummer, *A Critical and Exegetical Commentary on the Gospel According to S. Luke*, 285.
56 Plummer, *A Critical and Exegetical Commentary on the Gospel According to S. Luke* 285-6.

In His other parables, Jesus usually refers to indefinite events and places. In this parable, He spoke definitely of a man going down to Jericho. The road that such a person would have traveled to Jericho was notorious for robbers and murderers. As Edersheim described it:

> Some one coming from the Holy City, the Metropolis of Judaism, is pursuing the solitary desert-road, those twenty-one miles to Jericho, a district notoriously insecure, when he 'fell among robbers, who having both stripped and inflicted on him strokes, went away leaving him just as he was, half dead.'[57]

That road was a major highway for trading caravans, military forces, and pilgrims on their way to Jerusalem, but it was not safe to travel alone. Jericho is 825 feet below sea level and its climate is more like Africa than the Mediterranean climate of Jerusalem. It is actually an oasis in the desert all around it due to the water source commonly called, "Elisha's spring." Surrounded by the rocky Judean desert, Jericho was a difficult and arduous walk to Jerusalem even without the marauding bandits that were around every corner. Yet, in this parable, there was now the horrifying scene of a half-dead man left on the side of the road. What were the other travelers to do? Jesus says, "And by chance a priest was going down on that road, and when he saw him, he passed by on the other side" (Luke 10:32. A Levite did the same thing. Finally, a Samaritan came that way and "he felt compassion", bandaged his wounds, put oil and wine on his wounds, and carried him on his beast to an inn (Luke 10:33, 34). At the inn,[58] the Samaritan took care of the man and gave two denarii to the innkeeper with instructions, "Take care of him; and whatever more you spend, when I return I will repay you" (Luke 10:35). Thus, Jesus asked the lawyer, "Which of these three do you think proved to be a neighbor to the man who fell into the robber's *hand*s?" (Luke 10:36). All the lawyer could say was, "The one who showed mercy toward him" (Luke 10:37a). What the lawyer did not do was to refer to the Samaritan as the one who showed that mercy. Yet, Jesus had made His point and gave a truly gospel parable that made a complete change of the Jewish principles of hatred towards the Samaritans.

---

57   Edersheim, *The Life and Times of Jesus the Messiah*, 639.
58   There is an inn, the Good Samaritan Inn or Khan al-Ahmar, which is an Ottoman era hostel, only a few kilometers from Bethany on the southside of that road. That inn marks the spot where there was a caravansera, or a way station for travelers, dating back to Jesus' days. No doubt, that was the reference to 'an inn' in Jesus' parable. Cf. Maura Sala, "The Road to Jericho", accessed at: www.bibleodyssey.org on September 7, 2023.

The parable is even more amazing in light of the very recent treatment of Jesus and His disciples when they traveled through Samaritan territory on their way to Jerusalem for the Feast of Tabernacles. Jesus' kindly rebuke of James and John for their indignation was a precursor to this epistle. Plummer gives the moral of the parable:

> Christ not only forces the lawyer to answer his own question, but shows that it has been asked from the wrong point of view. For the question, "Who is my neighbour?" is substituted, "To whom am I neighbour? Whose claims on my neighbourly help do I recognize?" All three were by proximity neighbours to the man, and his claim was greater on the priest and Levite, but only the alien recognized any claim . . . "The neighbouring Jews became strangers, the stranger Samaritan became neighbour, to the wounded traveler. It is not place, but love, which makes neighborhood" (Wordsworth).[59]

Martha and Mary (Luke 10:38–42)

The road to Jericho passed through the little village of Bethany on the slopes of the southeast side of the Mount of Olives. To the east of of that little town was the desert where no one lived. McClintock and Strong describe the view from that village:

> The view from it is dreary and desolate. Olivet shuts out Jerusalem and the country westward; and the eye roams eastward down the bare, gray, "wilderness of Judea" into the deep valley of the Jordan, and then up again to the long wall of the Moab mountains on the distant horizon. The houses are massive and rude, built chiefly of old hewn stone.[60]

That desert area of the whole Jordan Valley, which empties into the Dead Sea, is the lowest place on earth and is more foreboding than can be conveyed in words. Yet, that was the only view which was visible to the people of this small village. It was a scene that could lead people to despair of life.

Bethany likely received its name due to the date trees that flourished in its vicinity (i.e., *"house of unripe dates"*). Palm trees, which were rare in other parts of Israel, also flourished there. Having just given the parable of the Good Samaritan concerning the dangers that awaited men on that road, Jesus and His disciples stopped in Bethany for a visit where they were invited by a woman named Martha into her home (Luke 10:38).

---

59 Plummer, *A Critical and Exegetical Commentary on the Gospel According to S. Luke*, 288–9.
60 McClintock and Strong, *Cyclopedia of Biblical, Theological, and Ecclesiastical Literature*, 11:470.

Villages, like Bethany, were too small to have a synagogue and it was very unusual to have such a distinguished guest as Jesus—esteemed by many people to be a Rabbi—to visit them. Rather, "their inhabitants were supposed to go to the nearest township for market on the Monday and Thursday of every week, when service was held for them, and the local Sanhedrin also sat (*Megill. 1:1–3*)."[61] Yet, Martha and her sister, Mary, were unexpectedly visited by the One about whom everyone in Israel was conversing. As a good host, Martha quickly became busy in her preparations for her guests. Mary responded differently to Jesus' visit. She was soon "seated at the Lord's feet, listening to His word" (Luke 10:39). Hendriksen describes the scene:

> Up to this point what a scene of serenity, tranquility. All is well in the lovely home at Bethany. A moment ago Martha extended a hearty welcome to Jesus. And now, Mary, her sister, is already seated at his feet, those very feet which at a later occasion she is going to anoint (John 12:3; cf. Matt. 26:6, 7; Mark 14:3). Here she is now sitting eagerly listening to the words of life that are issuing from the Savior's heart and lips. "All is well. All is well."[62]

The seeming indifference of Mary to all the work that Martha had to do was too much for her sister. How quickly her countenance and disposition changed. She soon became "distracted with all her preparations" (Luke 10:40) and her temper just as quickly got the best of her. There was a party of at least 15 people who needed to be served and Mary was sitting on the floor. Geldenhuys' comments are instructive:

> Martha certainly meant well, but alas, her too great zeal to entertain the Saviour well, caused her to become sulky towards her sister who sat and listened, and also towards the Lord Himself because He did not tell Mary to go and help with the serving. She is so dissatisfied that she wants to instruct the Saviour as to what He should do, namely to command Mary to help her. In this way she disturbed the harmony between herself and her sister and between herself and the Lord through her unbalanced zeal to entertain Jesus as lavishly as possible.[63]

Martha's impatience of spirit and temper are evidenced by "her addressing the rebuke to [Jesus] rather than to her sister"[64] She was angry with Jesus for allegedly being so unconcerned with her own

---

61 Edersheim, *Sketches of Jewish Social Life in the Days of Christ*, 87.
62 Hendriksen, *Exposition of the Gospel According to Luke*, 598.
63 Geldenhuys, *Commentary on the Gospel of Luke*, 315-6.
64 Plummer, *The Gospel According to St. Luke*, 291.

plight. Thus, she rebuked the Lord: "Lord, do you not care that my sister has left me to do all the serving alone? Then tell her to help me" (Luke 10:40). Martha was naturally energetic and active; Mary was more retiring and contemplative. Both had believed in Jesus and rejoiced to have Him in their home. But Martha allowed her strengths to be her stumbling block, as Ryle notes:

> In so saying, this holy woman forgot what she was, and to whom she was speaking. She brought down on herself a solemn rebuke, and had to learn a lesson which probably made a lasting impression. Alas! "how great a matter a little fire kindleth." The beginning of all this was a little over-anxiety about the innocent household affairs of this world![65]

Jesus was continually full of the Spirit and His gentle, but firm rebuke of Martha exhibits that fact. In words of tenderness, He says to her: "Martha, Martha, you are worried and bothered about so many things; but only one thing is necessary, for Mary has chosen the good part, which shall not be taken away from her" (Luke 10:41, 42). Proverbs 15:1 says: "A gentle answer turns away wrath, but a harsh word stirs up anger." Jesus' rebuke of Martha was soft and gentle, but it was a rebuke nonetheless. Martha had allowed an agitated spirit to upset all the glory of this visit to her home by Jesus and His disciples. A rebuke of Mary by Jesus would not have made things better, but rather worse. Martha, not Mary, needed a kind admonition because she was guilty of two errors, according to Calvin:

> Although Martha's hospitality was praiseworthy and indeed is praised, yet Christ points out two faults in it. The first is that Martha goes too far and is extravagant. Christ preferred frugality and moderate meals, so that the godly housewife should not be put to a lot of work. The second fault was that Martha left Him and was busy with unnecessary tasks and so made Christ's coming useless so far as she was concerned.[66]

Yet, having said that, it would be a mistake to draw the wrong lesson that Jesus was endorsing the contemplative life. It was Aristotle—not Christ—"who placed the highest and ultimate good of the human life in contemplation, which he calls the fruition of virtue."[67] Mary was praised for sitting and listening at the feet of Jesus and, thereby, having "chosen the good part, which shall not be taken away

---

65 John Charles Ryle, *Expository Thoughts on the Gospels: Luke* (Edinburgh. Scotland and Carlisle, Pennsylvania: The Banner of Truth Trust, 1986), 1:385.
66 Calvin, *A Harmony of the Gospels Matthew, Mark and Luke*, 2:89–90.
67 Calvin, *A Harmony of the Gospels Matthew, Mark and Luke*, 2:89.

from her" (Luke 10:42). Yet, it was not indolent contemplation that Jesus praised. Her decision was tied to the Person of Christ—not to an action. Martha's decision was an action to the neglect of the Person of Christ.

17

Jesus' Ministry in Perea

Following His visit with Martha, Mary, and Lazarus in Bethany, Jesus continued on His journey to the territory of Perea which formed part of the kingdom of Herod Antipas. Perea is "a name given to a portion of the country beyond Jordan, or on the east side of the river, the ancient possession of the two tribes of Reuben and Gad . . . it was bounded on the west by Jordan, east by Philadelphia, north by Pella, and south by the castle of Machaerus. The country was fruitful, abounding with pines, olive-trees, palm-trees, and other plants, which grew in the fields in abundance; it was well-watered with springs and torrents from the mountains."[1] Bruce describes Jesus' return to this region of the Holy Land:

> After His final departure from Galilee, Jesus found Himself a new place of abode and scene of labor for the brief remainder of His life, in the region laying to the east-ward of the Jordan, at the lower end of its course. 'He departed Galilee, and came into the borders of Judea beyond Jordan.'[2] We may say that He ended His ministry where it began, healing the sick, and teaching the high doctrines of the kingdom in the place which witnessed His consecration by baptism to His sacred work, and where He gained His first disciples.[3]

This portion of Jesus' Perean ministry was conducted from about November of AD 29 through the end of February in AD 30. There certainly were various miracles that He performed, but there was very little that was new during these months. Jesus neither purposely provoked the Jewish leaders nor unnecessarily avoided them. The Sanhedrin knew where He was, though, even as they had always known where John the Baptist was preaching and baptizing. They maintained a watchful and suspicious eye on the Galilean at all times

Luke does not give us the place or the setting of the events that he chronicled in chapters eleven and twelve of his Gospel, but they

---

1 McClintock and Strong, *Cyclopedia of Biblical, Theological, and Ecclesiastical Literature*, 7:932.
2 Matthew 19:1.
3 Bruce, *The Training of the Twelve*, 250.

consisted mostly of discourses and parables. That was the way Jesus began His ministry in Galilee and He did the same in Perea. This period was interrupted by Jesus' brief return to Jerusalem for the Feast of Dedication in late December. Many of the discourses of Jesus during this time covered the same themes as the Sermon on the Mount with only a few additions. It is certainly reasonable to assume that Jesus could have and would have taught the Jews in Perea and Judea the same things He had earlier taught the Galileans. The Gospel of John gives us the majority of the incidents for this phase of Jesus' ministry. As Edersheim notes:

> It will be noticed that this section is peculiarly lacking in *incident* . . . And this, not only because the season of the year must have made itinerancy difficult, and thus have hindered the introduction of new scenes and of new persons, but chiefly from the character of His Ministry in Peraea . . . Besides, after what had passed, and must now have been so well known, illustrative Deeds could scarcely have been so requisite in Peraea. In fact, His Peraean was, substantially a resumption of His early Galilean Ministry, only modified and influenced by the much fuller knowledge of the people concerning Christ, and the greatly developed enmity of their leaders.[4]

Persevering in Prayer (Luke 11:1–13)

On one occasion during those months, Jesus "was praying in a certain place," and "after He had finished, one of the disciples said to Him, 'Lord, teach us to pray just as John also taught his disciples'" (Luke 11:1). The Lord then gave them the greatest model for prayer ever devised and it was a repetition of what He had taught in the Sermon on the Mount. He showed them that prayer requires devotion as well as the right form. We must pray with the Spirit and with the understanding (1 Corinthians 14:15). To enforce this model prayer on His disciples, He also gave them a parable on the necessity of perseverance in their prayers. It was customary in warmer climates to travel by night which also meant that one would arrive at the destination in the night also—an inconvenient time for those who are already asleep. In Jesus' parable, a man came at night to his friend's house after the whole family had already retired to bed. The owner of the house was reluctant to get up and help his friend, but finally was persuaded to do so by his perseverance in knocking. From that parable, Jesus commented:

> Now suppose one of you fathers is asked by his son for a fish; he will

---

4 Edersheim, *The Life and Times of Jesus the* Messiah, 610.

not give him a snake instead of a fish, will he? Or if he is asked for an egg, he will not give him a scorpion, will he? (Luke 11:11, 12).

Fishermen sometimes catch reptiles and amphibians rather than fish, which makes the first question understandable, but the reference to scorpions is not as clear. Ryle makes the following explanation:

> Bishop Pearce shows by a quotation from Bochart, that the large kind of scorpions, when coiled and rolled up, had a white body not unlike an egg.[5]

The point of this parable is that persevering prayer will be rewarded. The three commands in Luke 11:10 are all in the present imperative tense—continue asking, continue seeking, continue knocking. God rewards those who persevere.

Casting Out a Demon (Luke 11:14–28)
Following that parable on prayer, Jesus cast a demon out of a mute man. This miracle is similar to one performed by Him in Galilee for a blind and mute man who was also demon-possessed (Matthew 12:22–24). This miracle led to the same kind of charge that had been brought against Jesus on many different occasions: "He casts out demons by Beelzebul, the ruler of the demons" (Luke 11:19). It also resulted in the same amazement among the crowds (Luke 11:14) which followed His other exorcisms. The Jews had a quirky view of demonology in which they believed:

> [T]he power of evil is not contrasted with that of good, nor Satan with God. The devil is presented rather as the enemy of man, than of God and good.[6]

The Jews saw no contradiction in saying that Christ cast out demons by the power of Beelzebul. Their position was so inconsistent that it is hard to explain how they could hold it. Thus, Jesus simply stated: "Any kingdom divided against itself is laid waste; and a house divided against itself falls" (Luke 11:17).

Luke also gives the context for the woes that Jesus declared against the scribes, Pharisees, and hypocrites (more fully given in Matthew 23). A Pharisee had asked Him to have lunch and was offended when Jesus did not ceremonially wash His hands before eating. That set the stage for Jesus to chastise them for their hypocrisy in washing the

---

5 John Charles Ryle, *Expository Thoughts on the Gospels: Luke* (Cambridge and London: James Clarke & Co., Ltd., 1969), 2:14.
6 Edersheim, *The Life and Times of Jesus the Messiah*, 1024.

outside of cups and platters while their own hearts remained unclean. Jesus' words were so stern that a lawyer replied to Him, "Teacher, when You say this, You insult us too" (Luke 11:45). To which, Jesus responded: "Woe to you lawyers as well! For you weight men down with burdens hard to bear, while you yourselves will not even touch the burdens with one of your fingers" (Luke 11:46). It might seem surprising that a Pharisee would ask Jesus to a meal at this point in His ministry, but Edersheim explains how this would have happened:

> Bitter as was the enmity of the Pharisaic party against Jesus, it had not yet spread, not become so avowed in every place to supersede the ordinary rules of courtesy.[7]

While certain of the Pharisees would invite Jesus to their homes for a meal or to question Him on some theological matter, they also would pivot quickly and turn against Him if His answers did not please them. Thus, the closing verses of Luke 11 state: "When He left there, the scribes and Pharisees began to be very hostile and to question Him closely on many subjects, plotting against Him to catch Him in something He might say" (Luke 11:53, 54).

These Pharisees had taken seriously their responsibility to be hospitable to strangers, especially a well-known teacher of Israel as was Jesus. The invitation was probably sincerely given to a degree, but their sincerity was as superficial as Jesus revealed in His denunciations of them. Yet, despite the opposition of the Pharisees, Jesus continued to see the crowds increase to the point that "so many thousands of people gathered together that they were stepping on one another" (Luke 12:1). Even in semi-retirement and away from the larger cities, Jesus' ministry continued to grow in power and in popularity.

Repent or Perish (Luke 13:1–9)

In Luke 13:1–9, there are three exhortations to repentance. The first two are references to actual events that had happened, while the third is a parable. In the first occurrence, Jesus was informed about the sacrilegious act of Pilate in mixing the blood of certain Galilean worshipers with their sacrifices. Luke 13:1 states: "Now on the same occasion there were some present who reported to Him about the Galileans whose blood Pilate had mixed with their sacrifices." Such mixing of human blood with the sacrifices required by God was a desecration of

---

7 Edersheim, *The Life and Times of Jesus the Messiah*, 616.

the whole sacrificial system and was an abomination to the Jews similar to the desecration of the Temple during the invasion of Jerusalem by Antiochus IV Epiphanes, king of Syria, in 167 B.C. That pagan monarch desecrated the altar of the Temple by offering there a pig to Zeus. Pigs were considered the most abominable animals to the Jews and an offering to a heathen god made it even worse. It probably had happened at the most recent Feast of Tabernacles. Yet, "the turbulent character of the Galileans, and the severity of Pilate and other Roman governors, make the incident more than credible."[8] Josephus refers to either this event or a similar one where he records concerning Pilate:

> After this he raised another disturbance, by expending that sacred treasure which is called Corban upon aqueducts, whereby he brought water from the distance of four hundred furlongs. At this the multitude had great consternation; and when Pilate was come to Jerusalem, they came about his tribunal, and made a clamour of it. Now when he was apprised of this disturbance, he mixed his own soldiers in their armour with the multitude, and ordered them to conceal themselves under the habits of private men, and not indeed to use their swords, but with staves to beat those that made the clamour.[9]

The tower of Siloam that Jesus referenced was erected by Pilate in the rebuilding of the underground aqueduct which brought water from the nearby Gihon Spring. That spring was outside the Jaffa Gate on the west side of Jerusalem and it brought water to the city through an underground aqueduct built by Hezekiah. His workers had to cut through almost 2,000 feet of solid rock to build the aqueduct which protected the city from having their water supply cut off by invading armies. The pool of Siloam was fed by the aqueduct and was fifty-three feet long, eighteen feet wide, and nineteen feet deep.

The two events—mixing the blood of the Galileans with their sacrifices and the tower of Siloam falling on eighteen people—were fresh in the memory of the Jews in Perea. Concerning the first event, "probably the Galileans (who were particularly rebellious by nature) had contravened some Roman law or other and had given to Pilate the opportunity of venting his bloodthirstiness on them."[10] Pilate, who was a master of half-measures, then likely sent his soldiers among the crowds surreptitiously with orders to beat them to death

---
8 Plummer, *A Critical and Exegetical Commentary on the Gospel According to S. Luke*, 337.
9 Josephus, *Complete Works of Flavius Josephus*, 479.
10 Geldenhuys, *Commentary on the Gospel of Luke*, 370.

with their staves.[11] This resulted in a great deal of Galileans' blood being shed. The falling of the tower of Siloam on eighteen people was referenced by Jesus to dismiss the "generally accepted notion that whenever calamities visited people this was a proof that they were exceptionally sinful and for that reason God allowed them to be overtaken by such disasters."[12] That Jewish notion was the underpinnings of the argument Job's three friends had used against him, but God rebuked it. Jesus used both of these events to issue a call to repentance without which every unbelieving person will perish. While the subject of repentance is repugnant to the natural man, Philip Henry—the brother of Matthew Henry, the great commentator—once said:

> Some people do not like to hear much of repentance. But, I think it is so necessary, that if I should die in the pulpit, I should desire to die preaching repentance; and if I should die out of the pulpit, I should desire to die practicing it.[13]

The necessity of repentance in order to escape eternal damnation led Jesus to give a parable on the barren fig tree. It generally takes three years for a fig tree to attain maturity and to start producing ripened fruit. In Jesus' parable, a man had planted a fig tree in his vineyard but the tree had not produced any fruit after three years. Thus, he ordered his vineyard-keeper: "Cut it down! Why does it even use up the ground?" (Luke 13:7b). The response of the vineyard keeper was: "Let it alone, sir for this year too, until I dig around it and put in fertilizer; and if it bears fruit next year, *fine*; but if not, cut it down" (Luke 13:8, 9). This parable teaches both the patience of God in giving sinners time to repent and the necessity of repentance without delay. It was an excellent commentary on the nation of Israel during Jesus' life. The Jews had the leaves which, supposedly, proved they were alive, but they did not have the fruits of repentance. A similar parable of a vineyard was given in Isaiah 5:1–7 where the prophet identifies Israel as the vineyard of the Lord. When the Lord came looking for good grapes, He found only worthless ones on it (cf. Isaiah 5:2). God is long-suffering, but He will by no means clear the guilty, as Ryle notes:

---

11 The staves carried by Roman soldiers were about 3 feet long and made of hardened wood or a vine wood rod. They were primarily used for casual corporal punishment.
12 Geldenhuys, *Commentary on the Gospel of Luke*, 370.
13 Ryle, *Expository Thoughts on the Gospels, St.* Luke, 2:112.

It is very probable that all unconverted members of Christ's Church will be found at the last day to have had their special "time of visitation," and to have been "digged about" by special providences, at some period of their lives. Hence their final condemnation will be proved most just.[14]

Robert Murray McCheyne (1813–1843) once penned a poem about this parable, "The Barren Fig-Tree," in which the last three stanzas state:

> How many years has thou, my heart, Acted the barren fig-tree's part, Leafy, and fresh, and fair,— Enjoying heavenly dews of grace, And sunny smiles from God's own face! But where the fruit? Ah! Where? How often must the Lord have prayed, That still my day might be delayed
>
> Till all due means were tried! Afflictions, mercies, health, and pain, How long shall these be all in vain, To teach this heart of pride! Learn, O my soul, what God demands, Is not a faith like barren sands, But fruit of heavenly hue. By this we prove that Christ we know, If in His holy steps we go; Faith works by love, if true.

McCheyne's poem captures the essence of what Jesus taught in all His discourses and parables. True faith is a working faith. James wrote: "I will show you my faith by my works" (James 2:18). And Paul said essentially the same thing: "For in Christ Jesus neither circumcision nor uncircumcision means anything, but faith working through love" (Galatians 5:6).

Journey to the Feast of Dedication (Luke 13:22–35)

Luke does not specify the particular places where Jesus visited in Perea, but he does give a synopsis of the things He taught to the people. The time was drawing near for the end of Jesus' ministry on this earth and His teaching was more poignant and direct than ever before. The Scripture, therefore, says: "And He was passing through from one city and village to another, and proceeding on His way to Jerusalem" (Luke 13:22). What Luke records of that teaching is abbreviated versions of what Jesus had taught on other occasions in Galilee, as Edersheim notes:

> Their consideration may be the more brief, that throughout we find points of correspondence with previous or later portions of His teaching.[15]

---

14 Ryle, *Expository Thoughts on the Gospels, St. Luke*, 2:118.
15 Edersheim, *The Life and Times of Jesus the Messiah*, 681.

What Jesus taught during the Sermon on the Mount was woven into His teaching wherever He went because that sermon was His basic message to all those who would become His followers. Most of the people in Perea had not heard that sermon which partially explains why there was this overlap in Jesus' teaching. While the Sermon on the Mount was preached to His disciples, these words were taught in response to a question: "Lord, are there just a few who are being saved?" (Luke 13:23). Whether that question evidenced an understanding of eternal salvation or simply referred to the Pharisaic understanding of the supposed privileges of the Messianic Kingdom is a matter of indifference. Jesus' answer was certainly directed to the reality of personal salvation from the torments of hell and to the enjoyment of heaven. His reply to that question was: "Strive to enter through the narrow door; for many I tell you, will seek to enter and will not be able" (Luke 13:24). Matthew 7:13, 14, while longer, was essentially the same statement. Ryle comments concerning Jesus' answer:

> He addressed these words to the whole company of His hearers. He thought it not good to gratify the curiosity of His questioner by a direct reply; He chose rather to press home on him, and all around him, their own immediate duty. In minding their own souls the would soon find the question answered. In striving to enter in at the strait gates they would soon see whether the saved were many or few.[16]

Jesus' indirect answer was also the best way to unmask hypocrites and manifest true worshipers. It has always been the hope of the natural man that salvation can be attained with little effort and without the renunciation of sin or the pursuing after holiness. Samuel Davies once showed that Jesus' words were something of a parable even among the ancient philosophers before He was born. Socrates, renowned for his works on ethics, stated: "I urge men to virtue, to which the ascent is steep, and unfrequented by most."[17] Apollo is credited by Eusebius with the following oracle concerning knowledge: "The way of the blessed is extremely rugged and of difficult ascent. The entrance is secured by brazen gates—and the roads to be passed through impossible to be described."[18] The Roman poet, Virgil, wrote concerning hell: "The path that leads down to hell is easy: and the gate of the in-

---

16 Ryle, *Expository Thoughts on the Gospels: Luke*, 2:133
17 Thomas Clinton Pears, Jr., ed., Samuel Davies, "Charity and Truth United, or The Way of the Multitude Exposed in Six Letters", Journal of the Presbyterian Historical Society, Vol XIX (1941), 204.
18 Pears, ed., Davies, "Charity and Truth United", 221.

fernal deity stands wide open night and day; but few enjoy the happy Elysian Fields."[19] Hesiod, a Greek poet thought to be a contemporary of Homer, wrote concerning virtue: "The gods have annex[ed] sweat to the pursuit of virtue; and the way to it is tedious and very rough at first."[20] Horace, the leading lyric poet during the reign of Caesar Augustus, also spoke of "the difficult way of virtue."[21] Lactantius, advisor to the Roman Emperor, Constantine I, and author of one of the first books on Christian theology, summarized the teachings of the poets and philosophers: "The way of virtue is, at first entrance, difficult and very rough; but that of vice, is at first, very pleasant, and much beaten down."[22] Thus, Davies concluded concerning the pursuit of personal salvation:

> If to live among the Multitude, will carry a Man to Heaven; if that Degree of Virtue & Holiness is Sufficient, which the most of Mankind content themselves with; then the Way of Life is certainly broad & easy; & cannot be missed by fashionable Sinners. And what can be more acceptable than this to the numerous Friends of Sin, who cannot bear the Strictness of universal Holiness?[23]

Jesus' words to the questioner, and all those who heard Him, were a direct denunciation of the false idea that heaven may be gained with little or no effort and while continuing to live in sin. He, therefore, described a scene in which anxious people outside the gates will seek to have the doors opened to them. From within Jesus replies to them: "I do not know where you are from" (Luke 13:25). They answer Him: "We ate and drank in Your presence, and You taught in our streets" (Luke 13:26). Once again, Jesus answered them," I tell you, I do not know where you are from; depart from Me you evil doers" (Luke 13:26). This response by Jesus was a shock to these Jews, as Geldenhuys states:

> Their remorse will be so much the worse because while they, as members of the chosen people are excluded, even Gentiles from all parts of the world will enter the kingdom of God. It will be the exact opposite of their own ideas, which were that Gentiles would be excluded and that they, as members of the chosen people, would be the blessed and privileged ones. Thus the first shall be last and the last first.[24]

---

19 Pears, ed., Davies, "Charity and Truth United", 221.
20 Pears, ed., Davies, "Charity and Truth United", 221.
21 Pears, ed., Davies, "Charity and Truth United", 221.
22 Pears, ed., Davies, "Charity and Truth United", 221.
23 Pears, ed., Davies, "Charity and Truth United", 204.
24 Geldenhuys, *Commentary on the Gospel of Luke*, 380.

Jesus described people coming "from east and west and from north and south, and will recline at table in the kingdom of God . . . but yourselves being thrown out" (Luke 13:28, 29). That was a shocking idea to the Jews and probably is the reason that "at that same time some Pharisees approached, saying to Him, 'Go away, leave here, for Herod wants to kill You" (Luke 13:31). For many years, there had been a close connection between Herod and the Pharisees which is why they so often acted in concert with one another. No doubt, the Pharisees had urged Herod to imprison and kill John the Baptist. Now, whether they had recently conferred with Herod or not, the Pharisees urged Jesus essentially to run for His life. Nehemiah, likewise, had been tempted by his enemies to flee for his life, but his reply was, "Should such a man like me flee?" (Nehemiah 6:11). That was even more so the sentiment of Jesus who had come in the flesh for the purpose of dying for His people. Jesus always avoided those people who wanted to kill Him before His time, but was ready to lay down His life willingly when His time would arrive. Thus, His response to those Pharisees was this: "Go and tell that fox, 'Behold, I cast out demons and perform cures today and tomorrow, and the third *day* I reach My goal'" (Luke 13:32). Jesus did not mince words in describing Herod—he was a fox because of his cunning and scheming ways. He was also a weak-willed person who had been forced into executing John the Baptist by his even more cunning wife, Herodias.

Jesus' words to the Pharisees were an unmistakable prediction of His death, for He said, "Nevertheless, I must journey on today and tomorrow and the next *day*; for it cannot be that a prophet would perish outside of Jerusalem" (Luke 13:33). Everything would be done in accordance with God's eternal plan. "It was Jerusalem that killed the prophets. So Jesus must continue on his way today, tomorrow, and the next day."[25] In Jerusalem, the Sanhedrin wielded more influence than anywhere else. They could and would meet to condemn Him to death. Jesus knew all that beforehand. His words to the Pharisees, and through the Pharisees to Herod, were a clear indication that He would die on God's timetable and not at Herod's whim.

This section of the Gospel is concluded with one of the most poignant expressions of grief and love for Jerusalem found anywhere in the Scripture. Jesus exclaims: "O Jerusalem, Jerusalem, the city that

---

25 Hendriksen, *Exposition of the Gospel According to Luke*, 710.

kills the prophets and stones those sent to her! How often I wanted to gather your children together, just as a hen gathers her brood under her wings, and you would not have it! Behold, your house is left to you desolate: and I say to you, you will not see Me until the time comes when you say, 'Blessed is He who comes in the name of the Lord!'" (Luke 13:34, 35). Calvin eloquently unfolds the meaning of Jesus' lament:

> There is pathos in Christ's voice raised up at the monstrous sight—God's holy city so sunk in mental decay that it had long tried to extinguish God's teaching by the bloodshed of the prophets. This is the relevance of the name repeated, for no ordinary word of detestation was fit for such prodigious and incredible wickedness. Christ is not reproving any particular murder, but a city so steeped in the habit that it did not cease slaying as many prophets as were sent.[26]

The Feast of Dedication (John 10:1–42)

The tenth chapter of John contains Jesus' discourse on the Good Shepherd[27] and the reaction of the Jews to what He taught. John 10:22, 23 state: "At that time the Feast of Dedication took place at Jerusalem; it was winter, and Jesus was walking in the temple in the portico of Solomon." In 29 AD, the Feast of Dedication began on December 19th and ended on December 26th, a feast of eight days like the Feast of Tabernacles. The weather in Jerusalem is moderately cold in late December with the high temperatures ranging from the 40's to 50's Fahrenheit.

The Feast of Dedication, or Hannukah,[28] was instituted to celebrate and commemorate the cleansing of the Temple and the rebuilding of the altar by Judas Maccabeus in 164 BC. While this feast was not proscribed by the Lord, it was a natural response of the Jews to their return to the true worship according to Scripture. In many ways, it was a celebration similar to Thanksgiving in the US. Most Jews did not go up to Jerusalem for this feast, though, but those who did were filled with joy in the remembrance of God's past deliverance and their hope for the future. During the celebration of this non-scriptural

---

26 Calvin, A *Harmony of the Gospels Matthew, Mark, and Luke*, 3:67.
27 The whole of John 10 appears to have taken place during the Feast of Dedication. Some commentators divide the chapter into two sections with the first taking place during the Feast of Tabernacles and only the section beginning with verse 22 to the end of the chapter taking place during the Feast of Dedication. Yet, the unity of theme in Jesus' teaching on the Good Shepherd is a strong argument that His words were not separated by two months.
28 Hannukah is also called the Feast of Lights, as well as the Feast of Dedication.

feast, lights were placed in the Temple and every home for each day of the feast. It was a symbol that God had come to the people during their darkest period and had given them light. In many ways, there was a close similarity between the Feast of Tabernacles and the Feast of Dedication. Just a few months previously, Jesus had declared at the Feast of Tabernacles, "I am the Light of the world" (John 8:12). Many of those worshipers who gathered for this celebration probably remembered Jesus' earlier words.

Despite being counseled by the Pharisees to flee from Herod who was seeking to kill Him, Jesus promptly went up to the Feast of Dedication where His teaching in the portico of Solomon was more visible in light of the diminished crowds. He purposely chose a topic that was deeply rooted in the Old Testament, and one of the great themes of the Scripture, in the contrast between true and false shepherds. In Ezekiel 34, the Lord God had proclaimed that He Himself was the true shepherd and that He would "seek the lost, bring back the scattered, bind up the broken and strengthen the sick" (Ezekiel 34:16). In John 10, Jesus identified Himself as that Good Shepherd even as the Lord God had described Himself in Ezekiel. Thus, it was not surprising when Jesus said, "I and the Father are one" (John 10:30). If the Father is the Good Shepherd and Jesus is the Good Shepherd, then Jesus is also the Lord God and equal with the Father. Much of the first eighteen verses is a contrast between the Good Shepherd *and* the thieves and robbers who, by implication, the Jewish leaders had become. Whereas Jesus "came that they might have life, and have it abundantly," the thieves and robbers had come "only to steal and kill and destroy" (John 10:10). The way the Good Shepherd provides that abundant life is by laying down "His life for the sheep" (John 10:11). Instead of fleeing for His life, Jesus taught at the feast in Jerusalem that the hired hand "sees the wolf coming, and leaves the sheep and flees, and the wolf snatches them and scatters them" (John 10:12). The Good Shepherd, in contrast, lays down His life for the sheep most willingly (Cf. John 10:15, 17, 18). Jesus was more intent to teach that particular truth at that time, for two reasons: First, He wanted His sheep to know that He would not flee for His life, like the hireling does. Second, He wanted to comfort His sheep that His death was altogether voluntary and that He would raise it back up. At this Feast of Dedication, Jesus for the first time openly taught the people the

Jesus' Ministry in Perea

same things He had been teaching His disciples ever since His transfiguration on Mount Hermon. As Ryle commented on this section:

> The treachery of Judas, the armed band of priests' servants, the enmity of the Scribes and Pharisees, the injustice of Pontius Pilate, the rude hands of Roman soldiers, the scourge, the nails, and the spear—all these could not have harmed a hair of our Lord's head, unless He had allowed them.[29]

Jesus wanted all His followers, not just His disciples, to know that His imminent death was neither an accident nor the sole result of the malignancy of wicked men. What He taught at the Feast of Dedication, Peter affirmed on the Day of Pentecost: "This *Man*, delivered over by the predetermined plan and foreknowledge of God, you nailed to a cross by the hands of godless men, and put Him to death" (Acts 2:23). Jesus' words, though, went beyond what Peter proclaimed. Certainly, the death of Christ was by the predetermined plan and foreknowledge of God, but it was also by the submission of the will of Christ who chose to lay down His life for the sheep, even as Hebrews recorded concerning the eternal plan of God: "Sacrifice and offering You have not desired, but a body You have prepared for Me; in whole burnt offerings and sacrifices for sin You have taken no pleasure. Then I said, 'Behold, I have come (In the scroll of the book it is written of Me) to do Your will, O God'" (Hebrews 10:5–7). In the counsels of eternity, the Father and the Son made the covenant of redemption to save lost sinners through the death of the only begotten Son who would willingly lay down His life for His sheep. Thus, Jesus was never enticed by the Pharisees who counseled Him to flee for safety. He knew the purpose for which He had come into the world.

Knowing that the treachery and cunning of Herod was probably known to the crowds in Jerusalem, Jesus went there to comfort the hearts of His true followers. He stated to them: "I lay down My life so that I may take it again" (John 10:17). As usual, though, Jesus was being watched at this feast and a division was soon stirred up among the people. Some of them said, "He has a demon and is insane. Why do you listen to Him?" (John 10:20). Others responded, "These are not the sayings of one demon-possessed. A demon cannot open the eyes of the blind, can he?" (John 10:21). Jesus' words seemed utterly inconsistent, as Hendriksen notes:

---

29 John Charles Ryle, *Expository Thoughts on the Gospels: St. John* (Cambridge and London: James Clarke & Co., Ltd., 1969), 2:214.

It is not difficult to understand that to the mind of natural man the words of Jesus appeared to be foolishness. Why would a man lay down his life *in order to take it back* again? True some people desire to commit suicide, but surely not with the intention of coming back to life once more even if they could! Many (perhaps, the majority; see also on 9:16) were reasoning in this manner. Hence, they said, "He has a demon and raves." See on 7:20, 49, 52; 8:48. They did not mean to identify insanity with demon-possession, but intended to convey the idea that Jesus, being definitely under the control of an evil spirit, was uttering sheer nonsense. So, why should anyone continue to listen to him?[30]

Afterwards, there were those who came to Jesus, asking: "How long will You keep us in suspense? If You are the Christ, tell us plainly" (John 10:24). Jesus' response to those questions was: "I told you, and you do not believe; the works that I do in My Father's name, these testify of Me. But you do not believe because you are not of My sheep. My sheep hear My voice, and I know them, and they follow Me" (John 10:25–27). Jesus had told the Jews plainly that He was the Christ in John 5:17–47; 6:29, 35, 51–65; 7:37–39; 8:12–20, 28, 29, 42, 56–58, and 10:7–18. His works had testified of Him also. The Jews did not need more proofs.

When Jesus uttered the words, "I and the Father are one" (John 10:30), the Jews immediately understood the meaning of them. Unless those words were true, they were blasphemous. Thus, "the Jews picked up stones again to stone Him" (John 10:31), like they had done two months earlier at the Feast of Tabernacles (John 8:59). Instead of fleeing, Jesus calmly asked them: "I showed you many good works from the Father; for which of them are you stoning Me?" (John 8:32). Their reply was: "For a good work we do not stone You, but for blasphemy; and because You, being a man, make Yourself out to be God" (John 10:33). Those words indicate clearly that they had the ability to discern the meaning of His teaching. Yet, as Leon Morris wrote: "What they did not stop to consider was whether it was true."[31] Despite their spiritual blindness, their ultimate condemnation was "because the mind set on the flesh is hostile toward God; for it does not subject itself to the law of God, for it is not even able to do so" (Romans 8:8). Thus, it was both their unwillingness to come to Christ and their inability to do so that caused them to continue in their persecution of Him.

---

30 Hendriksen, *The Gospel of John*, 2:116.
31 Morris, *The Gospel according to John*, 525.

All of Jesus' words to the Jews had no effect on them. When He said, once again, that He was equal with the Father, it was more than they could accept. "Therefore, they were seeking once more to seize Him, and He eluded their grasp" (John 10:39). So, for the second time Jesus left one of the feasts in Jerusalem and "He went away again beyond the Jordan to the place where John was first baptizing, and He was staying there" (John 10:40). Jesus was able, once more, to elude the grasp of those who surrounded Him because it was still not yet His time to lay down His life. Instead, He continued His ministry in Perea where He had been for the previous two months. The result was: "Many came to Him and were saying, 'While John performed no sign, yet everything John said about this man was true. Many believed in Him there" (John 10:41, 42). Ryle aptly remarked on the results of Jesus' ministry during these next several months:

> It seems highly probable that this accounts for the great number converted at once on the day of Pentecost and at other times . . . The way had been prepared in their hearts long before, by our Lord's own preaching, though at the time they had not courage to avow it. The good that is done by preaching is not always seen immediately. Our Lord sowed, and His Apostles reaped, all over Palestine.[32]

Healing the Infirm Woman (Luke 13:10–17)

In the last days of December, Jesus traveled back to Perea from Jerusalem. The exact place where Jesus' healed the infirm woman mentioned in Luke 13 is unknown, but it was in one of the synagogues in Perea. This may have been the last time Jesus ever preached in a synagogue in Israel inasmuch as the synagogue officials had become so openly hostile to Him. Wherever He was known, the hierarchy simply refused Him the opportunity to preach. Luke says: "And He was teaching in one of the synagogues on the Sabbath" (Luke 13:10). Previously, Jesus had had controversies in synagogues in Galilee and Judea. Now there was a controversy in Perea that was similar to the ones in Galilee and Judea.

During the Sabbath service, Jesus observed a woman in the synagogue "who for eighteen years had had a sickness caused by a spirit and she was bent double, and could not straighten up at all" (Luke 13:11). The Scripture does not indicate that she was infirm due to her sinfulness and Jesus never said that her sins were forgiven when He

---

32 Ryle, *Expository Thoughts on the Gospels: John*, 2:255–6.

healed her. When He saw her, "He called her over and said to her, 'Woman, you are freed from your sickness'" (Luke 13:12). Then, He laid His hands on her and healed her completely so that she became erect again. She began rejoicing and praising God, but the real drama with the synagogue official then began. He rebuked neither Jesus nor the woman but began chastising the crowd of onlookers: "There are six days in which work should be done; so come during them and get healed, and not on the Sabbath day" (Luke 13:14a). He said these things because he was "indignant because Jesus had healed on the Sabbath" (Luke 13:14b). The position of that synagogue official was certainly supported by the Talmud and the Mishnah, but not by the Scripture (Cf. Mark 2:23–28). Edersheim notes concerning Jesus' position on the Sabbath:

> [N]o teacher in Israel nor Reformer of that time—not the most advanced Sadducee—would have defended, far less originated, the views as to the Sabbath which Christ now propounded.[33]

The Jewish views on Sabbath observance were supplemented by so many man-made rules that they became contradictory and circuitous. The unwise chief ruler of the synagogue would not confront Jesus directly, but the Lord was aware of his clumsy attempt to attack Him covertly. Jesus' response was immediate and unanswerable: "You hypocrites, does not each of you on the Sabbath untie his ox or his donkey from the stall and lead him away to water him? And this woman, a daughter of Abraham as she is, whom Satan bound for eighteen long years, should she not have been released from this bond on the Sabbath day?" (Luke 13:15, 16).

Their legalistic rules concerning the Sabbath allowed owners to consider the needs of their poor animals, but made no allowance for compassion to fellow humans. There were numerous ways to get around the rules at the pleasure of the individual, but the Sabbath laws were strictly adhered to when it came to Jesus' healing people. This synagogue official was probably embarrassed as well as indignant because he was the one who gave Jesus the right to teach in the synagogue. Yet, he was also a coward at heart by rebuking the crowds that witnessed the miracle rather than the One who performed the miracle. On an earlier occasion in Galilee, Jesus had quoted Hosea 6:6—"I desire compassion and not sacrifice"—against His opponents

---

33 Edersheim, *The Life and Times of Jesus the Messiah*, 629.

who were offended because He was eating with tax collectors and sinners. This synagogue official in Perea, and all those who agreed with him, were guilty of a lack of compassion. They were more interested in the sacrifice than compassion. In their minds, there seemed to be ample Scriptural support for their position. In Malachi 1:6–8, the Lord had rebuked the Jews for offering the blind, lame, and sick as offerings. Thus, the synagogue official must have reasoned: "If the Lord requires worshipers to bring unblemished sacrifices, then I cannot allow this desecration of the Sabbath to take place in this synagogue." Such a legalistic spirit hindered compassion in his heart. Thus, Hendriksen is correct in his comments on this matter:

> If then the needs of *animals may* be supplied even on the sabbath, *must* not *human* needs be met, on every day of the week, including certainly the sabbath? Is this "daughter of Abraham" of less importance than an ox or a donkey? Besides, is it really true that Satan must be allowed to keep the woman in bondage for still another day—on top of the eighteen years during which he has already held her captive—just because it happens to be the sabbath? Is not the sabbath the very day when more than ever one should exert himself to the utmost to destroy the works of the devil?[34]

Israel and Judah's inhumanity to fellow humans was the basic charge that the Lord brought against them in Amos 1:3–2:8. Those ancient nations were guilty of actively doing things to harm the surrounding nations. This synagogue official and the others were guilty of failing to be touched by the feeling of sympathy for with this woman, but that was still inhumanity. Edersheim rightly draws a picture with words of the character of this synagogue official:

> Confused, irresolute, perplexed, and very angry, bustling forward and scolding the people who had done nothing, yet not venturing to silence the woman, now no longer infirm—far less, to reprove the great Rabbi, Who had just done such a 'glorious thing,' but speaking at Him through those who had been the astounded eye witnesses. He was easily and effectually silenced, and all who sympathised with him put to shame . . .
>
> The retort was unanswerable and irresistible: it did what was intended; it covered the adversaries with shame.[35]

Thus, Luke 13:17 states: "As He said this, all His opponents were being humiliated; and the entire crowd was rejoicing over all the glo-

---

34 Hendriksen, *Exposition of the Gospel According to Luke*, 701.
35 Edersheim, *The Life and Times of Jesus the Messiah*, 630.

rious things being done by Him." The response of the crowds was a typical response to Jesus' miracles. They were glorifying God not only for the miraculous healing of the woman, but also for His words to the synagogue officials and all the other things He said and did.

Sabbath Day Dinner Invitation (Luke 14:1–24)

Luke 14:1 states: "It happened that when He went into the house of one of the leaders of the Pharisees on *the* Sabbath Supposing, then, that this invitation to dine with a leader of the Pharisees took place following the Feast of Dedication, the date was no earlier than December 31, 29 AD. This invitation was on the Sabbath which was a special meal among the Jews. All the preparations for it had been carefully made before sundown so as to avoid any work on the Sabbath. Alfred Edersheim describes the typical observance of the Sabbath in a Jewish home:

> The return of the Sabbath sanctified the week of labour. It was to be welcomd as a king, or with songs as a bridegroom; and each household observed it as a season of sacred rest and of joy. True, Rabbinism made all this a matter of mere externalism, converting it into an unbearable burden, by endless injunctions of what constituted work and of that which was supposed to produce joy, thereby utterly changing its sacred character. Still, the fundamental idea remained, like a broken pillar that shows where the palace had stood, and what had been its noble proportions. As the head of the house returned on the Sabbath-eve from the synagogue to his home, he found it festively adorned, the Sabbath lamp brightly burning, and the table spread with the richest each household could afford . . . Nor were the stranger, the poor, the widow, or the fatherless forgotten.[36]

Whether or not Jesus had been teaching in one of the local synagogues cannot be determined. However the invitation came to pass, Jesus was invited into the home of this man who was one of the leaders of the Pharisees. This was a special meal and a special invitation. Hospitality was the guise, the hospitality required of the Jews to provide for the stranger, the poor, the widow, and the fatherless. The real reason was more sinister. The leaders of the Pharisees wanted to watch "Him closely" (Luke 14:1). No doubt, the healing of the woman who had been bound for eighteen years on the Sabbath day in one of the synagogues in Perea (Luke 13:10–17) was the primary reason for this invitation. The hostility Jesus had encountered in Galilee and

---

36 Edersheim, *Sketches of Jewish Social Life in the Days of Christ*, 97.

Judea among the Pharisees was now facing Him in Perea. The primary nexus to that persecution was the proper interpretation of the Sabbath day. Thus, this leader of the Pharisees invited Jesus to dine with him and his family, at least partly, for the purpose of testing Him more on that point.

Jesus' simplicity of heart is manifested in His acceptance of this invitation while knowing that His enemies were seeking grounds for a charge against Him. The place where this leader of the Pharisees lived is also undetermined, but most of the chief men of that party lived in or around Jerusalem. Perhaps, word had filtered back to the Pharisees during the Feast of Dedication about Jesus' healing in a synagogue in Perea. Thus, the invitation could have been extended to allow the leaders of the Pharisees to judge for themselves. Intrigue began as soon as Jesus entered the Pharisee's house. There in front of Him was a man suffering from dropsy or the swelling of tissue which often has a heart condition as the underlying cause.[37] Whether this man came to the home of the Pharisee in the hope of being healed by Jesus or he was planted in that position is irrelevant to the events that happened next. Hendriksen describes how the religious leaders viewed people with dropsy:

> This poor man was afflicted with dropsy . . . Moreover, the rabbis were of the opinion that the person so afflicted had committed a grievous sin.[38]

Luke 14:3 continues: "And Jesus answered and spoke to the lawyers and Pharisees, saying, 'Is it lawful to heal on the Sabbath, or not?'" Jesus answered the thoughts of their hearts as they were gathered together to keep close watch on Him. And then He questioned them. Thereby, "Christ showed how the principle of Pharisaism consisted in self-seeking, to the necessary exclusion of all true love . . . this self-seeking and self-righteousness appeared even in what, perhaps, they most boasted of—their hospitality."[39] A prime example of this selfish spirit was the jaundiced eye with which all alike among these Pharisees and lawyers carefully watched Jesus. Once again, Jesus had outwitted His opponents, as Plummer insightfully describes:

> The dilemma, if they had planned one against Him, is turned against themselves. These lawyers were bound to answer such a question; and

---
37 Dropsy today is called edema (or, oedema) which is known as fluid retention. Heart failure causes the retention of fluid which builds up in the tissues of the body.
38 Hendriksen, *Exposition of the Gospel According to Luke*, 720.
39 Edersheim, *The Life and Times of Jesus the Messiah*, 685.

if rigorist Pharisees made no objection when consulted beforehand, they could not protest afterwards. They take refuge in silence; not in order to provoke Him to heal, but because they did not know what to say. They did not wish to say that healing on the sabbath was allowable, and they did not dare to say that it was not.[40]

While all the Pharisees and lawyers "kept silent . . . He took hold of him and healed him, and sent him away" (Luke 14:4). Jesus seems to have particularly chosen the Sabbath day as the day when He would do many of His great works. It was not for the purpose of simply refusing to give into the Jews but rather to magnify the Lord's Day above all others. God rested from His works of creation on that day, but He did not cease to work the new creation in the hearts of His people.[41] Thus, while His antagonists were silent, Jesus performed the miracle of healing this man of his dropsy and sent him back to his home. This miracle dumbfounded Jesus' opponents. Yet, Jesus was not satisfied with just healing the man. He then turned back to the religious leaders and said to them: "Which one of you will have a son or an ox fall into a well, and will not immediately pull him out on the Sabbath day?" (Luke 14:5). Calvin describes the reason why Jesus asked this question of them:

> Yet He does this, not so much to teach them as to vindicate Himself from their slanders. He knew that they were too blinded by their envenomed hatred to be teachable and reasonable; but He wished to triumph over their malice and force them to shamed silence. For if it is lawful to give help to animals on the Sabbath day, it is too shameful not to do the same to a man formed in God's image.[42]

The result of Jesus' action was that all His opponents were silenced. That made them, no doubt, even more vengeful towards Him. Their guilty silence showed that they had truly been plotting against Him. Instead of rejoicing with the man who was healed, they were seething with rage on the inside while becoming even more determined to find some charge against Jesus. They were like petulant children who can be satisfied with nothing except to get their way. Thus, as Luke wrote, "they could make no reply to this" (Luke 14:6).

---

40 Plummer, *A Critical and Exegetical Commentary on the Gospel According to S. Luke*, 355.
41 It is my conviction that eternity will reveal that more people were saved on the Lord's Day than any other day and, perhaps, than all the other days combined. The purpose of the Sabbath is not mere indolence, but to give every person time to reflect on the needs of their souls.
42 Calvin, *A Harmony of the Gospels Matthew, Mark and Luke*, 2:102.

This Man Receives Sinners (Luke 14:25–15:32)

Jesus continued to attract great followings wherever He went during this period of His ministry. Luke 14:25, 26 simply records: "Now large crowds were going along with Him; and He turned and said to them, 'If anyone comes to Me, and does not hate his own father and mother and wife and children and brothers and sisters, he cannot be My disciple.'" The cost of discipleship and the bearing of one's own cross were challenges that Jesus had made to His disciples at Caesarea Philippi after His transfiguration. Now He makes that demand for counting the cost once again and uses two examples to define it. The first is that of a man who started to build a tower but ran out of money after laying the foundation. The second example is that of a king going out to war without duly considering if his army is powerful enough to defeat his enemy. Without counting the cost, the builder will be embarrassed that he cannot finish the tower and the king will have to sue for peace with the other king. Ryle's comments on Jesus' warning are insightful:

> Our Lord spoke as He did to prevent men following Him lightly and inconsiderately, from mere animal feeling and temporary excitement, who in time of temptation would fall away. He knew that nothing does so much harm to the cause of true religion as backsliding, and that nothing causes so much backsliding as enlisting disciples without letting them know what they take in hand. He had no desire to swell the number of His followers by admitting soldiers who would fall in the hour of need. For this reason He raises a warning voice. He bids all who think of taking service with Him to count the cost before they begin.[43]

Jesus had previously warned His disciples to count the cost. Now, the larger group of followers in Perea are given the same admonition. A few days before this admonition, Jesus had been warned by the Pharisees, "Go away, leave here, for Herod wants to kill You" (Luke 13:31). Herod had been anxiously seeking to do something about Jesus ever since John had been beheaded. And our Lord was staying one step ahead of that "fox" until His time came. While Jesus did go away from where the Pharisees had warned Him about Herod, He moved methodically and with a purpose. He first accepted the invitation of one of the leaders of the Pharisees to eat bread on the Sabbath. Afterwards, Jesus continued on His last journey to Jerusalem where all His prophecies about His scourging, death, and resurrection would

---

43 Ryle, *Expository Thoughts on the Gospels: St. Luke*, 2:169.

come true. Along the way, "all the tax collectors and the sinners were coming near Him to listen to Him" (Luke 15:1). Such a scene was too much for the Pharisees and Sadducees who "*began* to grumble, saying, 'This man receives sinners and eats with them'" (Luke 15:2). Usually, it was the Sadducees who took the initiative to criticize Jesus, but this time that ignoble act was led by the Pharisees. Such a charge was, no doubt, calculated to leave the impression that Jesus preferred the company of sinners and tax collectors to the refined and respectable religious leaders. Just a little while earlier, those Pharisees and Sadducees had remained silent in the home of one of the leaders of the Pharisees when Jesus asked them, "Which one of you will have a son or an ox fall into a well, and will not immediately pull him out on the sabbath day?" (Luke 14:5). This charge against Him in Luke 15:2 was their belated attempt to make a response, but it was just the same old charge that had been levied against our Lord so often before. Yet, that charge set the parameters for the three parables Christ spoke in Luke 15. Those parables all underscore the necessity of seeking the lost—the lost sheep, the lost coin, and the lost son. In His response to the Pharisees and Sadducees, Jesus doubled down on His position laid out in Luke 14:5. Not only should all followers of Jesus pull the ox out of the ditch even on the Sabbath day, but the "poor and crippled and blind and lame" are invited to the great heavenly feast of the last day.

There was a great difference between Jesus' message of the gospel and the teaching of the Rabbis. While the latter taught repentance, they "placed acceptance at the end of repentance, and made it its wages. And this because it knew not, nor felt the power of repentance, and as the free gift of God's love. The Gospel places acceptance at the beginning of repentance, and as the free gift of God's love. And this, because it not only knows the power of sin, but points to a Saviour, provided of God."[44]

The message of Rabbinism was works salvation. The message of Jesus was salvation by God's sovereign grace. Edersheim unfolds the connections and distinctions among these three parables:

> In the first Parable . . . the main interest centres in the *lost*; in the seeond . . ., in the *search*; in the third, in the *restoration*. And although in the third Parable the Pharisees are not addressed, there is the highest personal application to them in the words which the Father speaks to

---

44 Edersheim, *The Life and Times of Jesus the Messiah*, 651.

> the elder son—an application, not so much of warning, as of loving correction and entreaty, which seems to imply, what otherwise these Parables convey, that at least these Pharisees had 'murmured,' not so much from bitter hostility to Christ, as from spiritual ignorance and misunderstanding.[45]

There is a progression in these parables, therefore, which unfolds the main points of the Gospel. Sinners are lost; they need to be sought after; and, they need to be restored to their heavenly Father. Rabbinism was unevangelistic and did not seek after the lost which is why the religious leaders of Israel took so much offense at Christ for doing so. They were self-righteous and wrongly assumed that their standing with God was a matter of fact. Thus, these parables are connected and allowed Jesus to set forth the many facets of the gospel. Indeed, the whole work of the Triune God in salvation is displayed in them. The first parable sets forth the work of the Good Shepherd (John 10) in leaving the ninety-nine to search for the one lost sheep. Jesus identified Himself as that Good Shepherd. The last parable shows the patient waiting of the father who is ever ready to receive the prodigal back into his fellowship. That is the picture of the Heavenly Father who is full of compassion and embraces us with open arms. The middle parable displays the work of the Holy Spirit who opened the heart of Lydia to respond to the things of the gospel (Acts 16:14) and does the same for all converted sinners. All such searching for lost sinners would be in vain without the ministry of the Spirit.

The jealousy of the older brother who became angry and would not go into the dinner prepared for the prodigal son who had returned home was a clear reference to the attitude of the religious leaders of Israel. They were offended that Jesus would have such seemingly promiscuous fellowship with wicked sinners. He could have harshly upbraided the Pharisees and Sadducees, but instead Jesus tried to woo them to the same invitation of the gospel. Yet, it was mostly in vain. That is why Jesus said in the first parable: "I tell you in the same way, there will be more joy in heaven over one sinner who repents than over ninety-nine righteous persons who need no repentance" (Luke 15:7). The prodigal was not received by his father without repentance, but neither is he received because of his repentance. The father's uncon-

---

45 Edersheim, *The Life and Times of Jesus the Messiah*, 651.

ditional love showered the son with embraces and kisses before the prodigal declared: "Father, I have sinned against heaven and in your sight; I am no longer worthy to be called your son" (Luke 15:21). Shepard's remarks on this passage are on target:

> Jesus loved sinners deeply, while the Pharisees were filled with the cold pride of virtue. There is much irony in the story. The Pharisees were greater sinners than the publicans. The picture Luke gives of the father's love for the lost son and his tender and patient dealing even with the elder brother, explains the reason for the coming of Christ to the world to save the lost.[46]

The conflict between Jesus and the religious leaders boiled down to a few principles. He loved sinners; they disdainfully rejected them. He called all sinners to repentance and faith; they denied that they themselves had any need of repentance. He dealt gently with both the Pharisees and the publicans; they desired to be favored and wanted the publicans to be shunned.

The Raising of Lazarus (John 11:1–57)

While Jesus was conducting His ministry in Perea at some central location, word was sent to Him by Martha and Mary, saying, "Lord, behold, he whom You love is sick" (John 11:3). When the messenger left the two sisters to go to Jesus, Lazarus was only sick, but he probably died later that same day.[47] He was, therefore, buried in a tomb that belonged to his family, as Edersheim notes:

> Not only the rich, but even those moderately well-to-do, had tombs of their own, which probably were acquired and prepared long before they were needed, and treated and inherited as private and personal property . . . In such caves, or rock-hewn tombs, the bodies were laid, having been anointed with many spices.[48]

Those rock-hewn or natural cave tombs were prepared in such a way that they could usually hold up to eight bodies, three on each side and two at the end of the opening. The traditional site of the tomb of Lazarus is located within the modern-day city of Al-Eizariya where Bethany was. The entrance to that tomb from the main street of the city is down a flight of uneven rock-cut stairs. Bethany was on

---

46 Shepard, *The Christ of the Gospels*, 423.
47 It was the custom in ancient Israel to bury a person the same day they died. Since Jesus remained where He was for two more days and it probably took another day's travel to reach Bethany, that would total the four days mentioned by Martha in John 11:39.
48 Edersheim, *The Life and Times of Jesus the Messiah*, 695.

the other side of the mountain from the Garden of Gethsemane and there was no level ground in that village for tombs.

When the news reached Jesus of Lazarus' serious condition, His response was: "This sickness is not to end in death, but for the glory of God, so that the Son of God may be glorified by it" (John 11:4). One of those who have written on Jesus' life, M. Ernest Renan, has suggested that the miracle was really just a "pious fraud" perpetrated by Lazarus and his sisters in order to hopefully cause the Jews to support the Savior:

> It may be that Lazarus, still pallid with disease, caused himself to be wrapped in bandages as if dead, and shut up in the tomb of his family . . . Jesus (if we follow the above hypothesis) desired to see once more him whom he had loved; and, the stone being removed, Lazarus came forth in his bandages, his head covered with a winding-sheet.[49]

Renan's theory would make Jesus a co-conspirator in the fraud and, thus, unworthy of our faith and trust. For instance, in John 11:14, Jesus told His disciples: "Lazarus is dead, and I am glad for your sakes that I was not there, so that you may believe; but let us go to him." If Jesus had any part in a "pious fraud," then He was a charlatan and a deceiver—which is exactly what His opponents called Him.

There is no doubt that Jesus knew exactly what was happening with Lazarus. He knew that his sickness and death would result in the raising of His friend, as the greatest type of His own death and resurrection. Jesus had raised others from the dead—the raising of the widow's son at Nain and the daughter of Jairus. Yet, the "raising of Lazarus marks the highest point . . . in the ministry of our Lord; it is the climax in a history where all is miraculous—the Person, the Life, the Words, the Work"[50] Thus, after two days, Jesus and His disciples began the day's journey from Perea to Bethany. His disciples were hesitant to do so, reminding Jesus: "Rabbi, the Jews were just now seeking to stone You, and are you going there again?" (John 11:8). Jesus replied to them: "Are there not twelve hours in the day? If anyone walks in the day, he does not stumble, because he sees the light of this world. But if anyone walks in the night, he stumbles, because the light is not in him" (John 11:9, 10). Despite Jesus' words,

---

49 Ernest Renan, *The Life of Jesus* (London and Paris: Trubner & Co., and M. Levy Preres, 1871), 251.
50 Edersheim, *The Life and Times of Jesus the Messiah*, 688.

Thomas, also called Didymus,[51] characteristically said to his fellow disciples: "Let us also go, so that we may die with Him" (John 11:16). The expectation of Thomas, and probably of the other disciples, was that the warning Jesus had given about His crucifixion and resurrection was now at hand. They appear to have had the resolve of bearing whatever came on them as followers of Christ.

It is noteworthy that at this point in the ministry of Jesus, all the disciples had begun to realize the great enmity that the Jews had against Him. Yet, only a few months later, they would be shocked at His crucifixion and initially unbelieving of the reports of His resurrection. The only plausible explanation is that they gained a false hope of Jesus' future ministry as a result of Lazarus' resurrection. In other words, they learned the wrong lesson from this miracle. They should have learned that Jesus would both die and rise from the dead, even as He had warned them repeatedly. Instead, they seemed to have thought that Jesus would be spared from death inasmuch as Lazarus was raised from the grave.

It was only after Jesus and His disciples arrived in Bethany that He learned that Lazarus had already been in the grave for four days. Since Bethany was so close to Jerusalem, there was a large crowd of the Jews who had gathered to console Martha and Mary. Martha, hearing that Jesus was coming, went out to meet Him and when she came to Him she said, "Lord, if you had been here, my brother would not have died. Even now I know that whatever You ask of God, God will give You" (John 11:21, 22). Jesus replied: "Your brother will rise again" (John 11:23). Martha affirmed that truth by saying, "I know that he will rise again in the resurrection on the last day" (John 11:24). Jesus then stated: "I am the resurrection and the life; he who believes in Me will live even if he dies, and everyone who lives and believes in Me will never die. Do you believe this?" (John 11:25, 25). Martha fully acknowledged Jesus' divinity with her marvelous reply: "Yes, Lord; I have believed that You are the Son of God, *even* He who comes into the world" (John 11:27). The greatness of Martha's confession is brought out to us by Morris:

> Her faith is not a vague, formless credulity. It has content, and doctrinal content at that. She brings out three points. First, Jesus is "the Christ" *i.e.* the Messiah of Jewish expectation . . . Secondly, He is "the

---

51 Didymus is the Greek equivalent of Thomas and both names mean "twin."

Son of God" . . . There can be no doubt but that Martha is giving the words their maximum content. Thirdly, she speaks of Jesus as "he that cometh into the world," *i.e.* the long awaited Deliverer, the One sent by God to accomplish His will perfectly. Taken together these three affirmations give us as high a view of the person of Christ as one may well have. Martha should be known to us from this moving declaration rather than from her worst moment of criticism and fretfulness.[52]

While Martha had sought out Jesus, Mary was still behind in the house, uncomforted and disconsolate. Martha was sent by Jesus to tell Mary: "The Teacher is here and is calling for you" (John 11:28). Hearing those words, Mary "got up quickly and was coming to Him" (John 11:29). The Jews who had been consoling her thought she was going to the tomb of Lazarus to weep there, so they followed her. Instead, she went to where Jesus was—still on the outskirts of the village. When she arrived there, she fell down at His feet and repeated what Martha had said, "Lord, if you had been here, my brother would not have died" (Luke 11:32b). Observing her tears and the weeping Jews who followed her, Jesus Himself was overcome with emotion, being deeply moved and troubled. Thus, He asked them, "Where have you laid him?" (John 11:34). Then He wept. To suggest that this was all play acting would be the cruelest joke of all-time. It also shows that Jesus experienced all the same emotions as other men, but without any sin. The difference between our passions and Jesus' passions is brought out by Calvin:

> The vanity of our mind makes us sorrow or grieve over trifles, or for no reason at all, because we are too much devoted to the world. Nothing like this was to be found in Christ. No passion of His ever went beyond its proper bounds. He had none that was not right and founded on reason and sound judgment . . .
>
> But Christ took upon Him human emotions, yet without ataxia.[53] For he who obeys the passions of the flesh is not obedient to God. Christ indeed troubled Himself and was strongly agitated; but in such a way that He kept Himself under the will of the Father. In short, if you compare His passions with ours, they are as different as pure, clear water flowing in a gentle stream from muddy and thick foam.[54]

Thus, Jesus was moved out of pure love to raise Lazarus from the dead, which even the Jews had to acknowledge: "See how He loved

---

52 Morris, *The Gospel According to St. John*, 551–2.
53 Ataxia is a Greek word which means 'to be out of order or uncontrolled.'
54 John Calvin, *The Gospel According to St John and The First Epistle of John* (Grand Rapids: Eerdmans Publishing Company, 1961), 2:12.

him!" (John 11:36). Others of the Jews wondered: "Could not this man, who opened the eyes of the blind man, have kept this man also from dying?" (John 11:37). For His part, Jesus came to the cave where a stone was rolled against the opening and commanded the men, "Remove the stone" (John 11:41). He then offered up this prayer: "Father, I thank You that You have heard Me. I knew that You always hear Me; but because of the people standing around I said it, so that they may believe that You sent Me" (John 11:41–2). After praying, Jesus "cried out with a loud voice, 'Lazarus, come forth'" (John 11:43). Lazarus was completely bound from head to foot with wrappings and cloths, but his dead body was quickened by the voice of Christ (cf. John 5:25, 26) and he came forth from the grave. Ryle unfolds the meaning of this great miracle:

> The greatness of this miracle cannot possibly be exaggerated. The mind of man can scarcely take in the vastness of the work that was done. Here, in open day, and before many hostile witnesses, a man, four days' dead, was restored to life in a moment. Here was public proof that our Lord had absolute power over the material world! A corpse already corrupt, was made alive!—Here was public proof that our Lord had absolute power over the world of spirits! A soul that had left its earthly tenement was called back from Paradise, and joined once more to its owner's body. Well may the Church of Christ maintain that He who would work such works was "over all, God blessed for ever."[55]

Once Lazarus came forth from the grave, climbing those twenty or thirty steps up to the street level, Jesus commanded those standing around: "Unbind him, and let him go" (John 11:44). The result was that the crowds, as on so many other occasions, were divided over what they observed. Many of them who "saw what He had done, believed in Him" (John 11:45). Others of them, "went to the Pharisees and told them the things which Jesus had done" (John 11:46). The raising of Lazarus was as nearly parallel to what Jesus would soon experience as possible.

Yet, the chief priests and Pharisees were overly troubled and quickly convened a meeting of the Council, saying, "What are we doing? For this man is performing many signs. If we let Him *go on* like this, all men will believe in Him, and the Romans will come and take away both our place and our nation" (John 11:47–8). One of the members, "Caiaphas, who was high priest that year, said to them, 'You know

---

55 Ryle, *Expository Thoughts on the Gospels: St. John*, 2:317–8.

nothing at all, nor do you take into account that it is expedient for you that one man die for the people, and that the whole nation not perish" (John 11:49–50). John, the beloved disciple, noted that Caiaphas without realizing it was prophesying how and for what Jesus would die—that He would die "not for the nation only, but in order that He might also gather together into one the children of God who are scattered abroad" (John 11:51–2). Thus, the Jews plotted to kill Jesus from that day forward. They had tried to stone Him to death on other occasions and had sent officers to arrest Him, but those earlier occasions were the result of deep passions of the moment. Now, the Council had reached the point where they realized that the great spiritual movement under Jesus could only be stopped by putting Him to death—or so they thought. Yet, the more these wicked men tried to countermand the purposes of God for their generation, the more they were unwittingly doing the very thing that God's predetermined plan had ordained (Acts 2:22, 23; 4:27, 28).

18

Jesus' Retirement Ministry in Ephraim

In his masterful work, *The Christian Ministry*, Charles Bridges wrote:

> In the midst of the incessant, pressing, and active avocations of the Christian Ministry, how seasonable is the considerate advice of our gracious Master—"Come ye yourselves apart into a desert place, and rest awhile." The spirit of prayer cannot breathe deeply in the atmosphere of constant and exciting employment. Not that we would seek retirement, like the contemplative monk, for the purpose of abstraction; but to recruit our spiritual energies for renewed exercises of self-denial and perseverance.[1]

When the reports of the Sanhedrin's plots to kill Him filtered back to Jesus, He withdrew from Bethany and "no longer continued to walk publicly among the Jews, but went away from there to the country near the wilderness, into a city called Ephraim; and there He stayed with His disciples" (John 11:54). This plan by the Sanhedrin to kill Jesus had been developing over time and there had already been various attempts on His life (cf. Luke 4:29; John 7:32, 45; 8:59; 10:31, 39). Some of those earlier attempts were reactions on the spur of the moment, but now there had been an official decision by the Jewish rulers that Jesus must be killed in order to spare the whole nation from the wrath of the Romans. Jesus' decision to leave the area of Jerusalem and to no longer walk publicly there was not an act of cowardice or a sign of fearfulness. Rather, Jesus knew that it was not yet His time to die for the sins of the world. Thus, He departed from there to Ephraim, a town in the wilderness hill country of Judah about thirteen miles northeast of Jerusalem. That village is probably the same place as the modern-day village of El-Taybeh in Israel which has a population of only 1,400. It is also probably to be identified with Ophrah (Joshua 18:23) and Ephron (2 Chronicles 13:19) of the Old Testament. John Kitto describes the scenery at Ephraim for us:

> It is on a high hill . . . north of Jerusalem, and a short distance north

---

[1] Charles Bridges, *The Christian Ministry* (London: The Banner of Truth Trust, 1967), 145.

of the rock of Rimmon to which the remnant of the slaughtered Benjamites fled for defence, and a little to the northeast of Bethel. It occupies a lofty site; and from it one overlooks the adjacent desert, the Jordan and its great valley, and the mountains of Perea beyond.[2]

Ephraim, "perched on a conspicuous eminence and with an extensive view,"[3] was about five hundred feet above the elevation of Jerusalem. It was remote, sparsely populated, and an excellent observation post for any hostile activity that would threaten Jesus and His disciples. It was also close to the regions of Samaria, Galilee, and Perea. Those days in Ephraim provided a time of rest and quiet conversation with His disciples before Jesus began His last journey to Jerusalem. There is no mention in the Scripture of any great work that Jesus performed in the little village of Ephraim which indicates that it was a base camp for the final months of His ministry before the Passover in AD 30. The time for this ministry was most likely between February and April. Scripture is silent about Jesus' time in Ephraim, but He seems to have traveled between Galilee, Samaria, and Perea during those months. The movements of Jesus during this period are even harder to chronicle than most any other period of His life. Ryle comments on Jesus' choice of Ephraim:

> It is worth noticing that our Lord chose a scene of entire quiet and seclusion as His last abode, before going up to His last great season of suffering at the crucifixion, It is well to get alone and be still, before we take in hand any great work for God. Our Saviour was not above this. How much more should His disciples remember it! . . It is the very essence of Christian retirement, if it is to be profitable, that it should be without parade, and should not attract the notice of men.[4]

Ten Lepers Healed (Luke 17:11–19)
On one of His trips from Ephraim to other regions of Israel, Jesus "was passing between Samaria and Galilee" (Luke 17:11) where He was met by ten leprous men in a village. Luke tells us that Jesus was "on the way to Jerusalem" (Luke 17:11) at that time. He was probably skirting the borders of Samaria while traveling eastward through Galilee towards Bethshean where He would cross the Jordan River. Along the way, he came to a village where there were ten lepers who met Him. Their dwelling place was virtually a leper colony outside

---

2 John Kitto, *Daily Bible Illustrations: The Life and Death of Our Lord* (New York: Robert Carter and Brothers, 1881), 7:359-360.
3 Archibald Henderson, *Palestine: Its Historical Geography* (Edinburgh: T & T Clark, 1893), 160.
4 Ryle, *Expository Thoughts on the Gospels: John*, 2:343-4.

the city. When the men saw Jesus, they stood at a distance, raised their voices, and cried out, "Jesus, Master, have mercy on us!" (Luke 17:12, 13).

There was no set formula that Jesus used to heal people. He dealt with them in various ways. In response to the cry of these lepers, Jesus simply commanded them: "Go and show yourselves to the priests" (Luke 17:14a). That was probably not what the lepers were wanting to hear because that was nothing more than what the Mosaic law required of them. Yet, "they went at Christ's bidding, even before they had actually experienced the healing! So great was their faith, and, may we not almost infer, the general belief throughout the district, in the power of 'the Master.'"[5] As a result of their obedience to Jesus' command, the Scripture records: "And as they were going, they were cleansed" (Luke 17:14b). Along the way, one of the lepers "saw that he had been healed, turned back, glorifying God with a loud voice" (Luke 17:15). Returning to Jesus, "he fell on His face at His feet, giving thanks to Him" (Luke 17:16). That leper was the one Samaritan among the group of ten. The others were all Jews, but none of them turned back. Jesus responded: "Were there not ten cleansed? But the nine—where are they? Was no one found who returned to give glory to God, except this foreigner?" (Luke 17:17, 18). While they were covered with leprosy, "their dreadful malady" had "broken down the barrier between Jew and Samaritan."[6] Had the natural enmity between them once more been aroused when they were all healed? Whatever caused the other nine lepers to not return to Jesus was certainly wrong. Moreover, they missed the blessing of hearing Jesus say to them, "Stand up and go; your faith has made you well" (Luke 17:19). Regardless of the reason for the other nine not to return, Jesus was greatly disappointed in them. Geldenhuys' comments are helpful:

> The Saviour is grieved at the revelation of gross ingratitude on the part of the other nine lepers, who do not glorify and thank God, but are so selfishly taken up in their cure that they (probably all Jews) do not even take the trouble of turning back to Him out of gratitude, as the Samaritans did.
>
> He thereupon commands the cleansed Samaritan to arise and assures him that his faith has saved him—not merely cured him of his bodily sickness, but saved him in the fullest sense of the word, because

---

5 Edersheim, *The Life and Times of Jesus the Messiah*, 702.
6 Plummer, *The Gospel According to S. Luke*, 403.

he really believes in Him and has entered into a personal relation with Him. Although the other nine had also received their healing, they had no further connection with Him, owing to the superficiality of their faith . . . and ingratitude.[7]

It was one thing to experience bodily healing through Jesus, as all the ten lepers did. It was quite another to be made well by faith, as only this one Samaritan leper did. Jesus healed a large multitude of people during His ministry of all kinds of diseases—deafness, dumbness, blindness, leprosy, lameness, demon possession, and many more maladies. Not all who were cured in their bodies were also cured in their souls. This Samaritan who was healed of leprosy also received the pronouncement from the Master, "your faith has made you well." That one declaration from the lips of Jesus was worth more than anything else He could have done for this man. The silence of the other nine lepers is a sure sign that they had not experienced that new birth which Jesus had once told Nicodemus was absolutely essential to salvation.

The Rich Young Ruler (Matthew 19:16–30; Luke 10:17–31; and, Luke 18:18–30)

After healing the ten lepers on the borders of Samaria and Galilee, Jesus departed for the last time from the region where He had spent most of His life on this earth. He and His disciples then traveled back to Perea "beyond the Jordan" where our Lord ministered in the same place He had been baptized three years earlier. Those days near the Jordan were filled with opportunities to heal the sick and teach the people. Matthew records that "large crowds followed Him, and He healed them there" (Matthew 19:2). And, Mark states: "crowds gathered around Him again, and according to His custom, He once more *began* to teach them" (Mark 10:1). Not all those who came to hear Him were true followers of His, though. The "Pharisees came up to Jesus, testing Him, and began to question Him whether it was lawful for a man to divorce a wife" (Mark 10:2). Thus, the last days of Jesus' ministry were spent in the same way the previous three years had been conducted—exhorting in sound doctrine and refuting those who contradict (1 Timothy 1:9). Bruce artfully describes what Jesus' ministry was like in that area:

> Jesus did not by any means live there a life of seclusion and solitary

---

[7] Geldenhuys, *Commentary on the Gospel of Luke*, 436.

meditation. On the contrary, during His sojourn in that neighborhood, He was unusually busy healing the sick, teaching the multitude "as He was wont" (so Mark states, with a mental reference to His past ministry in Galilee); answering inquiries, receiving visits, granting favors. "Many resorted unto Him" there on various errands. Pharisees came, asking entangling questions about marriage and divorce, hoping to catch Him in a trap, and commit Him to the expression of an opinion which would make Him unpopular with some party or school, Hillel's or Shammai's,[8] it did not matter which.[9]

Following His time in Perea, Jesus and His disciples probably returned to Ephraim. When the days for the Passover drew near, Jesus left the house where He was staying and "setting out on a journey" when "a man ran up to Him and knelt before Him, and asked Him, 'Good Teacher, what shall I do to inherit eternal life?'" (Mark 10:17). This question by the rich young ruler "is more remarkable because he is not a suppliant for material help. In His eagerness to obtain spiritual advice he shews no less zeal than if he had sought the greatest of temporal benefits."[10] Yet, this young man obviously thought of Jesus as just a man; just a human teacher. He did not see the glory of God in the face of Jesus. Moreover, his question implied "an imperfect standard of moral goodness."[11] He was looking for something extra—something more than the moral law which he already had. His question was of the utmost importance and his manner of asking it of Christ was certainly respectful. Yet, this young man was wrong at the fountainhead and wrong at every other point, as all the narratives disclose. Jesus first mildly rebuked the man for calling him good while not recognizing that He was God: "Why do you call Me good? No one is good except God alone" (Mark 10:18). This was not a denial of Jesus' essential goodness, but it was a summons for the man to consider the holiness of God. Interestingly, our Lord took a novel approach to make that summons—He reminded the young man of five of the six commandments of the second table of the law. Those commandments had to do with man's duties to his fellow man. Yet, the commandments of the first table of the law—having to do with man's duties to God—were completely left out. Thus, Jesus responded to

---

8 The school of Hillel represented the loose view on divorce and the school of Shammai represented the strict view.
9 Bruce, *The Training of the Twelve*, 252.
10 Swete, *Commentary on Mark*, 222.
11 Swete, *Commentary on Mark*, 223.

the man's queries: "You know the commandments: 'Do not murder, Do not commit adultery, Do not steal, Do not defraud, Honor your father and mother" (Mark 10:19). Jesus knew immediately that the young man was not thoroughly acquainted with his own sinfulness and, therefore, could not be shown the glory of God's holiness.

The response of the rich young ruler was exactly what Jesus anticipated: "All these things I have kept; what am I still lacking?" (Matthew 19:20). Though he was insufficiently acquainted with his own heart, yet he was different than the Pharisee in Jesus' parable who thanked God that he was not like other men. The rich young ruler was keenly conscious that something was lacking in his life. Edersheim eloquently describes that exchange between Jesus and this young man:

> And Jesus saw it all: down, through that intense upward look; inwards, through that question, 'What lack I yet?' far deeper down than that young man had ever seen into his own heart—even into depths of weakness and need which he had never sounded, and which must be filled, if he would enter the Kingdom of Heaven. Jesus saw what he lacked; and what He saw, He showed Him.[12]

Jesus then said to the young man, "One thing you lack: go and sell all you possess and give to the poor, and you will have treasure in heaven; and come, follow Me" (Mark 10:21). With those words, our Lord revealed to this youth the true meaning of the tenth commandment, "You shall not covet" (Exodus 20:17).[13] Mark's description of this event is very touching in what it reveals of the heart of Jesus towards the rich young ruler: "Looking at him, Jesus felt a love for him" (Mark 10:21). He was so close to the kingdom of God, but so far away. He was earnest, but ignorant of his own heart. He was willing to give up much and to do many things—even hard things—in order to obtain eternal life, but he did not expect the answer of Jesus. It went against everything that Rabbinism taught. Almsgiving was taught by the Rab-

---

12 Edersheim, *The Life and Times of Jesus the Messiah*, 710.
13 During seminary, I worked one summer with Dr. G. Aiken Taylor, editor of *The Presbyterian Journal*, in starting a new church in Asheville, NC. He once told me that he thought that the rich young ruler might have been Saul of Tarsus. There are certainly things in favor of that view: Saul was a young man; he was being trained by the Sanhedrin and was a student under Gamaliel; before his conversion to Christ, he thought that salvation could be obtained through moral works of righteousness (Philippians 3:9); his conversion was a result of learning the true meaning of the tenth commandment forbidding covetousness (Romans 7:7); and, the rich young ruler's rejection by Christ would explain psychologically why Saul was breathing out threats against the followers of Jesus. If Saul was not the rich young ruler, then the rich young ruler was someone similar in many ways to Saul—and vice versa.

bis, but never to the point of voluntary poverty. Poverty was considered by them to be "worse than all the plagues of Egypt put together;" worse "than all other miseries;" and, "the worst affliction that could befall a man."[14] Yet, for this young man, it was the one thing needful before He could become a true follower of Jesus. His love of riches was greater than all else. Thus, "he went away grieving, for he was one who owned much property" (Mark 10:22). Swete describes the inner turmoil that Jesus' cross caused for this young ruler:

> As he heard the sentence, his brow clouded over . . . the lighthearted optimism of his mood broke down . . . The answer did not exasperate, but it gave him pain which was visible on his countenance . . . His hopes were dashed; the one thing he wanted was beyond his reach; the price was too great to pay even for eternal life. For the time the love of the world prevailed.[15]

What the rich young ruler lacked is not what every other person lacks and the advice given to him is not appropriate for all others. His riches were only the symbol of something deeper—the unwillingness to surrender heart and soul to the service of God; the refusal to love the Lord God with all the heart, and all the soul, and all the mind, and all the strength, and to love one's neighbor as self. As Edersheim notes:

> What he lacked—was earth's poverty and heaven's riches; a heart fully set on following Christ: and this could only come to him through willing surrender of all. And so this was to him alike the means, the test, and the need. To him it was this; to us it may be something else.[16]

After the young man left Jesus, the Lord turned to His own disciples and said: "How hard it will be for those who are wealthy to enter the kingdom of God!" (Mark 2:23). Those words shocked the disciples because they had imbibed the Jewish belief that material riches were a sign of God's favor. Jesus then reiterated that truth: "It is easier to go through the eye of the needle than for a rich man to enter the Kingdom of God" (Mark 10:25). "To contrast the largest beast of burden known in Palestine with the smallest of artificial apertures is quite in the manner of Christ's proverbial sayings."[17] Thus, Jesus had taught similar things about riches in the Sermon on the Mount (cf. Matthew 6:19–21, 24). Once again, Swete illuminates the reaction of the disciples:

---

14 Edersheim, *The Life and Times of Jesus the Messiah*, 710.
15 Swete, *Commentary on Mark*, 226–7.
16 Edersheim, *The Life and Times of Jesus the Messiah*, 710.
17 Swete, *Commentary on Mark*, 229.

Their astonishment now passed all bounds and broke out into a cry of despair . . . "Who can be saved if the rich are excluded?" The Twelve have not yet grasped the special difficulties of the rich, who seem from their position to have the first claim to admission into the Kingdom. If they are excluded, they ask, who dare to hope?[18]

Yet, the willingness of the rich young ruler to choose his riches over following Jesus and heaven's eternal glories is clear proof that it is extremely difficult for the rich to get into the kingdom of God. Jesus replied to His disciples: "With people it is impossible, but not with God; for all things are possible with God" (Mark 10:27). Then, Peter, as the spokesman for them all, replied: "Behold, we have left everything and followed You" (Mark 10:28). Truly they had left everything to follow Jesus. That was the great difference between them and the rich young ruler. They had done the one thing that is universally required of all followers of Christ. Thus, Jesus comforted them that their reward would be one hundred times greater in this life and would result in eternal life in the age to come (Mark 10:30). All who have left everything for Christ will also receive far more on earth and in heaven than what they have given up.

The Journey to Jericho and Jerusalem (Matthew 20:17–19; Mark 10:32–34; and, Luke 18:31–33)

It was now the week of March 26th to April 1st, AD 30, and crowds of worshipers were traveling all the roads of Israel to get to Jerusalem in time for the Feast of Passover. Jesus and His disciples would have left the house where He was staying on the morning of March 30th and merged with those crowds at some point on their journey from Ephraim to Jericho. Those caravans were headed first to Jericho, the "City of Palms," and then on to Jerusalem. Mark simply states about their journey:

> They were on the road going up to Jerusalem, and Jesus was walking on ahead of them; and they were amazed, and those who followed were fearful. And He again took the twelve aside and began to tell them what was going to happen to Him . . . (Mark 10:32).

There were mixed emotions among the followers of Jesus, including the Twelve, but a sense of foreboding was too easily painted on the faces of most of them. A little while earlier in the day, Jesus had left the house where He was staying and was met by a young man with

---

18 Swete, *Commentary on Mark*, 229.

a very urgent question. Where they were going was not immediately apparent to the crowd of His followers, but now things had changed. "The issue of the journey (v. 17) now becomes apparent; the road leads to Jerusalem, and to the Cross."[19] The starting point for Jesus' last journey to Jerusalem was undoubtedly Ephraim which had been His home during His retirement ministry over the past several weeks. There are still the ruins of a road from Ephraim to Jericho that Jesus and His followers would have taken. It is marked "by Roman pavement"[20] and was probably the main trade route through that part of Judea. "The traveller from Ephraim who reached Jericho by this route would enter the city through a gate on the [north] side of the city, and in order to proceed to Jerusalem, he would cross to the west gate"[21]

Jesus was most likely walking in front of the twelve disciples and His other followers "with a solemnity and determination that foreboded danger."[22] His appearance and demeanor caused some of His followers to be amazed and others of them to be fearful. He was like a general leading His soldiers into battle. Aware of the impact this journey was having on them, Jesus then called the twelve to Him in order to give them one more warning of what to expect in Jerusalem. "There was the risk of a real panic, and the Lord therefore checks His course, till the Twelve have come up to Him."[23] This was now at least the third time that Jesus warned His disciples of His crucifixion and resurrection.[24] The account in Mark is easily the fullest statement in the Scripture of what awaited Him:

> Behold, we are going up to Jerusalem, and the Son of Man will be delivered to the chief priests and the scribes; and they will condemn Him to death and will hand Him over to the Gentiles. They will mock Him and spit on Him, and scourge Him and kill Him, and three days later He will rise again (Mark 10:33, 34).

There are six distinct steps that are laid out in Jesus' words: His betrayal; His judicial sentence; His being handed over to the Gentiles; His mocking; His scourging and crucifixion; and, His resurrection. "The prediction is the same as in former cases, but with a more dis-

---

19 Swete, *Commentary on Mark*, 233.
20 Smith, *The Historical Geography of the Holy Land*, 264, footnote 1.
21 Swete, *Commentary on Mark*, 241. Such a route would be consistent with the synoptic Gospels which have our Lord both entering the city through a gate and exiting through a gate.
22 Swete, *Commentary on Mark*, 233
23 Swete, *Commentary on Mark*, 233.
24 Cf. Mark 8:31; 9:12, 31; and, the parallel passages in Matthew and Luke.

tinct intimation that he was to suffer by judicial process, or by form of law."[25] Heretofore, the exact role that the Sanhedrin would play in His death had not been clearly stated, but the plotting of that ruling body to kill Jesus was now known by many people, including His followers. Jesus' purpose in giving this final warning of what awaited Him was to calm their spirits, but it did not have that immediate effect on them as Luke writes: "But the disciples understood none of these things, and the meaning of this statement was hidden from them, and they did not comprehend the things that were said" (Luke 18:34). It is still puzzling to many people how the disciples could fail to comprehend things that Jesus had now plainly foretold them three different times. Yet, their initial blindness meant that their emotions would become totally involved in all the events that soon would follow. It is to the advantage of believers everywhere that "the disciples understood none of these things." Once they did understand and did believe them, they propagated the truth as the zealous converts that they were. As Plummer wrote:

> Their dulness was providential, and it became a security to the Church for the truth of the Resurrection. The theory that they believed, because they *expected* that He would rise again, is against all the evidence.[26]

The Sons of Zebedee's Request (Matthew 20:20–28 and Mark 10:35–45)

Such initial unbelief by the twelve in Jesus' resurrection helps to explain what happened next when the sons of Zebedee and their mother came to Jesus with an unusual request: "Teacher, we want You to do for us whatever we ask of You . . . Grant that we may sit, one on Your right and one on *Your* left, in Your glory" (Mark 10:35b, 37b). Matthew records that it was the mother of the two disciples who first came to Jesus with this request (Matthew 20:20, 21). Jesus was walking ahead of the Sons of Thunder with His other followers who were fearful of what was going to happen in Jerusalem. Once again, Jesus had warned His disciples that He would be handed over to the Gentiles, condemned to death, mocked, scourged, spat on, crucified, and killed but would rise from the dead on the third day (Mark 10:33, 34). Salome, the mother of James and John, was a godly woman who was present at His crucifixion (cf. Matthew 27:55, 56) and, no doubt, was aware of Jesus' warnings. In coming to Jesus with that petition, she

---

25 Alexander, *A Commentary on the Gospel According to Mark*, 289.
26 Plummer, *A Critical and Exegetical Commentary on the Gospel According to S. Luke*, 429.

was respectful and submissive, bowing down before Him. Her request then became the request of her sons as well. While there was certainly a measure of vainglory associated with this request, there was also an element of faith. She and her sons expressed faith that, despite Jesus' repeated warnings of His departure, that He would soon be coming in His kingdom. The petition was probably prompted by Jesus' recent assertion: "Truly, I say to you, that you who have followed Me, in the regeneration when the Son of Man will sit on His glorious throne, you shall sit upon twelve thrones, judging the twelve tribes of Israel" (Matthew 19:28).

If there were going to be twelve thrones for the apostles to sit on, then their request was that they would be allowed to sit closest to Jesus—especially since they were among the inner circle of Jesus' disciples. The two disciples, and their mother, thought there was going to be a regal reign of Christ that was imminent which they identified with the time of His "glory." Alexander comments on this request:

> The two places here described are those of honour everywhere, not only in the east or in ancient times, but at any public dinner no less than in royal courts. The desire to be near him was not wrong in itself, but only as involving an unwillingness that others should enjoy the same advantage.[27]

Jesus did not vainly grant their request, but responded to them: "You do not know what you are asking. Are you able to drink the cup that I drink, or to be baptized with the baptism with which I am baptized?" (Mark 10:38). The two brothers quickly answered that they were able. This request became known to the other disciples and caused them "to feel indignant with James and John" (Mark 10:41). The spiritual failures of the sons of Zebedee, and their mother, were now on full display before the other disciples. "It was essentially the same spirit that now prompted the request which their mother preferred"[28] that had led to their uncharitableness towards the Samaritans a few months earlier.

This request by the two brothers through their mother was ill-advised—not innocent—but it was not sinister. Jesus had already placed honor on them by making them part of His inner circle. Now, they wanted an even closer relationship—a relationship that

---

27 Alexander, *The Gospel According to Mark*, 290.
28 Edersheim, *The Life and Times of Jesus the Messiah*, 713.

would openly display that closer relationship with their Lord. They came to Jesus and boldly stated: "Teacher, we want you to do for us whatever we ask of You" (Mark 10:36). To which, Jesus replied: "What do you want for Me to do for you?" (Mark 10:36). Then, the sons of Zebedee put forth their request very plainly: "Grant that we may sit, one on Your right, and one on *Your* left, in Your glory" (Mark 10:37). There are a few problems with this request. First, they still considered Jesus' kingdom to be an earthly kingdom. Second, it was right for them to want a closer relationship with Jesus, but not such an exclusive relationship with Him. Their request, if honored, would have left others on the outside looking in. Third, they had no right to ask Jesus to do for them whatever they requested of Him. They needed to ask Jesus what He would have them to do for His kingdom. Jesus' response, therefore, was to inform them that "you do not know what you are asking. Are you able to drink the cup that I drink, or to be baptized with the baptism with which I am baptized?" (Mark 10:38). James and John probably thought Jesus' reference was to "[t]he cup which belongs to the royal banquet at which the King sits between His most honored guests."[29] And, that His question about baptism was a reference to the royal baths of a king. Despite Jesus' attempts to forewarn them of His crucifixion and resurrection, they were still focused on His crown and His kingdom. They were enchanted by the thoughts of a crown, but not the cross. They wanted the glory of His kingdom, but they were ignoring Golgotha and the path of suffering. His cup was the cup of God's wrath against sinners which He had to drink for His people. Jesus was trying to let His disciples down gently with these questions, but they confidently blurted out: "We are able" (Mark 10:39). Yet, their blind spot veiled from them the true meaning of Jesus' questions. They clearly were not able to suffer what Jesus would suffer nor were they even yet able to suffer for Jesus—not yet, at least—as subsequent actions revealed. Someday, Jesus told them, they would drink His cup and be baptized with His baptism, but the honor they requested could only be given to "those for whom it has been prepared" (Mark 10:40). Jesus could only dispense the honors which His Father had predestined.

The other disciples became indignant with James and John when

---

29 Swete, *Commentary on Mark*, 236.

they heard their request of Jesus. Peter, James and John had worked together in harmony hitherto, but this situation produced "bitter feelings" and "threatened the harmony and spiritual life of the Apostolate, and called for immediate correction."[30] It is easy to fault the brothers and their mother, Salome, but Jesus corrected them with the gentleness that was characteristic of Him. He addressed His words to all the disciples when He advised them: "whoever wishes to be first among you shall be slave of all. For even the Son of Man did not come to be served, but to serve, and to give His life a ransom for many" (Mark 10:44, 45). Those words were necessary for all His disciples, as Bruce explains:

> Pride and selfishness may vex and grieve the humble and self-forgetful, but they provoke resentment only in the proud and selfish; and the best way to be proof against the assaults of other men's passions is to get similar affections exorcised out of our own breasts.[31]

The indignant response of the other ten disciples to the request of James and John proved that the same spirit of vainglory and selfishness was in their hearts also. Thus, Jesus gave advice to all the twelve as well as all His followers. He was a servant of others and so His followers are to be the same. Jesus taught them all that they were not to lord it over others like the Gentiles, but to follow His example to them of humility and service. As he said: "But it is not this way among you. But whoever wishes to become great among you shall be your servant; and whoever wishes to be first among you shall be slave of all. For even the Son of Man did not come to be served, but to serve, and to give His life a ransom for many" (Mark 9:43–45). Jesus' words could not be mistaken as a rebuke of any kind, but "show the greatness of [His] condescension and self-sacrificing love as manifested to his enemies."[32] The disciples were not above their Master. Jesus' example affords "a constraining motive for an infinitely less degree of self-denial on the part of his followers towards one another."[33]

---

30 Swete, *Commentary on Mark*, 239.
31 Bruce, *The Training of the Twelve*, 289.
32 Alexander, *The Gospel According to Mark*, 294.
33 Alexander, *The Gospel According to Mark*, 294.

Jesus' Retirement Ministry in Ephraim

The Healing of Blind Bartimaeus (Matthew 20:29–34; Mark 10:46–52; and, Luke 18:35–43)

Jericho was a gateway city for travelers coming from either the area of the Jordan River or from Galilee. It was an oasis in the midst of the wilderness area of Israel where dates, springs, aromatic gums and spices were in abundance. The very name, Jericho, means "place of fragrance" which is probably a result of the fragrant Balsam trees that grow plentifully there. Yet, it was a city that could never defend itself and was bereft of heroes. One of the oldest inhabited cities in the world, Herod the Great and his son, Archelaus, had beautified and enlarged it in the days of Jesus. Herod had constructed an enormous winter palace there which spanned the Wadi Qelt Gorge via a bridge and had courtyards, sunken gardens, and swimming pools. The temperatures at Jericho were warm in the winter and it was close to Jerusalem. Moreover, the city was only a days' ride from Jerusalem by horseback. Smith describes the beauty and fame of ancient Jericho:

> Jericho was the gateway of a province, the emporium of a large trade, the mistress of a great palm forest, woods of balsam, and very rich gardens. To earliest Israel she was the city of Palms; to the latest Jewish historian 'divine region,' 'fattest of Judea.' Greeks and Romans spread her fame, with her dates and balsam, all over the world, and great revenue was derived from her. Her year is one long summer; she can soak herself in water, and the chemicals with which her soil is charged seem to favour her peculiar products.[34]

As Jesus and His disciples were approaching Jericho, there was a blind beggar on the side of the road who heard the sound of the crowd passing by him and he inquired of those around him what was happening. He was told that "Jesus of Nazareth was passing by" (Luke 18:37). Having heard of the many miracles Jesus had performed, blind Bartimaeus began to cry out, "Jesus, Son of David, have mercy on me!" (Luke 18:38). Bartimaeus recognized Jesus as the greater Son of David, the Messiah, who was to deliver His people from their bondage, but "those who led the way were sternly telling him to be quiet" (Luke 18:39). With his incessant cries for mercy, Bartimaeus was interrupting what was happening in that caravan of the followers of Jesus. Yet, Bartimaeus continued to beg Jesus for help. Then, "Jesus stopped and commanded that he be brought to Him; and when he came near, He questioned him, 'What do you want Me

---

34 Smith, *The Historical Geography of the Holy Land*, 266–7.

to do for you?' and he said, 'I want to regain my sight!'" (Luke 18:40, 41). Mark adds that when Bartimaeus heard the summons of Jesus he threw "aside his cloak, . . . jumped up and came to Jesus" (Mark 10:50).[35] Such eagerness to be healed was immediately rewarded by Jesus who said, "Receive your sight; your faith has made you well" (Luke 18:42). Mark adds that Jesus commanded him to, "Go," which probably was a command to return to his home. Yet, Bartimaeus immediately began following Jesus on the road, giving glory to God, while all the crowds were praising Him. Geldenhuys comments on this miracle:

> Whoever, like the blind beggar, in consciousness of his own misery, and believing in Jesus, cries to Him whole-heartedly will just as assuredly be healed of spiritual blindness through His word of power.[36]

The Conversion of Zaccheus (Luke 19:1–10)

Apparently, Jesus was intending to pass through Jericho and continue on to Jerusalem until he spotted a certain man in a sycamore tree, Zaccheus, a rich tax collector. Edersheim describes what the composition of the crowd in Jericho must have been like on that occasion in late March:

> And in the streets of Jericho a motley throng meets: pilgrims from Galilee and Peraea, priests who have a 'station' here, traders from all lands, who have come to purchase or to sell, or are on the great caravan-road from Arabia and Damascus—robbers and anchorites, wild fanatics, soldiers, courtiers, and busy publicans—for Jericho was the central station for the collection of tax and custom, both on native produce and on that brought from across Jordan . . .
>
> It was the custom, when a festive band passed through a place, that the inhabitants gathered in the streets to bid their brethren welcome. And on that afternoon, surely, scarce any one in Jericho but would go to see the pilgrim-band. Men—curious, angry, half-convinced; women, holding up their babes, it may be for a passing blessing, or pushing forward their children that in after years they might say that they had seen the Prophet of Nazareth; traders; soldiers—a solid wall of onlookers before their gardens was 'this' crowd along the road which Jesus 'was to pass.'[37]

---

35 Matthew and Mark place the healing of the blind man at the time when Jesus was leaving Jericho rather than when He was approaching it. Matthew also records that there were two men who were healed. With these minor differences aside, the accounts are completely consistent with one another otherwise. I will leave it to others to reconcile the differences.
36 Gendenhuys, *Commentary on the Gospel of Luke*, 466.
37 Edersheim, *The Life and Times of Jesus the Messiah*, 716–7.

Jesus had surely passed through these same streets of Jericho on many of His other visits to Jerusalem, but there was never before an occasion like this one. The reports of the conspiracy of the Sanhedrin against the Galilean would have filtered back to the common people by now. Like Jesus' disciples and many followers who were traveling with Him, the crowds in Jericho would have had some inkling that the great intrigue in Jerusalem concerning Him would soon have a tragic ending during the Passover feast. Everyone in the area, therefore, would have wanted to watch as Jesus and His festive band passed by—including a diminutive tax collector who had a bad reputation. For three years, great throngs of people had followed Jesus wherever He went. Thus, Zaccheus, unable to get a good look at the approaching "great Wonder of the ages" on the ground, "ran on ahead, climbed up into a sycamore tree in order to see Him, for He was about to pass that way" (Luke 19:4). Zaccheus' resourcefulness also made him noticeable to Jesus, "who looked up and said to him, 'Zaccheus, hurry and come down, for today I must stay at your house'" (Luke 19:5). While the chief tax collector of Jericho hurriedly obeyed Jesus' command, the crowd of onlookers just as quickly began to grumble, saying, "He has gone to be the guest of a man who is a sinner" (Luke 19:7). That had been a common complaint of the scribes and Pharisees against Jesus on many occasions. "It was not jealousy, but a sense of outraged propriety, which made them all murmur."[38] Nonetheless, as Jesus had once said, "wisdom is vindicated by her deeds" (Matthew 11:19). The wisdom of Jesus, who was greater than Solomon in that respect, was soon displayed when Zaccheus stopped and declared to Him, "Behold, Lord, half of my possessions I will give to the poor, and if I have defrauded anyone of anything, I will give him back four times as much" (Luke 19:8).

Just a little earlier that day, Jesus had exhorted the rich young ruler to "sell all you possess and give it to the poor" (Luke 18:22), but he was unwilling to do so. Zaccheus promised to give half of his possessions to the poor and to make restitution for anyone he had defrauded by repaying four times as much as he had taken. "And so the whole current of his life had been turned, in those few moments, through the joyous reception of Christ, the Savior of sinners; and Zaccheus, the public robber, the rich chief of the Publicans, had become an almsgiv-

---

38 Plummer, *The Gospel According to S. Luke*, 434.

er."[39] Jesus responded to Zaccheus' vows by saying, "Today salvation has come to this house, because he, too, is a son of Abraham. For the Son of Man has come to seek and to save that which was lost" (Luke 19:9, 10). The conversion of Zaccheus from a life of sin to a follower of Christ was one of the most magnificent acts of the ministry of our Lord. Outside Zaccheus' abode were bands of gossipers and slanderers. Inside was Christ with Zaccheus. Outside was condemnation. Inside was the redeeming love of the Master. Jesus' words on the purpose of His ministry was to dispel the idea in the minds of all Jews that the Messiah had come only to provide relief from the oppression of earthly enemies. Instead, the real purpose of Jesus coming in the flesh was "to seek and to save that which was lost." As Ryle commented on these verses:

> It is as a Saviour, more than as a Judge, that Christ desires to be known: let us see that we know Him as such; let us take heed that our souls are saved; once saved and converted, we shall say, "What shall I render to the Lord for all His benefits?" (Psalm cxvi. 12.) Once saved, we shall not complain that self-denial, like that of Zaccheus, is a grievous requirement.[40]

---

39 Edersheim, *The Life and Times of Jesus the Messiah*, 718.
40 Ryle, *Expository Thoughts on the Gospels: St. Luke*, 2:294.

19

Jesus' Triumphal Entry into Jerusalem

"How different was Messiah's entry into Jerusalem foretold in this prophecy, the accomplishment of which we read in the evangelists! He poured contempt upon the phantom of human glory . . . And though a secret divine influence constrained the multitude to acknowledge his character, and, with some accommodation to the times, 'to strew their garments in the way,' as they proclaimed the King who came in the name of Jehovah; yet he appeared unmoved by their applause. Had the history of Jesus, like those which we have of Socrates or Cyrus, been merely the work of a human writer, ambitious to adorn a favourite character with the most splendid qualities of a philosopher or a hero, we should never have known how his mind was engaged in this situation. The Saviour must be divine, his historian must be inspired, the fact must be true; for man could not have invented such a circumstance, that this meek and lowly Saviour took no notice of the zeal and homage of his friends, because his heart was filled with compassion for his enemies, who were thirsting for his blood. For it was then, amidst the acclamation of his disciples, that he beheld the city and wept over it, while he foretold the evils which the rejection of him bring upon it. 'Oh that thou hadst known, even thou, at least in this thy day, the things belonging to thy peace! But now they are hidden from thine eyes.'"[1]

The road from Jericho to Bethany was a treacherous and dangerous journey by "a steep, mountainous road with narrow, rocky defiles and blind turns, which made it a place to be wary of robbers."[2] For eighteen difficult miles, travelers wearied themselves with the nearly 4,000 foot climb and had to be ever vigilant against attacks. There was safety in numbers and those roads were usually traveled in the company of caravans during daylight hours.

Leaving the hospitality of Zaccheus on the morning of Friday, March 31st, Jesus and His disciples made haste to arrive in Bethany before the Sabbath began at sundown.[3] Martha had probably

---

[1] John Newton, *The Works of John Newton* (Edinburgh, Scotland and Carlisle, Pennsylvania: The Banner of Truth Trust, 2007), 4:128.
[2] https://www.onesteadfast.com/Blog/ScriptureStudy/The-Road-is-Not-Safe Accessed on January 17, 2024.
[3] John 12:1 says that Jesus arrived in Bethany "six days before the Passover." The evening of Nisan 14th would have begun in 30 AD on Thursday, April 6th. If the six days are counted by

already received news that Jesus would be visiting Bethany before proceeding to Jerusalem. Most of the caravan continued on to Jerusalem and probably started spreading the news that Jesus had remained behind in Bethany.

Mary Anoints Jesus for His Burial (Matthew 26:6–13; Mark 13:3–9; and, John 12:1–8)

In the home of Simon the leper, a large meal had been prepared for Jesus and His disciples. That would have been the Sabbath meal which was customarily prepared during the daylight hours of Friday before sundown. Martha, as usual, was the servant and Lazarus was also there—who had been raised from the dead only weeks before. While everyone was reclining at table, Mary took the occasion to anoint Jesus' head and feet with a very expensive jar of perfume and wiping them with her hair (John 12:3; Matthew 26:7; Mark 14:3). The perfume she poured on Him was a "pound of very costly . . . pure nard" in an alabaster jar—a white calcite mineral comparable to marble which was prized for its beauty. The whole house soon "was filled with the fragrance of the perfume" (John 12:3).

One of disciples, Judas Iscariot, soon objected to Mary's action as an ostentatious and extravagant waste of resources. He asked, "*Why was this perfume not sold for three hundred denarii and given to poor people?*" (John 12:5). Just the day before, Jesus had challenged the rich young ruler to sell all his possessions and give the proceeds to the poor. And Peter and the other disciples had questioned Jesus about the difficulty of entering the kingdom of heaven with such strict requirements. Later that same day, Zaccheus had proclaimed to Jesus: "Behold, Lord, half of my possessions I will give to feed the poor" (Luke 19:8). Thus, Judas' thievery and covetousness were easily veiled by his recommendation to help the poor which would have seemed very appropriate to the other disciples. The result was that all "the disciples were indignant when they saw this, and said, 'Why this waste?'" (Matthew 26:8). Once again, the same spirit about which Jesus had warned them just the previous day, that of indignancy, overtook them all. "All the disciples, it seems, disapproved of the action, the only difference between Judas and the rest being that he disapproved on hypocritical grounds, while his fellow-disciples were honest both in their

---

excluding the day Jesus arrived in Bethany, which seems most logical to me, then the Lord came to Bethany on Friday, March 31st, AD 30.

judgment and in their motives."⁴ Yet, their honest motives were still wrong. Instead of agreeing with His disciples, Jesus defended Mary, saying: "Let her alone; why do you bother her? She has done a good deed for Me. For you always have the poor with you, and whenever you wish you can do good to them; but you do not always have Me. She has done what she could; she has anointed My body beforehand for the burial. Truly I say to you, wherever the gospel is preached in the whole world, what this woman has done will also be spoken of her" (Mark 14:6–9).

It certainly appeared to the judgment of the disciples that Mary had wasted great resources. The perfume may indeed have had a value of three hundred denarii which would have been the wages of a laborer for three hundred days. In most circumstances, such a waste would have rightly deserved the response of the disciples. Those days were not ordinary circumstances, though. Mary's action was symbolically done to prepare Jesus' body for burial whether or not she had fully discerned the emblematical meaning of her actions. The disciples, despite being warned of Jesus' crucifixion, still had not yet understood what awaited Him in Jerusalem. Out of her great love for the Lord, Mary gave her very best to Him and probably would have done so on other occasions. Yet, there was still a realization on the part of many of Jesus' followers that dangerous times were at hand and the conspiracy of the Sanhedrin to kill Jesus was known by many. Bruce explains the narrative very well:

> As Mary broke her box of ointment and poured forth its precious contents, so Christ broke His body and shed His precious blood; so Christians pour forth their hearts before their Lord, counting not their very lives dear for His sake.. Christ's death was a breaking of an alabaster box for us; our life should be a breaking of an alabaster box for Him.⁵

The reaction of Judas to Mary's good deed "was because he was a thief, and as he had the money box, he used to pilfer what was put in it" (John 12:6). He took out small sums by and by for his own use, even though he was yet undetected by the other disciples and, thus, maintained their confidence. His perfidy is brought out eloquently by Edersheim:

---

4 Bruce, *The Training of the Twelve*, 298.
5 Bruce, *The Training of the Twelve*, 300.

It is ever the light that throws the shadows of objects—and this deed of faith and love now cast the features of Judas in gigantic dark outlines against the scene. He knew the nearness of Christ's Betrayal, and hated the more; she knew the nearness of His precious Death, and loved the more. It was not that he cared for the poor, when, taking the mask of charity, he simulated anger that such costly ointment had not been sold and the price given to the poor. For he was essentially dishonest, 'a thief,' and covetousness was the underlying master-passion of his soul.[6]

On the other hand, Mary's simplicity of faith and love is the reason she is well-remembered today and why her deed is proclaimed wherever the gospel is preached. True faith reaches into the subjective experiences of the believer and compels him to do great things for Jesus because He did great things for him.

The Large Crowd of Jews in Bethany (John 12:9–11)

The caravan of fellow travelers with whom Jesus and His disciples had journeyed from Jericho then evidently began reporting the whereabouts of the Lord to others. There was an excitement that soon compelled them to go to Bethany so that they could see both Jesus and Lazarus whom He had raised from the dead. Most likely, they traveled to that little village on the following day, Saturday, which would account for the large numbers of people who made up the entourage of our Lord on Palm Sunday.

The Sanhedrin had tried hard to squelch this interest in Lazarus' resurrection, but without success. Now, the numbers were growing of those who wanted to see that man who had been called out of the tomb after four days. The chief priests were now so jealous of the attention that Lazarus was receiving that they determined to put him to death also "because on account of Him many of the Jews were going away and were believing in Jesus" (John 12:11). The irrationality of those who are incensed by their hatred of the Lord has no greater example than these chief priests. They intended in their enmity to kill both Jesus and Lazarus. They wanted to put to death both the One who raised a dead man and the one whom He raised. The chief priests were Sadducees who did not believe in the resurrection so Lazarus was the problem they had to remedy.

---

6 Edersheim, *The Life and Times of Jesus the Messiah*, 722.

Jesus' Triumphal Entry (Matthew 21:4–9; Mark 11:7–10; Luke 19:35–39; and, John 12:12–16)

When Sunday morning, April 2nd, arrived, Jesus set out on His royal entrance into the Holy City. The little hamlet of Bethany was "perched on a broken, rocky plateau on the other side of Olivet."[7] The Lord and His followers would travel over that mountain in order to journey to Jerusalem. The growing crowds that went before Him and those who went with Him would soon be augmented by large numbers of those who anxiously awaited His arrival. Jesus sent two of His disciples on ahead of Him to a little village called Bethphage ("House of Figs"), which was situated in a fork of the road on the Mount of Olives between Bethany and Jerusalem. They were simply told, "Go into the village ahead of *you*; there as you enter, you will find a colt tied on which no one yet has ever sat; untie it, and bring it *here*. If anyone asks you, 'Why are you untying it?' you shall say, 'The Lord has need of it.'" (Luke 19:30, 31). Things happened just as Jesus had told them and the colt was brought to Him. He mounted the colt in fulfillment of Zechariah 9:9, "Behold, your king is coming to you; He is just and endowed with salvation, humble, and mounted on a donkey, even on a colt, the foal of a donkey." Morris points out the importance of Jesus' use of a colt, instead of a horse, for His grand entrance into Jerusalem:

> The words of this prophecy point to a distinctive mark of Christ's kingship. The ass was not normally used by a warlike person. It was the animal of a man of peace, a priest, a merchant or the like. It might also be used by a person of importance but in connection with peaceable purposes. A conqueror would ride into the city on a war horse, or perhaps march in on foot at the head of his troops. The ass speaks of peace. John sees accordingly not only a fulfillment of prophecy, but such a fulfillment of prophecy as indicates a special kind of king.[8]

The crowd following Jesus that day was a mixed lot. Some were true followers of His, such as Martha, Mary, Lazarus and His disciples. Others were those large crowds of Jews who had come to Bethany out of curiosity. Most of the other pilgrims who had followed Him were already in Jerusalem. At the Feast of Tabernacles six months earlier, the crowds had sought Him, asking, "Where is He?" (John 7:11). There was an excitement that pulsated through the crowds in

---
7 Edersheim, *The Life and Times of Jesus the Messiah*, 725.
8 Morris, *The Gospel According to St. John*, 587.

the Holy City as they realized their king was coming to them riding on a colt. The symbolism of Jesus riding on a colt did not seem to be comprehended by them. They anticipated that an earthly reign of the Messiah was at hand. Both the crowds who were following Him and those who came out to meet Him began to spread their coats and palm branches on the way (Matthew 21:8; Mark 11:8; Luke 19:35, 36; and, John 12:13). Some who were with Jesus "continued to testify *about Him*" (John 12:17) concerning the raising of Lazarus and the many other miracles He had performed. Those words were immediately reported to the leaders in Jerusalem, but nothing could suppress enthusiasm of the crowds to see Him on this particular day. Soon, they all together began to shout the words of Psalm 118:26, "Blessed is the King who comes in the name of the Lord; Peace in heaven and glory in the highest!" Yet, not everyone was pleased. The Pharisees began to grumble to one another: "You see that you are not doing any good; look, the world has gone after Him" (John 12:19). And others of the Pharisees said to Jesus, "Teacher, rebuke Your disciples" (Luke 19:39). The Lord replied: "I tell you, if these become silent, the stones will cry out" (Luke 19:40). Fearing the crowds, the Pharisees attempted to bring Jesus under their authority and directed Him to silence the multitudes. As Plummer opines:

> Having no power to check the multitude (Jn. xii. 19), and perhaps not daring to attempt it, they call on Jesus to do so. Possibly they wished to fasten the responsibility on Him, and they may have been sent by the Sanhedrin to spy and report. The Messianic homage was offensive to them, and they feared a tumult which might cause trouble with Pilate.[9]

Jesus did not give into their thinly-veiled demands for even a moment, but replied that such an action would be counter-productive and would result in the very stones crying out His praises. At this point, two groups were merged together—one from Bethany and the other from the City—with the latter now leading the way while the others were following Jesus. Slowly, steadily, the triumphant procession topped the mountain ridge "where first begins 'the descent of the Mount of Olives' towards Jerusalem."[10] When Jesus arrived at that spot and looked across at the City from that elevated perch, He burst forth in tears with those immortal words recorded in Luke 19:42–44:

---

9 Plummer, *A Critical and Exegetical Commentary on the Gospel According to S. Luke*, 448–9.
10 Edersheim, *The Life and Times of Jesus the Messiah*, 727.

> If you had known in this day, even you, the things which make for peace! But now they have been hidden from your eyes. For the days will come upon you when your enemies will throw up a barricade against you, and surround you and hem you in on every side, and they will level you to the ground and your children within you, and they will not leave in you one stone upon another, because you did not recognize the time of your visitation.

The weeping of a strong man is more affecting than the tears that flow too readily from the eyes of those whose heads are filled with fountains of water. The word used for Jesus' tears on this occasion means "loud and deep lamentation."[11] Having taken no thought of the adulation being poured out on Him, Jesus was now singularly focused on Zion, the city of God, whose praises are sung in the Old Testament. There before His view was that City where the Temple of God stood—the spot where successive generations of worshipers had offered the sacrifices required by the law. There before Him was the City where David and Solomon and numerous other kings had reigned. That city's time was now in the past, though they did not know it. Their sins had risen to the throne of God and a day was appointed when they would be leveled by a conquering nation. Their day of visitation had come and gone. They had not recognized the things that make for peace. The judgment of God would, therefore, soon be poured out on their impenitence. Yet, their greatest evil was soon to come and Jesus knew exactly what it was. He had thrice, at least, warned His disciples of what awaited Him on this occasion. A terrible time awaited them when they would publicly repudiate the Messiah sent by God and fill up the full measure of their sins. Within a few days that terrible deed would be done. Edersheim describes the essence of Jesus' broken sentences:

> The contrast was, indeed, terrible between the Jerusalem that rose before Him in all its beauty, glory, security, and the Jerusalem which He saw in vision dimly rising on the sky, with the camo of the enemy around it on every side, hugging closer and closer in deadly embrace, and the very stockade of the Roman Legions raised around it; then, another scene in the shifting panorama, and the city laid with the ground, and the very bodies of her children among her ruins; and yet another scene: the silence and desolateness of death by the Hand of God—not one stone left upon another![12]

---

11 Edersheim, *The Life and Times of Jesus the Messiah*, 729.
12 Edersheim, *The Life and Times of Jesus the Messiah*, 729.

After those tears over Jerusalem, Jesus and the great procession continued down the Mount of Olives, across the Kidron Valley, and entered into Jerusalem through one of the gates on the eastern side of the city—possibly the Horse Gate. The first thing Jesus did on that day, Palm Sunday, was to cleanse the Temple as He had done three years earlier. He, thereby, indicated that the worst of the sins of the Jews was their false worship and their profaning of the house of God. Matthew records what happened when Jesus arrived at the temple:

> And Jesus entered the temple and drove out all those who were buying and selling in the temple, and overturned the tables of the money changers and seats of those who were selling doves. And He said to them, "It is written, 'My house shall be called a house of prayer; but you are making it a robbers' den" (Matthew 21:12, 13).

Chamblin's comments on Jesus' actions and His quote of Isaiah 56:7 are enlightening:

> There is a further reason why Jesus, in Matthew 21:13, places quotations from Isaiah 56:7 ('My house shall be called a house of prayer') and Jeremiah 7:11 ('a den of robbers') alongside each other. Crowning his promises to Gentiles in Isaiah 56:3–7b, Yahweh declares in 56:7c that the house—his temple—'shall be called a house of prayer for all peoples.' As noted, the merchants and money-changers did their work in the Court of the Gentiles. The Gentiles had few privileges in the temple, but they were permitted in this remote area, to worship Israel's God. And now even that space is being usurped: these installed tradesmen are robbing Gentiles of their place of worship. So Israel's Messiah, the one appointed to proclaim peace to all the nations (Matt. 21:5; Zech. 9:9–10), now exercises his authority as Priest-King on their behalf. The preface to the quotation—"It has been written . . ."—shows that the prophecy of Isaiah 56:7 has lost none of its authority—that it 'stands written' until it is finally realized.[13]

Following this final cleansing of the temple, "the blind and the lame came to Him in the temple, and He healed them" (Matthew 21:14). The chief priests and scribes, always wary of Jesus' every move, could only raise a hypocritical, but indignant complaint as they "saw the wonderful things that He had done" (Matthew 21:15a) and the affect it was having on even the children who were shouting, "Hosanna to the Son of David" (Matthew 21:15b): "Do you hear what these children are saying?" (Matthew 21:16a). "And Jesus aid to them, 'Yes; have you never read, "Out of the mouth of infants and nursing

---

13 Chamblin, *Matthew*, 2:1015.

babies You have prepared praise for Yourself"'?" (Matthew 21:16b). Jesus, hereby, showed that He welcomed all people—Jews and Gentiles—into His kingdom; that He welcomed both the frenzied crowds who strewed palm branches along His path and the little children who were often neglected; and, that He welcomed the blind and the lame, as well as all those who were subject to all manner of sins as long as they repented and believed. After this exchange with the chief priests and scribes, Jesus "left them and went out of the city to Bethany, and spent the night there" (Matthew 21:17). A week of great intrigue awaited Him as Passover was at hand.

20

The Prelude to Jesus' Passion

"Socrates having expressed his idea of a perfect character, a truly virtuous man, ventured to predict the reception such a person, if such a one could ever be found, would meet with from the world. And he thought, that his practice would be so dissimilar to that of other men, his testimony against their wickedness so strong, and his endeavours to reform them so importunate and unwelcome, that instead of being universally admired, he would be disliked and hated; that mankind were too degenerate and too obstinate, to bear either the example or reproof of such a person, and would most probably revile and persecute him, and put him to death as an enemy to their peace.

"In this instance, the judgment of Socrates accords with the language of the Old, and with the history of the New Testament. Messiah was this perfect character. As such Isaiah describes him. He likewise foresaw how he would be treated, and foretold that he would be "numbered with the transgressors," despised and rejected by the very people who were eye-witnesses of his upright and benevolent conduct. And thus, in fact, it proved. When Jesus was upon earth, true virtue and goodness were visibly displayed, and thereby the wickedness of man became signally conspicuous. For they among whom he was conversant, "preferred a robber and murderer to him." They preserved Barabbas, who had been justly condemned to die for enormous crimes, and they nailed Jesus, in his stead. To the cross."[1]

Monday, April 3, AD 30, began early for Jesus and His disciples. The sun rose about 6:30 AM that morning and they probably set out on their journey soon thereafter. For the next few days, they would be traveling to and from Jerusalem each day. Across the Mount of Olives from Bethany and down the western slope of the mountain, they retraced the same path which Jesus had used for His triumphal entry into the city the day before when he was hailed as the King of the Jews by the adoring crowds. On this day, a "lone fig-tree" was conspicuous to the sight of Jesus "at a distance" (Mark 11:13) because it was unseasonably full of leaves. Jesus, being hungry, "came to it and found nothing on it except leaves only" (Matthew 21:19). Henry Baker Tristram explains the situation to us:

---

[1] Newton, *The Works of John Newton*, 4:198–9.

The event happened at the end of March, or beginning of April, a time of year when it would be most unusual for a fig on Mount Olivet to be in leaf. But if the tree exhibited its precociousness by having leaves so early, it might be expected to have fruit, although the time of figs was not yet, for the fruit appears before the leaves.[2]

What happened next has caused confusion for some people.[3] Jesus cursed the fig tree and said, "'No longer shall there ever be any fruit from you.' And at once the fig tree withered" (Matthew 21:19). Even "the disciples were amazed and asked, 'How did the fig tree wither *all at once?*'" (Matthew 21:20). There was a deeper lesson which Jesus would teach His disciples concerning this fig tree, but the immediate context is brought out well by Swete:

> The Lord had not broken His fast (cf. Jo. 4:32 ff.), or the morning meal had been scanty or hurried; a day of toil was before Him, and it was important to recruit His strength on which the spiritual exercises of the night had perhaps drawn largely. The wayside fig tree seemed to offer necessary refreshment.[4]

With unseasonably abundant foliage, the fig tree seemed to offer the sustenance that was needed for Jesus and His disciples. Such was not to be the case. "There were no figs under the leaves—not even the half-ripe figs which the peasants of Palestine ate with their bread in the fields."[5] In their surprise at Jesus' actions, the disciples asked, "How did the fig tree wither?" (Matthew 21:20); not why did Jesus curse it. The Lord answered their question by teaching the importance of praying with faith: "Truly I say to you, if you have faith and do not doubt, you will not only do what was done to the fig tree, but even if you say, 'Be taken up and cast into the sea,' it will happen" (Matthew 21:21).

Continuing on their journey, Jesus and His disciples arrived at Jerusalem. When He "entered the temple, the chief priests and elders[6] of the people came to Him, while He was teaching, and said, 'By what authority are you doing these things, and who gave you this author-

---

2 Henry Baker Tristram, The Natural History of the Bible (London: Society for the Promoting Christian Knowledge, 1867), 352. Fig trees in that area do not usually ripen with figs before May.
3 The author took a course on the survey of the New Testament at a junior college in which the professor stated that he thought Jesus' cursing the fig tree was an act of immaturity. *Au contraire.* If Jesus was immature in anything He ever did, then He was not qualified to be our Savior.
4 Swete, *Commentary on Mark*, 253.
5 Swete, *Commentary on Mark*, 254.
6 The elders and chief priests were augmented by the scribes per Mark 11:27 and Luke 20:1.

ity?'" (Matthew 21:23). They were obviously still seething in their hearts against Jesus because of the events of the previous day. Jesus' triumphant entry to the city had made it more difficult for them to carry out their plans to kill Him. This interrogation, therefore, probably took place in the colonnade of the Court of the Gentiles located on the southeast side of the temple grounds. Jesus might have been teaching while He was walking or, perhaps, could have sat down to teach as He often did. Swete's comments on the question of the Jewish leaders is helpful:

> The question in itself was a reasonable one, and the men who asked it felt that they had a right to do so. The Temple was in their charge, and by forcibly ejecting the vendors whom they allowed, Jesus had laid claims to a superior jurisdiction. They now ask Him publicly to produce His credentials, to state (1) the nature of His authority, (2) the name of the person from whom he received it.[7]

In His reply, Jesus promised to give them an answer if they would first answer one question: "The baptism of John was from what *source* from heaven or from men?" (Matthew 21:25). Jesus' question was not unrelated to the question of the authorities. He replied, therein, that His authority was from God and His baptism by John was the public confirmation of that authority. Both John and Jesus were called by God to their ministries. The authorities quickly discerned the corner into which Jesus had maneuvered them and refused to answer the Lord. They simply said, "We do not know" (Matthew 21:27). Of course, their answer was duplicitous. It was impolitic for them to speak favorably of John since he had been beheaded by Herod, but they could not denounce him in any way because the crowds regarded him as a prophet. Their dilemma enabled Jesus to refuse to answer their question as well. They had hoped to discredit Jesus before His followers, but were foiled once again in their attempts to do so.

Jesus' Parables in the Temple (Matthew 21:28–46)

With the Jewish leaders momentarily silenced, Jesus then spoke two parables to the crowds who were hanging on His every word. The first parable was about two sons. The first son initially said he would go work in his father's field, but did not. On reflection, "he regretted it and went" (Matthew 21:29). The second son initially said, "'I will, sir'; but he did not go" (Matthew 21:30). So, Jesus asked the crowds, "Which

---

7 Swete, *Commentary on Mark*, 262.

of the two did the will of his father?" (Matthew 21:31), who rightly replied, "The first" (Matthew 21:31). That gave Jesus the platform to praise the tax collectors and prostitutes for believing John and to condemn the leaders who "seeing this, did not even feel remorse afterward so as to believe him" (Matthew 21:32). The second parable was about a landowner and his vineyard which was an expansion on Isaiah's parable of the vineyard in Isaiah 5:1–7. The bloodshed that Isaiah foretold was the killing of the prophets and, finally, the Son of God. As Jesus stated: "When the harvest time approached, he sent slaves to the vine growers to receive his produce. The vine growers took his slaves and beat one, killed another, and stoned a third" (Matthew 21:34, 35). The same thing happened to the next group of slaves the landowner sent. Finally, he sent his son, expecting that they would respect him. "But when the vine-growers saw the son, they said among themselves, 'This is the heir; come, let us kill him and seize his inheritance'" (Matthew 21:38). Asking the crowds what they expected would be done to the vine-growers, the crowds responded: "He will bring those wretches to a wretched end, and will rent out the vineyard to other vine-growers who will pay him the proceeds at the *proper* seasons" (Matthew 21:41). Jesus then quoted from Psalm 118:22, "The stone which the builders rejected, this became the chief corner *stone*," before announcing that "the kingdom of God will be taken away from you and given to a people, producing the fruit of it" (Matthew 21:43). While Jesus spoke those parables to the larger crowds, He was obviously aiming His denunciations against the chief priests, scribes and Pharisees. And that band of conspirators, all too well, "understood that He was speaking about them. When they sought to seize Him, they feared the people, because they considered Him to be a prophet" (Matthew 21:45, 46). Jesus' parables against the Sanhedrists were effective in exposing "the true character of their hostility"[8] and "for the moment they had no alternative but to accept defeat and return to their council-chamber to mature their plots."[9] As Edersheim comments:

> Once more was their wrath roused, but also their fears. They knew that He spake of them, and would fain have laid hands on Him; but they feared the people, who in those days regarded Him as a prophet. And so for the present they left Him, and went their way.[10]

---

8 Swete, *Commentary on Mark*, 265.
9 Swete, *Commentary on Mark*, 273.
10 Edersheim, *The Life and Times of Jesus the Messiah*, 768.

The scribes and chief priests did not accept defeat easily, though. As a result of their consultations in private, they decided to watch Jesus closely and to send "spies who pretended to be righteous, in order that they might catch Him in some statement, so that they could deliver Him to the rule and authority of the governor" (Luke 20:20). While they were watching Jesus, He spoke another parable to the crowds about a marriage feast a king gave for his son. It was similar in some respects to the parable of the landowner and the vineyard. In both parables, the focus is on how the son was treated by those who should have honored him. Both parables describe the father as sending several servants to gather the harvest or to gather the invited guests. Both parables describe the cruel treatment that the servants, and the son, received. Of course, the son in both instances is Jesus, the Son of God. This parable of the wedding feast describes the invited guests as "unwilling to come" (Matthew 22:3) Rather, "they paid no attention and went their way, one to his farm, another to his business, and the rest seized his slaves and mistreated them and killed them" (Matthew 22:5, 6). This parable is a dire warning of God's judgment. In Luke 14:16–24, Jesus gave a similar parable which has more of the element of invitation, whereas this parable "sounds the note of judgment much more strongly."[11] In both Matthew 22 and Luke 14, the invited guests make excuses and so the servants are sent out to gather guests everywhere they could. As Calvin opines on the harmony of the two parables:

> After He had shown that they who contemptuously reject God's grace are unworthy, He now says that others are substituted for them, and those the meanest and most contemptible. And here is pointing to the calling of the Gentiles which would provoke the Jews to jealousy, as it says in the Song of Moses: 'They have provoked me by those who were not gods, and I will move them to jealousy with those which are not a people; I will provoke them to anger with a foolish nation' (Deut. 32.21). Because they were the first to be chosen, they thought His grace was bound to them and that He could not do without them. It is well known how they despised others. Therefore He makes a concession and compares the Gentiles to beggars, to the blind and the lame. And He says that they were called from the street-corners and lanes like outcasts and strangers, yet that they supply the place left empty by the friends and relations. Thus what the prophets foretold more obscurely of the creating of the new Church, He expressed more clearly. And certainly

---

11 Chamblin, *Matthew*, 2:1058.

this shaming was the consummation of divine wrath. He renounced them and received the polluted and unclean Gentiles into His house. But if He did not spare the natural branches, the same vengeance awaits us today if we do not respond to His call.[12]

These parables of Jesus prophesied of the coming judgment of the Jews and the taking of the kingdom of God away from them. Yet, those prophecies are not the end of the story for them. In Romans 11:23–26, Paul wrote about their future ingrafting into the church: "And they also, if they do not continue in their unbelief, will be grafted in, for God is able to graft them in again. For if you were cut off from what is by nature a wild olive tree, and were grafted contrary to nature into to a cultivated olive tree, how much more will those who were the natural branches be grafted back into their olive own olive tree? For I do not want you, brethren, to be uninformed of this mystery—so that you will not be wise in your own estimation—that a partial hardening has happened to Israel until the fullness of the Gentiles has come in; and so all Israel will be saved." William S. Plumer gives the correct interpretation of those verses in Romans:

> The rejection of the Jews was an awfully dark event, displaying in a manner suited to every man the severity and sovereignty of God. But it is capable of being understood, and it is instructive that Paul would not have the Gentiles ignorant of the lessons it teaches. When understood aright, it is very well suited to take the self-conceit out of men, and it contains an awful warning against unbelief . . . The fulness of the Gentiles then means the whole number determined on by God, who were to live before the conversion of the Jews.[13]

Thus, there was a warning and an invitation to all parties alike, whether Jews or Gentiles, for God is impartial. The general call goes out to all people everywhere to repent and believe, but as Jesus stated: "For many are called, but few are chosen"(Matthew 22:14). The parable includes an illustration of a man who was called, but not chosen. He entered into the wedding feast, but when the king came in "he saw a man who was not dressed in wedding clothes" (Matthew 22:11). When the king asked him how he got into the wedding party without the wedding clothes, "the man was speechless" (Matthew 22:12). As a result, "the king said to the servant, 'Bind him hand and foot, and throw him into the outer darkness; in that place there will be weeping

---

12 Calvin, *A Harmony of the Gospels Matthew, Mark and Luke*, 2:108-9.
13 William S. Plumer, *Commentary on Romans* (Grand Rapids: Kregel Publications, 1971), 552.

and gnashing of teeth'" (Matthew 22:13. D. Martyn Lloyd-Jones' sermon on the twelfth verse of this parable is instructive:

> To my mind there is only one great principle taught in this parable . . . And that is, that ultimately and finally, there is but one test that God applies to us—whether we have given our wills, our very selves to Him or not. I say "ultimately and finally" because that is the exact point which is made here, for we are shown with awful, terrifying clearness that unless we have actually done this, all else is of no value whatsoever. Here is a man who is actually in the banquet hall, seated at the table with the food placed before him, ready to eat, who suddenly, at the critical, all-important moment is condemned, bound hand and foot and cast into outer darkness! And all because of just one thing. Everything was right, except that he had no wedding garment on—that he had disobeyed the king in that vitally important respect!
>
> Nothing matters except this one thing of giving our wills to God. It determines whether we are destined for heaven or hell. How vitally, how terribly important it is! Is it not our one difficulty with the question of religion?[14]

It was that one thing that the rich young ruler was unwilling to do which caused him to go away saddened by Jesus' words. It was that one thing that Jesus told Martha was necessary and which her sister, Mary, had chosen. It was that one thing, that of submitting their wills to God, that the scribes, Pharisees, and chief priests refused to do.

While these parables had the effect of incensing the scribes, chief priests, and Pharisees, it was necessary for Jesus to forewarn both the Jews and His disciples of the coming apostasy of the chosen race from their covenant privileges. In these last few days before His crucifixion, Jesus became more and more exact and definite in prophesying every event that was going to take place. His warnings to His own disciples had become increasingly detailed and would continue to do so. When the Pharisees heard this parable of the wedding feast, they "went and plotted together how they might trap Him in what He had said" (Matthew 22:15). As a result, "they sent their disciples to Him, along with the Herodians, saying, 'Teacher, we know that you are truthful and teach the way of God in truth, and defer to no one; for You are not partial to any. Tell us then, what do You think? Is it lawful to give a poll-tax to Caesar, or not?" The party of the Herodians were supporters of that wicked and

---

14 D. M. Lloyd-Jones, *Evangelistic Sermons* (Edinburgh, Scotland and Carlisle, Pennsylvania: The Banner of Truth Trust, 1983), 92–3.

immoral ruler, Herod Antipas. For the Pharisees to join forces with them was a compromise of their professed allegiance to the Mosaic Law, but it shows to what lengths the enemies of Jesus would go in order to exterminate Him. They apparently lived by the adage, "The enemy of my enemy is my friend." For now, these parties who were natural enemies became friends in their zeal to rid the nation of this Galilean reformer. The question of this conniving group was easily dismissed by Jesus with His well-known response after He requested to be shown the image on a denarius: "Then render to Caesar the things that are Caesar's; and to God the things that are God's" (Matthew 22:21). As Plummer commented:

> The error lay in supposing that Caesar and God were mutually exclusive alternatives. Duty to Caesar was part of their duty to God, because for purposes of order and government Caesar was God's vicegerent . . .
> No one duty is to be understood to the exclusion of others, whether offerings in the temple, or penitence, etc.[15]

When the Pharisees and Herodians heard these words of Jesus, "they were amazed, and leaving Him, they went away" (Matthew 22:22). They had been convinced that their question would entrap Him as either a zealot opposed to taxes or one who served the king more than God. They were outwitted once again.

The Greeks Seek Jesus (John 12:20–26)

The only notice that John, the beloved disciple, makes to the public teaching of Jesus during His final Passover celebration is found in John 12:20–50. The opening verses of that section say: "Now there were some Greeks among those who were going up to worship at the feast; these men came to Philip, who was from Bethsaida of Galilee, and *began to* ask him, saying, 'Sir, we wish to see Jesus'" (John 12:20, 21). The time when these Greeks came to Philip cannot be accurately determined, but it seems likely that Jesus' parables about the kingdom of God being given to the nations prompted their interest.

Jesus' teaching during this week was performed in the Court of the Gentiles, a thirty-five acre area on the outside of the Temple grounds, as was His usual custom. That outer court was paved with marble, was shaded by the beautiful buildings, particularly the massive Herodian Temple, and was like an open air park where people congregat-

---
15 Plummer, *A Critical and Exegetical Commentary on the Gospel According to S. Luke*, 466.

ed, especially during the feasts. It was the perfect place for Jesus to teach in order to reach both Jews and Gentiles.

These Greeks who came to Philip seeking Jesus were undoubtedly proselytes to Judaism inasmuch as they had come up to Jerusalem "to worship at the feast" (John 12:20b). Gentiles were strictly forbidden from entering into the temple grounds proper, but were allowed to offer sacrifices just like the Jews (cf. Leviticus 17:8, 9 and Numbers 15:14–16). There were warning signs all around the Court of the Gentiles that commanded them not to enter the inner court area of the Temple on penalty of death. Yet, Jesus, the Galilean, was different. He taught all the people—Jews and Gentiles—and invited them all to come to Him. "These Greeks at the close of the Lord's life bring the Gentile world into fellowship with Him as the Magi had done at the beginning."[16]

After the Greeks came to Philip, he went first to Andrew and then they both went and told Jesus. Philip and Andrew were both from Bethsaida and the Greeks may well have been from one of the cities of Decapolis which were primarily inhabited by Greeks. When Jesus received this information, He responded, "The hour has come for the Son of Man to be glorified. Truly, truly, I say to you, unless a grain of wheat falls into the earth and dies, it remains alone; but if it dies, it bears much fruit" (John 12:23, 24). The reference to fruit is reminiscent of Jesus' parable concerning the landowner: "Therefore I say to you, the kingdom of God will be taken away from you and given to a people, producing the fruit of it" (Matthew 21:43). As Westcott commented:

> The answer involves far more than the mere admission of the Greeks to the Lord's Presence. The extension of the Gospel to the world rests on the Death of Christ, on His rejection by His own people . . .
>
> The inquiry of the Greeks heralded the proclamation of the Gospel to the Gentiles. For this the Passion and Resurrection were the necessary conditions.[17]

Jesus' initial reply, therefore, gave these Greeks hope that they would be admitted into His fellowship even as the Jews were. It was the perfect explanation of what Paul taught in Ephesians 2:11–14—"Therefore remember that formerly you, the Gentiles in the flesh, who are

---

16 Westcott, *The Gospel According to St. John*, 180.
17 Westcott, *The Gospel According to St. John*, 180-1.

called 'Uncircumcision' by the so-called 'Circumcision,' *which* is performed in the flesh by human hands—remember that you were at that time separate from Christ, excluded from the commonwealth of Israel, and strangers to the covenants of promise, having no hope and without God in the world. But now in Christ Jesus you who were formerly were far off have been brought near by the blood of Christ. For He Himself is our peace, who made *both groups* into one and broke down the barrier of the dividing wall." That work of breaking down the wall of separation was soon to be accomplished through His sacrificial death and resurrection.

Previously, Jesus had often said, "My hour has not yet come" (John 2:4; cf. John 7:6, 8, 30). Now, as He had forewarned His disciples, our Lord knew that His hour was at hand. It was only a few days before the great crisis would take place. With the crucifixion occupying His thoughts, Jesus said, "Now My soul has become troubled; and what shall I say, 'Father, save Me from this hour? But for this purpose I came to this hour. Father, glorify Your name" (John 12:27, 28a). Morris gives an explanation of Jesus' words:

> It seems clear that the words represent a rhetorical question, a hypothetical prayer at which Jesus looks, but which he refuses to pray. The words reveal the natural human shrinking from death. John does not record the agony in Gethsemane, and this is his equivalent of the Synoptic prayer in the Garden, "not what I will, but what thou wilt" (Mark 14:36).[18]

When Jesus finished His request, "Father, glorify Your name," "a voice came out of heaven, 'I have both glorified it, and will glorify it again'" (John 12:27b). The voice of the Father out of heaven was heard by the crowds standing around, but not understood. Some thought it had thundered. Others thought an angel had spoken to Him. Jesus replied to them, "This voice has come not for My sake, but for your sakes" (John 12:30). The Lord then explained the type of death He would undergo in which He would draw all men to Himself (John 12:32). It would be a death in which "the ruler of this world will be cast out" (John 12:31) even as that was the purpose for which Jesus came into the world (cf. 1 John 4:8). Hearing Jesus' references to His death, "the crowd then answered Him, 'We have heard out of the Law that the Christ is to remain forever; and how

---

18 Morris, *The Gospel According to John*, 595.

can You say, "The Son of Man must be lifted up?" Who is this Son of Man?'" (John 12:34). The crowd questioning Jesus at this point is primarily composed of those quibbling Jews who were continually doubting everything He said. They would be so pliable just a few days later. While they claimed that the Law taught the Messiah would remain forever, they were probably referring to the Old Testament. "The passages which they had in mind were probably the following: Ps. 110:4; Isa. 9:7; Ezek. 37:25; Dan.7:14. These they interpreted literally, as if they taught that the Messiah would remain on earth forever as king of the Jews."[19]

Detecting the hostility of the crowd, Jesus urged them, "While you have the Light, believe in the Light, so that you may become sons of Light" (John 12:36a). He responded to them without directly answering their question about the Son of Man. He had used that title about Himself on other occasions already and now He does so again. Then, "He went away and hid Himself from them" (John 12:36b). Jesus had hidden Himself on earlier occasions (cf. John 8:59) as a result of their unbelief and efforts to kill Him. He was cautious, not cowardly. He was careful, but He did not cower before the Jews in fear. He knew they were still unbelieving. As John wrote: "though He had performed so many signs before them, yet they were not believing in Him" (John 12:37). "Nevertheless, many even of the rulers were believing in Him, but because of the Pharisees they were not confessing Him for fear that they would be put out of the synagogue; for they loved the approval of men rather than the approval of God" (John 12:42, 43). Whereas, they were unwilling to profess Jesus before men, their faith in Him proved to not be true, saving faith (Cf. Matthew 10:32). As Westcott wrote:

> This complete intellectual faith (so to speak) is really the climax of unbelief. The conviction found no expression in life . . .
> The belief only lacked confession, but this defect was fatal.[20]

At the unwillingness by the rulers to openly confess Him, Jesus cried out once more with great urgency to the crowds, "He who believes in Me, does not believe in Me but in Him who sent Me" (John 12:44). He appealed to the crowd to believe in Him before it was too late. In the final words of this discourse, Jesus contrasted the simplic-

---

19 Hendriksen, *The Gospel of John*, 2:203).
20 Westcott, *The Gospel According to St. John*, 185-6.

ity of His service to the Father with the scheming, cowardly, intellectual belief of the rulers who refused to confess Him. Jesus fulfilled the mission given to Him by His Father.

The Sadducees' Question about the Resurrection (Matthew 22:23–33; Mark 12:18–27; and, Luke 20:27–40)

Matthew notes that "on that day some Sadducees (who say there is no resurrection) came to Jesus and questioned Him" (Matthew 22:23). Prior to this occasion there had only been one other time when Jesus had any conflict with the Sadducees. That was when they asked Him for a sign from heaven after He had fed the multitudes (Matthew 16:1). Most all of Jesus' previous conflicts had been with the Pharisees. Yet, Jesus had prevailed in each instance. As our Lord sat teaching in the Temple courts day after day, the Sadducees observed an opening for them to gain "a signal triumph for their tenets" and to defeat both Jesus and "their own Pharisaic opponents."[21] Their question appears to have "been well-planned"[22] and the men who asked it were no doubt the delegates from the party of the Sadducees. Edersheim describes the setting:

> Their object was certainly not serious argument, but to use the much more dangerous weapon of ridicule. Persecution the populace might have resented; for open opposition all would have been prepared; but to come with icy politeness and philosophic calm, and by a well-turned question to reduce the renowned Galilean Teacher to silence, and show the absurdity of His teaching, would have been to inflict on His cause the most damaging blow.[23]

Their question was not a serious question and everyone who heard it would have immediately recognized it as a mere cavil. In the Mosaic law, there was a provision for raising up a posterity for a deceased brother who died while still childless. Deuteronomy 25:5 says: "When brothers live together and one of them dies and has no son, the wife of the deceased shall not be married outside the family to a strange man. Her husband's brother shall go in to her and take her to himself as wife and perform the duty of a husband's brother to her." It had been intended to protect the laws of inheritance and to further the blessings of the Abrahamic covenant to the next generations. These Sadducees hypocritically referenced that passage only in a superfi-

---

21 Edersheim, *The Life and Times of Jesus the Messiah*, 747.
22 Edersheim, *The Life and Times of Jesus the Messiah*, 747.
23 Edersheim, *The Life and Times of Jesus the Messiah*, 747.

cial manner. Additionally, they raised a hypothetical situation about whose wife she would be if she had married seven brothers in succession. Their question was: "In the resurrection, therefore, whose wife of the seven shall she be? For they all had *married* her" (Matthew 22:28). The Sadducees were the party that did not even believe in the resurrection, so their hypocrisy was manifestly evident to Jesus. Chamblin gives us what the purpose of the Sadducees must have been:

> Better to say that they deliberately present an imagined and highly improbable (and almost comical) series of events in order to show how awkward life in a resurrected state would be, and thus how foolish are those who embrace such a doctrine.[24]

Jesus "did not need anyone to testify concerning man" (John 2:25), but these Sadducees, like other cavilers before them, never really took full measure of the Galilean Teacher. They kept thinking that they could entrap Him and He kept foiling their ill-advised plans. Thus, Jesus retorted to them along two lines. First, He showed them that they were thinking of the resurrection in too much of a materialistic manner. "For in the resurrection, they neither marry nor are given in marriage, but are like angels in heaven" (Matthew 22:30). As Edersheim notes:

> In His argument against the Sadducees Christ first appealed to the *power* of God (Matthew 22:29. 30, and parallels). What God would work was quite different than they imagined: not a mere re-awakening, but a transformation. The world to come was not to be a reproduction of what had passed away—else why should it have passed away—but a regeneration and renovation; and the body with which we were to be clothed would be like that which the Angels bear.[25]

After easily brushing aside that "flimsy cavil"[26] with a few words, Jesus then addressed the more important issue of whether there even is a resurrection. He found undeniable proof for the resurrection in the words of Yahweh to Moses from the burning bush: "But regarding the resurrection of the dead, have you not read what was spoken to you by God: 'I am the God of Abraham, and the God of Isaac, and the God of Jacob.' He is not the God of the dead but of the living" (Matthew 22:32). Jesus' argument turned on the tense of the verb used by God in those words to Moses—the present tense as opposed to any form

---

24 Chamblin, *Matthew*, 2:1088.
25 Edersheim, *The Life and Times of Jesus the Messiah*, 750.
26 Edersheim, *The Life and Times of Jesus the Messiah*, 751.

of the past tense. Abraham, Isaac, and Jacob had all died, but they were still living before God which is proof of the resurrection. Since these Sadducees had cited Moses and repudiated the prophets, Jesus also referred back to Moses to prove His point. He could have listed many proofs for the doctrine of the resurrection, such as Daniel 12:2, but one verse was sufficient. His reply was so effective that the mouths of these quibblers were shut and they offered no more objections to Him. "When the crowds heard this, they were astonished at His teaching" (Matthew 22:33). Whether the Sadducees stuck around or not, we simply do not know. Yet, the Pharisees soon "heard that Jesus had silenced the Sadducees" (Matthew 22:34) which gave them new hope and one of them, a lawyer, asked Him a question to test Him: "Teacher, which is the great commandment in the Law?" (Matthew 22:36). Most of the scribes, the great interpreters of the Mosaic law, "did not have courage to question Him any longer about anything" (Luke 20:40), but could simply reply: "Teacher, You have spoken well" (Luke 20:39). The Pharisees had gathered together in one place to develop a strategy for answering Jesus, but they were almost at their wit's end. This question offered them little hope to severely damage Jesus. Yet, this one lawyer still hoped to test Jesus with some question He could not answer. No doubt, the lawyer thought that the question he put to Jesus was unanswerable. This scribe probably had mixed emotions in putting forth this question. He was happy that Jesus had completely silenced the Sadducees, but he still wanted Jesus Himself to be silenced.

Jesus' reply to the lawyer was masterful. He reduced all the laws to two:

> "And He said to him, 'You shall love the Lord your God with all your heart, and with all your soul, and with all your mind.' This is the great and foremost commandment. The second is like it, 'You shall love your neighbor as yourself.' On these two commandments depend the whole law and the prophets" (Matthew 22:37–40).

Thereby, Jesus summarized the two divisions of the Ten Commandments into two just laws—the love of God and the love of your neighbor. Chamblin's comments are helpful:

> The second commandment is like the first, but does not rank with it. The term 'greatest' (megale) is reserved for the first. God alone is worthy to be loved with one's whole heart, soul, mind, and strength. Yet

for this very reason, there is a sense in which the second command is as important as the first. Though distinguishable, the two are inseparable. As is clear from the Decalogue (Deut. 5:6–21), loving one's neighbor is a primary means for showing one's love for God . . . . Will not a failure to love my neighbors, especially those who know and love God, demonstrate that I do not really love God?[27]

"Now while the Pharisees were gathered together, Jesus asked them a question: 'What do you think about the Christ, whose son is He?'" (Matthew 22:42). With this question, Jesus turned the tables on them in order to show them just how little they really understood about the Law. They rightly answered, "*The* Son of David" (Matthew 22:42), but they were still short of true spiritual insight. Thus, Jesus followed up with another question: "Then how does David in the Spirit call Him 'Lord,' saying, 'The Lord said to my Lord, sit at My right hand, until I put Your enemies beneath Your feet?' If David then calls Him Lord, how is He his son?" (Matthew 22:43–45). They were completely unable "to answer Him a word, nor did anyone dare from that day dare to ask Him another question" (Matthew 22:46). Yet, neither did they understand that Jesus had just given them the proof that He was the Messiah—the Son of David and the Son of God—the very proof that they said they wanted from Him.

---

27 Chamblin, *Matthew*, 2:1105.

21

Jesus' Parting Words

"We are now beginning a chapter which in one respect is the most remarkable in the four Gospels: it contains the last words which the Lord Jesus ever spoke within the walls of the temple. These last words consist of a withering exposure of the scribes and Pharisees, and a sharp rebuke of their doctrines and practices. Knowing full well that His time on earth was drawing to a close, our Lord no longer keeps back His opinion of the leading teachers of the Jews. Knowing that He would soon leave His followers alone, like sheep among wolves, He warns them plainly against the false shepherds by whom they were surrounded."[1]

Following the silencing of both the Sadducees and the Pharisees, Jesus no longer had any enemies who were willing to debate Him openly. Matthew 22:46 states: "No one was able to answer Him a word, nor did anyone dare from that day on to ask Him another question." They had plotted and schemed various ways to entrap Him, but were unable. They had asked Him questions which they thought were unanswerable, but He had revealed an otherwordly wisdom in each of His replies. They could not answer His questions and they dared not ask Him anymore. The verbal contest was over. All that remained at this point was for the Sanhedrin to carry out their plans to kill Jesus—even if they had been unable first to effectively discredit Him.

In His parting words, Jesus evidenced the true qualifications of a Shepherd of souls and minister of the Word—i.e., the ability to "seek the lost, bring back the scattered, bind up the broken and strengthen the sick; but the fat and the strong I will destroy. I will feed them with judgment" (Ezekiel 34:16). His parting words, therefore, were addressed to both His followers and His detractors. The Beloved disciple gives us those tender words Jesus spoke to His disciples and all who would believe in Him thereafter. Matthew and the other synoptic Gospels give us those terrible warnings to the enemies of the cross. The first of those warnings is contained in Matthew 23 wherein Jesus scathingly denounces the Pharisees. Hitherto, Jesus had nev-

---

1 Ryle, *Expository Thoughts on the Gospels: St. Matthew*, 256–7.

er spoken so directly or so fully against the Pharisees. Indeed, some people think that such polemics should be strictly avoided at all costs by God's shepherds. Yet, Paul wrote that an elder must hold "fast the faithful word which is in accordance with the teaching, so that he will be able both to exhort in sound doctrine and to refute those who contradict" (Titus 1:9). The warning against false shepherds is one of the chief warnings in Scripture and is sounded in every major section of Scripture (Cf. Deuteronomy 18:18–20; Jeremiah 23:16–22; Matthew 7:15, 16; Acts 20:28–31; 2 Peter 2:1–3; 1 John 4:1; Jude 3, 4; and, Revelation 2:14, 15, among many other passages). Jesus did not shrink from warning His followers against the sect that would prove to be the most virulent enemy of His Church. And His scathing words against the Pharisees anticipate the final judgment when the King will say: "Depart from Me, accursed ones, into the eternal fire which has been prepared for the devil and His angels" (Matthew 25:41). As shocking as Jesus' words in this chapter are, they were as necessary as His words in the Sermon on the Mount or His words in Matthew 24 and 25. As Chamblin states:

> By means of the dire woes and warnings of verses 13–39, Jesus shows his love for these his enemies (5:44) and pleads with them to flee the coming wrath. But his primary concern remains the crowd and his disciples. Acutely aware of the scribes' and Pharisees' true condition and baleful influences, Jesus unrelentingly exposes their manifold sin in order to deter his listeners from emulating them and thus incurring the same judgment.[2]

Denunciations of the Pharisees (Matthew 23:1–39; Mark 12:38, 39; and, Luke 20:45–47)

Jesus first compares the pride of the scribes and Pharisees with the humility that His disciples are to emulate in Matthew 23:2–12. The scribes and Pharisees, as those who "have seated themselves in the chair of Moses" (Matthew 23:2), "are responsible for studying, teaching, interpreting and applying the Mosaic law."[3] No doubt, they thought they were doing so admirably, but Jesus warned against their approach. Their failings were that they told others what to do, but failed to do the things they taught; they tied heavy burdens on the shoulders of others, but were unwilling to move them; they did their deeds to be noticed by men; and, they loved the places of honor, re-

---

2 Chamblin, *Matthew*, 2:1119.
3 Chamblin, *Matthew* 2:1119.

spectful greetings, and to be called Rabbi (Matthew 23:3–7). C. S. Lewis noted concerning "the entry of the supernatural into a human soul,"[4] that it:

> Opens to it new possibilities both of good and evil. From that point the road branches: one way to sanctity, love, humility, the other to spiritual pride, self-righteousness, persecuting zeal.... Of all bad men religious bad men are the worst.[5]

While the scribes and Pharisees superficially seemed to be closer to the kingdom of God than the Sadducees, they were in reality the worst of bad men. They were inconsistent hypocrites, they were ostentatious, and they loved pre-eminence. They were legalists whose righteousness consisted only of outward deeds performed before men, but whose obedience was not from the heart. The spirit of Pharisaism and legalism has always been the greatest danger to the Church. Thus, Jesus devoted a whole chapter to dire warnings against the Pharisees, but only a few verses of warning against the Sadducees, the theological liberals of His day.

Jesus' disciples are to be known by their humility. They are to possess a brotherly spirit and eschew being called Rabbi; they are not to call others father, because God alone is their Father; the One who is their Leader is Christ; and, "the greatest among you shall be your servant" (Matthew 23:11). "For disciples, as for their Master, greatness lies not merely *beyond* service but precisely in it."[6] Jesus modeled such humility of service to His disciples throughout His ministry and would do so even more as His hour approached.

From verses 13 to 39 of Matthew 23, Jesus pronounces eight woes on the scribes and Pharisees (whom He repeatedly calls "hypocrites"). These woes covered everything that could be said against them. "Step by step, with logical sequence and intensified pathos of energy, is each charge advanced, and with it the Woe of Divine Wrath announced."[7] They shut the kingdom of heaven to the people and did not even enter themselves; they devoured widow's houses and made long prayers; they traversed land and sea to make one convert to their party only to make him twice the child of hell; they made fine distinctions in

---

4 Chamblin, *Matthew*, 2:1120.
5 C. S. Lewis, *Reflections on the Psalms* (New York: Harcourt, Brace & Co, 1958), 162–9.
6 Chamblin, *Matthew*, 2:1130.
7 Edersheim, *The Life and Times of Jesus the Messiah*, 757.

order to cover their false oaths; they extended the law of tithing to ridiculous proportions while neglecting the weightier matters, such as justice, mercy and faithfulness; they had minute regulations for outward morality but inside were full of robbery and self-indulgence; they were like white-washed tombs full of dead men's bones; and, they revered the prophets of old while persecuting in every generation those who prophesied to them (Matthew 23:13–33). It was a scathing condemnation in the strongest words possible. As Ryle notes concerning these charges:

> We have in these verses the charges of our Lord against the Jewish teachers, ranged under eight heads. Standing in the midst of the temple, with a listening crowd around Him He publicly denounces the main errors of the scribes and Pharisees, in unsparing terms. Eight times, He uses the solemn expression, "Woe unto you;" seven times He calls them "hypocrites;" twice He speaks of them as blind guides—twice as "fools and blind,"—once as "serpents and a generation of vipers." Let us mark that language well. It teaches a solemn lesson. It shows how utterly abominable the spirit of the scribes and Pharisees is in God's sight, in whatever form it may be found.[8]

Jesus, though, did not conclude these last words He ever taught in public with that spirit of denunciation. He had not merely attempted to triumph over His enemies. Rather, He sought to woo them to come to Him. He ended His denunciations with a direful warning that the "all the righteous blood" of the prophets of all generations "will come upon this generation" (Matthew 23:35, 36). "The two verses together testify that God has long been storing up punishment for Israel's perennial sin, and that once the cup of iniquity is full (cf. 23:32), his vengeance will be swift and deadly."[9] That time had now arrived, Jesus warned the Pharisees. After those denunciations, Jesus yet appealed to them one last time with some of the most tender words possible:

> Jerusalem, Jerusalem, who kills the prophets and stones those sent to her! How often I wanted to gather your children together, the way a hen gathers her chicks under her wings, and you were unwilling. Behold, your house is being left to you desolate! For I say to you, from now on you will not see Me until you say, 'Blessed is He who comes in the name of the Lord!' (Matthew 23:37–39.

A more passionate plea for sinners to turn to Him cannot be found

---

8 Ryle, *Expository Thoughts on the Gospels: Matthew*, 301–2.
9 Chamblin, *Matthew*, 2:1154.

in Scripture. These were the worst of sinners because they were guilty of the blood of all the prophets and wise men that God had sent to them. Yet, Jesus tenderly entreated them to repent and believe while they had time, assuring them that He had often wanted to gather them together under His wings. Ryle's comments are on target:

> Let us understand that the ruin of those who are lost, is not because Christ was not willing to save them—nor yet because they wanted to be saved, but could not—but because they would not come to Christ . . . Christ would gather men, but they will not to be gathered; Christ would save men, but they will not to be saved. Let it be a settled principle in our religion, that man's salvation, if saved, is wholly of God; and that man's ruin, if lost, is wholly of himself.[10]

The Olivet Discourse (Matthew 24:1–51; Mark 13:1–37; and, Luke 21:5–36)

In *The Temple: Its Ministry and Service*, Edersheim wrote the following description of the view of the Temple from Olivet:

> From the Temple Mount to the western base of Olivet, it was not more than 100 or 200 yards across, though, of course, the distance to the summit was much greater, say about half a mile. By the nearest pathway it was only 918 yards from the city gate to the principal summit. Olivet was always fresh and green, even in earliest spring or during parched summer—the coolest, pleasantest, the most sheltered walk about Jerusalem. For across this road the Temple and its mountain flung their broad shadows, and luxuriant foliage spread a leafy canopy overhead . . . The stony road up Olivet wound along terraces covered with olives, whose silver and dark green leaves rustled in the breeze.[11]

Following his scathing words against the Pharisees, Jesus and His disciples left the temple and began to traverse that stony road to the summit of Olivet. They had not traveled far when "His disciples came up to point out the temple buildings to Him" (Matthew 24:1). No doubt, their questions were prompted by Jesus' words in Matthew 23:38—"Behold, your house is being left to you desolate." Would that glorious temple really be left desolate? Thus, Jesus elaborated on His earlier words: "Do you not see all these things? Truly I say to you, not one stone here will be left upon another, which will not be torn down" (Matthew 24:2). The idea "that the whole was about to be

---

10 Ryle, *Expository Thoughts on the Gospels: Matthew*, 310-1.
11 Alfred Edersheim, *The Temple: Its Ministry and Service* (Peabody, Massachusetts: Hendrickson Publishers, 1994), 7.

destroyed . . . sunk deeply into the minds of the disciples."[12] Thus, when they had reached the summit of Olivet and their Master had sat down, they came to Him with a further question: "Tell us, when will these things happen, and what *will be* the sign of Your coming, and of the end of the age?" (Matthew 24:3). Mark 13:3 identifies the questioners as Peter, Andrew, James and John. Their "question shows that in the disciples' minds the destruction of the temple and the consummation of the age are distinguishable but inseparable events."[13] Yet, Jesus' prophecies are better interpreted in light of the parables He taught during that last week, particularly what he said concerning the parable of the landowner: "Therefore I say to you, the kingdom of God will be taken away from you and given to a people, producing the fruit of it. And he who falls on this stone will be broken to piece; but on whomever it falls, it will scatter him like dust" (Matthew 21:43, 44). The disciple's questions, therefore, embraced "three points: one, the destruction of Jerusalem; another, the second personal advent; and a third, the end of the world. These three points are undoubtedly in some parts of the chapter so entwined together that it is difficult to separate and disentangle them: but all these points appear distinctly in the chapter, and without them it cannot be fairly explained."[14] Jesus' words in this chapter concerning the destruction of Jerusalem were an elaboration on the message that Gabriel gave to Daniel:

> Then after sixty-two weeks the Messiah will be cut off and have nothing, and the people of the prince who is to come will destroy the city and the sanctuary. And its end *will come* with a flood; even to the end there will be war; desolations are determined (Daniel 9:26).

In His initial reply (Matthew 24:4–14), Jesus gave various signs that "describe features of every generation . . . until the time of His glorious return."[15] Three times He uses the Greek word, *telos*, "the end" to describe the time towards which all these events are moving—cf. Matthew 24:6, 13, 14. The signs are general in nature and include false Christs appearing to "mislead many'; wars and rumors of war; nations rising up against one another; earthquakes and famines; the apostasy of many; false prophets and heresies; the increase of lawlessness; and, the preaching of the gospel to the "whole world as a

---

12 Ryle, *Expository Thoughts on the Gospels: St. Matthew*, 312.
13 Chamblin, *Matthew*, 2:1162.
14 Ryle, *Expository Thoughts on the Gospels: St. Matthew*, 312-3.
15 Chamblin, *Matthew*, 2:1164.

testimony." Most of the signs are negative in nature, except for the final one, which encourages world-wide evangelization. "Against the dark background of the preceding prophecies, the splendor of this one is all the brighter."[16] The end will not come until the mission of the church to evangelize the whole world has been accomplished, no matter how many other dark signs are being fulfilled. As Chamblin astutely comments:

> Just as the judgment on Israel in A.D. 70 would betoken rather than commence the final Day of Wrath, so too the progress of the gospel from Jerusalem to Rome before A.D. 70 would not fulfill the prophecy of 24:14 but rather prefigure its fulfillment at the close of the present age (28:20b).[17]

The primary point of Jesus' words in Matthew 24:15–31 concerned the destruction of Jerusalem and the Temple by the Romans in AD 70, forty years later. Josephus describes those terrible days of the Roman siege which lasted for three and a half years and his "writings are the best comment on our Lord's words; they are a striking proof of the accuracy of every tittle of His predictions."[18] "Jerusalem and the temple were the heart of the old dispensation; when they were destroyed, the old Mosaic system came to an end. The daily sacrifice, the yearly feasts, the altar, the holy of holies, the priesthood, were all essential parts of revealed religion, till Christ came,—but no longer."[19] The end of that system did not come with a whimper, but with a cataclysmic upheaval due to their impenitence. The Jews were given forty years to repent before the kingdom was taken away from them and given to a nation producing the fruits of it. Yet, as Paul wrote—"And they also, if they do not continue in their unbelief, will be grafted in, for God is able to graft them in again" (Romans 11:23).

One of the clearest signs Jesus gives in this section is the prophecy of the abomination of desolation. It is ironic that there seems so much controversy concerning a particular sign that Jesus told His listeners to look for in the near future, but this is probably to be expected since we are so far removed from that period.[20] Luke 21:20 gives an additional prophecy concerning those days: "But when you

---

16 Chamblin, *Matthew*, 2:1174.
17 Chamblin, *Matthew*, 2:1175.
18 Ryle, *Expository Thoughts on the Gospels: St. Matthew*, 316.
19 Ryle, *Expository Thoughts on the Gospels: St. Matthew*, 317.
20 Chamblin, *Matthew*, 2:1181.

see Jerusalem surrounded by armies, then recognize that her desolation is near." Chamblin agrees with the view of F. F. Bruce concerning the fulfillment of the prophecy of the abomination of desolation:

> When in the autumn of A.D. 70 'the temple area was taken by the Romans, and the sanctuary itself was burning, the soldiers brought their legionary standards into the sacred precincts, set them up opposite the eastern gate, and offered sacrifices to them there, acclaiming Titus as imperator (victorious commander) as they did so. The . . . offering of such sacrifices in the temple court was the supreme insult to the God of Israel. This action, following as it did the cessation of the daily sacrifice three weeks earlier, must have seemed to many Jews, as it evidently did to Josephus, a new and final fulfillment of Daniel's vision at a time when the continual burnt offering would be taken away and the abomination of desolation set up.'[21]

After answering the first of the disciple's questions about when the temple would be destroyed, Jesus then turns to the second question concerning His return. His first statement about such is that "of that day and hour no one knows, not even the angels of heaven, nor the Son, but the Father alone" (Matthew 24:36). Again, He said: "Therefore, be on the alert, for you do not know which day your Lord is coming" (Matthew 24:42). And finally, He said, "For this reason, you also must be ready; for the Son of Man is coming at an hour when you do not think He will" (Matthew 24:44). There is a stark contrast between the very definite signs and instructions Jesus gave to His disciples concerning the abomination of desolation and the perpetual readiness that they must have concerning His return. The time of the abomination of desolation could be observed by the signs Jesus gave them. The return of Christ will be sudden and unexpected and cannot be known ahead of time by anyone. "Uncertainty about this event calls for constant vigilance: since it could happen at any time, one must be watchful at all times."[22] Yet, the destruction of Jerusalem was marked by clearly discernible signs and could not happen until those signs were evident.

In Matthew 24:45–51, Jesus gives a brief statement about the end of the age. He describes the two different situations of the righteous and the wicked. The faithful slaves will be found doing their Master's will when He returns. The evil slaves will assume their Master's return will not be for a long time and, therefore, will "beat his fellow

---

21 Chamblin, *Matthew*, 2:1182. Chamblin quotes from F. F. Bruce, *Israel and the Nations*, 224.
22 Chamblin, *Matthew*, 2:1215.

slaves, eat and drink with drunkards" (Matthew 24:49). The faithful slaves will be rewarded, but the evil slaves will be "cut into pieces and assign[ed] . . . a place with the hypocrites; in that place there will be weeping and gnashing of teeth" (Matthew 24:51). The reference to the weeping and gnashing of teeth points to a judgment away from the presence of God (cf. Matthew 8:11, 12).

The answers Jesus gave to the second and third questions of the disciples are a prelude to His further elaboration on both matters in Matthew 25. There, He enforces the necessity of perpetual readiness through His parable of the wise and foolish virgins; He encourages the diligent use of one's talents for the glory of God; and, He gives even more detail about the day of judgment and the eternal separation of the sheep and the goats.

Parable of the Ten Virgins (Matthew 25:1–13)

When we come to Matthew 25, we find both a continuation and an apt conclusion of all the words of warning Jesus had given to the Pharisees about the coming judgments. Ryle summarized the twenty-fifth chapter of Matthew as follows:

> The chapter we have now begun is a continuation of our Lord's prophetical discourse on the Mount of Olives. The time to which it refers is plain and unmistakable: from first to last, there is a continual reference to the second advent of Christ, and the end of the world. The whole chapter contains three great divisions. In the first, our Lord uses His own second coming as an argument for watchfulness and heart-religion: this He does by the parable of the ten virgins. In the second, He uses His own second coming as an argument for diligence and faithfulness: this He does by the parable of the talents. In the third, He winds up all by a description of the great day of judgment: a passage which for majesty and beauty stands unequalled in the New Testament.[23]

The first of the parables is about the ten virgins at a wedding feast which is representative of the great wedding of the Lamb and the Bride found in Revelation 19:7–10:

> Let us rejoice and be glad and give glory to Him, for the marriage of the Lamb has come and His bride has made herself ready. It was given to her to clothe herself in fine linen, bright and clean; for the fine linen is the righteous acts of the saints. Then he said to me, "Write, 'Blessed are those who are invited to the marriage of the Lamb.'" And he said to me, "These are true words of God." Then I fell at his feet to worship

---

23 Ryle, *Expository Thoughts on the Gospels: Matthew*, 330.

him. But he said to me, "Do not do that; I am a fellow servant of yours and your brethren who hold the testimony of Jesus; worship God. For the testimony of Jesus is the spirit of prophecy."

In the parable of the ten virgins, Jesus is the bridegroom whom the virgins—representative of the whole professing church—are awaiting. Yet, not all who profess the faith truly believe it and that was especially true of the Pharisees whom Jesus had so severely rebuked in Matthew 23. There are both wise and foolish who make up the body of the professing church. The Pharisees, despite all their religious conceits, were like the foolish virgins, as Jesus said about them: "But woe to you, scribes, Pharisees, and hypocrites, because you shut off the kingdom of heaven from people; for you do not enter in yourselves, nor do you allow those who are entering to go in" (Matthew 23:13). In this parable, there are five virgins who have made all preparations and are completely ready to enter the wedding when the groom comes; and, there are five virgins who have not made such preparations. Jesus makes use of the figure of the "lamps" in order to illustrate the difference between the wise and the foolish. Those lamps are better understood as "torches." Chamblin describes them for us:

> These lampades are 'long sticks, around the tops of which are wrapped rags completely soaked with olive oil. A group of girls carry these burning torches in festive procession to the house where the wedding is to take place. There they perform all kinds of dances and figures until the torches go out.' A 'lamp would not stay lighted in a breeze, would not provide enough light outdoors, and would need an extra supply of oil. Torches resist a breeze, give a bright light, burn only about fifteen minutes, and then need to have the rags . . .soaked again in oil.'[24]

The failure of the foolish virgins is that they did not make sufficient preparations for the coming of the groom. They had oil in their "lamps," but "they took no oil with them" (Matthew 25:3). Their torches soon burned out before they could enter the door into the wedding feast. The wise virgins rightfully refuse to share their oil with the foolish virgins lest they also would have their torches burn out before the bridegroom came. While the foolish virgins were away trying to purchase more oil, the decisive moment of the bridegroom's arrival came. The wise virgins were ushered in, but the foolish virgins—when they arrived—were not allowed to enter. They pled with the host, "Lord, Lord, open for us" (Matthew 25:11), but were told, "Truly,

---

24 Chamblin, *Matthew*, 2:1224.

I say to you, I do not know you" (Matthew 25:12. Cf. Matthew 7:23 and Luke 13:25). The absence of their taking oil with them is symbolic of having no inner source of true spirituality—no true conversion to Christ. They have lived off of a profession, but have no sincere faith. They "are like whitewashed tombs which appear beautiful, but inside they are full of dead men's bones and all uncleanness" (Matthew 23:27). It is due to that fundamental failure on their part that the Lord says He does not know them. As Psalm 1:6 says: "For the Lord knows the way of the righteous, but the way of the wicked will perish." The foolish come to a realization of the one thing needful too late. Their lives are then filled forever with vain regrets and sorrowful reflection on the missed opportunities and the lost day of grace. They failed to "be on the alert" because they always assumed there would be sufficient opportunity to finalize their preparations at a later time. That is the great failure of the unbeliever and the primary reason he is lost. He continues to put off serious consideration of his soul until the door is closed, he is hopelessly lost, and it is too late.

Parable of the Talents (Matthew 25:14–30 and Luke 19:12–17)

The parable of the talents is one of the better known of Jesus' parables. Luke gives a slightly different version of this parable (Luke 19:12–17) that was taught in Jericho, but the main point remains the same in both. The parable of the talents also makes a similar point as the parable of the ten virgins and leads further to the last judgment taught in Matthew 25:31–46. The parable of the ten virgins addressed the problem of not being prepared. This parable addresses the problem of wasting one's talents. The setting is of a man going on a journey and entrusting "his possessions" to his servants. "To the one he gave five talents, to another two, and to another one, each according to his abilities" (Matthew 25:15). Ryle explains how these two parables in Matthew 25 are related to one another and how they are different from one another:

> The virgins and the servants are one and the same people,—but the same people regarded from a different point, and viewed on different sides. The practical lesson of each parable is the main point of difference: vigilance is the key note of the first parable, diligence of the second. The story of the virgins calls on the Church to watch; the story of the talents calls on the Church to work.[25]

---

25 Ryle, *Expository Thoughts on the Gospels: Matthew*, 336.

The problem with the foolish virgins is that they did not watch and were not prepared. They were not vigilant. The problem with the servant who received only one talent is that he did nothing with that talent. Thus, both the foolish virgins and the wicked, lazy slave are condemned for their failures to either be vigilant or to be diligent. The wise virgins were able to enter the wedding feast through the open door before them. The good and faithful slaves were rewarded by being put "in charge of many things" and invited to "enter into the joy of [their] master" (Matthew 25:21, 23). The wise virgins entered because they were vigilantly standing ready. The good and faithful slaves were able to enter into the joy of their master because they had been diligent in taking care of their master's possessions.

The Biblical usage of the word talent in this parable was a unit of weight that equaled about 75 pounds or 34 kilograms. When used concerning money it was valued at about 6,000 drachmas or twenty years of wages for a laborer. A single talent of money made a person very wealthy. Five talents made a person extremely wealthy. Even the slave who received one talent was in possession of great wealth. The failure and refusal by that slave to do anything with that wealth is what made his condemnation even greater. The underlying point of the parable is that even the worst of sinners have been given riches untold by the Lord which they have subsequently squandered. Therefore, their condemnation is just. The wicked, lazy responded to his master when he returned: "Master, I knew you to be a hard man, reaping what you did not sow and gathering where you scattered no *seed*. And I was afraid, and went and hid your talent in the ground. See, you have what is yours" (Matthew 25:24, 25). In those words, that wicked slave described the feelings of most people who refuse to come to Christ. They consider Him to be cruel and merciless. Thus, they consider it better to do nothing concerning the various appeals He makes through His Spirit to their hearts. They use many excuses. They say, "I do not want to be a hypocrite. Thus, I will do nothing with the talents He has given me. I can never please Him anyway." Such excuses are worthless before the Master. Chamblin notes concerning this wicked, lazy slave:

> He dreads failure and its consequences; one wonders to what extent this has affected his past conduct in office (cf. 25:15b). Assuming he will have no share in the profits, he has no counter-incentive to offset his fears. He thus concludes that the best investment is no investment; he buries the talent in the ground to preserve it for the master's return.

Now in the master's presence, the servant concludes by exclaiming, with an apparent note of satisfaction, 'Look, you have what is yours.'[26]

In applying Jesus' parable to believers, talents can be understood as the gifts or abilities God has given us. As Paul asked in 1 Corinthians 4:7—"What do you have that you did not receive?" The question we must ask ourselves is this: "How are we using the talents and abilities God gave us to glorify Him?"

The Last Judgment (Matthew 25:31–46)

The last section of Matthew 25 concerns the Last Judgment. It brings into focus what will happen when Christ returns. Verses 31 to 46 of this chapter give us the most direct and extensive teaching about that final judgment to be found anywhere in Scripture. This passage describes the whole scene of the judgment day when Christ returns in His glory. All the people who ever lived will be divided into two great camps—the sheep and the goats. The overwhelming majority of those who come before His throne on that day will have already been in their final place of destination ever since their death. This judgment will secure their fates for all eternity. Only those who are still alive when He returns will not be summoned from either Hades or Paradise. Matthew 25:32, 33 says: "All the nations will be gathered before Him; and He will separate them from one another, as the shepherd separates the sheep from the goats; and He will put the sheep on His right, and the goats on His left."

The first thing King Jesus does after separating the sheep and the goats is to declare concerning the sheep: "Come, you who are blessed of My Father, inherit the kingdom prepared for you from the foundation of the world" (Matthew 25:34). The idea that even believers will have to undergo a trial of their works before it is determined whether they shall be allowed into heaven is false. Jesus already knows our status because He knows all things. The same is true for the goats. Their eternal destiny is sealed when they are separated from the sheep at the beginning of the judgment.

In this passage, Jesus uses the same criteria to judge both the sheep and the goats. To the sheep He says: "For I was hungry, and you gave Me *something* to eat; I was thirsty, and you gave Me *something* to drink; I was a stranger, and you invited Me in; naked, and you clothed

---

26 Chamblin, *Matthew*, 2:1239.

Me; I was sick, and you visited Me; I was in prison, and you came to Me" (Matthew 25:35, 36). Hendriksen gives us a synopsis of these verses:

> What Jesus is saying is, "In your daily life and conduct, in what are often called 'the little things of life,' you have furnished proof that you are my true disciples. Therefore I call you blessed."[27]

The reply of the sheep to Jesus' open declaration about them indicates clearly that they are His disciples. They are incredulous and ask Him: "Lord, when did we see You hungry, and feed You, or thirsty, and give You *something* to drink? And when did we see You a stranger, and invite You in, or naked, and clothe You? When did we see You sick, or in prison, and come to You?" (Matthew 25: 37–39. By those questions, the righteous indicate the humility that is a necessary part of saving faith. They are His disciples in the same way that the publican went down to his house justified after beating on his chest and praying, "God, be merciful to me, the sinner!" (Luke 18:13). Therefore, Jesus will say to them: "Truly, I say to you, to the extent that you did it to one of these brothers of Mine, *even* the least *of them*, you did it to Me" (Matthew 25:40).

On the other hand, Jesus says the negative about the goats concerning all those same scenarios. He accuses them of not helping Him at all in those same situations. And, like the Pharisee in Jesus' parable, they are so conceited about their native goodness, that they reply to Him: "Lord, when did we see You hungry, or thirsty, or a stranger, or naked, or sick, or in prison, and did not take care of You?" (Matthew 25:44). One can almost hear the Pharisee's words being formed on their lips. "God, I thank You that I am not like other people: swindlers, unjust, adulterers, or even like this tax-collector. I fast twice a week, I pay tithes of all that I get" (Luke 18:11, 12). Thus, Jesus will say to the goats: "Truly, I say to you, to the extent that you did not do it to one of the least of these, you did not do it Me" (Matthew 25:45).

The judgment of God is not so much about specific acts of sin or righteousness, but the general tenor of one's life in all the day-by-day "little things of life." As Jesus said, "He who is faithful in a very little thing is faithful also in much; and he who is unrighteous in a very little thing is unrighteous in much" (Luke 16:10).[28]

---

27 Hendriksen, *Matthew*, 888.
28 There are people who attempt to interpret this whole chapter as teaching works salvation—

The great day of judgment will be a great proof of 1 Peter 5:5b,c: "and all of you, clothe yourselves with humility toward one another, for God is opposed to the proud, but gives grace to the humble." The truly humble are only humble because they have been humbled at the feet of Jesus their Lord and Savior. And, the proud remain proud only because they have refused to be humbled before Jesus. Thus, faith and works are found united before the judgment throne of Christ.

---

as though the wise virgins earned salvation through their efforts; the faithful servants earned Jesus' praise through their wise use of His talents; and, the judgment is based on what people have done. Matthew 25 must be interpreted in light of Matthew 23 where Jesus condemned the scribes and Pharisees for boasting that they knew God while their works proved that they did not know Him. Jesus is not teaching works salvation. He is teaching that true faith is displayed through works of love, as Paul said in Galatians 5:6—"faith working through love." And James said in James 2:18, "I will show you my faith by my works"; and, James 2:26, "faith without works is dead." Faith and works should be not be juxtaposed against one another. One cannot do works to earn salvation, but those truly saved through faith will do good works out of love for their Savior.

22

The Inner Sanctuary

"Jesus has completed his sojourn on earth, and the eve of the great and awful day of atonement has arrived. He assembles his followers once more, in the social chamber of a friend's house in Jerusalem. Once more they are permitted to look into the Master's faithful heart, and to feel how much God has given them in him. Never was the recollection of the affecting circumstances which took place that evening erased from their memory. The tranquil majesty displayed by their Lord and Master—the astonishing degree of ardent affection which manifested itself in every look, and every word—the heavenly peace which shone forth in his whole deportment—his cheerful and filial resignation to the will and counsel of God; and with all dignity, such amiable condescension, while in every expression of his lips, and in all his actions and conduct, there was something divinely profound, consoling and mysterious. The whole scene was overpowering and heart-cheering in a manner they had never before experienced. They felt themselves translated, as it were, into an inner-court of heaven, and would have felt infinitely greater blessedness . . . had it not been for the anticipation of the Master's approaching departure, which threw a melancholy gloom over their joy."[1]

On Wednesday, April 5, Jesus and His disciples returned to Bethany for their last evening in the home of Lazarus, Martha, and Mary. Along the way, Jesus told His disciples: "You know that after two days the Passover is coming, and the Son of Man is *to be* handed over for crucifixion" (Matthew 26:2). The Lord had been preparing His disciples for this very moment from the beginning of His ministry. At Cana of Galilee, He had told them, "My hour is not yet come" (John 2:4b). Over the previous year, He had warned them several times what awaited Him in Jerusalem at this Passover Feast. Now, the hour is almost at hand and He tells them exactly when it will be. It will be in two more days. He was aware of the malignancy of His enemies and their plans to kill Him, as Shepard tells us:

> His enemies were alert, watching thousands of pilgrims pouring into Jerusalem from all parts of the land, bringing them materials for their construction of their booths. They understood that among the Gal-

---

1 F. W. Krummacher, *The Suffering Saviour* (Grand Rapids: Baker Book House, 1977), 33–4.

ileans there would be many friends of Jesus. They had already been taking counsel how they might entrap Him. They now call together the chief priests and the elders in informal session of the Sanhedrin in the palace of Caiaphas, who had given utterance to the definite expression, that it was "convenient that one man die rather than the nation perish." This was to give the official sanction of the high priest to the idea of putting Jesus to death. They now met in informal session, not in the legal place of meeting, the Temple, nor within legal hours, but at night in the palace of Caiaphas to the west of the city. They had met for the purpose of arranging a secret plot to take Jesus by subtlety and kill Him. But they were restrained by their fear of the people and said: "Not during the feast, lest a tumult arise among the people."[2]

Judas' Conspiracy with the Sanhedrin (Matthew 26:1–5, 14–16; Mark 14:, 1, 2, 10, 11; and Luke 22:1–6)

It was the aim of the Sanhedrin to *not* kill Jesus during Passover, but it was God's plan to give His Son as "the Lamb who takes away the sin of the world" (John 1:29) during that feast—indeed, at the very time that the paschal lamb would be sacrificed. Despite all their scheming, these members of the Sanhedrin did not realize that they were like fish in a bowl and the Lord was directing their schemes to accomplish His purpose. Caiaphas' palace[3] was a large, luxurious edifice on Mount Zion, a little southwest of the Temple itself, and capable of accommodating all the people who would be involved in the intrigue over the coming days. On this night, the Sanhedrin was meeting there informally, "plotting together to seize Jesus by stealth and kill Him" (Matthew 26:4). Jesus' words against the scribes and the Pharisees, as well as His predictions of the coming judgments against them and the temple, finally drove the rulers to the point that they knew something had to be done concerning this Galilean as soon as possible. Then, suddenly, an unexpected visitor came to them—Judas Iscariot—one of Jesus' own disciples. Luke 22:3–6 tells us what happened:

> And Satan entered into Judas who was called Iscariot, belonging to the number of the twelve. And he went away and discussed with the chief priests and officers how he might betray Him to them. They were glad and agreed to give him money. So he consented and *began* seeking a good opportunity to betray Him apart from the crowd.

The amount of money Judas was offered was "thirty pieces of silver" (Matthew 26:15)—a paltry sum which amounts to only a few

---

2 Shepard, *The Christ of the Gospels*, 530.
3 The location and the remains of Caiaphas' home cannot be precisely determined.

hundred dollars in today's valuation. For that inconsiderable amount of money, though, Judas agreed to betray the Lord of glory. It was night and the "darkness had long been gathering"[4] in the heart of this disciple who had often pilfered the money box. Judas had now reached the crucial moment of his life. Perhaps, he had conversed with some of those officers or rulers on other occasions when the enmity of the Sanhedrin had made efforts to stop Jesus. Sin does not become full blown all at once. There had been incremental steps at several points along the way. Yet, now was the decisive time. Satan had entered Judas and was driving him headlong, like a herd of swine, into his destruction—and the death of the Lord. As Dorothy Sayers said concerning Judas' action in her book, *The Man Born To Be King*: "At the core of Judas are the devil's own sins of pride and unbelief, and beneath all his idealism is a rooted egotism."[5] Judas was not a believer, but a worshiper of his own idols of self-love and avarice. The devil twisted Judas' heart to the point of choking out any spiritual aspirations he had ever had. In the moment of the great crisis of his life, he chose silver over the riches of Christ. Edersheim describes what little we know about the life of Judas:

> We remember, that "Judas, the man of Keroth," was, so far as we know, the only disciple of Jesus from the province of Judaea. This circumstance; that he carried the bag, i.e. was the treasurer and administrator of the small common stock of Christ, and His disciples; and that he was both a hypocrite and a thief (John 12:5, 6)—this is all we know for certain of his history.[6]

Preparations for the Passover Meal (Matthew 26:17–19; Mark 14:12–16; and Luke 22:7–13)

After agreeing with the Sanhedrin to betray Jesus, Judas slipped back in among the other disciples in Bethany. Thursday, the first day of Unleavened Bread, was a day of rest and relaxation before the Last Supper by Jesus and His disciples. At some point, the disciples came to Jesus and asked: "Where do you want us to go and prepare for You to eat the Passover?" (Mark 14:12). Jesus then sent Peter and John to find a pace for the meal with these instructions:

> Go into the city, and a man will meet you carrying a pitcher of water, follow him; and wherever he enters, say to the owner, "The Teacher

---

4 Edersheim, *The Life and Times of Jesus the Messiah*, 799.
5 Dorothy Sayers, *The Man Born To Be King* (London: Victor Gollancz, 1943), 208.
6 Edersheim, *The Life and Times of Jesus the Messiah*, 799.

says, 'Where is My guest room in which I may eat the Passover with My disciples?'" And He will show you a large upper room furnished and ready, prepare for us there. (Mark 14:13–15)

Peter and John did just as Jesus had told them and made all the preparations for the Passover meal. Judas had most likely already bought everything that was necessary for the meal the previous evening which was the reason he was in Jerusalem that evening for the unplanned meeting of the Sanhedrin. When the disciples and Jesus gathered in the Upper Room on Thursday evening, April 6th, Judas was among them and was unsuspected by the others. John tells us what happened next:

> Now before the Feast of the Passover, Jesus knowing that His hour had come that He would depart out of this world, having loved His own who were in the world, He loved them to the end. During supper, the devil having already put into the heart of Judas Iscariot, the son of Simon, to betray Him, Jesus, knowing that the Father had given all things into His hands, and that He had come forth from God and was going back to God, got up from supper, and laid aside His garments; and taking a towel, He girded Himself (John 13:1–4).

Jesus Washes His Disciples' Feet (John 13:1–20)
John chapters 13 to 17 are filled with several discourses and events that are not found elsewhere. The first of those is the washing of the feet of the disciples. Before that, though, John focuses on the great love of Jesus for His disciples. Charles Ross, in *The Inner Sanctuary*, states: "Jesus was now to depart *out of* the world, but they were to be left *in it*; and therefore his heart turned towards them."[7] Much of the material given by John is for the purpose of showing how Jesus loved His disciples to the end and how He prepared them for everything that was going to happen. The Passover meal had not been eaten when Jesus got up from the table and began washing the feet of all the disciples, including Judas.

Jesus "poured water into the basin, and began to wash the disciples' feet, and to wipe them with the towel with which He was girded" (John 13:5). This was a great act of humility and an example to the disciples. He was among them as their servant and example, especially in light of their dispute at the meal over which one was to be considered as the greatest (Cf. Luke 22:24:-27), as they jock-

---

7 Charles Ross, *The Inner Sanctuary* (Edinburgh, Scotland and Carlisle, Pennsylvania: The Banner of Truth Trust, 2016), 6.

eyed to gain the places nearest to Him. Interestingly, Judas—the betrayer—took the seat to Jesus' left while John, the Beloved disciple, was on His right. When Jesus came to Peter, he said, "Lord, do you wash my feet?" (John 13:6). Jesus' reply was: "What I do you do not realize now, but you will understand hereafter" (John 13:7). Peter indignantly objected: "Never shall You wash my feet!" (John 13:8a), to which Jesus replied: "If I do not wash you, you have no part with Me" (John 13:8b). Then, Peter reversed his course and said, "Lord, then wash not only my feet, but also my hands and my head" (John 13:9). Peter was guilty of hastiness in his responses and ignorance of the true meaning of what Jesus was doing. As Ryle wrote:

> One moment we find him refusing to allow his Master to do such servile work as He is about to do... Another moment we find him rushing with characteristic impetuosity into the other extreme... But throughout the transaction we find him unable to take in the real meaning of what his eyes behold. He sees, but he does not understand... The heart may often be quite right when the heart is quite wrong.[8]

Thus, Jesus said to Peter: "He who is bathed needs only to wash his feet, but is completely clean; and you are clean, but not all *of you*" (John 13:10). The next verse clearly shows that Jesus' was giving a veiled hint that He knew what Judas had done and who was going to betray Him. Jesus' words could be interpreted simply as meaning that they were already clean except for their feet which was true of them. Yet, the whole context makes it clear that Jesus was already pointing out that one of them would betray Him. John 13:18, 19 is even more explicit:

> I do not speak of all of you. I know the ones I have chosen, but *it is* that the Scripture may be fulfilled, "He who eats My bread has lifted up his heal against me." From now on I am telling you before it comes to pass, so that when it does occur, you may believe that I am *He*.

Therein, Jesus distinguishes between those He chose and the one who will lift up his heel against the Son of Man. Shepard describes what must have been the inner working of the heart of Judas:

> Even now, as the traitor sat at the table with Jesus, he was seeking in his heart to trip Him up, like a wrestler taking advantage in a wrestling match. He was in a mortal grip with Jesus, to throw Him down into the power and grasp of His enemies. His close companionship made worse his sin of faithlessness.[9]

---

8 Ryle, *Expository Thoughts on the Gospels: St. John* , 3:13.
9 Shepard, *The Christ of the Gospels*, 539.

The Last Supper (Matthew 26:20–35; Mark 14:12–31; Luke 22:14–38; and, John 13:1–4, 21–38)

After washing the disciples' feet, Jesus returned to the table where they all shared in the Passover meal. Reclining at the table, Jesus said to them, "I have earnestly desired to eat this Passover[10] with you before I suffer; for I say to you, I shall never again eat it until it is fulfilled in the kingdom of God" (Luke 22:15, 16). After those words, Jesus then took the bread and the cup and gave them to His disciples, having given thanks, saying: "This is My body which is given for you; do this in remembrance of Me;" and, "This cup, which is poured out for you, is the new covenant in My blood" (Luke 22:19b, 20b). In that way, Jesus instituted the Lord's supper as a perpetual sacrament until He returns.

At some point during the Passover meal, there arose a dispute among the disciples as to which of them was the greatest. They had the same dispute following His transfiguration. Jesus had then told them: "The kings of the Gentiles lord it over them . . . But it is not this way with you, but the one who is greatest among you must become like the youngest, and the leader like the servant . . . I am among you as the one who serves" (Luke 22:25a, 26, 27b). It was that dispute that probably triggered Jesus' washing of their feet as an example of servant leadership.

While they were eating, Jesus, having become "troubled in spirit", informed them of the perfidy of one among them: "Truly I say to you, that one of you will betray Me" (John 13:21). Those were hard words to receive by the disciples and they "began looking at one another, at a loss to know of which one He was speaking" (John 13:22). John was resting on Jesus' bosom and Peter said to him, "Tell us who it is of whom He is speaking" (John 13:24). The betrayer was still in that "inner sanctuary" with Jesus' true disciples, but he escaped detection by the others despite our Lord pointing him out: "That is the one for whom I shall dip the morsel and give it to him" (John 1326a). Immediately after speaking those words, Jesus dipped the morsel and "gave it to Judas, *the son* of Simon Iscariot" (John 13:26b). The disciples remained blinded for the time being to the identity of the betrayer, though. Yet, Judas knew, as it is written: "After the morsel, Satan en-

---

10 The Passover meal of the Old Testament was transformed into the Lord's Supper and replaced by it in the New Testament through the sacrifice of Christ our Passover. Cf. 1 Corinthians 5:6–8.

tered into him" (John 13:27a). Judas knew what evil plans he had already agreed to do. His evil is what so troubled the spirit of Jesus as Ross notes:

> But oh! The deep emotion with which Jesus now approaches this painful subject . . . The words, 'When He had thus said,' connect this emotion with the preceding discourse, in which he had already twice referred to the treachery of Judas (verses 10 and 18); and thus they give us to understand the real cause of his trouble. Not the pain, which was soon to rack his body, nor yet the agony, which was so soon to seize upon his holy soul—it was not this which occasioned the sorrow with which his spirit was now troubled, but it was the sin—the aggravated sin—of the traitor . . . It was not merely the feeling of wounded friendship nor yet pity for the traitor, but it was a kind of holy shrinking, on the part of his pure nature, from the dread character of this most Satanic crime.[11]

Judas had been a trusted disciple—the treasurer—but now he had completely turned his back on the mission of Jesus. Darkness overwhelmed his soul and the Scripture properly notes that when he left the others that "it was night" (John 13:30). As Judas was leaving, Jesus simply said to him, "What you do, do quickly" (John 13:27). The other disciples did not discern anything unusual about Jesus' words to Judas since he was the treasurer and had the money box. They assumed "that Jesus was saying to him, 'Buy the things we have need of for the feast'; or else, that he should give something to the poor" (John 13:29). Jesus had appealed to whatever better nature still dwelt in Judas in every way that He could. Judas may very well have been given the chief seat at the table as Jesus made one "last appeal to the traitor."[12] Perhaps Judas had been the disciple who provoked the earlier debate over which one was the greatest among them. In his own demented way, Judas undoubtedly thought he was doing the right thing by betraying Jesus. Bruce has well-described the character of Judas:

> The false disciple was a sentimental, plausible, self-deceived pietist, who knew and approved the good, though not conscientiously practicing it; one who, in aesthetic feeling, fancy, and in intellect, had affinities for the noble and the holy, while in will and in conduct he was the slave of base, selfish passions; one who, in the last resource, would always put self uppermost, yet could zealously devote himself to well-doing when personal interests were not compromised—in short, what the Apostle James calls a two-minded man . . . Men of such type are by no

---

11 Ross, *The Inner Sanctuary*, 32.
12 Morris, *The Gospel According to John*, 626.

means so rare as some may imagine.[13]

To all outward appearances, Judas was the model apostle which is why none of the others suspected him of his evil deeds. He was conscientious in buying the supplies for Jesus and the Twelve, but the others did not know he was also pilfering from the money box for his own interests. Self-interest was his besetting sin. Hypocrisy was his hallmark. Deceitfulness was his tradecraft. It took a deceitful person to pull off the crime of all ages, to betray the Lord of glory—someone who was well-versed in how to make others think better of himself than they should and to prevent others from suspecting his secret plotting with the enemy. A person who was straightforward with the truth could never have done what Judas did. His evil did not begin at Jesus' last Passover meal or in the days just preceding it. He had proceeded in a downward direction through small, incremental steps for years until he reached the point where he could brazenly sell Jesus for thirty pieces of silver while saying with the adulteress woman, "I have done no wrong" (Proverbs 30:20). Solomon also described the character of a person like Judas as follows: "A worthless person, a wicked man is the one who walks with a perverse mouth, who winks with his eyes, who signals with his feet, who points with his fingers; who with perversity in his heart continually devises evil, who spreads strife" (Proverbs 6:12–14). Thus, Jesus said about His betrayer: "The Son of Man is to go, just as it is written of Him; but woe to that man by whom the Son of Man is betrayed! It would have been better if he had never been born" (Matthew 26:24). When Jesus spoke those solemn words, Judas had replied, "Surely it is not I, Rabbi?" (Matthew 26:25a). Jesus answered him, "You have said it yourself" (Matthew 26:25b). Thus, Proverbs 6:15 also says about such a worthless man: "Therefore his calamity will come suddenly; instantly he will be broken and there will be no healing." The price of those thirty pieces of silver Judas was to be paid was approximately the wages for a worker for 120 days or the equivalent of 120 denarii. Mary, the sister of Lazarus, had anointed Jesus with perfume valued at 300 denarii. Judas' betrayal in that light seems even worse. Mary's anointing of Jesus with that "very costly pound of pure nard" (John 12:3) was the final straw for Judas. He was peevish at not being able to pilfer from such a large sum of money. His self-interest finally defeated any good left in him.

---

13 Bruce, *The Training of the Twelve*, 370–1.

With Judas gone, Jesus turned His attention fully to the other disciples. This "inner sanctuary"—if only for a few brief moments—became the most perfect school of Christ that the disciples had ever experienced and the world had ever seen. These discourses in the Upper Room and the High Priestly prayer of Jesus form one of the most amazing sections of Scripture. There is no other part of Scripture that more completely unfolds the heart of Jesus than these chapters do. Thus, Jesus spoke to the eleven disciples who remained with Him—"Now is the Son of Man glorified, and God is glorified in Him; if God is glorified in Him, God will also glorify Him in Himself, and will glorify Him immediately. Little children, I am with you a little while longer. You will seek Me; and as I said to the Jews, now I also say to you, 'Where I am going, you cannot come.'" (John 13:31–33). The disciples still had very little comprehension that Jesus' life on this earth was quickly drawing to an end. Jesus had first described what the coming moments would be for Him. Bernard of Clairvaux accurately described the glory of Christ on earth in his well-known hymn, "O Sacred Head, Now Wounded" in which he penned these words; "O sacred Head, what glory, what bliss till now was thine!" Certainly, there was glory for Christ even during His state of humiliation in coming to earth as a man, but Jesus in John 13 speaks of a glory that God will bestow on Him as a result of His redemptive sacrifice. There is glory in the cross and even more glory in His powerful resurrection from the dead. Yet, the disciples are about to be left without their Master. Thus, Jesus comforted their hearts with these words: "A new commandment I give to you, that you love one another, even as I have loved you, that you also love one another. By this all men will know that you are My disciples, if you have love for one another" (John 13:34, 35). Westcott records an anecdote concerning John, the Beloved disciple:

> The well-known anecdote of St. John's extreme old age preserved by Jerome . . . is a striking comment on the commandment. It is related that the disciples of the apostles, wearied by his constant repetition of the words, "Little children, love one another." which was all he said when he was often carried into their assembly, asked him why he always said this. "Because," he replied, "it is the Lord's commandment; and if it only be fulfilled it is enough."[14]

Characteristically, Peter ignored everything Jesus said and focused

---

14 Westcott, *The Gospel According to St. John*, 198.

on the one statement that He was going where the disciples could not follow—at least at that time. He asked Jesus: "Lord, where are you going?" (John 13:36a). Jesus replied, "Where I go, you cannot follow Me now, but you will follow later" (John 13:36b).

Then, Jesus especially ministered to Peter, forewarning him of the trials that awaited him: "Simon, Simon, Satan has demanded permission to sift you like wheat; but I have prayed for you, that your faith may not fail; and you, when once you have turned again, strengthen your brothers" (Luke 22:31, 32). Luke alone includes those words of Jesus which tend "to mitigate Peter's guilt, by showing how sorely he was tried."[15] Unlike Job, though, Peter is told beforehand the source of his great trials. Thus, he would later warn other believers: "Your adversary, the devil, prowls around like a roaring lion, seeking someone to devour" (1 Peter 5:8b). Sadly, Peter was not aware of his own weakness and responded: "Lord, with You I am ready to go both to prison and to death!" (Luke 22:33). And again, "*Even* though all may fall away, yet I will not" (Mark 14:29). To those solemn declarations, Jesus replied, "Truly, I say to you, that this very night, before a rooster crows twice, you yourself will deny Me three times" (Mark 14:30). An incredulous Peter insisted: "Even if I have to die with You, I will not deny You!" (Mark 14:31a). Peter was not alone in that affirmation, but was joined by all the disciples.

Many Dwelling Places (John 14:1–4)
With Judas Iscariot's departure from the Upper Room, our Lord felt the unbounded freedom to minister to His faithful band of disciples in a way that He had never done before. "The exit of Judas into the darkness of the night, on his still darker errand, was a summons to Jesus to prepare for death. Yet He was thankful for the departure of the traitor. It took a burden off His heart, and allowed Him to breathe and speak freely."[16] No longer was there one among them who was being prompted by Satan. A year earlier at Capernaum, Jesus had warned His disciples that "one of you is a devil" (John 6:70). It is hard for two to walk together unless they are agreed (Amos 3:3). Judas had hindered the fellowship of the disciples with Jesus. It would be interesting to know how many times Judas was behind the divisions among them. Certainly, he had provoked the disciples

---

15 Plummer, *A Critical and Exegetical Commentary on the Gospel According to S. Luke*, 503.
16 Bruce, *The Training of the Twelve*, 378.

into being indignant at the supposed extravagant waste of resources when Mary anointed Him at Bethany. Now Judas was gone and would never return. Now Jesus could unfold comforting words to the other disciples in this inner sanctuary and teach them truths they had never understood. These five chapters of John's Gospel (thirteen through seventeen) represent the most spiritual teaching of Jesus' ministry. His words are like a slice of heaven on earth. As Ross notes:

> It would appear from the opening words of this remarkable passage that our Lord had spoken under a kind of painful restraint, so long as Judas was present among them. But now, on the departure of that traitor, all that is removed, and he pours forth his whole soul in one continuous stream, which only ceases as he is about to enter the garden of Gethsemane.[17]

To Peter's question, "Lord, where are You going?" (John 13:36b), Jesus now replies: "Do not let your heart be troubled; believe in God, believe also in Me. In My Father's house are many dwelling places; if it were not so, I would have told you; for I go to prepare a place for you. If I go to prepare a place for you, I will come again and receive you to Myself, that where I am, *there* you may be also. And you know the way where I am going" (John 14:1–4). Jesus' words are some of the most definitive concerning heaven to be found in Scripture. Heaven is a place where God abides. God is present everywhere (cf. Psalm 139:8), but He resides in heaven as the God of love and mercy. The Triune God will be present in heaven—Father, Son, and Holy Spirit. Heaven is a world of love and is described beautifully in Revelation 21 and 22. Jesus' comfort of His disciples focuses on two truths concerning heaven: 1. There will be a dwelling place in heaven for every believer; and, 2. Jesus is going before us into heaven in order to prepare that special dwelling place for each one of us. As Ryle commented:

> Heaven is a prepared place for a prepared people: a place which we shall find Christ Himself has made ready for true Christians. He has prepared it by procuring a right for every sinner who believes to enter in. None can stop us, and say we have no business there.—He has prepared it by going before us as our Head and Representative, and taking possession of it for all members of His mystical body. As our Forerunner He has marched in, leading captivity captive, and has planted His banner in the land of glory.—He has prepared it by carrying our names

---

17 Ross, *The Inner Sanctuary*, 45.

with Him as our High Priest into the holy of holies, and making angels ready to receive us. They that enter heaven will find that they are neither unknown nor unexpected.[18]

As our great High Priest (Hebrews 3:14), Jesus especially prepared us for heaven and heaven for us by His atoning death and His triumphant resurrection from the dead. As Hebrews 9:11, 12 says: "But when Christ appeared *as* a high priest of the good things to come, *He entered* through the greater and more perfect tabernacle, not made with hands, that is to say, not of this creation; and not through the blood of goats and calves, but through His own blood, He entered the holy place once for all, having obtained eternal redemption." When Jesus returned to heaven, He presented that perfect sacrifice for us and, thereby, gained that eternal redemption for us. That was the first and most important part of His preparing a dwelling place for us in heaven.

Jesus Comforts His Disciples (John 14:5–31)

Jesus' teaching on heaven raised the question by Thomas: "Lord, we do not know where You are going, how do we know the way?" (John 14:5). It was characteristic of Thomas at this point in his discipleship to have such doubts. His doubts were more seeming than real. While it was true that none of the disciples knew the way since they did not have a clear apprehension of the end, yet they were learning the necessity of walking by faith, not by sight. Jesus did not give Thomas and the others a roadmap of their destination. Rather, He replied to Thomas: "I am the way the truth, the life; no one comes to the Father but through Me. If you had known Me, you would have known My Father also; from now on you know Him, and have seen Him" (John 14:6, 7). Philip then replied, "Lord, show us the Father and it is enough for us" (John 14:8). Jesus responded: "Have I been so long with you, and yet you have not come to know Me, Philip? He who has seen Me has seen the Father; how can you say, 'Show us the Father'?" (John 14:9). Philip was the third disciple called by Jesus and had been with Him from the beginning of His ministry. He had seen everything Jesus had done. He had stated to Nathaniel: "We have found Him of whom Moses in the Law and *also* the Prophets wrote—Jesus of Nazareth, the son of Joseph" (John 1:45). Philip must have thought that Jesus intended to reveal the Father in some

---

18 Ryle, *Expository Thoughts on the Gospels: John*, 3:53–4.

outward manner because Jesus had said, "from now on you know Him, and have seen Him" (John 14:7b) Philip must have focused on the idea of seeing the Father with the eyes of the flesh—not with the eyes of faith. As Ross says:

> Most unquestionably Philip believed in Jesus to the saving of his soul, and in his heart of hearts, he desired to see God's face. Like Moses, he would say, 'Show me Thy glory' (Exod. 33:18). But it is undeniable, on the other hand, that, in this request, there was much weakness and imperfection.[19]

Heretofore, the disciples had never equated Jesus with the Father. The doctrine of the Trinity was still unclear to them. This was a new thought for them. Thus, Jesus expanded on what He had already told Philip: "Believe Me that I am in the Father and the Father is in Me" (John 14:11). Jesus' Unity with the Father was a new development in their understanding of God. To further emblazon this idea in their minds, Jesus said: "Whatever you ask in My name, that will I do, so that the Father may be glorified in the Son. If you ask Me anything in My name, I will do it" (John 14:13, 14). Praying in Jesus' name further illustrates that He is God, equal with the Father. Once again, Ross' comments are helpful:

> Praying in the name of Jesus is here declared to be the disciples' part in these greater works. The believer asks, and the exalted Redeemer answers from the throne of his glory. It is not, however, to *any* or *every* kind of prayer that this promise is given, but to prayer offered up *in his own name*.[20]

Jesus further comforted His disciples by foretelling the sending of the Holy Spirit. They would not be alone in the world. As He told them, "I will ask the Father and He will give you another Helper, that He may be with you forever; *that is* the Spirit of truth, whom the world cannot receive, because it does not see or know Him, *but* you know Him, because He abides with you and will be in you" (John 14:16, 17). The Greek translated as "Helper" is "parakleton" which means someone who is called alongside another to help them, to comfort them, to advocate for them, or to intercede for them. Of course, the Holy Spirit does all those things and more. He is the Person of the Trinity who dwells within believers and unites them with the Father and the Son. It is in that way that Jesus promised the disciples and all

---

19 Ross, *The Inner Sanctuary*, 81.
20 Ross, *The Inner Sanctuary*, 89.

believers: "I will not leave you as orphans; I will come to you" (John 14:18). Jesus' promise to disclose Himself to believers caused Judas (not Iscariot) to ask: "Lord, what then has happened that You are going to disclose Yourself to us and not to the world?" (John 14:22). He was told by Jesus: "if anyone loves Me, he will keep My Word,; and My Father will love him, and We will come and make Our abode with him" (John 14:23). Therein, Jesus confirmed that the whole Trinity would abide within every believer—a truth taught in Romans 8:9–11 and other parts of the New Testament.

Another important truth Jesus taught them was that the Holy Spirit would guide them into the truth. As He said, "But the Helper, the Holy Spirit, whom the Father will send in My name, He will teach you all things, and bring to your remembrance all that I said to you" (John 14:26). "The Spirit would make the absent Jesus present to them again, by bringing to their remembrance all His words, by testifying to them again, and by guiding them into an intelligent apprehension of the Christian truth."[21] No doubt, that was a promise to the disciples that the Spirit would guide them in remembering and writing Scripture, but there is also a promise for all believers throughout all time. As Ryle states:

> It is safer, wiser, and more consistent with the whole tone of our Lord's last discourse, to regard the promise as the common property of all believers, in every age of the world.[22]

Jesus concluded this portion of His dialogue with that wonderful promise: "Peace, I leave you; My peace I give to you; not as the world gives, do I give to you" (John 14:27a). He warns them of the coming of the "ruler of this world" who has nothing to do with Jesus. Far from comforting them that there would be no troubles for them in this world, Jesus does something so much better. He promises them that He will be with them in all their troubles and temptations. For that reason, He could say to them: "Do not let your heart be troubled, nor let it be fearful" (John 14:27b). At this time, their hearts were still too fearful and they would remain that way until Jesus rose from the dead. Then, they would gain fresh hope from their Lord. Before that point, though, the devil would make one more mighty effort to destroy Jesus. "He was mustering all his strength for one more tremen-

---

21 Bruce, *The Training of the Twelve*, 386.
22 Ryle, *Expository Thoughts on the Gospels: John*, 3:92.

dous battle."[23] Yet, that fiend would not be able to levy a single charge against Jesus that would stick. The Holy One of God was above reproach and could not be justly condemned.

---

23 Ryle, *Expository Thoughts on the Gospels: John*, 3:92.

23

The Garden of Gethsemane

"There is something strikingly heroic in this midnight visit to Gethsemane. Throughout His ministry Jesus had shown Himself sensitive to doing anything which might prematurely place Him in the hands of His enemies. But the moment His hour is come He advances to the closing scene with high determination and unfaltering step. All that was to happen was not only according to His knowledge, but according to His choice. Never did dying man give last directions with the lofty composure with which Jesus makes all preparations which lead Him down to death. The time, the place, the circumstances of His arrest are deliberately arranged.

"On His arrival at Gethsemane, He stations eight of the apostles as a watch near the entrance to the garden. 'Sit ye here, while I go and pray yonder' (Matt. 26:36). The remaining three, Peter, James, and John, He takes along with Him to some recess at a little distance."[1]

In the last words of John 14, Jesus said: "Get up, let us go from here" (John 14:31b). With that command, Jesus and His disciples "immediately left the supper room, as we believe, passed in silence through the streets of Jerusalem, and soon found themselves in some secluded spot on the slopes of Mount Olivet leading to the valley of the Kedron."[2] That spot has become known as the Garden of Gethsemane. It was a place with which Judas was familiar. Gethsemane was known as "the place of the olive press." The whole life of Jesus came down to this one place where He was now the olive in the press. Jesus had come here on other occasions with His disciples to pray. McClintock and Strong describe the place:

> The Kedron runs in the bottom of a deep glen, parallel with the eastern wall of Jerusalem, and about 200 yards distant. Immediately beyond it rises the steep side of Olivet, now, as formerly, cultivated in rude terraces . . . But Gethsemane has not come down to us as a scene of mirth; its inexhaustible associations are the offspring of a single event—the agony of the Son of God on the evening preceding his passion. Here emphatically, as Isaiah had foretold, and as the name

---

1 George Philip, *The Garden of Gethsemane* (London: Hodder and Stoughton, 1882), 18–9.
2 Ross, *The Inner Sanctuary*, 124.

imports, were fulfilled those words, "I have trodden the wine-press alone" (lxiii, 3).[3]

The Vine and Branches (John 15:1–26)

When they arrived at Gethsemane, Jesus changed His teaching methodology from dialogue to discourse. From John 15:1 to John 16:17, He takes up the theme of the disciples' relationship to Him and one another, their relationship to the world, and their relationship to the Holy Spirit.[4] During this extended discourse, Jesus is not so much answering their questions about the future, but teaching them about their lives on earth when He leaves them. Having gone to the Mount of Olives, Jesus had a natural example before Him. Thus, He said, "I am the vine and My Father is the vinedresser" (John 15:1). And, again: "I am the vine, you are the branches." "What He meant was, that He, the Father, and the disciples, stood in exactly the same relationship as the Vine, the Husbandman, and the branches. The relationship was of corporate union of the branches with the Vine, the Husbandman, Who for that purpose pruned the branches."[5] In Isaiah 5:1–7 and Jeremiah 12:10, the vineyard or the vine was identified as Israel. One of Christ's last parables only a few days earlier was on the Landowner and the Vineyard. He now relates to the disciples that they and other believers are the vineyard of the Lord. As the branches of the Lord's vine, they must bear fruit for Him. Of course, that is what Jesus said in Matthew 21:43: "Therefore I say to you, the kingdom of God will be taken away from you and given to a people producing the fruit of it."

John 15:1–11 is a simple, straightforward parable. The analogy is easily understood. Like all parables, there is one primary point. In this case, the point is that those who are true disciples of Jesus will bear fruit. It is saying in parabolic form the same thing that Paul wrote in Galatians 5:16–24 where he lists the fruit of the Spirit. Those who have the Spirit bear fruit. Those who do not bear spiritual fruit or bear bad fruit do not have the Spirit. Thus, Jesus said, "he who abides in Me and I in him, he bears much fruit, for apart from Me you can do nothing . . .If you abide in Me, and My words abide in you, ask whatever you wish, and it will be done for you" (John 15:5, 7). Ryle summarizes this point well:

---

3 McClintock and Strong, *Cyclopedia of Biblical, Theological, and Ecclesiastical Literature*, 3:841.
4 Ross, *The Inner Sanctuary*, 124.
5 Edersheim, *The Life and Times of Jesus the Messiah*, 833.

"Fruit" is the only satisfactory evidence of saving union between Christ and our souls. Where there is no fruit of the Spirit to be seen, there is no vital religion in the heart. The Spirit of Life in Christ Jesus will always make Himself known in the daily conduct of those in whom He dwells. The Master Himself declares, "Every tree is known by his own fruit." (Luke vi. 44).[6]

In John 15:8–10, Jesus said: "My Father is glorified by this, that you bear much fruit, and so prove to be My disciples. Just as the Father has loved Me, I have also loved you; abide in My love. If you keep My commandments, you will abide in My love; just as I have kept My Father's commandments and abide in His love. These things I have spoken to you so that My joy may be in you, and *that* your joy may be made full." The Ten Commandments and spiritual fruitfulness are not in opposition to one another. The true life of holiness will be a life of obedience to God's commandments. An antinomian life—that is, a life that is lived contrary to God's commandments—will carry out those desires of the flesh that are the very opposite of the life of the Spirit which alone produces fruitfulness. Jesus' parable cannot be twisted in any way into teaching that there are those who have been united with Christ by the ceremony of baptism and that they are true branches of Christ for a season only. The true branches are those, and those only, who bear fruit for Christ.

Jesus takes up the relationship of the disciples to one another in John 15:12–17. Of course, His words are not restricted to the Twelve or even to the larger number of disciples during His life. He made statements that are just as true for disciples of all ages. The second great test of a disciple is very simple—it is his relationship to other disciples. In this section, Jesus reiterated what He had said when He summarized the two tables of the law. The first test is the love of God. The second test is the love of the brethren. Thus, Jesus said, "This is My commandment, that you love one another, just as I have loved you" (John 15:12). 1 John 4:7, 8 strikes the same note: "Beloved, let us love one another, for love is from God; and everyone who loves God is born of God and knows God, The one who does not love does not know God, for God is love." Three times in this section Jesus refers to His disciples—all believers—as "My friends" or "friends." Abraham—the father of believers—was called the friend of God in

---

6 John Charles Ryle, *Expository Thoughts on the Gospels: John* (James Clarke& Co., Ltd., 1969) 3:108.

Genesis and all his spiritual seed are called Jesus' friends. For His friends, Jesus laid down His life—the greatest act of sacrifice that a friend can make. "A man can show no greater regard for those dear to him than to give his life for them, and such love would they find in Jesus!"[7] Following those expressions of friendship, Jesus informed the disciples: "You did not choose Me but I chose you, and appointed you that you would go and bear fruit, and that your fruit would remain, so that whatever you ask of the Father in My name He may give to you. This I command you, that you love one another" (John 15:16, 17). Once again, Jesus promised that bearing fruit will result in answered prayers when those prayers are offered in His name. As Hendriksen notes:

> On earth friends generally choose each other, but the friendship of which Jesus speaks is different. It is one-sided in its origin. It was not brought about by gradual approach from both sides, as is often the case among men, but by Jesus alone! The words, "You did not choose me, but I chose you," emphasize the free, independent, and spontaneous character of Christ's love. The ground of God's love for us never lies in us, always in himself.[8]

The disciples' relationship with the world is covered next in John 15:18–16:4. Instead of expecting the world to receive them, Jesus warned them to expect the world to hate them. He said, "If the world hates you, know that it has hated Me before it hated you . . . If they persecuted Me, they will also persecute you" (John 15:18, 20b). Jesus had warned His disciples when He sent them out on their mission through Galilee" "But whenever they persecute you in one city, flee to the next; . . . If they have called the head of the house Beelzebul, how much more *will they malign* the members of his household!" (Matthew 10:23a, 25). Christians will be persecuted because Christ was and is persecuted. The world cannot love believers because they have hated Christ without a cause (John 15:26). As Ryle comments:

> Ridicule, mockery, slander, misrepresentation, still show the feeling of unconverted people against true Christians. So it was in Paul's day, so it is now. In public, at school and college, at home and abroad "all that live goldy in Christ Jesus shall suffer persecution." (2 Tim. iii.12.)[9]

This hatred of Jesus has its genesis in the hatred of the Father also.

---

7 Ross, *The Inner Sanctuary*, 140.
8 Hendriksen, *The Gospel of John*, 307.
9 Ryle, *Expository Thoughts on the Gospels: John*, 3:131.

As Jesus said, "He who hates Me hates My Father also" (John 15:23). The Jews hated Jesus because He had "come and spoken to them . . . and done among them the works which no one else did" (John 16:22, 24). As a result of His words and deeds, they have no excuse for their sin. That is true of all who persecute Jesus and His disciples even to this day. Ross' words are a reminder to believers and the true church in all ages:

> And woe to that church whenever she loses the heavenly character of being hated and persecuted by a sinful world, until that day come, when the world shall lie down at her feet, bowing down before the sudden appearing of her glory.[10]

The Promise of the Spirit (John 16:1–15)

After warning His disciples of the persecutions they will soon bear for His name, Jesus promises them that the Holy Spirit will come to them. The Spirit of God will give them strength in their days of tribulation. He will guide them into all the truth. He will dwell within them. He will give the words with which to respond to their persecutors. Jesus gave this warning, as He said, so they "may be kept from stumbling" (John 16:1). In the midst of their trials, they could take comfort that the Church was growing despite their persecution. Also, He warned them that their greatest enemies would be the religious Jews, as Bruce states:

> The world, against whose hatred the Master forewarns them in part of His discourse, is not the irreligious, sceptical, easy-going, gross-living world of paganism. It is the world of antichristian Judaism; of synagogue-frequenting men, accustomed to distinguish themselves from "the world" as the people of God, very zealous after a fashion for God's glory, fanatically in earnest in their religious opinions and practices, utterly intolerant of dissent, relentlessly excommunicating all who deviated from established belief by a hair's-breadth and deeming their death no murder, but a religious service, an acceptable sacrifice to the Almighty.[11]

"It was a dark, gloomy, repulsive picture which Jesus set before his disciples, of what they had reason to expect in the world. But having tenderly and faithfully warned them, he now proceeds, for their encouragement, to speak again—and in terms of greater clearness and fulness than before—of the mission of the Comforter."[12] In John

---
10 Ross, *The Inner Sanctuary*, 149.
11 Bruce, *The Training of the Twelve*, 428.
12 Ross, *The Inner Sanctuary*, 167.

16:8–11, Jesus set forth the great work of the Spirit in the conversion of souls and without Whom nothing can be done. The Spirit will convict the world of sin, righteousness, and judgment. All of the convicting work of the Spirit is for the purpose of leading sinners to saving faith in Christ. C. R. Vaughan describes astutely the convicting and awakening work of the Spirit:

> The relations of the Holy Spirit to the unconverted in the administration of the covenant of grace, are of inexpressible importance. There are two forms of conviction of sin, one previous to conversion, and the other subsequent to it. With the first of these, awakening is always and closely connected, so that it is not easy to consider them apart, even in thought. Awakening has its chief reference to the danger which sin has entailed; but this cause of the danger necessarily comes under view in considering the danger itself. The awakening, then, is really an awakening to sin as well as to its danger, although the reference to sin is secondary to the apprehension of the peril it has induced. This apprehension of both may exist on a wide scale of degrees, from mere uneasiness to tragic intensity of feeling; but in all its degrees it is the result of those awakening and partially convictive influences of the Holy Ghost which precede regeneration.[13]

Vaughan correctly states that there is a great difference in the intensity of feeling among those convicted of their sin. Some will be simply annoyed enough to take action and others will be overwhelmed. Yet, the necessity of a true conviction of sin is "because they do not believe in Me" (John 16:9). Whatever degree of conviction that results in fleeing from the wrath to come and exercising saving faith is the work of the Spirit. The Spirit, though, continues to minister to believers after their conversion and continues to convict them of their sin, of the righteousness of Christ, and of the coming judgment. One of the great works of the Holy Spirit is to guide believers into all the truth. That is a promise for all believers—not just the apostles.

Jesus' Death and Resurrection Foretold (John 16:16–22)

Having warned the disciples several times of the events leading to His crucifixion, He now tells them of His coming death and resurrection once more. In John 16:16, He said, "A little, and you will no longer see Me; and again a little while, and you will see Me." Those words were very puzzling to the eleven remaining disciples. They began to

---

13 C. R. Vaughan, *The Gifts of the Holy Spirit* (Edinburgh and Carlisle: The Banner of Truth Trust, 1975), 41.

reason among themselves what Jesus meant by those words, but it was like a darkened parable which they could not interpret. Jesus was aware that they wanted to question Him more closely, so He said: "Truly, truly, I say to you, that you will weep and lament, but the world will rejoice; you will grieve, but your grief will be turned into joy. Whenever a woman is in labor she has pain, because her hour has come; but when she gives birth to the child, she no longer remembers the anguish because of the joy that a child has been born into the world. Therefore you too have grief now; but I will see you again, and your heart will rejoice, and no one *will* take your joy away from you" (John 16:20–22). The pain and agony that the disciples would soon feel would just as quickly be forgotten by their joy at Jesus' resurrection. He would be gone from them for a little while—three days—but then He would rise from the dead and evermore dwell in their hearts through the Holy Spirit (Romans 8:9–11). He would see then again and they would see Him again. Despite Jesus' very plain words, the disciples' eyes were still veiled from the truth. The more distant reference in Jesus' words is to His return which is the hope for all believers, as Ryle explains:

> There is something, even in the hearts of the most eminent saints, that will never be fully satisfied so long as they are on earth and Christ is in heaven. So long as they dwell in a body of corruption, and see through a glass darkly,—so long as they behold creation groaning under the power of sin, and all things not put under Christ,—so long their happiness and peace must be incomplete. This is what Paul meant when he said, "We ourselves, which have the first-fruits of the Spirit, groan within ourselves, waiting for the adoption, to wit, the redemption of the body." (Rom. viii. 23)[14]

Prayer Promises (John 16:23–33)

Having previously taught the disciples a formula to use in praying (Cf. Matthew 6:9–13; Luke 11:2–4), Jesus now encourages them by these words: "Truly, truly, I say to you, if you ask for anything in My name, He will give it to you. Until now you have asked for nothing in My name; ask and you will receive, so that your joy may be made full" (John 16:23b-24). Hitherto, Jesus had not made known to them that prayer was to be offered to the Father in His name. Now He does. This was a step forward in their training as disciples, as Bruce explains:

---

14 Ryle, *Expository Thoughts on the Gospels: John*, 3:168

The time had not yet come for asking anything in Christ's name; they could not fitly or naturally make "Christ's sake" their plea till Christ's work was completed, and He was glorified. But Jesus meant more than this by His remark. He meant to say, what was in fact most true, that hitherto His disciples had been petty, their ideas of what to ask obscure and crude; any wishes of large dimensions they had cherished had been of a worldly character, and therefore such as God could not grant. They had been like children, to whom a penny appears greater than a thousand pounds to a wealthy man. But Jesus hints, though He does not plainly say, that it will be otherwise with the apostles after the advent of the Comforter.[15]

While some would extend Jesus' promises of prayer to those childish, worldly matters which dominate the hearts of the unbelieving and immature, Bruce rightly shows that is not so. True prayer is with the Spirit as the teacher. Then, Jesus explained the words with which He opened this section: "I came forth from the Father and have come into the world; I am leaving the world again and going to the Father" (John 16:28). The disciples finally understood Him and replied: "Lo, now You are speaking plainly and are not using a figure of speech" (John 16:29). In conclusion, Jesus foretold their immediate future: "Behold, an hour is coming, and has *already* come, for you to be scattered, each to his own *home*, and to leave Me alone; and *yet* I am not alone, because the Father is with Me. These things I have spoken to you, so that in Me you may have peace. In the world you have tribulation, but take courage, I have overcome the world" (John 16:32, 33). Earlier that evening, they all had said they would never deny Him, but would fight for Him and with Him. Now, Jesus forewarns them they will all be scattered, so that Jesus would be left alone. A poem describes what Jesus would soon feel. In his hymn, *It Was Alone the Savior Prayed*, Ben H. Price wrote the following:

> It was alone the Savior prayed in dark Gethsemane
> Alone He drained the bitter cup and suffered there for me.
> Alone, alone, He bore it all alone,
> He gave Himself to His own,
> He suffered, bled, and died alone, alone.

---

15 Bruce, *The Training of the Twelve*, 441.

Jesus' High Priestly Prayer (John 17:1–26)

Psalm 109 "discovers to us how the Redeemer was affected by the treachery of Judas."[16] Verse four of that psalm says: "In return for my love they act as my accusers; but I am *in* prayer." It is at Gethsemane[17] on this very night that we get the clearest window into the prayer life of Jesus. Matthew, Mark, and Luke record only a small portion of Jesus' prayers that evening. John 17 gives us the greatest prayer of the Scripture—the only extended prayer of Jesus ever recorded in Scripture. This chapter has become known as Jesus' high priestly prayer. Just as He had been concerned about the disciples in His own hour of greatest need, so He first turned His attention to them in His prayers to the Father. The Scripture paints an unmistakable picture of Jesus' life as a life of prayer. Yet, in this chapter alone do we get a true sight of what His prayer life was really like. In the previous three chapters, Jesus had spoken such comforting, consoling, and instructive truths to His disciples—unparalleled words. He spoke with unbounded freedom after Judas left the others and went into the darkness of the night. Now, our Lord prays the most wonderful prayer—a prayer which reveals to us the kind of communion that Jesus had with His Father while on earth. Only after this prayer, does Jesus pray those better remembered words—"My Father, if it is possible, let this cup pass from Me; yet not as I will, but as You will" (Matthew 26:39).

Jesus' life was already being poured out as a drink offering for His people while He was at Gethsemane. To Peter, James and John, He said, "My soul is deeply grieved, to the point of death; remain here and keep watch with Me" (Matthew 26:38). His heart was in such agony that "He was praying very fervently; and His sweat became like drops of blood, falling down upon the ground" (Luke 22:44). His life was being pressed out of Him as he was experiencing that brokenness of heart that Psalm 69:20 describes—"Reproach has broken my heart and I am so sick. And I looked for sympathy, but there was none, and for comforters, but I found none." Yet, in all of His own travails, Jesus

---

16 George Smeaton, *Christ's Doctrine of the Atonement* (Edinburgh, Scotland and Carlisle, Pennsylvania: The Banner of Truth Trust, 1991), 83.
17 Where Jesus prayed this prayer in John 17 is disputed. John 14:31 indicates that Jesus and His disciples left the Upper Room at that time. John 18:1 indicates that they all came to Gethsemane after this prayer was prayed. It is one of many things in the life of Jesus that cannot be determined exactly.

continually kept His main focus on His disciples and all who would believe in Him through their testimony.

There are a couple of things that stand out immediately about Jesus' prayer in John 17. First, as throughout His whole life, Jesus' prayer expressed no consciousness of sin. He taught His disciples to pray: "And forgive us our debts, as we also have forgiven our debtors" (Matthew 6:12). Yet, Jesus never confessed any wrongdoing—neither at this time nor on any other occasions. So, He was not like the publican in His parable who "was unwilling to lift up his eyes to heaven, but was beating his breast, saying, 'God, be merciful to me, the sinner!'" (Luke 18:13). Second, neither was Jesus like the Pharisee who "stood and was praying this to himself, 'God, I thank You that I am not like other people: swindlers, unjust, adulterers, or even like this tax collector" (Luke 18:11). All other people that have ever lived are in one or the other of those categories. Everyone else is ether begging for mercy from God or they pridefully think they need no forgiveness. Jesus alone was and is in a different category and His high priestly prayer reveals that. He was neither making confession of sin nor was He boasting of His purity while disdainfully viewing others. His prayer was humble while revealing the intimacy between the Father and Himself. Indeed, it is the only extensive prayer of the Scripture in which there is no confession of sin on the part of the petitioner. The Puritan preacher, Robert Traill, said these words about Jesus' prayer:

> Men's hearts are best known by their prayers. And by the same way we may know Christ's heart. Whosoever would know how deeply his heart is concerned in the saving of his people, let them read and believe this prayer. And indeed, unless people do know how Christ's heart stands affected to their salvation, their hearts will never stand well affected towards him, in their employing him for salvation. A clear and strong persuasion of Christ's hearty concern in and about saving of sinners, will make a poor sinner hearty in trusting him with his own salvation.[18]

Never did a man speak "the way this man speaks" (John 7:46) and never did anyone else pray like Jesus did at Gethsemane. While the cares of all the ages were pressing on His heart, He unfolded His affections for His disciples and for His people to His heavenly Father. Only after offering this prayer did Jesus turn His attention to His own sufferings, about which Hebrews 5:7 states: "In the days of His flesh,

---

18 Robert Traill, *The Works of Robert Traill* (Edinburgh, Scotland and Carlisle, PA: The Banner of Truth Trust, 1975), 2:94.

He offered up both prayers and supplications to the One able to save Him from death, and He was heard because of His piety." Jesus' piety breathes as a sweet smelling incense throughout John 17. He prayed first for His own consecration as our great high priest (cf. Leviticus 29:1–9); then, for His disciples; and, finally, for all "those also who believe in Me through their word" (John 17:20). A more beautiful prayer cannot be imagined than this one. Yet, Christ, as our great high priest, continues even now to pray such prayers in heaven for all believers since He "always lives to make intercession for them" (John 17:25). Christ's work as a heavenly intercessor for His people will continue as long as this world remains and until the sun sets for the last time. George Newton sets forth the reasons this prayer is for all Christians of all time:

> So that this prayer of our Saviour Christ, you see, is very full. It is for himself the head of the church, and it is for the church which is his body, of which alone he is the Saviour and Intercessor. It is for the present church, it is for the church to come. It is for the apostles and the ministers, the officers and teachers of the church; and it is for the ordinary members of the church, who believe through their words. So that whoever appertaineth to the church; let him live in what time he will, be of what condition or estate he will, he hath a share in this prayer.[19]

Jesus Prays for His own Consecration (John 17:1–5)

This prayer, the most majestic and beautiful in all of Scripture, breathes a heavenly spirit. Jesus lifted up His eyes to heaven and said, "Father, the hour has come; glorify Your Son, that the Son may glorify You, even as You gave Him authority over all flesh, that to all whom You have given Him, He may give them eternal life" (John 17:1, 2). In petitioning the Father that He would be glorified, Jesus stipulated two things: First, He requested to be glorified so that He could glorify the Father; and, second, He asked that He be able to use His authority over all flesh for the salvation of those given to Him by the Father. His prayer was submissive to His Father's will and was completely devoid of all self-interest and vainglory. As Psalm 40:7, 8 prophesied of the Messiah: "Then I said, 'Behold, I come; in the scroll of the book it is written of me. I delight to do Your will, O my God; Your Law is within my heart.'" Jesus did not ask for great things for Himself only. He asks to be glorified so that He can fulfill the purpose for which He

---

19 George Newton, *An Exposition of John 17* (Edinburgh, Scotland and Carlisle, PA: The Banner of Truth Trust, 1995), 6–7.

came to earth. Thus, He asks His Father to glorify Him in the work of redemption, His death on the cross. Once again, Newton's words are helpful:

> It is true that, to a carnal eye, this was the place of his humiliation; but, to an eye of faith, it was the place of his triumphant exaltation. The world sees nothing but dishonor in the cross of Christ; but they that are enlightened see the great work of man's redemption finished there, sin and his kingdom broken there, and the devil vanquished and led captive there, to Christ's honour, and their eternal ignominy and confusion.[20]

In verse 5 of this prayer, Jesus refers to the "glory which I had with You before the world was." In other places in John, Jesus claimed to be the great "I AM" of Scripture—the One who existed from all eternity. And, John 1:1–3, teaches that Jesus, the Word of God, was "with God, and the Word was God. All things came into being through Him." Jesus had glory in eternity as the eternal God and Creator of the Universe; and, glory on earth, "glory as the only begotten from the Father, full of grace and truth" (John 1:14). Yet, His glory was hidden to most people while He was on earth. Jesus, therefore, prays that the Father would give such glory to Him that He had in eternity through His work on the cross. It is noteworthy that Jesus makes no reference to His own forthcoming sufferings in this prayer. There "is no mention of the cup of suffering, but only of the crown of glory."[21]

Jesus Prays for His Disciples (John 17:6–11)

In John 17:6–19, Jesus especially prays for the disciples whom He has sent into the world. His greatest work of ministry on earth was to train the disciples and empower them to evangelize and write the New Testament. Jesus referred to them as "the men whom You gave Me out of the world; they were Yours and You gave them to Me, and they have kept Your word" (John 17:6). Bruce elucidates Jesus' prayer for the disciples:

> He acknowledges that they were good when He got them . . . He testifies that since they had been with Him they had sustained the character they had when they joined His company . . . And finally, He bears witness that the men whom His Father had given Him had been true believers in Himself, and had received all His words as the very truth of God, and Himself as one sent forth into the world by God. Here, surely, is a generous eulogy on disciples, who, while sincere and devoted

---

20 Newton, *An Exposition of John 17*, 23.
21 Bruce, *The Training of the Twelve*, 450.

to their Master, were, as we know, exceedingly faulty in conduct, and slow to learn.[22]

In His infinite wisdom, Jesus saw His disciples for what they were in their hearts and what He knew they would become. He did not judge them for their petty jealousies, their disputes over which one was the greatest, or even their coming incontinence in fleeing from Him through fear for their lives. They were not yet finished in their preparation to take His words to the nations, but soon they would be. The Holy Spirit, as He had promised, would come to them and He would guide them into all the truth while reminding them of the things Jesus had taught them.

Jesus also referred in His prayer to the disciple who was no longer with them—Judas Iscariot. He said, "I guarded them, and not one of them perished but the son of perdition, so that the Scripture would be fulfilled" (John 17:12). Judas was lost through no failure of Jesus. He was lost because he was the son of perdition. He was lost because he always had been ruled by self-interest more than the will of God.

Later in this section concerning the disciples, Jesus also prays for two other important points. First, He asked His Father to leave them in the world, "but to keep them from the evil one" (John 17:15). It was important that they be left as lights and salt to the world. There was a mission to be accomplished in the establishment of the gospel to all the nations. It would be difficult with many temptations and much suffering. Thus, Jesus also prayed that they would be sanctified in the truth which is the Word of God (John 17:17). What Jesus prayed for His apostles—the sent ones—is necessary also for all ministers and all Christians. Holiness is a necessary prerequisite for the office of a minister and for Christians. As Hebrews 12:14 says, "Pursue peace with all men, and the sanctification without which no one will see the Lord."

Jesus Prays for All Believers (John 17:13–26)

Finally, Jesus prayed for "those who also believe in Me through their word" (John 17:19). Once again, there are two great requests Jesus made for all believers. First, He prayed that true believers will be "perfected in unity" (John 17:23). There will never be true unity among the saints on this earth until the day comes when they cease to be

---

22 Bruce, *The Training of the Twelve*, 455.

"carried about by every wind of doctrine" (Ephesians 4:14) and "all attain to the unity of the truth, and of the knowledge of the Son of God, to a mature man, to the measure of the stature which belongs to the fullness of Christ" (Ephesians 4:13). Jesus did not pray for the visible, external, or mechanical unity of believers, but for their spiritual unity, as Ross declares:

> It is when the Spirit shall be poured out upon us from on high, as the Spirit of truth and love, taking out of the way for ever sinful differences, jealousies, and heart-burnings; producing astonishment, humiliation and shame, at past unfaithfulness and unprofitableness; drawing forth living, loving desires after a holy catholic union; and awakening deep yearnings of soul after a lost and perishing world . . .it is then, and only then, that we may expect the effect here announced to be produced.[23]

The second thing Jesus prayed for all believers is that "they also, whom You have given Me, be with Me where I am, so that they may see My glory which you have given Me, for you loved Me before the foundation of the world" (John 17:24). All true believers "are protected by the power of God through faith for a salvation ready to be revealed in the last time" (1 Peter 1:5). There will not be one true believer who will be missing in the last day because the Good Shepherd gives "eternal life to them, and they will never perish; and no one will snatch them out of [His} hand" (John 10:28). The comfort of all believers is that Christ is stronger than all others and, therefore, not even the evil one can cause a saint to fall unto eternal destruction.

Jesus' Arrest at Gethsemane (Matthew 26:47–56; Mark 14:43–50; Luke 22:47–53; and, John 18:1–11)

In the garden of Gethsemane, Jesus "said to His disciples, 'Sit here until I have prayed.' And He took with Him Peter and James and John, and began to be very distressed and troubled. And He said to them, 'My soul is deeply grieved to the point of death; remain here and keep watch'" (Mark 14:32b-34). There was a sense in which the events of this night were a kind of replaying of what had happened at Jesus' transfiguration on the Mount. Everything was calm and serene when they were in the Upper Room. Now, they have left that place of ease and are in the outside world with the coming crisis at hand. Jesus

---

23 Ross, *The Inner Sanctuary*, 257.

called on the inner circle of His disciples—Peter, James, and John—to watch with Him while He prayed. Persecution was at hand and they needed to be prepared. Temptation was at hand and they needed the spiritual strength that only the Father God could give them. Yet, they all miserably failed as Bruce notes:

> The passages cited describe the part they played in the solemn scenes connected with the Master's end. That part was sadly an unheroic one. Faith love, principle, all gave way before the instincts of fear, shame, and self-preservation. The best of the disciples—the three who, as most reliable, were selected by Jesus to keep Him company in the garden of Gethsemane—utterly failed to render the service expected of them. While their Lord was passing through His agony, they fell asleep, as they had done before on the Mount of Transfiguration. Even the picked men thus proved themselves to be raw recruits, unable to shake off drowsiness while they did duty as sentinels.[24]

Their self-confidence was borne, not of prayerfulness, but of thinking too highly of themselves. Such over-confidence easily slides into fearfulness and a failure to trust in God. Peter, James, and John did not play the role of true sentinels because they were secretly afraid of what awaited them, particularly when they observed the changed attitude of Jesus towards the coming events. If Jesus was "deeply grieved to the point of death"—One whom they had never seen grieved in that way before—then how were they to respond? Before leaving the three disciples alone, He warned them: "Pray that you may not enter into temptation" (Luke 22:40). Jesus then "went a little beyond *them*, and fell to the ground and *began* to pray that if it were possible, the hour might pass Him by" (Mark 14:35). He prayed, "My Father, if it is possible, let this cup pass from Me; yet not as I will, but as You will" (Matthew 26:39b). "Now an angel from heaven appeared to Him, strengthening Him. And being in agony He was praying very fervently; and His sweat became like drops of blood, falling down from the ground. When He rose from prayer, He came to the disciples and found them sleeping from sorrow, and said to them, 'Why are you sleeping? Get up and pray that you may not enter into temptation'" (Luke 22:43–46). Three times Jesus prayed for that cup of God's wrath to be removed from Him, but always in submission to His Father's will.

There were defects in the character of all the disciples at this time.

---

24 Bruce, *The Training of the Twelve*, 464.

The warnings Jesus gave to His inner circle applied to all of them alike. Their breakdown at His moment of crisis was due to a failure to prepare ahead of time, to a lack of prayerfulness, and to unclear perceptions of the truths of the gospel. Their thoughts of the Messiah were still bound up with the false Jewish notions of His kingdom. Thus, they could not really imagine that Jesus would suffer and die—that He would be conquered, even for a little while, by His opponents. All His miracles had convinced them that He was able to overcome any situation. Yet, their imperfect knowledge of their own hearts was their chief problem at this time, as Bruce comments:

> A third radical defect in the character of the disciples was self-ignorance. He who knows his weakness may become strong even at the weak point; but he who knows not his weak points cannot be strong at any point. Now the followers of Jesus did not know their weakness. They credited themselves with an amount of fidelity and valor which existed only in their imagination, all adopting as their own the sentiment of Peter: "Though I should die with Thee, yet I will not deny Thee." Alas! They did not know how much fear of man was in them, how much abject cowardice in presence of danger.[25]

This self-ignorance on the part of all the disciples was the cause of their prayerlessness in their own time of greatest need. Whatever other armor they attempted to put on to prepare for this coming battle, they did not arm themselves with "all prayer and petition pray[ing] at all times in the Spirit" (Ephesians 6:18) as Jesus had modeled for them. If the Messiah, the Son of God, was fervent in prayer, then how could they justify the neglect of such? How could they continue in their prayerlessness after both His warnings and His rebukes of them?

After He finished praying, Jesus went to His disciples and said, "Get up, let us be going; behold, the one who betrays Me is at hand. Immediately, while He was still speaking, Judas, one of the twelve, came up accompanied by a crowd with swords and clubs; who were from the chief priests and the scribes and the elders" (Mark 14:42–3). That crowd included the Roman cohort which normally would have about 600 soldiers, the size of a battalion. They "came there with lanterns and torches and weapons" (John 18:3). There were also many of the Pharisees among them. Judas was leading the whole proces-

---

25 Bruce, *The Training of the Twelve*, 469–70.

sion which, evidently, was his way of informing every one of his own self-perceived greatness. The first thing Judas did was to go to Jesus and kiss Him after saying, "Rabbi" (Mark 14:45). Judas had told the soldiers, "Whomever I kiss, He is the one; seize Him and lead Him away under guard" (Mark 14:44b). Jesus responded to Judas, "Judas, are you betraying the Son of Man with a Kiss?" (Luke 22:48). Then, the Lord stepped towards the soldiers and asked, "'Whom do you seek?' They answered Him, "Jesus the Nazarene." He said to them, 'I am *He*.' And Judas also, who was betraying Him, was standing with them. So when He said to them, 'I am *He*,' they drew back and fell to the ground" (John 18:4–6). The picture of Jesus standing over that large crowd and all those soldiers is one of the most glorious in the Scripture. Jesus claimed once again to be Jehovah God with the words, "I am." Through the miraculous power of the Lord, He caused all those soldiers to fall down at His feet. Ryle describes the scene:

> A secret invisible power, no doubt, accompanied the words. In no other way can we account for a band of hardy soldiers falling prostrate before the voice of a single unarmed man . . . A real miracle was wrought, though few had eyes to see it. At the moment when our Lord seemed weak, He showed that He was strong.
>
> Let us carefully remember that our blessed Lord suffered and died of His own free will. He did not suffer because He could not escape. All the soldiers of Pilate's army could not have taken Him, if He had not been willing to be taken. They could not have hurt a hair on His head, if He had not given them permission.[26]

When the soldiers told Him that they wanted "Jesus the Nazarene," Jesus then demanded that they leave His disciples alone: "I told you that I am He; so if you seek Me, let these go their way" (John 18:8). While the soldiers were still prostrate on the ground, Peter took the opportunity to cut off the ear of a slave named, Malchus, who belonged to the high priest. He, no doubt, thought that the war was starting and He intended to fight on Jesus' side. Jesus told Peter: "Put the sword into the sheath; the cup which the Father has given Me, shall I not drink it?" (John 18:11) "Or do you think that I cannot appeal to My Father, and He will at once put at My disposal more than twelve legions[27] of angels?" (Matthew 26:53). Then, He touched the

---

26 Ryle, *Expository Thoughts on the Gospels: John*, 3:235–6
27 A legion in the Roman army was anywhere between 3,000 to 6,000 soldiers. Twelve legions would have been 36–72,000 soldiers. Such an army of angels would have completely swamped what Pilate and the Jews considered to be an insurmountable force that they had sent to arrest

ear of the slave and restored it immediately. Turning to the crowds, Jesus said, "Have you come out with swords and clubs to arrest Me as you would against a robber? Every day I used to sit in the temple teaching and you did not seize Me. But all this has taken place to fulfill the Scriptures of the prophets" (Matthew 26:55–56a). "But this hour and the power of darkness are yours" (Luke 22:53). With those words, "all the disciples left Him and fled" (Matthew 26:56b). Then, Jesus permitted the soldiers to seize Him and lead Him away.

Having warned them that they would all be scattered when He was arrested, "He expected His disciples to be panic-stricken, just as one should expect sheep to flee on the appearance of a wolf . . . From this leniency, we should infer that, in the view of Jesus, the sin of the disciples was one of infirmity . . . Jesus regarded the eleven men whose attachment to Himself was above suspicion, but who were liable to fall, through the weakness of the flesh, on being exposed to sudden temptation."[28] Their Master did not expect more of them than they were able to give at that time and He also knew what a difference His resurrection and the outpouring of the Holy Spirit would make in their lives.

Jesus.
28 Bruce, *The Training of the Twelve*, 468.

24

Jesus' Arrest and Trial

"We shall confine our present meditation to the state of resignation in which we left our great High Priest, at the close of the last chapter. He yields himself up to his adversaries, and suffers them to act with him as they please; and this very circumstance is for us of the greatest importance. His situation is deeply affecting. Imagine, as might easily have been the case, that immediately after the occurrences at Gethsemane a messenger hastened to Jerusalem to inform his mother Mary of what had befallen her son, outside the gates of the city."[1]

It was now the third watch[2] of the night on Friday evening, April 7th, when Jesus was escorted into the presence of Annas. The Passover Feast had begun at sundown earlier that evening. The Jews had plotted to avoid killing Jesus during the Passover, but their plans had been foiled by God's sovereign will. Jesus was now securely in the custody of the Roman cohort and the officers of the Sanhedrin. He was being led back by the same route He had traveled to the Garden of Gethsemane. His destination now was Annas' palace, a little south of the Upper Room. The tranquil, joyous experiences of Jesus and His disciples in that sacred place were all now behind them. All the agony and sufferings that Jesus had predicted now awaited Him.

"A young man was following Him wearing *nothing* but a linen sheet over his naked *body*; and they seized him. But he pulled free of the linen sheet and escaped naked" (Mark 14:51, 52). Of the disciples, only Peter and John followed the procession back to the Annas' luxurious home "on the slope between the Upper City and Tyropoeon" Valley.[3] Edersheim describes the working relationship between Annas and the Romans:

> His influence with the Romans he owed to the religious views which he professed, to his open partisanship of the foreigner, and to his enormous wealth. The Sadducean Annas was an eminently safe Church-

---

[1] Krummacher, *The Suffering Saviour*, 149.
[2] The third watch of the night is the period between 12 midnight and 3 AM.
[3] The valley or rugged ravine which separated the Temple Mount area from Mount Zion—the western hill—and the Valley of Hinnom, south of the city and outside the walls of it.

man, not troubled with any special convictions nor with Jewish fanaticism, a pleasant and useful man also, who was able to furnish his friends in the praetorium with large sums of money.[4]

Annas' two-story palace of 13,000 square feet—the largest private residence in Israel at that time—had a courtyard and a large reception hall where guests were received and various functions were held. It was to that reception hall that Jesus was led with Peter and John following at a distance. For some reason, John "was known to the high priest, and entered with Jesus into the court of the high priest, but Peter was standing at the door outside. So the other disciple, who was known to the high priest,[5] went out and spoke to the door-keeper, and brought Peter in" (John 18:15–16).[6] Annas was the father-in-law of Caiaphas, who was the high priest that year, and Annas as well had been the high priest in the past. So Annas first questioned Jesus about two things: "about His disciples, and about His teaching" (John 18:19). "Jesus answered him, 'I have spoken openly to the world; I always taught in synagogues and in the temple, where all Jews come together; and I spoke nothing in secret. Why do you question Me? Question those who have heard what I spoke to them; they know what I said'" (John 18:20, 21). That reply was heard by one of the officers standing by and he "struck Jesus, saying, 'Is this the way you answer the high priest?'" (John 18:22). In actual fact, Annas was not still the high priest at that time, but Jesus ignored that point in His reply: "If I have spoken wrongly, testify of the wrong; but if rightly, why do you strike Me?" (John 18:23). The questions of Annas were obviously calculated to see if Jesus was teaching insurrection or if His disciples were going to lead a rebellion. It is likely that the officers of the Sanhedrin and/or the soldiers of the Roman cohort had already informed Annas of Peter's action in cutting off the ear of Malchus. Ryle's comments on the impropriety of an officer striking Jesus are helpful:

> We may learn from this circumstance what a low, degraded, and disorderly condition the Jewish courts of Ecclesiastical law must have been at this period, when such a thing as publicly striking a prisoner could take place, and when violence could be shown to a prisoner in a court of justice for answering boldly for himself. It supplies strong evidence of the miserably fallen state of the whole Jewish nation, when such an

---

4 Edersheim, *The Life and Times of Jesus the Messiah*, 851.
5 Annas was called the high priest in the same sense as former Presidents of the US are called President.
6 Peter was allowed inside the courtyard, but not inside the palace.

act could be done under the watchful eyes of a judge . . . Our Lord's assailant evidently held that a prisoner must never reply to his judge, however unjust or corrupt the judge might be.

Theophylact suggests that the man who struck our Lord was one who had heard our Lord preach,[7] and was anxious to free himself from the suspicion of being one of His friends.[8]

Peter's Denials of Christ (Matthew 26:69–73; Mark 14:66–72; Luke 22:55–6; and, John 18:12–27)

While Jesus was being interrogated inside Annas' home, Peter was standing with the officers and slaves who had built a charcoal fire to warm themselves on that unseasonably cold evening. One of the slave girls said to Peter: "'You are not also one of this man's disciples, are you?' He said, 'I am not.'" (John 18:17). A more detailed account of that exchange is given in Mark where the servant-girl states: "'You also were with Jesus the Nazarene.' But he denied it, saying, 'I neither know nor understand what you are talking about'" (Mark 14:67, 68). This was the first of Peter's denials.[9] Swete describes the situation:

> The first glance revealed the presence of a stranger; closer attention enabled her to recognize Peter. St. John tells us why—she was the portress who at his desire had let Peter in.[10]

Thus, Peter was attempting to deny the obvious for which He should have known better. When Annas was unable to find a charge that would stick against Jesus, He "sent Him bound to Caiaphas the high priest" (John 18:24). The equally magnificent palace of Caiaphas was close to where Annas lived. The whole Sanhedrin met there in a hastily called and illegal meeting in the middle of the night at a residence. It was not permissible for them to conduct ecclesiastical trials there, but they did so anyway. In the courtyard of Caiaphas's house, Peter twice more[11] denied knowing Jesus. An hour passed between the second and third denials, when a man said to Peter, "'Surely you too are one of them; for even the way you talk gives you away.' Then

---

7 Cf. John 7:32, 45–49, ff. The officers sent by the Sanhedrin were mesmerized by the preaching of Jesus. If this officer had been among the number who had been sent to arrest Jesus in John 7—and it is likely that he was—then it would explain why he struck Jesus on this occasion.
8 Ryle, *Expository Thoughts on the Gospels*, 3:266.
9 The order of the denials are not exactly the same in all accounts, but the order of them is irrelevant.
10 Swete, *Commentary on Mark*, 362.
11 Peter's first denial was obviously at Annas' palace and his last denial, at least, was where the Sanhedrin was meeting at Caiaphas' house because immediately afterwards the cock crowed. But his second denial also fits better at Caiaphas's house.

he began to curse and swear, 'I do not know the man!' And Peter remembered the word which Jesus had said, 'Before a rooster crows, you will deny Me three times.'" (Matthew 26:73–75). Peter's cursing was satisfaction enough to convince his questioners that he was not one of Jesus' disciples. Even the world recognizes that Jesus' followers are supposed to be different than that. When the rooster crowed, "the Lord turned and looked at Peter . . . And he went out and wept bitterly" (Luke 22:61a-62).

It might be asked why Peter denied Jesus, but John did not. After all, both had asserted that they were willing to follow Jesus to death. Bruce is undoubtedly correct in his response to that question:

> The difference in conduct between the two disciples corresponded to a difference of their characters. Each acted according to his nature. It is true, indeed, that the circumstances were not the same for both parties, being favorable for one, unfavorable for the other. John had the advantage of a friend at court, being somehow known to the high priest. Peter, on the other hand, not only had no friends at court, but might not unnaturally fear the presence there of personal foes . . .one of the persons who charged Peter with being a disciple of Jesus was a kinsman of the man whose ear Pete had cut off . . .It is therefore every way likely that the consciousness of having committed an offence which might be resented, made Peter anxious to escape identification as one of Christ's disciples . . .
>
> Peter's disposition laid him open to temptation, while John's, on the other hand, was a protection against temptation. Peter was frank and familiar, John was dignified and reserved; Peter's tendency was to be on hail-fellow-well-met terms with everybody, John could keep his own place and make other people keep theirs . . .
>
> To protect himself from inconvenient interrogation by such dignified reserve, is beyond Peter's capacity . . . he is too frank, too familiar, too sensitive to public opinion, without respect to its quality.[12]

Neither Peter nor John had yet attained the spiritual maturity that their status demanded of them. They both needed to grow in grace. "In Peter it would take the form of concentration; in John expansion."[13] Peter did not have enough discretion; John was too aloof at first. Peter needed to become more reserved; John needed to become less reserved. Peter was too impetuous; John, once aroused, too quickly became a son of thunder. Both apostles needed more of the ministry and indwelling of the Holy Spirit in their hearts.

---

12 Bruce, *The Training of the Twelve*, 484–485.
13 Bruce, *The Training of the Twelve*, 486.

The Trial Before the Sanhedrin (Matthew 26:57–68; Mark 14:53–65; and, John 18:12–14)

At the palace of Caiaphas, the whole Council had gathered to conduct this trial of Jesus. All the elders and scribes were there. Both Sadducees and Pharisees were there. "Now the chief priests and the whole Council kept trying to obtain false testimony against Jesus, so that they might put Him to death" (Matthew 26:59). The actual truth was unimportant to the Council because they already knew what they wanted to do to Jesus. They yearned for His death. When the necessary number of witnesses came forward, their testimony was disappointing, contradictory, and frivolous. By this time, morning was already beginning to break and the Council knew that the time was short to accomplish their goal. Jesus had been in their possession for several hours already and they were no closer to a *fait accompli* than they were the previous evening. They could not present Jesus before Pilate on such flimsy evidence. Then, two witnesses came forward who said, "We heard Him say, 'I will destroy this temple made with hands, and in three days I will build another made without hands.' Not even in this respect was their testimony consistent" (Mark 14:58, 59). Certainly, Jesus had uttered some such words when He cleansed the Temple at the Passover Feast in AD 27. Yet, He was referring to His own resurrection—He was not boasting that He Himself would be able to rebuild the Temple in three days. As the Creator of the Universe in six days (Cf. John 1:1–3), He certainly had done much more than the mere erecting of a building. Those words, though, did not give the Council the proof they needed of Jesus' intention to incite insurrection. Such words could not convince Pilate to act for the good of the nation by putting Jesus to death.

There was one person who was not called as a witness and it would seem that he should have been, if there was any legitimacy to their proceedings—that was Judas. Judas knew more about Jesus' activities than anyone else the Sanhedrin could have examined. Yet, his conscious was already troubled. All the events that took place in the garden had, no doubt, made him into a faithless witness for the purposes of the Sanhedrin. "Bad as he was, he could prove nothing against Christ; wicked as he was, he knew well that his Master was holy, harmless, innocent, blameless, and true . . .The absence of Judas Iscariot at our Lord's trial is one among many proofs that the Lamb of God was without blemish,—a sinless man." [14]

At that point, Caiaphas took matters more directly into His own hands. He "stood up and came forward and questioned Jesus, 'Do you not answer? What is it that these men are testifying against You?'" (Mark 14:60). For His part, Jesus "kept silent and did not answer. Again the high priest was questioning Him, and saying to Him, 'Are you the Christ, the Son of the Blessed *One*?'" (Mark 14:61). Caiaphas attempted to extort a confession from Jesus since all other efforts to prove His guilt had failed. Jesus, like a lamb before its shearers, initially remained silent (cf. Isaiah 53:7), but when challenged concerning His divinity, He replied: "I am, and you shall see the Son of Man sitting at the right hand of power, and coming with the clouds of heaven" (Mark 14:62). Of course, Caiaphas had placed Jesus under oath to tell the truth: "I adjure You by the living God, that You tell us whether You are the Christ, the Son of God" (Matthew 26:63). Chamblin well describes the impact of Caiaphas placing Jesus under oath:

> As the chosen witnesses have failed to produce testimony sufficient to convict Jesus, this question is meant to settle the issue before the Sanhedrin. 'If Jesus refuses to answer [as in v. 63a], he breaks a legally imposed oath. If he denies he is the Messiah, the crisis is over—but so is his influence. If he affirms it, then, given the commitments of the court, Jesus must be false. After all, how could the true Messiah allow himself to be imprisoned and put in jeopardy [cf. 16:22]? The gospel's evidence suggests that the Sanhedrin was prepared to see Jesus' unequivocal claim to Messiahship as meriting the death penalty, and their unbelief precluded them from allowing any other possibility.'[15]

Though Caiaphas placed Him under a legal oath, yet it was Jesus who willingly gave to the Sanhedrin the evidence that they were trying to find. It was another proof of what the Lord had said in John 10:17b-18—"I lay down My life so that I may take it again. No one has taken it from Me, but I lay it down on My own initiative. I have authority to lay it down, and I have authority to take it up again. This commandment I received from My Father." The Sanhedrin would have continued to search in vain for proof of some charge against Jesus without ever finding it unless the Lord had confirmed that He is the Son of God. In the end, their only charge against Him was the

---

14 Ryle, *Expository Thoughts on the Gospels: Matthew*, 350.
15 Chamblin, *Matthew*, 2:1346.

very thing that should have brought rejoicing to their hearts—God in the flesh was in their midst. Instead, they responded by condemning Jesus of blasphemy. Caiaphas tore his clothes and said, "'What further need do we have of witnesses? For you have heard the blasphemy; how does it seem to you?' And they all condemned Him to be deserving of death" (Mark 14:63, 64).

After condemning Jesus to death according to Mosaic law—not Roman law—the members of the Sanhedrin "began to spit at Him, and to blindfold Him, and to beat Him with their fists, and to say to Him, 'Prophesy!' And the officers received Him with slaps in the face" (Mark 14:65). Leviticus 24:16 says: "Moreover, the one who blasphemes the name of the Lord shall be put to death; all the congregation shall certainly stone him. The alien as well as the native, when he blasphemes the Name, shall be put to death." Yet, Jesus did not blaspheme the Name of God—He glorified His Father and proved by His mighty works that He truly was the Son of God. Once again, Chamblin guides us in the right direction:

> Moreover, if Jesus' claims are true, then Caiaphas and the Sanhedrin are themselves guilty of the worst possible blasphemy—blasphemy against the Holy Spirit (Matt. 28:19). They directly revile and dishonor the Son of God (cf. Luke 22:65); and in so doing they also blaspheme the Father who sent his Son into the world, and the Spirit who empowered him for service . . . In this assembly, religion both condones and conceals great evil.[16]

The charge brought against Jesus by the Council was actually the sin of which they themselves were guilty. They blasphemed Jesus by considering Him as only a man—despite all the miracles He had performed, including the miracle of healing the ear of Malchus the evening before. Jesus was not a blasphemer—the whole Council was guilty of blasphemy for not believing in Him. It is often true that the false charges the world brings against Jesus and His followers are the things of which they are guilty. The Jews, though, were unable to execute their judgment against Jesus because it was, supposedly, a capital crime. Moreover, their hastily called meeting of the Sanhedrin did not represent a true decision of the Jewish court. "[T]he trial and sentence of Jesus in the palace of Caiaphas would . . . have outraged every principle of Jewish criminal law and procedure. Such causes

---

16 Chamblin, *Matthew*, 2:1352.

could only be tried, and capital sentence pronounced, in the regular meeting place of the Sanhedrin . . .not, as here, in the High Priest's Palace . . .Again, no process could take place on Sabbaths or Feast-days . . ., or even on the eve of them."[17] Thus, the Sanhedrin was in the midst of a great conundrum. This was their opportunity to kill Jesus, but their own laws and their subordination to the Romans did not allow them to take that step at this time. If Jesus was to be crucified, Pilate would have to issue that decree. The Sanhedrin was powerless to move forward without his complicity.

"Now when morning came, all the chief priests and the elders of the people conferred together against Jesus to put Him to death; and they bound Him, and led Him away and delivered Him to Pilate the governor" (Matthew 27:1, 2). This decision by the Sanhedrin was the outworking of the plan that the Council had agreed on after the resurrection of Lazarus just a few weeks earlier.

Judas' Remorse and Suicide (Matthew 27:3–10)

Lurking in the shadows during Jesus' mock trial before the Sanhedrin was that despicable character, Judas Iscariot. When Judas "saw that He had been condemned, he felt remorse and returned the thirty pieces of silver to the chief priests and elders" (Matthew 27:3). What did Judas expect was going to happen when he betrayed the Son of Man into the hands of the Roman cohort and the officers from the Sanhedrin? As Chamblin notes:

> If Judas was a fervent nationalist who sought to force Jesus into becoming a warrior-messiah, his present action reflects profound disenchantment with that supposed way of salvation, or at least deep regret that the innocent Jesus has become a pawn in a political struggle.[18]

Judas was "a double-minded man, unstable in all his ways" (James 1:8). Only hours before, he had declared his loyalty to Jesus in the presence of all the apostles. Then, he led the armed posse to arrest the Lord at Gethsemane. Now, he is once again full of conflicts as he has viewed the unfolding events and witnessed the Sanhedrin declare Jesus to be a blasphemer worthy of death. The chief priests had no such doubts. They were full of hypocrisy, but they were united in their hearts that Jesus had to die. Thus, they "show not the slightest awareness that they have sinned by taking this money from the

---

17 Edersheim, *The Life and Times of Jesus the Messiah*, 858.
18 Chamblin, *Matthew*, 2:1365.

temple treasury to secure the arrest and execution of Jesus."[19] Judas had spent too much time in the presence of the Son of God to be unaware of the hypocrisy of his own heart. Thus, he tried in vain to return the money to the chief priests. Under a hypocritical guise, they refused to accept the money, saying, "What is that to us? See *to that* yourself!" (Matthew 27:4). The chief priests were against putting that money back into the temple treasury, asserting that it was "the price of blood" (Matthew 27:6). Why was that blood money to them? It was the Sanhedrin that had contracted with Judas to betray Jesus and took the money out of the Temple treasury. If those thirty pieces of silver had become blood money, they were blood money when they were counted out to pay the son of perdition. Judas then threw the silver into the area of the temple courts where only the priests were allowed to be and went out and hanged himself.

The exact order of what happened next, and when, cannot be known for certain. It is unlikely that the chief priests would have taken the thirty pieces of silver and bought the Potter's Field during the Passover Feast, but Acts 1:18, 19 clearly indicates that a field, Hakeldema or Field of Blood, was bought with that money and Judas died there. Hakeldema was "a useless clay-bed outside the city walls,"[20] south-southwest of the Old City of Jerusalem across the Valley of Hinnom which fulfilled several prophecies of Scripture. Psalm 69:25 prophesied that no one would dwell there and Matthew 27:7 says that it became "a burial place for strangers." Strangers is a reference to the Gentiles who would be visiting Jerusalem. Their burial place would be where Judas killed himself. As Chamblin wrote: "unclean money buys an unclean place."[21]

The difference between Peter and Judas is underscored by the way they both dealt with their sins. Peter repented. Judas was remorseful, but only remorseful. He declared to the chief priests, "I have sinned by betraying innocent blood" (Matthew 27:4). But he never truly repented. Instead, his life seemed hopeless to him and he ended it. At that field bought with the blood money, he hung himself, fell "headlong . . .burst open in the middle and his intestines gushed out" (Acts 1:18). No doubt, his body became prey to the wild animals and the birds of the air. Ryle's comments are apt and important:

---

19 Chamblin, *Matthew*, 2:1369.
20 Shepard, *The Christ of the Gospels*, 581.
21 Chamblin, *Matthew*, 2:1370.

It is a common saying, "that it is never too late to repent." That saying, no doubt, is true, if repentance is true.; but unhappily, late repentance is often not genuine. It is possible for a man to feel his sins, and be sorry for them,—to be under strong convictions of guilt, and express deep remorse,—to be pricked in conscience, and exhibit much distress of mind,—and yet for all this, not repent with his heart. Present danger, or the fear of death, may account for all his feelings, and the Holy Ghost may have done no work whatever on his soul.[22]

Judas was sorry for the consequences of his sins. He was remorseful at the sight of Jesus being handed over to Pilate, but his first thought was the effect that his actions had on himself. He did not mourn for Jesus. He certainly did not mourn "as one mourns for an only son" (Zechariah 12:10). Nor, did he look on Jesus as One whom his sins had pierced and caused to suffer. If he had looked at Jesus with the eye of faith, he would have truly repented. His feelings were neither faith nor repentance. "It was despair, and his a desperate resolve."[23] Those who had enticed him to sin were no comfort to his pained, guilty conscience. "They turned from him in impatience, in contempt, as so often the seducer turns from the seduced—and, God help such, with the same fiendish guilt of hell."[24] Thus, having betrayed innocent blood and being unwilling to repent, Judas had nowhere to go except into the darkness. Passover was the feast that proclaimed God's grace in passing over sins through the sacrifice of the Paschal Lamb, but for Judas that Passover was the most hopeless and helpless of times.

Jesus Before Pilate (Matthew 27:1–14; Mark 15:2–5; Luke 23:2, 3; and John 18:29–38)

The residence of Pilate was the beautiful marble palace erected by Herod the Great from 37 to 4 BC. It was well-guarded with soldiers and "became the property of the State . . . Roman Procurators resided there, and took their seats in front of the Palace on a raised pavement to pronounce judgment . . .Pilate, especially as he was accompanied by his wife, resided there also."[25] A description of the splendor and magnificence of that building is given by Josephus:

> [T]he king had a palace thereto adjoined, which exceeds all my ability to describe it; for it was very curious as to want no cost or skill in its construction, but was entirely walled about to the height of thirty cu-

---

22 Ryle, *Expository Thoughts on the Gospels: Matthew*, 380-1.
23 Edersheim, *The Life and Times of Jesus the Messiah*, 870.
24 Edersheim, *The Life and Times of Jesus the Messiah*, 870.
25 Edersheim, *The Life and Times of Jesus the Messiah*, 864, fn. 4.

bits, and was adorned with towers at equal distances, and with large bed-chambers, that would contain beds for a hundred guests a-piece, in which the variety of the stones is not to be expressed; for a large quantity of those that were rare of that kind were collected together.[26]

The bed-chambers had furniture made of gold and marble with walls of great height. Each room was given a different name, especially in recognition of other kings and governors.[27] Jesus, the Son of Man, who had no place to lay His head, was then bound and led away to that magnificent palace. The contrast between the opulence of Pilate and the other-worldly spirituality of Jesus could not have been more stark. The chief priests were anxious and impatient to have the problem of the Galilean resolved. "There was no time to be lost; the Feast had begun (cf. xiv. 2), and the multitudes would presently assemble; they must place the Lord in the hands of the Procurator before a rescue could be attempted."[28] The whole affair had to be managed very carefully.

The chief priests presented Jesus to Pilate while being careful not to enter his palace—which would have made them ceremonially unclean until sundown and would have prevented them from eating the Passover. At that early hour of the morning shortly after dawn, Pilate simply demanded of these Jews: "What accusation do you bring against this Man?" (John 18:29). Their response to him was: "If this Man were not an evildoer, we would not have delivered Him to you" (John 18:30). Yet, that was exactly the question at hand which the Jews were unable to establish. Jesus was not an evil-doer and their illegal show trial had failed to even justify a single accusation that was levied against Him. Pilate, who was reluctant to do anything about Jesus, replied to the Jews: "Take Him yourselves and judge Him according to your law" (John 18:31a). In reply, the Jews said, "We are not permitted to put anyone to death" (John 18:31b). The chief priests were now in a desperate position, so they responded with emotional energy. "And they began to accuse Him, saying, 'We found this man misleading our nation and forbidding to pay taxes to Caesar, and saying that He himself is Christ'" (Luke 23:2). Of course, the Sanhedrin had found no evidence to accuse Jesus of either of the first two charges or several others, but they made up for that deficiency by accusing Him harshly (Cf. Mark 15:3) in the presence of Pilate. Their intense urgency was

---

26 Josephus, *Complete Works of Flavius Josephus*, 553–4.
27 Josephus, *Complete Works of Flavius Josephus*, 330–331.
28 Swete, *Commentary on Mark*, 367.

a cover for their want of substantive charges. They put forward the charges of "misleading the nation" and "forbidding to pay taxes" as those that would appeal most to Pilate, while the last charge was the only one according to their laws which demanded the death penalty. Pilate, for his part, questioned Jesus about the charge of Him being the Messiah: "Are You the King of the Jews?" (Mark 15:2a). Jesus replied, "*It is as* you say" (Mark 15:2b). "Then Pilate said to the chief priests and the crowds, 'I find no guilt in this man.' But they kept on insisting, saying, 'He stirs up the people, teaching all over Judea, starting from Galilee even as far as this place.'" (Luke 23:4, 5).

Jesus Before Herod (Luke 23:6–12)

Pilate then sensed an opening to rid himself of this problem and "asked whether this man was a Galilean. And when he learned that He belonged to Herod's jurisdiction, he sent him to Herod, who himself also was in Jerusalem at that time. Now Herod was very glad when he saw Jesus; for he had wanted to see Him for a long time, because he had been hearing about Him and was hoping to see some sign performed by Him" (Luke 23:7, 8). That decision by Pilate was not what the Sanhedrin had desired when they mentioned Jesus supposedly inciting riots in Galilee, as Hendriksen commented:

> The accusers must have regarded their remark that Jesus was a man from Galilee as being a *coup de maître* (master stroke). Was not Galilee always the very hotbed of revolution?[29]

Yet, the Sanhedrin was temporarily defeated in their desire to get the case of Jesus wrapped up quickly. Pilate's decision to send the Galilean to Herod meant that He had to be transported in broad daylight through the streets of Jerusalem to the Hasmonean palace where Herod resided. The Praetorium where Pilate resided was in the lower part of the city whereas the Hasmonean palace was on the Western side of the Upper City. There was risk that the sight of Jesus being escorted through the city in bonds by Roman soldiers could spark a revolt, the very thing the Sanhedrin did not want. The Hasmonean palace sat on a promontory in front of the Temple and just north of the modern Jewish quarter. Worshipers from all over Israel would soon be gathering there on this great day of the Feast. They had heard Jesus teach in the temple courts several days that week already. Thus, the chief priests had to be concerned and anxious when Pilate sent Him to Herod.

---

29 Hendriksen, *Exposition of the Gospel According to St. Luke*, 1010.

Herod, though, could not have been more pleased. That wicked king had entertained John the Baptist—who was a faithful reformer and preacher—on many occasions, but now Herod had Jesus—who had performed so many miracles. He anxiously wanted to see some such sign from Jesus. Yet, the Lord did not perform miracles to astound onlookers and, thus, He did no miracles for Herod. That must have been displeasing to wicked, impenitent Antipas. Hendriksen well describes what happened next:

> Though Jesus did not perform any miracle in the presence of Herod, the latter seems to have thought that the captive would at least talk to him, would certainly answer his questions. But he did not, not at all. This is significant. To be sure, other silences on the part of our Savior are also reported. There was a time when he was silent before Caiaphas (Mark 14:60, 61), before Pilate (Mark 15:4, 5), and again before Pilate (John 19:9b). But those silences were balanced by testimonies. In the case of Herod it was different. *He* never heard Jesus say anything at all! This man had had his full opportunity. He had been talked to and reasoned with again and again (Mark 6:20). But he had ignored all these warnings. And even now his only interest in Jesus was that born of perverse, contemptuous curiosity. He received no answer and deserved none.[30]

Such a tyrant as Herod with such a wicked wife as Herodias did not take kindly to being ignored or treated as irrelevant. The crown sat very lightly on his head and he probably chafed at the thought that Pilate now occupied the throne where his father previously had reigned. Would this Galilean who had fallen into his hands through an unusual situation completely ignore him? John had boldly denounced his sin, but the forerunner did not ignore Herod. Yet, what had such politeness gotten John? His head was still severed and delivered on a platter to a feasting party of Herod's sycophants. There was nothing that Jesus needed to say to Herod. Our Lord knew Antipas to be a wicked, wily fox, so "He did not open His mouth," but was, once again, "like a lamb that is silent before its shearers" (Isaiah 53:7). Moreover, Herod would not make the final decision in this matter. Jesus knew, as He had foretold His disciples, that the Son of Man would be handed over "to the Gentiles to mock and scourge and crucify" (Matthew 20:19).

After pummeling Jesus for some time with many questions which received nary a word of reply by the Lord, Herod's patience wore thin

---

30 Hendriksen, *Exposition of the Gospel According to St. Luke*, 1012.

and the real feelings of his heart were directed towards Jesus with the utmost contempt. The chief priests were also there "accusing Him vehemently" (Luke 23:10), but Jesus remained silent. That was more than the wily, despotic ruler could stand. "Herod with his soldiers, after treating Him with contempt and mocking Him, dressed him in a gorgeous robe and sent Him back to Pilate" (Luke 23:11). What Herod's soldiers did to Jesus, Pilate's would do also and even more. The real character of Herod is described by F. W. Krummacher:

> But what a depth of inward corruption is betrayed in the fact that this man, in spite of his conviction of the Saviour's ability to perform divine acts, not only refuses his belief and homage, but even degrades him to the state of an object of scorn![31]

Jesus Before Pilate Again (John 18:33–40)

As often happens with enemies, Herod and Pilate became friends that day, even if for only a short while, due to their conspiracy against God's Anointed One. As Psalm 2:2 states: "The kings of the earth take their stand and the rulers take counsel together against the Lord and against His Anointed." Both before and after Jesus' crucifixion, the kings of the earth have fulfilled this psalm, but it was never fulfilled more completely than through this terrible conspiracy between Herod and Pilate. The best commentary on Psalm 2:2 is found in Acts 4:25–28. The early church gathered together and with one accord prayed these words after Peter and John were released from prison: "For truly in this city were gathered together against Your holy servant Jesus, whom You anointed, both Herod and Pontius Pilate, along with the Gentiles and the peoples of Israel, to do whatever Your hand and Your purpose predestined to occur."

Once again, Jesus was led in bonds from the Upper City to the Lower City through the same narrow streets of Jerusalem, past crowds of worshipers who were headed to the Temple grounds, and back to where He had started. Time was moving on rapidly and still no charge had proved Jesus to be worthy of death—the very thing the chief priests insisted that Pilate do concerning Jesus. After summoning the chief priests and rulers to return to the Praetorium, Pilate once again questioned Jesus, asking: "'Are you the King of the Jews?' Jesus answered, 'Are you saying this on your own initiative, or did others tell you about Me?' Pilate answered, 'I am not a Jew, am I? Your own nation and the

---

31 Krummacher, *The Suffering Saviour*, 276-7.

chief priests delivered You to me; what have you done?' Jesus answered, 'My kingdom is not this world. If My kingdom were of this world, then My servants would be fighting so that I would not be handed over to the Jews; but as it is, My kingdom is not of this realm.' Therefore Pilate said to Him, 'So You are a king?' Jesus answered, 'You say correctly that I am a king. For this I have been born into the world, to testify to the truth. Everyone who is of the truth hears My voice.' Pilate said to Him, 'What is truth?'" (John 18:33b-38). Pilate did not wait for the answer to his last question and, thus, Jesus did not reply.

When the officials from the Sanhedrin arrived, Pilate went out of the Praetorium and said to them: "You brought this man to me as one who incites the people to rebellion, and behold, having examined Him before you, I have found no guilt in this man regarding the charges which you make against Him. No, nor has Herod, for he sent Him back to us; and behold, nothing deserving death has been done by Him. Therefore, I will punish and release Him" (Luke 23:14–16). Now, there was a custom that the governor or king would release one prisoner at Passover. "A that time they were holding a notorious prisoner, called Barabbas. So when the people gathered together, Pilate said to them, 'Whom do you want me to release for you? Barabbas, or Jesus who is called Christ?'" (Matthew 27:16, 17). Pilate was aware that Jesus had been delivered to him by the Jews "because of envy" (Matthew 27:18), but he was sitting on his judgment seat awaiting their reply when he received a message from his wife: "Have nothing to do with that righteous Man; for last night I suffered greatly in a dream because of Him" (Matthew 27:19). Meanwhile, the chief priests and elders were busy persuading "the crowds to ask for Barabbas and to put Jesus to death" (Matthew 27:20). Pilate's wife, a Gentile, appealed to him to not condemn Jesus; meanwhile, the Jews were working feverishly to persuade the crowds to ask for Barabbas to be released. The hypocrisy of the position of the priests cannot be overlooked, as Chamblin notes:

> While they present Jesus to Pilate as a serious threat to political and social stability, the chief priests and the elders now persuade the crowd to ask for the release of an insurrectionist and murderer. Given their Jewish audience, and the course of the proceedings reported in 26:57–68, we may judge that the authorities press their case by portraying Jesus as a blasphemer against God, a law-breaker and a Messianic pretender of the worst sort.[32]

---

32 Chamblin, *Matthew*, 2:1382.

Jesus Scourged, Robed, and Crowned (Matthew 27:27–30; Mark 15:16–19; and. John 19:1–11)

While the mock trial was ongoing, Pilate had Jesus scourged. Edersheim's suggestions concerning Pilate's scourging of Jesus are instructive:

> Pilate seems to have hoped that the horrors of the scourging might move the people to desist from the ferocious cry for the Cross . . . the scourge of leather thongs was loaded with lead, or armed with spikes and bones, which lacerated back, and chest, and face, till the victim sometimes fell down before the judge a bleeding mass of torn flesh . . . scourging was the terrible introduction to crucifixion—'the intermediate death.' Stripped of His clothes, His hands tied and back bent, the Victim would be bound to a column or stake, in front of the Praetorium. The scourging ended, the soldiery would hastily cast upon Him His upper garments, and lead Him back into the Praetorium. Here they called the whole cohort together, and the silent, faint Sufferer became the object of their ribald jesting.[33]

Pilate made one last effort to spare Jesus when he asked Him: "Where are you from?" Jesus, at first, remained silent. Then, Pilate said to Him: "You do not speak to me? Do You not realize that I have authority to release You, and I have authority to crucify You?" (John 19:10). Coming from a ruler who had just had Him scourged, Pilate's words were of little comfort. Thus, Jesus answered, "You would have no authority over Me, unless it had been given to you from above; for this reason he who delivered Me to you has *the* greater sin" (John 19:11). Ryle's description of the moral weakness of Pilate is enlightening:

> We see a Roman governor,—a man of rank and high position,—an imperial representative of the most powerful nation on earth,—a man who ought to have been the fountain of justice and equity,—halting between two opinions in a case as clear as the sun at noon-day. We see him knowing what was right, and yet afraid to act up to his knowledge,—convinced in his own conscience that he ought to acquit the prisoner before him, and yet afraid to do it lest he should displease His accusers,—sacrificing the claims of justice to the base fear of man,—sanctioning, from sheer cowardice, an enormous crime,—and finally, countenancing, from love of man's good opinion, the murder of an innocent person.[34]

---

33 Edersheim, *The Life and Times of Jesus the Messiah*, 873.
34 Ryle, *Expository Thoughts on the Gospels: St. John*, 3:300.

Even with respect to the scourging, Pilate and the chief priests were unwittingly fulfilling prophecy concerning the Messiah: "I gave My back to those who strike Me, and My cheek to those who pluck out the beard; I did not cover My face from humiliation and spitting" (Isaiah 50:6). Pilate's soldiers stripped Jesus of His clothing; twisted together a crown of thorns that they drove into His head; placed a reed in His right hand to symbolize a royal scepter; put a purple robe on Him; slapped Him in the face; spat on Him; hit Him on the head with a reed; and, mockingly fell down on their knees, saying, "Hail, King of the Jews!" (Matthew 27:29). Then, Pilate brought Jesus out to them, saying: "Behold, I am bringing Him out to you so that you may know that I find no guilt in Him" (John 19:4). When Jesus was led out wearing the crown of thorns and the purple robe, Pilate said to the Jews: "Behold, the Man!" (John 19:5). "So when the chief priests and the officers saw Him, they cried out, "Crucify, crucify!" (John 19:6a). Pilate, in response, said, "Take Him yourselves and crucify Him, for I find no guilt in Him" (John 19:6b). At that point, the Jews replied to Pilate, saying: "We have a law, and by that law He ought to die because He made Himself out *to be* the Son of God" (John 19:7). That was the conundrum for the chief priests and officers. They wanted Pilate to crucify Jesus for matters that were not offenses under Roman law.

Thus, the chief priests and elders were emphasizing to the crowds the things that were immaterial to Roman law, but highly important under Jewish law. Though Pilate was no friend of the Jews, he was also on unsteady ground with the them and could not afford an uprising any more than the Sanhedrin could. Neither side wanted Rome to take control of a situation which had spiraled out of control. In that scenario, the priests and elders actually had more leverage than Pilate—if only they could persuade the crowds to ask for Barabbas. Pilate's weak will was displayed by his refusal to listen to his wife's warning. He wanted to release Jesus, "but the Jews cried out saying, 'If you release this Man, you are no friend of Caesar; everyone who makes himself out to be a king opposes Caesar'" (John 19:12b). At those words, Pilate "brought Jesus out, and sat down on the judgment seat at a place called the Pavement . . . And he said to the Jews, 'Behold, your King!'" (John 19:13–14). When the crowds were asked who they wanted to be released, they said: "Away with this man, and release for us Barabbas" (Luke 23:18). Pilate was surprised and flummoxed by their response as they kept crying out concerning Jesus: "Crucify, crucify Him!" (Luke 23:21). Pilate asked: "Why, what evil has this man done? I have found in Him no guilt demanding death; therefore I will punish Him and release Him" (Luke 23:22). But the crowd was "insistent, with loud voices asking that He be crucified. And their voices began to prevail" (Luke 23:23). Pilate asked them, "Shall I crucify your King?'" and the "chief priests answered, 'We have no king but Caesar'" (John 19:15). Of course, the chief priests were being hypocritical with those words. Jehovah God was their one true King according to their profession, though not in reality. Moreover, they chafed at the rule of the Romans in their land which was supposed to be a theocracy. "When Pilate saw that he was accomplishing nothing, but rather that a riot was starting, he took water and washed his hands in front of the crowds, saying, 'I am innocent of this Man's blood; see *to that* yourselves.' And all the people said, 'His blood shall be on us and on our children!'" (Matthew 27:25).

Pilate could have refused to release Barabbas for cause since he was a robber, an insurrectionist, and a murderer. Instead, he released a criminal and punished a righteous Man. Yet, Rome tried to accede to the laws of the lands where they governed in every way that they could without surrendering their civil authority over those countries. Thus, Jesus' trial ended with Pilate giving into the wishes of the chief priests and the crowd. Such cowardice, such double-mindedness, such instability were the weaknesses of that governor. The trial ended without a true judgment. Pilate failed to adjudicate the matter before him, but allowed the crucifixion to go forward just the same. Neither the witnesses before the Sanhedrin, nor Pilate, nor Herod could prove that Jesus had committed a crime. Pilate had declared: "I find no guilt in Him!" Yet, Jesus was now to be numbered with the transgressors. The Lord of glory would suffer, the just for the unjust, the ignominy of being crucified. Krummacher summarizes what ultimately caused Pilate to concede the matter to the chief priests:

> The outcry hit the governor's weakest and most vulnerable side. He knew his master, the Emperor Tiberius, too well, not to foresee that an accusation like that which had just been raised against him, if it

reached his ear, would find only too strong a response in his suspicious mind, and would cost him, the governor, his office, and who knows what beside. He, therefore, felt assured that the emperor who, as we are informed by a contemporary writer, regarded the crime of *leze majesty*[35] as the highest of all accusations, would, without previous inquiry, pronounce the severest sentence upon him so soon as he should be informed that his viceroy had set a man at liberty who had attempted to claim the title of king over Israel.[36]

---

35 A French phrase which means the insulting of a monarch or other ruler.
36 Krummacher, *The Suffering Saviour*, 320.

25

Jesus' Crucifixion

"But his crucifixion, and the whole of his sufferings from wicked men, cannot give us a just idea of what he endured for us. Grievous as they were, considered in themselves they were light if compared with the agonies of his soul. These extorted the blood from his body, before the hand of man touched him. And when he uttered his most dolorous cry upon the cross, it was not for anguish of his bodily wounds, but his soul felt, for a season, a separation from the presence and comforts of God."[1]

The Via Dolorosa—or, "the sorrowful way"—is the name of the route that Jesus would have taken from where He was tried before Pilate to Golgotha, the place of His crucifixion. Many Christians mark that route from the Antonia Fortress[2] through the Old City of Jerusalem to the Church of the Sepulchre—which, supposedly, encloses both Golgotha and the tomb where Jesus was laid. Of course, the Antonia Fortress was located north of the Temple Mount where it strategically overlooked the Temple courts. Yet, there is no evidence that Jesus was tried at the Antonia Fortress—nor that He began His journey to Calvary from that fortress. Jesus was tried and condemned to crucifixion at the Praetorium in Pilate's residence, southwest of the Antonia Fortress, near to the Tower of David. With that being the case—and we believe it is—then the Via Dolorosa for Jesus was a different route altogether than the traditional route. Normally, Roman law allowed a convicted criminal to have up to ten days before his execution, but Jesus was escorted to His crucifixion immediately after the judgment was pronounced.

Where was Golgotha? Many scholars fix on a different site than the Church of the Sepulchre. Edersheim, for example, rejects the traditional site for Golgotha with these words:

> We cannot here explain the various reasons for which the traditional site must be abandoned. Certain it is, that Golgotha was 'outside the

---

1 Newton, *The Works of John Newton*, 4:223.
2 Herod the Great named that fortress after Mark Antony and the chief function of it was to guard the Temple.

gate' (Heb. 13:13), and 'near the City' (John 19:20). In all likelihood it was the usual place of execution. Lastly, we know that it was situated near gardens, where there were tombs, and close to the highway. The three last conditions point to the north of Jerusalem . . . Here the great highway passed northwards; close by, were villas and gardens; and here also rockhewn sepulchres have been discovered, which date from that period . . .And the description of the locality answers all requirements. It is a weird, dreary place, two or three minutes aside from the high road, with a high, rounded skull like plateau, and a sudden depression or hollow beneath, as if the jaws of the skull had opened.[3]

Thus, the route of the Via Dolorosa may well have taken Jesus from the southwest part of the Old City to a spot due north and outside the City walls, through the crowded streets and past closed shops. "The procession was composed of a great multitude, embracing the High Priests and their servants, who would want to witness the end of their enemy and victim; the crowd of the street rabble and the merely curious spectators; the two malefactors, also bearing their crosses; all proceeded by the centurion in charge of the bloody business, with four soldier-guards detached for each prisoner. None of the disciples were present except John, who records the fact that Jesus started out on the Via Dolorosa to Golgotha 'bearing the cross for Himself.'"[4]

Jesus quickly gave out of strength and the soldiers "seized a man, Simon of Cyrene, coming in from the country, and placed on him the cross[5] to carry behind Jesus. There were several reasons for Jesus' weakness, as Dr. Mark Eastman has written: "Jesus had not drunk since the night before, so the combination of the beatings, the crown of thorns, and the scourging would have set into motion an irreversible process of severe dehydration and cardiorespiratory failure. All of this was done so that the prophecy of Isaiah would be fulfilled: 'I gave my back to the smiters, and my cheeks to them that plucked of the hair; I hid not my face from shame and spitting.' Isaiah 50:6.'"[6]

---

3 Edersheim, *The Life and Times of Jesus the Messiah*, 877. J. W. Shepard in *The Christ of the Gospels* agrees with Edersheim. Andrew Bonar agrees with that location for Calvary.
4 Shepard, *The Christ of the Gospels*, 593–4.
5 All the criminals were required to carry was the cross piece, which weighed 75 pounds, on which his hands would be nailed—not the post that was permanently fixed into the ground. Yet, Jesus had suffered so greatly that even that cross piece was far too much for Him.
6 Mark Eastman, "The Agony of Love: Medical Aspects of the Crucifixion," accessed at www.khouse.org on June 14, 2024.

The Via Dolorosa and the Daughters of Jerusalem

Following Jesus was a large crowd of people and many women who were mourning and lamenting Him. These "daughters of Jerusalem" were the professional mourners whose job was to lament and wail at funeral processions and whenever criminals were crucified. These women had no special relationship with Jesus. They were simply carrying out their duties. So Jesus turned to them, saying: "Daughters of Jerusalem, stop weeping for Me, but weep for yourselves and your children. For behold, the days are coming when they will say, 'Blessed are the barren, and the wombs that never bore, and the breasts that never nursed.' Then they will begin to say to the mountains, 'Fall on us,' and to the hills, 'Cover us.' For if they do these things when the tree is green, what will happen when it is dry?" (Luke 23:26–31). Jesus' kindly rebuke of these "daughters of Jerusalem" is explained by Edersheim:

> [M]ere sympathy with Christ almost involves guilt, since it implies a view of Him which is essentially the opposite of that which His claims demand. These tears were the emblem of that modern sentiment about the Christ which, in its effusiveness, offers insult rather than homage, and implies rejection rather the acknowledgement of Him . . . all mere sentimentalism is here the outcome of unconsciousness of our real condition. When a sense of sin has been awakened in us, we shall mourn, not for what Christ has suffered, but for what He suffered for us. The effusiveness of mere sentiment is impertinence or folly: impertinence, if He was the Son of God; folly, if He was mere Man.[7]

When they arrived at Golgotha, Jesus was to be crucified between two notorious thieves "and the middle cross was assigned Him as the vilest of the three."[8] It was about 9 AM, the third hour of the day, when Jesus was finally nailed to the cross bar and lifted up. The Romans did not invent crucifixion, but they became the masters of using it effectively. Crucifixion caused such terrible suffering and pain that a new word to describe it was invented—excruciating, "out of crucifixion." By the time that Jesus arrived at Golgotha, His body was already in irreversible death throes. His journey to Calvary was, perhaps, as much as a mile.[9] James Stalker describes what this spot represents:

---

7 Edersheim, *The Life and Times of Jesus the Messiah*, 876.
8 John Brown, *Expository Discourses on 1 Peter* (Edinburgh, Scotland and Carlisle, PA: The Banner of Truth Trust, 1975), 2:137.
9 Mark 15:22 says, "Then they brought Him to the place Golgotha, which is translated, Place of a Skull." The verb translated as 'brought' can indicate that they gave Him support in going to Golgotha. Or, it may simply mean that they led Him to Golgotha.

This spot to which we have come is the centre of all things. Here two eternities meet. The streams of ancient history converge here, and here the river of modern history takes its rise. The eyes of patriarchs and prophets strained forward to Calvary; and now the eyes of all generations and of all races look back to it. This is the end of all roads. The seeker after truth, who has explored the realms of knowledge, comes to Calvary and finds at last that he has reached centre. The weary heart of man, that has wandered the world over in search of perfect sympathy and love, at last arrives here and finds rest.[10]

Jesus' Horrific Suffering (Matthew 27:33–44; Mark 15:22–32; Luke 23:33–43; and, John 19:17–24)

Crucifixion was first invented by the Persians and was brought back to Europe by Alexander the Great in the 4th century BC. The Persians executed their enemies by impaling them on a sharpened pole where the victims hung until they expired. Wicked Haman, in his jealousy and enmity towards Mordecai, a Jew, erected a "gallows fifty cubits high" (Esther 5:14) on which he hoped that righteous man would be executed.[11] Behind Haman was the devil and the intended crucifixion of Mordecai had its object in attempting to thwart the promise of God that the Messiah would come from the tribe of Judah. Additionally, Haman had already received permission from King Ahasuerus to exterminate all the Jews throughout the 127 provinces under his reign from India to Ethiopia. Crucifixion, in the plans of the devil, had its ultimate aim against Jesus—both in an attempt to prevent His birth and now to end His life. As Revelation 12:4 says concerning the red dragon at the birth of the Christ child: "And the dragon stood before the woman who was about to give birth, so that when she gave birth he might devour her child." Ever since Yahweh cursed the serpent in the Garden of Eden, that wicked fiend has known that his great battle was with the seed of the woman—the Son of God—and that his only hope was to defeat Him. It was fitting, therefore, that Jesus would suffer for the sins of the world according to the worst form of punishment ever imagined. The Romans further developed the practice of crucifixion and used it in punishing malefactors as a warning to others. Thus, their crucifixions were at places where people would

---

10 James Stalker, *The Trial and Death of Jesus Christ* (New York: A. C. Armstrong and Son, 1894), 157-8.
11 McClintock and Strong, *Cyclopedia of Biblical, Theological, and Ecclesiastical Lit*erature, 2:588. In an article on "Crucifixion," Esther 7:10 is referenced concerning the Persians which points to the 'gallows' or, more accurately, the tree Haman had prepared for impaling Mordecai.

readily observe the criminals. Golgotha, or the 'Place of the Skull,'[12] was at the convergence of the roads on the north and west sides of old Jerusalem. Many travelers to and from this Passover would have observed Jesus hanging on the cross. Eastman describes how the victims were nailed to the cross:

> The victim was then placed on his back, arms stretched out and nailed to the cross bar. The nails, which were 7–9 inches long, were placed between the bones of the forearm (the radius and ulna) and the small bones of the hand (the carpal bones).
>
> The placement of the nails at this point had several effects. First, it ensured that the victim would indeed hang there until dead. Secondly, a nail placed at this point would sever the largest nerve in the hand called the median nerve.
>
> The severing of this nerve is a medical catastrophe. In addition to severe burning pain the destruction of this nerve causes permanent paralysis of the hand. Furthermore, by nailing the victim at this point in the wrist, there would be minimal bleeding and there would be no bones broken![13]

Once the cross bar was raised and fastened to the pole, the victim's feet were then attached to the post in such a way that it would be very difficult for him to hang on the cross through his own strength. The bottom of the right foot was placed flat against the pole with his knee at a 45 degree angle and nailed in place with the left foot on top of the right foot. "An iron nail about 7–9 inches long was driven through the feet between the 2nd and 3rd metatarsal bones. In this position the nail would sever the dorsal pedal artery of the foot, but the resultant bleeding would be insufficient to cause death."[14] All of these things were designed to inflict as much suffering as possible on the victims while extending their lives for up to nine days longer. "The result is that within a few minutes of being placed on the cross, the shoulders become dislocated."[15] The legs are flexed in such a way that the victim could not push for very long and neither could he hold himself up by his arms and shoulders. Nor could he adequately supply his body

---

12 Alfred Plummer notes concerning the 'Place of the Skull' that it was: "A rocky protrusion, resembling a skull in form, is no doubt the meaning. Thus Cyril of Jerusalem speaks of it as 'rising on high and showing itself to this day, and displaying even yet how because of Christ the rocks were then riven.' (Cyril of Jerusalem, *Catechetical Lectures*, XIII, 39)." Plummer, *The Gospel According to S. Luke*, 531. Cyril lived from AD 313–386. His description of the 'Place of the Skull' fits with the picture given in this chapter, but not with the traditional site under the Holy Sepulchre.
13 Eastman, "The Agony of Love: Medical Aspects of the Crucifixion."
14 Eastman, "The Agony of Love: Medical Aspects of the Crucifixion."
15 Eastman, "The Agony of Love: Medical Aspects of the Crucifixion."

with the needed oxygen which, therefore, caused an irreversible rise in his heart rate. Thus, most victims of this cruel punishment died of cardiac arrest and/or suffocation. Some victims also had their hearts burst as a result of this combination of problems. In their pretended kindness, the Romans put a small wooden seat on the poles that would allow the victims to put their weight on their buttocks. If the Romans ever wanted to speed up the process of dying, they would simply break the bones of the victim and spear them in the side to cause more bleeding.

At Golgotha, "the Place of a Skull" (John19:17),[16] Jesus was offered "wine mixed with myrrh; but He did not take it" (Mark 15:23). "The wealthy ladies of Jerusalem had the practice of providing for those condemned to the awful punishment of crucifixion a soporific draught, composed of wine mixed with some narcotic like gall or myrrh, to dull the senses and deaden the pain. It was a benevolent custom; and the cup was offered to all criminals, irrespective of their crimes."[17] This was the first offer to Jesus of something to supposedly assuage His thirst, but "after tasting it, He was unwilling to drink" (Matthew 27:34. The solution of wine mixed with gall or myrrh was intoxicating and if it had been prepared the previous day would have been as impossible to drink as gasoline or vinegar. Jesus rejected this drink because He intended to suffer on the cross with full consciousness of the painful ordeal. The relief that solution would give to His suffering was only a small shortcut to the terrible ordeal awaiting Him.

The Crowd Around the Cross (Matthew 27:32–44; Mark 15:21–32; Luke 23:26–32; and, John 19:17–25)

There were several different groups of people who gathered at Golgotha to witness the terrible death of Jesus, the Messiah. "The sight which the crowd came to see was, we now know, the greatest ever witnessed in the universe. Angels and archangels were absorbed in it; millions of men and women are looking back to it to-day and every day."[18] Lucifer, the Prince of darkness, was keenly interested in what was happening at the cross. There were Roman soldiers and members

---

16 "The name has been held to come from the look or form of the spot itself, bald, round, and skull-like; and therefore a mound or hillock, in accordance with the common phrase 'Mount Calvary.'" McClintock and Strong, *Cyclopedia of Biblical, Theological, and Ecclesiastical Literature*, 3:918.
17 Stalker, *The Trial and Death of Jesus Christ*, 159.
18 Stalker, *The Trial and Death of Jesus Christ*, 173.

of the Sanhedrin who were nearby. There were the daughters of Jerusalem and the holy women who had faithfully followed Jesus were present at the scene. At least one of the disciples, John, was there. Simon of Cyrene was there, inasmuch as he had carried Jesus' cross. Then, there were the various passersby who were traveling on the nearby road.

The Roman soldiers were the ones who were closest to the scene. They had nailed Him to the cross bar and raised Him on it to fasten it to the post. Part of their responsibility was to ensure that every victim was "stripped before being affixed to the cross—a trait of revolting shame."[19] Jesus, like all others punished in that cruel way, hung on the cross completely naked. There were thirteen soldiers, especially, who were tasked with the whole procedure. The person being crucified would usually have a few items of clothing that would be valuable to the soldiers—an outer garment, an undergarment, a girdle, and a pair of sandals. While the soldiers watched Jesus from beneath the cross, "they divided up his garments among themselves by casting lots" (Matthew 27:35). When they came to Jesus' tunic which was worn next to the skin, since it was "was seamless, woven in one piece . . .they said, 'Let us not tear it, but cast lots for it, to *decide* whose it shall be'" (John 19:23b-24a). Their actions unwittingly fulfilled the prophecy about the Messiah's sufferings in Psalm 22:18. They also nailed the charge against Jesus on His cross that Pilate had made, "Jesus the Nazarene, the King of the Jews" (John 19:19). When the chief priests saw that inscription, they hastily went to Pilate and implored him, "Do not write, 'The King of the Jews,' but that He said, 'I am King of the Jews.' Pilate answered, 'What I have written I have written'" (John 19:21, 22). Pilate's reply to the chief priests probably gave him much inner delight for them having forced him into crucifying Jesus against whom they were no valid charges. It is most likely that this exchange with Pilate took place before the sign was affixed to the cross. But, Pilate at last had developed a little bit of backbone and refused to budge from what he had written—"partly to avenge himself on, and partly to deride, the Jews."[20] There were at least thirteen soldiers, including the centurion, at Golgotha, who were there both to guard the whole proceedings and to prevent a riot

---

19 Stalker, *The Trial and Death of Jesus Christ*, 174.
20 Edersheim, *The Life and Times of Jesus the Messiah*, 881.

which the chief priests greatly feared.

Then, there were the Sanhedrists—the chief priests, scribes, Pharisees, and Sadducees—who were there as malignant, sinister witnesses of all that would happen with Jesus. They had plotted to kill Jesus and that time was then at hand. They also did not want a riot to break out. The inscription Pilate had written for Jesus' cross made them "afraid the Jews who passed by might be influenced"[21] by it, as Edersheim elaborates:

> We imagine, that the Sanhedrists had originally no intention of doing anything so un-Jewish as not only to gaze at the sufferings of the Crucified, but to even deride His agony—that, in fact, they had not intended going to Golgotha at all. But when they found that Pilate would not yield to their remonstrances, some of them hastened to the place of Crucifixion, and, mingling with the crowd, sought to incite their jeers, so as to prevent any deeper impression which significant words of the inscription might have produced.[22]

The daughters of Jerusalem followed Jesus to Calvary in their role as professional mourners primarily to feign sympathy for the Galilean, but it is not known how long they remained there. It was different with the faithful women—Mary the mother of Jesus; Mary Magdalene; Mary the wife of Clopas;[23] and, Salome[24]—who were also gathered around the cross. Those four godly women had hearts of true sympathy for the Messiah. Also, there were many women there "looking from a distance, who had followed Jesus from Galilee while ministering to Him" (Matthew 27:55). Some of those women had financial means and had helped to support the work of Jesus. The only disciple who is mentioned as being at Golgotha was John the beloved disciple. All of the followers of Jesus who were there were incredulous at what was happening to their Lord. "Bewildered as were their ideas, He had as firm a hold as ever on their hearts. They loved Him; they suffered with Him; they could have died for Him."[25]

Then, there were the two criminals who were crucified with

---

21 Edersheim, *The Life and Times of Jesus the Messiah*, 881.
22 Edersheim, *The Life and Times of Jesus the Messiah*, 881.
23 Eusebius states that Clopas was the brother of Joseph, the father of Jesus. Clopas' wife was the mother of James the Less and Joses (or Joseph).
24 Salome was the sister of Mary the mother of Jesus, the wife of Zebedee, and the mother of James and John. James and John were thus the cousins of Jesus. Salome is also referred to as the sister of Mary, the mother of Jesus, in John 19:25.
25 Stalker, *The Trial and Death of Jesus Christ*, 182.

Him, one on each side. Luke refers to them as "evil-doers" or "criminals." Mathew and Mark refer to them as "robbers" or, perhaps "bandits." They were not thieves in the sense of being people who break into homes and steal the valuables. If so, another Greek word would have been used to define them as kleptomaniacs. They were not just thieves, they were violent thieves. They took things by force and hurt or killed their victims. Chamblin remarked that the Greek word used by Matthew "can mean 'robber' or 'bandit,' and also 'revolutionary' or 'insurrectionist.'"[26] Barabbas was also called a "robber" in John 18:40, whereas Luke 23:19 says about him: "He was one who was thrown into prison for an insurrection made in the city, and for murder." Thus, Jesus was falsely accused of inciting an insurrection while the real insurrectionist was released instead of Him. It is possible that these two "robbers" had been involved in that insurrection with Barabbas and that is why they were in prison with him and why they were now being crucified with Jesus. Barabbas was released and Jesus took the punishment of that insurrectionist.

The Roman soldiers who were at Golgotha were, initially at least, without any compassion for Jesus, or any of those suffering by crucifixion; the Sanhedrists were against any show of compassion for Him; the women and friends of Jesus were overwhelmed with sympathy and compassion for Him; while the two robbers were a mixture of all those emotions.

"Father, Forgive Them" (Luke 23:34)
The first words Jesus spoke from the cross were these: "Father, forgive them; for they do not know what they are doing" (Luke 23:34). The immediate context might make it seem that Jesus was praying only that the Romans soldiers, and perhaps even Pilate, would be forgiven for their sins in condemning Him to such a cruel death. Yet, the wider context of the Scripture points in a different direction. The primary focus of Jesus' prayer was for the sins of the Jews, and especially the Sanhedrin, who had forced Pilate's hands, so to speak.

Jesus' prayer was not a blanket request that all those who had participated in this terrible deed would be forgiven. Forgiveness is granted in no other way than through faith and repentance. Yet, His prayer

---
26 Chamblin, *Matthew*, 2:1402.

was answered with the conversions of thousands in Jerusalem. Acts 6:7 even records that "a great many of the priests were becoming obedient to the faith." This prayer issued in the conversion of many Jews who otherwise would not have believed. In this respect also, Jesus "interceded for the transgressors" (Isaiah 53:12f). Ryle's comments on Jesus' prayer are worthy of careful consideration:

> Whether our Lord included the chief priests and scribes, Annas and Caiaphas and their companions, who had heard His declaration that He was the Christ, and yet formally rejected and condemned Him, I think more than doubtful. I believe they were given over to judicial blindness, and most of them probably perished in their sins. We never read of any of them being converted. The priests who were "obedient to the faith" (acts vi. 7) were probably of a different party from those who condemned Christ.
>
> Let it be noted that the union of a clear head knowledge of Christ with wilful heart rejection of Him is the nearest approach that can be made to a definition of the unpardonable sin.[27]

During His first three hours on the cross, from 9 AM to noon, various passersby who traveled the nearby road "were hurling abuse at Him, wagging their heads and saying, 'You who are going to destroy the temple and rebuild it in three days, save Yourself! If You are the Son of God, come down from the cross" (Matthew 27:39, 40). The charge that the Sanhedrin rejected because the testimony of the witnesses was inconsistent became the slur thrown at our Lord by the unthinking multitudes. "In the same way the chief priests also, along with the scribes and elders, were mocking *Him* and saying, 'He saved others; He cannot save Himself. He is the King of Israel; let Him now come down from the cross, and we will believe in Him. He trusts in God; let God rescue *Him* now, if He delights in Him; for He has said, 'I am the Son of God'" (Matthew 27:41–43). Unwittingly, the chief priests and scribes affirmed several things that are true about Jesus—that He had saved others (His raising of Lazarus was still on their minds); that salvation is through believing in Him; and, that He said, "I am the Son of God." Their demand that He come down from the cross before they would believe in Him was simply a falsehood and a malevolent attack inspired by the devil. That wicked fiend had from the beginning tried to entice Jesus to disobey the Father's mission for

---

27 Ryle, *Expository Thoughts on the Gospels: St. Luke*, 2:468.

Him, but now "the devil acts with greater urgency. By the same token, were Jesus now to come down from the cross, the evil one would experience his greatest triumph."[28]

The Soldiers Mock Jesus (Matthew 27:40–44; Mark 15:27–32; and, Luke 23:36, 37)

With the passersby and the Jewish officials openly reviling Jesus, the Roman soldiers were enticed to join in this blasphemy of the Son of God, saying, "If You are the King of the Jews, save Yourself!" (Luke 23:36, 37). One of the thieves also joined in the mocking of Jesus, "hurling abuse at Him, saying, 'Are You not the Christ? Save Yourself and us!'" (Luke 23:39). By hurling abuse at Jesus, that criminal manifested that his request to be saved by Jesus was not sincere. Indeed, Matthew 27:44 and Mark 15:32 state that both criminals were initially hurling abuse at Jesus, but one of the thieves had a change of heart and said to the other: "'Do you not even fear God, since we are under the same sentence of condemnation? And we indeed are suffering justly, for we are receiving what we deserve for our deeds; but this man has done nothing wrong.' And he was saying, 'Jesus, remember me when You come in Your kingdom!'" (Luke 23:40, 41). While suffering excruciating pain, the impenitent thief foolishly reviled and mocked Jesus, thus proving that "pain, suffering, and the approach of death, are not sufficient, without grace, to convert a soul."[29] Yet, the grace of God opened the heart of the other thief to petition Jesus to remember him when He comes in His kingdom. The acknowledgement of his sin and the appeal to Jesus for mercy represent the two requisite elements of true conversion: repentance and faith. Thus, Jesus replied to His petition: "Truly, I say to you, today you will be with Me in Paradise"(Luke 23:43). Ryle, in *Holiness*, describes the strength of the thief's faith in Christ:

> He saw no sceptre, no royal crown, no outward dominion, no glory, no majesty, no power, no signs of might. And yet the dying thief believed, and looked forward to Christ's kingdom.[30]

The penitent thief's saving faith was none too soon. In a few hours he would be dead and, without Christ, his unbearable pain on the cross would have become infinitely and unendingly worse in hades. Instead, Jesus spoke some of the most incredible words in Scripture

---

28 Chamblin, *Matthew* (Ross-Shire, Great Britain: Christian Focus Publications, 2010), 2:1404.
29 Ryle, *Expository Thoughts on the Gospel: St. Luke*, 474.
30 J. C. Ryle, *Holiness: Its Nature, Hindrances, Difficulties and Roots* (Cambridge and London: James Clarke & Co., Ltd., 1956), 189.

when He promised the thief that he would be with Him in Paradise that same day. John Flavel unfolds the meaning of Christ's words to the dying, penitent thief:

> By paradise he means heaven itself, which is shadowed to us by a place of delight and pleasure. This is the receptacle of gracious souls, when separated from their bodies.[31]

Jesus' words must have seemed like a dream or a fairy tale to one who had deservedly been sentenced to the most cruel form of punishment then known to mankind. Yet, that thief had expressed great faith in the Lord when most were turning away from Him.

Darkness from Noon to 3 PM (Matthew 27:45, 51–54; Mark 15:33; Luke 23:44, 45)

Mid-day had now arrived, but it was a most unusual mid-day. Matthew 27:45 records that "darkness fell upon all the land until the ninth hour" (i.e., until 3 PM according to Roman time). Edward J. Schnabel makes the following comments about the darkness at mid-day:

> While some have defended the view that this was a solar eclipse . . . this is astronomically impossible, since solar eclipses do not happen at full moon (when Passover was celebrated), and they last only for a few minutes, not three hours. Still it is possible that the darkness was indeed a prolonged, terrifying eclipse of the sun resulting from God's direct intervention. It is equally possible that arranged by divine providence the darkening of the sun was due to the khamsin, the Mediterranean sirocco, a sand storm[32] which is capable of creating dusk—or night-like conditions. Some think of heavy clouds.[33]

During this period, darkness covered the entire rest of the time Jesus hung on the cross, Matthew records that "the veil of the tem-

---

[31] John Flavel, *The Fountain of Life* (New York: American Tract Society, n.d.), 387.
[32] Having served in Desert Storm as an Army chaplain, I can attest to the fact that such sand storms in Saudi Arabia produce darkness over the whole area in the middle of the day. It is easy for me to believe that a sand storm in Israel would have had the same effect.
[33] Eckard J. Schnabel, *Jesus in Jerusalem: The Last Days* (Grand Rapids: Eerdmans Publishing Company, 2018), 326–7. An article was widely circulated prior to Good Friday in 2025 that NASA had determined that a lunar eclipse happened on April 3, AD 33 that might pinpoint the day Christ died. Lunar eclipses take place at night and do not cause darkness during the daylight hours. Oxford University scholars, Colin Humphreys and W. Graeme Waddington, had previously suggested am eclipse theory for Jesus' crucifixion based on Acts 2:20 which quotes from Joel 2:31, "The sun will be turned into darkness and the moon into blood before the goat and glorious day of the Lord." The problem with tying that prophecy to Jesus' crucifixion, though, is that a lunar eclipse does not explain the darkness during the day of His death. There would need to be evidence of both a solar eclipse and a lunar eclipse on the Good Friday in AD 33 in order to support their theory. Thus, the lunar eclipse on April 3, AD 33 gives more confirmation to the date of April 7, AD 30 as the correct date of the crucifixion of Christ.

ple was torn in two from top to bottom; and the earth shook and the rocks were split;" and, that "[t]he tombs were opened, and many bodies of the saints who had fallen asleep were raised" (Matthew 27:51–2). The tearing of the veil of the temple which separated the holy place from the holy of holies symbolized that the access into the presence of God was now made possible through the blood of Jesus. "By this action God the Father declares that by the virtue of the new covenant established through the blood of his Son, his people have unprecedented access into his holy presence."[34] (cf. Jeremiah 31:31–34; Hebrews 6:19, 20; 8:8:13; 9:1–28; and, 10:15–22). McCheyne unfolded the full implications of the rending of the veil of the temple in a sermon on John 14:6:

> Not a shred of the dreadful curtain now remains to intercept us. The guiltiest, the vilest sinner of you all, has now liberty to enter through the veil, under the light of Jehovah's countenance, to dwell in the secret of his tabernacle, to behold his beauty, and to enquire in his temple.[35]

The tearing of the veil of the Temple was also a testimony to the Jews that Jesus had accomplished by His death what all the blood of their animal sacrifices never could. It was torn from the top to the bottom to indicate that this was the action of Jehovah in heaven. The members of the Sanhedrin mistakenly thought they had triumphed over Jesus of Nazareth when He was sentenced to be crucified, but Paul rightly said about His death: "When He had disarmed the rulers and authorities, He made a public display of them, having triumphed over them through Him" (Colossians 2:15). That public display of the rulers and authorities—and God's triumph over them—was accomplished at the cross, as the context of Colossians shows. Thus, the moment of the Sanhedrin's supposed triumph was the moment when they were made into a public display of scorn and ridicule. That was what the tearing of the veil of the temple indicated.

Not only was the whole land under a cloud of darkness for three hours, there were other unusual events that were taking place. One of those was the earthquake that soon followed. "The earthquake provides a geological counterpart to the darkness that enveloped the land, and similarly portends divine judgment."[36] The darkness may

---

34 Chamblin, *Matthew*, 2:1425–6.
35 Robert Murray McCheyne, *The Sermons of the Reverend Robert Murray McCheyne* (New York: Robert Carter, 1848), 11.
36 Chamblin, *Matthew*, 2:1426.

Jesus' Crucifixion

well have been a result of the earthquake. Another unusual event was the opening of the tombs of many of the saints who then were raised from the dead following Jesus' resurrection. The Scripture does not give us the names of any of those saints, but their appearance in Jerusalem manifested the power of Christ to raise the dead. The earthquake provided the geological event that tore open the tombs of those saints who became the fruits of His own resurrection.

During those three hours of darkness, there were several other notable things that happened. Seeing "His mother, and the disciple whom He loved standing nearby, He said to His mother, 'Woman, behold your son!' Then He said to the disciple, 'Behold, your mother!' From that hour the disciple took her into his own household" (John 19:26b-27). Such composure of thought in a time of extreme suffering is rare. While suffering in behalf of others, Jesus did not forget that charity begins at home. At this time, Mary was already a believer in Jesus as the Messiah, but none of His brothers were. Joseph was already deceased. So, Jesus commits the care of His mother to the beloved disciple, John, who was immediately obedient 'from that hour.'

Towards the end of that period of darkness, Jesus cried out, "I am thirsty" (John 19:28). "A jar full of sour wine was standing there; so they put a sponge full of the sour wine upon a branch of hyssop and brought it to His mouth" (John 19:29). Scripture does not identify who brought that sponge to Jesus, but simply says, ""Someone ran and filled a sponge with sour wine" (Mark 15:36).This matter was in fulfillment of Psalm 69:21, one of the most important Messianic psalms. George Smeaton describes the relevance of Psalm 69 to the sufferings of Christ:

> This psalm unfolds to us how the Saviour during His crucifixion reflected on His present sufferings, and how he lamented and prayed. He declares that the reproaches of them that reproached God had fallen upon Him (ver. 9); that He had been the song of the drunkard, doubtless when He went about doing good, mighty in deed and word (ver. 12); and that in the exercise of strict severity, though not too severe, a dread doom was impending over those who rejected their Messiah (ver. 23–29). Bright prospects breaking out from behind the terrible gloom of His sorrows, sustain His soul after these complaints (ver. 30–37); and there is a joyful end to these sorrows both for the sufferer and for all the earth. Under all these woes He was perfectly innocent, sustain-

ing them for others (ver. 5–6); for He restored what He took not away (ver. 4).[37]

A feeling of great thirst results from such loss of blood that Jesus had experienced at Gethsemane, in His scourging, and now in His crucifixion. The physical suffering of Jesus from this loss of blood was prophesied in Psalm 22:15— "My strength is dried up like a potsherd, and My tongue cleaves to my jaws; and You lay me down in the dust of death." Sour wine could not assuage the thirst resulting from such a great loss of blood. Jesus had refused the drugged wine offered to Him at the beginning of His crucifixion, but now He drunk some of this sour wine.

Jesus Quotes Psalm 22:1 (Matthew 27:46–49 and Mark 15:34–38)

Another of the sayings was Jesus' quote of Psalm 22 which was about the ninth hour or 3 PM. "Jesus cried out with a loud voice, saying, 'Eli, Eli, Lama Sabachthani?' that is, 'My God, My God, why have You forsaken Me?'" (Matthew 27:46). Intellectually, Jesus knew exactly why God had forsaken Him and had known it for quite some time already. He had always known why God would forsake Him throughout His entire public ministry. Yet, this separation from His heavenly Father was why He had agonized so much in His prayer at Gethsemane. Jesus' quote from Psalm 22 expressed the experience of the wrath of God against sin which He was then feeling. He did not merely think that He was forsaken by His Father—He really was forsaken during His suffering on the cross. Indeed, Jesus prayer from the cross was addressed to "God" rather than to "Father." All Jesus' other prayers in the Scripture are addressed to the One with whom He had been intimate before the foundations of the world. Yet, as He suffered at Calvary, Jesus felt estranged from His Father while He was bearing the sins of the world. This is a mystery that cannot be fully plumbed to its depths. Calvin's comments on this matter are very helpful:

> There appeared to be more than human vigour in Christ's cry, but it is certain that intensity of grief forced it from Him. This was the chief conflict, harder than any other agony, that in His anguish He was not given relief by His Father's aid or favour, but made to feel somehow estranged. He did not only offer His body as the price of our reconciliation with God, but also in His soul bore our due pains: He was truly made the Man of sorrows, as Isaiah says (53.3). They are unenlightened who make stress of the torment of the flesh outwardly, and hold back

---

37 Smeaton, *Christ's Doctrine of the Atonement*, 84–5.

this part of redemption: for Christ to make satisfaction for us He had to stand trial at God's tribunal. There is nothing more dreadful than to feel God as Judge, whose wrath is worse than all deaths . . . It is an inner sadness of soul, with violent fire that drives Him to break out a cry . . . Those who reckon that Christ took on the office of Mediator on condition of bearing our guilt in soul as in body will not wonder at the struggle He had with the pangs of death; as though under the wrath of God, He were cast into the labyrinth of evil.[38]

Jesus' cry from the cross was not mere play-acting or the quoting of Scripture on cue. He really felt such agony of soul when He suffered the wrath of God against sinners. How could it have been otherwise? Jesus' tragic and heart-wrenching lament was the experience of His own soul in that hour of suffering and was just as much a reflection of His true feelings as the laments of Job and Jeremiah were (Cf. Job 3:1–26 and Jeremiah 20:7–18).

Following Jesus' plaintive cry for God's help, some people in the crowd were confused and mistakenly thought He was calling for Elijah to come to His rescue. Some said, "This man is calling for Elijah" (Matthew 27:47). "Either they do not hear some of Jesus' words (as recorded in v. 46), or else they do not recognize them to be a quotation from Psalm 22:1 . . . Their own statement reflects popular belief that Elijah might be summoned to aid persons in grave danger or sore distress."[39] "But the rest of *them* said, 'Let us see whether Elijah will come to save Him.'" (Matthew 27:49). That last statement was first made by the soldier who gave Jesus the sour wine (Mark 15:36) and then was reiterated by the other soldiers. Those soldiers were not waiting on the miraculous appearance of Elijah, but were using Jesus' prayer for help as another opportunity to ridicule Him. They were, in effect, saying, "See, there is no help for this man. He is completely abandoned." They were doing what the passersby, the chief priests and scribes, and even the other thieves had done in hurling abuse at Jesus. Their actions were prophesied in Psalm 22:7, 8— "All who see me sneer at me; they separate with the lip, they wag the head, *saying*, 'Commit *yourself* to the Lord; let Him deliver him; let Him rescue him, because He delights in him.'" Even the soldiers were now involved in that cruel treatment of Jesus, as Chamblin notes:

---

38 Calvin: *A Harmony of the Gospels Matthew, Mark and Luke and the Epistles of James and Jude*, 3:207–8.
39 Chamblin, *Matthew*, 2:1418.

> The purpose is not to prevent the soldier from giving drink to Jesus (this has already happened), but to continue the mockery. To judge from the context, there is not the least expectation that Elijah will heed Jesus' call. On the contrary, the statement is itself part of the ridicule: God has not delivered Jesus (27:43, 46); what folly to expect *Elijah* to do so.[40]

The reality was that "the latter-day Elijah [had] already come and declared that Jesus is indeed the promised Messiah."[41] Elijah the Tishbite had appeared with Moses *to* Jesus on the Mount of Transfiguration and talked with Him. John the Baptist had preceded Jesus in martyrdom at the hands of Herod Antipas, so he could not come to the Messiah's aid. Moreover, Jesus could have called on legions of angels to help Him—if that had been His Father's will. Jesus was without help at this hour because that was part of His work of atonement for sins. He had to be accursed by God in that moment when He took the punishment for the sins of His people. Yet, the emotional experience by the Suffering Servant was still heart-wrenching. Even Isaiah 53 speaks of "the anguish of His soul" when He rendered "Himself as a guilt offering" and when the Lord was pleased to crush Him "putting Him to grief" (Isaiah 53, 10, 11). Anguish and grief were the experiences of Jesus' soul when He realized that His Father had momentarily forsaken Him. As John Brown wrote on these verses found in Isaiah 53:

> That this was the bitterest ingredient in our Lord's sufferings—that they were the expression of the displeasure of God against the sin of those whom he was, as it were, identified—that this was the greatest of all those aggravations, there can be no reasonable doubt. These sufferings of his soul were the soul of his sufferings.[42]

While Jesus felt abandoned and forsaken as He suffered on the cross, "the Lord was pleased to crush Him, putting Him to grief" (Isaiah 53:10). Jesus felt anguish of soul and grief. His Father felt pleasure that finally the Messiah had become a guilt offering in the place of His spiritual offspring. The darkness of those hours unveiled the worst of experiences for Jesus, but they were the joyous experience for "the Father of Lights, with whom there is no variation or shifting shadow" (James 1:17). The satisfaction of the Father

---

40 Chamblin, *Matthew*, 2:1421-2.
41 Chamblin, *Matthew*, 2:1422.
42 John Brown, *The Sufferings and Glory of the Messiah* (U.S.A.: Sovereign Grace Publishers, 1959), 298.

would soon become the experience of Christ Jesus "who abolished death and brought life and immortality to light through the gospel" (2 Timothy 1:10). Never was it truer in any respect that the darkest hour is just before dawn. Of course, Jesus' sufferings on the cross did not end with the excruciating pain He endured. He suffered more. After His plaintive cry to His Father, Jesus uttered those words: "It is finished" (John 19:30) and "Father, into Your hands I commend My Spirit" (Luke 23:46). And with those final words, Jesus "bowed His head and gave up His spirit"(John 19:30) and "He breathed His last" (Luke 23:46). Yet, John records for us that Jesus received the sour wine and gave up His spirit only when He knew "that all things had already been accomplished to fulfill the Scripture" (John 19:28). His arduous mission had been fully completed. He had fulfilled every requirement that was needed for Him to be the Savior of the world. His life's work was now "finished" because all that was written about Him "in the Law of Moses and the Prophets and the Psalms" (Luke 24:44) was now fulfilled. Jesus alone, of all men who have ever lived, could utter as His last words: "It is finished!" (John 19:30).

The end of Jesus' life was as shocking as His birth was surprising. Men and angels exulted at His birth, but it was different at His death. "Now when the centurion saw what had happened, he began praising God, saying, 'Certainly this man was innocent.' And all the crowds who came together for this spectacle, when they observed what had happened, began to return, beating their breasts. And all His acquaintances and the women who accompanied Him from Galilee were standing at a distance, seeing these things" (Luke 27:47–49). Matthew supplements what Luke records: "Now the centurion, and those who were with Him keeping guard over Jesus, when they saw the earthquake and the things that were happening, became very frightened and said, 'Truly, this was the Son of God!'" (Matthew 27:54). Edersheim states concerning the affirmations of the centurion:

> Many a scene of horror must he have witnessed in those sad times of the Crucifixion, but none like this. Only one conclusion could force itself on his mind. It was that which, we cannot doubt, had made its impression on his heart and conscience. Jesus was not what the Jews, His infuriated enemies, had described Him. He was what He had professed to be, what His bearing on the Cross and His Death attested him to be:

'righteous,' and hence, 'Son of God.' From this there was only a step to personal allegiance to Him.[43]

There were three groups of people around the cross. The Roman centurion, and his companions, had often witnessed crucifixions, but the death of Jesus was so different for them that they proclaimed His innocence and His divinity. While it cannot be known to us what affect this experience had on this centurion and the soldiers, it is possible that one or more may have been a part of that "whole praetorian guard" (Philippians 1:13) who later became saints through faith in Jesus (Philippians 4:22). Perhaps, these soldiers were comprehended in Jesus' prayer for forgiveness for those who did not know what they were doing. The expressions of the centurion and the soldiers make us hopeful that they may have been converted. The second group was the crowd "who came together for this spectacle" (Luke 23:48). Their interest was sinful curiosity for most of them, but the death of Jesus had a sobering effect on them all. When Jesus breathed His last, they returned to the city while "beating their breasts" (Luke 23:48). The final group was composed of the women and the various acquaintances of Jesus. Scripture does not tell us the response of the last group to these events, but it had to have been grievous and deeply troubling. Ryle comments on the responses of the first two groups:

> We know not exactly the nature of the feelings here described: we know not the extent to which they went, or the after-fruit which they brought forth. One thing at all events is clear: the Roman officer felt convinced that he had been superintending an unrighteous action and crucifying an innocent person; the gazing crowd were pricked to the heart by a sense of having aided, countenanced, and abetted a grievous wrong. Both Jew and Gentile left Calvary that evening heavy-hearted, self-condemned, and ill at ease.[44]

The Jewish onlookers to the crucifixion may well have been some of those who later "were pierced to the heart" (Acts 2:37) on the day of Pentecost. Certainly, Joseph of Arimathea and Nicodemus would have been there at Calvary. Some of them, also, may have been in the group that "were cut to the quick, and they *began* gnashing their teeth" (Acts 7:54) at Stephen when he finished his sermon to them. While conscience alone is never sufficient to lead a person to salvation, a seared conscience through resisting the Holy Spirit is a dangerous situation.

---

43 Edersheim, *The Life and Times of Jesus the Messiah*, 895.
44 Ryle, *Expository Thoughts on the Gospels: St. Luke*, 2:481.

Those who were at Calvary left that day with consciences sufficiently pricked by the events that they should have asked, "Brethren, what shall we do?" There is hope for those whose consciences are pierced to the point that they become sincere seekers of salvation. As Jeremiah 29:13 says: "You will seek Me and find Me when you search for Me with all your heart." Being heavy-hearted, self-condemned, and ill at ease never saves anyone until it issues in true repentance and saving faith. Hearts can only be "sprinkled clean from an evil conscience" (Hebrews 10:22) by the application of the blood of Christ. Only eternity will testify whether those first witnesses to the atonement of Christ became recipients of the grace of God in the gospel.

When Jesus gave up His spirit, it was about 3 PM on the day of preparation. Passover was at hand and would begin at sundown. Knowing this, the Jews hastily went to Pilate and asked that the bodies of the three men would be removed before the Passover was celebrated. It was customary for the Romans to speed up the death of those being crucified when necessary by breaking their legs. That was the method used by the soldiers on this occasion. They broke the legs of the two criminals, but when they came to Jesus "they saw that He was already dead," and "they did not break His legs" (John 19:33) which was according to prophecy: "They pierced my hands and my feet. I can count all my bones" (Psalm 22:16b-17a). Instead, "one of the soldiers pierced His side with a spear, and immediately blood and water came out" (John 19:34). That also was according to prophecy in Zechariah 12:10—"they will look on Me whom they have pierced." "The spontaneous spouting of 'blood and water' (John 19:34) suggests cardiac tamponade:[45] the heart was penetrated, which allowed the fluids and blood that had accumulated between the heart muscle and the pericardium to flow out ."[46] When the two thieves died soon afterwards, the bodies of all three men were taken down and removed from the "Place of a Skull."

The sufferings of Jesus on the cross cannot be quantified, as John Brown summarizes:

> The sufferings were sufferings to death . . . His death was a violent death; and of all violent deaths that probably which inflicted most pain on the

---

45 Cardiac tamponade is the compression of the heart caused by fluid collecting in the sac surrounding the heart. That fluid puts pressure on the heart and keeps blood from filling the atrium properly. Thus, there results a dramatic drop in blood pressure that can be fatal, shortness of breath, and lightheadedness.
46 Schnabel, *Jesus in Jerusalem: The Last Days*, 340.

sufferer. During those tedious hours He suffered every moment more than the agonies of an ordinary death. It was of all modes of punishment, too, the most ignominious. No Roman citizen, however foul his crime, could be legally crucified. It was the punishment appropriated to felonious slaves. In being nailed to the cross, our Lord was exhibited as an outcast from society, a man who had no rights, a person unworthy of being treated as an ordinary criminal; a worm, and no man.

What his sufferings were, none knew, none can ever know, but He who endured and he who inflicted them . . . Never was there a sufferer like Christ, the just One . . . To borrow the words of an old divine, "If hunger and thirst, if revilings and contempt, if sorrows and agonies, if stripes and buffetings, if condemnation and crucifixion, be sufferings, Jesus suffered. If the infirmities of our nature, if the weight of our sins, if the malice of man, if the machinations of Satan, if the hand of God could make Him suffer, our Saviour suffered."[47]

The Crucified Bodies (John 19:31–37)

It was typical for the Romans to leave the bodies of those who were crucified hanging on their crosses until the birds of prey had sufficiently ravaged them that only the bones remained. Roman sentries were stationed to guard the bodies and to prevent the family members from taking them down. Yet, the Passover caused a change in this instance. The Sabbath was approaching and it was a particularly "high day" since it was on the weekly Sabbath when that Passover began. The Jews, therefore, did not want to defile that holy feast with the cursed bodies hanging just outside the gates of the city. While Scripture does not mention what happened with the bodies of the two thieves, they were probably deposited at Gehenna, the valley of Hinnom. McClintock and Strong describe Gehenna for us:

> [A] deep narrow glen to the south of Jerusalem, where, after the introduction of the fire-gods by Ahaz, the idolatrous Jews offered their children to Moloch (2 Chron. xxviii, 3; xxxiii, 6; Jer. vii, 31; xix, 2–6). In consequence of those abominations the valley was polluted by Josiah (2 Kings xxiii, 10); subsequently to which it became the common laystall of the city, where the dead bodies of criminals, and the carcasses of animals, and every other kind of filth was cast, and . . . the combustible portion consumed with fire. From the depth and narrowness of the gorge, and, perhaps, its ever-burning fires, as well as from its being the receptacle of all sorts of putrefying matter, and all that defiled the holy city, it became in later times the image of the place of everlasting punishment.[48]

---

47 Brown, *Expository Discourses on 1 Peter*, 2:137–139.
48 McClintock and Strong, *Cyclopedia of Biblical, Theological, and Ecclesiastical Literature*, 3:764.

Jesus' Crucifixion

Yet, Gehenna was not the place for the Messiah—the Son of David—to be laid to rest. Consequently, Joseph of Arimathea—a rich member of the Sanhedrin—gathered his courage and went to Pilate to request "that he might take away the body of Jesus; and Pilate granted permission. So he came and took away His body" (John 19:38). His act of kindness was also a fulfillment of prophecy: "His grave was assigned with wicked men, yet He was with a rich man in His death, because He had done no violence, nor was any deceit in His mouth" (Isaiah 53:9). Without Joseph's intervention, Jesus would have been buried in the same place—Gehenna—where the wicked men with whom He was assigned were laid. The perpetual burning fires at that place would have charred His body and the birds of the prey would have ripped away His flesh. Joseph's act of kindness was none too soon. Before granting Joseph's request, though, Pilate summoned the centurion to testify that Jesus was dead (Mark 15:44, 45). Joseph, like Nicodemus, had been a secret disciple of Jesus for fear of the Jews, especially the members of the Sanhedrin, with whom they both served. Nicodemus joined Joseph in preparing he body of Jesus for burial and brought with him "a mixture of myrrh and aloes, about a hundred pounds *weight*" (John 19:39). They wrapped the body in linen cloths together with the spices and laid Him in "a new tomb in which no one had yet been laid" (John 19:41). That tomb was in a garden which was in the same place where His crucifixion took place.[49] Standing at a distance were Mary Magdalene and Mary, the mother of Joses, watching closely as Jesus was buried. An interesting fact is that the body of Jesus was being prepared for burial "about the same time, that a noisy throng prepared to follow delegates from the Sanhedrin to the ceremony of cutting the Passover sheaf."[50] Edersheim once again unfolds the meaning of these events at the Temple and in the garden-tomb:

> But, as this festive procession started, amidst loud demonstrations, a small band of mourners turned from having laid their dead Master in His resting-place. The contrast is as sad as it is suggestive, And yet, not in the Temple, nor by the priest, but in the silence of that garden-tomb, was the first Omer[51] of the new paschal flour to be waved before the

---

49 Having investigated the two main sites for the tomb of Jesus, it is my decided opinion that what is known as Gordon's tomb or the Garden Tomb is the place where Jesus was buried. It is in a garden connected to the site of Calvary which fits all the criteria laid out earlier in this chapter.
50 Edersheim, *The Life and Times of Jesus the Messiah*, 899. Cf. Leviticus 23:9–11.
51 An omer was 1/10 of an ephah which was equal to our modern bushel.

Lord.[52]

On that Sabbath day of the Passover, having begun at sundown, "the chief priests and scribes gathered together with Pilate, and said, 'Sir, we remember that when He was still alive that deceiver said, "After three days I *am* to rise again." Therefore give orders for the grave to be made secure until the third day, otherwise His disciples may come and steal the body away and say to the people, "He has risen from the dead," and this last deception will be worse than the first'" (Matthew 27:62–64). Pilate, thus, commanded them to make the grave "as secure as you know how" (Matthew 27:65), which they did and "set a seal on the stone" (Matthew 27:66). The soldiers who guarded the grave were those who were under the authority of the Sanhedrin—"a 'custodial guard' from the temple police."[53] Yet, Pilate had to approve their "custodial guard" since it consisted of Roman soldiers under his command that he provided to the Sanhedrin. Even in His death, Jesus continued to trouble the Sanhedrin and the Jewish leaders. They had accomplished their desire in having Him crucified, but their fears concerning Him still rushed to the forefront of their thoughts in the most ironic manner. Thus, they sealed the grave with a heavy stone that was rolled to the entrance of the tomb and, then, placed the Roman imperial insignia on the stone as a warning to all that any tampering with it was a criminal act. The stone probably weighed between 1 or 2 tons. Removing such a stone have would required several strong men who first would have had to have overtaken the guards. After first checking to make sure the body of Jesus was still in the tomb before sealing it, the Jewish officials were finally confident that the Galilean was no longer any trouble for them. The posted guards were a guarantee that the grave would not be robbed. And there was no robbery of His grave. Instead, there was an even greater challenge concerning the body of Jesus that awaited them.

---

52 Edersheim, *The Life and Times of Jesus the Messiah*, 900.
53 Chamblin, *Matthew*, 2:1452.

26

Jesus' Resurrection and Ascension

Early on Sunday morning, April 9th, AD 30, the chief priests of the Sanhedrin were visited by several panic-stricken Roman soldiers from the "custodial guard" who were assigned to guard the tomb of Jesus. Unimaginable events had just happened in the garden where Jesus had been laid. These soldiers were desperate for help. Jesus' tomb was now empty and their punishment for failing at their post was death under Roman law. Thus, these soldiers ran to the Sanhedrin where they were assigned—not to Pilate—for help. With breathless anxiety, they told the chief priests about the earthquake; and, the dazzling appearance and strength of the angel who rolled away the stone (Matthew 28:2, 3). They reported how they "shook for fear of him and became like dead men" (Matthew 28:4). The chief priests hastily called a meeting of the elders and agreed to give "a large sum of money to the soldiers" (Matthew 28:12) with these instructions, "You are to say, 'His disciples came by night and stole Him away while we were asleep.'" (Matthew 28:13). "The soldiers account 'could have been enough to cause the Jewish authorities to rethink their estimate of Jesus had not their minds been irreversibly made up. Thus their guilt is intensified.'"[1] It is amazing that the Sanhedrin was so blinded against the truth that their first response was to spin a lie for which they paid the soldiers handsomely. They could have sent a deputation to the grave and examined the matter themselves, but they accepted the empty tomb as fact and attempted to mitigate the situation with a lie that was full of holes. How could all of the soldiers have all been asleep at the same time? Even that "admission" by the soldiers was still incriminating. Indeed, there has never been any serious attempt to disprove the empty tomb because it is so clearly based on indisputable fact. How could soldiers who were asleep give any credible testimony to who and how the body of Jesus was stolen away? As A. B. Bruce wrote in *The Expositor's Greek Testament* on Matthew 28:11–15:

---

1 Chamblin, *Matthew*, 2:1475. Also, Donald A. Hagner, *Matthew 14–28* (Dallas: Word Books, 1995), 876.

> The lie for which the priests paid so much money is suicidal; one half destroys the other. Sleeping sentinels could not know what happened . . . The ordinary punishment for falling asleep on the watch was death. Could soldiers be persuaded by any amount of money to run such a risk? Of course they might take the money and go away laughing at the donors, meaning to tell their general the truth.[2]

The question which has never been answered is why those soldiers did not meet with the mandatory punishment that deserters of their posts deserved? The solution may be simpler than what has been imagined. The soldiers knew the truth of what happened. The chief priests and the whole Sanhedrin soon learned that truth also—which is why they were never able to mount an effective campaign to silence the apostle's clear and open proclamation that Jesus had indeed risen from the dead. And, thus, Pilate and Herod also must have learned the facts very quickly. With a conscience already troubled by his part in Jesus' crucifixion, Pilate was not the man to force the Roman garrison to execute the soldiers. The whole situation was an extraordinary conundrum which neither the Sanhedrin nor the Roman rulers could solve. For that reason, the story—or lie—that the disciples of Jesus stole His body was reported widely and believed by many. The reason so many believed such an incredible story is explained by Chamblin:

> Probably some, perhaps most, of those people willfully suppressed the strong evidence for Jesus' resurrection; for, were he actually risen from the dead, the consequences for those who rejected and killed him were too terrifying to contemplate.[3]

In his *Dialogue with Trypho, a Jew*, Justin Martyr (AD 100–165) accused the Jews of sending "chosen and ordained men throughout all the world to proclaim that a godless and lawless heresy had sprung from one Jesus, a Galilean deceiver, whom we crucified, but his disciples stole him away by night from the tomb, where he was laid when unfastened from the cross, and now deceive men by asserting that he has risen from the dead and ascended to heaven."[4] This lie of the Sanhedrin was still promiscuously being circulated by the Jews more than a hundred years later during Justin Mar-

---

2 Bruce, *The Expositor's Greek Testament: The Synoptic Gospels*, 1:338.
3 Chamblin, *Matthew*, 2:1479.
4 Alexander Roberts and James Donaldson, eds., Justin Martyr, *Ante-Nicene Fathers: Dialogue to Trypho, a Jew* (Peabody, Massachusetts: Hendrickson Publishers, 1999), 1:253.

tyr's lifetime and continued to be propagated for hundreds of years more. As time continued, most Jews adopted the "vision theory" to explain the empty tomb of Jesus. That theory tried to account for the renewed hope of Christians and their dogmatic insistence that Jesus had risen from the dead on a common vision. Group visions or hallucinations simply do not exist. There is no recorded evidence of groups of people having common hallucinations concerning anything. Moreover, the "vision theory" still does not provide a credible answer for why the tomb of Jesus was empty on Sunday morning, April 9th. The only other explanation for the empty tomb is the "swoon theory." It asserts that Jesus was close to death, but He revived afterwards. Of course, how would Jesus in such a weakened condition have the strength to push away the stone and give renewed hope to the disciples? The period of convalescence Jesus would have needed to overcome the very serious wounds He had received does not fit with the timeline of Scripture. Indeed, if Jesus merely swooned, then where did He live after His revival? Only the literal resurrection of Jesus from the dead explains the empty tomb.

The efforts to deny or suppress the truth of Jesus' resurrection by the Sanhedrin and the Roman officials only serve to make their condemnation greater. They knew that the Lord of Glory rose from the dead. They knew that His tomb was empty. They knew that His body could nowhere be found. They knew that He was no longer on earth. Yet, they perpetuated and protected a lie because of their own self-interest. The consequences of doing otherwise, as Chamblin stated, were "too terrifying to contemplate." This palace intrigue quickly spread through the Sanhedrin like wildfire. It helps us to understand why the chief priests persecuted those who preached that Jesus had risen from the dead, but refused to mount any effort to refute the claim. They could not refute it because they knew the tomb was empty and their own soldiers had testified to them about all the events they saw. Whether those soldiers saw Jesus after He had risen or they only saw the angel is a matter not covered by the Scripture. But, they certainly knew the body was gone and that the linen wrappings were unrolled. They knew enough to deduce that the body had not been stolen by the disciples. The facts they knew pointed to some other explanation—an explanation which must have caused panic in the hearts of the chief priests.

It is an interesting fact that the Scripture never gives any information about the actual moment of resurrection. It can only be because that moment was so stupendous that our human minds could not comprehend it. Instead, the New Testament repeatedly bears testimony to the *fact* of Jesus' resurrection and not the mere moment of it. Even the apostles did not see Jesus rise from the dead, but they did see Him after He had risen. The evidence of Christ's resurrection comes to all believers, including the apostles, in the same way. There are incontrovertible facts that supply all the proof that is needed. Chamblin's comments about Jesus' resurrection are helpful:

> Jesus' emergence from the tomb did not require the removal of the stone. That does not mean his resurrected body was less substantial than his crucified body; he made it clear in Luke 24:38–43 that he had not become a *pneuma* (v. 39), a pure spirit or ghost (cf. 1 Cor. 15:1–58). There are suggestions, on the contrary, that Jesus' body had become (if one may put it so) more substantial than before. John 20:19 and 26 appear to say that Jesus came into his disciples' presence by *passing through* locked doors. That suggests in turn that he did not require the removal of his graveclothes, but that instead he *passed through* the clothes, leaving them neatly in place (John 20:5–7; contrast 11:44); and that he likewise *passed through* the stone, or the wall of the tomb. In that case, the heavier or denser matter passed through the lighter, as when water passes through air, or a steel pipe through water.[5]

It is better, therefore, to realize that the angelic involvement in rolling away the stone was for the benefit of believers—particularly for those first witnesses who would go to the tomb and see that Jesus was not there.

The Darkest Hour

The time between the crucifixion and the resurrection was a very dark time for the disciples and all the followers of Jesus. From Friday afternoon to Sunday morning, their hopes had been thoroughly dashed. "They had painful misgivings that all was lost; that he in whom they had trusted had for some unknown reason failed in the hour of trial; and been forsaken of God; that all their fond dreams of the return of Israel's ancient glory were now dashed, the victims of some strange delusion or some fearful failure . . . They saw only the descending night and the unopened grave, and felt themselves in the valley and shadow of death, without the comforting rod and the supporting staff

---

5 Chamblin, *Matthew*, 2:1467.

of the Shepherd."[6] Their souls were in despair, but they had not yet spoken to their hearts, as David did in Psalm 42:5, "Hope in God, for I shall again praise Him *for* the help of His presence." Their new day had not yet broken and, thus, they were comfortless. Yet, the greatest and best attested miracle in the history of the world was only a few hours away.

The Dawn of a New Day (Matthew 28:1; Mark 16:1–4; Luke 24:1–3; and, John 20:1–10)

It was early in the morning on the first day of the week when the women—Mary Magdalene; Mary, the mother of James; and, Joanna—arrived at the tomb with the spices with which they would prepare the body of Jesus. The previous day had been the Jewish Sabbath and these righteous women had been delayed by that day's required rest. They probably started their journey from different points that morning and intended to meet where Jesus' battered body had been laid in Joseph's sepulcher. While John 20:1 records that Mary Magdalene "came early to the tomb, while it was still dark," Luke 24:1 says it was "early dawn," and Mark 16:2 says "the sun had risen." No doubt, the women started out when it was still dark or early dawn, but the sun had risen by the time they arrived at their destination. "Grey dawn was streaking the sky, when they who had so lovingly watched Him to His Burying were making their lonely way to the rock-hewn Tomb in the Garden."[7] Even these women, who had never forsaken Jesus for a moment, were not prepared for what they would find there. "They found the stone rolled away from the tomb, but when they entered, they did not find the body of the Lord Jesus. While they were perplexed about this, behold two men suddenly stood near them in dazzling clothing" (Luke 24:2–4). Mary Magdalene, finding the tomb empty, immediately ran away to Peter and told him and John: "They have taken away the Lord out of the tomb, and we do not know where they have laid Him" (John 20:2b). Both Peter and John began at once to run to the tomb with John arriving there first. The beloved disciple stooped and "saw the linen wrappings lying there, but he did not go in" (John 20:5). Then Peter arrived and immediately He entered the tomb where he saw

---

6 T. V. Moore, *The Last Days of Jesus* (Edinburgh, Scotland and Carlisle, Pennsylvania: The Banner of Truth Trust:1981), 14–5.
7 Edersheim, *The Life and Times of Jesus the Messiah*, 907.

not only the linen wrappings and "the face-cloth which had been on the head, not lying with linen wrappings, but rolled up in a place by itself" (John 20:7). What Peter and John saw convinced them that Jesus had indeed risen. Until that moment, they had "not understood the Scripture, that He must rise again from the dead" (John 20:9). As Shepard elaborates:

> All the cloths, with which the body had been wrapped, were lying there in order. The napkin was rolled up. Evidently, there was no evidence of grave-robbers, as Mary had surmised. There had not dawned on Maty, and until now on them, any idea of the resurrection. They face a puzzling situation. If His enemies, or even His friends had removed the body, they would not have left the grave cloths at all, much less in an orderly state. It remained for John, who had followed Peter down to the lowest level of the niches of the tomb, to grasp the meaning of all the combined circumstances.[8]

Peter and John then "went away again to their own homes" (John 20:10), without having yet seen the risen Christ. John, at least, had seen "the evidence' of Jesus" resurrection and had believed, but neither of them could yet say, "I have seen the Lord. He is risen indeed!" "In the heart of John there is rejoicing, and this is true also with respect to Peter."[9] Yet, there would be even greater rejoicing for both of them and the other disciples before the day was over.

The Angelic Announcement (Matthew 28:2–8; Mark 16:5–8; and, Luke 24:4–10)

While Mary Magdalene was running with perplexed concern to tell the disciples that the body of Jesus was not in the tomb, the other Mary and Joanna were visited by two angels who "suddenly stood near them in dazzling clothing; and . . . *the women* were terrified and bowed their faces to the ground" (Luke 24:4b-5a). Then the angels announced to them: "Why do you seek the Living One among the dead? He is not here, but He has risen. Remember how He spoke to you while He was still in Galilee, saying that the Son of Man must be delivered into the hands of sinful men, and be crucified, and the third day rise again" (Luke 24:5b-7). Not only the disciples, but all the followers of Christ—including these women—were privy to the various warnings of the crucifixion and the promises of the resurrection. All of them alike had refused to consider the possibility of Jesus' crucifixion and,

---

8 Shepard, *The Christ of the Gospels*, 614.
9 Hendriksen, *The Gospel of John*, 451.

therefore, they had failed to realize that He must rise from the dead. The grave could not contain Him. "No bonds of grave or death could keep Him bound, and it is the spontaneous outcome of His whole being as perfect Man and Son of God, that, after He had accomplished full expiation through His suffering and sacrificial death, He arose from the dead in triumph."[10] This announcement by the angels was both a proclamation of glad tidings—as at His birth—and a gentle rebuke for their failure to believe. The other Mary and Joanna saw the two angels, but they did not see the risen Lord. Like Mary Magdalene, they also ran to the eleven disciples and reported the empty tomb and what the angels had told them. "But these words appeared to them as nonsense, and they would not believe them" (Luke 24:11). "The words of the women concerning the empty sepulchre and the tidings of the angels, seemed to the perplexed group of disciples like senseless women's talk, and they would not believe them."[11]

Jesus Appears to Mary Magdalene (John 20:11-18)

The first appearance of Jesus from the dead was not to the Roman soldiers; nor, to disciples; nor, to the company of the women together. Rather, He appeared first of all to one woman—a woman who had once been possessed of seven demons. She was a woman from whom Jesus had gained forever her undying love and faithfulness. The intensity of her love, having been forgiven much, was extraordinary and is, no doubt, the reason that our Lord appeared to her first. After reporting the empty tomb to the disciples, she returned to the garden to look for the body of Jesus. The order of events is hard to set down with accuracy, but she probably was alone when she ran to the disciples and when she returned to the tomb. Her return to the tomb was, no doubt, after Peter and John had run there and had deduced that Jesus had risen. Mary Magdalene had probably not looked into the tomb when she first came there in the morning. So, now she returned there to investigate the matter more closely. When Peter and John returned to their homes, she remained "outside the tomb weeping; and so, as she wept, she stooped and looked into the tomb; and she saw two angels in white sitting, one at the head and one at the feet, where the body of Jesus had been lying" (John 20:11, 12). The angels asked her, "Woman, why are you weeping?" (John 20:13a). She replied, "Because they have taken away my

---

10 Geldenhuys, *Commentary on the Gospel of Luke*, 623.
11 Geldenhuys, *Commentary on the Gospel of Luke*, 624.

Lord, and I do not know where they have laid Him" (John 20:13b). As soon as she uttered those despairing words, she turned and found herself in the presence of Jesus without realizing who He was. She thought He was the gardener. He asked her, "Woman, why are you weeping? Whom are you seeking?" (John 20:15). Mary replied to Him without recognizing Him, "Sir, if you have carried Him away, tell me where you have laid Him, and I will take Him away" (John 20:15). Her eyes were still blinded until Jesus spoke her name, "Mary," in such a way that this grieving lamb heard the voice of her Shepherd and replied with tender affection, "Rabboni!" (John 20:16). Jesus then mildly admonished her, "Stop clinging to Me, for I have not yet ascended to the Father, but go to My brethren and say to them, 'I ascend to My Father and your Father, and My God and your God'" (John 20:17). Hendriksen unfolds the meaning of those words to Mary:

> Jesus did not object to being touched. Otherwise how can we explain his word to Thomas? ... What he condemned was Mary's mistaken notion that the former mode of fellowship was going to be resumed, in other words, that Jesus would once again live in daily visible association with his disciples, both men and women. The fellowship, to be sure, would be resumed; but it would be far richer and more blessed. It would be the communion of the ascended Lord in the Spirit with the Church.[12]

Jesus probably appeared first to Mary Magdalene because He knew her heart was about to break due to her great emotion and grief. "Mary, with the fearfulness of a mourning love, too intense to give room for any other feeling, was addressed with words directed not to fear, but to grief, 'Why weepest thou?'"[13] Our Lord has a heart of tender affection towards all those who grieve His seeming absence from them. He was the same when He rose from the dead as when He conducted His ministry for three years. He is present with His people even when they are not aware that He is near to them. He gathers His lambs in His arms and carries them in His bosom (Isaiah 40:11). "A bruised reed He will not break and a dimly burning wick He will not extinguish" (Isaiah 42:3). Jesus' words to Mary Magdalene are instructive for all believers. Mary's "tears were needless. Her anxiety was unnecessary ... How often we mourn over the absence of things that are within our grasp, and even at our right hand!"[14]

---

12 Hendriksen, *The Gospel of John*, 455.
13 Moore, *The Last Days of Jesus*, 32.
14 Ryle, *Expository Thoughts on the Gospels: St. John*, 3:412.

Jesus Appears to the Women (Matthew 28:9, 10)

Jesus' second resurrection appearance was to the women who went to the tomb with Mary Magdalene, the other Mary and Joanna. Matthew 28:9, 10 says, "And behold, Jesus met them and greeted them. And they came up and took hold of His feet and worshiped Him. Then Jesus said to them, 'Do not be afraid; go and take word to My brethren to leave for Galilee, and there they will see Me.'" As Mary Magdalene had done, the other women immediately recognized the voice of Jesus. Calvin helps us with a timeline of these events:

> The three Evangelists pass over what John says of Mary Magdalene, that before she saw the angels, she returned to the city and complained with tears that Christ's body had been removed. Only the second return to the city is treated here, in which she and her companions announced to the disciples that Christ had risen, as they had learned from the voice and testimony of the angels, and from the sight of Christ Himself.[15]

There was a lot of feverish, excited activity on this first day of the week and the emotions of the disciples and followers of Jesus were running the whole gamut from depression to unrestrained joy. When these women met Jesus on their journey back into the city, they immediately fell down and worshiped Him—proving that they considered Him divine. Yet, in Jesus' first appearances to women, He sanctions the important role that women have in the kingdom of God. It was these godly women who announced to the disciples that Jesus was risen from the dead even as the first living voices that bring the good news to little children are often their mothers. Thus, these women were honored to be the first heralds that Jesus was alive. Mary Magdalene reported to the disciples that she had seen the Lord, but "they refused to believe it" (Mark 16:11). When the other women made their report to the disciples, "they did not believe them either." (Mark 16:13). Regrettably, women were considered unreliable witnesses in antiquity and were not allowed to testify in court. Therefore, the disciples remained gloomy and sad despite the verifiable testimonies of at least three women.

Jesus Appears to Peter (Luke 24:34 and 1 Corinthians 15:4, 5)

The Scripture declares that Jesus made His third appearance to Peter. Scripture is silent when and where that happened, but it is not difficult to determine why Jesus appeared to Peter before the other apostles. Peter had denied Jesus three times just a few days earlier. He was the

---

15 Calvin, *A Harmony of the Gospels, Matthew, Mark and Luke*, 3:226.

"lost sheep" who had to be searched for by the Shepherd and brought back into the fold. Peter repented of his sins when he went out after the rooster crowed and wept bitterly. Yet, he needed to be restored to fellowship with Jesus. "Peter was a penitent backslider, with a heart all broken and bleeding in remorseful anguish, and he who signalized his death on the cross by forgiving a penitent thief, would signalize his resurrection by forgiving a penitent disciple."[16] That appearance to Peter must have happened sometime around mid-day.

Jesus Appears to Two Disciples Traveling to Emmaus (Mark 16:12, 13 and Luke 24:13–35)

With all the excitement happening in Jerusalem on that Sunday, two disciples—one named Cleopas and the other unnamed—set out for the village of Emmaus where one of them at least had a home. These disciples were probably among the Judean followers of Jesus like Martha, Mary, and Lazarus; Nicodemus; and, Joseph of Arimathea, among others. The village where they were going has remained obscure, but most modern scholars today fix on a place northwest of Jerusalem that is the right distance—"about seven miles from Jerusalem" (Luke 24:13). As Plummer notes:

> *El Khubeibeh*, which is about 63 stadia[17] from Jerusalem, on the road to Lydda, is probably the place. It is about 7 miles N.W. from Jerusalem, in the beautiful Wadi Beit Chanina, and the tradition in its favor dates from the crusades.[18]

Cleopas and his fellow disciple were probably returning to their homes in Emmaus after the Feast of the Passover was over. Behind them was "[t]he blood-stained City; and the cloud-and-gloom-capped trysting-place of the followers of Jesus"[19] known as the Upper Room. After twenty-five to thirty minutes of vigorous walking, they reach "the edge of the plateau"[20] on which Jerusalem was built. In another half hour, they are "beyond the dreary, rocky region, and are entering on a valley."[21] Edersheim describes this part of their journey:

> What an oasis this in a region of hills! Along the course of the stream,

---

16 Moore, *The Last Days of Jesus*, 50.
17 The distance of a stadia is somewhat indefinite, but a stadia roughly translates to about 600 feet. 63 stadion (the plural) would be 37,800 feet and, therefore, 7.15 miles.
18 Plummer, *A Critical and Exegetical Commentary on the Gospel According to S. Luke*, 551–2. Cf., also, Geldenhuys, *Commentary on the Gospel of Luke*, 636, n. 3.
19 Edersheim, *The Life and Times of Jesus the Messiah*, 913.
20 Edersheim, *The Life and Times of Jesus the Messiah*, 913.
21 Edersheim, *The Life and Times of Jesus the Messiah*, 913

which babbles down, and low in the valley is crossed by a bridge, are scented orange—and lemon-gardens, olive-groves, luscious fruit trees, pleasant enclosures, shady nooks, bright dwellings, and on the height lovely Emmaus. A sweet spot to which to wander on that spring afternoon; a most suitable place where to meet such companionship, and to find such teaching, as on Easter Day.[22]

As the disciples traveled home, they were discussing among themselves all the things that had happened over the past few days. Suddenly, an unknown stranger came alongside them and began to travel with them. The spot where this stranger met them might well have been at the convergence of "the two roads from Lifta and Kolonieh."[23] The stranger was Jesus, "[b]ut their eyes were prevented from recognizing Him" (Luke 24:16). Jesus asked them, "What are these words that you are exchanging with one another as you are walking" (Luke 24:17). Sadness came over their countenance before Cleopas replied, "Are you the only one visiting Jerusalem and unaware of the things which have happened here in these days?" (Luke 24:18). "Jesus knew the cause of their sadness more deeply than they knew it themselves. Yet he required them to declare it."[24] Ironically, He also knew better than anyone else what things had happened in Jerusalem over the last several days, but He was anxious to teach them truths that would turn their sadness into rejoicing. Thus, He asked them very simply: "What things?" (Luke 24:19a). They once again replied, "The things about Jesus the Nazarene, who was a prophet mighty in deed and word in the sight of God and all the people, and how the chief priests and our rulers delivered Him to the sentence of death, and crucified Him. But we were hoping that it was He who was going to redeem Israel. Indeed besides all this, it is the third day since these things happened. But also some women among us amazed us. When they were at the tomb early in the morning, and did not find the body, they came saying that they had also seen a vision of angels who said that He was alive. Some of those who were with us went to the tomb and found it just exactly as the women also had said: but Him they did not see" (Luke 24:19b-24). In those words, "[t]here was the chilling doubt that all hope of deliverance through Jesus

---

22 Edersheim, *The Life and Times of Jesus the Messiah*, 913
23 Edersheim, *The Life and Times of Jesus the Messiah*, 913. Lifta was a hillside village north of Jerusalem overlooking Wadi Salman and was destroyed in 1948. Today it is like a ghost town on the hillside. Qalunya or Colonia or Kolonieh was a village about 3.7 miles west of Jerusalem, but was also destroyed in 1948.
24 Moore, *The Last Days of Jesus*, 60.

was perhaps a dream or delusion."[25] Their hopes had been so dashed by the crucifixion that they could find little solace in the interesting reports that the tomb was empty and that angels had announced His resurrection. Thus, Jesus mildly rebuked them, "'O foolish men and slow of heart to believe in all that the prophets have spoken! Was it not necessary for the Christ to suffer and to enter into His glory?' Then beginning with Moses and with all the prophets, He explained to them the things concerning Himself in all the Scriptures" (Luke 24:25–27). "A temporal redemption of the Jews by a conqueror appears to have been the redemption which they looked for: a spiritual redemption by a sacrificial death was an idea which their minds could not thoroughly take in."[26] Like most Jews of all ages, they had completely glossed over the idea of a suffering Savior. They looked instead for a Warrior Prince. Thus, Jesus had to correct their erroneous thoughts by quoting copiously from the Old Testament Scriptures concerning the sufferings and glory of the Messiah. Without a doubt, our Lord saw many things in the Scripture concerning the Suffering Servant which even the greatest of expositors have never fully observed. That unrecorded sermon was certainly one of the best sermons ever preached. It was preached, not to a crowd, but to two obscure Judean disciples who otherwise were completely unknown to us.

When they arrived at their home in Emmaus, Cleopas and the other disciple extended their hospitality to this still unknown stranger and urged Him, "Stay with us, for it is getting towards evening, and the day is now nearly over" (Luke 24:29). Jesus accepted their offer and went in to break bread with them. As he blessed and broke the bread and gave it to them "their eyes were opened and they recognized Him; and He vanished from their sight" (Luke 24:31). As soon as they knew Him to be the Lord, he was gone. Yet, a great change had come over them as they had experienced joy of being in the presence of the risen Christ. Thus, they said to one another, "Were not our hearts burning within us while He was speaking to us on the road, while He was explaining the Scriptures to us? And they got up that very hour and returned to Jerusalem, and found gathered together the eleven and those who were with them" (Luke 24:32, 33). Geldenhuys unfolds the effect of this appearance of Christ to these two disciples:

---

25 Moore, *The Last Days of Jesus*, 60.
26 Ryle, *Expository Thoughts on the Gospels: St. Luke*, 2:500.

All of a sudden everything became clear to the two men and they realized why they had been so moved by the manner in which the Stranger had expounded the Scriptures to them on the way. Although Jesus had departed so soon after they had recognized Him, all doubt was now banished from their hearts. They know now that He is risen and that He lives as the Messiah, the promised Redeemer. And this certainty immediately brings such a light and joy into their hearts, that they have an irresistible urge to give others also a share of their joy.[27]

Since these two disciples had not yet heard of any other disciple who had actually seen the risen Lord, they hurried back to Jerusalem to share the glorious news with the eleven and the others in the Upper Room. They knew that joys shared are doubled and they had the greatest joy of all.

Jesus Appears to the Disciples in the Upper Room (Mark 16:14–18; Luke 24:36–49; and, John 20:19–25)

Cleopas and his fellow disciple knew exactly where to find the disciples who were huddling together in the Upper Room with the doors tightly shut. Outside was danger, whether real or perceived, as the Romans and the Sanhedrin were desperately trying to deal with the problem of the empty tomb. The whole city was in a state of uproar and news was spreading like wildfire. When they arrived where the eleven and those who were with them "were gathered together" (Luke 24:33), they were greeted with the news: "The Lord has really risen and has appeared to Simon" (Luke 24:34). Cleopas and the other disciple then "began to relate their experiences[28] on the road and how He was recognized by them in the breaking of the bread" (Luke 24:35). The eleven now had the testimony of three unimpeachable witnesses to Jesus' resurrection, but they were soon to see the risen Lord themselves. "While they were telling these things, He Himself stood in their midst and said to them, 'Peace be to you.' But they were startled and frightened and thought they were seeing a spirit" (Luke 24:36, 37). To comfort their hearts and convince them He was really risen, Jesus said, "Why are you troubled, and why do doubts arise in your hearts? See My hands and My feet, that it is I Myself; touch Me and see, for a spirit does not have flesh and bones as you see that I

---

27 Geldenhuys, *Commentary on the Gospel of Luke*, 635.
28 The other disciple with Cleopas was probably the one who soon after this experience wrote down what was said between them and Jesus. That document was used by Luke to write this chapter. It was customary for an author to refer to himself in the third person only, even as John in his Gospel calls himself "that disciple whom Jesus loved."

have" (Luke 24:38, 39). Even beholding His hands and His side with their wounds, the disciples, while filled with joy and amazement, simply could not believe that it was Him. To convince the disciples that He was not a spirit, Jesus asked them, "Have you anything here to eat? They gave Him a piece of a broiled fish; and he took it and ate *it* before them" (Luke 24:41–43). Their joy was borne of faith and also was a hindrance to their faith as Matthew Poole stated:

> *Believed not for joy*; yet if they had not believed, they doubtless would not have rejoiced, but their faith was the cause of their joy; yet the excess of their joy was the hindrance of their faith; so dangerous are excessive motions of our affections.[29]

When the disciples were then convinced that Jesus had really risen, He said to them once again: "'Peace *be* with you; as the Father has sent Me, I also send you.' And when he had said this, He breathed on them and said to them, 'Receive the Holy Spirit. If you forgive the sins of any, *their sins* have been forgiven them; if you retain the *sins* of any, they have been retained'" (John 20:21–23). The forgiving or retaining of the sins of anyone is called the power of binding and loosing which Christ gave to His church to be exercised through the apostles and the elders. It is a *declarative power* today whereby the elders receive members on the basis of credible faith and remove them from the church when they remain impenitent for their sins. Once again, Matthew Poole is helpful:

> The question therefore amongst divines is, Whether Christ in this text hath given authority to his ministers actually to discharge men of the guilt of their sins; or only to declare unto them, if their repentance and faith be true, their sins are really forgiven them? . . . What knowledge the apostles might have by the Spirit of discerning, we cannot say. But certain it is, none hath any such certainty of knowledge now of the truth of any man, declaring his faith and true repentance; from whence it is to me apparent, that no man hath any further power from Christ, than to declare to them, that if indeed they truly believe and repent, their sins are really forgiven.[30]

Before Jesus gave such declarative power to the apostles—and to His church,—He breathed on them which symbolized the outpouring of the Holy Spirit. The declarative power of binding and loosing

---

29 Matthew Poole, *A Commentary on the Holy Bible* (Edinburgh, Scotland and Carlisle, PA: The Banner of Truth Trust, 1975), 3:275.
30 Poole, *A Commentary on the Whole Bible*, 3:381.

depends on having Spirit-filled officers who receive and dismiss members. Otherwise, the elders will either be too strict or too loose in carrying out their duties either way. Goats will be too easily received into the church while true sheep are hindered. And, discipline will be too harsh towards some and too lax toward others. It takes the Spirit of God leading the elders for them to strike the right balance in this matter.

There was one of the eleven disciples who was not there on the first appearance of Christ to them—Thomas Didymus, a disciple who was naturally prone to doubting and to fearing the worst. He has become known as Doubting Thomas. Though "the other disciples were saying to him, 'We have seen the Lord'" (John 20:25a), he remained incredulous, saying: "Unless I see in His hands the imprint of the nails, and put my finger into the place of the nails, and put my hand into His side, I will not believe" (John 20:25b). By that time, there were a large number of witnesses to the resurrection of Jesus—including the other ten disciples, the two disciples on the road to Emmaus, the three women, and the group of other followers of Jesus who had gathered in the Upper Room. Thomas refused to believe any of them or all of them. Instead, he said: "Unless I see . . . I will not believe" (John 20:25b). Jesus had offered to let the other disciples do exactly what Thomas stated was the acid test of proof for him. None of them had put their fingers in the nail prints or His side. Thomas asserted that he would do so and settle the matter in his mind. He, without a doubt, spent another week of gloomy doubts and misery as a result of his incredulity. "He missed the meeting with Jesus, and the peace, faith, hope, and joy that were connected with it. He remained in darkness for another week, and doubtless in sorrow, for unbelief is but another name for unhappiness."[31] He brought such heartache on himself because he was not with the other disciples on that first resurrection Sunday. By missing their fellowship, he missed Jesus also. Yet, he was a true disciple and Jesus would not allow him to remain in doubts.

What is also interesting about this first Lord's Day is that there is no mention of Mary, the mother of Jesus. She probably had returned to Bethany after the crucifixion. If she was among the group of followers who were in the Upper room when Jesus appeared there, she was not singled out in any way.

---

31 Moore, *The Last Days of Jesus*, 79.

Jesus Appears to Doubting Thomas (John 20:26–29)

A lonely week passed between resurrection appearances by Jesus. The other ten disciples were probably in constant contact with Thomas, encouraging him to remain with them for such a time when Jesus would appear once again. What Jesus did during that week can only be a matter of conjecture. Why did He not seek out Thomas earlier? Why did He make the skeptical disciple wait a whole week? For one thing, that is the Lord's way. He answers at the appropriate time when we have waited on Him because that is best for our souls. There is probably a deeper answer, though. Jesus honored the Lord's Day—the new Sabbath—by appearing again on the first day of the week. "That hallowed day was again to be distinguished by the cure of a sceptical disciple, in the establishment of the great fundamental fact of Christianity, the resurrection of Jesus."[32] Like the previous Lord's Day, the disciples and followers of Jesus were huddled together in the Upper Room with "the doors having been shut" (John 20:26). Then, Jesus suddenly appeared in their midst and spoke the same words he had spoken the week before: "Peace *be* with you" (John 20:26). On that Sunday, April 16th, Thomas was with all the others. While that disciple was "naturally, a man of gloomy and saturnine spirit, prone to look on the dark side of everything,"[33] there was also enough of a spark of true faith in his heart that he was not going to be absent in case the reports of the other disciples were true. He would test things for himself, but he would have to be gathered with them to test anything. The only thing that is recorded about this appearance of Jesus was His ministry to Thomas.

Thomas had already clearly set out his position and what was essential for him to believe. Thus, Jesus made that offer immediately to his doubtful disciple: "Reach here with your finger, and see My hands; and reach here your hand and out it into My side; and do not be unbelieving, but believing" (John 20:27). The same gracious spirit with which Jesus had always ministered to His disciples was manifest in this matter also. He had not changed in any way as a result of the resurrection. He was perfect on earth and is perfect still. Jesus' offer was sincere. Thomas' doubts were misdirected. "If ten men could be deceived, could not one? . . . If Jesus or any other agent could deceive

---

32 Moore, *The Last Days of Jesus*, 79.
33 Moore, *The Last Days of Jesus*, 79.

the senses of sight and hearing, might he not that of touch? Hence to reject this evidence and demand that of his own touch alone, was absurd. It was, as a German writer quaintly observes, to trust his ten fingers more than the testimony of ten other apostles."[34] Faith had come slowly but surely to Thomas, who replied simply: "My Lord and my God!" (John 20:28). He made no attempt to put Jesus' resurrected body to the acid test. Thus, Jesus replied to him: "Because you have seen Me, have you believed? Blessed *are* they who did not see, and *yet* believed" (John 20:29). T. V. Moore's comments about this whole matter are on target:

> Yet it is well that it was so, for we are thus assured that the evidence was well sifted. The fact that the ten were incredulous to the statement of the women, and that Thomas was equally so to theirs, proves that the evidence must have been irresistible, and gives us an ample guaranty that this fundamental fact must have been fully and thoroughly tested, before it was believed and proclaimed to the world.
>
> But still it is not the less true, that all scepticism is unreasonable in its rationalism, and credulous in its unbelief. It demands an evidence for which it has no right, and in doing so betrays its weakness. Men who cannot believe Moses and Paul, believe Voltaire and Paine...They make their own notions or senses the rule, instead of some tried and sure standard.[35]

Jesus' words to Thomas were essential to the spread of the gospel. Only a small number of believers would ever be able to see Jesus in the flesh after His resurrection. The rest of us would be required to believe even though we have not seen. Yet, we believe on the basis of the recorded testimonies of those who saw Him after His resurrection. "Faith which results from seeing is good, but faith which results from hearing is more excellent."[36] Thus, the greatest sense is that of hearing because "faith *comes* from hearing, and hearing by the word of Christ" (Romans 10:17; Cf. also, 1 Corinthians 1:21). Thomas, and all the other apostles, had chosen the wrong sense to trust in the beginning and all of them needed to see the evidence for themselves before they would believe. Thomas may have been more headstrong than the others on that point, but he was not fundamentally different than them. Their belief in Christ's resurrection had also required seeing the risen Savior.

---

34 Moore, *The Last Days of Jesus*, 81.
35 Moore, *The Last Days of Jesus*, 81–2.
36 Hendriksen, *The Gospel of John*, 466.

Jesus Appears on the Shore of Galilee (John 21:1–23)

After Jesus' appearances to the disciples in the Upper Room on the first two Lord's days, they left Jerusalem and headed to Galilee as He had commanded them to do so. Most of the eleven were poor fishermen who had lived off the gifts of those who supported the Lord's ministry before His crucifixion. Everything was different now. Back along the Sea of Galilee, several of the disciples returned to their former occupations while they awaited the great meeting that was promised. The Scripture is silent about Jesus' activities during the forty days before His ascension other than the few appearances He made to His disciples and individuals. In Galilee, there were at least seven disciples gathered near where they had often fished—Simon Peter, Thomas, Nathaniel, James and John, and two others who are unnamed. On one occasion, Peter said to them all: "I am going fishing" (John 21:3a). All of them replied to him: "We will also come with you" (John 21:3b). As they had done on many other occasions, they went out at night and fished through the hours of darkness until the sun rose the next morning. "[T]hat night they caught nothing" (John 21:3c). Two years earlier they had done the same thing on the evening before Jesus called them to be "fishers of men."

As the wearied disciples were rowing back to shore while the morning was breaking, there was a man standing "on the beach, yet the disciples did not know that it was Jesus" (John 21:4). They had seen His resurrected body twice before, but they were never able to recognize Him without the enlightenment of the Spirit. "There was something strange and almost suspicious in the sight"[37] of this mysterious man whose form was peeking through the dawn. Then, He courteously and kindly said to them, "Children, you do not have any fish, do you?" (John 21:5a). Of course, the Lord knew the answer to that question and anticipated their despondent answer, "No" (John 21:5b). It was all part of His plan to not only provide them once again, with a great catch, but to complete and confirm their calling as "fishers of men." Thus, He said to them, "'Cast the net on the right-hand side of the boat and you will find a *catch*.' So they cast, and then they were not able to haul it in because of the great number of fish" (John 21:6). William Hendriksen unfolds the event very well:

> Experienced fishermen usually do not permit a perfect stranger to give

---

37 Moore, *The Last Days of Jesus*, 92.

them directions...But they did nothing of the kind...Instead—so deeply impressed were they by the compelling tone of the stranger's voice—they obey immediately with soldierly promptness. They cast their net on the right hand side, and at once it enclosed so many fishes that though these fishermen kept on exerting themselves (note the force of the imperfect), that they were unable to pull the net up into the boat.[38]

John was the first disciple to realize that the stranger on the shore was Jesus. He was the disciple who most possessed the grace of spiritual reflection and understanding. Thus, he simply said to Peter, "It is the Lord" (John 21:7). Peter, being the impetuous man of action, immediately "put his outer garment on (for he was stripped for work), and threw himself into the sea" (John 21:7). Impetuosity is not always a virtue. The disciples in the boat were not far from land and they quickly rowed ashore, dragging the net of fish with them. The net was unbroken and there were 153 large fish enclosed. This great catch, though, was a prelude to what would happen next.

When the fishermen came ashore, Jesus already had some fish on a charcoal fire which He was preparing for their breakfast, along with some bread. The Lord then said to the disciples, "Bring some of the fish which you have now caught" (John 21:10). Their catch was so large that they could have fed the whole towns of Capernaum and Bethsaida. "Jesus said to them, 'Come and have breakfast.' None of the disciples ventured to question Him, 'Who are You?' knowing that it was the Lord. Jesus came and took the bread and gave it to them, and the fish likewise" (John 21:12, 13). There was a symbolism in what Jesus was doing and how He was restoring His disciples, especially Peter, for the great work ahead of them.

The events described in John's last chapter took place in late April or early May of AD 30. The verdant countryside of Galilee and the beautiful, blue waters of the Sea of Tiberias were in their splendor, sparkling "like a gem in its setting."[39] The whole scenery recalled "the early days and history"[40] of their ministry with Jesus in this same area two years earlier. For all of them, their work had officially begun at Capernaum—not Jerusalem—when Jesus spent a whole night in prayer and then called then to be His twelve disciples. Some of them had earlier been called to become "fishers of men" or chal-

---

38 Hendriksen, *The Gospel of John*, 481.
39 Edersheim *The Life and Times of Jesus the Messiah*, 918.
40 Edersheim *The Life and Times of Jesus the Messiah*, 918.

lenged to leave the tax-booth and follow Jesus. So, it was most natural for them to be back in Galilee by the Lake once again. But what did the future hold for them? How were they to serve Jesus now that He had risen from the dead? Thus, Jesus focused His attention on that disciple who had boasted that He would never forsake the Lord with three important questions, all slight variations of one question, "Do you love Me?" Jesus' question to Peter is one which every follower of Him must answer. Edersheim unfolds the scene for us:

> Turning to Peter, with pointed though most gentle allusion to the danger of self-confidence—a confidence springing from only a sense of personal affection, even though genuine—He asked' 'Simon, son of Jona'—as it were with fullest reference to what he was naturally—'lovest thou Me more than these?' Peter understood it all. No longer with confidence in self, avoiding the former references to the others, and even with marked choice of a different word to express the affection from that which the Saviour had used, he replied, appealing rather to the Lord's, than to his consciousness.[41]

Peter was already a changed man before this enquiry by his Master. Jesus had appeared to Peter alone on the first day of His resurrection and had restored him to the apostleship. No longer was he brimming with self-confidence that is easily replaced by fearfulness when countered. Jesus knew Peter's heart more than he did. Yet, He asked Peter three times to confess his love for Him, even as he had three times denied Him. He asked Peter in front of the others if he indeed loved Him more than these—that is, the other disciples. As Peter had denied Jesus before charcoal fire, now Jesus made him confess Him before a charcoal fire in the presence of those very men of whom he had once said: "Even though all may fall away because of You, I will never fall away" (Matthew 26:33). They had all been scattered after Jesus' crucifixion, but Peter had also. So, our Lord queried Peter about his love in comparison to the others. Did he really love Christ more than they did? Jesus did not refer to him as Peter, though. "He received his name Cephas, or, in its Greek form, Peter, because of his confession of Christ; but having denied that confession, the name was denied to him"[42] on this occasion—until he made the good confession before witnesses again. No longer did Peter boast about his faithfulness in comparison to the others. With each answer, Peter appealed to the

---

41 Edersheim, *The Life and Times of Jesus the Messiah*, 920.
42 Moore, *The Last Days of Jesus*, 102.

knowledge of Jesus: "Lord, You know all things. You know that I love You" (John 21:17). Surely, Peter did love Jesus more than anything else. Jesus fully knew that, but confession is good for the soul. Peter's humility in avoiding any comparison of himself to the other apostles was as much a sign of his new found spirituality as was his grief that Jesus queried him three times as a reminder of His previous failure. Self-distrust is as much an indication of spiritual growth as is godly contrition for sin. Peter was now ready to undertake the solemn task of feeding Jesus' sheep, a task which he later exhorted all elders to do by being "examples to the flock" (1 Peter 5:3b). Jesus' charge to Peter on this occasion was to do exactly what He had set as an example on the night of His betrayal—to wash the feet of others.

The final exchange on this occasion concerned the circumstances of Peter's life and death. Jesus told him, "Truly, truly, I say to you, when you were younger, you used to gird yourself and walk wherever you wished, but when you grow old, you will stretch out your hands and someone else will gird you, and bring you where you do not wish to go" (John 21:18). The man of action, the man of industry would someday be dependent on others. Peter turned around and seeing John asked the Lord what would happen to him. Jesus replied, "If I want him to remain until I come, what *is that* to you? You follow Me!" (John 21:22). The saying then went out that John would not die; "yet Jesus did not say to him that he would not die, but *only*, 'If I want him to remain until I come, what *is that* to you?'" (John 21:23). Jesus was teaching Peter and all the disciples what David stated in Psalm 31:15, "My times are in Your hand." There was a work for each of the apostles to perform; a time for everything, even the days of their deaths. Jesus wanted Peter simply to focus on what his mission was and not to be concerned about what would happen to the other apostles. All of them were under the providential government of the Lord and there was an exact number of days appointed for each of them "when as yet there was not one of them" (Psalm 139:16d).

Jesus Appears to the Disciples and the Five Hundred (Matthew 28:16–20)

Jesus' appearance to the five disciples by the Sea of Galilee was an interlude before the appointed meeting at the mountain in Galilee which He had designated as the place where He would meet them (Matthew 28:16, 17). The particular mountain is undesignated, but it was undoubtedly either one of two mountains—the mountain where He preached the "Sermon on the Mount" or the mountain where He was transfigured. A strong case could be made for either as the mountain which He had designated, but the strongest case—in my opinion—is that the mountain was where Jesus preached His magnificent sermon. That site would have allowed people who had followed Jesus to be present there. Not only the eleven disciples were there, but more than five hundred people also (1 Corinthians 15:3). "When they saw Him, they worshiped *Him*; but some were doubtful" (Matthew 28:17). Those who were doubtful were not the disciples, but the people who comprised the five hundred. They had heard of Jesus' crucifixion and the reports of His resurrection. They gathered at the mountain out of curiosity more than certainty. Their doubts were understandable. There was something different about the resurrected Christ. He was the same and had all the same features. "But . . . He was not easily recognizable even for those who had walked with Him for three and a half years. 'There was a mystery about Him which even those who knew him best were now unable to penetrate.'"[43] It was that mystery which caused the doubts of those who saw Him. Could it really be that Jesus of Nazareth was risen from the dead? Was this man before them the same Person they had followed on other occasions? True faith sometimes comes slowly and can be mixed with many doubts. Yet, these five hundred people became witnesses to the resurrection of Christ, according to Paul, and their doubts must have been transformed into faith.

It was at this meeting on the mountain that Jesus delivered what is known as the Great Commission found in Matthew 28:18–20 and Mark 16:15. Chamblin's comments are instructive:

> The Lamb who was slain, the Lion who has conquered, is judged worthy to govern the whole future course of history (Rev. 5:1–10). The Son will now exercise 'all authority' . . . Having earlier refused the devil's offer of 'all . . . the kingdoms of the world and their splendor' (Matt. 4:8–10, Jesus now receives these from the Father. Since Jesus has been given 'all authority . . . on earth . . .,' his people 'will inherit the earth . . . ,' not just 'the land' of Israel. . .Furthermore, Jesus will henceforth rule 'in heaven' . . . as well. This 'comprehensive sovereignty over the whole of the created order' is the Father's bequest to his victorious Son. And whereas Jesus earlier sent the twelve on a mission to Israel . . ., he now

---

43 Chamblin, *Matthew*, 2:1485.

authorizes these eleven to make disciples of all nations (28:19)."[44]

Though neither in Matthew 28:18–20 nor Mark 16:15 does Jesus actually command the disciples to go into the world, that is certainly the sense of the commission. They are being sent out on a mission and so, in their going, they are to do certain things—make disciples, baptize, and teach—or "preach the gospel to all creation" (Mark 16:15). What they had done concerning the lost sheep of Israel before Jesus' resurrection, they are now to do with respect to the whole world. Through this Great Commission, Jesus established the permanent missionary nature of the Church between His ascension and His second coming. The Church is to evangelize with the goal of making disciples who will then be baptized into the visible church through their good confession made in the presence of many witnesses and then they will be continually nurtured in the faith through the teaching of the Word. There is never an end of the imperative for this Great Commission until Jesus returns. It is a perpetual commission for the whole Church in every generation.

Jesus Appears to James (1 Corinthians 15:7)

I Corinthians 15:7 states: "then He appeared to James." This particular James was, without a doubt, the brother of our Lord. Where Jesus appeared to James and what He said to him is not mentioned in the Scripture. Only the bare fact of this special appearance of Jesus to His brother, James, is mentioned. James and the other brothers of Jesus had not believed in Him while He was carrying out His ministry. Yet, James was a man of sterling character and great promise. Jesus saw in His brother things that would make him useful for the future church. Thus, Jesus appeared to James for the purpose of eliciting faith from him. This appearance of Jesus to James was that special preparation which God always gives to those whom He calls. James would become the leader of the Jerusalem church; the first Moderator of the Jerusalem Synod; the author of the Epistle of James; and, a martyr for the faith. Eusebius, the early church historian, recorded that James died by being cast down from the pinnacle of the temple. The devil was unable to destroy the Son of God in that way, so he killed the Messiah's brother from that pinnacle instead.

---

44 Chamblin, *Matthew*, 2:1487.

Jesus' Apostolic Commission (Matthew 28:19, 20; Mark 16:15–20; Luke 24:44–49; Acts 1:6–8)

It would appear that the order of these events in Galilee was, first, that Jesus appeared to the apostles and to more than five hundred on the mountain where He promised He would meet them. Then, He appeared to James in an unknown location—probably also in Galilee. Finally, He appeared to the disciples on the day when He ascended into heaven. All the resurrection appearances of Jesus took place between April 9th and May 19th, AD 30, a forty day period—which always represents a period of testing in the Scripture. His appearances in Galilee by the Sea and on the mountain took place sometime between April 16th and May 19th, when he met His disciples in Jerusalem. The day of that last meeting was a Thursday, ten days before the Feast of Pentecost for that year. This final appearance took place on the Mount of Olives where Jesus reiterated the commission He had given previously to the disciples gathered in the Upper Room on the first day He rose from the dead (Luke 24:44–48) and once again to the eleven and the great crowd on the mountain in Galilee (Matthew 28:18–20 and Mark 16:15, 16). It was the practice of Jesus to repeat Himself when there were great truths He was conveying. He had warned the disciples several times concerning His coming death and resurrection before they traveled there for the Passover. Now He once again made it very clear what the great mission of the Church is. He said to them: "It is not for you to know times and epochs which the Father has fixed by His own authority; but you will receive power when the Holy Spirit has come upon you; and you shall be My witnesses both in Jerusalem; and in all Judea and Samaria, and even to the remotest part of the world" (Acts 1:7, 8). The great task before them, world-wide evangelization, was a work so great that it required a monumental effusion of the Holy Spirit on them. They were commanded to wait in Jerusalem until that outpouring of the Spirit had equipped them for their great calling.

Jesus' Ascension (Mark 16:19; Luke 24:50–53; and, Acts 1:9–11)

It was on that same day that Jesus was taken away from them in a most glorious way. There was no hugging, kissing, or shaking of hands as is typical for close friends who are parting from one another. After Jesus had given His final words to the disciples, "He was lifted up while they were looking on, and a cloud received Him out of their sight" (Acts 1:9). He had disappeared before, but never by being lifted up into the clouds. His ascension is shrouded in darkness in the same way that His transfiguration was. The disciples were unprepared for His ascension. "And as they were gazing intently into the sky while He was going, behold two men in white clothing stood beside them. They also said, 'Men of Galilee, why do you stand looking into the sky? This Jesus, who has been taken from you into heaven, will come in just the same way as you have watched Him go into heaven'" (Acts 1:10 11). At the end of the world, Jesus will come again riding on the clouds. His return will be sudden, visible, bodily, personal and every eye shall see Him. He "will appear a second time for salvation *without reference* to sin, to those who eagerly await Him" (Hebrews 9:28b). Until then, He will reside in heaven while He puts all things under His feet so that at the end of the world He can hand over the kingdom to the Father (Cf. 1 Corinthians 15:20–28).

All the resurrection appearances of Jesus provided the Church, and even the world, with infallible proof that the grave could not contain the Lord. The tomb was empty, not because the disciples had stolen the body away, but because Jesus was no longer there. The soldiers who guarded the tomb, though they did not see Jesus rise, witnessed the majesty of the angels who rolled away the stone and observed that the body was gone. They were witnesses to the Sanhedrin, whether from faith or fear. The whole Sanhedrin was willing to participate in a lie—the lie that the disciples stole the body away while the soldiers slept—in order to not arouse the suspicion and ire of Pilate and the Roman officials. Yet, the whole city was soon abuzz with the reports of Jesus' resurrection from Sunday, April 9th AD 30 onwards. The dam completely broke just ten days after Jesus ascended into heaven when Peter boldly proclaimed on the day of Pentecost, "This Jesus God raised up again, to which we are all witnesses" (Acts 2:32). Peter's words were not spoken in the Upper Room with the doors tightly closed, but in the midst of the city before a mixed crowd of people from various places in Europe, Asia, and Africa. He addressed not the followers of Jesus alone, but also the men of Judea and Israel as well as all those who lived in Jerusalem. Following that sermon, it became impossible to stifle the witness of the followers of Jesus as they did not fear the persecution of the officials. Even the unbelieving members of the Sanhedrin could not deny the reports of the resurrection since they *"began* to recognize them as having been with Jesus" (Acts 4:13b)—i.e., Peter and John who proclaimed that their power to heal the blind beggar came from "the name of Jesus Christ the Nazarene, whom you crucified, whom God raised from the dead—by this *name* this man stands before you in good health" (Acts 4:10). There was no corner of Jerusalem where the resurrection of Jesus could any longer be effectively countered—and soon there would be no place in the inhabited world where that news would not be spread. Kings and rulers would soon hear the testimony. Jewish synagogues throughout the dispersion would soon have the followers of Jesus to proclaim Him as the Messiah. The apostles faithfully proclaimed the death and resurrection of Christ throughout Asia, Africa, and Europe wherever they labored in those regions. Thus, the resurrection is a fact that cannot be denied, as Richard William Dickinson wrote:

> It but remains, therefore, for men of a speculative cast of mind, or averse to the distinctive features of the gospel, to undermine by sophistry what cannot be overthrown by logical reasonings; to explain away by fanciful analogies or preconceived notions, what by no well-known law of literary criticism, nor by any legitimate principle of hermeneutics, can be consistently denied; to supersede by ingenious theories what must be admitted either as a historical, or a truth according to the fait and obvious import of the phraseology in which it is couched.[45]

Nearly two millennium have passed since Jesus rose from the dead and the unbelieving world has still not decided on any effective way to deny His resurrection. There simply is no way to do so and the world will never move beyond their own circular reasoning in their attempts to salvage their unbelief—until some of them come to faith. The great dividing point of all humanity will always be between faith and unbelief. Abraham, the father of all believers, believed in "hope against hope" (Romans 4:18) that God would fulfill His promise to make him a father of many nations. The unbelief of those who deny the resurrection of Christ is unbelief in the face of all the evidence that should point them towards faith. When the world disbelieves, we who believe that God raised Jesus from the dead must be ever more diligent in holding Him up to the world as the only refuge from the

---

45 Richard William Dickinson, *The Resurrection of Jesus Christ Historically and Logically Viewed* (Philadelphia: Presbyterian Board of Publication, 1865), 127.

coming storm of God's wrath against sin. As Edersheim closed his magnificent book on the life of Christ:

> Our task is ended—and we also worship and look up. And we go back from this sight into a hostile world, to love and to live, and to work for the Risen Christ. But as earth's day is growing dim, and, with earth's gathering darkness, breaks over it heaven's storm, we ring out—as of old they were wont, from church-tower, to the mariners that hugged a rock-bund coast—our Easter-bells to guide them who are belated, over the storm-tossed sea, beyond the breakers, into the desired haven. Ring out, earth, all thy Easter-chimes; bring your offerings, all ye people; worship in faith, for—'This Jesus, Which was received up from you into heaven, shall so come, in like manner as ye beheld Him going into heaven.' 'Even so, Lord Jesus, come quickly.'[46]

Or, once again, the first stanza of McCheyne's eloquent poem "I am Debtor":

> When this passing world is done,
> When has sunk yon glaring sun,
> When we stand with Christ in glory,
> Looking o'er life's finished story,
> Then, Lord, shall I fully know—
> Not till then—how much I owe.

Peter proclaimed concerning Jesus on Sunday, May 29 AD 30 "that God has made Him both Lord and Christ—this Jesus whom you crucified" (Acts 2:36). The Feast of Unleavened Bread, which immediately follows Passover, was filled with worshipers from all over when the first witnesses to Jesus' resurrection began reporting the good news. All of Jerusalem soon heard the news. You were not there when Jesus was crucified, but your sins contributed to His sufferings and death. You were not there when Jesus rose from the dead, but that message of hope and joy is the only consolation for sinners that the Lord ever gives. There is only one way that you ever will be able to stand with Christ in glory and fully know how much you owe to Him—you must come to Him. You must humbly bow your hearts before Him in repentance for your sins that caused His suffering and you must believe that God indeed raised Him from the dead for your justification. The Easter message still resounds: "Christ is risen, indeed!" That truth changed the ancient world and it is powerful enough through the ministry of the Holy Spirit to still change hardened hearts today.

---

46 Edersheim, *The Life and Times of Jesus the Messiah*, 922.

Bibliography

Alexander, Joseph Addison, *The Gospel According to Matthew: Explained*, Lynchburg, VA: James Family Christian Publishers, n.d.

Alexander, Joseph Addison, *A Commentary on the Gospel of Mark*, London: The Banner of Truth Trust, 1960.

Angus, Samuel. *The Environment of Early Christianity*, London: Duckworth & Co., 1914.

Bagster, Samuel. *Bagster's Bible Handbook*, Old Tappan, New Jersey: Fleming H. Revell Company, 1983.

Blomberg, Craig L., *Matthew*, Nashville: Broadman Press, 1992.

Bonar, Andrew A., *Leviticus*, London and Carlisle, PA: The Banner of Truth Trust, 1972

Bridges, Charles, *The Christian Ministry*, London: The Banner of Truth Trust, 1967.

Brown, David, *The Four Gospels*, London, England: The Banner of Truth Trust, 1969.

Brown, John, *Expository Discourses on 1 Peter*, Two Volumes, Edinburgh, Scotland and Carlisle, PA: The Banner of Truth Trust, 1975.

Brown, John, *Hebrews*, London, England and Carlisle, PA: The Banner of Truth Trust, 1972.

Brown, John, *The Sufferings and Glory of the Messiah*, U.S.A.: Sovereign Grace Publishers, 1959.

Bruce, Alexander B. *The Humiliation of Christ*, Grand Rapids: Eerdmans Publishing Co., 1955.

Bruce, A. B., *The Training of the Twelve*, Grand Rapids: Kregel Publications, 1971.

Bunyan, John, *The Pilgrim's Progress: From This World To That Which Is To Come*, Oxford, England: Oxford University Press, 1960.

Calvin, John, *A Harmony of the Gospels Mathew, Mark, and Luke*, Three Volumes, Grand Rapids: Eerdmans Publishing Company, 1972.

Calvin, John, *The Gospel According to St John and The First Epistle of John*, Two Volumes, Grand Rapids: Eerdmans Publishing

Company, 1961.

Candlish, Robert S., *A Commentary on 1 John,* London and Carlisle, PA: The Banner of Truth Trust, 1973.

Case, Shirley Jackson. "Jesus and Sepphoris," *Journal of Biblical Literature,* 1926.

Chamblin, J. Knox. *Matthew,* Two Volumes, Fearn, Tain, Ross-Shire, Great Britain: Christian Focus Publications, 2010.

Danby, Herbert, *The Mishnah. Translated from the Hebrew with Introduction and Brief Explanatory Notes,* London: Oxford University Press, 1964.

Davies, Samuel, *Sermons by the Rev. Samuel Davies,* Three Volumes, Pittsburgh: Soli Deo Gloria Publications, 1993.

Deilitzsch, Franz, *A Day in Capernaum,* New York: Funk & Wagnalls, 1887.

Dickinson, Richard William, *The Resurrection of Jesus Christ Historically and Logically* Viewed, Philadelphia: Presbyterian Board of Publication, 1865.

Edersheim, Alfred. *Sketches of Jewish Social Life in the Days of Christ,* London: James Clarke & Co., 1961.

Edersheim, Alfred. *The Life and Times of Jesus the Messiah,* Peabody, Mass.: Hendrickson Publishers, Inc., 1995.

Edersheim, Alfred, *The Temple: Its Ministry and Service,* Peabody, Massachusetts: Hendrickson Publishers, 1994.

Fairbairn, Patrick, ed., *Fairbairn's Imperial Standard Bible Encyclopedia,* Six Volumes, Grand Rapids: Zondervan Publishing House, 1957.

Farrar, Frederic. *Life of Christ,* USA: Bibliotech Press, 2020.

John Flavel, *The Fountain of Life,* New York: American Tract Society, n.d.

Flavel, John, *The Works of John Flavel,* Volume Three, London: The Banner of Truth Trust, 1968.

Geldenhuys, Norval. *Commentary on the Gospel of Luke,* Grand Rapids: Eerdmans, 1960.

Godet, Frederick Louis, *Commentary on the Gospel of John,* Two

Volumes in One, Grand Rapids: Zondervan Publishing House, 1970.

Henderson, Archibald, *Palestine: Its Historical Geography*, Edinburgh: T & T Clark, 1893.

Hendriksen, William, *The Gospel of John*, Edinburgh, Scotland and Carlisle, PA: The Banner of Truth Trust, 1976.

Hendriksen, William. *Exposition of the Gospel According to Luke*, Grand Rapids: Eerdmans Publishing Company, 1981.

Hendriksen, William, *The Gospel of Mark*, Edinburgh, Scotland and Carlisle, PA: The Banner of Truth Trust, 1976.

Hendriksen, William, *Matthew*, Edinburgh: The Banner of Truth Trust, 1976.

Henry, Matthew, *Commentary on the Whole Bible*, Six Volumes, Old Tappan, New Jersey: Fleming Revell, n.d.

Hooker, Morna D., *The Gospel According to Saint Mark*, Peabody, MA: Hendrickson Publishers, 1991

Huizenga, Lee Sjoerds, *Unclean! Unclean! Or, Glimpses of the Land Where Leprosy Thrives*, Grand Rapids, Michigan: Smitter Book Company, 1927.

Josephus, Flavius, *Complete Works of Flavius Josephus*, Grand Rapids, Michigan: Kregel Publications, 1960.

Keil, C. F. and Deilitzsch, F., *The Pentateuch*, 3 Volumes in One, Grand Rapids: Eerdmans Publishing Company, 1975.

Kitto, John. *Palestine: The Physical Geography and Natural History of the Holy Land*, Two Volumes, London: Charles Knight and Co., 1841.

Kitto, John, *Daily Bible Illustrations: The Life and Death of Our Lord*, Volume Seven, New York: Robert Carter and Brothers, 1881.

Krummacher, F. W., *The Suffering Saviour*, Grand Rapids: Baker Book House, 1977.

Lane, William L., *The Gospel According to Mark*, Grand Rapids: Eerdmans Publishing Company, 1974.

Latham, Henry, *Pastor Pastorum of the Schooling of the Apostles by our Lord*, New York: James Pott & Co. Publishing, 1891.

Leahy, Frederick S., *Satan Cast Out*, Edinburgh, Scotland and Carlisle, PA: The Banner of Truth Trust, 1975.

Levine, Lee I., ed., *Ancient Synagogues Revealed*, Jerusalem, Israel Exploration Society, 1981.

Lewis, C. S., *Miracles*, New York: Touchstone, 1996.

Lewis, C. S. *Reflections on the Psalms*, New York: Harcourt, Brace & Co, 1958.

Lightfoot, J. B. *The Epistle of St. Paul to the Galatians*, Grand Rapids: Zondervan Publishing House, 1974.

Lloyd-Jones, D. M. *Evangelistic Sermons*, Edinburgh, Scotland and Carlisle, PA: The Banner of Truth Trust, 1983.

Lloyd-Jones, D. Martyn, *Studies in the Sermon on the Mount*, Two Volumes in One, Grand Rapids: Eerdmans Publishing Company, 1972.

Machen, J. Gresham, *The Virgin Birth of Christ*, Cambridge: James Clarke & Co., 2022.

Martin, Hugh, *Simon Peter*, Edinburgh, Scotland and Carlisle, PA: The Banner of Truth Trust, 1984.

Mason, Mike. *Jesus: His Story in Stone*, Victoria, BC, Canada: Friesen Press, 2017.

McCheyne, Robert Murray, *The Sermons of the Reverend Robert Murray McCheyne*, New York: Robert Carter, 1848.

McClintock, John and Strong, James. *Cyclopedia of Biblical, Theological, and Ecclesiastical Literature*, Twelve Volumes, Grand Rapids: Baker Book House, 1981.

Moore, T. V., *The Last Days of Jesus*, Edinburgh, Scotland and Carlisle, PA: The Banner of Truth Trust, 1981.

Morris, Leon, *The Gospel According to St. John*, Grand Rapids: Eerdmans Publishing Company, 1971.

Newton, George, *An Exposition of John 17*, Edinburgh, Scotland and Carlisle, PA: The Banner of Truth Trust, 1995.

Newton, John, *The Works of John Newton*, Six Volumes, Edinburgh, Scotland and Carlisle, PA: The Banner of Truth Trust, 2007.

Olsen, Ted Olsen. "The Life & Times of Jesus of Nazareth: Did You Know?" *Christianity Today*. Accessed on October October 10, 2023 at: https://www.christianitytoday.com/1998/07

Onion, Amanda Onion. "Researchers Diagnose Herod the Great," (ABC News, January 7, 2006). Accessed on May 26, 2021 at: https://abcnews.go.com/Technology/story?id=98107&page=1

Pears, Thomas Clinton, Jr., ed., Samuel Davies, "Charity and Truth United, or The Way of the Multitude Exposed in Six Letters", Journal of the Presbyterian Historical Society, Vol XIX (1941).

Pfeiffer, Charles F. and Vos, Howard F. *The Wycliffe Historical Geography of Bible Lands*, Chicago: Moody Press, 1978.

Philip, George, *The Garden of Gethsemane*, London: Hodder and Stoughton, 1882.

Pink, Arthur W., *An Exposition of the Sermon on the Mount*, Grand Rapids: Baker Book House, 1974.

Plumer, William S., *Commentary on Romans*, Grand Rapids: Kregel Publications, 1971.

Plummer, Alfred, *A Critical and Exegetical Commentary on the Gospel of S. Luke*, Edinburgh: T & T Clark, 1960.

Plummer, Alfred, *An Exegetical Commentary on the Gospel According to S. Matthew*, London: Elliott Stock, 1909.

Poole, Matthew Poole, *A Commentary on the Holy Bible*, 3 Volumes, Edinburgh, Scotland and Carlisle, PA: The Banner of Truth Trust, 1975.

Renan, Ernest, *The Life of Jesus*, London and Paris: Trubner & Co., and M. Levy Preres, 1871.

Reynolds, Barbara, ed., Dorothy Sayers, *The Letters of Dorothy Sayers*, Cambridge: Dorothy L. Sayers Society, 1997.

Roberts, Dewey, *Historic Christianity and the Federal Vision*, Destin, Florida: Sola Fide Publications, 2016.

Robertson, Archibald, T., *John the Loyal: Studies in the Ministry of the Baptist*, New York: Charles Scribner's Sons, 1911.

Robertson, Archibald Thomas, *Word Pictures in the New Testament, The Gospel According to Matthew, The Gospel According to Mark,*

Nashville, Tennessee: Broadman Press, 1930.

Ross, Charles, *The Inner Sanctuary*, Edinburgh, Scotland and Carlisle, PA: The Banner of Truth Trust, 2016.

Robinson, Edward. *Biblical Researches in Palestine, Mount Sinai and Arabia Petraea*, Two Volumes, Boston: Crocker and Brewster, 1841.

Ryle, John Charles, *Expository Thoughts on the Gospels: John*, 3 Volumes, Cambridge and London, James Clarke & Co., Ltd., 1969.

Ryle, John Charles, *Expository Thoughts on the Gospels: Luke*, 2 Volumes, Cambridge and London: James Clarke & Co., Ltd., 1969.

Ryle, John Charles, *Expository Thoughts on the Gospels: Luke*, 2 Volumes, Edinburgh. Scotland and Carlisle, PA: The Banner of Truth Trust, 1986.

Ryle, John Charles, *Expository Thoughts on the Gospels: Matthew*, Cambridge: James Clarke & Co., 1974.

Ryle, J. C., *Holiness: Its Nature, Hindrances, Difficulties and Roots*, Cambridge and London: James Clarke & Co., Ltd., 1956.

Sayers, Dorothy, *The Man Born To Be King*, London: Victor Gollancz, 1943.

Schnabel, Edward J., *Jesus in Jerusalem: The Last Days*, Grand Rapids: Eerdmans Publishing Company, 2018.

Schurer, Emil, *A History of the Jewish People in the Time of Jesus Christ*, Five Volumes, London: Bloomsbury T & T Clark, 2000.

Shepard, J. W. *The Christ of the Gospels*, Grand Rapids: Eerdmans Publishing Company, 1939.

Smeaton, George, *Christ's Doctrine of the Atonement*, Edinburgh, Scotland and Carlisle, PA: The Banner of Truth Trust, 1991.

Smith, David, *The Days of His Flesh: The Earthly Life of Our Lord and Saviour*, New York: A. C. Armstrong & Son, London: Hodder and Stoughton, 1905.

Smith, George Adam. *The Historical Geography of the Holy Land*, London: Hodder and Stoughton, 1900.

Spurgeon, Charles Haddon, *The Metropolitan Tabernacle Pulpit*, Volume Sixteen, London: Passmore and Alabaster, 1870.

Spurgeon, C. H. *The Treasury of David*, Three Volumes, Grand Rapids: Zondervan Publishing House, 1974.

Stalker, James, *The Trial and Death of Jesus Christ*, New York: A. C. Armstrong and Son, 1894.

Stewart, James S. *The Life and Teaching of Jesus Christ*, Nashville and New York: Abingdon Press, n.d.

Swete, Henry Barclay, *Commentary on Mark*, Grand Rapids, Michigan: Kregel Publications, 1977.

Tarbell, Martha Tarbell. *The Geography of Palestine in the Time of Christ*, Indianapolis: The Bobbs-Merrill Company, 1907.

Thornwell, James Henley. *The Collected Writings of James Henley Thornwell*, Edinburgh, Scotland and Carlisle, Pennsylvania: The Banner of Truth Trust, 1974.

Tristram, Henry Baker, *The Natural History of the Bible*, London: Society for Promoting Christian Knowledge, 1868.

Tristram, Henry Baker, *The Natural History of the Bible*, London: Society for the Promoting Christian Knowledge, 1867.

Traill, Robert, *The Works of Robert Traill*, Volume Two of 4 Volumes, Edinburgh, Scotland and Carlisle, Pennsylvania: The Banner of Truth Trust, 1975.

Justin Martyr, *Ante-Nicene Fathers: Dialogue to Trypho, a Jew*, Peabody, Massachusetts: Hendrickson Publishers, 1999.

Vaughan, C. R., *The Gifts of the Holy Spirit*, Edinburgh and Carlisle, PA: The Banner of Truth Trust, 1975.

Westcott, Brooke Foss. *The Gospel According to St. John*, Grand Rapids, Michigan: William B. Eerdmans Publishing Company, 1971.

Young, Edward J., *The Book of Isaiah*, Three Volumes, Grand Rapids: Eerdmans Publishing Company, 1978.

www.ingramcontent.com/pod-product-compliance
Lightning Source LLC
Chambersburg PA
CBHW050327010526
44119CB00050B/698